Hells Canyon and the Middle Snake River
A Story of the Land and Its People

Hells Canyon and the Middle Snake River
A Story of the Land and Its People

Carole Simon-Smolinski

Confluence Press

Copyright © 2008 by Carole Simon-Smolinski. All rights reserved.
Published by Confluence Press, Lewiston, Idaho

No part of this publication may be reproduced, stored in a retrieval system, or transmitted in any form or by any means, electronic, mechanical, photocopying, recording, scanning, or otherwise, except as permitted under Section 107 or 108 of the 1976 United States Copyright Act, without the prior written permission of the Publisher. Requests to the Publisher for permission should be addressed to the The Permission Company, 47 Seneca Road, P.O. Box 604, Mount Pocono, PA 18344. Phone: 570-839-7477; fax: 570-839-7448, or on the web at www.permissionscompany.com.

Book design by Brian Kolstad
Cover design by Tamara Schumacher & Brian Kolstad
Cover photo courtesy of Nez Perce County Historical Society
Map illustrations by Sarah Moore

Library of Congress Cataloging-in-Publication Data:

Simon-Smolinski, Carole
    Hells Canyon and the Middle Snake River: A Story of the Land and Its People / Carole Simon-Smolinski.—1st ed.
    Includes bibliographical references and index.
    ISBN: 978-1-881090-07-6 Paperback
    Printed in the United States of America
10 9 8 7 6 5 4 3 2

Dedicated to
the Spoken Word,
who brings order out of chaos.
Remember.

CONTENTS

List of Maps	viii
Acknowledgments	ix
Author's Note	xiii
Abbreviations	xiii
1 Frowning Precipices, Mad River, and the Sidehill Gouger	1
2 According to the Rocks	5
3 A Land Diverse and Bountiful	13
4 The Winds of Change	25
5 Mackenzie and the Captain	37
6 Steamboat Pioneers	49
7 War Threatens Hells Canyon	61
8 Gold, Greed, and Murder	75
9 Bull-headed Fools	89
10 Success to the Enterprise!	103
11 Eureka!	119
12 The Daniel Webster Mote Interlude	143
13 When the Roll Is Called	159
14 Stewards of the Land	171
15 Ranch Hands, Dogs, and Dadburn Predators	187
16 Ties That Bind	203
17 Rubbering, Neighboring, and Tolerating	215
18 Events Memorable and Heartbreaking	229
19 Up, Down, Out, and Across	245
20 Flirting with Angels	263
21 Into the Modern Era	283
Epilogue	295
Appendix A: Clearing the Channel	299
Appendix B: Fraud or Just Poor Business Practices?	301
Appendix C: The End of an Era	307
Notes	317
Bibliography	363
Index	373

Maps	*Sarah Moore, Cartographer*	
1.1	Hells Canyon and the Middle Snake River	xiv
2.1	Geographic Features of Eastern Oregon and Idaho	6
3.1	Home to the Nez Perce Indians	21
4.1	Area Covered by Members of the Lewis and Clark Corps of Discovery	26
4.2	Wilson Price Hunt Expedition Route through Idaho	31
5.1	Benjamin Bonneville Expedition Route	44
6.1	The Steamboat Shoshone's Route through Hells Canyon	56
7.1	The 1877 Nez Perce War in Idaho	64
7.2	The 1878 Bannock War	70
8.1	Chinese Massacre of 1887	78
9.1	South Canyon Mining and the Norma	93
10.1	Central and Northern Mining in Hells Canyon	106
10.2	James Brewrink's Sketches of the AAI Mine	109
11.1	Eureka Mining, Smelting and Power Company Properties	121
12.1	Daniel Mote's Canyon	146
13.1	Sheep and Cattle Ranches	163
20.1	Route for Mailboats from Lewiston to Johnson Bar	244
20.2	Mountain Trails along the Snake River	256
C.1	Dams and Proposed Dam Sites	306

ACKNOWLEDGEMENTS

With the exception of my husband, who is always first, the following names appear in alphabetical order. I am grateful to you all for helping throughout this long labor of love. Forgive me if I inadvertently omitted anyone's name.

Max Smolinski, my husband and best friend, inspired me, encouraged me, and frequently pushed me as I wandered through the production of this book. His love for this region's history, for this land we call home, and for the Creator who designed Hells Canyon—we share it all. To Max, I shall forever be grateful.

Grace Bartlett spent her lifetime recording the history of Wallowa County, Oregon. Her daughter, Ann Hayes, carries on that commitment through her work at the Wallow County Museum. I thank Grace and Ann for the advice and source references they shared, especially for Grace's laboriously typed copy of Daniel Mote's diaries.

While working in the canyon for Ken Johnson, Dick Rivers, and Wally Beamer, Helen Beard grew to love the place and collected a wide range of historical information about it. She generously shares her material with anyone interested in Hells Canyon history. I appreciate her inspiration and generosity.

I thank Johnny Carrey, Cort Conley, and Ace Barton for writing *Snake River of Hells Canyon*, a valuable and needed contribution to the history of Hells Canyon. This book attempts to complement, not replace, their 1979 publication.

Janice Cochrane and Barbara Bush patiently transcribed most of the interviews collected on tape and video. Without the transcriptions, the task of incorporating interviewees' stories into this narrative would have been prohibitive.

Elizabeth Cunningham took on the formidable task of helping shorten a long, unwieldy manuscript. She encouraged me to trust my voice and my ability to tell a good story. Thanks, Liz.

Andrew Dahlquist, a good friend, helped me learn the ins-and-outs of sheep ranching and straightened me out on confusing Hells Canyon family relationships.

Steve Evans, Connie Evans, and Allen Pinkham took me to the edge of Wapshilla Ridge between the Salmon and Snake Rivers to better visualize the Lewis and Clark Expedition route into Hells Canyon. Steve and Allen are writing a book about the Nez Perce perspective of the expedition, a valuable study.

Lora Feucht, archivist for Nez Perce County Historical Society, helped in many ways on this book, especially by securing information about the Eureka Mining, Smelting and Power Company.

Anne R. Gibbons smoothed the rough passages, clarified obscure phrases, and caught errors. I respect her professionalism, appreciate her advice, and enjoy the friendship we developed through the editing process.

I am indebted to Susan Gibbons Harris for agreeing to index this book. It was a hard job, but without an index, a comprehensive history is useless. Susan provided the final ingredient for a reader-friendly, meaningful book.

Jim Hepworth, director of Confluence Press, Lewiston, pushed me to keep-on-keeping-on for more than twenty years. He has awed me with his talent, surprised me with his enthusiastic endorsement of my abilities, and helped me through the last stages of this book's production.

Mary John helped during early research stages of this book.

I cherish the times Patricia Keith, my dear friend, and I shared in the canyon and Patricia's quiet, respectful appreciation for the canyons' many attributes. I thank her for editing a revised manuscript and for her visual and literary inspiration and help as we waded together through the production of two Hells Canyon videos.

Marilyn Levine, a scholar of Chinese history, language, and culture, helped with the chapter on Chinese miners in the canyon.

Mindful of both the reader's needs and the author's and publisher's requirements, Brian Kolstad successfully transformed an unwieldy manuscript into this skillfully and attractively designed book. Thanks Brian for a job well done.

Aldyth Logan gave me a copy of *Topping Out*, a fictitious account of an early 1900s Hells Canyon teacher written by her friend Kathryn Harris, and a copy of her 1975 interview with Harris. The book is out of print.

Bob McGrady generously loaned me his parents' albums and scrapbooks filled with a vast array of articles and photographs documenting Kyle McGrady's time on the river as a mail carrier.

James Miller, grandson of the president and cofounder of the Eureka Mining, Smelting and Power Company, realized after a trip into Hells Canyon the importance of his grandfather's papers and photographs. By donating the collection to the Nez Perce County Historical Society, he has helped clarify many questions about that mining venture.

Working with obscure places and imprecise locations, Sarah Moore produced maps for this book. Without her maps, the book would be incomplete.

I have admired for years Keith Petersen, a Pacific Northwest historian whose writing and scholarship are dedicated to preserving our region's history. He set my path in the pursuit of regional history and encouraged me at every step. PNW history has no greater friend than Keith.

Barbara Powell produced Citizens of North Idaho, a two-volume compilation of biographical data and articles from Lewiston's earliest newspapers. When I asked for help from her continued work with more recent Lewiston newspapers, she generously provided it.

Virgil Purviance shared a 16-mm, colored, silent film that his father, Norman Purviance, took in 1940 while traveling into the canyon with Kyle McGrady. His film captures images that complete the pictures and descriptions shared by others. I also thank Ace Barton, Darrell Bentz, and Art Seamans, who helped identify the people and places in the Purviance movie.

I thank Jane Rohling for being a friend and inspiration throughout this project. While she worked as an HCNRA interpretive specialist, we collected pictures and stories from Hells Canyon residents.

Christy Shaw helped me by interviewing pilots Bud Stengle and Ted Grote.

Tracy Valier, THE geologist of Hells Canyon, has spent a lifetime peeling away the mystery of Hells Canyon origins. He encouraged me to write the canyon's history and twice edited the geology chapter. Tracy's passion for the canyon is contagious.

Steve Wassmuth and Herald "Frog" Stewart of Holiday River Expeditions, Grangeville, Idaho, generously provided Patricia Keith and me with a three-day float trip through Hells Canyon, always stopping when we wanted to take pictures and explore a site. The trip enabled me to better understand the places about which I was writing.

Bill Wilson and Kay Coffman, descendants of the Pete and Ethel Wilson clan of Saddle Creek, I thank for sharing their parents' stories and photographs. I also thank Bill for publishing *A Hells Canyon Romance*, the account by his mother, Murrielle McGaffee Wilson, of growing up and working in the canyon.

Bruce Womack, retired HCNRA archeologist, interviewed many canyon residents. Through his foresight, those oral history sources are preserved. From him I learned much anthropological and archeological history of Hells Canyon.

I spent many years gathering data but carelessly neglected to write down the names of the archivists who helped me at public, state, and university libraries. Forgive me, and thank you all for your invaluable help.

I thank the Idaho Humanities Council for a 1995 research fellowship to support my research for this book and for the smaller subsequent grant the council awarded to support collecting oral histories. I also thank the Charles Redd Center for Western Studies, Utah, for a 2003 research grant.

I especially want to thank all the people who shared their life stories through interviews. As pieces of each individual story mesh, a mosaic of canyon life emerges. I am indebted to all of you. Your shared experiences enrich us now and will continue to enrich the future: you tell of a way of life nearly forgotten in a land barely known. Your willingness to entrust your life stories to my pen humbles me; I pray that I have properly valued their worth.

People interviewed by the author:
George Allen
John A. K. Barker
Ace Barton
Ralph Beard
Marjorie Wilson Chadwick
Jess Earl
Arvid Elson
Theo "Ted" Grote
Catherine "Kitty" Grunig
Horace Henderson
Esther Hibbs
Polly Johnson Hollandsworth
Dick Rivers
Francis "Bud" Stengle
Winifred "Janie" Stone
Doug Tippet
Erma VanPool
Sharon Horrocks Wing

People interviewed by Patricia Keith and the author:
Ace Barton
Dennis Brown
Martha Cooper
Esther Hibbs
Greg Johnson
Oliver McNabb
Walter W. Seibly
Violet Wilson Shirley
Carmen Winniford Yokum

People interviewed by Bruce Womack and HCNRA staff:
Ace Barton
Elmer Earl
Jess Earl
Hazel Johnson
Len and Grace Jordan
Violet Wilson Shirley
Max Walker
Murrielle (McGaffee) and Jim Wilson

Thank you all.

AUTHOR'S NOTE

Much of the material in the book is from personal recollections obtained through interviews. Names and pertinent information regarding interviews—those conducted by me as well as by others—are given in the bibliography. When quotations or descriptions are clearly attributable to an individual, I have often relied on the reader's intelligence in determining the source of the information, rather than providing the citation in an endnote.

In the mid-1800s the fur traders called the indigenous people of north-central Idaho "Nez Perce" (pronounced "nes purse"), a word derived from French for "pierced nose." The word is a misnomer, for they did not, as a people, pierce their noses. Nonetheless, the name stuck. Members of the Nez Perce Tribe now ask to be called Nimiipuu, meaning "the people." But because the historical sources used in this book consistently refer to the Nimiipuu as Nez Perce, to avoid confusion I have used that historical term throughout this book.

Whether spelled Shoshone or Shoshoni (either is correct), the final vowel is pronounced like a long e. The people identified themselves according to what their band ate, Agaidikas (salmon-eaters), Tukudikas (sheep-eaters), Kucundikas (buffalo-eaters), and so on. For clarity and consistency, I have used the name Shoshone throughout.

ABBREVIATIONS

CSN	California Steam Navigation Company
FPC	Federal Power Commission
HCNRA	Hells Canyon National Recreation Area
IPC	Idaho Power Company
OR&N	Oregon Railroad and Navigation Company
OSL	Oregon Short Line
OSN	Oregon Steam Navigation Company
PIN	Pacific and Idaho Northern
PNPC	Pacific Northwest Power Company
PNW	Pacific Northwest
TVA	Tennessee Valley Authority
UP	Union Pacific
USFS	U.S. Forest Service
USGS	U.S. Geological Survey
WPPSS	Washington Public Power Supply System

Map 1.1. Hells Canyon and the Middle Snake River.

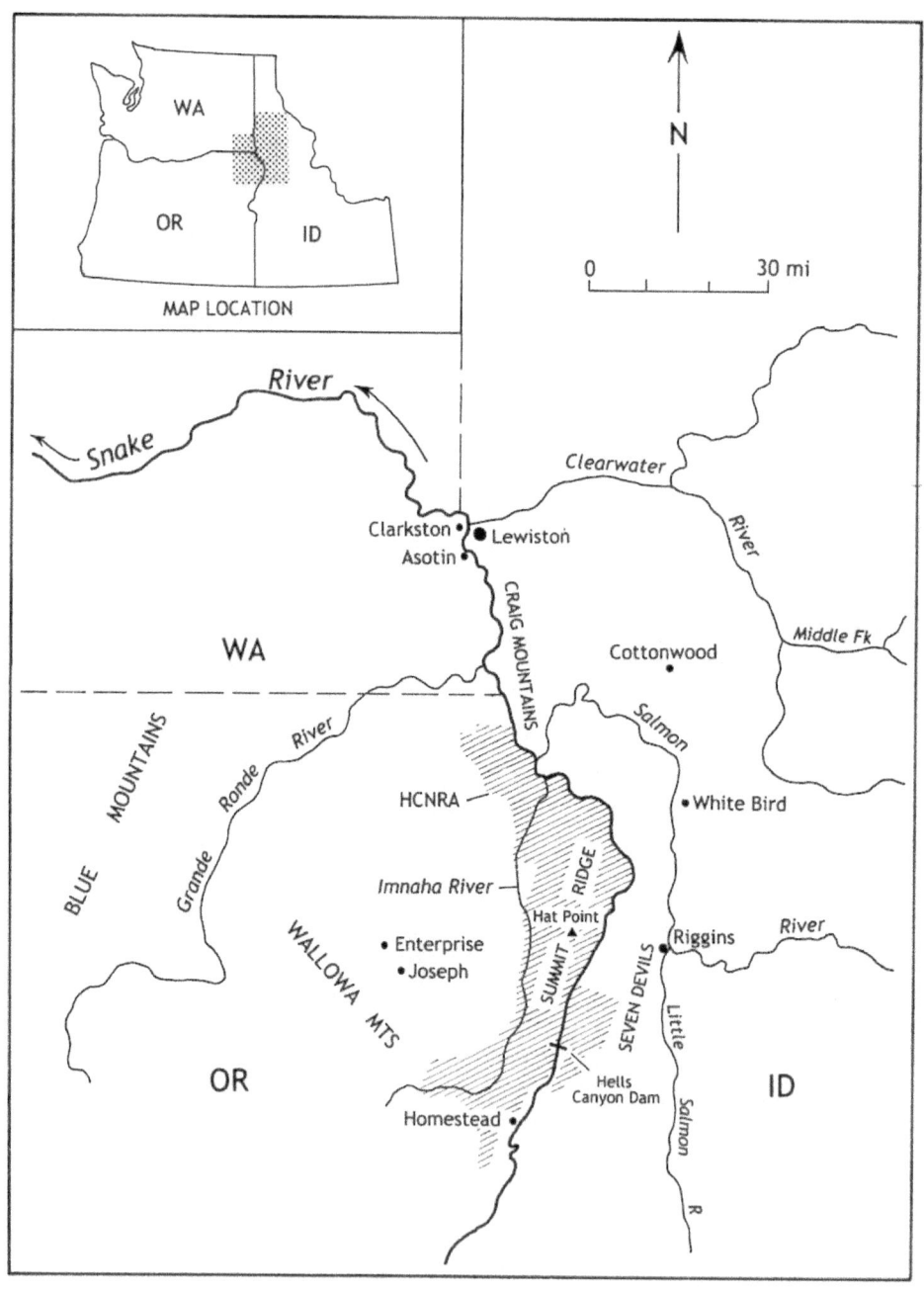

Chapter 1

Frowning Precipes, Mad River, and the Sidehill Gouger

Until the 1970s very few people had the opportunity to visit Hells Canyon and the middle Snake River of Idaho, Oregon, and Washington. Gravel roads provided limited public access at the extreme north and south of the canyon. People living and working in the canyon entered and left by horseback on narrow, winding, often precariously positioned trails, or they used the mailboat. A few ranchers built marginal roads to tie their river homes to small communities across the breaks. In later years some resorted to airplanes, with the accompanying challenge of landing and taking off on rocky benches. Tourists enjoyed the luxury of floating the canyon, or they went in with the mailboat on hunting, fishing, or sightseeing trips, but they never came in large numbers. Most of us simply did not have the opportunity or resources to enter the depths of the canyon.

I grew up in Clarkston, Washington, during the 1950s. Clarkston is at the northern end of what I call the middle Snake River.[1] My surroundings hinted at the type of terrain, climate, and vegetation I would find farther south in the canyon. My land is hot in the summer and pleasant the rest of the year. Layers of basalt and rock formations that stir my imagination terrace the gentle hills—hills that are barren of trees yet boast luxuriant crops of cheatgrass, prickly pear, thistle, and sage. Gnarly netleaf hackberry and sumac grow in the ravines, dotting tan hillsides with spots of brown and red. Bright golden coyote willow embellish the autumn riverbanks. My town and its neighbors—Lewiston, Idaho, and Asotin, Washington—are blessed by the joining of the beautiful Snake and Clearwater Rivers in the heart of the valley. Few places rival the valley's grandeur. Yet in my mind, when I was growing up, Hells Canyon was a place best avoided. When my family left the valley for a change of scene, if we didn't go "to the coast," we took day trips up the Clearwater River or to Camas Prairie. There we could expect to see green fields and timbered mountain slopes. The road-accessible, twenty-six-mile section of Snake River canyon south of Clarkston failed to attract our family outings. But none of those reasons fully explains why as a kid I had such a negative image of Hells Canyon.

I remember a book my parents had: *Hells Canyon: Seeing Idaho through a Scrap Book*, by Robert G. Bailey. On its red cover was a drawing of the state of Idaho. On the sketch, just south of my town, THE DEVIL—silhouetted in black—thrust his three-pronged fork into the edge of Idaho. It targeted Hells Canyon. A kid does not forget that image. Why would

Figure 1.1. Flowing north through the center of the picture, the Snake River passes Swallows Nest rock before joining the Clearwater River at the foot of the distant hills. From there the combined rivers continue west. In the foreground is the village of Asotin; the new town of Clarkston emerges beyond Swallows Nest on the west bank; the older community of Lewiston is on the east bank. c. 1900. (Photo courtesy of the Asotin County Historical Society.)

that land have such a name and the book such a cover unless it was justified? To me the name fit the canyon's inaccessibility, its notorious summer heat, its barren hills, and treacherous waters. It fit impressions I picked up through reading and hearing about the canyon. The true nature of the great canyon of the middle Snake River was long ignored in print and speech. I would not begin to learn that nature for many years, and then only slowly and never completely.

Hells Canyon—the name for the deepest section of middle Snake River canyon—certainly suggests images of doom in biblical proportions. In the minds of many, including me, that impression applied to the entire river stretch from Homestead, Oregon, to my home at Clarkston, Washington. Descriptive writing of the middle Snake River, especially the Hells Canyon section, conjured up the image of a grand yet grim and foreboding land. In my mind the authors painted a place both heroic and horrifying. It was sinister, foreboding, somber, barren, treacherous, and dark—all words that belie the incredible, dynamic, and captivating surroundings. We were told that at the canyon's greatest depth daylight is fleeting, that after the sun's brief appearance somber black cliffs of basalt slip back into the shadows, returning the canyon to its sinister mood. The image is dark and frightening. Names like the Seven Devils, which shape the eastern edge of the canyon, denote a fearsome presence of evil that underscores the region's darker image. One can easily imagine devils dwelling in the parapets, granted escape from their captivity in hell so long as they remain confined to places like Devils Throne, Twin Imps, Purgatory Lake, the Ogre, or the Goblin. Occasional names such as Horse Heaven, Heaven's Gate, or Paradise Lake are but futile attempts to make the region less horrific.

Words that paint the canyon's negative image go back as far as the colorful writing of Washington Irving, who described the 1811 Hells Canyon tragedy of the Wilson Price Hunt expeditionary party and the later canyon misfortunes of Capt. Benjamin Bonneville. Irving's tales of those two exploring parties fed popular mythology and formed the nucleus of an image that lingers today. That "accursed mad river" forced Hunt and his ragged, starving men into the winter mountains.[2] Bonneville's party encountered many "sharp and rocky ridges" projecting into the stream and "perpendicular precipices," which "rendered it impossible" for them to stay along the riverbank. The deeper they penetrated, the more "frowning in bleak and gloomy grandeur" their surroundings grew, causing the men's hearts to "quail under their multiplied hardships."[3] The ominous tones of later writers perpetuate the image. A 1903 author wrote about the "mysterious cavern" at Mountain Sheep Rapids, where "rockwalls of tremendous height" were crowded so close together that the canyon assumed the "darkness of evening." In 1977 William Ashworth described rapid following rapid "in stupefying succession" and the "sense of impending doom" one experiences while surging toward "the vortex of a maelstrom." Once caught in the rapid "there is a pounding and surging and an overwhelming sensation of brute strength."[4] And a momentary gripping fear; I remember it well.

From the pit of Hells Canyon come embellished stories to help frame the image of the land. Neither beast nor man escapes those stories. Take for example the sidehill gouger, a relative of today's cow but unique to the steep canyon country because of its adaptation to the environment. With legs longer on one side than the other it can safely graze the hillsides that are "steeper than a cow's face." According to Clem Stretchett, there were two species, some with long legs on the left side, and some with long legs on the right side. One animal grazed clockwise, the other counterclockwise. Stretchett wondered how the two animals avoided "a head-on impasse."[5] Crazy, yes, but would such a silly story be told if the land did not invite it? One rancher frequently claimed that Hells Canyon was the only place on earth where he could sit in his cabin and watch his cattle herd through his smokestack.[6]

Most of the stories had a kernel of truth but grew more bizarre with the telling. Some were bald-faced lies. I overhead this tale in the mid 1980s. About a hundred years ago a reclusive cannibal lived deep in the canyon. Over the years his grisly behavior explained the disappearance of many settlers and miners. Though I've seen no other reference to this tale, the storyteller spoke with the assurance of one who knew. After all, an old-timer who lived in the canyon told him it was true. It's the kind of tale you might expect from such "accursed" country. Gently undulating green hills of a "civilized" landscape do not spawn those kinds of stories. But frowning basaltic precipices and brutish rivers do. That is the kind of place that transformed my childhood fear into my adult curiosity, luring me on to learn more about the stories of larger-than-life characters.

A few canyon folk are remembered for their unconventional behavior. People seem willing to accept others' eccentricities; nonetheless their stories are told across the miles and over the generations. As they were remembered in the telling, they have become an important part of canyon lore. Most of the canyon people were just plain folk, but they too seem to have emerged from canyon lore in hyperbole. They are friendlier and more hospitable, hardier or stronger-willed there than anyplace else. Everyone likes everyone; everyone can do anything they put their mind to; and everyone willingly endures the tough life the canyon offers. Canyon mythology rarely admits that some of the people were lazy, some inhospitable, some unhappy, some just not likable. The land molded the image if not the reality.

The place that so indelibly marked both residents and visitors surprisingly resisted the name Hells Canyon until quite recently. The authors of *Snake River of Hells Canyon* suggest that the first reference to Hells Canyon appeared in McCurdy's *Marine History of the Pacific Northwest*, published in 1895. But the name was not widely accepted for another forty years.[7] Before then, though some locals called it Hells Canyon, people also knew the canyon regionally as Box Canyon, Seven Devils Gorge, or Grand Canyon of Snake River. The Oregon Board of Geographic Names claims that the name Hells had nothing to do with Hades, but was a corruption of Heller's Canyon, a small side gorge entering from the Oregon side at river mile 246. But as William Ashworth noted, "the fact was that for this dark, narrow crack in the earth a name suggesting the netherworld was singularly appropriate." Alfreda Elsensohn, Idaho County historian of the 1930s and '40s, thought that the canyon should be called Haller's Canyon, honoring "an old sea captain" who in the late 1800s was the "first man to attempt navigating the full length of the Snake canyon between Weiser and Lewiston." Elsensohn also credits a 1911 government surveyor for naming a small section of the gorge Hells Canyon.[8] About the same time, Lewiston author Robert G. Bailey published the book that scared me so as a child—*Hells Canyon: Seeing Idaho through a Scrap Book*—and helped popularize the name throughout the region. The book's circulation, however, was limited and probably had little to do with establishing the name beyond the interior Pacific Northwest. Otherwise, the canyon was virtually unknown until the 1940s, when the dam-building controversy and Oregon's journalist-turned-statesman Sen. Richard Neuberger thrust the region and its name into the national spotlight.

There was also no agreement as to the precise location of Hells Canyon. All that I knew was that it was some mysterious place far to the south of my home. Bailey described the canyon as beginning fifty miles below the northern bend of the Snake River and ending at Johnson Bar, a distance of forty miles, with today's Hells Canyon Dam in the middle. The title of Grace Jordan's book, *Home Below Hells Canyon*, clearly indicates that she located her 1930s Kirkwood Bar home downstream from or "below" Hells Canyon. The geologist Tracy Vallier, who refuses to get caught in the naming controversy, defines Hells Canyon as the stretch between the Oxbow and the mouth of the Grande Ronde River.[9] Congress settled the matter in 1975 by establishing Hells Canyon National Recreation Area (HCNRA). Legally, Hells Canyon now begins at Hells Canyon Dam and ends at the HCNRA border one mile south of the Washington-Oregon line, seventy-two miles total. The great canyon is now labeled, confined within established borders, and managed.

For forty miles, Hells Canyon averages a depth of fifty-five hundred feet; it is a mile and a half at its deepest point from the summit of He Devil to the edge of the Snake River. The steep walls, rock-strewn hill slopes, and narrow finger of a gorge through which surges the wild Snake River all contribute the physical attributes that lend themselves to the canyon's freedom and imagery. It is a serious land of unprecedented depth, wildness, and majestic grandeur, free to define its own borders and its own degree of human control. That unruly nature plus the hardships and heartache many people knew and associate with the canyon, the stories of those difficulties and the exaggerations they spawned, help explain why the middle Snake River resisted a name and established borders for so long.

Today the great Snake River canyon is less shrouded in mystery, less subject to overblown imagery. For nearly fifty years it has been studied, surveyed, probed, explored, filmed, photographed, and written about by an annual parade of visitors. Their arrival in increasingly larger numbers reflects our changing national attitudes toward nature. Wild lands are no longer places to be avoided or developed. Our national psyche does not demand a gently undulating landscape with verdant vegetation for a place to be acceptable and inviting; nor does it demand four-star resorts. A dry, hot, barren, rugged, and remote place like the middle Snake River now draws thousands of people from around the globe, people who come to it for its restorative powers and the lessons the natural landscape teaches. The canyon's history first drew me there; the rocks I pick up each time I visit, take home, and treasure now pull me back time after time. There is indeed much to learn from the rocks, where our story begins.

Chapter 2

According to the Rocks

Some people may think that a geologist's explanation about the canyon's origins is as bizarre as the tale of the Hells Canyon cannibal. But the canyon's whispers tell geologists a fascinating and imminently plausible tale. Its substantiation lies in the canyon rocks. Layers of basalt, sandstone, limestone, and bold outcrops of granite speak loudly and clearly to those scientists who take the time to listen; they reveal the intrigue of a good detective story and the mystical element of an ancient legend.

Tracy Vallier is one scientist who listens to the rocks. To him, the land of Hells Canyon is dynamic and alive, and has been since his romancing the canyon began in 1963 when dissertation research first took him there. Over the years he and others have gradually revealed the layers of the canyon's prehistoric origins. An amazing story comes to life. It begins 300 million years ago, with the formation of the oldest rocks in the canyon. They, however, were not formed at or even near their present location, but thousands of miles away in the equatorial zone of the Pacific Ocean.[1]

To understand the setting, imagine yourself millions of years ago looking down on the ancestral Pacific Ocean from a position high above. By dramatically accelerating time, you will see a chain of volcanoes emerging from the ocean floor. An arc of islands takes shape. It rides on the back of a tectonic plate, drifting in a northeasterly direction toward North America. Along its journey this exotic terrane amalgamates with other exotic or drifting terranes of island arcs.[2] The composite terrane ultimately meets ancestral North America, where it becomes "wrapped in the embrace of [the] more ancient continent and [in time] stroked by rapids of Snake River."[3]

Riding the Tectonic Plates

How have Vallier and others come to such a hypothesis? The answer lies in the relatively new theory of plate tectonics. Scientists began to connect pieces of the river canyon's puzzle by examining geological processes at the "ring of fire," Pacific islands of the Tonga, Mariana, Kurile, and Aleutian chains, and comparing their findings to the fossil records, rock types, and alignment of the rocks' magnetic particles they found in Hells Canyon.

The oldest rocks in the land that now encompasses the Blue Mountains of southeastern Washington, eastern Oregon, and western Idaho, through which natural forces carved the dramatic Hells Canyon, are part of a geological formation known as the Blue Mountain Island Arc. The arc's violent origins were on the equatorial seafloor of the Pacific Ocean, where tectonic plate movement caused two or more slabs of the earth's lithospheric plates to collide. The younger, lighter mass forced the older, heavier slab below it, forming a subduction zone. As the subducted slab was pulled down, the upper

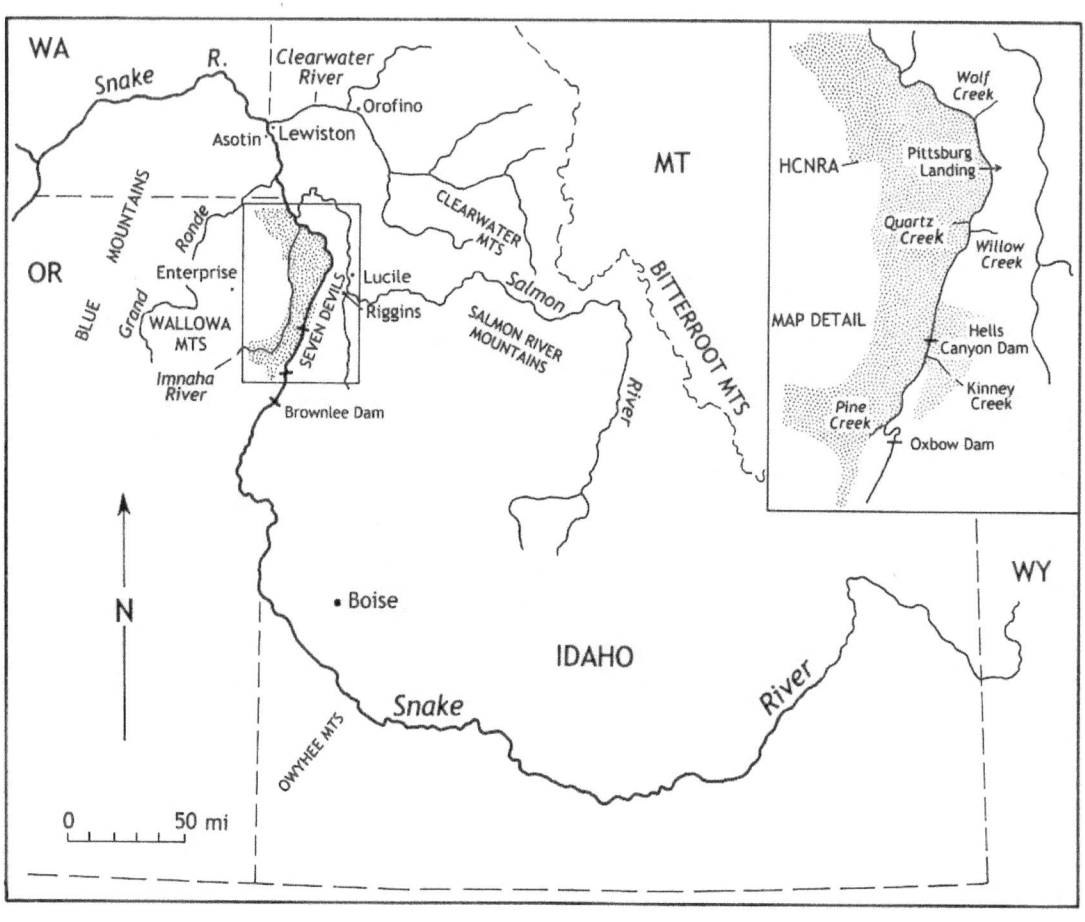

Map 2.1. Geographic features of eastern Oregon and Idaho. Map detail shows some sites mentioned in chapter 2.

slab lifted and in places partially melted. Lava erupted out of volcanoes, and magmas crystallized deep under the growing volcanoes to form plutons, or large rock bodies. At times, the volcanoes spewed volcanic ash into the atmosphere. The entire process resulted in an uplifted, curved string of mountainous islands.

Increased pressure from colliding oceanic plates ultimately caused the arc to fragment, forming islands of older rocks that lifted along faults. Basins also formed between the islands; they grew, deepened, were partly filled with sediment, and migrated with the wandering islands. Today if you examine Hells Canyon near Pittsburg Landing and the Coon Hollow Creek area south of the Washington-Oregon border, you can still see the rocks formed from sediments that filled those basins. Sedimentary rocks also formed on the quieter ocean floor at some distance from the volcanic activity and evolved into thick deposits of limestone and shale. A portion of the vast Martin Bridge Limestone deposit that formed in that manner extends from the Snake River across the Nez Perce reservation nearly to Orofino, Idaho. Most of the limestone is now buried under younger lava flows of the Columbia River basalt, but the limestone is visible near the mouth of the Grande Ronde River on both the Washington and Idaho sides. Another more visible and dramatic example of the Martin Bridge Limestone deposit is near Kinney Creek on the Snake River, about 120 miles upriver from Lewiston. That same deposit forms cliffs high in the Wallowa Mountains and along the Salmon River near Lucile, Idaho.[4]

Traveling with the movement of the lithospheric plates at a rate of two to three inches a year and changing in size and composition as they amalgamated with other exotic terranes, sections of the Blue Mountain Island Arc ultimately reached the shore of the old North American continent. About 120 to 130 million years ago, as ocean waves lapped the shoreline of what is now Idaho, the islands collided with the continent. The islands and the continent were zippered together along a suture zone that is exposed near Riggins, Idaho. The zone continues through the South Fork of the Clearwater River before arching westward to the confluence of the Snake and Clearwater Rivers near Lewiston, Idaho. With that fusing of the Blue Mountains Island Arc and other terranes adrift along the continental margin, North America expanded 350 to 400 miles westward and acquired valuable real estate—Washington, Oregon, California, and British Columbia.

Scientists estimate that it took as long as another 100 million years, from about 130 to 30 million years ago, for the present size and shape of the West Coast to emerge. As the exotic terranes collided with the continent the region lifted, and the ocean was displaced westward. Forces were so great that mountains of central Idaho thrust upward, probably to greater heights than today.

The theory postulating the formation, moving, and colliding of the island arcs explains the mysterious origins of many Snake River anomalies—the Martin Bridge Limestone at the mouth of the Grande Ronde River, the unique sedimentary rock formation exposed at Pittsburg Landing and Coon Hollow, pillow lava high up in the Seven Devils that could only have been formed in the ocean, and tropical fossils embedded in limestone and shale thousands of feet above sea level in what is now a temperate, northern climate. Evidence of the islands is visible at sites where later erosion exposed these original rocks—the dark, massive rocks at Hells Canyon Dam that now tower thousands of feet above the river, for example. They were all part of the Blue Mountains Island Arc, all formed far away and under the ocean.

Rivers of Lava and Water

Yet many more forces were called upon to mold the canyon's unique configurations. Even today's most casual observer of the rocks and forms of Hells Canyon can see striking evidence of the subsequent plateau basalt stage of geological transformation. Between about 17 and 14 million years ago, volcanic lava flows transfigured the gentle landscape of the eroded and welded island arcs, leaving in their wake intriguing shapes of jagged, black basaltic flow rocks arranged, as if by a sculptor, on the otherwise level plateau.

The earth opened and belched forth massive flows of liquid rock—lava that is said to have moved like a river, sometimes as fast as forty miles an hour. Known collectively as the Columbia River Basalt Group, successive lava flows spread indiscriminately across more than seventy thousand square miles of the ancient land, filling in and leveling off the old terrain as it deposited layer upon layer of molten lava.[5] A vast tableland formed on the pile of lava flows—some as much as ten thousand feet thick—spreading from the Bitterroot to the Cascade Mountains. An upward tilt of its southeastern corner forced many of the ancient, meandering rivers into a northwesterly course.

Figure 2.1. Two of Wally Beamer's tour boats docked at Beamer's Heller Bar restaurant and boat landing just downriver from the confluence of the Grande Ronde and Snake River. The background hill provides an excellent example of basalt terracing characteristic of the canyon. (Photo by author, 1981.)

The oldest of the lava flows—the first stage of the Columbia River Basalt Group—is the Imnaha Basalt. For more than 500,000 years, from its origins near Oregon's Imnaha River, molten rock spewed forth from long fissures. The second stage, the Grande Ronde Basalt, lasted much longer, nearly 2 million years. During that time more than sixty flows "erupted at a greater average rate than is found either before or after this period."[6] Single lava flows of the Grande Ronde Basalt, each one lasting an average of about 10,000 years, flooded the entire Columbia Plateau as the center of the volcanic activity gradually moved north to the Oregon, Washington, Idaho juncture. The younger formations had short eruptive histories; some were localized, like the Pomona flows that form the bent columns near Asotin, Washington, on the Snake River.

With each eruption the lava belched forth, covered the land, and then cooled. A layer of soil gradually formed over the cooled rock before the next outpouring of lava thousands of years later, trapping the soil between the two basalt layers like a sandwich. The cycle continued, layer upon layer upon layer. Look high on the canyon walls to see the most dramatic examples. Strata delineated in different colors, thicknesses, and compositions pile one upon the other, creating a distinctive spectacle in nature's muted array in tones of black, brown, gold, and tan. In a few places—near the mouth of the Grande Ronde River and north to Lewiston, between the Imnaha River and Wolf Creek, and between Oxbow and Brownlee Dams—those layered lava flows reach the canyon floor.

Depending on the configuration of the earlier topography, the lava flows assumed shapes other than simple layering. In some places the slow-moving liquid rock filled old stream canyons. It then cooled and formed columns at right angles to the older surface. Spectacular polygonal columns resulted. Multilayered and radiating, these tilted columns resemble the spokes of an old wagon wheel. An excellent example is found across the Snake River from Asotin. In other places, such as the Lewiston/Clarkston valley, repeated lava flows and subsequent erosion tended to smooth out the topography, removing most of the rough terrain and giving the land soft, wrinkled contours of an aging face. An occasional prominent basalt landmark, like Swallows Nest Rock, which stands as a sentinel over the valley, erupted from a nearby fissure and filled a preexisting low area, probably a stream channel. Evidence of the earth's groaning and wrenching shows in a variety of locations throughout the entire Snake River canyon, each exhibiting its own unique design in a stark, commanding beauty. Along some slopes the lava cooled perpendicular to the surface, forming crystallized clustered columns of five- to eight-sided polygonal shapes, creating a hillside design that contrasts starkly with its surroundings. Excellent examples of that type of columnar jointing also appear at the Asotin site and far to the south at the Oxbow opposite Pine Creek.[7]

The basaltic rock forms created during this period of geological activity invite creative interpretations. All along the river, I see forms that suggest human or animal shapes preserved in motion. I imagine places where grand battles between contending factions occurred, where man or beast hid in ambush behind the rocks or met in open combat along the slopes. As I look upward to the canyon rim, I see ancient fortresses, crumbling castles, or terraced fields and vineyards. Let the land's configurations give wings to your own flights of fancy. Enjoy those somber, jagged, dark rocks that speak of the geological formations that so uniquely characterize the inland Northwest.

Scientists admit they know nothing about geological processes that occurred after the main phase of basalt eruptions and before the third—Wanapum—phase, a period of about 8 million years. The evidence is gone. It's as if the land rested, enjoying what was, in geological terms, a brief period of time until measurable geological forces relentlessly resumed their molding of the landscape with the fourth and final—Saddle Mountains—basalt eruption. It began approximately 6 million years ago and continues to the present. During this period the Seven Devils, Wallowa Mountains, and Blue Mountains were slowly uplifted, and the Snake River cut its canyon home. The land we know today gradually evolved, but the evolution was not always gentle.

It remains a matter of conjecture as to where ancient Snake River originally flowed. Some speculate that it moved in a relatively straight westward line through southern Idaho and Oregon toward the California coast.[8] If that is true, it seems reasonable to assume that a sudden cataclysmic event altered its course and forced the river into a ninety-degree turn to the north. One suggestion is that the same internal pressures that created the Wallowa and Seven Devils Mountains also thrust the Owyhee Mountains in southwest Idaho directly into the Snake River's westward path. The river became a lake—known in geological circles today as Lake Idaho. Numerous tributaries, melting glaciers, and heavy rainfall fed the growing lake to an ever increasing volume and size. Then a breach in the lake's natural boundaries about 2 million years ago transformed that huge volume of water into an immense earth-wrenching flood.

Others theorize that the flood spilled north through what had been a north-flowing tributary to the Salmon River. That tributary stream eroded its way headward and essentially captured the large lake, opening a northern outlet for the maelstrom. The surge of water began cutting through the faulted rock in search of its new riverbed. Over the next 2 million years torrents ebbed and flowed, carving with each flow a deeper and wider gorge as tectonic forces lifted the surrounding mountains.[9]

The Snake River then was not the river we know today. Sometimes swollen by melting glaciers and heavy rainfall, its volume grew great and its flow intense. Other times natural blockages formed temporary lakes. One especially notable flood occurred about 15,000 years ago when ancient Lake Bonneville (predecessor of Salt Lake in Utah) spilled its waters north through the gorge of the Snake River. The lake left its banks at Red Rock Pass and flowed into the Snake River in the vicinity of American Falls, Idaho, increasing the volume about one thousand times greater than present spring runoffs.[10] The swollen river surged north, eroding and widening its banks. In places, where the canyon is narrow, accumulated debris formed temporary dams. Briefly held in quiet captivity, while sediment filtered down to the riverbed, the dam then collapsed leaving the sedimentary deposits high above the river's water level. Scientists now believe the Bonneville Flood lasted for a very short period, possibly only a few months, a remarkably brief time for such visible change to be permanently etched on the canyon slopes. Scattered all along the river are the terraces and benches, as the locals call them, formed during that and other floods. One of the best examples is the high terrace at Temperance Creek. Some benches are visible from the river or from above; others are hidden in the many gulches and canyons that feed into Snake River. On some of those benches—many large enough to support a small Indian village or settler's homestead—humans, much, much later, made their homes.

These ancient floods also deposited sand and gravel, especially evident throughout the river valley. In places where deposits are accessible, as in Lewiston, Idaho, mining marketable sand and gravel is a lucrative business, and has been for 60 years.[11] To me those deposits provide rich material for my imagination. Did the Lewiston/Clarkston valley then look as if it had dropped into an immense, deep depression, as it now does? Would I have liked the valley then? Or the canyon?

Mystifying Colors, Curious Features, and Enduring Change

It is also challenging to imagine what it must have been like to be living in the depth of Hells Canyon when Mt. Mazama exploded. Crater Lake, a blue gem of a lake in the Cascade Mountains of western Oregon, is a caldera of a once towering Mt. Mazama. The ancient mountain dwarfed the snowy peaks of today's Cascade Range. When it erupted about 6,900 years ago, endless blankets of ash descended on people and animals as far away as Hells Canyon and throughout the entire Pacific Northwest, utterly disrupting their lives. Unlike ash from Mt. St. Helens' 1980 eruption, which fell in a light skiff at the northern end of the Snake River canyon and within a few weeks disappeared, Mazama's heavy ash storm left traces that are visible to this day.

The ash most likely fell in an even blanket, covering the land like a heavy yet gentle snowfall. Over time rain, melting snow, and wind erosion carried the ash to gullies and streambeds, which concentrated the deposits on alluvial fans and terraces. Today you see the thick deposits sparkling white amid black and brown rocks and tawny vegetation. Some ash deposits are near the river margin; others are high up the canyon slopes and tributary canyons.

Patches of red and orange sometimes shout out from the canyon's dark, muted colors. For years people have speculated that these colorful rocks high on both the Idaho and Oregon slopes near Willow and Quartz Creeks (about twenty-two miles below Hells Canyon Dam), were alum deposits. Actually they are residual mineral deposits called gossans, formed by hot, circulating fluids from a deep magma chamber. Iron-rich minerals precipitated along faults and in crushed zones. Pyrite, chalcopyrite, and other sulfide minerals formed, then the iron and sulfur in those minerals oxidized to produce the yellow and red colors we see today. It is that dumping area—gossans—that told the miners to look deeper, for chances were good that the hot fluids also penetrated the interior rocks, creating veins of gold, copper, or silver.[12]

Snake River canyon looks like a place where by simply turning the shovel or sluicing a stream you could get lucrative mineral returns. To the novice's eye, the rocks hugging the river margin look the most promising, not the muted rocks higher up the hills to which a seasoned miner would turn. Along the river, highly polished rocks glisten in the sun, their glimmer reflecting in the water pools below. Surely, vast amounts of silver or gold must lie trapped within the rock to give off such shine. No, say the geologists. Those are the same as the dull rocks above the high water line. Two different processes give those river rocks their unique coloration and glimmer. Some retain their original color—brown, green, black, or maroon—but the river's polishing action during high water enhances the color. It is not the water itself that does the polishing, but the suspended sand and silt. In some places, if the water is forced into a circular pattern or other repetitive movement, the abrasive action even carves curious grooves and depressions into the rocks.

The rocks' metallic luster, which is even more eye-catching, is a coating of manganese and iron minerals. There is some debate over how that coating is formed, but the river is clearly the catalyst. Apparently the process is similar to desert varnishing, in which night dew moistens the rocks and then the warmth of the morning sun rapidly evaporates the water. The sequence of hot dry air and rapid evaporation draws the manganese or iron-rich minerals and moisture form the rock to its surface. In Hells Canyon some of the minerals may also be carried in the water and deposited on the rock before evaporation.[13] The visual results are splendid.

Today when we observe the gossans, ash, basalt, granite, limestone, polished rocks, and all the other miraculous changes nature has brought to the canyon over an inconceivably long period of time, we assume that the work must be finished. It looks finished. But we occupy only milliseconds on the geological clock. Unless we witness a cataclysmic change like the eruption of Mt. St. Helens or a high-magnitude earthquake, how can we possibly see those changes? Nonetheless, it is possible to observe one less dramatic but still significant geological transformation, and enjoy some great recreation in the process.

Think about rapids. How are they made?

At the mouth of most every small, tributary stream, or often at the bottom of a steep, unstable slope, there are rapids. They range in degrees of difficulty from insignificant riffles to class 5 rapids. The great rapids, the ones you hear roaring in the distance, make your heart pound a little faster and your adrenaline flow and give the river canyon its unique, distinguishing signature. Many of those rapids were formed hundreds, maybe thousands, of years ago. Annals and tales of river travelers repeatedly recorded and warned against some we still consider to be the worst, like the rapids at Wild Sheep, Granite Creek, or Waterspout.

At any moment an equally treacherous rapid could quickly materialize through the same conditions that created those infamous obstacles. Frozen slopes, suddenly thawed after a heavy snowfall, or a torrential cloudburst can convert a gentle creek into a gully washer within minutes or instantly loosen the rocks of an unstable hillside and send them crashing downward. Boulders, rocks, gravel, dirt, trees, and bushes wash down the streams and canyon walls. If the debris dumps into the river and the boulders are large and numerous, with angry, relentless determination the impeded river races over and around them, creating another turbulent rapid. If gravel, dirt, and small rocks end up in the channel or along the margin, the river is perhaps less dramatically but nonetheless significantly changed. New gravel bars reconfigure the water's flow and depth.

Geologic forces constantly build up and tear down just as they have always done and will continue to do. When we see some dramatic transformation, we are reminded that the canyon—its face and its many moods—might change instantly or at a pace slower than any human can fathom; nonetheless it is in a state of perpetual alteration.

We humans now contribute to river changes. Even though our participation has been insignificant on the geologic clock, our contribution is measurable, obvious, and, I believe, unfortunate. On my first trip into the canyon, in 1980, a few sandy beaches still graced the river margin above its confluence with the Salmon River. Pictures taken decades earlier show inviting beaches on both sides of the river through the entire canyon. Now there are almost no beaches, not even below the free-flowing Salmon River. Snake River dams at the upper end of the canyon block the natural movement of South Idaho's sediment, which would otherwise augment the river beaches. The dams also release different amounts of water hourly, daily, weekly, and annually. That frequent and inconsistent release flushes sand from the tributaries below the dams almost as quickly as it is deposited. Nature's cycle of deposit and flush has been replaced by the dam's capricious schedule, and dams don't build beaches. Many believe that each jet boat roaring through the canyon contributes to the tearing away of the beaches. I think the dams are the bigger offender, but it is obvious that as the number of powerboats increase the wave action pounding the shoreline will increase proportionately and something will change.

Possibly, the erosion of the shoreline by river craft and water fluctuation is minimal when viewed in geological terms. It is difficult, however, for those of us bound by a small sliver of time, to view the intrusion of three dams—Hells Canyon, Brownlee, and Oxbow—as anything but a major impediment to the natural flow of the river and certainly a blemish on the natural beauty of the landscape. How long the dams will be there we cannot say; how great a role they play in the canyon's continuous geological transformation is also difficult to assess. What we do know is that for the first time in the canyon's geological history, humans have contributed in an overt and deliberate way to changing the natural character of the canyon even though their period of activity is minuscule in a geological sense. In earlier times human activity either harmonized with the canyon's natural cycle or lacked the technology to make dramatic change. The canyon's geological evolution barely acknowledged the presence of such people. Indeed, land forms, seasonal cycles, plants and wildlife, and river features had a powerful influence on human activity, not the reverse.

Figure 2.2. An excellent example of varied geological formations along the Kirkwood to Pittsburg Landing trail. Idaho is on the right; Oregon on the left. (Photo by Sheri Worle, 2000.)

Chapter 3

A Land Diverse & Bountiful

It was a hot July afternoon. One hundred four degrees I heard someone say. We were standing at the confluence of the Snake and Imnaha Rivers. The heat was suffocating, the air still. There were no birds in flight, no sounds of nature save the rivers' roar. Stunted hackberry and willow trees lethargically hugged the shoreline. Bunchgrass and fescue—long since turned from green to a golden tan—looked thirsty and tired along the adjacent slopes. I had been sharing a bit of the site's history with others in my party when we saw him.

Across the Imnaha River from where we stood, a shirtless, hatless young man clad only in shorts and boots walked down the trail and into the water, woefully disoriented and oblivious to everything around him save his need for immediate relief from the heat. He was alone. Our offers to help fell on deaf ears. Back through the old Mountain Chief mine tunnel we went, boarded our jet boat, and drifted downstream to where he was. By then he had waded into water up to his shoulders. We pulled him into the boat and gradually pieced together his story.

He was a Californian with an Australian accent having a wilderness experience in Oregon. He had hoped to hike down the Imnaha River trail to the Snake River and then upstream along the Oregon shoreline to Dug Bar, where his friends would pick him up. Confident that they would be there, he refused our offers to take him to Lewiston, despite his possible need for medical help. We therefore ferried him three miles back to Dug Bar and left him. That was the last we saw or heard of him.[1]

The man obviously knew nothing about the canyon's geography. His Imnaha River trail dead-ended at the Snake River confluence. Cactus Mountain, projecting like a pyramid of stone directly into the two rivers, blocked his intended upstream route. Had he walked a few miles downriver, he would have found a barricading rock jungle there as well. Even worse, he ignored the temperature extremes that a few hundred feet in elevation bring. That ignorance nearly cost him his life.

In Snake River country, climatic conditions range from desert to alpine over a relatively short vertical distance. With the temperature comfortably warm at higher altitudes, it can be dangerously hot at river level, as our unsuspecting traveler discovered. Conversely, while freezing storms rage in the mountains above, winter touches the canyon floor but lightly. The stark elevation contrast is greatest in the heart of Hells Canyon. There, in the pit of the chasm, which even at midday lies in shadows, the eastern rim projects 8,043 feet above sea level. Seven miles in the distance, He Devil—the tallest peak of the Seven Devils Mountain Range—reaches heavenward another 1,350 feet. On the Oregon side a myriad of perpendicular rock outcroppings that extend the western rim 5,632 feet above sea level cast deep shadows across the river, blocking the afternoon sun from painting all but the very top of the opposite rim. Two miles back from the river and one mile above it, Hat Point—the highest promontory—towers above. Gradually, the elevation contrast diminishes toward the

Figure 3.1. The passengers are preparing to board Wally Beamer's mailboat at China Bar on the Oregon side of the river, a short distance upstream from Eureka Bar and the Imnaha River/Snake River confluence. (Photo by author, 1981.)

northern and southern ends of the canyon. Still, marked vegetation and climate differences remain. Even in Lewiston and Clarkston, where the canyon widens into an expansive amphitheater 2,700 feet below the surrounding uplands, the diversity in temperature, rainfall, and vegetation is pronounced.[2]

That elevation difference today provides wintertime outdoor recreational opportunities ranging from golf in December at the lowest elevations to a variety of winter sports in the mountains. During earlier times the contrast in elevations provided prehistoric and native populations with a way of life that followed a seasonal round of food gathering from low to high elevations and back. Unlike the young Californian, those people knew how to live in Hells Canyon.

The Seasonal Cycle

For thousands of years the Nez Perce and people of antiquity, who the Nez Perce believe were their ancestors, followed a seasonal life cycle well adapted to the region's elevation, vegetation, and climatic changes. Northern Paiute, Western Shoshone, and their ancestors made their homes in the southern reaches of the canyon as well. When cold winter winds ravaged the high country and heavy snowfall made trails impassable, the river canyon and tributary streams offered shelter and a constant supply of driftwood to burn. Wandering herds of deer, elk, mountain goats, and bighorn sheep sought food and winter refuge in the canyon and became easy prey for the Nez Perce atlatl, bow and arrow, or later rifle. Migratory fowl—Canada geese, ducks, the great blue heron, and the stately osprey—and spawning fish also supplemented the people's food reserves or provided them company and entertainment.

Far above the river valley, as winter's blanket of snow transformed blue, tree-covered mountains into white promontories glimmering in the morning sun, daytime canyon temperatures rarely dropped below freezing. If snow fell, it generally came in a light skiff. Grasses, bent and cushioned with age, cloaked the hillsides in a robe of velvet that gradually turned from tan to a muted green with the winter rains. Yet even in the dead of winter, when extravagant washes of lavender painted the distant hills, brilliant splashes of deep orange cocklebur clusters, golden coyote willow branches, and bright red osier dogwood highlighted the river margin. It was a time for the Nez Perce and their ancestors to relish the winter beauty surrounding them while making preparations for spring.

At winter's end, as the meadowlark proclaimed spring's debut, the air warmed and freshened with the clean smell of recent growth. New grasses emerged—first near the riverbanks, then gradually transforming the hillside and mountain slopes into a yellow green blanket—providing feed for the wild game that grazed from the lower hills to alpine and subalpine regions. The seasonal cycle had begun for the native people, who followed the grazing game and harvested the maturing plants. Their upward trek took the families over canyon slopes painted with yellow arrowleaf balsamroot and sagebrush buttercups, over blue and white tonella flowers, the rust-red heads of Indian paintbrush, and past contrasting shades of blue camas and wild hyacinth. They moved through stands of white serviceberry and syringa blossoms surrounded by white and purple vetch—vivid reminders of nature's beauty and abundance. Climbing ever upward, the people gazed down on the Snake River as it was gradually transformed into a narrow, silver ribbon. The large yellow flowers of the prickly pear cactus covered rocky slopes; blue purple upland larkspur and deep pink Snake River phlox dominated the panorama.

Once out of the canyon, the native people left behind the raw days of summer. Yellow hues of clover, flannel mullein, and sunflower had gently changed the character of the slopes and river margin by the time the people reached their hunting and harvest camps. Green grasses on the canyon slopes had already turned to a golden tan and would soon bear the parched appearance of desert vegetation. There, in the higher elevations, the people could enjoy the cooler weather and abundance the land had to offer, briefly returning to the hot canyon to catch migrating fish and harvest roots. Even then, as the men fished and the women dug the roots, they avoided the hottest days of July and August, when the sun seared the parched land and midday temperatures hovered near one hundred degrees.

Then, as the night air changed from chilly to cold, falling leaves washed the surroundings with a new color palette and proclaimed the completion of another year's seasonal cycle. It was time to return to the sheltered winter villages. The people reached the canyon in late September in time to gather lower-elevation plants, such as serviceberries, black raspberries, chokecherries, blackberries, and red rose hips. Seed pods from yellow salsify, horehound, cocklebur, and teasel attached themselves to the people's clothing—nature's way of ensuring next summer's plant proliferation. Moving on through grasses gracefully arched under heavy seed heads and patches of buckwheat, yellow sunflowers, and dull red sumac, the people returned to their winter villages near tributary streams where thorny, woody, and multi-stemmed shrubs like snow gooseberry, wild rose, blackberries, western clematis, and red osier dogwood grew in abundance. As nature prepared for rest and rebirth, the village residents shared their winter sanctuary with the canyon's small creatures—raccoons, badgers, skunks, weasels, ferrets, beavers, and river otters. Black, brown, and grizzly bears; bobcats, coyotes, and cougar sought refuge from the winter along with deer, elk, mountain goats, and big-horned sheep. Another seasonal cycle had ended.

People of Antiquity

Archeologists tell us people have lived in Hells Canyon for at least seven thousand and possibly as long as ten thousand years.[3] For perhaps four thousand years, small groups of aboriginal people—extended families of ten to fifteen members—made their homes in cave-like depressions at the base of rocky cliffs near the Snake River or along tributary streams. These were secure yet accessible areas where the rock walls provided warmth and protection. A hide-covered, porchlike structure with a wood frame projected from the mouth of these shelters, providing covering from the sun and rain.[4]

Then, from three to five thousand years ago, pithouses replaced the rock shelter homes, giving the people a greater variety of sites to accommodate a growing population The villages varied in size according to the size of the extended family; the larger villages consisted of from thirty to thirty-five structures often arranged in stair-step fashion on a naturally terraced bench with the larger homes situated at the top. The individual family's home—a circular depression in the ground two to three yards in diameter and approximately three feet below ground level—had a level floor with the dirt sides cut at a slight outward slant. A willow, alder, cottonwood, or syringa wood frame surrounded the pit in a conical shape, with the wood arranged tepee style at the top. Mats made from grasses, tule, Indian hemp, or cattails—all of which grew along the waterways—covered the frame. (Domestic objects such as mats, baskets, snowshoes, cradle boards, and similar items were made from the same natural materials.) People entered their homes from above, using a ladder. Inside, a fire circle occupied the middle, with family and personal items stored along the outside walls. Menstrual huts, sweat bath houses, storage and refuse facilities also had a pithouse design.[5]

Scientists date those prehistoric sites through stratigraphy and radiocarbon dating of organic remains. They also look for other clues of when and how long people occupied a specific location. Volcanic ash deposits, for example, can fingerprint an erupting mountain. Mt. Mazama erupted about 6,900 years ago. Consequently, evidence of human occupation found above a Mt. Mazama ash deposit dates the site more precisely. After the eruption, the American West experienced, first, a period of great drought lasting more than two thousand years that would have had an obvious impact on food sources. Then a long, wet period followed, destroying many fish spawning beds, thus reducing fish populations and forcing the people to use a broader range of food resources over a greater geographic range.[6] The native people thus began to follow the seasonal food cycle more extensively. Evidence of a changed lifestyle due to those gradual yet profound climatic changes helps scientists more precisely pinpoint human activities at archeological sites.

Archeologists can also look at the types of tools found at an archeological site. For example, spear points found at a specific location help to date that site before 2,500 years ago, when canyon hunters used the atlatl with a spear point. They are known to have been in existence for about 20,000 years. The six-foot-long hunting tool enabled an expert hunter to throw the short shaft and cut-rock spear point at the tool's end with precision and accuracy.[7] Then as the people adapted the bow and arrow, introducing "one of the most significant inventions" of North America to their subsistence technology, they further facilitated adaptation to the seasonal cycle.[8]

What was life like so long ago? To formulate an educated but fragmented guess about daily life in those prehistoric villages, anthropologists find clues in archeological evidence and apply them to what they have learned about native culture from contemporary Native American people. Were the ancient people primarily hunters or did they also harvest the land's abundance as their descendants did? Animal and fish bones found at archeological

Figure 3.2. The author is describing prehistoric village life to a Lewiston 4th grade class. The location high above the Snake River illustrates the ideal village site with a sheltered creek (left front) and ample expansion space on the bench. (Photo by Barry Kough, *Lewiston Morning Tribune*.)

sites provide important clues about some of their food sources, but with limited evidence concerning whether vegetation was part of their diet, the answer remains vague. Suckers and squawfish appear to have made up a larger portion of their diet than salmon. The people ate mussels when other resources were depleted. Boiled deer bones provided bone grease to make soup. Obsidian projectile points suggest that they engaged in early trade outside the canyon; copper trade items attest to later outside trade. To find both items at one site indicates that the site had been a pithouse-type village site for many generations. Several prehistoric sites, in fact, had extensive, uninterrupted use until someone either accidentally or intentionally destroyed it. Then, years later, another family rebuilt at the same location.

No clear evidence remains regarding prehistoric people's use of dugout canoes and rafts on the Snake River. Some scholars suggest if they did use them, they would have been made from driftwood.[9] During the historic period the Nez Perce crossed the river with rafts of hide stretched tight across a circular wooden frame.[10] Prehistoric people may have used them as well. Before they had horses, the people swam with the rafts to guide them across the river. Certainly, like their Nez Perce descendants, ancient travelers followed an intricate network of trails to convenient and safe river crossings, and in and out of the canyon on both sides of the Snake River.[11]

Canyon Art

Today's canyon visitor will rarely see evidence of rock shelters or pithouses, which so blend with the landscape they are all but invisible to the untrained eye. Nonetheless, nearly everyone hiking the trails or riding a boat sees numerous petroglyphs or pictograph rock art designs throughout the middle Snake River country.[12] Although scholars cannot date the rock art with precision, they believe most sites are only from 500 to 1,000 years old, due to the relatively fast rate of deterioration. Exceptions are pictograph fragments at Bernard Creek Rockshelter and the "highly patinated humans and mountain sheep at Buffalo Eddy,"

Figure 3.3. Prehistoric rock art at Buffalo Eddy on the Idaho side of the river. Rock art should never be chalk-highlighted, as it is here. When this picture was taken in the 1960s, people did not realize that chalking damaged the art. (Photo courtesy of Robert Hoyle.)

where evidence suggests they could have been painted between 6,000 and 8,000 years ago.[13] One hunting scene at Buffalo Eddy, for example, shows men using atlatls rather than bows and arrows, indicating that it was painted more than 2,500 years ago.

Petroglyphs—designs carved into the rock—are the older of the two art forms. Only a few are painted (although possibly paint on others simply wore off with time). Most petroglyph figures are abstract or anthropomorphic. No petroglyph shows horses, and there are no petroglyphs in the deepest part of the canyon south of Pittsburg Landing. There are, however, numerous sites downriver from that point, with major sites at Buffalo Eddy, Dug Bar, and Pittsburg Landing.[14]

Pictographs—designs painted onto the surface of the rock—are more numerous throughout the middle Snake River, appearing in small groups of fewer than fifty and in some places no more than ten.[15] They are colored red, green, yellow, black, white, or sometimes blue and are stained in such a way that the colors literally become part of the rock. The colors derive from naturally occurring minerals like red iron oxides made by quarrying the mineral from a convenient rock outcrop, pulverizing it, and possibly mixing it with an organic substance such as fish oil or bear grease to congeal the paint. The artist most likely applied the paint with his finger and used a feather or stick for extremely fine lines. Many pictograph images show bison, known to have lived in the region before the historic era, and horses with mounted riders, thus dating the art after the late 1600s.[16]

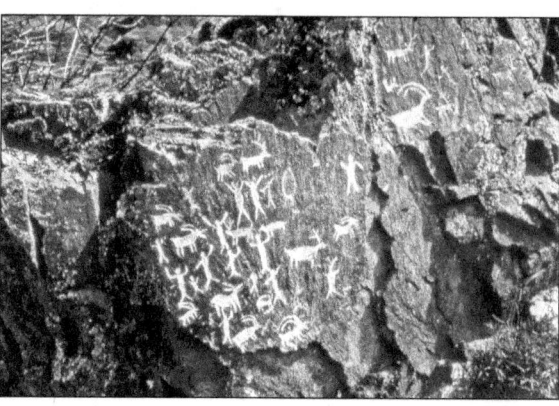

Buffalo Eddy, eighteen miles south of Asotin, is one of the most famous rock art sites. On large rock outcroppings along both sides of the Snake River are more than five hundred separate petroglyphs and a few pictographs. On the Idaho side of the river, on an extensive floodplain and alluvial fan deposit, both pictographs and petroglyphs depict images of geometric designs, anthropomorphic figures, animals, and men on horseback.[17] Interestingly, only petroglyphs appear on the less spacious Washington side of the river. All the images on both riverbanks demonstrate artistic skill and creativity. A fifty-foot-long snake carved into the cliff, for example, blends into the rock unless the light is exactly right. Some images are either too high to see well or are situated at such improbable locations one wonders how the artist managed to access the place. It's obvious the people who took the time to make the designs put considerable effort into their work and no doubt took pride in the finished product.

On the Washington side of the Buffalo Eddy site, the rock outcrop projects into the river; the county road from Asotin to the Grande Ronde River passes directly behind. In 1941, when a WPA crew built that stretch of the road, they destroyed two images and may have damaged others by cleaning off construction debris with an air compressor. The *Lewiston Morning Tribune* reported the loss but gave no description of the destroyed pictures. The article did describe the "most outstanding" picture that remained. It was a "set of three angular dotted lines, ranging in size, with a large circle at the end of each group. The upper tangent [had] parallel lines of ten small circles on the left arm and fourteen dots on the right side. The next two angles decrease[d] in size but [were] of similar construction." The author

Figure 3.4. Prehistoric art at Buffalo Eddy on the Washington side of the river. The picture was taken c. 1960. (Photo courtesy of Robert Hoyle.)

concluded that it was a map of a journey. The article identified other images at the site: "a coyote leaping at a deer, a brave spearing an elk, scenes of cougars and elk, and several writings which had nearly vanished under high water."[18] In the 1980s an Asotin County road crew damaged more rock art along the road, and on the Idaho side about the same time someone used an iron bar to pry off and steal part of one panel.

Many images from the Middle Snake River country are similar to art of the Columbia Plateau, indeed they are similar to ancient art found throughout North America. Unfortunately for scholars (but fortunately for those of us who love the mystery), few if any of the images can be interpreted with any degree of accuracy. Because there is no Rosetta Stone for North American rock art, we cannot make an educated guess about the meaning of Snake River art based on similarities elsewhere. Even the Nez Perce, whose ancestors probably created the art, have lost to time the stories the images tell. However, human nature being what it is, individuals feel obliged to offer explanations. One of the most moving interpretations came from an elderly woman of the Spokane tribe, who said that the designs "spoke of troubles, of seasons, of rain and of the passing of time."[19] Specific designs frequently reappear, suggesting that the images are celestial observations or travel instructions. Perhaps they are personal messages that document a successful hunt, help locate a good fishing hole, or report on the wildlife in the area. There might be a mystical connection to the birds, animals, or reptiles depicted in the designs. Possibly they reflect a vision quest or other spiritual experience. Then again, the art could be nothing more than a person's creative outlet or, as a few suggest, the prehistoric equivalent of modern graffiti. Unquestionably, the mystery of the rock art contributes to the mystery of Hells Canyon in an unforgettable way.

The Nez Perce and the Historic Period

I remember listening to a talk by Sandi McFarland, a member of the Nez Perce tribe and archeologist on the Clearwater National Forest. She held up a small purse, about the size of a fist; it was beautifully beaded into an intricate rose design. This wasn't the work of a night or a weekend but of eleven or twelve weeks, she explained. McFarland reminded us that long before the Nez Perce applied beading to clothes and personal items, they decorated their possessions with ornamentation made from feathers, quills, bones, shells, animal teeth and claws, or hair. If her people grubbed out a hand-to-mouth existence in an endless quest for food, she asked, would they have had the leisure to pursue such intricate, time-consuming work? No. In other words, the constraints of the environment did not *force* the Nez Perce into a seasonal round of hunting, fishing, and gathering, as so many scholars imply. Rather, the unique diversity and abundance of the land *blessed* the Nez Perce people.

The seasonal round served them well. True, there were times when the resources were limited, as Lewis and Clark discovered on their return trip in 1806, but the Nez Perce could always count on a renewed food source with the onset of spring. They also recognized the necessity of preserving the continuation of that source, whether by engaging in agricultural practices to ensure next year's crop or by burning an area to create abundant pasture. In so doing they adopted a relationship with their environment that was respectful, appreciative and sustaining. They were not at odds with an environment that forced them into an undesirable lifestyle; they lived in harmony with a uniquely diverse and abundant land.

When, in the early 1800s white explorers first reached the middle Snake River country—inaugurating the so-called historic period—they found very few native people living in the depths of Hells Canyon. Archeological evidence supports their find.[20] The explorers could not have known that some time beginning in the late 1700s and into the early 1800s a smallpox pandemic reached the Nez Perce, reducing their total population by a third or more.[21] Neither could they have known that approximately one hundred years earlier the Nez Perce acquired the horse, thus revolutionizing their culture. The deepest sections of the canyon could obviously not accommodate horses and were, therefore, no longer desirable places to live.

Sometime between the late 1600s and 1730, the Nez Perce traded with the Shoshone of southeast Idaho for their first horses and then rapidly became expert at raising and breeding the animals, building up "some of the largest horse herds on the continent."[22] Their ideal land and terrain provided ample grasslands to pasture the enormous herds as well as mild, protected valleys to shelter and corral the animals during winter. With horses, entire families could travel to distant buffalo plains and trade centers, exposing more people to a greater variety of cultures. Religion, dress, dances, games, family ties, even Nez Perce homes gradually reflected these outside influences.

The mobile tepee, adopted from the Great Plains, suited the temporary hunting, gathering, and fishing camps and provided the Nez Perce with a more versatile, semipermanent winter village home than the earlier pithouses. The new longhouse, for example, that might be up to 150 feet long, comfortably housed a number of married couples through the cold season. The Nez Perce built tepee frames from tall, straight, and abundant lodgepole pines, covered them with hides or tule mats, and anchored the covering to the ground with a ring of stones.[23] They pitched the more permanent structures over a shallow excavation.

Horses and tepees made the seasonal round much easier for the women, who did most of the work and were responsible for village and camp homes.[24] Using horses to transport themselves, their children, homes, and camp gear, the women selected the time and location of each move. Horses provided them with an ideal means of transporting the roots, berries, meat, hides, and fish they gathered and processed during the seasonal round.

Camas, a high percentage of the Nez Perce diet, grew in marshy prairies of higher elevations. When the plants bloomed in the spring—a sight once seen and never forgotten—the women marked the edible, blue flowered plants by bending the stems over, to distinguish them from the deadly, white-flowered death camas. Then in the fall they dug and processed

Map 3.1 Hells Canyon and the Middle Snake River country, home to the Nez Perce Indians.

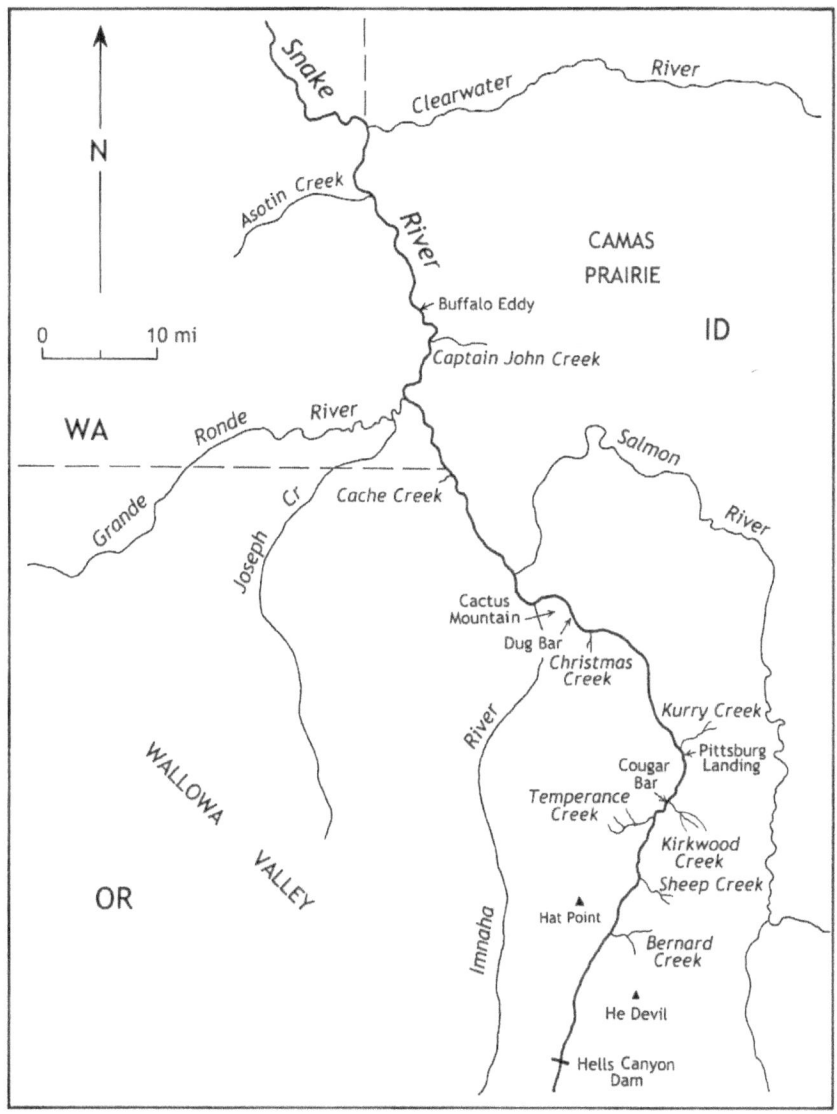

hundreds of pounds of the highly nutritious root.[25] After baking and steaming the roots in oven pits dug near the meadow camps, the women prepared roots as porridge for immediate consumption and shaped the rest into small cakes to store for the winter.

Other root staples included kouse, bitterroot, and yellow bell corms—all of which grew in the dry, rocky soil of Snake River valley.[26] For medicines and ointments the women also gathered canyon plants such as arrowleaf balsamroot, cattail, yarrow, horsetail, showy milkweed, and prickly pear. Medicines ranged from laxatives to digestive aids, skin ointments, and eyewash; they were used to dress wounds and stop bleeding, even to relieve run-down conditions. When food was otherwise scarce, the Nez Perce ate inner bark, or cambium, of lodgepole pine trees—peeled and mashed; when traveling in the spring where horse feed was scarce, the Nez Perce peeled the bark of black cottonwood trees and fed the inner bark and sap to the animals. Woven items or mats came from grasses; tobacco from kinnikinnick and red osier dogwood; "Indian ice cream" from beaten and sweetened buffalo berries; and tea or chewing gum from a wide variety of plants.[27] While women directed the camp activities and prepared their food, the men hunted elk, mule deer, and white-tailed deer, sometimes even mountain sheep, mountain goats, moose, bison, or antelope. Occasionally the women hunted small game like birds and rabbits.

From the first salmon run in June until the last runs in early fall, the men fished the rivers and high mountain creeks, using nets, spears, or weirs made of willow brush and poles,. At one of their most popular Snake River sites, just north of the mouth of Captain John Creek on the Idaho side, the Nez Perce fishermen built rock walls into the river to slow the current and create resting places for the migrating fish.[28] Besides salmon—their most important and abundant fish—the Nez Perce men caught steelhead trout, cutthroat trout, Dolly Varden, whitefish, sturgeon, western lamprey, chiselmouth, squawfish (pikeminnow), and suckers. The women cleaned, dried, and pounded most of the salmon for storage and baked, broiled, boiled, or smoked the rest.[29] Asotin Creek, or Hasotino—place of collection and "one of the largest and most important villages on Snake River"—supplied a great lamprey eel fishery when the migrating eel ascended Asotin Creek.[30] The Nez Perce also caught both green and white sturgeon in the Snake River until 1937, when Bonneville Dam on the Columbia River blocked the fish migration to the Pacific. Today, the Middle Snake River is one of the last strongholds of the great white sturgeon that have adapted to freshwater living, and although they do not have the longevity of their migratory predecessors, Hells Canyon sturgeon sometimes live to be fifty years or older and are almost equal in size to those reported from the early 1900s.[31]

Having horses to ride and pack shortened the travel time and eased the difficulties of the Nez Perce seasonal travels. Distances varied with the terrain and the day's activity. In the high country, Nez Perce camps were only five to six miles apart; across the prairie the people moved camp every thirty to forty-five miles. When traveling light, the Nez Perce could cover forty-five to sixty miles a day over good traveling country.[32] Long-established, heavily used trails that followed the ridge lines, open slopes, or tributary valleys guided their routes from lower camps and river crossings to the upper country. Pittsburg Landing— "throw off place" in Nez Perce—was one important river crossing along the main route from Idaho into the Grande Ronde country of Oregon. According to legend, Bannocks captured a lone Nez Perce man, beat him up, and there threw him off a bluff into the Snake River. The man survived, floated downstream out of sight, and returned to his people to recount his ordeal.[33] Cache Creek, another popular Nez Perce river crossing site, received its name from an 1876 military scout who recognized that the Nez Perce used the chalky (Mazama ash) soil to cache their dried salmon.[34] (Since antiquity the native people commonly cached food reserves at strategic locations like river crossings. Women dug a pit, placed baskets or hide bags of food on a lining of leaves or grass, and covered them with more grass or leaves and dirt. A pile of rocks marked the cache.[35]) Dug Bar a few miles upriver from the Imnaha River was another ancient Snake River crossing, sadly remembered since the spring of 1877 as the place where Chief Joseph's Wallowa band made their forced river crossing to the Lapwai reservation—the last time Joseph's people made their time-honored journey into Idaho.[36]

Nez Perce Society

From today's perspective, one might envy the seasonal round enjoyed by the Nez Perce and their predecessors. At fishing and seasonal camps the people renewed old acquaintances, met new people, shared ceremonies, held foot- or horse races, played games and gambled, learned about distant people and cultures, courted a prospective spouse, or sat around the campfire and listened to the elders' stories. Because of the abundance the land had to offer at different altitudes and different times of year, and the social interaction among family groups and bands, the seasonal round enriched their lives and molded their culture.

The natural environment also molded their social organization. The Nez Perce people lived in loosely affiliated bands scattered throughout their homeland, which originally encompassed approximately twenty-seven thousand square miles of what is now north central Idaho, northeast Oregon, and southeast Washington. Snake River canyon divided the land near its center. Each band became identified with a specific geographic area where separate villages—consisting of seventy-five to eighty people—wintered. Although each band respected the other's geographic claim to their winter village sites, they shared communal fishing spots, gathering grounds, and hunting areas. Each village elected a headman, who usually held that office for life. But all the villages within that specific geographic area formed an alliance, or band, and elected a notable village headman as "chief."[37] Often within each band a different man would rise to prominence if his individual talents met a specific need; otherwise the band chief was the recognized leader. Each chief of a band, or geographic alliance, would also contribute his individual talents to the entire nation should such a need arise. For example, one band's chief might be an excellent warrior and thus placed in charge of all the other bands when at war.[38] No single chief, however, spoke on behalf of the entire Nez Perce nation—a cultural nuance regularly ignored by white outsiders. The chiefs from the different bands occasionally held a council to make decisions on matters affecting the entire nation, but each individual was at liberty to oppose the action.

Geographic differences of the land served to divide the Nez Perce nation into two sections. The Upriver group included Idaho's Clearwater River bands from Ahsaka and Orofino to Kooskia and Stites; the Downriver people lived along the Clearwater River below Lapwai and along the Snake River. A slight difference in dialect and diet distinguished the two groups. The Downriver people—mostly salmon people—went to the Celilo trade center on the Columbia River, where they took and traded *tonnut*, their most expensive and cherished food. (*Tonnut* was pounded dried salmon mixed with huckleberries.) The Upriver people—buffalo people—were more inclined to cross the Bitterroot Mountains and visit the Salish and Great Plains people. Because the two Nez Perce groups exchanged salmon and buffalo with each other, the Upriver people could introduce the Salish and Plains people to salmon and eel, and the Downriver people could introduce buffalo products to their trading partners at the Celilo trade emporium.[39]

On rare occasions, the two Nez Perce groups were rivals; they fought each other at least once. More common for Snake River Nez Perce bands were occasional flare-ups between them and their Bannock or Western Shoshone neighbors, whose homelands included the southern reaches of Hells Canyon. Despite its rugged character, Hells Canyon served as one of the most important contact points between the contesting people, who were openly antagonistic and in constant, usually undeclared, warfare. "The more powerful Nez Perce normally had the upper hand."[40]

The Nez Perce bands making their homes in the open areas of the Snake River canyon during the 1800s included a band known as Te-maun-muh and identified as the people of High Bear. They lived near the mouth of Salmon River.[41] Another band, under the headmanship of Tu-hul-hul-sut during the mid-1800s, had long ties to the canyon. They made their homes from the Imnaha River to the upper reaches of Hells Canyon, with their main winter villages at Temperance Creek, Kirkwood Creek, Kurry Creek, Christmas Creek, Dug Bar, and Pittsburg Landing.[42] The Gorge People of the Wallowa band wintered along the Imnaha and Grande Ronde Rivers, in Joseph Creek canyon, and at Sheep Creek and Cougar Bar on the Snake River.[43] From late spring through early fall they lived in the Wallowa Valley of northeastern Oregon. The War of 1877 changed everything for the Nez Perce who made their winter homes in the canyon, as it did for all Nez Perce bands living outside the Lapwai reservation (see chap. 7).

The consequences of the Nez Perce War ended the Nez Perce people's choice of where they would make their homes, bringing an end to the underreported but very important chapter of Hells Canyon and Middle Snake River history, the years of the Nez Perce. After the war the Nez Perce occasionally returned to the benches and valley that had been their home for countless generations, but only for fishing or hunting, for spiritual reasons, or simply for remembering. Years later, when environmental issues such as dam construction and the preservation of fish migrations became a national debate, the Nez Perce Tribe took an active role in the controversy as it unfolded in Hells Canyon. Until then, the land that outsiders had taken from them so many years earlier awaited new people, different activities, and profound change.

Chapter 4

The Winds of Change

Change usually comes as a thief in the night. Harbingers of change emerge, subside, then reemerge with greater acceleration. But in the early stages a clear picture of what is to come rarely takes form. Then, suddenly everything is different.

Perhaps that is how the Nez Perce felt during the 1800s. At first it seemed innocent enough. Small parties of white explorers moved through their land. The strangers were a curiosity, usually in need of help, yet a potential source of trade goods and highly prized guns and ammunition. What harm was there in welcoming them, guiding them, befriending them, or providing them with food and information? Next came Canadian, Hawaiian, and American fur traders. Most Nez Perce welcomed them; some women took trapper husbands; and generally the two groups established amicable, mutually beneficial working relationships. When Henry and Eliza Spalding came to the Nez Perce as missionaries in the 1830s, they too seemed relatively harmless. They brought the white man's Book of Heaven and knowledge about power associated with it. Some of the people accepted the Spaldings' religious teaching and adopted the agricultural practices they advocated. Others did not. It was a personal choice that, at the time, did not seem to have a profound influence on the nation as a whole.

Transformation came in the wake of the missionaries' work among the native people. It came first to Nez Perce neighbors to the west and south as missionaries paved the way for thousands of settlers bound for the Willamette Valley in Oregon. Soon Oregon Country became part of the United States. Congress divided it into two territories and sent government officials to guide the growing populations west of the Cascades. They believed that improved physical connections to the East required protected rights-of-way through interior Indian land. Government officials oversaw, and Congress sanctioned, the dismemberment of Indian land claims and the creation of reservations, opening the way for railroad access and future settlement. Most Nez Perce headmen signed the first interior treaty in 1855. It had little effect on their land holdings or traditional ways. They were able to remain relatively untouched by change for a few more years. Then Pacific Slope farmers responded to E. D. Pierce's gold discovery and initiated a gold rush into the Clearwater and Salmon river basins of the Nez Perce reservation. By the 1860s indelible change had transformed the Nez Perce country and made its mark on the people themselves. A second treaty in 1863 reduced their land to slightly over a quarter of the original five-thousand-square-mile reservation in the newly created Idaho Territory. Many headmen refused to sign. They did not feel bound by its provisions and consequently did not move their people to the new reservation. Over time tensions rose, finally culminating in the Nez Perce War of 1877.

Throughout that entire sweep of nearly seventy-five years between the Lewis and Clark expedition of 1805–6 and the 1877 war, Hells Canyon and the Middle Snake River re-

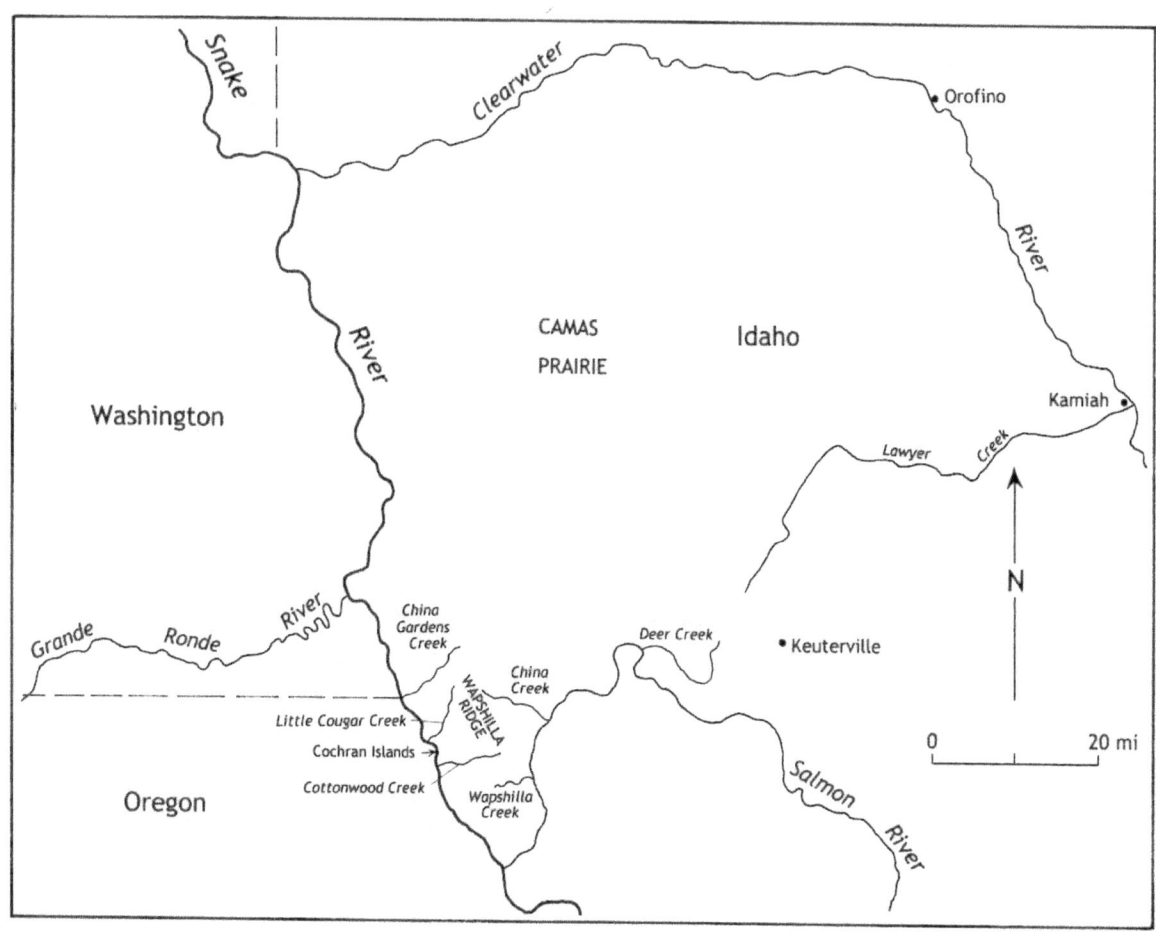

Map 4.1. The area covered in 1806 by John Ordway, Robert Frazer, and Peter Weiser, members of the Lewis and Clark Corps of Discovery. They were the first white men to visit Hells Canyon.

mained relatively unscathed by outside intervention. Intruders sporadically ventured into the canyon to test the terrain but soon found a better route, a better home, and an easier land. Only at the end of the nineteenth century did the land undergo observable modification. Nevertheless, it is important to follow those early nineteenth century incursions into the canyon country to understand its later history.

Lewis and Clark in Uncharted Land

It began with an early 1800s American expeditionary party known as the Corps of Discovery. In June 1803, President Thomas Jefferson commissioned Meriwether Lewis to head a fact-finding expedition across the continent to the Pacific Ocean. He ordered Captain Lewis to locate the "most direct and practicable water communication across this continent, for the purposes of commerce." Jefferson dreamed of the commercial and travel benefits that such a route would bring his young country. Connecting the Mississippi and Missouri system to the Columbia and its tributaries would provide American fur companies overland access to the rich fur-bearing regions of the Oregon Country. It would also strengthen Robert Gray's 1792 claim to American ownership of the Columbia River and all that it drained. The Nez Perce homeland was at the headwaters of a Columbia tributary and directly in the path of the Lewis and Clark expedition.

Jefferson's plan was sound. His only mistake was that he did not know the topography of the continent's interior. He—and everyone else associated with the venture—underestimated the vast mountain expanse that separated those two river systems. Consequently, two years later, when the men of the expedition reached the Rocky Mountains, under the leadership of Captains Meriwether Lewis and William Clark, they anticipated a brief and relatively easy mountain crossing. Instead, they encountered not only the Rocky Mountains but also the unexpected Bitterroot Range. After enduring 220 miles of travel through inhospitable terrain, some of which to this day is barely penetrable, the hungry, demoralized, cold, and frustrated travelers met some Nez Perce people at a mountain prairie in the heart of present-day Idaho. The Nez Perce gave them food, friendship, and guidance. In return the native people hoped to procure weapons, ammunition, and valuable trade items.

During their westward trek, no members of the Corps of Discovery ventured into the Middle Snake River canyon. They were in a hurry to reach the mouth of the Columbia River and had no time for side trips. About forty miles east of the Clearwater/Snake River confluence, the desperately ill men prepared for water travel to the Pacific Ocean. On October 7, 1805, the small party boarded their five ponderosa pine canoes and headed down the Clearwater River. At its junction with the Snake River, aided by a map drawn by Nez Perce headman Twisted Hair, Lewis and Clark calculated the location of the Salmon, Grande Ronde, and Imnaha Rivers south of them. That is the first documentation of the Snake River and its tributaries in the canyon.

The following spring the Corps of Discovery was again in the land of the Nez Perce. Once back on the Clearwater River, they hoped to visit briefly with the people who had been such a help the previous fall, then gather their horses and gear—left behind in Nez Perce care—and continue across the Bitterroot Mountains. Instead, heavy snow in the mountains forced them to remain at their river camp near present-day Kamiah, Idaho, for over a month. During that stay the expedition members and Nez Perce people struck warm and lasting friendships. While Lewis negotiated diplomatic matters and Clark doctored needy patients—who suffered primarily from eye problems—the rest of the men either hunted or traded for enough food to see them across the mountains. No one wanted a repeat of the previous fall's debacle.

The hunt for food took Sergeant John Ordway and Privates Robert Frazer and Peter Weiser into the area now known as Hells Canyon. They were the only members of the expedition to see the canyon and the first non-Indians to see and document a portion of that magnificent terrain. The two captains dispatched Ordway, Frazer, and Weiser to a Nez Perce fishery on the Salmon River to buy salmon. What was supposed to be a brief, half-day trip turned into a seven-day expedition over some of the most difficult terrain the three men had thus far experienced.[1]

A brief description of the region's somewhat confusing geography will help readers better understand the difficulties the men faced. Camas Prairie is a high, open expanse of what were then lush grasslands and camas fields. Small prairie streams, gentle hills, and scattered stands of timber define its contour. Encircling the prairie are deep canyons cut by three separate river systems. To the east and north of the prairie flows the Clearwater River. The Salmon River drains the prairie to the south. To the west the prairie rises to the Craig Mountains, a high, narrow ridge of timbered, rugged mountains that drop abruptly to the Snake River. North of the Salmon/Snake River confluence is Wapshilla Ridge, rising precipitously from both riverbeds.

On May 27, 1806, under the guidance of three young Nez Perce men, Ordway, Weiser, and Frazer left the expedition's main camp on the Clearwater River and headed west. They ascended Lawyer's Creek west toward Camas Prairie, passed one lodge, and proceeded another eight miles to Twisted Hair's village.[2] They stayed there for the night, with a "hard Thunder Shower" pounding their grass house.[3]

The next morning the young guides returned to the Clearwater River; the three explorers, the "chief," and another man continued west across Camas Prairie, then left the "road" and headed south through "unlevel timbred country."[4] Scattered patches of snow, fallen

Figure 4.1. Allen Pinkham is barely visible on the ridge at the center of the picture between the Salmon and Snake River drainage. Based on his knowledge of Nez Perce trails, he is locating a trail possibly used by three men of the Lewis and Clark Expedition, 1806, from the Salmon River canyon to Hells Canyon. (Photo by author, 2006.)

timber, and a severe thunderstorm complicated the journey. Near evening they descended a "bad hill down on a creek," and followed it some distance before arriving at a village a short distance above the creek's juncture with the Salmon River. There they spent the second night.[5]

That evening Robert Frazer traded "an old razer" to a woman for "2 Spanish mill dollars."[6] Here is evidence of Nez Perce participation in an extensive trade network that reached deep into the Southwest. Jefferson had ordered Lewis and Clark to establish trade connections with tribes across the continent. Evidence of Nez Perce trade demonstrates their role in fulfilling Jefferson's plans for expanded American trade and, more importantly, illustrates that the Nez Perce people were far from isolated.

The next morning, Ordway, Frazer, Weiser, the chief, and the fourth man proceeded down the creek to the Salmon River (the "East branch of Lewis's river.")[7] Either the salmon had not yet arrived or the Nez Perce had not caught any for the explorers to purchase. Ordway failed to describe the terrain; his captains, however, provide this first written description of the lower Salmon River: "The East fork of Lewis's river . . . [is] one Continued rapid of about 150 yards wide, it's banks are in most places Solid and perpindicular rocks, which rise to a great hight; it's hills are mountanious high."[8]

The explorers needed to buy salmon, so their Nez Perce guides took them back into the Craig Mountains.[9] The travelers' trail took them to a lodge on the east slope of Wapshilla Ridge, then across "a steep bad hill" and down "a long hill" to another larger lodge on the west slope of the ridge. Ordway's description fits the Cottonwood Creek/Cougar Creek drainage into the Snake River at the southern tip of Wapshilla Ridge. Steep but gentle hills extend from the Salmon River to the ridgetop—no wider than a jeep road—before dropping down a series of abrupt, open, grassy ridges on the western slope. The land transitions from the combined, expansive heights of the Cougar and Cottonwood Creek drainages into narrow, rock and brush-strewn declivities near the Snake River.[10] It was that final few miles into Snake River that Ordway described as "the worst hills we ever saw a road made down."[11] (If a seasoned traveler like Ordway described a trail in such extreme terms, it surely was a terrible route.)

That evening they arrived at the Snake River fishery, located at "a bad rapid." Both Lewis and Clark described the rapids as being "nearly as Great from the information of Sergt. Ordway as the Great falls of the Columbia," a reference to Celilo Falls on the Columbia River.[12] Because no Snake River falls approximate in size or magnitude those of the Columbia River, the three explorers' exact location in Hells Canyon remains a mystery.[13] Had Ordway been comparing a similar configuration of the rapids to Celilo Falls, rather than the size, the description best fits the Rock Island arc, also known as Cochran Island, at the base of Cougar Creek. There the river is shallow on the Oregon side and forty to sixty feet deep on the Idaho side. Even today, it is a good sturgeon fishing location. Archeological studies and current Nez Perce teaching tell us that both sides of the river have been important Nez Perce fisheries for a long time.

When Ordway, Frazer, and

Figure 4.2. A view from Wapshilla Ridge down to the Cottonwood Creek and Snake River juncture and across to Oregon. Cochran Island Rapids are at the center of the picture. (Photo by author, 2006.)

Weiser reached the fishery, they found that most of the men were fishing and the women were collecting kous roots. Not one of the journals mentions how many people were at the camp. They do mention, however, a "common house... about 150 feet long and 35 feet wide, made of split timber and flat on top."[14] What follows is simply speculation, but it might help substantiate the fishery location at Cochran Island. In 1881 Lieutenant Thomas Symons of the Corps of Engineers surveyed the Snake River south of Lewiston. He and three other men began the survey at the mouth of the Salmon River, where they built a small raft "of all the drift-wood we could find in the vicinity" and floated downstream to Cochran Islands. There they built "a large raft... of sufficient size to go safely over the rapids below." Symons did not elaborate on where they found the wood for the raft. Could they have dismantled the vacant "common house" that the Nez Perce used only seasonally? Otherwise, how did they have enough lumber to build a large raft for four men when earlier they used driftwood to build an inadequate raft?[15]

At the fishery, the "old chief" told the travelers to wait outside the lodge. Once invited inside, the three explorers received a meal of roasted salmon and white bread, called "uppah."[16] Ordway said they ate heartily of the fat fish but did not even consume a quarter of it. He also noted that the Nez Perce had caught very few salmon.

The following morning, May 30, 1806, many of the Nez Perce left camp early with nearly all of the day's catch. The three men had to wait an additional day while the remaining fishermen caught more fish, mostly on the opposite side of the river along the rocks.[17] The catch must have been good that morning, for by the afternoon the three visitors could buy as many salmon as they "thought were necessary to take home."[18] They hung their fish outside the tent that night. The next morning they awoke to find some of their recently purchased fish missing. Ordway said that some young men "stole" them. Nez Perce elder Allen Pinkham explains that it was customary for the headman to ensure a fair distribution of the day's catch to everyone at the fishery. Probably, he suggests, when the young people prepared to leave, they had a disproportionate number of fish for their people and the headman told them to take some from the visitors to equalize the distribution. The three visitors would not have understood that custom and thus assumed their fish were "stolen." It was simply a cultural misunderstanding.

Despite the loss, the next morning the three explorers prepared for early departure with seventeen good-size salmon and some kous roots. Without a guide's help, they followed the same road back over the mountains toward the Salmon River.[19] At the Deer Creek village, which they had visited earlier, the headman suggested that they follow a different but better road and assigned two boys to escort them to the next village. The boys took them "over a verry bad hill" and down to the Salmon River, then up a creek along a "high long hill near the top of which is a large village."[20] There they spent the night, ending an excruciatingly long and hard day's trip.

The next day the travelers recrossed Camas Prairie and dropped down to a village on the Clearwater River. There they bought "considerable uppah and couse" before proceeding on to another village at the forks, where they camped.[21] Seven days after leaving the main party, Ordway, Frazer, and Weiser were back at the Corps of Discovery's Clearwater camp with seventeen, mostly rotten salmon. Eight days later, June 10, 1806, the entire expedition broke camp and resumed their journey east across the Bitterroot Mountains.[22] Of all thirty-three members of the Lewis and Clark Expedition, only those three men—John Ordway, Robert Fraser, and Peter Weiser—had ventured into spectacular Hells Canyon at the heart of Nez Perce country. They and their entire Corps of Discovery were undeniably harbingers of considerable change on the Nez Perce horizon—but none realized it at the time.

Map 4.2. The Wilson Price Hunt Expedition route though Idaho to the Pacific Ocean, 1811–12. Map detail 1 shows the area covered by Donald Mackenzie; detail 2 shows Hunt's November meanderings.

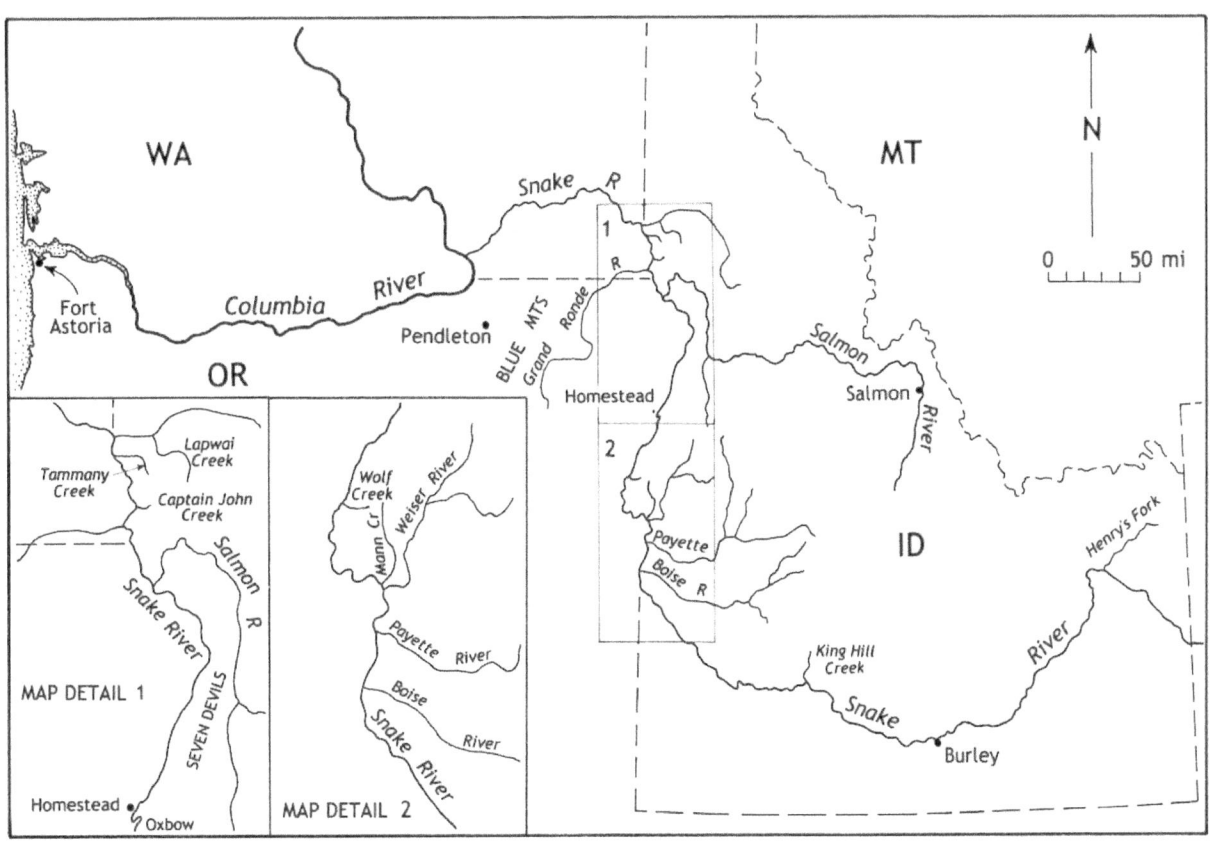

The Hunt Expedition: An American Fur Trade Venture

Hells Canyon played a near-disastrous role in the second expedition that traveled west through the land of the Nez Perce. Under the leadership of Wilson Price Hunt, the expedition was part of a great commercial venture planned and funded by New York merchant John Jacob Astor and the implementation of a dream shared by numerous visionaries before and during Astor's time.

By the late 1700s, John Jacob Astor had amassed considerable wealth in the Missouri fur trade. His business contacts included partners of the North West Company of Montreal, men who influenced Astor's decision to form his own fur trading company—the Pacific Fur Company—to capitalize upon a lucrative beaver fur trade on the West Coast.[23] In 1810 John Jacob Astor set his plan in motion by sending forth two expeditions to the Columbia River. One party traveled by sea aboard the *Tonquin* under the command of U.S. navy lieutenant Jonathan Thorn; the second traveled overland with merchant and would-be adventurer Wilson Price Hunt. The men had orders to build and staff a major fur-trading depot at the mouth of the Columbia River, as well as minor trading posts along navigable rivers in the interior. The success of Astor's plan hinged on good relations with the native people, minimal competition from Canadian companies, competent company men, and the good fortune Lewis and Clark enjoyed. Unfortunately for Astor and many of his men, the scheme failed. Good fortune eluded them at every juncture, especially throughout Hunt's foray into Hells Canyon. Washington Irving, using expedition journals and company correspondence, described in near-melodramatic prose that Hells Canyon venture in his fifteen-volume account of the Astor enterprise, published in 1848–49.

September 1811 found Wilson Price Hunt and his party of sixty-five at the juncture of the Hobach and Snake Rivers in present-day Wyoming. They crossed Teton Pass and on October 9 reached Henry's Fort on Henry's Fork of the Snake River, where they cached supplies and built canoes to continue their western trek by water.[24] Hunt's belief in a safe water route to the Pacific Ocean kept him on the Snake River until they reached Caldron Linn, twenty-three miles above present-day Burley, Idaho. From then on, water travel was impossible.

There in late October, 1811, Hunt "dispatched eleven men, including John Reed, Robert McClellan, and Donald Mackenzie, to explore toward the north in the hope of finding an easier way to the Columbia."[25] He remained at Caldron Linn with the larger group. However, because they lacked the necessary supplies to stay there through the winter, Hunt divided that group into two smaller groups and sent them west along the north and south sides of the Snake River. Hunt led one party along the north bank, consisting of twenty-two men, a pregnant Marie Dorion, Iowa nation woman and wife of Sioux interpreter Pierre Dorion Jr., and her two- and four-year-old children. On the opposite bank were Ramsay Crooks and his group of nineteen men.

The two parties paralleled the river for about 150 miles through the hostile, barren plain of south Idaho. Snake River, deep in the gorge below, was inaccessible most of the time. Hunt's party came upon a small encampment of Shoshone near King Hill and learned that there was a shorter route northwest across the plain to the Boise River. The cutoff shortened their travel distance but took them through a desert with low water reserves. At the Boise River oasis they came to another Shoshone camp and supplemented their rapidly dwindling provisions with a few fish and dogs.

By that time it was late November. It was cold. They were so hungry they resorted to killing their horses, but on they pressed. After fording the Boise River, the ever-weakening band continued north to ford Idaho's Payette and Weiser Rivers near the modern towns of the same names.[26] They then followed the Weiser River, pushing farther north into increasingly more rugged terrain. "Before them was a wintry-looking mountain covered with snow on all sides."[27] They continued up the narrowing gorge of Mann Creek to two Shoshone lodges, where the people "seemed nearly [in] as great extremity as themselves." Hunt and his men tried to trade for food or horses, but hunger had just forced the Indians themselves to kill two horses. Although the native people had little to spare, they parted with a bag of seed and a few small pieces of horseflesh. Hunt continued up Mann Creek to Wolf Creek, then down that stream to its mouth on the Snake River in the southern end of Hells Canyon.[28]

It was now early December 1811. Hunt persisted in his belief that the Snake River would provide the best route to the Columbia River, but winter conditions at the higher elevations forced them to attempt travel at river level.[29] Food shortages remained critical. They lacked even the warmth of a fire. One evening after an entire day enduring horrible "toil," the cold, tired travelers had "the mortification" of discovering that they were only four miles from their previous night's camp.[30] They were at the Oxbow of the meandering Snake River.

The Adventures of Ramsay Crooks

Frustration followed frustration. On December 6, 1811, much to their surprise and dismay, Hunt's party spotted Ramsay Crooks and his men on the Oregon side of the river. Hunt had assumed that those men were safely past that horrible section of the country and well on their way to the Columbia River. Instead he found starving men further debilitated by their arduous journey into Hells Canyon. Hunt "immediately returned to camp, caused a canoe to be made out of the skin of the horse killed on the preceding night, and sent enough food to our famished companions."[31] Sardepie, one of Astor's many Canadian voyageurs, crossed the river in the "frail bark" with the horse flesh and returned with Crooks and Francois LeClerc.

Crooks had wretched news for Hunt. For three days they had ventured farther down the Snake River to a place where the river was "compressed into a canal not more than sixty to a hundred feet wide between precipitous rocks."[32] It was impossible for them to go deeper into the canyon. The only glimmer of hope Crooks could suggest to Hunt was that they had seen Mackenzie and Reed on the opposite side of the river (Idaho) a few days earlier. By yelling across the river, they learned that Mackenzie's and Reed's men were in much better condition, better provisioned, and pushing north along the Snake River breaks.

Crooks told Hunt that he and his men had followed the south side of the Snake River to beyond present-day Homestead before being forced back.[33] For the past six days they had eaten only the carcass of a dog. Three days before that they ate one beaver, a few wild cherries, and the soles of their old moccasins. In that deplorable condition, Crooks's men had attempted to travel along the banks of the Snake River by "frequently climbing over sharp and rocky ridges that projected into the stream."[34] They finally came to a place where a "perpendicular precipice . . . rendered it impossible to keep along the stream." Washington Irving captured the anguish of the experience: "The river here rushed with incredible velocity through a defile not more than thirty yards wide, where cascades and rapids succeeded each other almost without intermission. Even had the opposite banks . . . been such as to permit a continuance of their journey, it would have been madness to attempt to pass the tumultuous current either on rafts or otherwise." They pushed on through deep snow until they reached enough height to survey the lay of the land. There, not even halfway up the mountains, they could see that "mountain upon mountain lay piled beyond them, in wintry desolation."[35]

Hunt faced a difficult decision—stumble forward into this wintry desolation or return along the familiar dreadful path. He chose the latter. They would retrace their steps back to the Weiser, Payette, or Boise Rivers, hoping to find Indians willing to sell them some horses, and then push west across the Blue Mountains to the Columbia River. Crooks and LeClerc would stay with Hunt; the others in their party would keep up as best they could on the opposite side. Crooks, however, became violently ill that evening and was in no condition to travel the next day. Hunt left John Day and J. B. Dubreuil behind to care for him and pressed on in search of some Shoshone.

Leaving the Snake River Canyon

Numbed by cold and hunger, the Astorians stumbled through a kind of "mountain nightmare."[36] At one point they surprised a small party of Shoshone and, as the startled Indians fled, stole five of their horses. One horse immediately became food. Hunt sent a horse and some horseflesh back to Crooks. When Crooks finally rejoined them, he was shocked to learn that no food had been ferried across the river to his men and immediately demanded that someone build a skin canoe. The starved men on the opposite shore had water boiling by the time the canoe was finished, but none of Hunt's men volunteered to cross over with the meat. Finally, Ben Jones took the meat across, and Joseph Delaunay returned with the canoe a second time, carrying additional supplies. Jean Baptiste Prevost, "whom famine had rendered wild and desperate," frantically tried to board the canoe in an effort to get to Hunt's side of the river.[37] He upset it. The angry Snake River swept the poor man away.[38]

Back on the Weiser River, the Hunt party was again in the company of some Shoshone. They told Hunt that there was a good road across the Blue Mountains to the land of the Cayuse, where the explorers could buy horses for the rest of the journey, but it would be foolish to attempt the crossing this time of year. Hunt ignored their warnings. He cajoled the reluctant Shoshone until finally three men agreed to guide them across the mountains.[39]

They left the Weiser camp on December 21, 1811, and traveled toward the Snake River. Three men were too weak to travel and remained behind with the Shoshone. Near the Weiser and Snake confluence the others found the rest of Crooks's men, crossed the river to join them, and with five wretched horses for food headed toward the Blue Mountains.[40] The bedraggled party—consisting of thirty-two white men and three Shoshone Indians, as well as Marie Dorian and her two children—moved northwest into Oregon's Grande Ronde Valley. On Christmas day, Marie Dorion gave birth. The travelers did not stop for either the birth or the holiday. Nor did they stop for the infant's death two weeks later. On they pressed, pausing only on New Year's Day, 1812—a "favorite festival" for the French Canadians—for a much-needed rest. While Marie Dorian agonized in silence, the men sang and danced "in defiance of all their hardships" and dined on a "sumptuous banquet of dog's meat and horse flesh."[41]

What kept them going? Perhaps the slight warmth to the air or the sun that finally appeared. Perhaps their three guides kept up their spirits with talk of the large Cayuse horse herds. Certainly having those men as guides made a difference, for six days after leaving the Shoshone camp the starving expedition came upon a large encampment of Cayuse near present-day Pendleton, Oregon.[42] Nearly two thousand horses ranged the grasslands around the Cayuse encampment. Inside the lodges, Hunt found "brass kettles, axes, copper tea-kettles, and various other articles of civilized manufacture"—confirmation that these Indians communicated with the people of the Pacific coast who traded with the white seafarers.[43]

Finally Hunt acknowledged the gravity of their earlier situation and his depth of gratitude. "I cannot sufficiently express my gratitude to Providence for having let us reach here; because we all were extremely fatigued and enfeebled."[44] The Astorians spent six days with that band of Cayuse, eating, renewing their strength, and trading for horses. They joined another Cayuse Indian band on the Umatilla River a few days later, learned the region's geography, and proceeded on to the Columbia River. In February 1812, the tattered, tired, disheartened men, Mrs. Dorion, and her two children reached Fort Astoria—the fort that John Jacob Astor's seabound expedition members had already built at the mouth of the Columbia River. What would have been the Astorians' fate had the Shoshone and Cayuse not helped them? Did Donald Mackenzie and his men find similar help in Hells Canyon?

"Perpetual Motion" Mackenzie

At Caldron Linn on the Snake River, Wilson Price Hunt had divided the expedition into three groups in late October 1811. Donald Mackenzie and his ten men went north through present-day Idaho in search of a route to the Columbia River. Speculation surrounds the route that they followed. Either they faced the inhospitable terrain of the high Seven Devils Mountains that frame the east side of Hells Canyon or their route took them along the Salmon River farther to the east.[45]

I believe they followed the east mountain ridges that parallel Hells Canyon, then crossed the Salmon River near the Nez Perce fishery, visited five years earlier by Lewis and Clark Expedition men Ordway, Frazer, and Weiser. Washington Irving's account of Donald Mackenzie's adventure after he and his men left Caldron Linn described a landscape that mirrors Hells Canyon's mountainous country. "The river had worn its way in a deep channel through rocky mountains, destitute of brooks or springs. Its banks were so high and precipitous that there was rarely any place where the travelers could get down to drink of its waters."[46] The travelers never had enough water, and severe snowstorms encumbered their travel. Their journey—equally as daunting as Hunt's and Crooks's travels through that harsh terrain—grew tolerable under the inspired guidance of Donald Mackenzie.

Alexander Ross, one of Astor's Pacific Fur Company partners, captured the essence of the human dynamo, Donald Mackenzie, as he led his men north through the Seven Devils Mountains. Ross described the dark days that Mackenzie and his men shared on the trail and the difficult journey they faced, how Mackenzie, "that bold North-Wester," called together "his little band" and assured them that "there is still hope before us." Mackenzie admonished his men that "to linger on our way, to return back, or to be discouraged and stand still, is death—a death of all others the most miserable." If they would just "take courage . . . persevere and push on ahead" then "all will end well." When Mackenzie's men heard those words "the poor fellows took off their caps, gave three cheers, and at once shot ahead." Ross wrote that the travelers "kept as near the river as possible, and got on wonderfully well, until they came into the narrow and rugged defiles of the Blue Mountains [Seven Devils]."

Their suffering was intense. One time they traveled for five days without a mouthful to eat. Then, one beaver nourished eleven men. Of all those men, Mackenzie alone "stood the trial well." He encouraged the others with a cheery countenance, frank words, and inspiring example. A giant of a man, nothing seemed to slow him down or diminish his zest for life.[47]

Ultimately, after "twenty-one days of toil and suffering," Mackenzie and his men made it through the miserable mountains and dropped down to "a tributary stream"—the Salmon River.[48] They gazed upon a herd of "wild horses, the first they had seen west of the Rocky mountains," and soon met "a friendly tribe of Indians." The travel-hardened men had come upon a most welcome sight—one of the many enormous herds of Nez Perce horses grazing on the Salmon River breaks and a nearby Nez Perce winter village. The travelers might have then crossed Camas Prairie and Wapshilla Ridge to descend to the Snake River at any number of locations, including Captain John Creek or Tammany Creek. Alternatively, they might have continued north across Camas Prairie and the Clearwater River via Lapwai Creek, then on downstream to the Snake River.

Regardless of their precise route, Mackenzie and his men were in the midst of Nez Perce country at the time of year when the people resided in their canyon and valley winter villages. The Nez Perce provided those eleven men the same kind of help and friendship they had earlier bestowed upon the Lewis and Clark Expedition members. Their hospitality was manifest in food, canoes, and travel instructions. Once physically revitalized, with transportation and an idea of distances and directions, Mackenzie and his men "dropped down" the Snake River "to its confluence with the Columbia, then down that river to Astoria." They reached Astoria in January 1812, a month before Wilson Price Hunt and his party. As was characteristic of other explorers who kept journals, Alexander Ross failed to credit the Nez Perce people for helping Donald Mackenzie on that final segment of their long and difficult journey. He did, however, recognize that a higher power preserved the expedition members during their nearly impossible winter trip through the mountains of Hells Canyon: "To that Being alone who preserveth all those who put their trust in Him, were in this instance due, and at all times, our thanksgiving and gratitude," he wrote.[49]

Although the Wilson Price Hunt 1811 expedition encountered its most tormenting stretch of travel in Hells Canyon, the travelers had limited contact with the Nez Perce. But the work of the Astorians had just begun. John Jacob Astor had instructed his company men to establish fur trading posts in the interior where the native people would bring beaver pelts in exchange for trade items. Donald Mackenzie, one of Astor's business partners, was in a position to decide where posts would be located and who would staff them. Possibly because of his acquaintance with the Nez Perce and the goodwill he felt for them, and almost certainly to discourage the North West Company—Astor's Pacific Fur Company competitors—from moving farther south into Idaho, Mackenzie decided to locate an interior post among the Nez Perce people. Furthermore he would build it. That second harbinger of change implied a more immediate transformation of Nez Perce culture than had the Corps of Discovery. The pace had accelerated.

Figure 4.3. Donald Mckenzie's 1811 north bound trek would have taken him across the mountains on the left side of the canyon.(Photo courtesy of the Nez Perce County Historical Society, Miller Collection.)

Chapter 5

Mackenzie and the Captain

In June 1812, Pacific Fur Company partners Donald Mackenzie, David Stuart, and John Clarke, with a small group of fur trappers, left Fort Astoria at the mouth of the Columbia River and ventured inland. They were initiating phase two of John Jacob Astor's business plan for beaver trade in the Pacific Northwest—to locate fur trading posts along navigable interior streams. On the Columbia River near its juncture with the Walla Walla and Snake Rivers, the travelers parted company. Mackenzie and company clerk Alfred Seton, with three Canadians and some Hawaiians, boarded one boat and two canoes for the Clearwater River in present-day Idaho.[1] Young Seton kept a journal of their activities and his impressions of the experience.

The small party reached the Snake and Clearwater River confluence sixteen days later. Had they continued up the Snake River and found a good trading post location, their adventure would probably have been oriented toward Hells Canyon. Instead they continued east up the Clearwater River. Consequently, what follows is an account of Mackenzie's activities outside the Middle Snake River country. While on the Clearwater River, however, those Astorians interacted extensively with people from the canyon country. This was the first semipermanent occupation of whites in Nez Perce land: an important contribution to understanding the dynamics between the two groups of people and the dynamics within the Nez Perce tribe itself.

The fur traders went up the Clearwater River across from the mouth of the North Fork, where Lewis and Clark had built their canoes seven years earlier.[2] There they camped; Seton took charge of the encampment while Donald Mackenzie and four employees traveled on upstream for two days, hoping to find good beaver country.[3] They were disappointed. There were few signs of beaver and the food resources were limited. Mackenzie decided to relocate their camp forty-five miles downstream near the Snake and Clearwater River confluence "in the center of a numerous nation of Indians" that owned large horse herds. They had grown dependent on horses for food and found inadequate herds farther up the Clearwater River. Washington Irving described the new site on "the great thoroughfare" where tribes from the Columbia River passed through on their way to "make war upon the tribes of the Rocky Mountains; to hunt buffalo on the plains, or to traffic for roots and buffalo robes."[4] The Nez Perce nation, ideally situated between the Coastal people and the Plains people, had developed an extensive trade network with both groups. The new location should serve the Astorians well.

Fur Traders in Their Midst

At their new location on the Clearwater River, five miles above its confluence with the Snake River, there "was not a tree to be seen."[5] Mackenzie ordered his men to build the fur trading post out of driftwood. Three weeks after selecting the site, their trading post—consisting of a store, a house for the men, and a third building for Mackenzie and Seton—modestly graced the banks of the Clearwater River. Now they must acquaint themselves with their Nez Perce neighbors.

The Astorians did not identify the Nez Perce as a single nation nor did they use any variation of the word "Nez Perce." Rather, they divided the nation into three separate groups. Two of the groups they called Sahaptian. One group lived along the upper reaches of the Clearwater River (Seton called it the Shahaptin River), where Mackenzie made his initial reconnaissance. Their lives were directed through trade and travel with the people east of the mountains.[6] A second group of Sahaptians lived near the Astorians' post at the Clearwater and Snake River confluence. They were "quiet and peaceable folks who devoted themselves to the rearing of numerous herds of horses." Providing horses for their neighbors—the Snake, Kootenai, and Salish people—formed their main economy.[7]

The third group of Nez Perce—whom Seton called the Tashepas—lived along the Snake River south into Hells Canyon.[8] They were "a very powerful and warlike nation divided into many tribes." A "chief" (headman) held authority over each "tribe" (band) and the size of his horse herd determined his wartime power. The Tashepas possessed "almost innumerable horses." The Tashepas' main enemy, the "Snakes" (Bannock or Shoshone), lived farther up the river and "were separated from the Tashepas by a ridge of mountains."[9] In war, the Tashepas took scalps; with each scalp taken the warrior garnered greater respect.[10] Seton observed that among the canyon Nez Perce, only the chiefs owned guns. Conversely, the upper Clearwater Sahaptians, who fought the Blackfeet, commonly owned guns, suggesting that they had a more extensive trade with Canadian and American fur traders on the Great Plains.[11]

By early September 1812, the Astorians had settled into their new post near the rivers' confluence. From there they planned to trap and trade throughout the winter, but outside forces soon dictated otherwise. For one thing, the fur traders had grown dependent on the natives' horses for food but found the price rising so fast they doubted if their trade goods would hold out until spring. Initially the Nez Perce charged forty to fifty loads of ammunition per horse. Within a few months the price also included blankets, axes, and other necessary items. Additionally, while Donald Mackenzie was visiting partners at Fort Spokane, he learned that the United States and England were at war.[12] He even saw a copy of President Madison's declaration of war. Back on the Clearwater River, he immediately made plans to abandon the Clearwater post and return to Astoria.[13]

In the dead of winter, "Perpetual Motion" Mackenzie hurried to Astoria with news of the war and a warning of an armed British ship, the *Isaac Todd*, en route to assault the American fort.[14] Seton attempted to take their trade goods and extra supplies to John Clarke's post on the Spokane River. Heavy snow and bitter cold stopped him. Back on the Clearwater River, Seton sent word to the trappers scattered throughout the region to return to the post by Christmas Day. One man refused. He had no intention of going to Fort Astoria and fully intended to stay with his new wife and her Nez Perce people.[15] He and his wife lived at a Snake River village four day's ride from the post, deep in the canyon. Seton went there to persuade the man to change his mind. Seton was well acquainted with the headman, whom the French Canadians called Le Grand Coquin, for the Nez Perce man had frequently visited the fur trading post with others from his band and spent many hours in target practice with Seton.

Seton proved persuasive, for on Christmas Day he and the wayward hunter were back at the Clearwater post. All the other men had returned and were preparing to move. In order to travel quickly and unencumbered, they cached all their trade goods and unnecessary supplies by first packing the goods in bales, then digging a hole under the floor of one of the buildings. They stashed the baled goods in the hole, covered it, and replaced the floor boards. After celebrating New Year's Day with "a famous horse pye & a couple of quarts of real Boston particular"—with which the entire group of trappers "regaled" themselves "*pas mal*"—they vacated the buildings and prepared to burn them, hoping to allay Nez Perce suspicions that there were any goods at the site. After dropping the clay caulk from the rafters onto the floor, they torched the buildings. The next morning Seton, his twenty men, a Nez Perce woman, and a child boarded their canoes and proceeded five miles down the Clearwater to the Snake River and on to the Pacific Ocean.

On January 16, 1813, the Clearwater contingency reached their ocean fort. "Almost at once the senior partners decided to abandon Astoria."[16] In early April, Mackenzie and a party of twenty men returned east with letters outlining the partners' decisions for John Clarke and David Stuart at their Spokane and Okanogan River posts. Before traveling on to the two northern posts, Mackenzie's party would stop on the Clearwater River to retrieve their cached goods and purchase enough horses from the Nez Perce for an overland evacuation of all the interior posts.

As planned, they reached the site of the Clearwater River post on April 21, 1813, and "had the extreme mortification" to find that their cache "had been lifted" and all their property stolen.[17] The Nez Perce living in the vicinity told them that a band of Tashepas had been poking around the abandoned post for weeks; they had stolen the goods.[18] Mackenzie dispatched John Reed and two men to the Spokane River with the letters while the remaining men set out in pursuit of their stolen property. For the next two months they searched Sahaptian villages for the missing goods, finding themselves more than once "in dangerous and trying situations." They retrieved very few items. The Sahaptian people, however, were "united" in blaming a band of Tashepas who lived along the banks of the Snake River, "in a small savannah hedged in by rocks and precipices," where there were "fearful rapids above and below [that] forbade the approach of canoes."[19] (The description unquestionably fits any number of village sites in the Hells Canyon country.)

Mackenzie's search for the missing goods took the Astorians to a temporary Tashepa encampment on the Clearwater River. There they expected to find most of their property. When they arrived, about twenty-five young men greeted them, guns in hand, bullets in their mouths, ready to shoot Mackenzie and Seton as they got out of their canoe. Mackenzie ordered the other men on shore while he advanced toward the warriors. He "examined each and every gun," and emptied each of its priming, all the while reminding the young men that the Astorians had come to the country to supply them with arms.[20] Mackenzie then told Seton to smoke with the young men while he and his aide "ransacked their lodges." They found three or four bales of goods. Mackenzie then ordered his men back into the canoes, fired four or five times into the air, as a show of contempt, and brazenly set up camp about five hundred yards away.[21] His bluff worked; the band of Tashepas returned to their "own firesides among the crags and precipices of the tumultuous" Snake River.

A few days later a large band of "friendly" Cayuse rode into Mackenzie's camp. They and the Astorians were enjoying a hospitable exchange when a second band of Tashepas arrived, dressed in war regalia. It was Le Grand Coquin with sixty of his armed men—

and Seton.[22] Mackenzie "recognized them at once and divined their purpose," but he and everyone else ignored the mounted warriors.[23] The intruders waited, mounted, and still as statues. No one greeted them nor appeared to notice them. Le Grand Coquin covertly tried to convince the Cayuse to join them in taking up arms against Mackenzie's small group. The Cayuse headman replied that ever since Wilson Price Hunt's party had arrived in their land, destitute and hungry, they were bound in friendship with the whites. Mackenzie got wind of the Tashepas' conspiracy and ordered his men to fix their bayonets and load their guns. The band "remained in their statuelike posture for four or five minutes, then suddenly wheeled and left" the camp.[24]

After this incident the Cayuse continued their journey east, but before departing, an old Cayuse man advised Mackenzie to move twenty miles down the river to a village of friendly Sahaptians. "We bade the old man a cordial farewell, and took his friendly counsel." The fur traders relocated near the mouth of the Clearwater River and remained there until June 1813.[25] Provisions grew dangerously low; even the friendly Sahaptians refused to sell them any horses. The desperate Astorians resorted to ill-advised behavior; at the time they saw no other options. They periodically stole a horse and slaughtered it for food. Seton commented: "This displeases the Indians very much for we sometimes killed a favorite animal, but necessity has no law." He left off abruptly with these words: "We started on 1st June on our way again to the Fort [Astoria]." Thus, men representing the interests of John Jacob Astor forever took leave of the land of the Nez Perce. Within a few years, though, Donald Mackenzie returned, but only briefly.

"The Passage by Water Is Now Proved Safe"

By spring of 1814 the threat of war and the collective misfortune of Astor's Pacific Fur Company forced Donald Mackenzie and the other partners to sell all of Astor's Columbia operations to his Canadian competitors, the North West Company. Mackenzie and many of Astor's other employees switched allegiance to the new owners and remained in the Pacific Northwest.[26] Mackenzie had already worked for Canada's North West Company. At the age of seventeen he had moved to Canada from Scotland. Nine years later he began working for the North West Company and remained with them one year before John Jacob Astor hired him. Four years later, Mackenzie again found himself working for the Canadian company. He did well. By 1816 he had moved up the ranks to command their Columbia River fur trade and changed the way the company did business. No longer would they depend on the Indians for beaver pelts. Instead they used the brigade system, which Mackenzie invented, whereby company trappers made annual forays throughout the interior to trap marketable pelts. Each man carried equipment and supplies on packhorses and often traveled with his native wife and children. The company assigned him a "store"—one of five forts in the interior country—where the trapper would return once a year for supplies and to deposit his furs. All imported supplies and exported furs moved along the navigable waterways of the Columbia River drainage to and from Fort George (Astoria) at the mouth of the Columbia River—the main trading depot.

Mackenzie considered both Fort Okanogan and Fort Spokane as a possible interior post, but neither site proved acceptable. He required a place closer and with better transportation access to the "Snake Country" of south Idaho, eastern Oregon, and western Wyoming.[27] He therefore selected a site on the south side of the Columbia River near the Walla Walla River and eleven miles south of the Snake River confluence. Mackenzie called the new post

Fort Nez Perces, although it was not located in Nez Perce country. It had the necessary features: easy access to the grasslands of Walla Walla Valley, an ideal location at the northern end of a well-traveled route across the Blue Mountains to the Snake River Plains, and river access to Fort George. Also, should the Snake River prove navigable, it was on an all-water route to South Idaho. Mackenzie received authorization from company headquarters at Fort Williams, Canada, to put one hundred men to work building the new fort. By July 1818, Fort Nez Perces was ready to do business.

Before sending brigades to Central and South Idaho streams, however, Donald Mackenzie required Nez Perce permission for his North West Company brigades to travel through their land.[28] Although apprehensive about how the Nez Perce would accept the Hawaiian trappers traveling with him—they "did not half relish the swarthy aspect of these invincibles"— Mackenzie and his small group of men found a hospitable welcome, despite his men's having stolen and butchered Nez Perce horses four years earlier.[29] The Nez Perce promised Mackenzie that future brigades traveling through their land would have safe passage.

Donald Mackenzie led the first three Snake River brigades. He scheduled the third brigade for the fall of 1818, so he could examine the country during the winter, see some of the principal chiefs, and determine the possibility of using the Snake River as a water highway. Mackenzie left Fort Nez Perces with fifty-five men—including some Iroquois hunters, 195 horses, and three hundred beaver traps—bound for the Blue Mountains and southwest Idaho. There he left the Iroquois hunters to work the rich beaver creeks and continued east toward the headwaters of the Snake River.[30] Peace among the tribes ensured the trappers' well-being and throughout that twenty-five-day journey, Mackenzie conveyed a message of "welcome tidings of peace" from the Nez Perce to the several bands of Shoshones whom they met. From the Snake River headwaters, Mackenzie and six men returned west while most of the trappers remained behind to work the streams. Traveling in the winter, the small group retraced their route along the Snake River, crossing and recrossing much of Mackenzie's 1811 route. When he rejoined his Iroquois hunters, Mackenzie discovered that they had scattered about and were not hunting. Instead, they were "living with the savages" and "were perfectly destitute of everything I had given them." Mackenzie left them as he found them and continued with his six men across the Blue Mountains to Fort Nez Perces, concluding an incredible six-hundred-mile trip primarily on snowshoes. Donald Mackenzie, an enormously powerful man more than six feet tall and weighing 312 pounds, had already proved his physical strength and mental resolve time and time again. This trip merely confirmed those attributes, but the success of his next venture has people dumbfounded even today.

Figure 5.1. This view shows Snake River above Johnson Bar, determined to be the head of navigation by 20th century mailboat captains. However, Donald Mackenzie's triumphant 1819 ascent of Snake River went this far and beyond, or so he reported. (Photo courtesy of Robert Hoyle.)

Seven days after Mackenzie returned to Fort Nez Perces, he and his six men were again on the move, this time to test the extent of Snake River navigation. One of the most remarkable episodes in the annals of Hells Canyon navigation resulted. Regrettably, the only

Figure 5.2. This 1935 picture of a National Geographic Society scow descending the Salmon and Snake rivers gives some indication of how difficult Mackenzie's trip against the current would have been. (Photo courtesy of the Nez Perce County Historical Society.)

account, written by Alexander Ross, is based almost entirely on a brief letter Ross received from Donald Mackenzie after he cleared the Hells Canyon obstacle.

In February 1819 Donald Mackenzie's party of seven left Fort Nez Perces. They successfully paddled and poled a cumbersome, loaded barge against the current for 11 miles up the Columbia River to the Snake River and another 147 miles to the mouth of the Clearwater River. They then continued south for more than 100 miles through Hells Canyon to a place Donald Mackenzie called "Point Successful, head of the narrows."[31]

Mackenzie described their adventure, beginning with the positive—no doubt intending to allay concerns about that route's impracticality. "The passage by water [on the Snake River, from its mouth to Point Successful] is now proved to be safe and practicable for loaded boats with one single carrying place or portage. Therefore, the doubtful question is now set at rest forever." (Perhaps a topic of considerable debate up to that point.) The rest of his brief account painted a gloomier picture. Mackenzie admitted they "often" had to use a line and drag the boat from the shore. There were two especially threatening places in the depth of the canyon where "bold cut rocks" compressed "a great body of water" into a narrow confine, rendering it unsafe during spring flood. But, he added, there were only two such places, and they were not long. (It was late winter, before spring runoff had begun.) At this point, businessman reluctantly ruled adventurer. Mackenzie explained, "From the force of the current and the frequency of rapids, it may still be advisable and perhaps preferable to continue the land transportation while the [fur trade] business in this quarter is carried on upon a small scale." Hells Canyon constituted too great an obstacle; the profit margin did not justify the risk.

Often overlooked is the follow-up descent through Hells Canyon by four of Mackenzie's men. After successfully inching up the wild and turbulent Snake River through the heart of the canyon, four of the seven men turned around—no doubt using the same bateau—and descended that raging river to deliver Donald Mackenzie's letter to Alexander Ross at Fort Nez Perces. It was critical that Ross learn Mackenzie's travel plans, for he and the other two men were about to embark on a "doubtful and dangerous undertaking"—a twenty-day journey through dangerous Indian country, a place so dangerous they would have to "adopt the habits of the owl, roam in the night, and skulk in the day" to avoid their enemies. Mackenzie hoped to join the trappers he left behind the previous fall, and he wanted Ross to send additional supplies and men for reinforcement.

Ross immediately dispatched the men and all ended well for Mackenzie and his fellows. Donald Mackenzie's reconnaissance of the Snake River through Hells Canyon proved that the brigades could not use the river to transport furs out of south Idaho, thus ending all fur trade activities in the canyon country. Also, since the brigades would not use the Snake River as a main transportation route and Nez Perce country had a limited beaver population, the Nez Perce played only a minor role in North West Company fur trafficking. The trappers were harbingers of transitory change followed by a brief calm. The only other whites to enter Hells Canyon during this early era came not as fur trappers but as explorers, members of Captain Benjamin Louis Eulalie de Bonneville's expedition, "a rambling kind of enterprise, [which] strangely engrafted the trapper and hunter upon the soldier."[32]

The Captain and the Canyon

In 1831 Captain Benjamin Bonneville asked Major General Alexander Macomb for a leave of absence from the U. S. Army to visit the American West. He intended to "examine the locations, habits, and trading practices of the Indian tribes, visit the American and British establishments, and study the best means of making the country available to American citizens."[33] Either he hoped to initiate a fur trade business, as he publicly claimed, or he engaged in a covert fact-finding expedition for the American government. While no proof exists for the later supposition, many historians subscribe to that motive. With the waning of the western fur trade, early indications of America's infection with "Oregon fever" began to surface. Since 1816, the United States and Great Britain had jointly occupied the Pacific Northwest. It became increasingly apparent that the United States intended to take and hold as much of the country as possible. Gathering information to facilitate that objective may well have been Bonneville's prime directive.

In the spring of 1832, traveling with 120 men and twenty wagons of trade goods, Bonneville left Fort Osage on the Missouri River. He headed west on the well-traveled trappers' Platte River route and crossed the Continental Divide at South Pass—demonstrating that heavily loaded wagons could cross the pass, an important bit of intelligence for Americans later bound for the Oregon Country.

By September 19, 1832, Bonneville's expedition had reached the upper waters of the Salmon River where they came upon some Nez Perce hunters. They remained in each other's company for two days; "The most amicable intercourse prevailed and they parted the best of friends."[34] Bonneville established winter quarters near the present-day site of Salmon, Idaho, where they were surrounded by encampments of Salish and Nez Perce Indian people. The following year, 1833, the Americans' adventures and intrigue culminated with a winter expedition into the heart of Snake River canyon country. First, Bonneville established their second winter camp at Portneuf on the Snake River, near present-day Pocatello, Idaho. Feeling secure at leaving his main expedition and supplies among the Bannock Indians who lived there, "a tribe as honest as they were valiant," Bonneville decided to undertake a "reconnoitering expedition of great extent and peril" to Fort Walla Walla (old Fort Nez Perces) in the heart of the Hudson's Bay Company on the Columbia River. He selected three "companions," a small stock of provisions, and five horses and mules to pursue a route

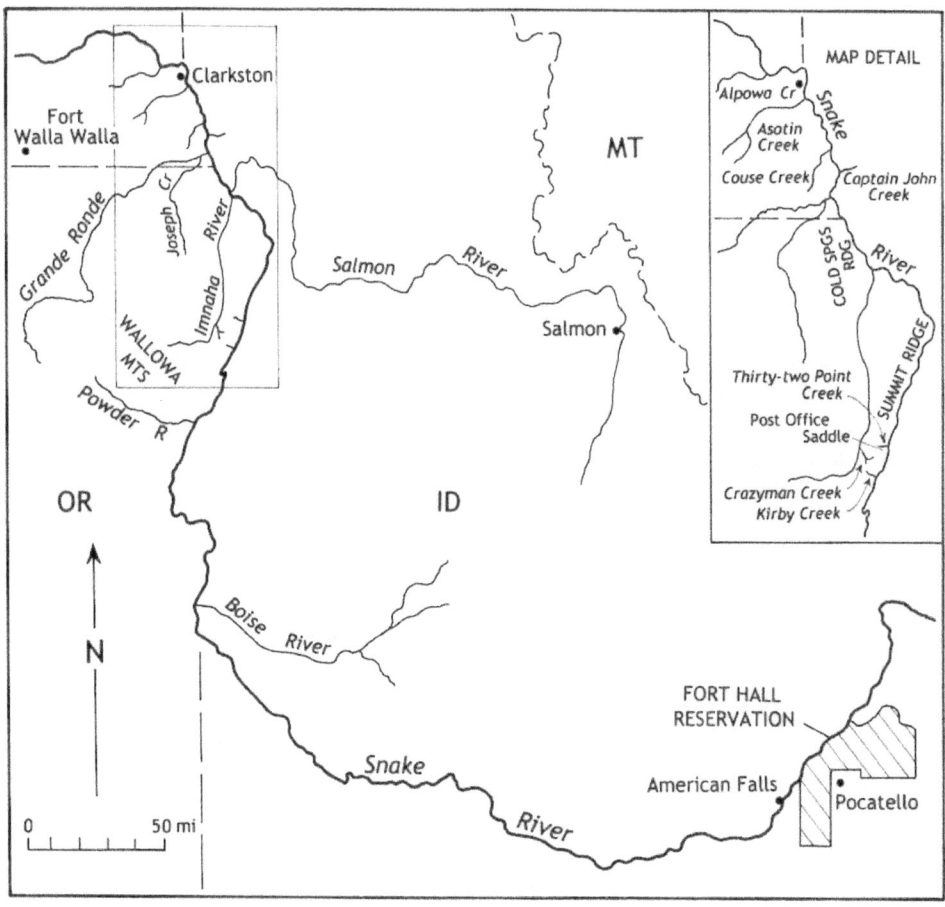

Map 5.1. The route followed by the Benjamin Bonneville expedition in 1834. The map detail shows the area of Hells Canyon where he decided to leave the Snake River.

through the Snake River country to that Hudson's Bay Company fort. They intended to return in March 1834.[35]

In January 12, 1834, Bonneville and his three men reached the Powder River, at the southern end of Hells Canyon, about three miles above its convergence with the Snake River. Sparse snow dotted the landscape; a biting cold permeated the atmosphere. Gradually the weather grew warmer and more pleasant as they ventured farther north; the ice sheets on the once frozen river had broken free and floated along with the current.[36] The men ultimately came upon a group of "Root Digger" (Shoshone) Indians returning from the Boise River plains who gave them a "considerable supply of fish and an excellent and well-conditioned horse." The Shoshone advised the travelers to stay along the Snake River for it was unimpeded by snow. "An excellent guide" agreed to travel with them. For the next two days the guide crossed and recrossed the Snake River in search of food before meeting a friend and departing "without the ceremony of leave taking."[37]

Again on their own, the explorers continued to a small village of people whom Bonneville described as "extremely kind and honest." They spoke a language totally different from the Shoshone but one the men recognized as a dialect of Nez Perce, a language they knew from their earlier acquaintance with the Nez Perce. The people gave the four men important travel information and a small quantity of meat, but no one would agree to act as a guide.

Still on their own in foreign land, the group of Americans continued northward toward a high mountain. They stumbled to its summit, surveyed the landscape, and saw nothing but dismal prospects wherever they looked. "The loftiest peaks" of the Wallowa Mountains rose in the distant west. Far below, the Snake River dashed "through deep chasms, between rocks and precipices, until lost in a distant wilderness of mountains, which closed the savage landscape."[38] Needing an evening camp site, they swiftly but laboriously descended through deep snow drifts to the valley—about twenty miles long—known among trappers as the "Grand Rond." They were in the Imnaha Valley, possibly in the vicinity of the mouth of Crazyman Creek.

The next morning the explorers scaled the hills to find a "more eligible route" north. Finding none, they returned to the Snake River intending to travel on the ribbon of ice that edged the river, should the banks prove impassable. Instead, they found the river almost entirely free of ice. Their travels ultimately brought them into the depths of Hells Canyon "where the river forced its way into the heart of the mountains." Tremendous walls of basaltic rock rose perpendicularly from the water's edge, "frowning in bleak and gloomy grandeur." The soft, unyielding snow, two or three feet deep, provided no foothold for the horses. At times crags and promontories crowded the travelers onto a band of ice. Impassable rock ledges either forced them to the opposite shore on hazardous bridges of ice and snow or onto a narrow trail with a "shouldering wall of rock on one side, a yawning precipice on the other." Two horses fell into the river; they were able to rescue only one.[39]

On they pushed. At Thirty-Two Point Creek, where the "river narrowed to a mere chasm with perpendicular walls of rock," they had no recourse but to climb the barricade. Near the summit, travel there too became impossible, leaving them the sole option of turning around and retracing their route to their Kirby Creek campsite of the previous night. The day's travel, perilous in the extreme, left "their hearts quailing under their multiplied hardships."[40]

Somewhat refreshed after a meal, a hot fire, a "tranquilizing pipe," and a night's rest they were ready to pursue an alternative route up the ridge and into the Imnaha Valley to the west. Should that prove impossible, they would kill their horses, "make horse-hide boats," and trust their lives to the hostile river.[41] Along the divide to the Imnaha Valley, encumbered by either heavy snow drifts or melting snow and slippery slopes, their provisions gave out.

Figure 5.3. Above China Bar and the Imnaha River confluence. Captain Bonneville's travels along the Imnaha River canyon were to the west but parallel to the Snake River. (Photo courtesy of Robert Hoyle.)

For three days the men traveled without food; the horses were without feed even longer. One mule, unable to continue, became nourishment for the weakened men. Desperate to know what lay ahead, Bonneville sent one of his men to inspect the area. Three days later he reported back that the Snake River, impossible to reach, lay immediately below the ridge they were on. He advised that they continue across the rim and down into the Imnaha Valley.[42]

The destitute party headed northwest, topping out just south of Post Office Saddle.[43] Although snow had blown off the summit, deep, melting snowdrifts, piled high in the draws, blocked their descent. Totally without food and with spent animals, it was only when they saw the "smooth valley" of the Imnaha "stretched out in smiling verdure below them" that they could muster the momentum to continue.[44] Dragging their jaded horses, the captain and his men finally reached the river valley. While the horses devoured the young spring grass, numerous nearby Indian trails relieved the men's anxieties. Help was near.

Fifty-three days since leaving the main party at Portneuf, Bonneville and his bedraggled men again set forth, debilitated but filled with hope. Their spirits soared when a Nez Perce man approached them, gave them directions to his nearby camp, and departed.[45] The travelers continued toward his camp, until, after about two miles, Bonneville's "energies suddenly deserted him." The ordeal of all that he had been through, plus the added burden of responsibility not only for these three men but the others left behind, had finally caught up with him. The captain threw himself on the grass and "sank into a profound and dreamless sleep." The other three men set up camp as he slept.

The next morning the explorers traveled in the company of a group of Nez Perce, who had arrived with fresh horses, to a village of about twelve families and a meal of roots. (All of the Nez Perce, whom they met in the days to come, were aware of the expedition's progress. Runners traveling as fast as the man could run constantly carried information back and forth among the Nez Perce people throughout their vast territory.) The village headman befriended Bonneville in a most affable manner. Throughout their remaining acquaintance, the "ancient and venerable chief" confirmed his friendship to Captain Bonneville, "the bald chief," and his three men. (With his bald head and bearded face, Bonneville might also have been called "the man with his face on upside down.")[46] Friendship aside, the men craved food—meat not roots. Unwilling to break into their winter reserves, the Nez Perce tried to assure them that roots were nourishing. Frustrated, Bonneville offered his "trusty plaid," a favorite article of clothing, in exchange for some meat. He cut the cloak into strips of material and distributed them among the women. In return Bonneville and his men received an abundance of dried salmon and deer hearts.

As they prepared to depart the following morning, the "venerable patriarch" presented his new friend, Bonneville, with a beautiful brown horse as pledge of his friendship. In return, Bonneville gave him a rifle. Bonneville knew Nez Perce culture well enough to recognize the concept of reciprocal obligations. He seemed unaware, however, that when travelers moved through Nez Perce territory all the Indian people also expected to receive gifts. An exchange of one gift for another did not meet that cultural decree. Bonneville's new friend explained to Bonneville how much the horse meant to his wife—Bonneville gave her some glittering earbobs—and to his son—Bonneville gave him a hatchet. Finally the chief indicated that Bonneville had given him a nice but—without powder and ball—"dumb" rifle. Bonneville's gift of some much-needed powder and ball would satisfactorily conclude the gift giving.[47]

Refreshed and invigorated, Bonneville and his men continued their descent along the Imnaha River to about four miles above its juncture with the Snake River, when they came upon another Nez Perce encampment.[48] The headman, who had already learned about the strangers from his "Buffalo brethren" (the Upper Nez Perce), enthusiastically welcomed the travelers. Although appreciative of the welcome, Bonneville attempted to avoid another round of gift-giving by claiming that he had a mule loaded with gifts for the Lower Nez Perce but that the poor animal fell into the Snake River and was swept away. The headman accepted their destitute state, satisfied the travelers' appetite for meat with a freshly killed colt, and agreed to join them on their journey the next day.

Traveling with the headman and a Nez Perce guide, the captain and his companions continued north over rugged and broken country—Cold Springs Ridge—before dropping down Horse Creek to Joseph Creek and on to "the valley of the Way-lee-way"— the lower Grand Ronde River—"a considerable tributary of Snake River."[49] There, near the union of Joseph Creek and the Grande Ronde River, they reached a large Nez Perce village. Villagers "arrayed in all their finery" greeted the visitors, extending them every courtesy, and fed their guests a banquet of deer, elk, and buffalo. (Their Nez Perce guides had secretly gone ahead to this large village to announce their arrival.)[50] Afterward, when the chief—possibly Old Joseph—asked about the United States, Bonneville conveyed "important facts . . . about the merits of his nation" to the men in the lodge. The "village crier" then dispatched Bonneville's words throughout the rest of the village. (Irving described the village criers as "walking newspapers . . . who go about proclaiming the news of the day, giving notice of public councils; expeditions, dances, feasts, and other ceremonials, and advertising any thing lost.")[51]

The explorers continued their travels, still with their original guide and chief, down the Grande Ronde River to the Snake River, traveling along an open and easy route. Bonneville was "charmed" by the area's beauty. "The grandeur and originality of the views, presented on every side," he wrote, "beggar both the pencil and the pen." Nothing they had previously "grazed upon in any other region could for a moment compare in wild majesty and impressive sternness" with the "series of scenes" before them that "astonished" their senses, and filled them "with awe and delight."[52] Bonneville's words not only convey the scenery's magnificence and beauty but also suggest the comfortable circumstances that allowed him to appreciate that grandeur. A full stomach, a good night's sleep, a competent guide, and fresh horses made enjoyment of the surroundings easier.

Bonneville, his men, the chief, and their guide continued north along the Snake River a considerable distance before the "old chief" suggested they stop to graze the horses. He summoned a cousin from a village across the river, possibly near the mouth of Captain John Creek on the Idaho side, who jumped into a light cottonwood canoe and vigorously paddled across the river. The cousin visited briefly, crossed back to his village, then returned with tobacco and provisions, and joined the travelers on their continued trek.

On down the Snake River they went, meeting other Nez Perce along the way. A man with whom Bonneville had become acquainted the previous winter greeted the captain with open arms. When they reached the vicinity of Couse Creek—their guide's home—the guide took his leave while others crossed the river to meet the old chief, his cousin, and the strangers. A trivial incident marred their otherwise sociable evening. One of Bonneville's men displayed a small, rare animal hide to their guests, who "examined it with looks of lively admiration and pronounced it great medicine."[53] The next morning it was missing; suspicion fell on a "gallows-looking dog" that belonged to a Nez Perce man who lived nearby. Certain of the dog's guilt, Bonneville's man killed the poor animal and "rigorously scrutinized" his intestines. No skin. The Nez Perce believed the Americans had accused them of thievery—although supposedly Bonneville's men never made such charges—and the agitated Nez Perce broke camp to return to their village across the river. Bonneville and his men continued on down the Snake River. Although mortified at what had occurred, the "old chief" remained with them. Ultimately he returned to his genial self.

They next came upon the village of a great chief near the mouth of Asotin Creek.[54] There the Nez Perce greeted the travelers with the same hospitality they had earlier received at the Grande Ronde village. "The whole population [appeared] in the field, drawn up in lines, arrayed with the customary regard to rank and dignity." The explorers fired salutes and shook hands with every member of the village. Afterward the residents honored the travelers with a smoke, banquet, displays of agility, and horse races. The Nez Perce asked numerous questions about the United States and requested the healing services of the captain. (Bonneville's reputation as a healer followed him on his travels throughout Nez Perce country, as had William Clark's thirty years earlier.)

When Captain Bonneville and his three explorers left the Asotin village, their continued travels took them out of Snake River country. They probably did not reach the confluence of the Snake and Clearwater Rivers, an added eight miles downstream, but most likely took one of the routes across what is now Clarkston Heights to the mouth of Alpowa Creek on the Snake River. There they visited a Nez Perce village, nine miles below the present town of Clarkston, where Chiefs Timothy and Red Wolf resided, before continuing on to Fort Walla Walla. The land's agricultural potential in the vicinity of present-day Lewiston and Clarkston impressed Bonneville. "What a delight it would be," he wrote, "just to run a plough through such a rich and teeming soil, and see it open its bountiful promise before the [plow] share."[55] His words heralded the region's future, but not before another wave of intruders entered the country that belonged to "this kind and hospitable, scrupulously honest, and remarkable" Nez Perce people. That wave arrived thirty years after Captain Bonneville's visit, not as farmers with a desire to plow the teeming soil, but as gold seekers intent upon extracting its precious metals. The early stages of change brought by outsiders to the Nez Perce nation, once subtle and nonintrusive, suddenly turned irreversible.

Chapter 6

Steamboat Pioneers

Gold enticed people by the thousands to the heart of the Nez Perce reservation. Easterners fleeing a civil war, Willamette Valley settlers, California miners, plus first- and second-generation European and Canadian immigrants—they all came, drawn by rumors of prodigious mineral deposits in the Clearwater and Salmon river country in what was soon to become Idaho Territory. By the spring of 1861, stern-wheel riverboats of the Oregon Steam Navigation Company (OSN) had pushed east up the Columbia and Snake Rivers to the mouth of the Clearwater River, carrying prospectors, entrepreneurs, animals, and a wide variety of supplies from Portland stores. The arrival of the first riverboat, the *Colonel Wright*, immediately transformed the barren, tranquil Clearwater/Snake River confluence into Lewiston, a full-fledged, ripsnorting mining supply town and commercial center.[1]

Throughout Lewiston's first three years as a mining supply center, the town experienced a robust and growing economy. The infant community sought to capitalize on its favorable location by extending steamboat navigation into Hells Canyon with road access from river landings to the expanding central Idaho mining regions. Then, in mid-1863, the boom shifted south to the goldfields of Boise Basin. John Scranton, the editor of Lewiston's first newspaper, the *Golden Age*, who both reflected and influenced the views of his adopted community, tried to recapture Lewiston's dying economy by pushing even harder for a river highway through the canyon to tap the promising south Idaho trade. Scranton, with his unbridled enthusiasm—infectious and highly characteristic of a time when people disdained the word "can't"—predicted that soon steamer whistles would "reverberate along the banks" of the Snake River and would be heard "for ages yet to come" throughout the "ravines, gorges and canyons" as a symbol of "ambition and perseverance."[2]

Figure 6.1. The first picture taken of Lewiston, Washington Territory, 1862. Located at the head of steamboat navigation from Portland, Oregon, the town grew quickly as a supply center for mining camps to the east. The Snake and Clearwater confluence is on the left; earliest steamboats docked at the confluence. (Photo courtesy of the Oregon Historical Society.)

A Corridor to the South

When valley residents and OSN officials first conceived the idea of creating a river highway through Hells Canyon, they assumed that they knew the Snake River. They had already proved, despite prevailing opinion, that stern-wheel riverboats could navigate the Snake River from its mouth to Lewiston. Promoters of a canyon highway could not anticipate the river's character south of Lewiston where it dropped from slightly over 2,000 feet at today's Brownlee Dam to only 925 feet at China Garden, a distance of slightly over one hundred miles, creating a raging class 3 river. They had no reason to expect a boulder-riddled channel, a channel altered in a flash by landslides, sheer rock cliffs dropping perpendicularly into the river, or a threadlike channel barely permitting a steamboat's passage. Even if the promoters had known the river's unique characteristics, they almost certainly would have pursued their dream undaunted. They were intent on conquering nature, on molding it to serve their needs. The optimists simply needed a way to surmount the canyon barrier.

First, OSN company officials had to determine the stream's navigational feasibility. In the spring of 1862, they hired Levi Allen and Edmund Pearcy, Lewiston shingle manufacturers, and a Mr. Stubadore to lead an exploratory expedition.[3] On March 14, with the river high from a heavy snow melt, Allen, Pearcy, and Stubadore, plus ten other men, set sail for Lewiston from Fort Walla Walla near the mouth of the Snake River. Their heavily loaded bateau drew eighteen inches of water, forcing them repeatedly to tow the cumbersome craft. Once in Lewiston the party laid over two days, then continued south, following the east (Idaho) side of the Snake River to its juncture with the Salmon River, still dragging the boat most of the route. The task must have been exhausting but would have given the surveyors an intimate look at the shoreline.

At the Snake/Salmon River confluence, all thirteen men turned left to ascend the Salmon River. In twelve miles they reached Wapshalee (Billy Creek) and a Nez Perce camp. There navigation ceased and the party separated. Allen, Pearcy, and four other men returned overland to the Snake River by crossing the northern spur of the Seven Devils Mountains that separates the Snake and Salmon Rivers. They determined that the mountain "was not so steep as to prevent a good wagon road."[4] Once back on the Snake River, the explorers retraced their land route back to the Wapshalee village, where they obtained a Nez Perce canoe, paddled down the Salmon River to its mouth, turned left, and proceeded south up the Snake River. For the first seven miles they walked along the banks, towing the canoe. They then paddled and portaged the boulder-strewn, turbulent river through the entire canyon to, by Allen's reckoning, a few miles north of the Weiser River confluence. There they left the river and continued overland to the "Boise mines."[5]

When back in Lewiston, Allen shared his assessment of the Snake River's navigational potential through the canyon with the *Golden Age* editor, John Scranton. At the upper end, he claimed, "steamers can go between Powder and Weiser [Rivers] and have a fine landing." Scranton listened intently; he wanted news about the river farther north. Allen estimated that the channel depth from Lewiston to the Salmon River confluence was from three and a half to twelve feet deep with "no obstructions of any kind to successful navigation of the river." He and his companions also were convinced that they had proved "conclusively" that a trail existed "close by Snake River" along that section. Then Allen provided what Scranton had been waiting to hear: "The river would probably be navigable the entire year" unless there was "an extraordinary cold winter." Lewiston would be within four days, Allen promised, of "the greatest mining country yet discovered in extent in our Territory [the Boise mines]." Allen's report guaranteed Lewiston's continued future as an important river port and mining supply center. It was "only a question of time," Scranton added. Both he and Allen, however, had ignored the fact that the water had been abnormally high during the survey. Allen's exploratory party had failed to experience normal river conditions.[6]

Nevertheless, Levi Allen and Edmund Pearcy's party had ascended the Snake River to Pittsburg Landing and possibly beyond, a feat known to have been accomplished only by Donald Mackenzie and his fur trappers more than forty years earlier. Two important chains of events resulted from Allen and Pearcy's 1862 journey. First, their optimistic report of the feasibility of steamboat navigation through the canyon inspired subsequent exploration and development schemes throughout the region.[7] Second, the surveyors brought back word of copper and gold in the Seven Devils, a discovery that would be critical to later events in the canyon.[8]

Based in part on that initial, positive report, riverboat Captain A. P. Ankeny sent out a second reconnaissance party to examine Hells Canyon. With navigational obstructions most obvious during low water, the surveyors—Charles Clifford, Washington Murray, and Joseph Denver—planned to travel overland to the mouth of the Boise River, then raft downstream to Lewiston. They left Lewiston on September 20, 1862, walking along the Snake River to the mouth of the Grande Ronde River—an "open river with no obstructions"—then continued their land route through the Grande Ronde Valley to the "old emigrant road" (the Oregon Trail). Once on the trail they continued to the confluence of the Snake and Boise Rivers.[9]

At Fort Boise, the abandoned Hudson's Bay Company post near the mouth of the Boise River, the three men prepared for the hazardous journey downstream to Lewiston. They built a raft, lashed their provisions to it, said good-bye to the skeptical onlookers, and "came dashing and foaming down the wild, tortuous Snake." The banks of the first twelve-mile-long canyon exhibited clear evidence of a sixty-foot or greater fluctuation in the water level. Drifting next through an eight-mile valley, the explorers observed expansive "glorious open country" before entering the next fourteen-mile gorge that "penetrated the two ridges of the Blue Mountains" (Seven Devils and Summit Ridge).

Sixty miles later they arrived at the mouth of Salmon River, that they estimated was "inside of 100 miles" from Fort Boise. Forty more miles, according to their estimates, and they docked at Lewiston. The surveyors generally relied on guesswork through a confusing terrain, thus their figures were off. That is understandable. However, with such a low river level, they should have seen possible navigational impediments. Consequently, their concluding assessment, as reported by *Golden Age* editor John Scranton, seems dubious. "They found nothing in the river to impede navigation, whatsoever, and pronounced it feasible at any season of the year unless it be by ice." He then concluded that the river was "much safer to travel than from Lewiston to the mouth of the Snake." Those words surely heartened a community frequently frustrated by OSN claims that the Snake below Lewiston was not navigable much of the year.

Scranton's boosterism further embraced the future of Lewiston's expanding trade as he suggested potential business far beyond the Boise River. "We shall penetrate Nevada and Utah territories by steam," Scranton envisioned. Steamboats could continue on to Salmon Falls "only 90 miles from Fort Boise" and open a "new avenue of trade" with road connections to the south. To those who believed Scranton's boastings, Lewiston's future looked bright.

Brigadier General George Wright, stationed at Fort Vancouver, also read Scranton's article with some interest. In a letter to the adjunct general of the army, Wright requested that a military post be built at or near the abandoned fur trading post of Fort Boise, "in the very heart of the mining districts of the north" and on the route used by "the vast emigration from the East." To support his request, Wright enclosed the *Golden Age* interview "relative to the navigation of Snake River" and the "probability" that steamers would ascend "as far as Boise or Salmon Falls."[10] On December 23, 1862, the *Official Record of Union and Confederate Armies in the War of Rebellion* published Wright's letter and the *Golden Age* article. As *Golden Age* editor John Scranton interpreted the events, people with some sway were finally aware of central Idaho Territory's potential. During the Civil War, however, the federal government and the U.S. Army had a much bigger agenda. They needed western gold. If the Snake proved navigable, moving gold from south Idaho downriver to the Columbia solved a critical transportation problem.

Captain A. P. Ankeny, who sent out that second 1862 reconnaissance party, was at the time competing with Portland's Oregon Steam Navigation Company. He, along with W. H. Corbett, Dorsey S. Baker, Ephraim Baughman, and several others built the *Spray*, a 116-foot, 235-ton sternwheeler. They put the small craft on the rivers from Celilo to Lewiston hoping to break the OSN's monopoly on that lucrative stretch. The *Spray* reportedly paid for itself within its first five months.[11] If it could only push on south to the Boise River, the investors would have a commanding edge over the Portland-based river giant.

The *Spray* attempted the canyon run in the fall of 1862, but only fifteen miles above Lewiston, Ankeny's dream was shattered. The mission was aborted, but why it was aborted has not been discovered. The effort, however, prompted the OSN to buy the steamboat for twice its initial cost. About the same time, a group of Lewiston businessmen—the group might have included Ankeny and his partners—envisioned putting a line of boats on the Snake River south of town with landings at or near intersecting trails. The first boat landing would be near the mouth of the Salmon River. From there travelers would have direct access east to the Salmon River mines while bypassing the Nez Perce reservation.[12] The businessmen planned to build additional landings throughout the canyon. The scheme would have steamboats plying the river at least as far as the Boise Basin mining district, and optimistically beyond, up the Snake River to where they could establish a link to Salt Lake City.[13] "Pie in the sky," folks would say today. At that time such farsighted development schemes went with the territory—and took on definite urgency by mid-1863.

The mining business turned fickle. Gold strikes in the Boise Basin, eastern Oregon, and western Montana enticed a growing number of prospectors away from central Idaho, threatening the support businesses that provided Lewiston's stability. The town's population dropped dramatically as town merchants, Portland suppliers, and the OSN scrambled for ways to revitalize their once lucrative markets.[14]

An 1863 exploration of Hells Canyon sparked one of the most creative schemes. Five men under the leadership of Captains Molthrop and Collins built a small boat at Buena Vista Bar above Hells Canyon and continued down the stream sixty miles. By March 1864, results of their survey had inspired Portland incorporators to form the Snake River Portage Company to construct a portage bridging the nonnavigable stretch of river above and below "the rapids" of Hells Canyon. (The report failed to indicate which rapids.) The portage would include a "macadamized, plank or clay road, a pack trail and a railroad" and accommodate "all kinds of property, goods, wares and merchandise, and passengers." Travelers would pay the company toll, and the company would own the right-of-way.[15]

When *Golden Age* editor John Scranton reported the plans, although he questioned the logic of the proposed project, his alternative was equally grandiose. Scranton wondered if the incorporators had the foggiest idea of the hurdles they faced. Although he agreed that the difficulties impeding navigation below the canyon were "by no means insurmountable" for nine months out of the year, and that the two stretches of navigable waters could be connected with a considerable capital outlay "in due time," he doubted that "any one of the incorporators ever made even a casual observation of the line of their portage." Instead, Scranton proposed two portages, one between the Salmon and Powder Rivers and a second below the mouth of Burnt River. He implied that a portage through the entire stretch of the canyon might not be necessary. "Navigation to the mouth of Salmon River has been tested," he reminded his readers, and "serious men who have been up and down the river in small boats" are convinced that steamers can run "successfully" to a point eighteen miles above Pittsburg Landing. Scranton admitted that some others did not believe it could be done, and he called for someone with a steamboat of "proper construction and capacity" to put it to a test.[16]

Against the Current?

In mid-June 1865, Captain Thomas Stump accepted the challenge. His tough little *Colonel Wright*—a 110-foot craft often described as a cross between a sloop and a steamer—had proved its worthiness four years earlier under the command of Captain Len White. The *Colonel Wright* pioneered navigation of Snake River as far as its confluence with the Clearwater, then pushed an additional twenty-two miles up that mountain stream.[17] Now Stump, a riverman with Sacramento River experience under his belt, rode at the helm with young William Polk Gray at his side. Others on board the *Colonel Wright* included Alphonso Booke, mate; Peter Anderson, chief engineer; John Anderson, assistant engineer; "Old Titus," the cook; and two passengers, William's father, the venerated riverboat captain W. H. Gray; and J. M. Vansyckle, promoter and developer of Wallula Landing on the Columbia.

From Lewiston the *Colonel Wright* triumphed over the turbulent Snake River to about twenty-five miles above the Salmon River, where Stump attempted a "dangerous eddy" that caught the boat and threw it into the current. "It carried away eight feet" of her bow, keel, and deck sides. "Things looked desperate for a moment." Stump ordered his crew to get a line to shore. "You never saw such a universal willingness" to leave the boat, William Gray remembered. He, Stump, John Anderson, and "Old Titus" remained aboard the deteriorating craft while the crewmen ashore attempted to secure the line. They failed. The current caught the boat and dragged it half a mile downriver. Finally Stump beached the boat. The crewmen walked down to meet their captain, then set about repairing the forward bulkhead.[18]

In the meantime, Captain Stump, young Gray, and the two passengers crossed the river in a small boat and began to climb the hill to see what lay beyond, expecting to return in a couple of hours. Instead, after "a steady climb of four hours" they reached the crest of the hill and as the sun set, looked over "into the beautiful Wallowa Valley." Darkness overtook them, so they stayed there through the night.[19] The next day, with the bulkhead repaired, the *Colonel Wright* returned to Lewiston, covering the same distance "in three and a half hours" that had taken them "four and a half days" pushing against the current. Gray gave no detailed description of the trip in either direction.

Although no *Golden Ages* have survived to authenticate the story, a Corps of Engineers 1875 report provides additional confirmation of the *Colonel Wright*'s venture. Major Nathaniel Michler wrote that the *Colonel Wright* ascended the Snake eighty miles "at a low stage of water" as far as Twin Rock, "about 20 miles above the junction of the Salmon," to search "for a trail leading from the river to the mining regions of the Idaho Basin." Michler concluded that "no important benefits were derived from the examination."[20] Captain Stump even reportedly saw little value in his accomplishments, as he recalled the venture years later.[21] But the *Colonel Wright* was probably the only steamboat to successfully ascend the Snake River to Pittsburg Landing or a point nearby, and that indeed makes Stump's accomplishment noteworthy.[22]

Despite the *Colonel Wright*'s success, the Oregon Steam Navigation Company and any real or potential competitors realized that regular, reliable commerce through the canyon was unrealistic. The OSN, however, did not intend to give up on the lucrative South Idaho trade, even if it meant bypassing Lewiston. "We must leave 'no stone unturned' to divert all the Boise and Owyhee trade this way [to Portland]," announced company man Simeon G. Reed. "It is not a matter of choice but of necessity."[23]

With the Current?

The Oregon Steam Navigation Company felt the sting of competition from the south, competition that they could not eliminate with a buyout. The California Steam Navigation Company (CSN), which previously ran central Idaho traffic by sea to Portland and up the Columbia/Snake Rivers on OSN boats to Lewiston, now used the Sacramento River, Red Bluff, and Chico land routes to reach south Idaho gold and silver mining camps. The route was closer and cheaper. The OSN's only way to compete was to transfer cargo at Umatilla Landing on the Columbia River to freight wagons, then haul it diagonally across the Blue Mountains and Baker Valley of northeast Oregon to the Snake River at Olds Ferry, ninety miles west of the booming town of Boise City and above Hells Canyon. There the company would transfer the boat cargo back to one of their riverboats, ship it 120 miles upstream to the Boise/Ruby City road, and make another land transfer to either town.

In January 1866, the OSN began phase one of the plan. At Fort Boise, twenty men under the supervision of Captain John Gates, consulting engineer for all OSN operations, began construction on a large, light-draft steamboat, 136 feet long and weighing 300 tons. Coal from nearby deposits would supplement its cordwood fuel supply.

Fate frowned on the ambitious venture from the onset. The western Shoshone Indians, no longer content to watch the incursion of outsiders into their land, were at war and would be for the next two years. The hardworking construction crew found themselves in the midst of the conflict with the threat of attack plaguing both them and their suppliers. A lumberman, on his way back to Portland after delivering lumber and cordwood at the shipyard, "came near losing his life." One time Indians shot his horse from under him; other times they "brushed his hair" with bullets. However, from the OSN's perspective, the real problems came not from the "Snakes" but from company suppliers. The lumberman, for example, received nineteen thousand dollars for his delivery, "frightful figures but there is no back out now," OSN President J. C. Ainsworth wrote. Another supplier refused to cross the Blue Mountains with the boat's machinery until the roads dried out unless Ainsworth paid him seven hundred dollars extra. Ainsworth was "more and more disgusted" with him but knew the boat could not be launched without the cargo he carried.[24]

On April 20, 1866, the grand venture began with the launching of the *Shoshone*. That worthy craft proved itself with each of thirteen successful runs between Olds Ferry (Farewell Bend) and Owyhee Ferry. Nonetheless, the business was doomed. The Portland company simply could not compete in price or service with the California-based CSN. The total charge for moving goods from Portland over the Blue Mountains to Boise City was

$123 per ton. Even though the OSN's Umatilla, Boise, and Idaho Express and Fast Freight Line periodically readjusted their rates to make the company more competitive, still the Californians had the advantage. CSN could move freight earlier in the spring and with fewer cargo transfers. The Oregon company, on the other hand, unloaded and reloaded cargo seven times from Portland to the Boise/Owyhee ferry, costing them lost time and money.[25] Even the fuel supply, upon which the riverboat depended, proved to be low grade and inadequate coal.

Company officials ultimately halted all riverboat shipments. For three years the *Shoshone* lay idle, tied up at the Owyhee Ferry while the company decided its fate. At length an angry, frustrated President Ainsworth called it quits. He ordered the *Shoshone* to be taken down the Snake River to go into service below Lewiston.

Captain Cyrus Smith was willing to pilot the *Shoshone* on a first-of-its-kind run north through the canyon. "A more perilous and uncertain adventure has never been undertaken in these waters," a May 1869, Silver City newspaper proclaimed.[26] John Anderson, earlier on board the *Colonel Wright*, signed on as engineer.[27] The river immediately challenged Smith and Anderson's assault. Shortly after launching from Owyhee Ferry the *Shoshone* entered the unexplored section below the mouth of Powder River, where the water was "too rough and swift to be considered safe" even for skiffs.[28] The crew momentarily tasted victory as they safely eased the sturdy craft through the Big Canyon below Olds Ferry and into a wide basin above Lime Point. Ahead loomed Copper Ledge Falls, a deadly, three-hundred-foot-long cataract with a full eighteen-foot drop.[29] Smith weighed his options. With insufficient rope to ease the boat down over the rapids, his choices were either to abandon the venture or conquer the rapids. Smith's crew made the decision for him. They deserted him.[30] Smith ordered the *Shoshone* tied to a nearby tree, left two men behind to keep watch, proclaimed that the vessel could "rot where she lay,"[31] and he and Anderson "descended the remaining distance to Lewiston in a small boat." The two doubtless sensed failure as they made that final descent. Fame had eluded them.[32]

The Oregon Steam Navigation Company was not as quick to abandon the *Shoshone*. The following spring, 1870, they hired Captain Sebastian "Bas" Miller, "one of the old and experienced Willamette River pilots," and Daniel E. Buchanan, "an experienced engineer," to bring the little steamer on downriver.[33] Their task would prove daunting, but no less so than simply reaching the *Shoshone* in that godforsaken stretch of the canyon. The two rivermen left Portland on March 21, 1870, traveled by steamboat from Portland to Umatilla, and then boarded the stage for Union Town (now Union), Oregon. Near Union Town they hired John McCam and his packhorses to guide them to the *Shoshone*, following the Powder River to its confluence with the Snake River and proceeding north.[34]

The Snake River rarely invites land travel along its banks. Soon rocky cliffs forced them away from the river and across a spur of the mountain, around Indian Cave, then back to the Snake River.[35] The travelers briefly paralleled the river before again climbing "a very bad and miry" trail to Pine Creek Valley before returning yet again to the river. At McGrath's cabin, just above Lime Point, the horses could go no farther. Guide McCam, the packers, and horses returned to Union Town. McGrath provided the rivermen with some "small Cayuse ponies." Miller and Buchanan loaded their heavy packs on the ponies and drove them down the trail "by the ordinary appliances of much shouting and many stones to urge them forward." The men walked a three-mile ascent along "the worst road of the whole route" around a perpendicular wall of rocks opposite Lime Point, and "finally re-crossed the Snake" to a miner's camp. From there they boated on down the river. Sixteen days and 150 miles after leaving Union Town, Miller and Buchanan reached the *Shoshone*.[36.]

Map 6.1. In the 1860s steamboat companies hoped to navigate the rivers from Umatilla, Oregon, to Shoshone Falls, Idaho, using a series of portages. The steamboat *Shoshone*, initially part of that scheme, became the first of two steamboats to descend the Snake River through Hells Canyon.

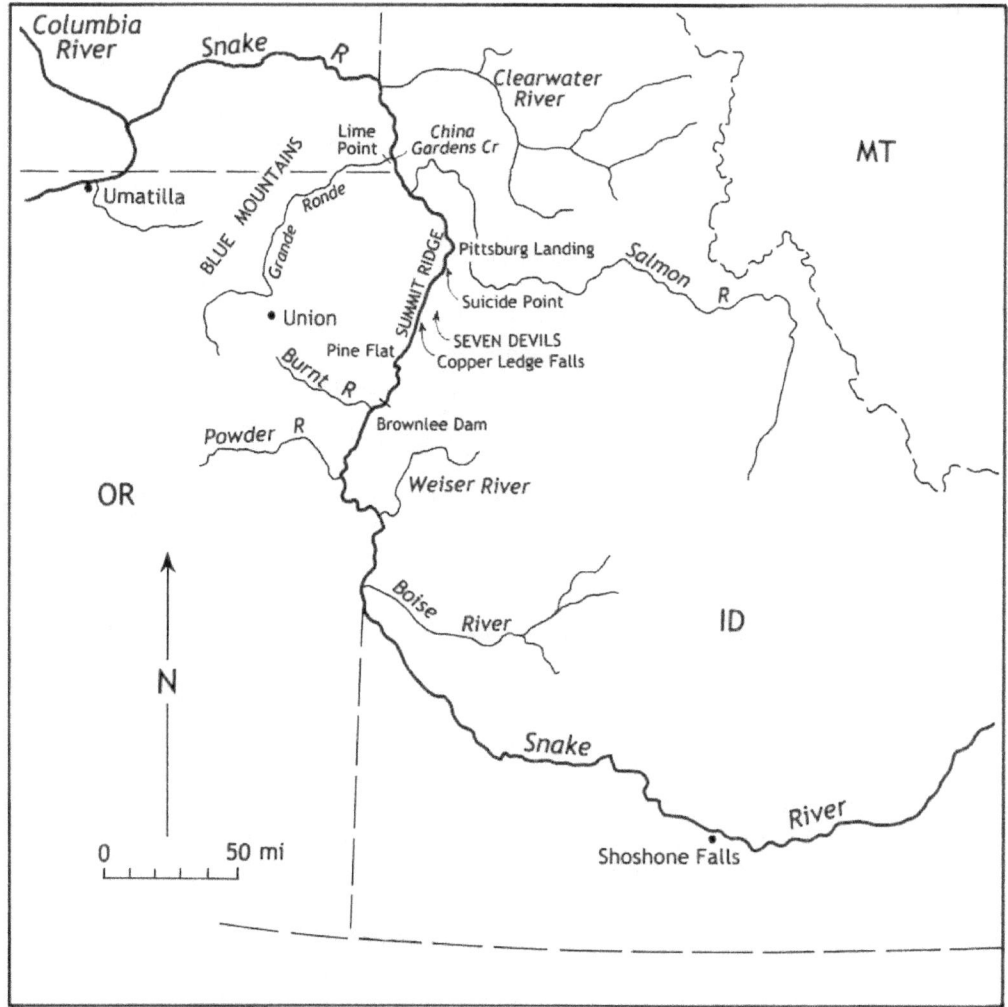

At Lime Point, Buchanan and Miller met Livingston and Smith, the *Shoshone*'s "keepers" for the past few months. Livingston signed on as mate for the upcoming voyage, Smith as fireman, and W. F. Hedges joined the crew as "general utility man."[37] For four days the men worked to make the *Shoshone* river worthy. Buchanan got the machinery in working order, tested it under steam, and found it satisfactory. He rigged hoses and pumped water over the hull to swell the pine planking, since he lacked both time and supplies to caulk the boat. As a safety precaution they attached a small boat to the stern for the engineer and for the rest of the crew lashed a larger boat to the bow.

As the crew worked, spring melt gradually swelled the river, raising it to optimum height for departure. Even with the distraction of preparations, for four days the men were beset by uneasiness. Cut off from the world, the men had no clear idea what lay ahead. The thunderous roar from Copper Ledge Falls, two hundred yards below where they were working, constantly reminded them that once they cast off they would plunge immediately into the maelstrom. But there was no turning back. On April 20, 1870, Miller announced their departure. They fired up the boiler, got up a full head of steam, loosed the lines, and launched. As a precaution Buchanan placed lighted candles in the hold to detect leaks.

Miller planned to "drift" the *Shoshone* down the river by keeping the bow downstream with the engines running in reverse. The force of water would build pressure against the wheel rudders to give the captain some control over the steering. "To steam ahead the boat would be lost against the rocks," Buchanan explained.[38] Unfortunately, Miller misjudged the power of the eddy above the falls. As if already tired of this new nuisance, the river caught the boat and swirled it around three times. Then, just as Miller regained some control and prepared to line out the steamboat, the angry water of Copper Ledge Falls ripped the boat from him, pulled the bow to the crest of the eighteen-foot falls, tilted it briefly on the brink, then plunged it straight down. Up shot the paddle wheel into the air. Freed from the slowing effects of the water, it spun faster and faster, casting broken pieces up as high as the upper deck, or so claimed the miners gathered to witness the disaster.[39] Then the wheel plunged down. The section that had been weathering all year shattered against the rocks. The Snake River now completely controlled the *Shoshone* but had not yet finished with her. It crashed the bow into the rocks at the foot of the rapids and ripped off eight feet of the hull. Captain Miller, drawing upon his years of experience to keep the boat intact and regain some semblance of control, finally managed to land the boat.

In the meantime, engineer Buchanan had his own problems. "Things were becoming complicated down in the engine room. As the boat danced and buckled, the cabin set up a caterwauling as it strained and creaked."[40] The signal gong clanged ceaselessly. Buchanan could not tell whether Miller was signaling him or not. When the boat hit the rocks the weight on the safety valve broke loose. Shrieking steam added to the pandemonium until Buchanan finally wrestled the weight back on the rod and the valve closed.

Figure 6.2. Hells Canyon Dam tamed the turbulent Snake River, as seen here in the 1960s, and inundated Copper Ledge Falls. Nevertheless, one can imagine the formidable task facing Captain Bas Miller and his crew as they began their 1870 descent in the steamboat *Shoshone*. (Photo courtesy of Robert Hoyle.)

Everything happened quickly. One moment the men were fighting for their lives, the next they were safely ashore. Considering their ignorance of Copper Ledge Falls, it was a miracle. The river channel coursed around a sharp elbow then flowed with a torrent of water against a solid rock wall on the opposite side. There the channel divided. On one side was the basin of the eddy that caught the *Shoshone*; on the other side the river followed a natural course over boulders and through falls of surging waves. Even with cool heads, a steady hand at the helm, machinery in perfect control, and an engineer who could hear and promptly obey the call of the bell, the cataract would test the best of rivermen. The men aboard the *Shoshone* were handicapped with a crushed stem, damaged wheel, waves washing over the deck, and an engineer unable to discern the signals.[41]

The next day the crew repaired damage to the wheel and hull. They cast off the following morning, continuing through the narrow canyon of steep perpendicular cliffs and a series of difficult rapids and whirlpools. That afternoon the *Shoshone* hit two of the worst rapids yet—probably Wild Sheep and Granite. The boat shipped so much water it poured into the boiler deck and chased Buchanan out of the hold. The rapids' roar drowned out every noise, even the creaking and splintering of the cabin.[42] The *Shoshone* barely held together through the rest of the day—requiring another day's delay while the crew made paddle buckets for the wheel "out of any plank they could find."[43]

Back on the river, Captain Miller successfully navigated two miles of bad bends until high winds funneling through the narrow fissure forced him to land. They pressed on the next morning, making frequent stops to examine the channel ahead, and beached midday to cut cordwood at Pine Flat. There Miller nearly lost his life. A log rolled on him, rendering him unconscious. For two days a concerned crew waited at Pine Flat while Miller recuperated.[44]

Midmorning on June 26, 1870, the *Shoshone* reached Suicide Point. With the engines backing at half throttle they continued for another thirty miles to the mouth of the Salmon. The increased velocity of the combined Salmon and Snake Rivers enabled the *Shoshone* to travel at three minutes per mile over the foaming cascades to where the Grande Ronde meets the Snake River. There Miller, Buchanan, and their crew spent the last night of what would become a historic first feat of navigation—the initial steamboat adventure north through Hells Canyon.

When the *Shoshone* reached Lewiston, the townspeople were surprised to see the battered steamboat and her crew. Days earlier someone had pulled the *Shoshone*'s jackstaff out of the Columbia River at Umatilla. Everyone thought the boat and crew had fallen victim to the river's wrath. One Lewistonian even hoped to profit from the adventurers' foolhardiness. Stationed a few miles above town, each day he kept watch over the river, waiting for pieces of floating wreckage to salvage. But that bright spring morning when he saw the boat, with her bow staved in, her house wrecked and frayed at the seams but intact, he joined with the rest of the citizens "in manifestations of joy on their successful journey."[45]

As the *Shoshone* rounded-to at the Lewiston landing, Miller shouted through the speaking tube to Buchanan. "I say, Buck, I expect if this company wanted a couple of men to take a steamboat through hell, they would send you and me!"[46] For a riverman, that experience in Hells Canyon was probably as close to hell as he would want to get. At Lewiston, Miller turned over command of the *Shoshone* to Captain Holmes, agent for the Oregon Steam Navigation Company, who took her on down to Celilo on the Columbia River. Miller finally had the chance to heal properly from his accident.[47] The Snake River had a respite before the next riverboat assault more than two decades later.

"A Stupendous Piece of Work"

The *Shoshone*'s successful voyage might explain why Major Nathaniel Michler, head of the Portland District U.S. Army Corps of Engineers, received orders in 1874 to include a reconnoiter of the Snake River between Lewiston and Shoshone Falls in his Columbia and Snake Rivers channel improvement work.[48] Clearly, the *Shoshone*'s ordeal influenced Michler's opinion of the requested examination. He thought it was a waste of time. "The object to be attained is not very apparent," he wrote, since "the impossibilities of rendering this section of the river navigable are already too well authenticated."[49] In short, the major resisted ordering the survey and made a persuasive case against it. But he promised to examine the stream next fall to determine "whether the necessities of commerce" would justify the enormous outlay of money required for "such a stupendous piece of work."[50]

In Michler's estimation, the "best plan" for the survey was to ascend the Snake River from Lewiston while collecting "all available information by inquiry and by actual observation" on the way. Otherwise, his survey crew would have to build suitable boats in Portland, transport them by steamboat from Portland to Umatilla, and then freight them an estimated 508 miles across the Blue Mountains to Shoshone Falls. Michler already knew that there were "several crossings and ferries" and "many Indian rancherias" along a thirty-mile trail south from Lewiston. He knew that there was an Indian trail "seldom used by white men" from the Grande Ronde River to the "Boise Crossing," that there were "occasional" Nez Perce fishing trails touching the river "at a few particular falls or rapids," and that the native people used trails—"few and far between"—to herd their horses and cattle to water. Beyond that, Michler's only knowledge of human activity in the canyon was what he had learned from the *Shoshone* engineer, Daniel Buchanan, and Buchanan's method of acquiring information was, to Michler, foolhardy.

Alonzo Leland, editor of the Lewiston *Teller*, who also opposed the Shoshone Falls–to–Lewiston survey, reflected the town's diminishing interest in a river highway to south Idaho. In a lengthy July 1874, editorial, Leland conveyed his irritation with Idaho representative John Hailey, who urged that the Idaho portion of the Snake River be included in the U.S. House River and Harbor Committee's $75,000 appropriation. Instead, Leland requested that federal money be put into Snake River improvements below the city, "that our people would have . . . continuous steamboat navigation" from the Columbia River to Lewiston. Deriding Hailey, Leland commented that "no man who is at all acquainted with that pass [south of Lewiston] would ever think of asking Congress" to allocate money just "to remove boulders through the canyon." Leland, usually regarded as the "eternal optimist," concluded that even "five million dollars" was not enough to make that stretch of the river navigable. The whole project "was conceived through ignorance or for pure bumkim." Hailey wanted the money to benefit only southwest Idaho, not Lewiston. (Washington Territory's McFadden would not support the bill because it would benefit only its "eastern terminus"—Lewiston.) Leland had another reason to suspect the Idaho Territory representative's motives. North Idaho wanted to become annexed to the emerging state of Washington. Leland, a most vocal proponent, admitted that the region he championed, Lewiston and its surrounding communities, suffered because Idaho could not present a united front in Congress.[51]

Whether Michler or his replacement, Major John Wilson, even ordered the 1875 survey is uncertain. One brief mention of a Snake River survey appears in the April 21, 1877, edition of the *Teller*. A Lieutenant Doane and his party were ordered to explore the Snake River from its source in Wyoming to Lewiston. They left their Wyoming headwaters in December 1876; the following April they were overdue in Lewiston. No one knows what happened to them.

Figure 6.3.
Swallows Nest rock and the Lewiston Hill appear as the area might have looked when the north bound *Shoshone* reached Lewiston in 1870. Note the cable ferry in the foreground. (Photo courtesy of the Asotin County Historical Society.)

Throughout the 1870s, regional development through various Hells Canyon navigation schemes clearly had lost its earlier appeal. Only a very few white people even attempted to make a living in the canyon. The Kurry family settled at Pittsburg Landing in 1877. Farther south near Pine Creek, Andy Culver made a marginal living raising horses to sell to the Indians and to whites. At Salmon Falls, a Mr. Williams and his two associates built a decked flatboat "with a comfortable cabin." They used the boat as their home while descending the river to Lewiston, occupying "much time trapping for furs at different points on the route." They were "quite successful," the *Teller* reported.[52] Otherwise, placer miners and fur trappers, using small boats to move from place to place in their search for gold or pelts, were the only non–Nez Perce on the river. Their stories would help flesh out this period of canyon history. But unless a local newspaper made mention of miners and trappers when they passed through town, the lives and work of those men escaped notice.

The meager success that newspaper articles document was a world away from John Scranton's 1864 prediction that steamer whistles would "reverberate along the banks" of the Snake River and be heard "for ages yet to come." Triggered during the heady days of a mining boom and nourished at a time of economic downturn, the dream of making the Snake River a major commercial corridor to south Idaho with all the regional development the scheme promised was now gone.[53] On the whole, newspapers in the 1870s were silent about the comings and goings in Hells Canyon. Enterprises would later disrupt the tranquility of the canyon and again fill the news reports, but for a time, life in the canyon remained constant.

Chapter 7

War Threatens Hells Canyon

After the *Shoshone*'s exhilarating run through the canyon in 1870, Lewiston's frenzy to turn Snake River into a commercial highway moderated temporarily. The little village settled into a period of quiet respectability. It remained yoked to Portland and outside markets by the Snake and Columbia Rivers, served by two or three steamboats a week during suitable river levels.[1] However, farming and ranching gradually replaced mining as the region's economic foundations. The riverboats' manifests showed an increase in fruit and grains; cattle, wool, and hides; farm implements; domestic goods; and a growing number of immigrants hoping to shape a living out of the interior's fertile soil—all at the expense of Nez Perce land. The settlers did not look south to the canyon of Snake River for economic development. They looked to the open valleys and prairies of central Idaho Territory and northeast Oregon, productive land that would yield to the farmers' plow as it had yielded for centuries to the Nez Perce *tuk' es* (digging stick).

To ensure uncontested access to historic Nez Perce properties, the prospective settlers demanded that the federal government enforce the Nez Perce treaty of 1863—known to the Nez Perce people then and now as the "steal" treaty. The treaty had mandated that the Nez Perce abandon 90 percent of their 1855 reservation land and settle on a small tract of reservation property near Lewiston. In actuality, many native bands of people ignored the treaty and continued living where they always had. During the mining era, the Nez Perce people's failure to comply with the treaty mattered little to outsiders who were bent on finding gold in Nez Perce country, for once the diggings played out, they moved on. Settlers, however, were permanent farmers and ranchers. By the late 1870s, they were in the region to stay. Similar events happened far to the south and east, forever changing the lives of the Bannock Indian people.

The clash of cultures resulted in the Nez Perce War of 1877 and the Bannock War of 1878, wars that covered a vast geographic area on both sides of the Snake River. The river and Hells Canyon barricade became center stage for the initial phase of the Nez Perce War. Throughout the two wars, it remained a mental and physical barricade both to the settlers who were frightened by unfolding events and to the military that was trying to protect them.

No Longer Welcome

The middle Snake in the 1870s continued as homeland for many Nez Perce bands, people who had been living there peacefully since the incursion of the first outsiders. That is, until 1877 when the canyon life they had cherished for centuries ended. In the spring of that year the government ordered all "nontreaty" bands onto a reservation at Lapwai, Idaho

Territory. Nontreaty—a term used by both Nez Perce and whites—designated Nez Perce bands who had refused to sign the 1863 treaty. Because they did not sign the treaty, they believed they were not obligated to abide by its terms and consequently refused to comply with the treaty's directive to move from their traditional grounds to the Lapwai reservation east of Lewiston.[2] By 1877, outside pressure to enforce the treaty grew so great that General Oliver O. Howard, acting on orders from his superiors, mandated that all nontreaties move to the Lapwai reservation. The people complied, but their orderly move turned tragic and a war resulted. The retelling of events— well documented in numerous sources—is beyond the scope of this study. However, the prominent role that the Snake River, the lower Salmon River, and the surrounding country played in the early events of this momentous juncture of history merits attention.

The nontreaty Nez Perce bands in Oregon included the Imnaha, Walwama, Inantoinu, Koiknmapu, and Isawisnemepu bands. They wintered on the Imnaha and Wallowa Rivers, Joseph Creek, and the lower Grande Ronde River at its mouth and north.[3] On the Idaho side of Snake River, Toohoolhoolzote's band wintered south of the Salmon River confluence to Pittsburg Landing. The mandate to move followed a failed government effort to establish a second Nez Perce reservation in the Wallowa Valley.

In 1871, President Grant issued an executive order establishing the proposed Oregon reservation. Its eastern boundary bordered Snake River from the mouth of the Grande Ronde River to the mouth of Sluice Creek, due east of the present-day town of Enterprise. Using today's reference points, it embraced part of Enterprise, all of the town of Lostine and some land to the south, and "all of the town of Wallowa and the surrounding lower valley." It excluded Wallowa Lake and the Wallowa Mountains, the town of Joseph, and Prairie Creek, Alder Slope, and the Hurricane Creek drainage.[4] Even though the white population at that time numbered only 115, the proposed reservation included many previously established homesteads and wagon roads. The prospect of uprooting and relocating upset those folks. Additionally, as Lapwai Indian agent John Monteith observed, the Nez Perce were unwilling to move to the newly designated lands because it meant losing access to some longtime hunting and fishing grounds. Monteith expected the Nez Perce people to adopt an agrarian lifestyle, and as happened throughout the country at this time, he focused his attention wholly upon Chief Joseph. Monteith contended that Joseph and his band were not "entitled to the Wallowa" unless they settled there as farmers. Once they did that, the "upper portion of the valley" would be "sufficient for farming and grazing" and would have ample fishing sites. Joseph's people would no longer require access to hunting grounds, he argued.[5]

In truth, however, no one was willing to endorse a second Nez Perce reservation, neither Monteith, nor the Wallowa Valley settlers, nor most interior Pacific Northwest settlers. The settlers' intractable position supported by Oregon congressional delegates, plus numerous additional obstacles, voided the proposed reservation. The nontreaty bands were to move to the Idaho reservation and it fell to General Oliver O. Howard to make sure they were on the reservation by mid June 1877.

After their final May 15, 1877, meeting with General Howard, Joseph and his brother Ollokut returned to the mouth of Joseph Creek. Their people were waiting. Toohoolhoolzote and his band had joined them. Nearby on the Grande Ronde River, Captain Stephen C. Whipple, 1st Cavalry, had also set up camp. Tension and great sadness filled the air in the Nez Perce camp. Some of the young men, alarmed by Whipple's presence, urged that they fight. The council of elders reluctantly advised against it. Joseph said, "It required a strong heart to stand up against such talk, but I urged my people to be quiet, and not to begin a war."[6] That decided, the entire group left Joseph Creek and headed back to the upper Imnaha valley, a more open expanse where the vast Nez Perce livestock herds had already ranged from their winter canyon confinement. (Two years earlier, Agent Monteith had estimated that the Nez Perce collectively owned from two thousand to four thousand horses, but no one knows for sure how many horses and cattle those bands had that spring.)[7] The young men gathered what livestock they could find as the people returned north through the valley toward Snake River. The Nez Perce bands would cross the Snake River a few miles south of the Imnaha River. In the meantime, General Howard sent Companies E and L to "occupy the Wallowa in the interest of peace." They had moved from Fort Walla Walla to establish a permanent camp near what is now Elgin, Oregon. At the same time, Howard ordered Company H from Fort Walla Walla to establish camp opposite Lewiston. The general prepared for war while praying for peace.

It was the worst possible time of year to ford the turbulent canyon rivers. The Nez Perce knew the crossings well and they knew the rivers' many moods—when to cross, how to cross, and when to wait. Had it been earlier, in March or April, winter runoff would not yet have swollen the rivers. But the rivers raged in early June. Thirty days. General Howard had given the Nez Perce people thirty days to move after their final and failed May 15th negotiations. The people had "to do in thirty days what would have taken half a year."[8] Move all their people—from infants to the infirm—all their supplies and possessions, and that boundless herd of livestock.

The Nez Perce tribe's oral tradition maintains, and most historians agree, that the Wallowa band made their Snake River crossing at Dug Bar, about three miles upstream from the mouth of the Imnaha River. It was one of the best sites to herd and swim livestock. An easy trail drops to the river, where the shoreline is confined enough to corral the animals. During spring's high water, two adjacent eddies guide animals and boats northeast across the river to smooth banks on the Idaho side. There the animals can get their footing to pull themselves out of the river and climb a ridge along Divide Creek that extends to Joseph Plains, a high tableland south of the Snake and Salmon River juncture.[9]

The river at flood stage formed a dreadful crossing. For two days the Nez Perce loaded and transported all their possessions aboard rafts and buffalo-hide bullboats. The young and old rode on top the baggage. "Three or four ponies, guided by riders and swimmers, towed each of the tossing craft across the torrent."[10] Others either rode across or swam with their horse. Pandemonium perhaps, certainly rage and anguish, must have exacerbated those arduous chores of moving livestock, building and packing boats, and organizing people. Imagine the sounds—certainly the river's relentless roar, but also cattle bellowing, horses snorting and whinnying, children crying, dogs barking, and men and women screaming out orders loud enough to be heard above all the hubbub. Remarkably all the people crossed safely, but it cost them the loss of treasured animals and baggage.

On the Idaho side they traveled across Joseph Plains to the headwaters of Billy Creek, then down to the Salmon River and another difficult river crossing north to Camas Prairie. The bands left their cattle on the south side of the river attended by a few young men and crossed the Salmon River with most of the horses in the same manner as before. They continued up Rocky Canyon to an ancient rendezvous site near Tolo Lake on the Camas Prairie, a few miles east of Cottonwood. There they waited—one final moment of freedom with friends and family from neighboring bands before confinement and dependency.

Map 7.1. The 1877 Nez Perce War in Idaho. Note the difference in size between the 1855 and 1863 Nez Perce Reservation boundaries. Map detail shows Joseph Plains, Idaho, where the Nez Perce befuddled General Howard.

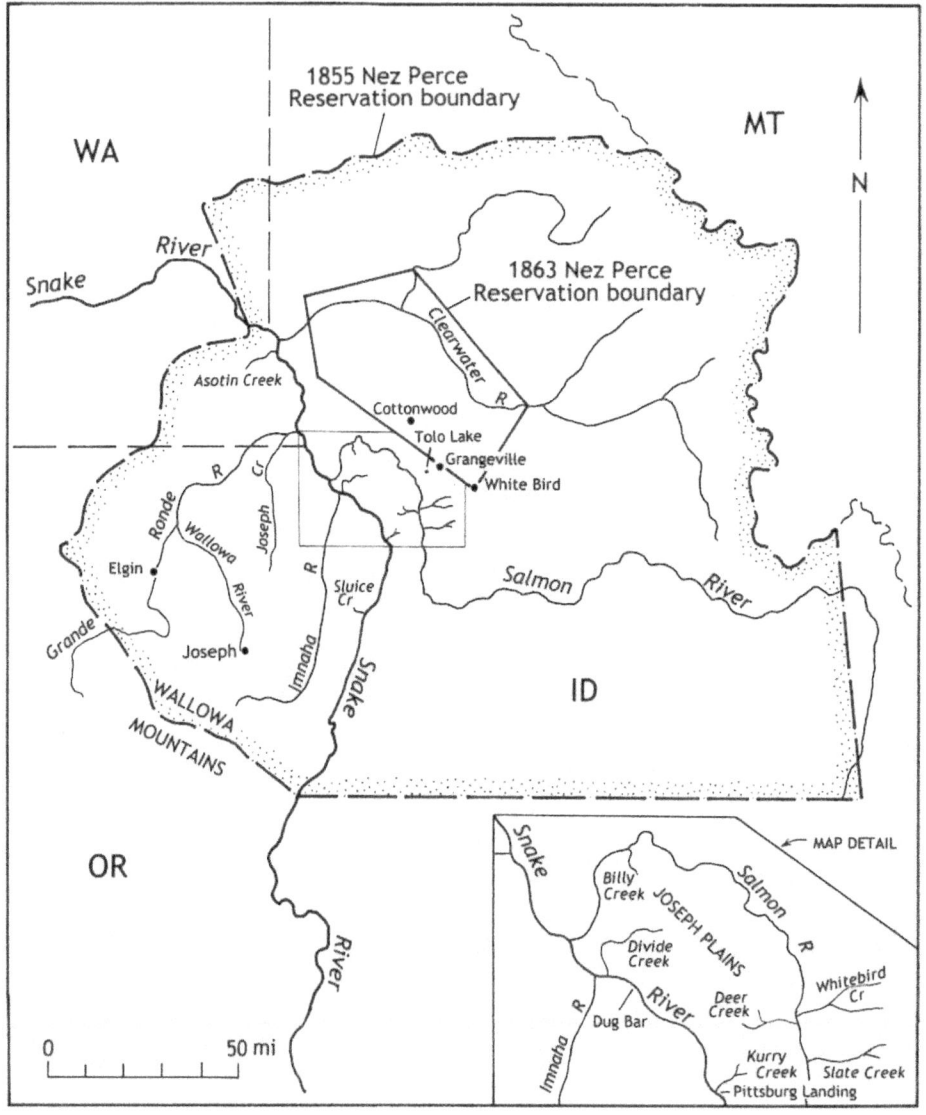

Hostilities Begin

That pause would prove fatal. With Joseph and his brother Ollokut on the south side of the Salmon River butchering some cattle, a "warlike spirit crept across the camp" of more than six hundred people. The evening of June 12, 1877, two days before their final move to the reservation, three young men rode south out of camp toward the Salmon River. Enraged by past injustices and their current circumstances, the young men sought blood retribution. Three whites were killed, then more when other Nez Perce learned what had happened. Joseph and Ollokut returned from across the Salmon River to confront news of the tragedy. They immediately counseled peace. Others tolerated no such talk. There was no turning back—for either side.[11]

News of the killing spread like a raging fire throughout the white communities. The settlers had long feared the worst from this forced Nez Perce relocation and had prophesied its outcome. A careful study of regional newspapers reveals that people anticipated war months before it happened. Once the first whites were killed, no one asked if war was warranted. Their own had died and they too called for blood. That's what they got. The first military encounter occurred June 17, 1877, on the grassy slopes of White Bird Hill near present-day Grangeville. From the hill summit a dazzling vista of river valley, grass-covered hills, and distant forested mountains suggests a place of peace. Not a place for neighbors, once friends, to turn enemies. As events unfurled over the next few weeks, the nontreaty Nez Perce realized that as long as they remained in Idaho they would not know peace. The council decided they would leave Howard's relentless pursuit by retreating to Montana. There they would join their friends the Crows. That was not to happen.

Once the fighting started, the settlers all over the interior anticipated a tragedy. Some feared that other northwest tribes would join the melee. They kept a close eye on reservation Nez Perce, expecting them also to turn from their peaceful ways. Homesteaders and townsfolk alike fortified themselves, sent volunteers to Howard, and demanded that he call

Figure 7.1. The Salmon River a few miles before it enters the Snake River. Near the center of this picture members of the non-treaty bands of Nez Perce crossed the Salmon River from Joseph Plains (right) to Camas Prairie before fighting began and a second time while giving chase to General Oliver O. Howard. (Photo by author, 2006.)

in more troops to protect them. Soldiers, officers, supplies, arms, and horses disembarked at the Lewiston steamboat landing from throughout the west. The *Teller* reported their arrival. On June 14, seventeen tons of freight, horses, and cavalry gear arrived aboard the *Almota*; the same day the *New Tenio* docked with sixty tons of freight for the quartermaster. A month later seventeen men and ten officers from San Francisco disembarked. On July 28, four hundred troops appeared from the east. And on August 4, 1877, four hundred more officers and men of the Second Regiment of Infantry joined the assembled force along with forty packers and eighty-five mules.[12]

Company H from Fort Walla Walla camped opposite Lewiston at the present-day site of Clarkston, Washington, while settlers on that side of the river abandoned their homes, fortified Jerry Maguire's house on Asotin Creek, and prepared to defend themselves from imminent attack.[13] Lewiston residents dug a series of rifle pits to prepare for an attack from the southeast while Howard ordered Colonel Alfred Sully and the 21st Infantry to their defense.[14]

Panic grew as rumors swept south throughout Idaho. L. P. Brown, a pioneer of Mount Idaho, sent a false report to the *Teller* that well-armed tribes were going to join the warriors, with plans to "kill and capture all the country about Weiser, Piette [sic] and Boise valley." Brown claimed that the Nez Perce also had sent runners "to Palouse, Spokane, Columbia river and Umatilla tribes." The united tribes would "capture the whole country about the Snake and Clearwater rivers."[15] People who might otherwise have remembered traditional Nez Perce goodwill toward the whites, now swayed by similarly irresponsible rumors, fed the fear spreading throughout the region.

After fighting began June 17, 1877, at White Bird Hill—a short fifteen-minute skirmish that ended with a humiliating rout of the volunteers and U.S. troops—the Nez Perce crossed the Salmon River below Horseshoe Bend, ascended a saddle and made camp on Deer Creek. Yellow Wolf, a Nez Perce man who fought with the nontreaties and later described the war as he remembered it, provided a detailed picture of the Indians outmaneuvering General Howard in the Salmon and Snake River country. From their position west of the Salmon River, the Nez Perce scouts kept close watch over activity at Howard's camp on the east side of the Salmon River, near the mouth of White Bird Creek. Howard was making preparations to cross the Salmon River in pursuit of the fleeing Nez Perce. A volley of gunfire followed some verbal exchange between the scouts—"hostiles" as the *Teller* referred to the nontreaty Nez Perce—and "Howard's Christian Nez Perce scouts"—Yellow Wolf's term for Nez Perce tribesmen fighting with the army. The retreating chiefs told their scouts to let the soldiers cross. "We are not after them. They are after us. If they come to our side we can fight them if we want."[16]

Camas Prairie pioneer Frank Fenn described General Howard's failed strategy at that stage of the war. After crossing the Salmon River to Joseph Plains, the general planned to "get in Joseph's rear and drive him south," thus trapping the hostiles "between two bodies of troops and crush them."[17] Major John Greene's troops were marching north from Fort Boise with three companies of cavalry and twenty Bannock Indian scouts.[18] Howard, who based his tactics on imperfect intelligence, later acknowledged the superb strategy employed by the retreating Nez Perce bands. "No general could have chosen a safer position [than Joseph]." The Nez Perce had placed themselves where they could "puzzle and obstruct a pursuing foe." Should the general "present a weak force," Joseph could turn upon the army. If Howard directly pursued the Nez Perce, they could outmaneuver the army by moving south along the Salmon River breaks "for at least thirty miles" before turning east. Alternatively, the Nez Perce could move north along the Salmon River, pass Howard's flank, and threaten the army's line of supply while all the time keeping the Salmon River, "a wonderful natural barrier," between them and Howard.[19]

While encamped at Deer Creek, the war chiefs had watched Howard prepare to cross the Salmon River. The Nez Perce women in camp, however, grew uncomfortable so near the soldiers, so on July 1, 1877, the bands broke camp on Deer Creek and moved north. Some of their scouts stayed behind to observe the army's progress.[20] While skillfully maneuvering herds of up to three thousand horses along with all the women, children, aged, and infirm, the chiefs oversaw the move north through Joseph Plains high above the Salmon River. They traveled for thirty-six hours over nearly twenty-five miles of "steep, rugged country" before descending to the Salmon River "at a place known as the Craig Billy Crossing."[21] Yellow Wolf described their move as "good." Immediately the bands crossed the Salmon River a third time and camped high in a mountainous region, in "the country of the *pottoosway*, the medicine tree."[22]

The next day, July 2, well to the south of the Nez Perce, Howard's soldiers and volunteers methodically crossed the Salmon to Joseph Plains. Using a small skiff, a few of the men carried a ferry line to the west bank then returned to help rig two boats as ferries. After loading equipment and supplies on the boats, a few soldiers lined them across the river with the aid of the current. Some men were aboard while others forced their horses and mules into the current. It was a time-consuming operation.

Once across, Howard immediately dispatched Colonel George Hunter and his Dayton, Washington Territory volunteers, who were among the first to cross the river, southwest toward Pittsburg Landing, about twenty river miles above Dug Bar where the Nez Perce had crossed just a few days before. Howard, believing that the Nez Perce were moving in that direction, had ordered Hunter to "examine the country thoroughly . . . especially in the direction of Joseph's reported encampment."[23] Hunter and his men left the Salmon River and struggled up a "steep, hard-to-climb mountain" to its summit. There they came upon "Joseph's trail"—broad and easily followed. Hunter and his volunteers followed the trail south for some distance before returning north. After a short distance they left the main summit trail and dropped down to Snake River at Pittsburg Landing, then returned to the summit trail and continued north. At one point, Hunter was about fifteen miles above the army headquarters, which was still on the Salmon River. He tried to attract someone's attention to relay his report, but failed. Hunter's report, however, was erroneous. Although he was "fully" satisfied that the Nez Perce bands had gone toward "Canoe Encampment" (perhaps the same location as Pittsburg Landing) and had from there crossed the river to Oregon, Hunter was dead wrong.[24]

As soon as Hunter returned to camp, Howard ordered him to guide the troops "to the trails of the hostiles" at the "top of the mountain." Hunter led them up "a spur of the mountain." It was a hard, ten-mile route that, Howard complained, took three times as long to march as "an ordinary road." Pouring rain, thick clouds, and slippery slopes complicated the march. Several pack mules rolled down the mountain to their death. Clearly, the U.S. Army did not have Nez Perce expertise in negotiating the trails of Hells Canyon country.

Once at the summit, Howard found clear evidence of recent Nez Perce presence: caches of clothing, flour, and other supplies. This indicated the headmen's intent to retrace their route home once the hostilities abated. The soldiers destroyed it all. Hunter paused to consider the area's ranching potential and describe it in his journal. He saw a "grand grazing country. Thousands of broad acres of rich and abundant grass, with water [aplenty]"—ideal summer ranges—"while the deep canyons, with little bottoms, rank with shrubbery and tall grasses, furnish food and shelter for cattle and horses during the winter season."[25] Hunter viewed the land through a rancher's perspective. Howard was interested in Nez Perce whereabouts, not ranching potential, and what he saw there frustrated him. He could not tell whether the Nez Perce had turned left toward Canoe Encampment or moved north to a lower Salmon River crossing.

On July 3, 1877, and still without a clear understanding of what the Nez Perce intended, the main military body reached the trails. They traveled north along a clearly defined route only to again descend to the Salmon River, this time opposite Rocky Canyon where the Nez Perce had already crossed. That night Howard's scouts reported that the hostiles had crossed the Salmon River and were on Camas Prairie preparing to move east. Howard made immediate plans to cross the Salmon River—this time at the northern bend of the Oxbow—and continue his pursuit of the hostiles across Camas Prairie to the Clearwater River. His pursuit and the Nez Perce retreat then took them east to Weippe Prairie, the Bitterroot Mountains, and on into Montana. Ultimately, the U.S. Army prevailed. On October 5, 1877, the surviving Nez Perce surrendered at Bear Paw Mountains in Montana, thirty miles from the Canadian border and seventeen hundred miles from their Wallowa Valley and Hells Canyon homes.

Confusion in the Canyon

The conflict as it played out across the Snake River in Idaho Territory caused considerable agitation in Oregon's Wallowa country. Throughout this period Companies E and L stood ready "in the interest of peace." Since early May 1877, ninety-seven men and one Gatling gun had headquartered near the present-day town of Elgin, Oregon.[26] Before the fighting began, the cavalry under Captain Whipple received orders to go to the Lewiston trail crossing near the mouth of the Grande Ronde River, three days from base camp. While in the Elgin camp, and before Joseph's people crossed to Idaho, Whipple thought Howard would want him to "watch the trails leading into Wallowa Valley from Snake River and the lower Grande Ronde." He dispatched Second Lieutenant Servier M. Rains to Fort Lapwai to make inquiries about troop placement in the event of war. Rains left with veterinary surgeon S. G. Going. A guide and an enlisted man accompanied them. They anticipated a safe Snake River crossing. They were wrong. Near the opposite bank, Going, separated from his horse and unable to negotiate the swollen Snake River alone, drowned. The horse made it safely to the opposite bank.[27] A few weeks later the Nez Perce would make a much more difficult Snake River crossing without any loss of human life. Whipple's cavalry and the Gatling gun went on to join Howard.

Once word of the war in Idaho spread, Oregonians were convinced the Nez Perce would return to reclaim their land. Exaggerated reports frightened the settlers. Wallowa's *Mountain Sentinel* received news July 6, 1877, from Captain Elliott of the Pataha Rangers. He and his twenty men were scouting the Imnaha River when they came upon a well-armed band of nine hundred warriors. "We don't know how many we killed, as we had to retreat." Elliott's questionable report added that his troops had captured seventy-five Nez Perce cattle and forty horses. He was certain that the "Indians are mostly between the Snake and Salmon rivers."[28]

On July 12, twenty-six days after the war commenced with fighting concentrated in the Clearwater country, Captain W. R. Booth sent a communiqué back to Wallowa headquarters with a report from acting First Lieutenant John W. Cullen. Ordered to take thirty-two men to the Snake River, Booth's company was to make a reconnaissance of the

Figure 7.2. A view from Pittsburg Saddle, on the Idaho side, looking northwest. The mountain pass between the Snake to Salmon rivers provided a relatively low and easy travel route, one used extensively by Nez Perce people for generations. (Photo by author 2005.)

country and possible Nez Perce activities. Rough travel caused twenty-three men, including Booth, to turn back. Cullen and his men forged on, reaching the Snake River near the mouth of Sluice Creek. Canyon walls "from 4000 to 6000 feet in height" surrounded them.[29] The canyon continued for twenty miles to Pittsburg Landing, where the soldiers found "a low pass" across the mountains to Salmon River. It was in the direction of Whitebird and Slate Creek and "not more than ten miles distant." They spotted two small ranches at Kurry Creek and Pittsburg Landing, and a "plain trail leading direct from Snake river across the pass." About ten miles on downstream, they came upon "a small valley on the river and a good place for swimming the river." Cullen described Dug Bar, which was, unbeknownst to him, the same place that Joseph's band had crossed a month earlier. Across the river they spotted some forty head of cattle and four Indian ponies—one saddle-marked and jaded. Cullen felt certain that more cattle ranged in the surrounding gulches, but could not see them. He also saw "a plain trail leading across the river in the direction of Salmon river." Cullen's report concluded with the assurance that, "having followed all of the windings of the river," that they had located the "only two practicable crossings"—Dug Bar and Pittsburg Landing. Probably by the time Cullen and his men returned to Wallowa Valley with this report, fear that the Nez Perce would return had been tempered. By that time the Indians had reached Weippe Prairie, soon to cross the Bitterroots to Montana.

Ultimately the nontreaty Nez Perce did return to the Pacific Northwest. Some settled on the Lapwai reservation in Idaho; some, on the Colville reservation in northeast Washington; some joined distant relatives on the Umatilla reservation in Oregon.[30] Despite treaty promises to the contrary, the government and many local residents denied Nez Perce use of most traditional fishing, hunting, and root gathering locations, including sites in the Wallowa Valley and the Snake and Salmon river canyons. Over time, however, white resistance to Nez Perce use of traditional food-gathering locations tempered; the Nez Perce returned to the Snake River canyon for short visits and in small numbers. However, before the nontreaty Nez Perce returned to the Pacific Northwest around 1885, another war scare had swept through Hells Canyon country.

Map 7.2. The 1878 Bannock War and the three reservations from which the warriors came. Speculation that they would cross the Snake River at Hells Canyon kept a military presence in the canyon and alarmed central Idaho residents.

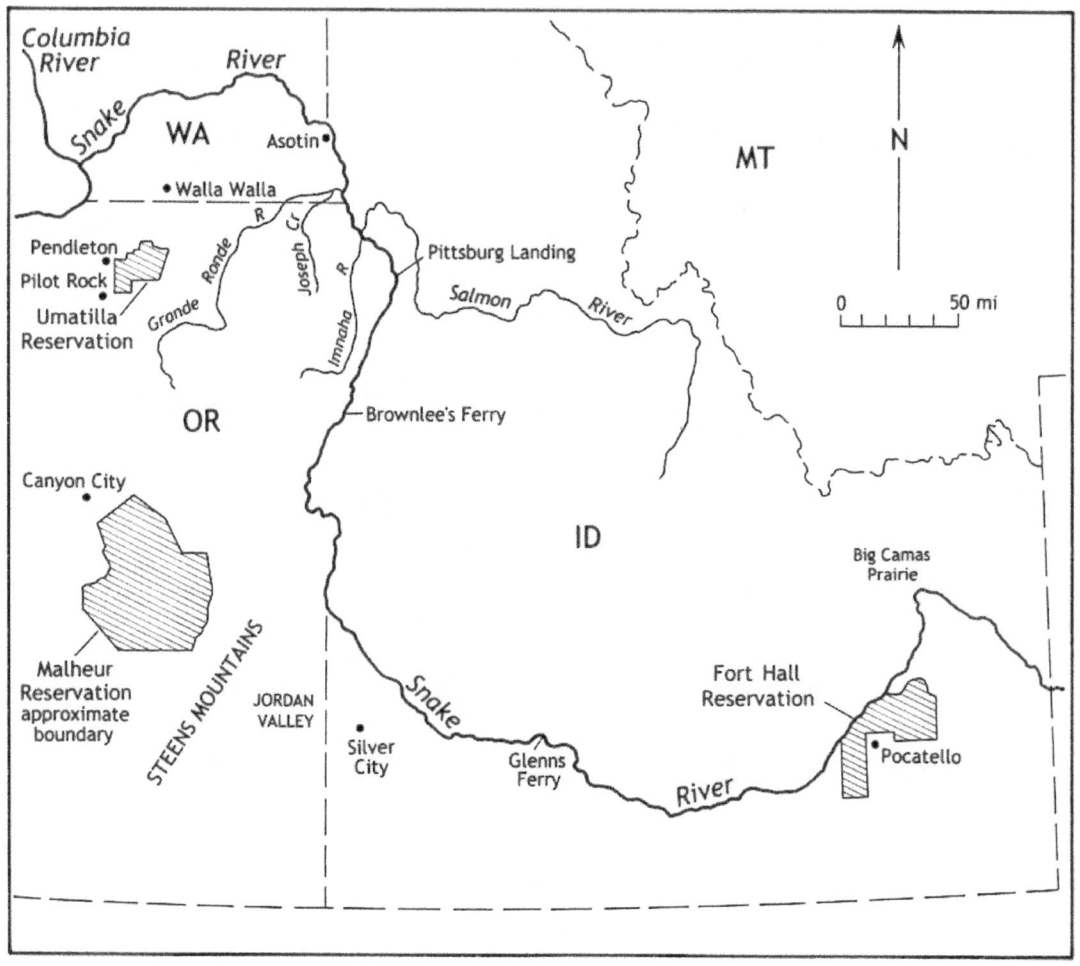

Background to the Bannock War

In the southeastern corner of Idaho Territory, the U.S. government's flawed Indian policy set in motion another chain of events that resulted in war in the spring of 1878. The Bannock Indians' circumstances had grown so intolerable that a few warriors retaliated, igniting skirmishes that spread from south central Idaho throughout most of eastern Oregon. Once again the settlers of the middle Snake region lived in fear of imminent attack, and the native people faced another dilemma of how to respond.

Reasons for the Bannocks' resorting to war are complex and numerous and can be traced back to the Treaty of 1868. That treaty assigned members of the Bannock and Shoshone tribes to the Fort Hall reservation northeast of present-day Pocatello, Idaho. The two tribes shared the reservation land and a vast expanse beyond. However, the unique lifestyles and customs of each tribe often strained their relationship. The Indian agent's behavior aggravated existing tribal differences. When the two agreed on their shared reservation borders, both tribes expected the reservation to include Big Camas Prairie, where camas bulbs, their food staple, flourished.[31] Characteristic of the government's shameful Indian policies, however, the authorities reneged on their promise and excluded the prairie from the final reservation. The Bannock and Shoshone people could still harvest the camas crop on Big Camas Prairie, but they must share the land with the ranchers. Even as camas became an increasingly more critical supplement to the Indians' inadequate reservation diet, it grew scarcer. Settlers converted the prairie to grazing land. Ultimately, an intolerable incident triggered a war.

Some pig farmers drove their herds to Big Camas Prairie to root out the spring camas crop. Then, before the land had a chance to heal, three stockmen pastured their cattle and horse herds in the same area. Two Bannock men arrived on the scene, feigned friendship with the cowboys, had supper with them, returned the next morning for breakfast, then shot and wounded the cowboys. As the cowboys rode away, they looked back to see a "large band of Indians bearing down on their camp."[32] War began immediately after the Big Camas Prairie shooting incident, when Buffalo Horn organized two hundred warriors and struck back. Buffalo Horn, a scout for General Howard during the Nez Perce War, had spent the winter of 1877–78 "stirring up" the Paiutes, Cayuse, and Umatillas—all of eastern Oregon—to seek revenge upon the whites.[33] Whether he had intentionally formed a confederacy or the dissatisfied tribesmen took advantage of the uprising to vent their own anger is not clear. Regardless, before the war's end in midsummer 1878, Buffalo Horn's original confederation had grown significantly.[34]

After insulating themselves in the protection of the lava beds near south Idaho's Camas Prairie, Buffalo Horn's entourage rode southwest to the Snake River and crossed the river at Glenns Ferry (about halfway between present-day Mountain Home and Twin Falls) in south central Idaho. From there an ever-growing wave of warriors swept southwest through Idaho into Oregon, leaving dead settlers and destroyed property in their wake. Buffalo Horn led people seeking retaliation for nearly four decades of white misdeeds. Unlike the Nez Perce, they refused to retreat from the U.S. Army.

Word reached General Howard at his home in Portland that war was again brewing in central Idaho and eastern Oregon. "Is it possible that we must go through another such ordeal as that of last year?" he asked his wife.[35] Yes, it was possible, and his ordeal would be quite similar: more of a wild goose chase than conventional combat.

On June 8, 1878, four days before General Howard reached the Boise Barracks, Captain R. F. Bernard from the barracks, Captain J. B. Harper's citizen volunteers from Silver City, and some Paiute scouts had already responded to the attacks and engaged Buffalo Horn in the "first real skirmish of the war."[36] Buffalo Horn was killed, possibly at the hands of a Paiute scout known as Joe. With Buffalo Horn's death, an unknown number of followers returned to their reservations. Fighting, however, moved west, engaged more warriors, and embroiled the U.S. Army and regional volunteers in sporadic skirmishes for the next two months.

Before Buffalo Horn died, most reports speculated that he would move north through Idaho's Long Valley into the Salmon River country. The Lewiston *Teller* characteristically cautioned its readers that "it will be important for our people north to be on the alert and ready to check the first movement in the approach of Salmon River."[37] When Paiute headmen Egan and Oytes took command of the "militant traditionalists after Buffalo Horn's death," the Indians' movements generated even greater consternation among people in both Idaho and Oregon.[38]

As it happened, Egan and Oytes led their followers west across the territorial border to Oregon's Jordan Valley and the Steens Mountains before they turned north, skirting the foothills along their way to the Malheur reservation, Egan's home. (In published reports, by now Egan, like Joseph the year before, was receiving sole credit for directing the war.) Presumably Egan was returning home to recruit more followers, though he might have had more personal reasons for his return. If the reports were accurate, he commanded four hundred men by the time he reached the reservation. Within the next month, that number had increased to one or two thousand followers. Since the figures were subject to settler hysteria, how many Indians the soldiers were really pursuing or fighting is unknown.

During the next few weeks the roving Bannock-Paiute army vented its wrath on isolated ranchers in Harney, Malheur, Grant, Baker, Union, Umatilla, and Morrow Counties of Oregon. Scattered widely throughout the region and moving "like twisters with tornadic fury," they killed freighters, plundered wagons, stole livestock, frightened settlers, and burned the settlers' buildings.[39] Their northbound route toward the Umatilla reservation took them past the mining community of Canyon City, through the foothills of the Blue Mountains, and near the settlements of Pilot Rock and Pendleton. Never knowing the Indians' exact location; finding that they moved not as one large unit but dispersed into small, scattered attack forces; and fearful that an ever-expanding number of Indian tribes would join them, the settlers of Snake River country daily expected the worst. So did General Howard.

Howard wanted to retain peaceful relations with the main body of Bannock, Paiute, Umatilla, and Cayuse bands while he worked simultaneously to convince the rebellious members to return to their reservations. As the campaign continued north, Howard's tactics evolved to prevent the Indians from crossing either the Columbia or Snake Rivers.[40] The army's fear of a Snake River crossing and the efforts to prevent it brings the Bannock War into the narrative of middle Snake River history.

Unfounded Fears

During the campaign, Alonzo Leland, the editor of the *Teller*, was attending Washington's constitutional convention in Walla Walla, Washington Territory. (He was lobbying for North Idaho's inclusion in the new state of Washington.) With fighting moving ever closer to Walla Walla, Leland was well-positioned to telegraph news of the hostilities back home to Lewiston. His information, however, replete with conjecture regarding Egan's intentions, agitated rather than reassured readers of the *Teller*. On July 6, 1878, Leland reported that General Howard, situated at Pilot Rock, Oregon, about fourteen miles southwest of Pendleton, had expected that Egan would move in the direction of the Columbia River. Leland disagreed with the general. He thought Egan's warriors would leave the Blue Mountains and go north "via the mouth of the Grande Ronde river and cross the Snake." Once across the Snake River, Leland postulated, the Indians would cross the Camas Prairie south of Lewiston, move into the Clearwater Valley, and continue north to Montana or Canada via the Potlatch River. Alternatively, Leland postulated, Egan and his warriors might cross the Snake River at either Pittsburg Landing in the heart of Hells Canyon or Brownlee's Ferry at the upper end of the canyon. Later that day Leland verified that the Indians indeed planned to cross the Snake River near the mouth of the Grande Ronde River. He cautioned the settlers south of Asotin to be on their guard.[41]

Figure 7.3. The meandering Snake River at the center of the picture and the Blue Mountains in the background provide some perspective on the altitude difference in Hells Canyon. Although most of the fighting was west of the mountains, rumors flourished that on their way to Montana the Bannock Indians and their allies would cross the Snake River either near the Grande Ronde River to the north of this picture or Pittsburg Landing to the south. (Photo by author, 2006.)

On July 12, 1878, General Howard was in Walla Walla with a new strategy. He now agreed that Eagan was indeed heading for the Grande Ronde and Snake Rivers. Based on that assumption, Howard made arrangements to move seventy soldiers by water to the mouth of the Grande Ronde River while sending one column overland to the Grande Ronde Valley, one to the Salmon River country, and one "on the trail of the Indians as they roam Umatilla country . . . towards the mouth of the Grande Ronde River." The next day Howard and his seventy soldiers boarded the paddle wheeler *Northwest* at Wallula Junction on the Columbia River and, "with all dispatch," steamed past Lewiston toward the Grande Ronde River. With troops in place, Howard could either intercept Egan as he prepared to cross Snake River near the mouth of the Grande Ronde River or, in the event that Egan instead moved through Wallowa Valley to Pittsburg Landing, Howard's troops would be ready to join the cavalry and intercept Egan at a Snake River crossing farther south. Editor Leland could not resist assessing Howard's plan: "He thinks by this means to corral or bag them as you would snipe. But it is the generally conceded opinion that the driving into the bag is the most difficult part of the job. They don't bag worth a cent."[42]

Special correspondent Penseroso of the *Portland Oregonian* accompanied General Howard and the troops aboard the *Northwest*. At the mouth of the Grande Ronde River they disembarked, marched up the river a few miles, then veered to the left to climb south up Joseph Creek. Traveling through Chief Joseph's winter quarters, Penseroso described the land as "so rugged" that the only appropriate words for it were "confusion worse confounded." Everywhere they looked, evidence of recent Nez Perce occupation spoke to them. Joseph Creek's rocky bottom was "literally honeycombed with holes used as caches." A few caches still held "tons" of provisions and clothing; most of the caches had been robbed. Clearly, the Nez Perce had been unable to pack many of their possessions as they hurriedly prepared to vacate the land. Conversely, the caches testified to Joseph's people's assurance that they would one day return to reclaim their possessions.[43]

Howard's soldiers pushed up Joseph Creek, then left the creek and ascended a "very steep mountain." They camped on its summit. The countryside through which the men passed evoked a flow of descriptions from the *Oregonian* correspondent—luxuriant grass-covered hills where "pines and firs abound," a prairie "thickly strewn with innumerable wild flowers of various hues and descriptions." The region's natural beauty awed Penseroso. As the party of travelers continued their southward trek, it began to drizzle and grow cold. The men donned overcoats and pushed on. Finally, at a "very high altitude" they reached a narrow ridge on the Wallowa Trail. To their right Penseroso looked down to the Imnaha River Canyon, where "the mountain falls away to heavily timbered ravines and gulches." To their left, he gazed into Hells Canyon, "an immense terrible looking gorge, suggestive of the bottomless pit." To Penseroso, the journey had been a "chain of sublimities from Alpha to Omega."[44]

Penseroso wrote his descriptive report while encamped along the trail at a Nez Perce campsite called Sis A Nim-Max Howit.[45] He wrote the rest of the report at Union Town, Oregon, 150 miles from the mouth of the Grande Ronde River. His characteristically nineteenth-century writing captures the beauty of Joseph's Wallowa country and the majestic Wallowa Mountains. A "black, steep, rugged" mountain range "covered with timber" rose "to a prodigious height" above the valley. The peaks "soared high above the clouds," their summits "clothed in the chaste grandeur of glittering snows and bathed in purple twilight." Altogether "a scene of intense, bewildering majesty" assailed Penseroso's senses.[46]

Did the soldiers with whom Penseroso traveled see that same beauty? Perhaps, for they were never distracted by enemy encounters along the route. Reminders of war, however, confronted them as they passed many "unnecessarily deserted" ranches that the residents had abandoned either in anticipation of an attack or when they joined a local volunteer unit. Once in Union Town, the soldiers saw that war and fear of war dominated the community. Penseroso reported that a "record of terrible atrocities still increases," but he did not elaborate. Perhaps repeating Howard's assessment, Penseroso concluded that the general's move up the Snake River and into the Wallowa Valley had successfully prevented the warring factions from crossing the river at the southern end of Hells Canyon. In fact, by the time Howard reached Union Town, the retreating Indians had already realized the futility of their resistance and were on their way home.

By mid-August most of the Paiutes had returned to the Malheur reservation; "traditionalists" from the Umatilla reservation were home; and the Bannocks were on their way to Fort Hall.[47] The war had ended. For the people in and about the middle Snake River country, it amounted to nothing but a series of rumors that fed the flames of fear and mistrust. Although one last "war"—the so called Sheepeater War—created a similar hysteria before the turbulent 1870s decade closed, it was confined to the Salmon River drainage well to the east of Hells Canyon. Ultimately peace reigned in the region, but at a heavy price. With the conclusion of the 1870s wars, the Nez Perce, Bannock, Paiute, and other inland northwest reservation tribes entered almost a century of an enforced and debilitating dependency upon the government.

Throughout the Indian Wars, Hells Canyon was an ally for the native people. They used the terrain to their military advantage to confuse the U.S. Army officers and volunteers, who were never sure where the Indians were or what they intended to do next. For a time after the war, Hells Canyon remained geographically isolated from the cultural changes transforming the neighboring country. Settlers who either claimed or hoped to claim Indian land ultimately got what they wanted, but at a dreadful price to the native people. Utilizing a variety of homestead laws over the next twenty years, farmers and ranchers moved to the vacated lands, including the northern and southern reaches of the middle Snake River. If we could step back through the pages of history, however, to Hells Canyon of the late 1870s and 1880s, we would find the canyon as it had been centuries earlier—but without the Nez Perce.

Chapter 8

Gold, Greed, and Murder

The earliest miners to reach Hells Canyon were Chinese immigrants. They arrived almost anonymously after a frenzied gold rush that swept the region in the early 1860s, searching river bars and tributary streams for surface deposits of flour-fine gold dust. Their work with pans, rockers, and sluice boxes was slow and methodical. The nearby communities knew little about those first placer miners—not their names, their origins, or their personal stories. All they knew was that the prospectors, beginning in the late 1860s and continuing through the 1880s, traveled in and out of the canyon usually in small groups. Then in 1887, a grisly event occurred in the depths of Hells Canyon that stunned the country.

The remote inaccessibility of the canyon attracted another group of men as well: brutal men who stole horses, cattle, and gold. Those men used the hostile terrain to their advantage, moving undetected back and forth across Snake River through the conflicting legal jurisdictions of Oregon State and the territories of Idaho and Washington. These men preyed on anyone who got in the way of their greed and passions. At this time in western history, Chinese immigrants were frequently hated, feared, and treated with contempt. They were also resented for their mining success and their willingness to work demanding jobs for little pay.

In the heart of the canyon greed and racial prejudice drove evil men to commit murder. Such men felt no remorse because they were incapable of it, thought their victims were unworthy of such soul searching, or both. The Chinese miners had safely isolated themselves in the depths of the canyon and were spared the hostility from townspeople who sometimes displayed signs such as "No dogs or Chinamen allowed." Generally, such isolation gave the miners a degree of peace. For thirty-one of these Chinese miners, however, Hells Canyon became a tomb.

Skilled Miners by Culture and Craft

By the time they reached Hells Canyon, Chinese miners were already contributing to the mining economy of the inland Northwest. They came on the heels of the gold rush that gave birth to Lewiston, but only after territorial legislators had rewritten the earlier laws that prohibited Chinese people from owning or leasing mining claims. On February 17, 1865, Portland's *Daily Oregonian,* reported "a very large immigration of Chinese miners may be expected in the upper Country [in] the coming season." The writer estimated their numbers would be between two to five thousand. The next month the same paper reported that the "first installment of Chinese miners"—fifteen or twenty—were "on their way to the Snake River and Oro Fino Mines."[1] After reaching Lewiston most of the men fanned out to gold camps vacated by earlier miners in the Clearwater and Salmon river mountains. The Chinese were free to either purchase existing mineral claims or acquire them through preemption.

By the end of the 1870s, the interior country was experiencing a severe economic decline. In fact, had it not been for Chinese people working the region's claims and providing support services in town, Lewiston might have collapsed as a community. Lewiston had yet to establish either its agricultural or its lumber base. The estimated fifteen hundred Chinese living in Lewiston during the 1870s worked as merchants, vegetable farmers, and laundrymen, and they ran packing services in and out of the mines.[2] In eastern Oregon, Chinese miners likewise dominated the mining communities and helped buoy up the economy of Baker City and surrounding towns. By 1867, for example, Chinese had acquired many of the claims in and around the Granite Creek gold strike in northeastern Oregon and remained there until at least 1891.[3]

Precisely how early the Chinese ventured into Hells Canyon in pursuit of gold is difficult to know. Supposedly a "party through Hells Canyon" arrived as early as 1877.[4] However, the first documentation—found in a published report of a Corps of Engineers river survey—does not appear until 1881. Thomas Symons, while conducting a survey from Lewiston to the mouth of the Salmon River, observed "a number of Chinese washing the sands and gravel of the bars for gold" along the Snake River "between Lewiston and the Grande Ronde."[5] He probably would have noted Chinese miners beyond the Grande Ronde River had they been there that early in the decade. Chinese miners did work the Snake River during the late 1880s. Farming imprints and remnants of rock structures, identified by archeologists as temples and dugout houses, remain as silent indicators of a Chinese presence in the canyon.[6] Place-names like China Garden, China Gulch, and Garden Creek, as well as local lore, also linger, but they too leave unanswered questions. How many Chinese miners worked in the canyon? Did they leave a site each winter and return the following spring, or did their gardening skills and general self-sufficiency enable them to live there year round? How successful were they?

The historical record reveals that those Chinese immigrants traveled in small groups and by boat wherever possible. Presumably they followed similar travel and settlement patterns throughout the region's valleys and canyons. On April 19, 1885, the *Lewiston Radiator* reported that some Chinese "found good diggings" along the banks of the South Fork of the Clearwater River. When word of their discovery reached Lewiston's Chinese community, many prepared "with all possible haste" to join the miners either by foot or by boat.[7]

A year later, about forty Chinese men journeyed from Lewiston through Grangeville on their way to the Salmon River where they "built skiffs and voyaged up the river on a prospecting trip" to a site above Salmon City, a considerable distance away. There they wintered, supplied by a Chinese-operated pack train from Mt. Idaho, a small community near Grangeville. "The Chinese hereabouts are very reticent about the diggings," the report continued.[8] We can reason that Chinese miners heading south up Snake River also traveled by boat, sent word of their strikes back to their kinsmen to join them, and were equally secretive about their diggings.[9]

The Chinese miners' practice of traveling in groups differed significantly from the practice of American and European miners who often traveled alone. Consequently, local newspapers faithfully reported movements and numbers of Chinese miners. Newspaper reporters, however, failed to grasp the logic or the long history of this practice. Chinese miners had already immigrated to Southeast Asia's diamond and gold mines a hundred years before they appeared in the American West. To protect themselves, Chinese men traveled in groups that evolved into mining companies. For more than a century company methodology and efficiency remained fundamental to Chinese mining success throughout the Pacific Rim. Usually twelve to fifteen men from the same family, village, or district formed a company. Because the men were usually related, they shared the common goal of providing income for their families back home in China. Members of the mining community bolstered each other's resolve to persevere while contributing their diverse talents to the community's work. While some men mined, others built and maintained shelters, fished and hunted, doctored, planted and tended gardens, or prepared and preserved food.[10]

Placer or surface mining involves using water to separate rock and sediment from the heavier gold dust or nuggets. The method can be as elementary as swirling water and sediment around in a pan. It can also be as complex as draining an entire riverbed or blasting away a mountainside with hydraulic pressure. Each method involves some understanding of aquatic management, and Chinese miners in the American West had such knowledge in abundance. It derived from a heritage of farming tropical rice fields in southeast China where they learned various techniques for moving water on and off the land. The Chinese miners then adapted that expertise to the inland Northwest goldfields. But so far we have no archeological studies of placer mining in the canyon to tell us which skills they utilized.[11] At a later time in canyon history, ranchers often used ditches to distribute water from tributaries to terraces and river bars for their hay fields, orchards, and vegetable gardens. Did the ranchers adapt portions of ditches built by their Chinese predecessors? Possibly, if the miners had been prospecting the higher terraces. Repeated damming and draining of colossal prehistoric floods often deposited gold at those locations. But finding gold there would be sheer luck.[12]

Experienced miners looked instead along the shorelines of the Snake River. They paid special attention to the widely scattered alluvial fans where for eons fine gold dust had been washed down the tributaries or the main river and deposited along the bank. To start their search for gold, prospectors read the flow of the eddies to find "hot spots" of gold deposits.[13] They searched, using the most rudimentary technology—the gold pan, sluice box, and rocker. It was demanding physical work—frustrating. Even when they did find "colors," each pan or rocker load usually bore only minute traces of the elusive prize. Often, colors flicked into view and then immediately washed away. Surely the patience and dogged determination that Chinese miners exhibited throughout the American West were as critical to a miner's success as skill and knowledge.

To sustain their communities, Chinese miners used available natural resources in ways similar to the Nez Perce. Their shelters, the only remaining artifacts, reflect the miners' adaptation to the resources and environment of the canyon. Chinese miners built rock walls "above a rectangular pit" and piled dirt "against the outside of the walls for support and insulation." The homes were cool during a hot summer afternoon and, if the men wintered over at the mining site, as some reports suggest they did, the dwellings were adequate in the canyon's mild winter climate. In a region devoid of timber, the men collected driftwood for cooking and heating. They hunted and "fished extensively, often catching salmon, steelhead, trout, and whitefish." One effective but dangerous and environmentally destructive fishing method was to set off explosives in the stream. The *Hailey (Idaho) Wood River News* reported in September 1881 that "a Chinese had both hands blown off, trying to kill salmon with giant powder at Camas on the South Fork of the Salmon River."[14] They may have resorted to that method in Hells Canyon as well.

Sites in Hells Canyon bearing names such as China Gardens suggest that the miners not only had vegetable gardens but also a gardening talent noteworthy enough to be remembered long after their departure from the canyon. In fact, throughout the West,

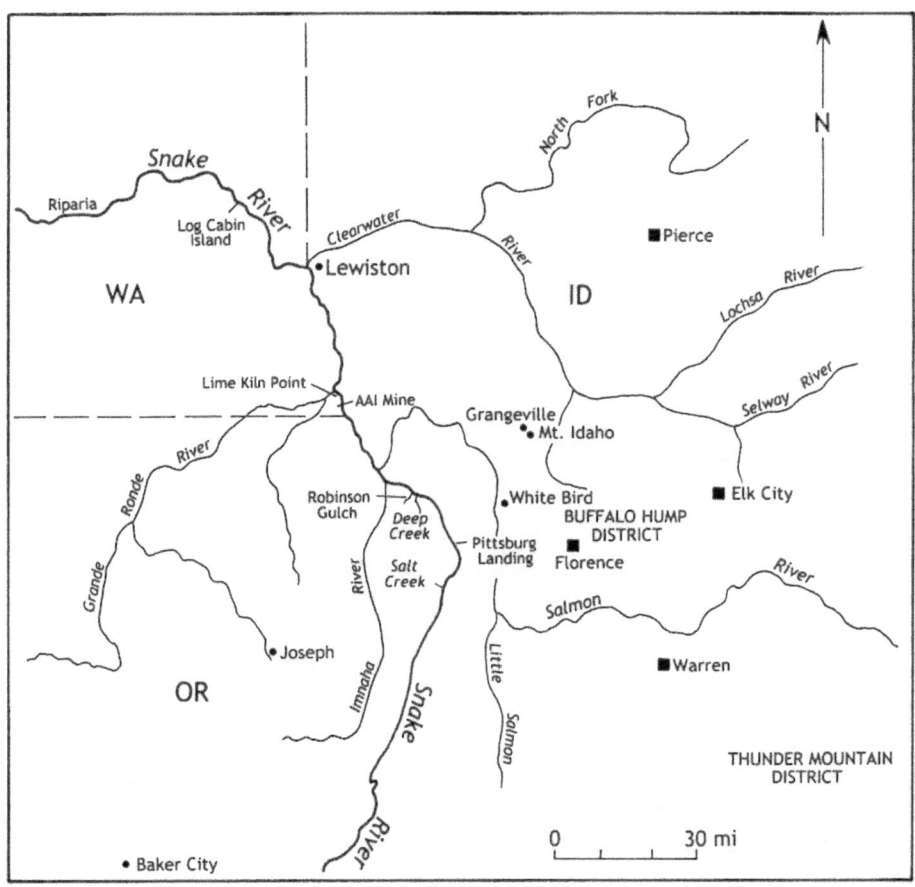

Map 8.1. Beginning in the 1860s, gold miners flocked to northeast Oregon and north central Idaho. By the 1880s most of the miners were Chinese immigrants. In 1887 criminals murdered a group of those miners in Hells Canyon at Deep Creek.

Chinese miners acquired a reputation as the "most thorough gardeners in the world."[15] They adapted their water management knowledge to irrigate the barren land. By taking advantage of the canyon's long growing season and mild climate, they could produce enough food for immediate consumption *and* off-season provisions. Most important, their healthy, balanced diet helped them avoid scurvy, the bane of non-Chinese miners in most western mining communities. The "Chinese commercial network" distributed imported herbal medicines to distant communities (towns such as Lewiston or Baker City), providing the miners with "access to resident herbal doctors" and a place to buy medicines for camp use.[16]

Thus, despite the many disadvantages Chinese miners faced in the American West, their mining experience, willingness to work cooperatively together, knowledge of water management, and general self-sufficiency all "ensured Chinese competitiveness in the American west."[17]

Cowardly Treachery

Chinese miners' success did not go unnoticed. Throughout the West, rumors circulated that the immigrants had unearthed vast quantities of gold (often at locations abandoned or ignored by their white contemporaries) and stashed the gold in camp until it was time to move on. Some outsiders probably admired their skill and success; others simply acknowledged it. But when such rumors were fueled by the anti-Chinese sentiment and the racism that was rampant throughout the West at that time, unscrupulous individuals often acted without fear of reprisal, which is exactly what happened in Hells Canyon.

By the spring of 1887, the Chinese miners' site at Deep Creek, Oregon, was "at its best as a producer." Rumors spread that a crew of Chinese miners, believed to be in Hells Canyon as contract laborers employed by the Sam Yup Company of San Francisco, had for many years washed out "great quantities of gold" in the vicinity of Deep Creek. Some claimed there was $5,000 worth of gold in the Chinese camp. Or was it $30,000? Others insisted they had

Figure 8.1. The mouth of Deep Creek on the Oregon side, where thirty-one Chinese miners were murdered in 1887. In June 2005 the Oregon Geographic Name Board named this site Chinese Massacre Cove to more accurately reflect the history of what happened here. (Photo by author, 1981.)

seventeen or eighteen flasks filled with the valuable dust, each flask worth $500 to $1,000.[18] Was there any truth in those stories?

While the Chinese miners probably found gold, that they collected anything near the amounts reported is unlikely. Historian William Ashworth explained that gold, although present, was "neither abundant nor easily worked." The placer deposits "occur as highly localized lenses called 'skim bars,'" along which "the gold content averages less than .0015 ounces per cubic yard." Nearly "seven hundred cubic yards of sand" would have to be sifted "to obtain one ounce of glitter."[19]

The probability of the rumors being false meant nothing to men consumed by greed. At the time, Hells Canyon was "overrun with outlaws, rustlers, and fugitives."[20] One gang of rustlers headquartered in the canyon heard scuttlebutt of the miners' wealth. Maybe they believed the stories and decided to steal the gold; maybe they were not interested in the gold at all but wanted to eliminate intruders who might report their illegal activities; or maybe their prejudices against the Chinese were enough to spur unprovoked acts of violence. Hells Canyon was one of the most remote places in the West. Who would know? Who would care? Since no one witnessed the event at Deep Creek that fateful week of May 1887, the story that unfolds is shrouded by conflicting information. Exactly how many Chinese died? Where were they killed? Did they all die the same day at the same location? Historians can only theorize about what happened.

We do know that the story began in October 1886, when a group of Chinese prospectors passed through Lewiston on their way to Deep Creek. Burdened by heavy supplies, Chea Po and Lee She led as many as four boatloads of their countrymen (with approximately ten men per boat) up Snake River from Lewiston. They rowed, poled, and portaged their way south, "trying their luck at a number of sites" until they reached a sandbar at Deep Creek, six miles above the mouth of the Imnaha River.[21] There in the vicinity of Deep Creek and Robinson Gulch, a quarter mile downstream, beside the thundering river and a world away from the nearest town, the Chea Po party set up camp and began mining operations. (Thirty-one is often cited as the number of miners at Deep Creek, but scholars disagree on the exact number.) Ashworth described that general area as "an austere and spectacular spot of closed vistas and little vegetation, perched on a tiny shelf beside a deep, narrow side canyon."[22] Lee She and his party of at least ten members of the original group continued deeper into the canyon to work the bars near Salt Creek.[23]

In the meantime, a gang of hooligans and thugs—described by historians as everything from "cowhands" working for a nearby rancher to "rustlers" and "thieves"—had set up temporary headquarters a few miles downstream from Deep Creek at an abandoned cabin near Dug Bar. At the time, rancher George Craig was using the area for winter range but had moved his cattle to higher ground. Thomas J. Douglas, who had built the abandoned cabin some seven years earlier, was himself purportedly a thief. He had allegedly robbed a Montana stage of gold bars then disappeared into Hells Canyon with the gold, which he reportedly buried near his cabin. There, in 1883, someone ambushed and killed him.[24] Maybe that gold rumor later drew the rustlers to set up headquarters at Douglas's cabin. Although many shady characters drifted in and out of their headquarters, the gang ringleaders were Bruce Evans and fellow horse thieves J. T. (Tigh) Canfield and C. O. (Homer) LaRue. Others included Frank Vaughn and Carl (Hezekiah) Hughes, "who operated more-or-less legitimate" ranches in Wallowa Valley; Hiram Maynard, who also had local ranching connections; and fifteen-year-old Robert McMillan.[25]

In late May 1887, the criminals worked out a plan to murder the nearby Chinese for their gold dust and agreed that if anyone divulged what they were about to do, the others would kill him.²⁶ While Frank Vaughn stayed behind in the cabin to prepare dinner, the others rode to the steep slopes above the Chinese camp. Historian David Stratton envisioned what took place at Robinson Gulch. "Hughes and Maynard were posted along the river as lookouts, one upstream and the other downstream . . . while young McMillan was left in charge of the horses. Canfield and LaRue, who stood above the rim . . . and Evans, who was stationed below, began shooting down at the unsuspecting miners on the gravel bar." Ten prospectors, working that site when the shooting began, tried desperately to escape. One by one each fell to his death. They were the fortunate ones. Shortly afterward, the murderers brutally tortured other hapless victims to get them to reveal the location of the gold cache before they died an agonizing death.²⁷

Before killing the last man, the thugs ran out of ammunition. (By then they must have worked their way down to the river from their higher vantage point.) They broke the surviving man's arm; he nevertheless made a frantic run to the river and attempted to escape in the boat. When the murderers caught him, they beat his brains out with a rock. The killers returned to Douglas camp that evening for more ammunition. The next morning "the three principal killers"—Evans, Canfield, and La Rue—returned to the massacre site.

Simultaneously, eight unsuspecting Chinese miners paddled into camp, undoubtedly arriving from one of the other nearby encampments. The horror of what they stumbled into may not have even registered before they suffered the same fate. Stratton conjectured that "the white men then traveled by boat to another Chinese camp about four miles away where thirteen Chinese were mining on a river bar" and brutally murdered each of them. So over the course of two days, at two different locations, at least three of the "cowhands" committed up to thirty-one premeditated, heinous crimes in what seems to have been an almost methodical and indifferent manner.²⁸

Many years later Jim Chapman, an early resident of Hells Canyon and a self-described "hiker by habit and collector of Indian lore by hobby," told James Brewrink's father that around 1909, twelve years after the massacre, he found human skeletons and evidence of a miners' camp at Lower Deep Creek. There were "at least seven skulls and scattered remains." The next year, James's father took James, his mother, and some AAI mine crewmen to the place Chapman described. Brewrink remembered seeing clear evidence of "broken iron pots and tools scattered at a cooking area." There was a nearby sleeping shelter that consisted of a recess dug into the bank with "clear remains of double decks on both sides" that provided eight bunk spaces. Most of the "shelf parts" of the bunks had fallen, probably because the leatherlike binding had rotted or been destroyed by rodents. Brewrink speculated that the bands holding the end-post frames had been made from bark or vines and noted that they were in good enough shape to reveal the original structure. He added that his father and the crew "collected five skulls and other bones and buried them as best they could with the tools available."²⁹ That happened more than twenty years after the murder. It is surprising that no one had taken care of the bodies before that date, because the canyon was swarming with prospectors. On the other hand, there is no reason to question the authenticity of the report.

Within days of the massacre, word of a crime in the canyon reached the outside world. Initial reports were sketchy and highly speculative, describing badly decomposed and mutilated bodies found along the river above and below Lewiston. The first body found had floated ashore at Lime Kiln Point near the mouth of the Grande Ronde River. The corpse had a bullet hole in the back and two ax wounds in the head. Driftwood snared the second body at Log Cabin Island below Lewiston. The head and one arm had been chopped off, wrapped in a coat, and tied to the body at the waist. On June 9, 1887, the *Lewiston Teller* reported that the body of a third Chinese victim also appeared floating down Snake River a number of miles below Lewiston. The victim had been shot and "his head mashed in." He was "stark naked, save a leather belt around his waist." Hideous reports continued to pepper the weekly papers. Explanations for the mysterious appearances of these bodies over many miles in the river began to emerge. The first explanation came from friends of the deceased.

Ten miners who had been working the Oregon shoreline at Salt Creek under Lee She decided to visit their countrymen downriver at Deep Creek.[30] They found their friends murdered or missing and their camp destroyed. Frantically the miners raced downriver to Lewiston to report their discovery. Along the way they came upon a boat wedged in some rocks. It contained a load of blankets and provisions. A hole had been chopped in the bottom. Lee She and his party recognized the boat, then spotted the bodies of three of their friends floating nearby. They retrieved two of the bodies and ascertained that they had been shot; the third body drifted beyond their reach. Because Lee She and the others assumed that only one of the original three boat crews had been working the Deep Creek site, they were unaware that possibly members of all three crews had died. Consequently, Lee She's report to authorities in Lewiston mentioned only the death of ten men. As soon as the Chinese filed their report, a coroner's inquest established the fact that a crime had been committed.[31]

Lee She and his party reached Lewiston with news of the massacre on Saturday, June 11, 1887. The *Teller* featured the shocking news in two articles in their next edition—June 16. One article reported that ten Chinese miners had been murdered near Pittsburg Landing and three thousand dollars in gold dust had been stolen. The second article, in the same issue, explained that the miners had reached Lewiston "on Saturday last" with news that ten Chinese had been murdered "about 150 miles above here by some unknown parties" and that the killers had stolen "upwards of $3000" worth of gold that the miners had collected the past year. The newspaper editor, Alonzo Leland, speculated: "Some think the Chinamen murdered them, while others think Indians or whites, but the mystery may never be solved."

Why would the editor prematurely speculate that "the mystery" might "never be solved"? Perhaps because in 1887 people knew little about Hells Canyon. At the time even locations of landmarks were still vague, mileages imprecise. The region was generally regarded as tough and dangerous; even an atrocity of such magnitude might be better left alone. Of course, had it been a party of ten white miners who had been murdered, Leland probably would never have passed it off so lightly. Instead of his modest appeal, which appeared two weeks after the original article—"We hope the guilty parties can be found and brought to justice"—he might well have demanded an immediate manhunt and called for the killers to be promptly brought to trial and properly punished.[32]

The Hunt

Although initial newspaper and verbal accounts were confusing and contradictory, and some had lacked the outrage that one might have hoped for, the crime had immediately made local and national headlines. In Washington, D.C., Chinese ambassador Tsui Yin read about the deed and "immediately dispatched a high embassy official, Pung Kwang Yu, to the Snake River country." Yu's thorough investigation of the crime caused a "considerable local sensation."[33] The *Lewiston Teller* reported that word of the massacre had also reached San Francisco. "Chinese in San Francisco have sent up [two] parties here to have them take all steps necessary to ferret out the facts . . . and have provided the means to pay for the investigation."³⁴ The article did not identify the two "parties" but possibly Pung Kwang Yu was one of them and came from San Francisco rather than Washington, D.C. The San Francisco delegation was prepared to offer a detective one thousand dollars, and the Lewiston Chinese community raised a like amount.³⁵

The Chinese consul in San Francisco had requested that the Sam Yup Company look into the case. The company "immediately dispatched Lee Loi to Lewiston." (The second "party" perhaps.) He signed a John Doe complaint with the justice of the peace who, in turn, certified the description of the three bodies found.³⁶ Lee Loi then hired U.S. commissioner Joseph K. Vincent as a special investigator."³⁷ Vincent, along with James McCormick and an unidentified Chinese man, went into the Snake River canyon to investigate.³⁸ Vincent left the others on a river bar "with instructions to return to Lewiston if he wasn't back within 10 days," disguised himself as a miner, borrowed a few gold nuggets to look more legitimate, and headed on upriver.³⁹ Near Douglas's cabin Vincent met a group of "drifters" and befriended two young members of the group, whom he covertly queried "with innocent questions." He learned that Canfield, Evans, and La Rue were the group's "leaders," and he noticed "sacks of flour with Chinese markings" in the camp. He estimated there were about thirty men in the gang, but never more than a handful of men in camp at any one time. Most were elsewhere transporting stolen horses between Oregon and Idaho Territory.⁴⁰ After observing the camp for a few days, Vincent returned to his companions.⁴¹

Two weeks later the *Lewiston Teller* learned that J. K. Vincent and party had returned to town, but before the reporter could interview them, Vincent had again headed upriver and McCormick had left on a prospecting tour to the Bitterroot Mountains.⁴² Documents later revealed that, while at Lewiston, Vincent received an inquiry from Liang Ting Tsan, consul general, and F. A. Bee, consul of San Francisco, about his investigation. In his response of July 19, 1887, he summarized his investigation to that point, then added: "It was the most cold-blooded, cowardly treachery I have ever heard tell of on this coast, and I am a '49er. Every one was shot, cut up, and stripped and thrown in the river." He added a brief recommendation regarding the direction the investigation should take from that point forward. "The Chinese here have paid me for what I have done so far, but the Government ought to take it in hand, for with actions like this none are safe."⁴³

Nevertheless, Vincent relentlessly pursued the case as long as he could, employing stealth, intelligence, and determination to solve the crime and bring the killers to justice. After his first trip into the canyon, Vincent went into Salmon River country to investigate activities of outlaws in that area. He soon came back to Lewiston and then returned to Salmon River towns to "learn whether the gold dust and nuggets had been sold by members of the gang." Finding nothing, he crossed the ridge from White Bird into the Snake canyon, borrowed a boat from a rancher, and quietly approached the camp of the suspects. In the shadow of night he eavesdropped on camp conversations. Vincent knew that if they discovered him, "his life wouldn't be worth a holler in a box canyon." He nevertheless persisted long enough to learn that some of the Chinese miners' gold had indeed been found and that the conspirators planned to convert it to cash some place far enough away from the crime to avoid suspicion. He also learned that the killers knew an investigator was on their trail and that they had to disband soon.⁴⁴

Back in Lewiston, apparently troubled by the fact that he "lacked sufficient evidence for an arrest," Vincent was unable to answer numerous inquiries from the Chinese consul general about his investigation. What could he report beyond what he had already said? He needed people with political clout behind him if the incident were ever going to reach a trial. That help came early in 1888 after the "Chinese minister to the United States, Chang Yin-huan, sent a detailed report of the crime to Secretary of State Thomas F. Bayard." After reviewing the facts of the case and emphasizing the brutality of the killings, the minister then pointed out the likelihood that unless the criminals were brought to justice, "other wicked persons may from their hatred of the Chinese, follow [this example] which will affect the interest and safety of the Chinese residents there and elsewhere in the United States."[45]

Secretary Bayard contacted officials of Oregon State and the territory of Idaho. In Lewiston, Vincent "had already issued a 'John Doe' warrant for the arrest of the unknown murderers" and was ready to follow up on new information about the killers' identities if he had some compensation. "Most of us here are too poor to work for glory, [even] in tracing up such brutal murders," he wrote to Idaho's governor Edward Stevenson. He also told the governor that the Lewiston sheriff was ready to arrest the guilty men. The crime, however, had happened in Oregon; Idaho had no jurisdiction in the case.[46] Nevertheless, Vincent went to Wallowa County where he met with Carl (Hezekiah) Hughes and Frank Vaughn, the two men who "operated more-or-less legitimate ranches" in the county. He persuaded Vaughn to turn state's evidence.[47]

About the same time, James Slater, a former U.S. senator residing in Joseph, Wallowa County, Oregon, wrote to federal authorities in Portland that "six gang members were under indictment in Wallowa County for the murder and robbery of the Chinese miners." Three were in jail and the fourth had turned state's evidence. Unfortunately the principal culprits—Evans, Canfield, and LaRue—were nowhere to be found.[48] Slater petitioned the Justice Department to hire detectives to track those three down because the governor of Oregon could not request the suspects' extradition without knowing their location. The response from the Portland office revealed just how casually the federal government looked at this case; the State Department suggested that Wallowa County request help from the Chinese government in hiring special detectives "to pursue this matter 'in which Chinese interests are so deeply concerned.'"[49]

Chinese minister Chang Yin-huan remained apprised of the developments in the investigation. He requested that the State Department take some action against the identified criminals. In May 1888, almost one year after the killing, the under secretary of state responded: "There is no present occasion for federal jurisdiction in the premises, or for interference to procure testimony on the part of the judicial officers of the United States."[50] It was Wallowa County's responsibility to follow up on the case.

The Trial

In the spring of 1888, with testimony from Frank Vaughn before the grand jury, Wallowa County, Oregon, had enough information to issue an injunction against "J. T. Canfield, Bruce Evans, C. O. Larue, Heyram [sic] Maynard, Carl Hughes, and Robert McMillan for the crime of murder."[51] Unfortunately only Hiram Maynard, Carl (Hezekiah) Hughes, and Robert McMillan actually came to trial later that summer. The county never tried the three worst offenders, even though a year earlier Wallowa County had arrested Bruce Evans and J. T. Canfield on charges of altering horse brands. Held in the Wallowa County jail at Joseph—a "chicken coop of a jail"—it was not long before the two escaped. "Evans hoodwinked Sheriff Thomas Humphreys into taking him to the outhouse where someone had hidden a six-shooter for the outlaw." He used the gun and escaped from the sheriff, jail, county, and state—leaving a family behind. "Canfield either shot his way out of jail or was released on bail—accounts differ—and promptly disappeared." Homer LaRue, who disappeared almost immediately after the massacre, was never apprehended.[52]

Very little was known about the Maynard, Hughes, and McMillan trial until early in 1995 when the Wallowa County clerk found court records of the trial.[53] Although the records did not include trial transcripts, they did contain depositions taken earlier that year from Vaughn, Maynard, Hughes, and McMillan. Surprisingly, based on those depositions and the testimonies of the three defendants, the Wallowa County jury found that they were innocent of any collusion in the barbaric events that transpired that fateful spring day in 1887. Vaughn, whom detective Vincent earlier persuaded to turn state's evidence, testified to the following: Vaughn and his six associates—Hughes, Maynard, Canfield, LaRue, Evans, and McMillan—were staying at a cabin three miles from the Chinese camp. One afternoon all except Maynard and Hughes decided to visit the miners to rent their boat. (Stratton's sources suggested that it was Maynard and Vaughn, not Hughes, who remained behind.) No one mentioned robbery or murder until they approached the Chinese camp. Then Bruce Evans, J. T. Canfield, and Homer LaRue began to talk. "I don't recollect just what [the talk] was," Vaughn claimed. "I didn't understand from this talk that there was any killing to be done." Later, however, when asked if he recalled the conversation between Evans, Canfield, and LaRue, Vaughn replied, "I knew it was about the killing, but do not remember the words."

Vaughan then told Wallowa County judge Patrick O'Sullivan that Canfield and LaRue left the others behind and advanced on the camp. He and McMillan were about two to three hundred yards away when they heard shooting; Evans was nearby. None of them could "stop the affair." When they reached camp after the shooting, Vaughn saw "four or five dead Chinamen" but did not go to the boat. He knew that those men who did the killing were "desperate men" and he was later afraid to "make the matter known." When the judge asked Vaughn why, in his appearance before the grand jury, he implicated Maynard, Hughes, and McMillan in the killing, he replied: "I didn't implicate them there anymore than I have now." He then assured Judge O'Sullivan that he did not talk with Maynard and Hughes about the killing after returning to the cabin.[54]

In his testimony, Robert McMillan, who claimed to be in the canyon in the employ of Bruce Evans, confirmed Vaughn's account. Hughes and Maynard were at the cabin the whole time and knew nothing about the crime. McMillan also knew nothing about it "until just a few minutes before the shooting" when he heard LaRue, Canfield, and Evans "speak something about it." McMillan assured the judge that he "had no way of preventing it, and had no hand in it." He explained that they left for the Chinese camp in the afternoon and returned to their cabin in the evening, a little after dark. When Judge O'Sullivan asked the young man, sixteen at the time of the trial, why he never told anyone about the killing before the trial, McMillan replied, "Because I was afraid to." He did not recall any specific threats made if he told, but he "didn't think it was safe." Other sources charge McMillan with taking care of the horses during the crime. That coincided with his testimony, *if* he was telling the truth. He probably was some distance from the massacre and probably did not consider horse tending connected to the crime.

Hezekiah Hughes testified that he was residing at the Douglas cabin near Snake River in May 1887. When asked to tell what he knew about the murder of the miners and his own, Maynard's, and McMillan's guilt or innocence, he responded, "I can say Maynard and myself are innocent." He did not know about McMillan because, as he explained, he and Maynard were at the Douglas cabin at the time the miners were supposed to have been killed. He claimed he did not even know how far downriver his cabin was from the mouth of Deadline

(Deep) Creek, where the murders occurred. All he knew was that the Douglas cabin was about three miles from the river. He also claimed that he had never been up Snake River beyond the cabin trail.[55] "No sir, I know of no Chinese being killed." The *Teller*, May 16, 1888, stated that Hughes "did not like the idea at all and would have no hand in the matter," whereas Stratton conjectured that Hughes and Maynard were posted as lookouts at the crime scene.

Thirty-eight-year-old Hiram Maynard—fellow resident of Wallowa County—gave a testimony similar to Hughes. He was at the Douglas cabin "about three days" during the last of May when "a number of Chinamen are said to have been killed on Snake river." He admitted to having heard of the atrocity but denied ever having been on the Snake at or near the crime scene. As with Hughes, the closest he had ever been was at the head of Big Eddy trail. He knew Hughes was innocent because he was with him all the time but did not know about McMillan.

The judge's questions to Vaughn and the three defendants seem inadequate. Based on the incomplete trial records, it appears that the judge never asked any of the defendants exactly how many Chinese died. Nor did he ask if anyone returned to the murder scene the next day or at any later date. Did anyone visit any nearby Chinese camp that day or later? Granted, any answers he might have received from Hughes and Maynard would have been hearsay—and might not have been truthful. But with additional examination he might have learned enough to guide his interrogation of Vaughn and McMillan. Why didn't he ask those two what they overheard as they rode toward the Chinese camp with Evans, Canfield, and LaRue? What, more specifically, did Vaughn see at the camp besides the four or five dead bodies? Where were the horses, and who took care of them? Or did everyone ride directly into camp and remain with their mounts?

Given that so little information surfaced during the testimonies of Vaughn, Hughes, Maynard, and McMillan, it may have seemed that none of the four was guilty of murder, but too many questions went unasked and therefore unanswered. Although the judge called others to testify, they apparently did not provide enough additional information to bring a guilty verdict.[56] In fact, that testimony may have swayed the jury's decision. Wallowa County historian Bill Rautenstrauch, who also examined the court records, believed that the jury initially brought in a verdict of guilty but after listening to more testimony "was reinstructed by the court, and retired to deliberate again."[57] Their second verdict—not guilty.

So many questions beg for answers. How many Chinese immigrants were in the canyon that spring? If just the ten miners whose names were listed in the 1888 injunction had been killed, were the 1887 reports of from thirty-one to thirty-four murders inaccurate? If that was the case, what happened to the other Chinese miners who had been working in the canyon that spring? If up to thirty-four men died, who were they and why were they not named in the injunction or mentioned during the trial? Clearly, some of those miners who went into the canyon the autumn before the murder—Lee She's group—were the same men who reported the crime in Lewiston, specifically claiming that ten men died. Lee She's group then disappeared from the records. Why? And why were none of these questions asked at the trial? Too many questions remain unanswered—perhaps because they were never asked. Special investigator Joseph K. Vincent must have been extremely disappointed to learn that of the seven suspects he identified, only three were brought to trial and none received even token punishment for the crime.

George Craig, the Wallowa County cattleman and banker who owned the cabin appropriated by the rustlers, submitted the following testimony March 2, 1936—forty-nine years after the massacre. He said he was present at the trial when Maynard, McMillan, and

Hughes told their stories. Because he knew all the men except LaRue, Craig was curious to hear "what the facts were." He learned that first the ringleaders had posted Hughes and Maynard—"one up the river and one down the river"—to see that nobody came. Vaughn stayed in the house to get dinner. "Bob McMillan held the horses and watched them kill the Chinamen." Obviously Craig's version does not agree with the testimonies. Later, when Fred Lockley of the *Oregon Journal*, asked Craig about the case, his assessment of it cast a negative light on both the trial and jury members. "I guess if they had killed 31 white men something would have been done about it, but none of the jury knew the Chinamen or cared much about it, so they turned the men loose."[58]

From any perspective, the massacre in Hells Canyon was tragic; the failure to apprehend and try the three murderers—Evans, Canfield, and LaRue—reprehensible; and a community's unwillingness to confront the crime for so many years unsettling. From a Chinese perspective, equally tragic was that the deceased never found rest with ancestors in their native villages. Even those who had a proper burial in America—like the bodies Vincent and others brought back from Riparia on the lower Snake and buried in the Lewiston Chinese cemetery—had no one to tend their graves, no one to placate their spirits unless someone from a Chinese company or association collected the bones and returned them to China. In 1896, Fang Chung of Six Companies collected bones from San Francisco north into Idaho and Washington. There is no way to know if that collection included bones of the men murdered in the canyon.[59] The real horror of this episode—according to Chinese beliefs—is that the bodies were mutilated and body parts dispersed, condemning the victims to eternal wandering as ghost spirits.

The end of the nineteenth century concluded the era of Chinese miners—that last wave of freelance gold seekers to scour the American West. Chinese immigrants mining in the wilds of Oregon and Idaho gradually left the backcountry to abide in the safer havens of West Coast Chinese communities, joining fellow immigrants during those decades of anti-Chinese bigotry. A few individuals remained in the region to live out their lives, some as miners, most as gardeners, houseboys, launderers, laborers, or restaurateurs. But in Hells Canyon their stay ended with the tragedy at Deep Creek.

Chapter 9
Bull-headed Fools

As Chinese mining in Hells Canyon drew to a close, fundamental change came to America. In the late nineteenth century, the nation stood on the threshold of industrial development with new methods of production, distribution, and resource extraction. Electricity became basic to a way of life as Americans moved faster and farther through time and space with improved transportation. New markets placed increased demands on natural resources, especially copper for electrical wiring, and technological innovations accelerated the extraction of those resources. Copper connected Snake River to that national shift. The mining industry shifted from entrepreneurial ventures by a few individuals in search of surface gold to a sophisticated, expensive business dedicated to finding marketable metals deep within the earth. New ways of doing business demanded corporate organization, capital expenditures, modern equipment, sophisticated transportation, and large crews of wageworkers. Promoters willingly invested money, muscle, time, and sometimes lives on speculation for the elusive gold, silver, or copper. Difficult-to-extract minerals and poor transportation doomed Hells Canyon quartz mining ventures to an era of comparatively short duration, but driven by technological innovations, growing market demand, and a do-or-die mind-set, miners and promoters ventured into dreams and schemes they might otherwise have discarded. Although this brief period in canyon history affirmed man's dogged determination to ignore the dictates of the landscape and force nature to yield to their exploitive demands, ultimately the natural environment would prevail.

By today's standards, environmental damages resulting from methods used in accessing, extracting, processing, and dumping the ore were irresponsible; then, however, very few people had knowledge of what environmental consequences their actions would create. To most, a potential bonanza promised the investors unlimited wealth, not unlike the stock market today. More important, if a venture proved successful, it would guarantee community and regional growth to the neighboring cities and counties. So as a new wave of mining activity swept through the region, community leaders promoted the development and eagerly awaited the rewards their towns would reap.

Montana Money to the Devils

Hells Canyon did not escape the frenzy. The earliest, biggest, and most successful quartz venture was at the upper end of the canyon in the heart of the Seven Devils Mountains—too far to the south to benefit Lewiston but a potential asset to southwestern Idaho and eastern Oregon towns. (The waters of the reservoirs behind Hells Canyon and Oxbow dams now cover the lower mines of the south canyon mining region.) Success at the Seven Devils district inspired others to venture into the risky enterprise elsewhere. The search for gold, silver, copper, or any other marketable mineral or rock swept through the entire canyon and precipitated efforts to find new ways to navigate the Snake River and improve its navigational channel. It also fueled the dream of building a railroad through the canyon, finally connecting north and south Idaho.

In 1862, while traveling with a reconnaissance party to survey Snake River and adjacent land for a transportation link to south Idaho and to prospect the surrounding country, Levi Allen discovered a gold and copper producing area in the Seven Devils when a snowstorm on July 4 stranded Allen's small party on White Monument Mountain adjacent to the Seven Devils peaks.[1] Near their shelter an outcropping of vividly blue rock, 550 feet long and 80 feet wide, caught Allen's eye and stirred his ambitions. The men staked out the area and, because of its rich colors, called it Peacock.

Each year Allen returned to the Peacock Mine to do assessment work. His search for investors to help develop the strike took him, in 1877, to Professor Isaac R. Lewis, superintendent of several Montana mining companies. Lewis examined the Peacock and found an impressive copper deposit, then joined Allen in locating a second copper lode three miles from the Peacock. They called it the White Monument.[2] Allen convinced other Montana mining magnates to invest in the claims: Marcus Daly, owner of the Anaconda smelter in Montana; Granville Stuart, who discovered the ore-rich Alder Gulch strike in Montana; and S. T. Houser, a wealthy Helena miner and later governor of Montana Territory. They paid Allen $12,500 for one-quarter interest in his claims, but they never developed them.[3]

Years later, in 1885, a fourth Montana investor, Albert Kleinschmidt, purchased shares in the Peacock and White Monument as well as the new claim of Helena. He added nearby Blue Jacket, Mountain Queen, and Alaska Legal Tender claims. Prussian-born Albert Kleinschmidt was one of the earliest and most successful men of this modern mining era. Kleinschmidt, who had already made a fortune grubstaking Montana gold miners, believed enough in modern technology and knew the market well enough to gamble on the Seven Devils copper investment. Kleinschmidt adapted his mercantile, construction, farming, and mining background to the development of the copper district in the heart of the Seven Devils Mountains of Idaho and transformed undeveloped mineral claims into a paying venture.

Although success required time, money, and creativity, one of Kleinschmidt's biggest challenges was to find the best way to transport the ore from the mountains to the nearest smelter. At first he packed the ore on the backs of horses and mules, hauling it seven miles east over the Idaho mountains from the Blue Jacket Mine, his most productive claim, to the closest road at Bear Creek. From Bear Creek he freighted the ore to the nearest railhead, then shipped it first to the smelter at Anaconda, Montana, and later to St. Louis, Missouri. When that proved costly and inefficient Kleinschmidt briefly adopted "a rather unique method of transporting copper ore from the 'Devils' mines to the smelters." On September 13, 1889, the *Weiser (Idaho) Leader* interviewed Kleinschmidt's manager and learned of his plans to ship one hundred tons of ore from Portland, Oregon, to Swansea, England, "for treatment." The manager claimed that it would cost no more to deliver ore to England than to St. Louis. "This seems incredible," the writer editorialized; "still we believe it, as many lumber-laden ships require heavy ballast."[4]

No matter the eventual destination, Kleinschmidt's main problem remained the need for an efficient means of transporting ore out of the canyon, be it by water or rail. Like all Hells Canyon miners and investors, Kleinschmidt kept a close eye on reports of railroad surveys and construction proposals. A rail line to the Seven Devils mines presented an obvious solution. In 1883, the Northern Pacific Railroad Company, in partnership with the Union

Figure 9.1. A spectacular aerial view of the Seven Devils Mountains in Idaho. The mining district named after this mountain range sweeps from its foothills to the Snake River. (Picture source and date unknown.)

Pacific, had completed its transcontinental line from the Great Lakes to Puget Sound. This initiated a frenzy of speculation regarding the location of subsequent transcontinental and connector lines. When the Union Pacific and Northern Pacific later became competitors, UP's subsidiary company, the Oregon Short Line, built a shortcut from Wyoming to Huntington, Oregon, at the southern end of Hells Canyon. There it joined the Oregon Railway and Navigation Company line that crossed Oregon's Blue Mountains to Portland. On the Idaho side, the Pacific and Idaho Northern railway approached Weiser with promises to continue north, if there was enough business. Should the copper mining district prove productive, that would guarantee PIN extension north, and it might even convince a railroad company from either side of the river to run an extension line into the mines.

Speculation swept Hells Canyon country. Which company would extend the railroad north through the canyon—OSL or PIN? People in the Seven Devils mines expected someone to at least build a feeder line to them, if not from Weiser then in from Oregon. A notation written on an 1890 map of eastern Oregon mining districts gave them reason to hope: a railroad to "several mining camps" would "terminate at Seven Devils, Idaho," it read.[5] That would certainly benefit the southern reaches of the canyon. But what about the north? For seven years the folks in Lewiston had hoped for a railroad north along the Snake; they dreamed it would tap the canyon's entire mineral potential and give Lewiston a badly needed jump-start. Then on April 3, 1883, a Lewiston newspaper article confirmed that a survey of Snake River canyon was "proof positive" that the OSL was going to build a line to Puget Sound "by way of Snake River."[6] The editor ignored a company report stating that they would build no farther north than the mouth of Burnt River, Oregon.[7] Shortly after the newspaper's publication, the OSL survey crew met their death in the Snake's turbulent rapids; the railroad, however, ultimately reached that Burnt River site, giving birth to Huntington, Oregon

Until 1889 the copper market was solid. That year it faced a serious setback when French capitalists tried to corner the market. They failed, but sent share values into a downward spin. The drop in futures, however, fazed neither Kleinschmidt nor his on-site manager, who that July assured the *Weiser Leader* that they had "the fullest confidence in [the market's] future." In their view there was no reason to stop plans for improving transportation in and out of the district. Consequently, in 1890, while waiting for rail service to reach the Seven Devils

Mining District, Albert Kleinschmidt, his brother Carl, and James Millich organized the American Mining Company to build a twenty-two-mile road from Helena, Idaho, down the steep grade to Little Bar on the Snake River. Levi Allen, who had discovered copper in the area more than twenty-five years earlier, was a shareholder.[8] The road ultimately cost Kleinschmidt more than a thousand dollars a mile to build. No wonder it became known as Kleinschmidt Grade.[9]

Located on the forks of Copper Creek, the new town of Helena, Idaho—a small settlement situated on a twenty-acre bench below Peacock Mine—existed to serve the Seven Devils Mining District. Little Bar was downhill from Helena on the Snake River and opposite the area later known as Ballard's Landing, Oregon. There Kleinschmidt envisioned having steamboats pick up the ore and haul it approximately seventy miles south to the railroad at Huntington, Oregon. Should steamer service not be available, the Baker City–Seven Devils wagon road would provide a temporary, although slower and more expensive, route out of the canyon.

For more than thirty years, steamboats had proved their worth on the Columbia and lower Snake Rivers, hauling passengers, equipment, supplies, minerals, and crops. Despite the *Shoshone*'s 1870 failure to capitalize on the trade above what is now Hells Canyon Dam, the approaching century brought promise for a successful steamboat venture over the seventy-mile stretch between Huntington and Ballard's Landing. The region's growing population and its quartz-mining activity should provide business for a riverboat shuttle service. Communities on both sides of the river had everything to gain from a riverboat, as did Kleinschmidt.

Kleinschmidt needed to persuade others to invest in the construction and operations of a stern-wheeler. He convinced James Kerr, James Miller, and Jacob Kamm—all men who knew the boat business and believed in the venture—to go into partnership with him.[10] The four men formed Snake River Transportation Company and on March 15, 1890, began building a 488-ton, 160-foot stern-wheeler at Bridgeport, Idaho—at a cost of thirty thousand dollars. They christened it *Norma* after Kleinschmidt's oldest daughter and launched the boat August 1, 1890. The river was low. The *Norma* could go only half a mile downriver to Whiskey Rapids before returning to the Snake River railroad bridge. After that maiden run, the *Norma* laid up at the bridge for the winter under the care of a watchman.[11]

In the spring of 1891 the *Norma* made two trips. That was all she would make that season. Low water forced her onto rocks that caved in her hull.[12] But what actually kept her out of commission that year was the boat company's failure to generate profitable business—not the damaged hull. In essence, the *Norma* had been "penned into the 30 mile stretch of river between Huntington and the head of the canyon."[13] The Union Pacific bridge two miles from Huntington had no draw span, thus preventing the boat from reaching the agricultural regions and the more populous areas farther south. She hauled only ore and supplies to and from the Seven Devils mines. No steamboat could succeed without diverse cargo and work assignments and certainly not in a remote location like Hells Canyon. As soon as Kleinschmidt's seventy-five-man crew finished work on the Helena to Little Bar grade, the *Norma* was supposed to begin hauling ore south to Huntington. Instead, when they finished the road, on July 31, 1891, the *Norma* was out of commission for the year.

The federal government, however, had committed to improving that stretch of the Snake River channel to provide the *Norma* a longer season. In 1892, Congress appropriated twenty thousand dollars for work on the Snake from Huntington to the Seven Devils. Two years later the figure was increased by five thousand dollars. Work crews removed ledge rock and boulders and cleared obstructions from the channel.[14] Nevertheless, the *Norma* remained

Map 9.1. In the late 1800s, the discovery of copper, gold, and silver attracted a flurry of activity at the southern end of Hells Canyon. Plans included using the steamboat *Norma* to transport the ore. Instead, *Norma* was the last steamboat to descend the Snake River through Hells Canyon.

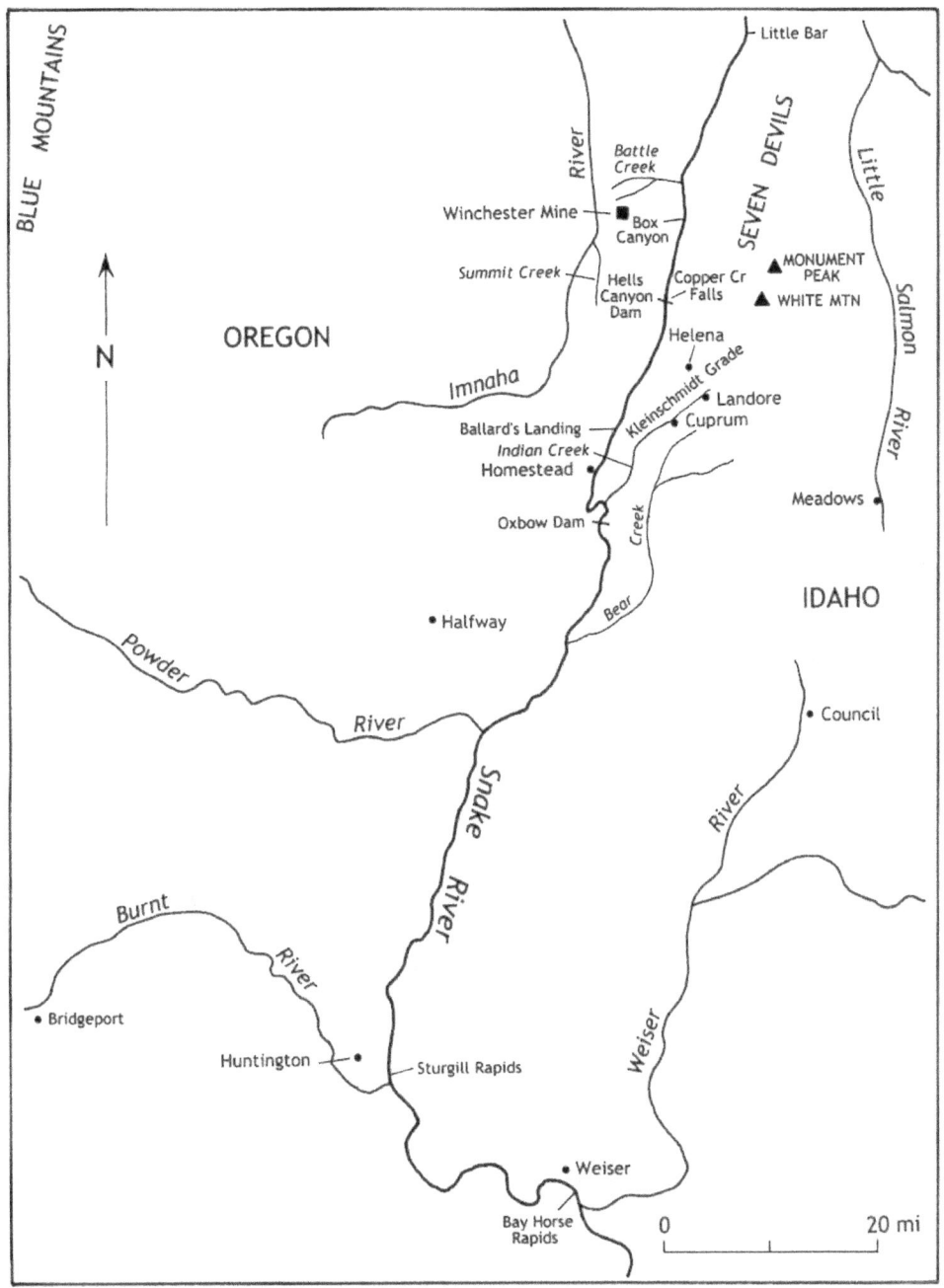

trapped by a railroad bridge. The government expended money to improve the channel but failed to require Union Pacific to put in an opening bridge span.

While Kleinschmidt's Snake River Transportation Company awaited the speedy completion of channel improvements, C. W. Williams, on behalf of the company, tried to force the Union Pacific into modifying the bridge. He took his case before the federal court and petitioned the secretary of war but failed to convince anyone to order construction of the opening span.[15] To make matters worse, an economic depression swept the nation, slowing the demand for copper and further hindering the *Norma*'s chances of getting back to work. Moving the *Norma* to the more lucrative lower Snake River and Columbia River trade remained the boat company's only option for recouping its investment.

"I Was Afraid They Would Jump the Jib"

In the spring of 1895, Jacob Kamm instructed Captain William Gray to "bring the [*Norma*] down to Lewiston at all hazards."[16] Many years later, seventy-five-year-old Captain Gray wrote an account of the trip in a letter to the director of the U.S. Geological Survey.[17] Considering his many adventures over a long, illustrious career on a variety of rivers, he found it hard to "remember the details of one short trip." Nevertheless, the account Gray left conveys a vivid picture not only of the drama of the voyage but also of the strength of his resolve and his ability to coax cooperation from reluctant crewmen. A shorter account of the trip appeared in the *Teller* after the *Norma* safely reached Lewiston.[18] The story from these two sources follows.

On May 15, 1895, the *Norma* left "the unused wharf" near the Huntington bridge to begin her trip north. Kamm had earlier ordered the crew to strengthen and overhaul her in preparation "for her perilous voyage."[19] Gray was in command, with his brother A. W. as first mate and Ed Lyons second mate. Twelve other men made up the crew, including F. D. Farwell, who doubled as clerk and newspaper reporter. At Bay Horse Rapids, three miles from their departure point, "while drifting in a channel improved by Government engineers," the *Norma* ran into a piece of two-inch drill steel left behind by the engineers. It ripped some holes in the bottom of the boat and damaged the wheel. The crew limped on to Gray's Landing, "put some household goods" ashore, and repaired the boat. Two or three days later they were ready to proceed.

Eighteen miles downstream, with Gray steering and the mate reading the government navigation chart, Gray looked ahead and said, "It don't look good, what does the chart say?"

"All clear."

Gray wasn't satisfied. He rang the bell ordering the engineer to stop—just as the *Norma* "struck the starboard knuckle," resulting in a thirty-one-by-three-foot hole in the hull.[20] Gray immediately grabbed the government chart and "flung it out of the window." From then on he "found his way by reading the character of swift water."

Gray's account conveyed his insight into the mood of the crew and his ways of dealing with their apprehension. He feared that the crew, already a "little discouraged at the 'Bay Horse' trouble," might decide to "jump the jib" if he landed above Sturgill Rapids. They knew it was an easy return back to the railroad bridge from above the rapids, but once they cleared those rapids it was another matter. As Gray slowly moved the *Norma* toward the rapids, the men gathered on the forward deck. One man asked Gray if he was going to land. "I made no reply and soon we were below the rapids where we landed." They remained at Sturgill Bar the next three days repairing the damages. When they finished, Gray knew that the men still expected to return to the bridge, so that night he "sounded the men as to going on or going back." Every man chose the first option.

Then, on the q.t., he approached the engineer, Charlie Jennings, and said: "Charlie, this boat is worthless up here, what do you think about going back?"

Charlie replied, "We came up to here, I say go on or put her where they can't find her."

"Charlie, you're my man. The boys think I am going to make a short trip down a few miles to test our new bulkhead, but we will forget to come back."

On the afternoon of May 21, 1895, they left Sturgill Bar.[21] Ten miles downstream "the boys accepted their fate." As evening approached, they rounded a bend in the river and immediately confronted a steel ferry cable stretching across the river eight feet above the water line. Gray stopped the boat and tried backing it. A strong current carried them "down to certain decapitation of everything above the main deck." But Gray knew that the boat was "a good backer." He landed the boat head down against a rocky cliff, kept the engines running, and held her in place with several ropes, waiting for the ferryman to acknowledge his whistles and lower the cable. No response. No doubt irritated, although he did not mention it, Gray sent the mate and two crewmen across the river to lower the cable. The ferryman, Brownlee, told them why he refused to honor the steamer whistle. "I am doing it to prolong your lives. You have a bull-headed fool running that boat and not a soul will live to go through that canyon."

Brownlee had seen the torrent that Gray was about to tackle. From the top of cliffs where the canyon was so narrow he could "jump across," Brownlee often watched as the angry stream below effortlessly flung hundred-foot drift logs against the cliffs. When he could not convince Gray to turn back, he finally relented. Brownlee lowered the ferry cable.

The *Norma* continued in the dark, in search of a landing. The risks they took that night still haunted Captain Gray many years later. "I wonder if you can imagine the strain on a pilot on a strange river known to be swift and treacherous, on a dark night, over-shadowing mountains throwing impenetrable gloom over all, and no searchlight."

Early the next morning they took off, en route to Steamboat Landing above Copper Ledge Falls. Probably near Homestead or Ballard's Landing they took aboard a Seven Devils prospector whom the crew later nicknamed Calamity Bill. Because the prospector boasted of "intimate knowledge of the river," Gray thought his expertise might come in handy and resumed the journey. Ahead, as the *Norma* entered a chute of "leaping foam," Gray's prospector pilot assured the captain of safe passage. "But he was soon dumb with fright." The current hurled the boat from side to side. Water poured over the deck. The timbers creaked; the hull cracked. Gray righted the boat, and they safely cleared the chute. But after that experience, the prospector "discovered he was out of his element in the pilothouse." He raced down to the lower deck, looked at the rock-walled cliffs, cursed, and then begged to go to shore. No sooner had the prow touched the beach, than Calamity Bill disappeared "over the lonely trail."[22]

About noon, the *Norma* reached the landing above Copper Ledge Falls, where in 1870 "the crew deserted the *Shoshone*" as Captain Smith was about to undertake the same perilous run.[23] While the *Norma* laid up for nearly a day, everyone walked down on the Oregon side to inspect the falls. Gray described them as more of a "pour" than a fall and estimated their drop at eighteen feet. "For an hour I watched and studied the currents, eddies, and back-lash of the water," Gray remembered. Ultimately he decided that his safest option was to "drop over the fall on the Idaho side and let the back-lash" hold them away from the cliff. Back on the boat, Gray sketched that stretch of the river to show his fellow officers the strategy he planned. He would jam the prow of the boat against the rock. It risked crushing the hull but seemed his only recourse. That was the newspaper reporter's version. Gray didn't recall having had that conversation; all he remembered was telling the carpenter, Thomas Wright, where he figured the damage would occur.

"I want you to run in a bulkhead six feet back of that to the midship keelson, then have the mate back it up with cordwood in case the water should rush in hard enough to tear away your bulkhead."

The carpenter objected, "You will drown us all."

Gray retorted, "If that should happen, our names will appear in every paper in the United States and Europe."

After finishing the bulkhead, Gray said he heard Tom muttering, "Damned old fool, going to be drowned for excitement because a damned fool wants notoriety."

The next morning, before attempting the falls, Captain Gray made his one and only quarterdeck speech. Knowing that the crew feared for their lives, he assured them that there was "not a particle of danger." The boat was built of enough wood "to float her machinery" and had forty cords of wood in the hold. Even if they knocked in her bow and side, she would float long enough for the crew to board small boats and head for shore. He warned the crew to keep calm and not jump overboard. "Snake River never gives up her dead." Typical of the times, the *Teller* reported the exchange between captain and crew in heroic terms. "The men were steadfast. The order was given to distribute life preservers, but the men said they were there to work and refused them." They set forth to meet their fate at Copper Ledge Falls.

"The staunch steamer darted forward like a battering ram straight on toward the impregnable wall of ever lasting rock." Gray recalled that they faced "certain destruction on the cliff below." He slowly backed the boat to within ten feet of the rock. Her bow passed near the mouth of Copper Creek, where an eddy gave the *Norma* a slight swing out. Gray then backed the helm hard to starboard. He could take a chance with the bow but must protect the stern at all cost. Instantaneously the bow touched the cliff "just hard enough to break three guard timbers without touching the hull." Gray skillfully avoided disaster as the *Norma* "bounded into the still water below."

Gray's technical description lacks the colorful conclusion that the reporter provided. "The crew sent up an earnest cheer. It was a pathetic cheer. It was a benediction. The boat quivered, rolled and was tossed on the heavy torrent as it shot into hell canyon."[24]

Safely over the falls, Carpenter Wright—with two life preservers securely strapped around him—stepped out in front of the pilothouse and called up to Gray, "Hurrah, Cap! You start her for hell, and I'll go with you from this on!"

The *Norma* hurled on through the thirty-mile chute of Box Canyon, where "winds like a serpent" gathered strength for greater speed. The boat seemed frail; the men felt helpless. Towering walls blocked out the sun. White foam spilled from the torrent, filling the "labyrinthine passage with perpetual rain" and a deafening roar. The *Norma* shot down the chute "like a meteor from the sky." In some places the fall was upward to 25 percent. "The waters glided smoothly in too much haste to hear a ripple or a wave on its surface." Gray, too busy watching the river, failed to notice, but the men insisted that they saw stars through the gloom of the dimly lit canyon.

After a victorious run through Box Canyon, the *Norma* plunged into a straight cataract cut through a plateau of blue clay and granite boulders. The narrow canal, not more than sixty feet wide, was a mile or two long. Gray guessed that it dropped at one hundred feet to the mile. Even though they emerged unscathed, heavy wind forced them to tie up for the rest of the day and night at Johnson Creek.

Figure 9.2. Six men, including mailboat captain Kyle McGrady, repeated the *Norma's* successful downstream run through the depths of Hells Canyon. The *Helles Bell*, pictured here at Buck Creek Rapids was one of the two boats the men used in their July 1939 venture. (Photo courtesy of Robert McGrady.)

The next day, May 24, 1895, the *Norma* journeyed on north to Lewiston. Gray wrote nothing about that river section, and the newspaper noted only that "the run was uneventful." All of Lewiston anxiously awaited their safe arrival. When the *Norma* reached town, "The brave officers and men were warmly congratulated upon their arrival." After resting a day and visiting old friends, the crew took the *Norma* on down the Snake to Riparia, Washington. The steamer remained in Snake River service, with frequent visits to Lewiston and occasional runs south of town as far as Wild Goose Rapids, until 1906.

Idaho's Boom to Bust

The *Norma's* 1895 absence from the upper canyon was not the only change to come to the Seven Devils mining district. High county taxes on patented claims, levied at a time of economic downturn, left the mine owners with "nothing to show for the investment."[25] Both Albert Kleinschmidt and Levi Allen had sold their shares in the Peacock, Helena, and White Monument in 1891, leaving Allen out of the American Mining Company alltogether and Kleinschmidt in the process of restructuring it. In the transactions, however, Kleinschmidt lost controlling interest in the Seven Devils mines. Since the *Norma's* ill-fated venture proved the impracticality of steamboat transportation, the American Mining Company's new directors favored construction of a railroad into the Seven Devils District. The railroad, scheduled to reach the Blue Jacket Mine by August 1897, would surely solve transportation problems, but without other revenue sources it would be at the expense of company development.[26]

Then in 1897, Metropolitan Trust Company, a group of "New York Capitalists," gave the industry a shot in the arm by leasing the Blue Jacket mine from Kleinschmidt and announcing plans to build a smelter and railroad to Snake River.[27] Isaac B. Blake, former president of Continental Oil Company, was the primary investor.[28] The renewed activity and apparent commitment by the investors "started a stampede of thousands into the area."[29]

Around the new smelter blossomed the town of Cuprum, halfway between the older town of Helena and the Snake River and thirty miles by road from Council, Idaho. The August 1898 issue of the *Weiser Signal* described Cuprum as "quite a little town [with] a store, post office, two saloons and a number of substantial dwellings."[30] It also included a miners' hospital. The Seven Devils mines promised jobs for mining "bindlestiffs"—men who traveled throughout the Northwest looking for employment. More important, it provided a refuge for miners "fleeing from the murderous tensions and bloodshed in the miners' union of North Idaho."[31] The entire Seven Devils region held promise for workers and investors alike. PIN railroad was advancing north from Weiser. The Ford brothers from Cripple Creek, Colorado, announced plans for a cyanide mill in the Black Lake area. And a new company—the Boston and Seven Devils Copper Company—had purchased claims five miles upstream from Cuprum. "Money flowed in fantastic sums."[32] One slight setback happened in 1898. When the Metropolitan Trust Company fired up their new "water-jacket type smelter," it suffered a 40 percent loss of copper. They tried again; again it failed. Consequently the company sold the smelter to the owners of the new Iron Dyke Mine across the river in Oregon, where it operated successfully.[33]

Still, the mining companies needed good transportation to sustain growth. Until a railroad feeder line could reach them, developers again decided to use a steamboat shuttle to the OR&N station at Huntington. But they expected an existing transportation company to pick up the trade. OR&N entertained the idea and even commissioned Captain Harry Baughman to explore the Snake River from "the Big Canyon" to Huntington and test navigation feasibility. Baughman, a well-respected captain on the lower Snake, was frequently asked by both individuals and companies to examine a river channel and make necessary improvements. In this instance he let it be known that if he ruled the river navigable for OR&N, he planned to return with a crew to "improve the stream and prepare for the immediate opening of the river for boats."[34]

The next year, 1898, Captain Baughman made several trips aboard the steamer *Mable* from Huntington to Ballard's Landing, successfully carrying "heavy cargoes both ways." That stretch of the river was not the maelstrom the *Norma* encountered farther north, but it did present its own kinds of challenges: namely, low water and big boulders. Longtime resident John Flynn did not remember the *Mable* being particularly successful. She was a "snazzy little" stern-wheeler, considerably smaller than the *Norma*, and low enough to pass easily under the railroad bridge that had bedeviled the *Norma*. Consequently, the *Mable* was able to reach Weiser on her maiden voyage. She made two more successful upstream trips before attempting to go downriver. Then, on each trip north to Ballard's Landing, rocks punched holes in her bottom. In the end, the little steamer hit a rock at the mouth of Powder River, and on that bar she stayed. She came to an undignified end as, piece by piece, salvagers packed her off.[35] Baughman returned to Snake River navigation in the Lewiston area.

Elsewhere, trouble was brewing. As early as 1897, Isaac E. Blake, once identified as a key investor of the Metropolitan group, proved to be nothing but a con man. He had raised seventeen thousand dollars, supposedly money enough for a smelter, an engine, a partially set boiler, an assay office, a two-story bunkhouse with attached kitchen, four stoves, cooking utensils, a stable, three acres of partially cleared ground, a ditch, and a small amount of work on three mines. All of that should have cost no more than four thousand dollars. Blake skipped town in 1897 with the investors' remaining thirteen thousand dollars.[36]

Nonetheless, based on the activity at the Peacock mines, the Seven Devils district looked solid in 1897. Thirty-five carloads of high-grade ore consigned to a New York smelter showed a profit, attracting new discoveries and even more investors. Under the leadership of president Lewis Hall, the Boston and Seven Devils Copper Company expanded the district. Towns grew, while others were born. Landore, a new town of five hundred people, mushroomed five miles upstream from Cuprum, near the company's best claim. The town of Deborah appeared on Garnet Creek just below Landore. Cuprum, Landore, and Deborah mirrored each other's services and "competed for the trade," with Landore eventually evolving as the dominant supply center.[37]

Activity at the Blue Jacket was also encouraging. The Boston developers continued the road from Kleinschmidt Grade to the Blue Jacket and other properties. They built cabins, shore houses, and bunkhouses and covered the approaches to the tunnels and shafts. Then news reached the area that "a wealthy lumberman of New York and Michigan" was building the railroad "alone and unaided" from Weiser through Council and on to Meadows.[38]

Gradually the railroad inched north from Weiser and on toward the Seven Devils. At an elevation of eight thousand feet, "scores of Austrians" dug a grade around White Monument to connect the railroad with the Weiser line at Council.[39] But in spite of repeated promises to the contrary, construction on the proposed short line to Landore stopped. Unable to pay its taxes, Lewis Hall's Boston and Seven Devils Copper Company was forced to dissolve, ending railroad construction for all the mines.

At Black Lake, however, business still looked promising. The Ford brothers had eliminated the horrible Kleinschmidt Grade wagon haul by building a bucket tramway three and a half miles from the Peacock Mine down to the river landing. They kept their cyanide mill and new tram operating through the summer of 1902, when the mill burned to the ground. Despite the setback, the brothers continued mining operations until 1914. This time international politics, not advances in technology, brought change to Snake River. World War I cut off the mine's supply of cyanide from Germany.[40]

In 1904 Ladd Metal Company of Portland moved their smelter from Mineral (near Weiser) to Landore, precipitating a renewed flourish of activity around the young town. The company began operating the smelter in September but soon realized that wood did not burn hot enough to fuel the smelter and installed new boilers and furnaces to burn coke. Unfortunately, the expense of importing coke and iron flux prevented the company from making a profit. Ladd Metal Company soon shut down their entire operation.

Other companies were stymied by one setback after another, not the least of which was litigation. The state mine inspector explained that the Seven Devils district "has been badly handicapped since its discovery by title litigation and some of the rankest kind of mining mismanagement." The district attracted "large amounts of capital," but the money resulted in very little "intelligent development."[41] Still, many investors and miners clung to the hope of a railroad down Snake River canyon, a hope sparked by Union Pacific surveys of 1911 and 1912. Nearly a hundred years later the railroad has yet to arrive.

Oregon's Copper Lode

While the miners on the Idaho side reaped rewards from the copper belt, discovery of a copper lode on the Oregon shore drew even more attention to the upper canyon. In 1897, two cattle ranchers, Jake and Bert Vaughn, scratched a rock ledge and discovered copper. They got "pretty excited," dropped what they were doing, and started to follow the ledge. After tunneling in about fifty feet and down about twenty feet, they discovered their "Glory Hole," a forty-foot-long copper ledge.[42] The Vaughn brothers named their strike the Iron Dyke Mine and sold it within six months for a substantial profit. In 1898, using

Metropolitan Trust Company's temperamental smelter from across the river, mining at the Iron Dyke began in earnest.[43] The Iron Dyke owners doubtless used Harry Baughman's boat services that year as well; he was then operating the *Mable* on that stretch of the river.

Soon the new town of Homestead grew up to service the nearby development. Kitty Grunig's childhood memories are of a young, exuberant town during its heyday when the Iron Dyke flourished.[44] Theresa Amrich, Kitty's widowed, Czechoslovakian-born mother, moved there with her four children in 1915; Kitty was four years old. Theresa created a business washing the miners' "filthy" clothes, then married a miner, Carl Veranek, also a Bohemian, and they moved into "one of the old brown shacks" used by most of the miners' families. Homestead also had "big houses where the big shots lived" and a store (the company commissary) that doubled as a boardinghouse. Most of the bachelor miners boarded there.

A short time after her second marriage, Kitty's mother began running a boardinghouse at Homestead. Kitty's stepfather, like so many miners, often worked at one of the other mines on either the Oregon or Idaho side of the river, and he was not always home. Her mother's boardinghouse guests were "the townspeople or people that would come in" (usually on the train), and she cooked for the railroad crew when they were in town. Homestead was a "turntable."[45] A train from Huntington arrived three days a week—Monday, Wednesday, and Friday—to drop off passengers and supplies and pick up ore before returning south. Kitty did not remember Homestead's population when she lived there, maybe five hundred, but she had vivid memories of its rowdiness, with saloons, prostitutes, and "lots of shootings and knifings." Because Kitty's mother had once been a nurse's aide, one of her many side jobs involved nursing the victims back to health. Homestead was twenty-five miles away from the nearest doctor at Halfway, Oregon, and she was the only person trained to care for the injured and ill.

Homestead couples took their children and their "lunches" to all-night dances and danced the night away. Something exciting always seemed to happen at the dance, like the time a "handsome" man brought one of his prostitutes—"a gorgeous looking babe"—to the community dance. As soon as the pair started to dance, Kitty's mother and the other proper women instructed the "orchestra to stop playin' and they started gatherin' up their kids to go home." The offending couple danced a complete circle around the room, then left. They were only there "for orneriness." Kitty's parents went to all the dances; they even ferried across the river at Ballard's Landing and climbed Kleinschmidt Grade to attend the Cuprum dances. They went for business as well as fun. Kitty's mother and stepfather were "bootleggers, same as a lot of other people." Her mother specialized in peach and apricot brandy.

When Kitty's mother moved to Homestead, Theron and Halsted Lindsay from Colorado owned the Iron Dyke. In 1917 they installed a flotation plant, which along with the smelter gave Homestead the largest copper concentrator in the state.[46] As the level of mining activity increased, so did the population and civic services. Kitty was too young to go to Homestead's first school up Irondyke Creek canyon, but she remembered a second school being built in 1918. By then Homestead's population of married supervisors and miners was enough to support a school of around forty students.[47] Homestead remained a small but vibrant town so long as the Iron Dyke continued to produce.[48] The mine closed during World War II, despite an effort to keep it operational for war production. In the late 1950s, when construction began on Oxbow Dam, the railroad tracks that had brought business to Theresa Amrich Veranek's boardinghouse were removed, and by the time

Hells Canyon Dam inundated the Homestead site, nothing much remained of the town. Nevertheless, Homestead in the early 1900s provided Kitty, and probably many others who lived there while the mines were operating, with vivid lifelong memories.

Later investors occasionally showed an interest in resurrecting mines in the upper Hells Canyon gold- and copper fields.[49] Even today, there is enough copper in Hells Canyon's southern reaches to keep investors interested. To be sure, poor transportation remains a challenge, but modern technology could overcome that obstacle. It is the land itself—Hells Canyon and the Snake River—that limits the region's mineral development. The geographic combination of a turbulent, unpredictable river, rugged hillsides, deep canyons, and high surrounding mountains prevents access and keeps mining companies from extracting most of the potential ore. Whether the miners were drawn to the canyon by an almost irrational devotion to the idea of striking it rich or were there merely as hardworking, family men just trying to keep the family going, they have never persuaded the land to release its mineral wealth.

Chapter 10

Success to the Enterprise!

In Hells Canyon's southern reaches, the mineral wealth was abundant but transportation a problem. Although mining activity gave birth to a few small communities, most of the towns were too far from the canyon mines to profit directly from the ventures. That was not true for Lewiston at the north end of the canyon. City fathers believed that a renewed mining boom would produce the same kind of growth for Lewiston that Spokane, Washington, one hundred miles to the north, was enjoying. A combination of Silver Valley mineral discoveries in Idaho mountains east of Spokane, the region's expanding agricultural and lumber economies, and a network of interconnecting rail lines transformed the sleepy community of Spokane into the business heart and railroad hub of the Inland Empire. Promoters expected the same for Lewiston.

The little town urgently needed an end-of-century economic boost. Rail service eluded it until 1887.[1] It would take another thirty years before the lumber industry would spark economic growth, and unreliable, high-priced steamboat service inhibited agricultural development. Also, a large tract of arable land remained—in the minds of covetous developers—"locked up" by the Nez Perce reservation.[2] Lewiston lacked a solid economic base to build on. That is, until the resurgence of mining activity in the mountains and valleys of north central Idaho. Community leaders believed the boom would provide the incentive to bring transcontinental rail service and all resultant economic advantages to the Lewiston valley. And newspaper editors promoted that dream.

Potential mine investors from the East, Midwest, even Europe visited the region. Each new arrival prompted enthusiastic editorials heralding imminent development on the heels of one mining strike after the other. New technology and new markets revitalized the old districts of Pierce, Elk City, Warrens, and Florence in the Clearwater and Salmon river mountains of central Idaho. But the real bonanza awaited investors in the recently discovered mines of the Buffalo Hump district, "one of the last pell-mell mining stampedes in the western United States."[3] Beginning in the 1880s and lasting well into the next century, the stampede reached beyond Buffalo Hump into the Snake River canyon. An intense search for gold, copper, silver, and iron extended south from Lewiston through the canyon. Even less-exotic deposits of coal, lime, and granite also attracted attention.

Miners who were intent on extracting wealth from the rocks of Hells Canyon unwittingly learned the truth of Aldo Leopold's assertion that the characteristics of the land determined the course of history as "potently as the characteristics of the men who lived on it."[4] For nearly three decades, miners, promoters, and their well-wishers doggedly resisted the land's characteristics in their efforts to coax mineral wealth from Snake River canyon walls. Stories of the miners' resolve to succeed against the land's unforgiving ruggedness present a window into the resolute determination of people at that time and a newspaper's unashamed endorsement of the mining ventures from Lewiston 108 river miles south to Battle Creek.

Mines near the Grande Ronde

The earliest mining venture was near the mouth of the Grande Ronde River, twenty-eight miles south of Lewiston. The Grande Ronde River, after following a meandering course through Oregon's Wallowa Valley, plunges through a deep canyon to merge with the Snake River near the Washington-Oregon border. Here, in 1880 or earlier, a Mr. Simpson discovered lime at what would turn out to be one of the Pacific Northwest's finest lime deposits. Lime filled a regional demand for rock and brick masonry and a disinfectant whitewash for outbuildings. But, in ways reminiscent of Seven Devils mining to the south, the location of the lime handicapped Simpson's venture. Transporting lime from the quarry to the market presented an enormous problem that Simpson solved by rigging a scow with sails and towing it with mules.[5]

In 1884, a man by the name of G. W. (Cap) Lewis operated Simpson's Grande Ronde limekiln. Lewis predicted that by the end of the next year the quarry would be producing between a thousand and twelve hundred barrels per month.[6] At some point Lewis supplemented the Lime Point kiln with two additional kilns—one on the Idaho side about two miles downriver near the shore at Billy Creek; a second farther north and about three miles up Captain John Creek.[7] Throughout his remaining eighteen years in the business Lewis continued to use Simpson's less-than-adequate scow, presumably as his main method, for transporting the burned lime to market.[8]

In response to a growing regional lime market, developing the site to full capacity clearly required larger, more powerful watercraft and "river improvement." Congress authorized the U.S. Army Corps of Engineers to survey the river and estimate the costs of channel improvements, and on August 2, 1881, Surveyor Thomas W. Symons left Lewiston with three men and a "small boat" to begin the task.[9] It took them seven days to reach the mouth of the Salmon River, "a very hard journey" that involved crisscrossing the river, towing their boat along one bank, then ferrying the boat across to drag it along the other bank. They began the survey at the Salmon River. Symons started off with a negative impression. "Nowhere on earth can there be a scene more grand, gloomy and desolate than where these two rivers join their waters." They were back in Lewiston on August 11, and his impression had not changed. He found no reason to recommend channel improvement, thus hindering mining development of Hells Canyon but not discouraging a surge of miners, investors, assayers, and hangers-on.[10]

When, in 1885, the Union Pacific conducted a survey downstream from Huntington, Oregon, some men of the survey party brought out high grade ore from ledges on both sides of the river. Their failure to note precisely where they found the ore contributed to a myth about vast quantities of copper to be had somewhere in the canyon. A rush ensued. It began near the Grande Ronde and Snake river confluence, a ways upstream from Simpson's lime quarry. For a brief period a flurry of news articles reported one discovery after another; then word of mining progress disappeared from newspaper pages.

In the spring of 1888, six Lewiston-area men reported finding a six-foot-wide ore-bearing ledge of rock on the Idaho side, with indications of a "true fissure vein." They sent ore samples to Salt Lake City, Portland, Helena, "and other places" to have it assayed. The results showed the rock contained "gold, silver, copper and a small percent of nickel to the value of $100 a ton."[11]

The *Teller*'s editor, Alonzo Leland, the perennial optimist, pronounced "success to their enterprise," hoping their achievement would inspire a "thorough prospecting" of the canyon and the construction of a transcontinental railroad line into the Lewiston valley.[12] Then in 1890, word reached Lewiston that an investor in the London Lode group near Grande Ronde River was "looking for a place to have the ore smelted." Leland was thrilled. If the investor could not find a satisfactory smelter, "in all probability" the mine owners would locate one at Lewiston.[13] The outcome of the investor's quest failed to make the paper, and no smelter was ever located in Lewiston.

In the fall of 1890, the *Teller* announced the discovery of magnesia rock quarries at Idaho's Captain John Creek and Billy Creek, both downriver from the Grande Ronde. The quarries consisted of "the finest building rock known in the world today," rock that was so rare it had been found in only three other quarries worldwide, the *Teller* claimed.[14] The quarry owners formed the Magnesia Stone Company, sold more than ten thousand shares of stock at twenty-five cents per share, then reorganized under the name Idaho Stone Company.[15] In April 1891, some of the investors visited the Billy Creek quarry with a *Teller* reporter. The reporter filed a lengthy and detailed description of the quarry, but as with other ventures, this one then disappeared from newspaper updates.[16]

In 1900 a venture began near the mouth of the Grande Ronde with the discovery of a three-thousand-acre coalfield that included one vein of fine coal, ten feet wide.[17] Five years later there was still talk of "opening up" the coalfields with a forty-one-and-a-half-mile electric road from the Snake River up the south bank of the Grande Ronde River to the timber belt. None of those plans materialized.[18]

At Captain John—the other ore-producing site north of the Grande Ronde—the first reported mining venture was Perry Mallory's gold discovery in 1900. He located nine claims about four miles up Captain John Creek from the Snake River but had no assay results to report.[19] (At the same time Cap Lewis would have been working a lime deposit one and a half to two miles down the creek.) Nothing more about Mallory's Captain John activity made the newspaper, but in the winter of 1901 the *Lewiston Morning Tribune* briefly noted that the Wild Goose Rapids Mining and Milling Company was working some claims at Captain John.[20]

Then in 1904, Daniel, Ole, and Nels Hether, who were actively prospecting a number of claims throughout the canyon, discovered "wonderful leads" close to the bottom of Captain John Creek. (Earlier prospecting had been higher up the mountainsides.) By then, mining circles recognized Captain John as the beginning of what they called the Craig Mountain mineral belt. The mouth of the creek was easy to reach by steamboat, plus a road from Waha and Soldiers Meadows allowed horse and buggy entrance from Lewiston and Camas Prairie. Ore samples from the Hether claims assayed from $2.48 to $12.00 per ton. That favorable report plus monetary backing from "parties" in Vineland (later known as Clarkston), Washington, and Helena, Montana, ensured the brothers' continued work on the claims.[21] When the Craig Mountain mineral belt failed to produce as expected, the Lewiston newspaper responded as it had with all the earlier ventures. Rather than admit a claim's failure, the newspaper simply ended its fervent endorsement of one strike and immediately jumped to endorsing another strike—this time in the Idaho copper belt.[22]

The Idaho Copper Belt: Wild Goose to the Salmon

Despite considerable mining activity near the Grande Ronde River, most miners believed the fabled copper deposit lay somewhere between Wild Goose Rapids, about four miles south of the Grande Ronde, and the mouth of the Imnaha River, twenty-three miles farther upstream. The rush there began four years after the Union Pacific's 1885 survey, when a

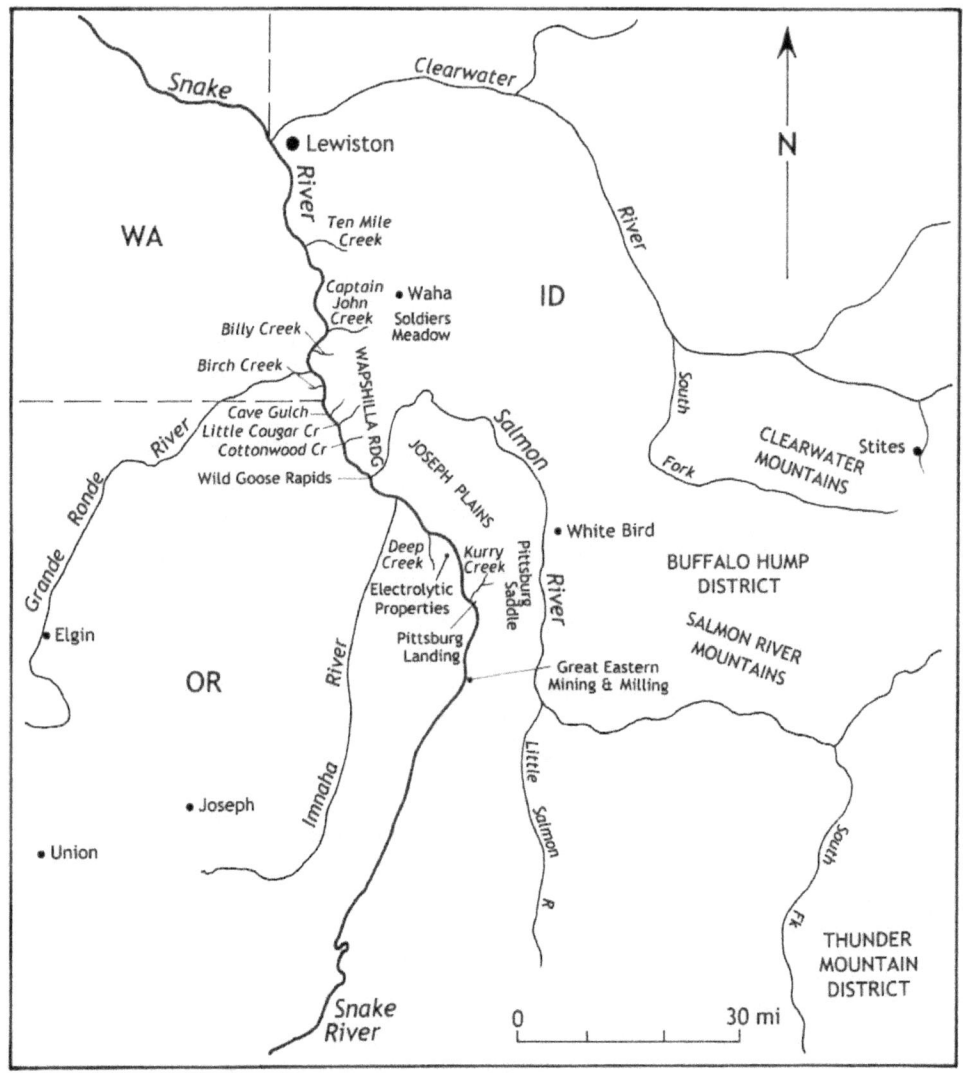

Map 10.1. Beginning in the 1890s the search for copper and gold attracted hundreds of miners and thousands of dollars to mining ventures throughout the central and northern sections of Hells Canyon.

group of Lewiston residents formed a company and located claims just beyond the Wild Goose Rapids. Their holdings became known as the Butcher Boy mines. In June 1889, a Lewiston correspondent to the *Portland Oregonian* described that area—the "Idaho copper belt"—as being at least as rich as the "famed" Seven Devils country to the south "with the added advantage of being accessible by steamers."[23]

Miners then had a limited understanding of the geological origins of the middle Snake. Who could have imagined the canyon's convoluted beginnings—the shifting of earth plates, South Pacific volcanoes drifting into North America, Idaho fronting the Pacific Ocean, or layer upon layer of volcanic rock belching its way out of the bowels of the earth from great distances? While those miners would have instantly dismissed such a tale as rubbish, they admitted that the copper belt's geology defied all reason and that it kept "a dozen experts exhausting their theories on its formation." Even though Butcher Boy looked promising, the experts acknowledged that the entire district exhibited "very interesting conditions." They could see that "volcanic, or other disturbances, [had] left a broken surface in the narrow mineral belt" and that the ore bodies that carried iron capping were "often broken and displaced by internal disturbances."[24] They failed, however, to recognize that Butcher Boy was a fault rather than a fissure. It cost nearly a decade of hard work, considerable expense, and broken dreams before they admitted failure.

Disappointment at Butcher Boy did not make other miners question the true nature of the Idaho copper belt. They doggedly continued their relentless search for copper. In 1896, a *Teller* headline read, "Another Big Bonanza." The strike was at the mouth of Cottonwood Creek, nine miles above Wild Goose Rapids, in the same Idaho copper belt as Butcher Boy. Described as "one of the most interesting districts to the prospector in all the northwest," the Cottonwood Creek strike was also certain to be "one of the few mining propositions that is a certainty."[25]

The huge, easily accessed ledge was a "mountain of ore" concealed only by "the mosses of age." It measured forty feet wide and assayed "as a whole" at $40 a ton in copper and silver. Owners figured that because pieces of the ledge broke off so easily, they could put ore aboard a boat for only $1 a ton. Within a month and a half, miners had swarmed into the area, "speaking with great confidence about the district." Even a "prominent capitalist" from Spokane showed interest in adjacent property.[26]

In the spring of 1900, the Wild Goose Rapids Mining and Milling Company, including investors from Duluth, Minnesota, incorporated in Lewiston. They owned the Anaconda group of ten claims near Wild Goose Rapids, claims that the men had been quietly developing since January.[27] Through the fall of 1900, packers hauled supplies to sustain the eight- to ten-man crew throughout the winter.[28] In November, the mine manager provided the *Teller* with a comprehensive report on the mine's progress. "We are certain to have a fairly good mine," the manager claimed, but admitted that to "put it on a paying basis" would require considerable capital and development. His optimism becomes more apparent when examining their plans to dig a three-hundred-foot tunnel with a seven-hundred-foot extension, given that his crew was only able to cut fifty feet of tunnel a month. Along with that, they had forty tons of freight, including an "assay outfit" and "a complete air conveyer plant," waiting in Lewiston for the river to rise.[29] Putting the mines "on a paying basis" was a challenge indeed. Nevertheless, reports that the mines showed "signs of merit" still appeared in the newspapers in 1913.[30]

The Chronicles of James Brewrink

Ample newspaper accounts of mining during this period fill the pages with names, places, and figures, but even the briefest account of life at one of these early mines is rare. For that reason, "the chronicles of James Brewrink" is a treasure. Around 1914, James lived with his mother and father at the AAI camp on the Idaho side. The camp was half a mile downstream from Pullman Mining and Milling Company's AAI mine at Wild Goose Rapids. Brewrink described the AAI mine as a "stock selling gamble" to probe an ore deposit at "Glory Hole, well up the mountain." The riverbank just below the site "had been worked extensively by Chinese placer miners with obvious persistence," which enhanced the mine's prospects of being a gold producer.[31]

When the Brewrinks lived there, "the mine was slowing down in favor of a new prospect at Salmon River." Nonetheless, James's father (who may have been the superintendent) and crew installed machinery for air compressor–operated drills. They dug and timbered an ore cart tunnel to replace the wheelbarrow method of carrying out the muck. "The compressor also provided air circulation to purge blasting gasses." The men further improved the air by adding a "low pressure pipe in addition to the high pressure one used for drill operation." Young James also had a job—to "keep oil cups filled on the big single cylinder engine that ran the compressors." Because it was hard to get the engine started, especially in cold weather, they kept the engine running—and James employed—most of the time.

Located just below the Wild Goose rapids, the camp doubled as a boat landing. It consisted of three cabins—a central storehouse, a bunkhouse for the crew, and a downstream house for James and his parents that they also used as a dining room for everyone. (About 1914, after a rock fall demolished the storage house near the Brewrink dwelling, James's father built them a new house closer to the mine at a safer location.) James didn't say, but his mother must have been the camp cook. It took at least three men to work the mine "and assure an outside man for emergencies," so there were usually three or four helpers around, plus James's parents. James described two of the men. John Gerbert, "an old time employee," was the handyman who maintained the wood supply and took care of the food suspended on wire-supported racks "or otherwise protected." Gerbert had "visions" of finding a rumored pocket of gold upstream. Another man, named Albert, was his father's "muscle man in handling machinery." He was also James's pal, who showed him how to make whistles from willow sticks. Rufus and Rastus, Airedale terriers that his father brought in to "keep down rodents and other native animals," completed the camp's population—until the dogs multiplied to the point that his father gave them all to a passing hunter.

James did not say how long his parents worked at the mine—maybe five or six years—nor how long the mine was operational. He mentioned that his father held supplemental jobs with shearing crews and that he hauled freight up the river during prohibition, which puts them there through the 1910s and possibly into the 1920s. Though he does not mention it in his chronicles, his father, William Pressly (Press) Brewrink, operated one of Hells Canyon's first mail and freight boats. It was that work, not his mining, that provided the family's main income source and granted Press his place in Hells Canyon history (see chap. 20).

Map 10.2. James Brewrink's sketches of the area around the AIA mine.

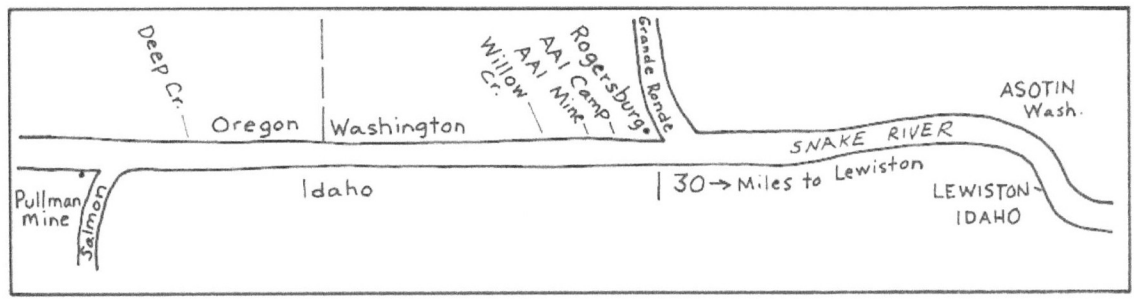

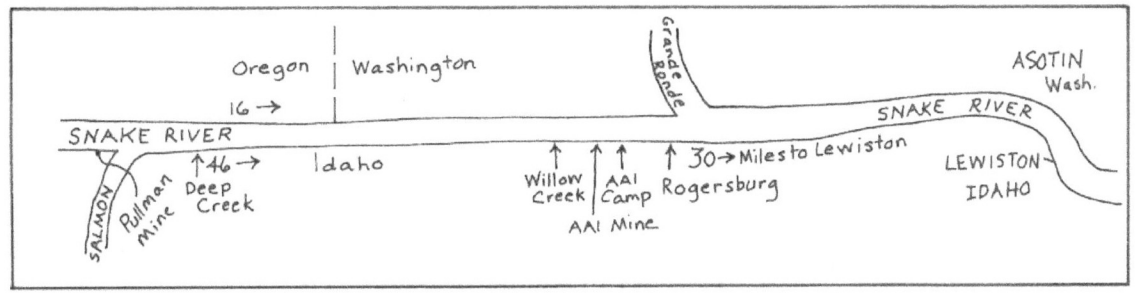

Cave Gulch Strikes

Farther upstream on the Idaho side, four miles above Wild Goose Rapids, is Cave Gulch, also part of the Idaho copper belt. In the spring of 1903, reports of recent gold and copper discoveries at Cave Gulch filtered down the canyon. Bordered a mile to the north by China Garden Creek and one and a half miles to the south by Little Cougar Creek, the entire Cave Gulch district encompasses a large tract of land. Grass-covered ridges and slopes, intermixed with small stands of timber, sweep west from Wapshilla Ridge. The sloping, broken expanse gradually narrows to deep canyons and gulches at the river margin. The upper sections of the region are readily accessible from the Waha, Idaho, road; access from the river is much more difficult.

Miners began probing the hills of Cave Gulch as early as the 1880s, and many Lewiston people filed claims over the next twenty years. But poor river transportation impeded the owners' ability to open the properties.[32] Then, in 1903, news of the upcoming construction of a small but powerful steamboat, the *Imnaha*, designed specifically for that stretch of the Snake, inspired renewed activity in the Cave Gulch district. One glowing report sent from the district, which appeared in the March 14, 1903, *Lewiston Morning Tribune*, sparked a rush.

The article claimed that Herman Wundrum and J. J. McDuff reached Lewiston about 9:00 p.m. with three packhorses "loaded with rich ore" and "a can of gold amounting to at least $400." The two men filed three claims, deposited the ore sacks at Lewiston's Gem Saloon, and put the can of gold in the saloon's safe. At a time when for ten cents each a man could buy a Rosewood pipe, a silk poplin four-in-hand tie, and a pair of lightweight suspenders, $400 was a huge sum of money. Wundrum and McDuff's activities that March evening attracted considerable attention.[33]

"The Gold Is Here," Lewiston residents read in the morning paper. Herman Wundrum,

Figure 10.1. Cougar Creek drainage on the Idaho side, part of the Cave Gulch District that was extensively examined by copper and gold miners in the early 1900s. (Photo by author, 2006.)

well-known to the people of Lewiston as an experienced miner, had found gold. This was more than a rumor. He had evidence and a convincing story. News of the Herman Wundrum strike reached "every section of the Inland Empire," enticing two hundred people to visit Lewiston's mining bureau to inspect the exhibited ore.[34] A Tacoma, Washington, refinery valued one hundred ore sacks from the Wundrum mines at $1,008 a ton.[35] One week after news of Wundrum's strike, the experts were in town ready to examine the claims. A "representative and expert of the New York Development Company" left Lewiston for the canyon on March 22, 1903, and returned with a glowing assessment. "The Cave Gulch country is destined to become one of the big gold camps of the west." To validate his findings, the expert assured the reader that "I have been in the bonanza districts of Australia and South America, but I have never seen such marvelously rich surface showings as are found in the section of Snake River Country."[36] By April 1903, an estimated five hundred "mining operators and experts" were in the Snake canyon, coming from "every section of the country."

In November 1903, the new Snake River steamer, the *Imnaha*, which had been launched in July of that year, wrecked. Property developers, who had come to depend on the boat, once again faced transportation problems.[37] They dumped large quantities of fine ore along the riverbank to await later shipment and set about planning for the future. At one claim, the Yellow Boy, work continued though the winter and there was talk of building a mill. If necessary, men and supplies could be brought in via Waha, twenty-two miles away, even though the onset of winter brought deep snow and fallen timber along the road. Work on the other Cave Gulch properties continued through the winter and the following year. In the spring, the *Mountain Gem* replaced the *Imnaha*. Once again, mine owners expected that they could transport ore out of the canyon with some regularity. The coming year looked promising.[38] From all indications at the time, the men working the Cave Gulch properties intended to keep the mines operational for years to come.[39]

In the end, investing in granite was a much more solid economic venture than sinking money and time into mining copper, silver, or gold. In late 1899, Niles and Vinson, two proprietors of a Walla Walla, Washington, marble works, claimed eighty-five acres on the Idaho side a mile below Cave Gulch. For twelve years the two men had been searching throughout the Northwest for quarries "that would provide a product that they could handle and market from Walla Walla." Vinson visited the site and "found an immense granite dyke" of both gray and black granite that crossed the river at a point a few miles above the rapids. A brief examination of the stone convinced Vinson and Niles that they had at last found the ideal quarry. Niles was especially pleased with the black granite. "We consider [it] to be as fine as the Quincy granite of Massachusetts. It is beautiful in the finished form." They began immediate preparations to open the quarries and soon had finished stone on the market. It sold well.[40]

Up to that time, distant Vermont had supplied their stones, but the two men believed they could transport granite slabs from their Snake River quarry to the reducing plant in Walla Walla "for less expenditure than the freight rate from Vermont to Walla Walla." They built two scows to haul the granite to Lewiston, where they transferred it to a steamer, shipped it down the Snake to Riparia, Washington, and then sent it by rail to their Walla Walla marble works.[41] The scows, however, proved to be an unnecessary expense. Soon they used the scows only to move the stone from the quarry to below the rapids where a steamboat picked it up. Vinson optimistically predicted that "the operation at the quarries will continue indefinitely." When asked about the inconvenience and expense of transportation, he responded that they must endure the "great inconvenience and expense" to have the granite "for the Northwest trade."[42] In fact, he expected to increase output once river transportation improved.[43]

Everywhere they displayed the granite, its "delicate and glossy" finish stimulated increased demand and value. Two monuments sold for eight hundred dollars each. Although the partners struggled to keep up with the demand through 1901 and 1902, it grew increasingly more difficult. Vinson briefly considered moving the partners' Walla Walla plant to Lewiston, then, in January 1903, with the river too low for steamboats to clear Wild Goose Rapids, they shut down the quarry. The product was still in demand and had value. It was simply too expensive to deliver.[44]

In June 1903, their circumstances changed. Three men affiliated with the Eureka Mining, Smelting and Power Company, the biggest mining venture on the river, had located granite quarries on eighty acres near the Niles and Vinson quarries. That same mining company, with whom the two Walla Walla men now found themselves in competition, was finishing construction of their new steamboat, the *Imnaha*.[45] This vessel would have solved Niles and Vinson's problems, but by the time the *Imnaha* made its maiden voyage, the Eureka Mining, Smelting and Power Company had bought the partners' marble quarries.[46]

Enthusiastic over their recent investment, one of the new Eureka Company owners predicted that with the "practically inexhaustible" Wild Goose granite supply, the "marble" industry in Idaho would doubtless become "a formidable rival to the celebrated Vermont product."[47] Their new ancillary company, the Idaho Granite Company, had their "marble" processed at Colfax and Walla Walla while negotiating with Lewiston city fathers to acquire 280 feet of Snake River waterfront to build their own polishing plant. Early in their venture the company sold granite slabs to the state of Idaho for an addition to Lewiston Normal School (now Lewis-Clark State College), then under construction.

In mid-July 1903, H. A. Nixon, a former store proprietor, and G. A. (Arza) Garlinghouse, recently of Sedan, Kansas, formed a partnership under the name Lewiston Marble and Granite House to build a reduction and finishing plant in Lewiston. Garlinghouse and Nixon were so impressed by the quality of upper Snake River granite that they negotiated with the Idaho Granite Company to finish their stone. (Apparently Idaho Granite Company had shelved their plans for a polishing plant.)[48]

The Nixon-Garlinghouse business opened later in 1903 and remained in the Garlinghouse family through the end of the century. Arza's son, Arthur, a skilled quarrier, worked on the Lewiston Normal School construction project. The builder sent him up the Snake River to cut granite for the window ledges and door sills, thus filling the order Idaho Granite Company had earlier negotiated.[49] By 1905, Garlinghouse either owned the quarry or was still finishing stone in the employment of others. Lewiston's Garlinghouse family remains in the stone-finishing business to this day.[50] Silver, copper, and gold lured investors to canyon mining, but granite proved to be the better investment.

Salmon River to Pittsburg Landing

Even the rugged, inaccessible area surrounding the Snake and Salmon river confluence attracted copper and gold mining ventures around the turn of the nineteenth century.[51] At that time, the steamer *Norma*, owned by the OR&N, was making infrequent runs upstream, usually only as far as Wild Goose Rapids. In November 1900, a Lewiston newspaper article announced that the *Norma* would go upriver with one hundred tons of freight "for the mines on the upper Snake river." The boat's cargo would include two carloads of coal and about fifteen tons of provisions destined for the Salmon River Mining and Development Company at Salem Bar near the confluence. The next month a company employee took his wife and child to the mining camp, which suggests that families occasionally lived in the Snake River camps. Then news of Salmon River Mining and Development Company at Salem Bar no longer made the paper. The next reference to the Salmon/Snake confluence mines appeared in 1913.[52] By then, gasoline launches had replaced the larger more cumbersome steamboats.

Many years later, in 1938, a man by the name of Bert Abbott reminisced about a winter experience at the Baker mine, located in the rocky point projecting between Salmon and Snake rivers. In the winter of 1919–20, the Snake River froze solid for fifty miles. It fell to Abbott to go to Lewiston for supplies. He remembered walking out of the canyon on the ice-covered river, over cracks two to ten feet wide. Looking down through twenty-foot-deep cracks, he sometimes saw "solid bare ground." At other places he gazed "down into open rushing water." It took Abbott three days to reach town. He spent the first night at a sheep ranch at Cache Creek and the second night below Captain John Creek, having walked about twenty-five miles, by his reckoning, on ice.[53]

Figure 10.2. The mouth of the Salmon River is at the center of the picture; the Snake River is in the foreground and extends to the right. Mine tailings from the Pullman Mine of the early to mid 1900s are lost in the brush above the confluence. (Photo by author, 2003.)

During the Depression, desperate times drove many people to the Snake riverbanks near the Salmon River confluence. Franklin Roosevelt's gold policies, which increased the value of gold, and a WPA program that trained men and women in placer mining methods encouraged potential prospectors' search for gold in the canyon. Conversely, the low price of copper discouraged their revisiting the old copper mines. Otis Freeman, then president of Eastern Washington College of Education, visited the canyon during the summers of 1935 through 1937. He found many prospectors along the Snake below the Salmon confluence working alone or in groups of two or three. Some used only a rocker "to supplement the pick and shovel." They exhibited, however, "considerable ingenuity" by installing both current- and wind-driven pumps "to raise water to wash out the gold."[54] Sometimes women, especially mothers raising their families alone, also tried their luck on the Snake. A compelling picture of Doris Sigler, a schoolteacher from Orofino, Idaho, shows her on the river near the mouth of the Salmon with her three children. She did very well. "Sometimes their three months' labor would be rewarded with about $1600 in gold."[55] At a time when a schoolteacher was lucky to make $60 a month, that kind of income for three months' work is impressive. As Freeman noted, however, most of the prospectors "obtained only a meager livelihood."[56]

About three miles above the Salmon, the Eureka Mining, Smelting and Power Company operations at the confluence of the Snake and Imnaha Rivers, received the most attention during the early 1900s, and has since captured the public's imagination in ways both positive and negative (see chap. 11). But three other somewhat extensive turn-of-the-century mining operations between the Salmon River and Pittsburg Landing deserve consideration: the Electrolytic Company about nine and a half miles below Pittsburg Landing and fifteen miles above the Imnaha River; nearby Copper Mountain and Milling Company; and Pittsburg Mining and Milling Company at Pittsburg Landing.

Early in 1903, three men from St. Paul, Minnesota, and three local investors purchased properties in the Imnaha District of Wallowa County, Oregon and named them the Electrolytic Company.[57] They believed the holdings contained "rich deposits of chalcopyrite ore [with] high values of gold and copper," but to reach them required taking the steamer *Imnaha* to Eureka Bar, just north of the mouth of Imnaha River, and then traveling twenty-five miles on a "rough trail along the breaks of Snake River."[58]

By July, the Electrolytic Company miners had dug three tunnels and planned a fourth tunnel to dissect "the two big veins." The veins, appearing as an outcropping "clearly defined on the surface," convinced the men that their tunnels would tap "one of the largest bodies of copper ore in the northern country." They used ore carts and rails to dig deeper and deeper through cracks and fissures until they reached a six-inch "stringer" of heavy sulfide ore "as good as any uncovered on the river."[59] Determined miners pursued the elusive veins for maybe another ten years. Then they closed the mines. An enterprising rancher converted the ore track rails into a "sturdy corral."[60]

Newspaper references to the Copper Mountain Mining and Milling Company eight miles above the Imnaha first appeared in 1903, when J. F. Tuttle was the superintendent. (Copper Mountain, a prominent geographic feature that separates Deep Creek drainage from the Snake River, still bears that name today.)[61] Superintendent Tuttle believed enough in the mine's potential that he began platting a town site on the Oregon side of the river eight miles above the Imnaha. He described the location as "one of the very best on the river." Steamers could easily ply the river, he contended, since once a steamboat got beyond Eureka Bar, there was no reason why it could not reach Tuttle's proposed town. A wagon road on the Idaho side would extend the boat's service to "the country lying between the Snake and the Salmon."[62] Tuttle's idea for a new town and shipping point, however, disappeared from local newspapers along with news of Copper Mountain Mining and Milling Company activity. The flurry of 1903 was over and nothing became of Tuttle's town.

William Rankin, another name associated with the Copper Mountain mining area, came to Snake River in 1889 to work on the family sheep ranch. Their winter range encompassed Copper Mountain and Copper Creek. Within a few years, mining took increasingly more of Rankin's time and attention. Working with partners, he began to extract copper ore, which he expected to ship out of the canyon on the *Imnaha*. In order to pay transportation costs, Rankin transferred some of his Copper Mountain claims to Eureka Mining, Smelting and Power Company, owner of the new steamer, in exchange for "$14,000 in shipping credit." He planned to charge the $12 per ton shipping cost against his credit. When the *Imnaha* sank in November 1903, "Rankin's credit went down with the ship."[63] Maybe J. F. Tuttle's dream went down with the ship too.

Pittsburg Landing grew into enough of a town that it appeared on a 1912 Rand McNally map of Idaho. In 1897, the Pittsburg Mining and Milling Company operated eight mining sites at Pittsburg Landing and had property reaching high into the mountains.[64] By 1903, a group of men planned to set aside 160 acres at Pittsburg Landing for a town site. They anticipated that it would become "one of the most prominent shipping points on the boat route."[65]

The Pittsburg Landing site was a likely one to develop into a community, for the Nez Perce band of Toohoolhoolzote and their predecessors had used it as a winter village until the war of 1877. Shortly after the war, a number of settlers took up homesteads on and

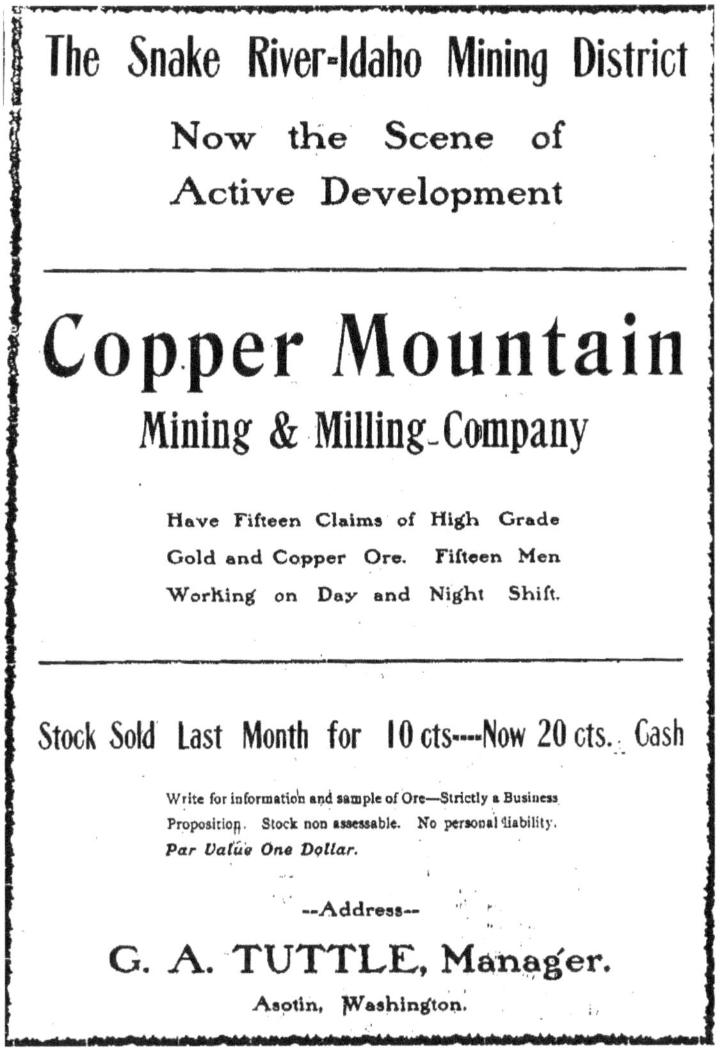

The Snake River-Idaho Mining District

Now the Scene of Active Development

Copper Mountain
Mining & Milling Company

Have Fifteen Claims of High Grade Gold and Copper Ore. Fifteen Men Working on Day and Night Shift.

Stock Sold Last Month for 10 cts----Now 20 cts. Cash

Write for information and sample of Ore—Strictly a Business Proposition. Stock non assessable. No personal liability. Par Value One Dollar.

--Address--

G. A. TUTTLE, Manager.
Asotin, Washington.

Figure 10.3. Numerous notices such as this appeared in regional newspapers or were circulated as broadsides during the early 1900s mining craze that swept Hells Canyon country. Here, G.A. Tuttle of Asotin hopes to encourage investors in his Copper Mountain Mining & Milling Company. (Courtesy of the Nez Perce County Historical Society, James Miller Collection.)

around the landing on both sides of the river. Mike Thomason, who arrived on the Oregon side around 1885, put in a ferry six years later where it remained until 1933.[66] The twelve-mile wagon road over Pittsburg Saddle on the Idaho side to the ferry, built the year before, presumably "opened the gate to new arrivals."[67] In 1903 folks even talked about putting in a stage line between the landing and White Bird, since the "upper river steamer on the Snake is making arrangements to run regular trips from Lewiston." The plan was to shorten the trip by two or three days between Lewiston, Thunder Mountain mining district, and Boise. Pittsburg Landing would thus become "one of the best shipping and receiving points and busiest places anywhere on the upper Snake." Promoters anticipated that trade should reach a hundred-mile radius through eastern Oregon and central Idaho.[68] Mining would constitute but a small part of what developers envisioned for the town's economic base. However, between 1905 and 1913, the post office periodically opened and closed, suggesting that the stability of the community and Pittsburg Mining and Milling Company was as shaky as most other mining ventures.

Mines in the Heart of the Canyon

The Great Eastern Mining Company, seven miles above Pittsburg Landing can be traced back at least to April 13, 1900. A news article of that date explained how owners of the Great Eastern were "not disinherited" by the failure of the steamer *Spokane* to reach Pittsburg Landing. Ezra Baird of Lewiston, one of the mine owners, when in Lewiston on an infrequent visit, simply announced a temporary, alternative plan to move ore sacks downriver. He would return to the mine with George Stonebreaker, "an accomplished riverman," where they would build large rafts to float the ore to Lewiston. Baird, however, insisted that if the state of Idaho intended to develop its Snake River mines, it better "seek to open lines of transportation." For the first time, a miner placed the responsibility of making the river navigable on the state rather than the federal government.[69] By June 1903, the Great Eastern still (or again) had several tons of copper and gold ore at the landing waiting for a riverboat. There was a mill on the site though, and work continued at the mine even though transporting the ore remained a problem. The miners had dug 300- to 440-foot tunnels and planned to extend an additional 100-foot tunnel to tap the main ledge.[70]

By 1913, however, the Great Eastern mining venture had ended. Captain MacFarlane used his gasoline launches, *Prospector* and *Flyer*, to haul four carloads of ore out of the canyon for shipment to the Tacoma smelter. At the time the ore "bore an average run of $52 to the ton of gold."[71] Today, clear evidence of most early canyon mining ventures is difficult to find, but behind Big Bar and plainly visible high above the river, gray tailings of the Great Eastern Mine sweep from the dark opening across steep, grass-covered slopes.

The Barton brothers, Ralph and Guy, settled at Battle Creek on the Oregon side in the heart of Hells Canyon seventeen miles above Big Bar.[72] With work opportunities available in the Oregon and Idaho copper and gold mines farther south (see chap. 9), one brother worked for wages while the other tended the livestock, garden, fruit trees, and alfalfa fields. Experience at the mines gave them "gold fever" and some knowledge about where to look for it. One can imagine their elation when they located a small gold vein about one and a half miles up Battle Creek canyon. The vein looked promising, and they were able to attract the interest of Sherman Winchester, a mining acquaintance from Cuprum, Idaho. Winchester had influential contacts in Boston who encouraged him to examine the mine. If he was satisfied with his findings, they would purchase the claim. He was and they did—for $12,500. The Boston investors hired Winchester as mine superintendent and raised enough money to cover his salary and buy six prospectors' "mule-back stamp mills" to separate the gold from the rock.[73]

Using a small, water-powered sawmill, Winchester built his cabin and a bunkhouse for a crew of four. Since they had enough waterpower from Battle Creek to run a Pelton waterwheel, their first big project was to bring in a proper sawmill to build an ore mill. The larger facility would serve them far better than the small mule-back stamp mills. It took eleven packhorses and a few extra men to move the equipment from Summit Creek to the new site. They freighted most of the mining equipment and all of the heavy equipment to Fred Himmelwright's place at the mouth of Summit Creek on the Imnaha River, then packed it by horse to Battle Creek. As the crow flies, Himmelwright's place was directly across the mountain from the mine, but rugged country made it a slow eight-mile trip up a steep mountain trail, then down the other side.

With the sawmill up and running, Winchester started building the foundation for the ore mill. Ace Barton, son of one of the founders, recalled that the mill once employed fifty men. Most of them lived there, "in a bunkhouse, in nooks and crannies," though

Figure 10.4. Ed Fisher, Goldie Winchester, Lenora Barton, Ralph Barton, and Sherm Winchester are pictured here with unidentified children. (Photo courtesy of Esther Hibbs.)

some lived on the Imnaha River and commuted across the ridge.[74] First, they freighted and packed in material for a tramway. And then, by 1911, they were ready for the enormous task of packing in the ore mill. Freighters hauled the mill by wagon from the railhead at Homestead to Himmelwright's place. Mornings the men would unload the wagons, pack the horses, and head for the mine, which they usually reached in early afternoon. After laying over one day to rest the horses, they headed back to Himmelwright's and arranged the packs for the next morning.

If a piece was too heavy to load by hand, they would set it on a pole tripod, raise the packs up with block and tackle, and move the horses under the packs. They packed huge wheels—like locomotive wheels—used in the mill to crush the rock. They were large enough to go around the body of the horse so the men guided the horse's hind feet into the wheel, then lifted it up over the horse's hips and onto the pack saddle. Not all horses would tolerate such a cumbersome load. There were eight wheels, so progress was slow. "The most troublesome pack was the center stand around which the wheel rotated. A cast iron stand about 275 pounds had to be moved in one piece. It stood about two and a half feet high with a base of eighteen inches diameter." Only one horse was strong enough to carry it, and even he needed frequent reprieves. So every quarter mile the men hoisted poles under the carrying platform, lifting the load off the horse's back to give it a break.[75] Moving in all that equipment took two packers and eleven packhorses nearly all summer.

Ace Barton's father told him that the mine made about fifty thousand to eighty thousand dollars, "but a lot more money went in than ever came out."[76] Unfortunately, as soon as the operation got running, problems developed in Boston. Stock sales went down. For two years, there was enough money to keep the crew, but when the money ran out, the crew left. Work fell to Winchester, his wife, Goldie, two of her brothers, and their wives. They all, including the Winchester's two young sons, resided at the mine. Fred Himmelwright packed in supplies and mail as long as they lived there, and he helped pack them out when tragedy struck. In November 1912 Goldie Winchester became ill. She left the cabin, rode horseback to the Himmelwright place, and boarded a wagon for Joseph, Oregon. There she caught a train to Weiser, Idaho, to see the doctor. She died in Weiser. After her death, the family lost

Figure 10.5. The Barton's second Battle Creek cabin as it looked in 2003. The cabin sits on a bench midway between the Snake River to the left and the Winchester Mine up the draw to the right. (Photo by author.)

all interest in the mine and had no desire to go back to the canyon. That was the end of the Imnaha Gold Mining Company, one of the last big mining ventures in the canyon.

A flurry of mining activity swept the canyon between the 1880s and 1920s, sparked by the unwavering belief that wealth was to be had in the rugged hills and fed by endless, excited reports and optimistic endorsements from regional newspapers. Most of those mining ventures involved extensive, backbreaking work by a crew of miners, a substantial capital outlay from the investors, and a determination to turn the enterprise into a paying endeavor. Their success, however, hinged on the achievements of one bold yet controversial venture undertaken at the dawn of the twentieth century where the Imnaha and Snake Rivers merge, which is the topic of the next chapter.

Chapter 11

Eureka!

"All the indications I get are that they got some money up, started the basic mining, and built the foundations for the stamp mill—and had nothing. They continued to sell stock, and everything, got all this money—and then when they had the stamp mill on the *Imnaha*, took it up there, and were at the point where they were going to have to start producing something for the stockholders, the *Imnaha* mysteriously is lost in the rapids and sunk. Obviously bankrupting the company, after somebody had lined their pockets very well." For many years, this statement by a well-known and respected Snake River outfitter reflected the conventional explanation for the rise and fall of the Eureka Mining, Smelting and Milling Company.[1]

A review of the company's history and correspondence reveals that many of those charges and implications are not true. But the damage has been done. Regional lore continues to perpetuate the belief that every aspect of that company's mining venture—at the juncture of the Imnaha and Snake Rivers—was nothing more than a swindle to milk gullible investors of their hard-earned cash. Callous and greedy company officials, so the story goes, intentionally arranged the wreck of the steamer *Imnaha*, the very riverboat that promised success to all the mining ventures up and down the canyon; they cared nothing about the people or the communities that pinned their hopes on the company's success. Endless repetition of the story has transformed an obscure bit of history into a regional myth.[2] The myth assumes a scam—that from its very inception the venture was a pernicious plan by company officials to "line their pockets." Consequently, it also resolves a puzzle: Why would anyone expend so much time and money on such an obviously worthless venture?

There may have been some substance to the accusations; there certainly were some unhappy investors. Moreover, some charges made it into the courts. But why was that mining company so much more maligned than any number of other failed Snake River mining ventures? Why did this particular story of a failed business metamorphose into a canyon myth? Why has this story continued to capture the attention of canyon visitors so long? The historical record might answer those questions, but only when it is put in the context of the dreams and schemes of that era and its people.

The Discovery

According to William Ashworth, author of *Hells Canyon: The Deepest Gorge on Earth*, "The story of the discovery was a masterpiece, with just the right blend of romance and realism to stir the imagination: Word of a fantastic new copper discovery near the mouth of the Imnaha River began to leak out of Hells Canyon country." For decades before, Nez Perce tales of "gold that glittered in the sun" had attracted prospectors to the mouth of the Imnaha who turned away in disappointment when they found out it was only chalcopyrite—copper iron sulfide. With this latest rumor in 1900, the race began. Two cowboys, M. E. (Elmer) Barton and Martin Hibbs, "mounted on swift horses, outrode their competitors in a night race over the roughest mountain trails in the northwest and at daylight reached and scaled the walls of the box canyon."[3]

That makes a good story. But like many a good story, the facts cannot withstand scrutiny. First, this certainly was not the first time word of a "fantastic copper discovery" had leaked out of the canyon. Newspaper articles for at least the previous twelve years were replete with accounts of one "leak" after another all up and down the canyon. Second, by 1900 almost all would-be Snake River miners knew about the famous Idaho copper belt, which encompassed both sides of the river from Wild Goose Rapids to above the Imnaha. It was not terra incognito in mining circles. Third, although cowhands may not have known its value, any serious miner by then knew the worth of chalcopyrite. Industrialized nations required an ever-increasing supply of copper wire; there was a considerable market for the ore. It was gold to them.

It is true that Barton and Hibbs originally discovered the Imnaha copper district. Martin Hibbs had a stock ranch on Horse Creek, a tributary to the Imnaha eleven miles above its juncture with the Snake. One day in 1898, so the story goes, a mining engineer stopped by the ranch, saw some rocks on the windowsill at Mart's blacksmith shop, showed interest in them, and asked where they came from. Neither he nor his friend and ranch hand, Elmer Barton, could remember.[4]

As soon as the man left, Hibbs and Barton rode north to the place where they had found the rocks and staked their claims. Elmer stayed on guard while Mart rode back to Joseph to record the claims. Soon news of the strike spread like wildfire through the hills. In mid-January 1900, Hibbs and Barton bonded their claims to the Idaho Exploration and Copper Company, an eastern company that by that time controlled thirty-two claims of the original Imnaha discoveries and claims on the Salmon.[5]

The mother lode was the Snake River Chief, "an immense dyke cutting the full length of three claims." At first, they did not find the anticipated primary ore, making the dyke disappointing in its early stages. However, by the end of January 1901, miners came upon "rich carbonate oxide and sulfur ore," a condition that in the judgment of the *Lewiston Morning Tribune* writer "assures permanence for the camp."[6] Then, about three miles up Imnaha River, three men from Joseph "discovered a five-foot ledge carrying a large percentage of native copper."[7]

The Imnaha copper mines continued to look promising throughout that year and the next. Positive reports streamed down the river and across the mountains into the local newspapers. One experienced miner said he thought the Imnaha district presented the greatest surface showings he had ever seen. On one trip back to Lewiston he met thirty prospectors heading into the canyon while other miners congregated in growing numbers at the Imnaha/Snake confluence. He believed that was "every indication of a big rush in the spring."[8] Another miner optimistically predicted permanence for the mining district, evidenced by the outside capital each district had attracted.[9] Properties frequently changed owners, usually from the original local and independent operators to out-of-region investment groups that could raise the necessary money for lode mining. Two such groups were the Fargo Company and the Eureka Mining, Smelting and Power Company—two corporations loosely affiliated but separately organized.[10]

Martin Hibbs and Elmer Barton sold their holdings to Fargo Company in the summer of 1901.[11] Immediately after the sale, the Fargo mining camp at the Imnaha/Snake confluence

Map 11.1. The Eureka Mining, Smelting and Power Company and the Fargo Company properties at the mouth of the Imnaha River, taken from an original sketch in the Eureka Company archives, Nez Perce County Historical Society, Lewiston, Idaho.

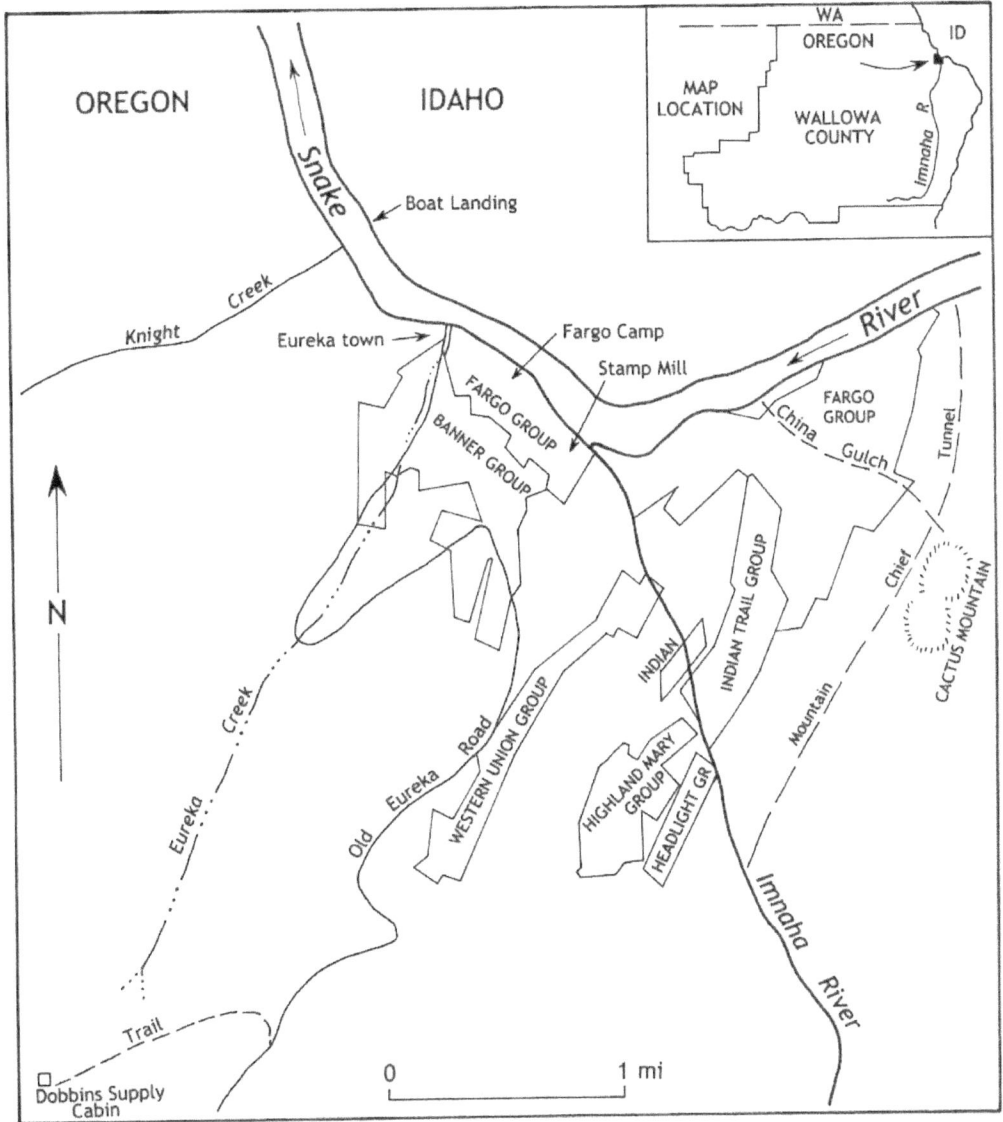

began bustling with activity. By 1902, when the Eureka Company came on the scene, the camp had grown into a small mining town with all the associated activities. The town reached its high point the following year when Eureka Company became the most visible and aggressive mining operation in the canyon. The Eureka Company rapidly achieved many of the failed plans of earlier investors.

A Company's Dream

Board of trustees member O. E. (Ell) Guernsey, a dapper gentleman of about fifty who sported a full, gray moustache and a white, black-rimmed straw hat, wrote to company president James T. Miller in September 1902: "We have reached the point in this business where it will take all the energy and brains that our combined board have, not only to put this business on its feet, but to run the business when once started."[12] At the beginning of the year, an idealistic group of midwestern investors had incorporated the Eureka Mining, Smelting and Power Company under the favorable laws of Washington State and elected James T. Miller, a tall, ample-waisted, middle-aged hardware salesman, as their president.[13] With their first company prospectus in hand, officers and trustees set about selling shares of stock. By midyear, they had already invested considerable money, time, and optimism in the mines. With the entire nation dabbling in "coppers," their timing was favorable. At the dawn of the twentieth century, the future of the copper market seemed solid; national demand for electric lights and trolley cars was seemingly insatiable and unsatisfied, as evidenced by the substantial profits Montana's Anaconda and Michigan's Calumet and Hecela mines had been generating for more than a decade. There was no end in sight.[14] When the Eureka Company incorporated, the founders had every reason to believe they were on target.

The "1902 Eureka Mining, Smelting and Power Company Prospectus" offers some idea of how the company officials convinced friends, family, and acquaintances to invest in a promise and a piece of paper. It described four hundred acres of "mineralized ore property" but failed to mention either its deep canyon location or the Snake River's turbulent nature. According to the prospectus, the property had a one and a half mile river frontage and access to Imnaha River waterpower capable of developing at least 20,000 hp. There was adequate space for a town site, a milling plant, and a smelting plant. Winters were so mild the miners could live comfortably in common tents, and they could operate the smelters 320 days out of the year. Most important, none of the shareholders' money would be used to prospect. Twenty full-size Eureka mining claims were already producing ore for processing. At each claim the ore veins were 1500 feet long and from 10 to 100 feet wide. The estimated value in copper was $140.48 per ton of each of these claims, which in addition showed some value in silver and gold. What's more, owners of the other canyon mines had agreed to pay Eureka for smelter and transportation services and to donate 10 percent of their own ore to the Eureka Company.[15]

Conventional wisdom in copper mining circles dictates a patient approach to developing a mine. First, a geologist explores the property, sinks a test shaft, and estimates the extent of the ore body. Then the company sinks a permanent shaft or, as in the case of the Eureka claims, runs a tunnel into the hillside. However, the Eureka founders demonstrated neither patience nor cautious planning. After all, as the company prospectus noted, "All of the prospecting has been done." Subsequent events proved they should not have relied so extensively on reports and results from those earlier developers. As Angus Murdoch, author of *Boom Copper: The Story of the First U.S. Mining Boom*, explained, "Only after the rock house fills with vein rock

Figure 11.1. From a view high on Cactus Mountain looking north down the Snake River, a portion of the "mineralized ore property" promoted in the Eureka Mining, Smelting and Power Company prospectus is visible. The company boarding house is in the center of the picture, the boat landing is out of sight around the river bend, and the stamp mill foundation is at the lower left. The Imnaha River enters the Snake River out of sight at the base of Cactus Mountain. (Photo by Henry Fair, 1903, courtesy of the Nez Perce County Historical Society, Miller Collection.)

does a sensible mining company begin building its machine shops, pump house, stamp mill, and smelter. And even then the board of directors prays nightly that the ore body will hold out long enough to repay the investment and leave enough [left] over for dividends."[16] Did the Eureka board members pray nightly? With hindsight, they may have wished they had, for by leaping whole hog into developing the property, it appears they put the cart before the horse and the horse got away from them.

Prospectus plans reflected their impatience. The plans called for the purchase of two one-hundred-ton smelters—one to reduce the company's own ore, the second to reduce ore from neighboring mines. The trustees also planned for a fifty-ton concentrating plant. Gravity trams would move the ore to the smelters and boat dock. Power to run two smelters and all the additional equipment, as well as provide power enough for the entire mining district, was to come from the Imnaha River. Until the OR&N built their rail line through the canyon from Huntington, Oregon to Lewiston, Idaho—they had already completed the survey—Eureka would send ore downriver by OR&N steamboats to the Northern Pacific railhead at Lewiston or on to the OR&N rail line at Riparia, Washington.[17]

When word first reached the people of Lewiston that a new company had been organized with capital of $2 million, the company representative told them it was "for the purpose of building a smelter" on the upper Snake. There was no mention of the company's owning and operating any mines, only that the electric smelter would be capable of reducing two hundred tons daily. It would first process ore from Fargo Company claims but ultimately reduce all the ores of Snake River and Imnaha districts. In addition, the representative promised Lewiston residents a company-owned steamboat to transport ore to the smelter.[18]

So, why did the Eureka trustees not simply operate a smelting and transportation service for other mining companies? Why did they pursue mining as well? National enthusiasm for "coppers" certainly swayed them; they must also have believed propaganda from the Snake River mining interests and neighboring communities. Although they had their claims assayed, apparently they believed only the positive reports.[19] Certainly the willingness of board members and officers to risk everything to make the company profitable is obvious, but so too is their naïveté. Operating on the assumption that the mineral content of the mines was much higher than it really was and leaping prematurely into the expensive development phase of the business proved their undoing. Add expensive delays, growing internal problems, and one serious accident, and we see why the company ultimately failed. What is amazing is that despite all the setbacks they accomplished as much as they did in those first two years.

Business as Usual

Most of the spring and summer of 1902 it was business as usual at the mines, and reports were positive. By October, workers had drilled in ninety feet from the Snake and sixty-five feet from the Imnaha for what would become the company's longest and largest tunnel—the Mountain Chief—cut through Cactus Mountain at the rivers' juncture.[20] The company also had work crews probing other potential veins on both the Idaho and Oregon sides of the Snake and along the lower Imnaha. However, beginning in the fall of 1902, company correspondence reveals serious problems. They were unable to meet the prospectus's promise of having even one of the two smelters on the ground and operational that fall. They were unable to get the boat built and operating in a timely fashion. Finally, the ore was not of the quality and amount they had anticipated. Ultimately, all those problems converged to cause the company's downfall, but for the men caught up in the day-to-day tasks of beginning and running a business, through most of 1902 the problems were mere inconveniences.

Company trustee O. E. Guernsey made his first visit to the mine in late August or early September 1902. He wrote that he was "satisfied that everything claimed in the prospectus and circulars was correct. We have a fortune in those mines." But transportation obstacles troubled him. Even though it would be expensive, a road from the smelter to the timber was essential. The timber was six miles away, straight up. With the road, it would also be cheaper to send in light machinery. However, like others before him, Guernsey realized that the river must be their main transportation corridor. The Corps of Engineers would have to remove rocks from above Wild Goose Rapids so OR&N company boats and Eureka's own "proposed boat" could reach the mine. "If we can erect our smelter and get it running between now and

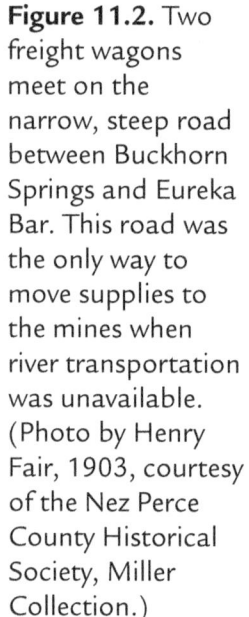

Figure 11.2. Two freight wagons meet on the narrow, steep road between Buckhorn Springs and Eureka Bar. This road was the only way to move supplies to the mines when river transportation was unavailable. (Photo by Henry Fair, 1903, courtesy of the Nez Perce County Historical Society, Miller Collection.)

January, I have great faith that we will be upon a dividend basis by January 1st, 1904. Your future," he wrote company president James T. Miller, "as well as mine…depends upon the success of this company, and in my opinion the success of the company depends upon the one proposition, transportation."[21]

A short time later company secretary G. A. Nehrhood, a wiry, dark-haired, take-charge sort of fellow, wrote to President Miller advising that he was on his way to Lewiston from Portland and ordering machinery for a boat along the way. He planned to organize a subsidiary boat company once he reached Lewiston.[22] Although both Fargo and Eureka investors would own the boat company, secretary Nehrhood was going to maneuver the company structure to ensure Eureka's control.[23]

With the Lewiston Southern Navigation Company formed, Nehrhood's next task was to find a way to send electric drills and an engine to the mine, since they could not get the steamboat on the river until mid-January. His solution was to transport the drills and engine by rail to Stites, Idaho, a small town on the Clearwater River at the end of the railroad, freight them across Camas Prairie to White Bird, and pack them another twelve miles across the divide to Pittsburg Landing. He hired the Rogers brothers of Asotin, Washington, who also needed to get supplies upstream to their mines, to build a twenty-two-foot-long, five-ton boat and bring it up to Pittsburg Landing. Meanwhile, Nehrhood was going to Spokane for some supplies, such as gasoline and dynamite. He expected to have the drills and supplies at Pittsburg when Rogers' boat arrived.[24]

Eureka's remote location mandated a plethora of similar problems and unanticipated expenses.[25] Nehrhood's approach to solving the problems hints at a certain amount of independent action outside of company sanction. For example, Nehrhood wrote Miller that the company was "sorely in need of telephone service to the outside world" and set about organizing a telephone company. All Nehrhood wanted from the Eureka Company was a five-year contract to use the line at customary rates, but anytime Eureka and Fargo wished to buy the company, they could. Nehrhood would sell to none other.[26] Convincing locals to invest in the proposed telephone company was harder than Nehrhood anticipated, but in his October 23, 1902, letter to Miller he reported that everything was ready to put in the telephone system. That promise never materialized.

Did they ever install a smelter? The documentation presents a contradictory picture. The raison d'être for Eureka Mining, Smelter and Power Company was to

Figure 11.3. Dobbin's supply cabin at Buckhorn Springs, the end of a rustic road from Joseph, Oregon, until the Eureka Company continued the road down to the Snake River. (Photo by Henry Fair, 1903, courtesy of the Nez Perce County Historical Society, Miller Collection.)

Figure 11.4. The Eureka Company sawmill at Buckhorn Springs, eight miles above the town of Eureka. (Photo by Henry Fair, 1903, courtesy of the Nez Perce County Historical Society, Miller Collection.)

Figure 11.5. The Eureka Company stamp mill under construction on the north side of the Snake and Imnaha river confluence. (Photo by Henry Fair, 1903, courtesy of the Nez Perce County Historical Society.)

provide smelter services for all the mines. Investors put money into the company on the assumption that would happen—and soon. However, as late as October 1902, there was no smelter. After attending the most recent board meeting, Guernsey had assumed the smelter was ready for shipment. Now it looked as if they would not have a smelter on the ground until February, when he hoped the boat would be finished. He was obviously unhappy that no one had told him otherwise. "I tell you Mr. Miller that you and I have got to see Eureka a success. Our whole future depends upon it."[27]

Ultimately, Guernsey's concern about transportation proved to be prophetic, but throughout 1902, poor transportation was more of an inconvenience than a serious impediment. The builders did not complete the boat on schedule, and the corps did not improve the channel as promised.[28] Finally, in mid October, the boat contractor received assurances from his eastern suppliers that all the machinery would be in Lewiston within ten days. The boilers would take more time. By early 1903, the boat should be on the river. In the meantime, they needed to locate a good riverboat captain. OR&N officials recommended Harry Baughman, the son of pioneer Snake River navigator Ephraim Baughman and the brother of another respected riverboat captain. He was a good choice indeed.

The Dream Takes Shape

Throughout 1903, Eureka Company officials concentrated on three critical tasks: installing and operating the mining and smelter equipment; providing transportation to the mines; and building and equipping a town. Unfortunately, they encountered one obstacle after another.

Obviously, the steamboat was a high priority. Until it was ready for use, the expensive alternative of shipping equipment and supplies by rail to Elgin, Oregon, freighting them to Buckhorn Springs, and packing them to Eureka Bar forced the company to hire a forty-man crew to build the proposed eight-mile road from the springs to the river.[29] With the road, freighters could also haul timbers down to the mines from the company sawmill, which they purchased in Portland and set up near Buckhorn Springs.[30] Meanwhile, work at the mines progressed throughout the winter with spring bringing expectations that the new boat would deliver more equipment, a power plant, and the long-awaited

Figure 11.6. The interior of the Eureka Company power generating tent. (Photo by Henry Fair, 1903, courtesy of the Nez Perce County Historical Society, Miller Collection.)

smelter. Until then freight wagons moved in the less cumbersome drills and a gasoline engine to power them.³¹ They would store smelter parts at the company's new river warehouse in Lewiston until the steamboat's completion.³² In the meantime, excavations for the smelter's stone foundation began in February.

From May 1 through early summer 1903, nothing more about the smelter appeared in the local papers. That no slag pile exists anywhere in the area of the mines suggests there never was a smelter. A 1904 company prospectus makes oblique, vague references to a smelter but never specifically claims that it is, in fact, operational or even on site. Had company correspondence from that period survived, we might have some idea what happened. Most certainly, we would be reading very frustrated and angry exchanges among board members regarding those elusive smelters.

If in fact there was no smelter, development continued, apparently, impervious to its absence. At the end of February 1903, men were "actively engaged" in developing six claims, including the Headlight, Delta, Mother Lode, and Mountain Chief. They "had enough ore blocked out in two of them to keep the smelter running day and night for an indefinite period."³³ One-third of the Mountain Chief's 740-foot tunnel was finished. The surface tram tying the various claims to the new smelter would run through the completed tunnel, which alone would furnish the smelter with one hundred tons of ore per day.

The long-anticipated town, which "ought to become a place of considerable importance in the near future," began to take shape in early February 1903, when engineer W. E. Adams surveyed the spacious, hundred-acre grass-covered river bar near the mouth of Eureka (Deer) Creek.³⁴ The bar slopes east to the Snake River; behind, steep brush-covered foothills flank Eureka Creek, defining the town's western border. About a mile north of town along the Snake River, the canyon narrows to the width of a wagon road before again opening to a protected, sandy beach sheltered in the sweep of a hillside curve. There the company's steamboat would one day dock. About one mile south of Eureka town, the rock foundation for what would be an enormous stamp mill climbed in stair-step configuration up the steep slope; the smelter was or would be nearby. Beyond that, where the smaller Imnaha River tumbles into the Snake River, were the blacksmith shop, electrical power station, and explosives storage. On south, across the Imnaha River, men were digging Mountain Chief Tunnel through Cactus Mountain from both the Snake River and Imnaha River sides.

Eureka town's first building, a combined general store and post office owned by A. R. Brecky of North Dakota, was under construction in Clarkston that February 1903 and would arrive in sections on the first boat, ready for assembly. In addition, lumber for the other buildings would arrive either by boat or from the Eureka Company sawmill in the mountains behind town. One of those buildings would be the boardinghouse—a large, wooden structure with a rock foundation built to accommodate up to forty men. (The boardinghouse may also have had a dining area and kitchen.)³⁵ In the meantime, miners, carpenters, and stone masons—all the men working at the mines and building the town—were living in tents at Fargo camp on Fargo Company's property halfway between Eureka town and the

Figure 11.7. Ore cart rails from the Mountain Chief Tunnel run parallel to the right bank of the Imnaha River. If the bridge under construction had been completed, the rails would have extended to the stamp mill around the corner. The Snake River is in the upper section of the picture. Company plans envisioned a power dam to be built above the bridge. (Photo by Henry Fair, 1903, courtesy of the Nez Perce County Historical Society, Miller Collection.)

stamp mill. Eureka Company employees would move to the new town of Eureka as soon the boardinghouse or their individual homes were ready. Although population figures vary, it appears that from one hundred to two hundred people—including a few families—lived at Eureka during its heyday.

In mid-June 1903, the town and company houses had electricity from an electric light and power plant that ran off a powerful gasoline engine. That engine would serve the town until the sawmill was operational, then a large, wooden flume would corral the Imnaha River and light the town while the company built its fifty-foot-long dam across the Imnaha River.[36] Telephone service connecting Eureka properties to company offices in Lewiston remained at the talking stage. In early July, the poles were still at Pittsburg Landing, but construction would begin "soon."[37] Did Eureka ever have telephone service? Probably the poles remained at Pittsburg Landing until some enterprising rancher put them to better use.

"It Was a Beautiful Sight"

While all that activity was taking place at and around the new town of Eureka, most people directed their attention toward the day-by-day progress of the company's steamboat, the *Imnaha*. Back in November 1902, George Supple, who molded the hull at his shipyards in Portland, sent the materials in five railroad cars to Riparia, Washington, and on to Lewiston by boat. Supple and his assistant reached town a short time later and began to assemble the boat. Captain Harry Baughman superintended the construction and suggested modifications as work progressed.[38] Eight experienced ship carpenters had the frame and deck "in position" by mid-December. A few weeks later an estimated seven hundred people visited the Snake River Avenue shipyard to watch the workers install the launching skids, and at one o'clock on January 6, 1903, two thousand people lined the road for the christening ceremony. "'I cristin [sic] thee *Imnaha*,' said Miss Lulu Kroutinger as with a graceful swing she broke a wine bottle on the bow of the craft." The crowds cheered. The 125-foot-long craft, decorated with the national colors and a large flag flying from a rear standard, started down the ways. She dipped faintly toward the river, righted herself, then floated "gracefully and proudly" into the current. "No prettier boat on the service of Snake River," someone proclaimed. The throngs of well-wishers had duly christened the enterprise, "which promises to do more towards the advancement of Lewiston than any project that has matured since the arrival of the railroads."[39]

Two months later carpenters put the finishing touches on the staterooms. Ship machinery arrived on schedule, including a Benton electric light plant and a two-thousand candlepower electric search light. The boiler had a locomotive firebox capacity of 225 pounds per square inch of pressure and was equipped to burn either cordwood or coal. The stern-mounted wheel was proportionately larger than others on the river, and the power of the engines was proportionately greater. A light draft enabled the boat to run at lower water levels than larger boats. In short, the *Imnaha* would outshine the *Spokane*, *Lewiston*, and *Norma*—three larger OR&N riverboats then in Snake River service.[40]

Although the *Imnaha* would be the most powerful boat on the Snake, Captain Baughman recognized the importance of making the river channel south of Lewiston more navigable. Early in 1903, Eureka Company president Miller had persuaded the U.S. Corps of Engineers to dynamite out some of the rocks at Wild Goose Rapids, even though the latest congressional appropriation had not authorized the work. Captain Baughman would like to have seen more channel clearing there and at Mountain Sheep Rapids, the other

Figure 11.8. The steamboat *Imnaha* at the Lewiston, Idaho, Snake River dock. Photographer Henry Fair possibly took the picture shortly before the boat's maiden upriver voyage in 1903. (Photo courtesy of the Nez Perce County Historical Society, Miller Collection.)

major navigational impediment on the Lewiston-to-Eureka run. But even without those improvements, he was eager to prove the *Imnaha*'s worth on her maiden voyage to Eureka.

At 5:15 p.m. on the last day of June 1903, two hundred people watched as Captain Baughman guided the stately craft into the current. Aboard were fourteen passengers including smelter and boat company officials and Baughman's father, Ephraim, one of the most accomplished pioneer pilots to run Snake River.[41] For local residents, one of the most important passengers was W. B. Stainton, editor of the *Lewiston Morning Tribune*. He would be their eyes and ears on this maiden voyage—which was really a test run. Baughman and the crew would select and prepare landings, take depth soundings, inspect the channel, and repair, alter, or adjust the "rough and stiff" machinery.

"She made a fight for progress and she won," proclaimed the *Tribune* headlines on July 4, 1903. What a splendid way to start Independence Day! Valley residents, who had been anxiously awaiting news of a successful trip, were treated to a detailed account of the voyage the day after she returned from her maiden run. For many, Stainton's vivid descriptions provided their first glimpse into the unknown, remote Snake River canyon. Below is a synopsis of what they read.[42]

As soon as the *Imnaha* left the Lewiston landing, she crossed the swells of Cox's rapids and sixty minutes later was at the small town of Asotin, Washington, where jubilant well-wishers waved hands, hats, even tablecloths as the boat passed. Near the upper end of town, the warehouse man beckoned the boat to shore. "Next trip," Baughman yelled back. At 6:45 p.m., the boat passed the warehouse at Waha Landing on the Idaho side and an hour later the Couse Creek Landing warehouse on the Washington side, where those on board were greeted by a family of fifteen. The children shouted; a herd of cattle stampeded through the orchard. When the river was high, OR&N boats picked up grain from the upland farms at each of the three warehouses and hauled it to Riparia. The *Imnaha* would give those boats some well-deserved competition.

At nine o'clock that evening, the steamer docked at the Earl place, one mile below Buffalo

Figure 11.9. Harry Baughman, captain of the sternwheel riverboat *Imnaha* in 1903, had been a well-respected Snake River captain and pilot for a number of years before working for the Eureka Mining, Smelting and Power Company. Here he is visiting with a lower Snake River resident. (Photo courtesy of the Nez Perce County Historical Society, Carol Wilson Collection.)

Rock. They had been moving at a speed of about 6 mph and traveled the last hour in darkness. The intense searchlight "danced on the bluffs hundreds of feet away" as it sought the deadman (or heavy post) buried on shore to which it could anchor. High above, black, jagged bluffs silhouetted the nighttime sky.

Early the next morning, in dawn's flickering light, the *Imnaha* resumed her journey. At Buffalo Rock, passengers had their "first peep at the grand canyon of Snake River." They looked upon "a beautiful sweep of green hills, ascending higher and higher, until capped by immense pyramids." Clumps of pine skirted the western range of Craig Mountain. "Far back on the higher slopes, numberless small herds of cattle, horses and sheep could be seen grazing while the first sun of morning flitted across the peaks miles in the distance."

Twenty-five minutes later, at 4:40 a.m., they reached Captain John Landing, "nestling beautifully at the foot of a great ravine that sweeps down from Craig Mountain." Next was Billy Creek, followed by Captain Lewis Rapids, Salmon Bar, and at 6:30 that morning the Grande Ronde River. Baughman drifted the boat into the smaller stream and took aboard a supply of freshwater. Three miles farther, Lime Point "stood as a sentinel" at the lower approach to Wild Goose Rapids. All eyes turned toward that "formidable sight," long considered a barrier to steamboat navigation. Immense bluffs crowded close on both sides. The channel narrowed, and then narrowed again because of an acre-size island in the middle. The full force of the stream centered on the huge boulders at the head of the island then rushed in heavier volume to the right. The main channel dropped 10 feet in a distance of 150 feet, forcing the *Imnaha* into the face of the steep, rough water climb.

Slowly Baughman guided the *Imnaha* along the right bank and then plunged into the rapid. With a steam gage reading 210 pounds, the boat crowded forward. Water dashed in rolls to the rim of the lower deck. Two minutes later, cheers rose from the deck as they reached the crest of the rapid. Then the gage dropped. Voices silenced. Slowly, inch by inch, the boat crept backward.

Baughman adjusted the boat's direction to the left channel slough, and in three minutes, they conquered Wild Goose Rapids, accomplishing with a shallow-draft boat what the inadequate coal had prevented in the main channel. Part of this test run was to see if coal from the Grande Ronde coalfield had good "steaming qualities." It didn't.[43]

They left the moorings above Wild Goose at 8:20 a.m., passing Niles and Vinson's marble quarries, currently under Eureka Company ownership, and the mining districts of Cave Gulch, Birch Creek, Garden Creek, and Corral Creek. Cougar and Coon Hollow rapids were formidable rapids, but the *Imnaha* cleared them with 182 pounds of steam. Along the way, canyon walls grew "more stately." Miners emerged from dark prospect tunnels, sometimes many hundreds of feet above the waterline, to wave their hats at the passing boat. Baughman obligingly tooted a greeting.[44]

The *Imnaha* tied up at the mouth of the Salmon for an hour while the captain, crew, and passengers mentally prepared to enter waters "that had been run but once by a steamboat." Nearly forty years earlier, the little *Colonel Wright* traveling south from Lewiston reached a point known as Farewell Bend a short distance beyond Pittsburg Landing. Except for the *Shoshone* and *Norma*, both traveling north with the downstream current, only the *Colonel Wright* had ever tested the ferocious Snake of Hells Canyon. Now, it was the *Imnaha*'s turn.

The *Tribune*'s account of this maiden voyage continued. The canyon "is marked by stately columns of weather-worn diorite that reach fully 800 feet above the stream." At this point, the river is about 225 feet wide. Then the channel gradually narrows, becoming more rapid. The canyon's walls, sparkling at their base with "blue-capped spray, stand almost perpendicularly to tremendous heights. From sparkling sunlight the scene is almost instantly changed to the gloom of evening."

On raced the *Imnaha*, through the "shadows of the gateway of the upper Snake." Then, in the distance, "a white sheet [spread] across the surface from shore to shore." They were entering the infamous Mountain Sheep Rapids, only two miles below their destination. The rapids were nearly one-quarter mile long and situated at an abrupt bend in the river. On the right bank "huge boulders" in the channel formed "innumerable cross cuts and swirls." At the upper rapids, "a chute of water pours down with a steep fall between a long ledge of rocks on the right and an immense rock" twenty feet from the left bank. This rock had a massive forty-by-thirty-five-foot surface. Water rushed against its surface before piling to the right, "forming at the point of the rock a fall of four feet." Directly behind the rock was a back eddy with a 5 mph current. "The water presented an innocent appearance to the passengers," but Captain Baughman and his father, both in the pilothouse, "saw trouble ahead."

An intense rain driven by strong wind complicated difficult maneuvering. "*Imnaha* poked her nose beyond the point of the rock to her left, but a swirl from the current veered her to the right." Crowded by the powerful forces, Baughman rang the order to go ahead. Instead, the wheel caught in the back current, turned the *Imnaha* completely around, and shot the boat to the opposite shore. Facing downstream, they landed on the right bank, where Baughman ordered the crew to string a three-quarter-mile cable. Using the cable as a winch, the boat again shot into the stream and got within forty-six feet of the rock before the heavy current again caught it. Darting straight toward the bluffs on the right side, "as the bow turned with the current, the cable dead man gave way." The bow grazed the bluff, swinging the boat across the stream and onto the sloping rock. For a few minutes, the boat lodged there, and then backed off. Finally, they headed to the opposite bank and tied up for the night.

Someone from the boat headed upriver two miles to Eureka camp to fetch a crew of miners to blast out the offending rock. At ten o'clock that night, mine engineer W. E. Adams showed up with the crew. Early the next morning, he and Baughman inspected the rock and decided it would take several days to blast it out. Baughman suggested instead that the miners cut out the projecting ledge on the right of the channel, a job that took all day Thursday. They then decided the big rock also had to go. Friday morning the mining crew was back at it. The senior Baughman took advantage of the slack time to visit mining properties at Cave Gulch while Harry made a trip to the head of the rapids. After inspecting the channel, he decided to take the boat through the narrows. "The *Imnaha* will run it, and we will not wait on that rock," he announced. Once again, they ran the cable to the rock on the right of the channel, attaching a line to the cable. A deckhand waited nearby.

"At exactly 10:00 o'clock, the *Imnaha* left the bank and tackled the current for a fourth time." Under Baughman's guidance, she "walked" up to the crest between the two rocks and remained in limbo for three minutes. "The man at the rock made an unsuccessful throw with the light [manila] line." Deckhands made two more unsuccessful attempts to catch it before Mate G. H. Bluhn "shot out a line that reached its goal." They pulled the cable aboard and tightened the line as "inch by inch the craft crept over the top of the torrent to smooth waters." The entire affair took only fifteen minutes. Forty-five minutes later they were at Eureka, tying up at 11:00 a.m. Actual running time from Lewiston to Eureka was eleven hours.

What a wave of emotions must have swept the canyon as the men, and a few women and children, first beheld that steamboat. They knew the boat had been trying to reach them. They knew the Mountain Sheep Rapids had doggedly tried to prevent it. In the distance, at first barely audible against the river's roar, they heard the rhythmic pounding of the engine reverberating off the canyon walls. It grew louder. Suddenly, they saw at the river's bend the glistening white *Imnaha* framed by the dark, majestic walls of the canyon. White smoke danced from her stack as it playfully floated toward the eastern cliff. In front of the stack, as if commanding the boat and all its surroundings, was the pilothouse, crowned with an ornate piece of decorative wooden trim. Inside stood Captain Baughman, guiding the craft toward the landing with one hand as he good-naturedly sounded the steam whistle to announce their arrival.

The *Imnaha* landed. Passengers disembarked. Two excited little girls raced to the river to greet the boat. A crew of spirited prospectors ready with handshakes and backslaps quickly surrounded the passengers. Along the hillsides on both sides of the Snake, miners joined the celebrations by waving their hats while yelling out congratulations and bravos. The crew unloaded the cargo and then boarded for another brief trip to Fargo Camp, one mile above the landing across Imnaha Rapids. Here too they discharged cargo as more congratulations "were sung on every hand." Shortly afterward, they returned to Eureka to pick up passengers

Figure 11.10. The steamboat *Imnaha* rounds the last river bend before landing at Eureka Bar. (Photo by Henry Fair, 1903, courtesy of the Nez Perce County Historical Society, Miller Collection.)

who wanted to go to Lewiston and were on their way downriver by three o'clock. That evening they docked in Lewiston, three hours and twenty-five minutes of actual running time from Eureka.

Three days after her successful maiden voyage up the Snake, the *Imnaha* set off for a second time with passengers and freight, which included supplies for Eureka camp as well as other mining camps along the way. The *Imnaha* crossed the slough at Wild Goose with little difficulty, but it took four hours and four unsuccessful attempts to line through Mountain Sheep rapids before the tedious job ended.[45] Once back in Lewiston, Baughman immediately telegraphed the Corps of Engineers requesting that government engineers blast out the Mountain Sheep rock. On the *Imnaha*'s third trip the captain tied up for the night at the Grande Ronde River, then early the next morning ran the main channel at Wild Goose for the first time; the river was too low to use the slough. There the boat lost considerable time while the crew established "facilities for permanent use in lining over the rapids"—embedding a heavy log in the shore above the rapids.[46] Using the line, they cleared Mountain Sheep Rapids in good time and, for the first time, reached Eureka late that same day. After dropping off sixty tons of freight, they returned to Lewiston.

Figure 11.11. The *Imnaha* docked at Eureka Bar, where the crew is unloading building materials and supplies. (Photo by Henry Fair, 1903, courtesy of the Nez Perce County Historical Society, Miller Collection.)

The *Imnaha* was proving herself everything Baughman, the boat's builders, and the Eureka Company hoped it would be. She was also gaining quite a reputation in outside circles. In mid-July 1903, the *Tribune* announced that Lewiston photographers Henry Fair and S. Leslie Thompson had received an order from a Chinese official of an unnamed port in China for six photographs of the *Imnaha*. Apparently, representatives of the Chinese government had inspected the boat, unbeknownst to the *Tribune* reporters and most everyone else in town, and recommended that their government model several steamers for use on Chinese rivers after the Snake River boat. It would be interesting to know if that ever happened.[47]

A week later, the paper noted that Captain Baughman had prepared a description of the boat for the Chinese minister. The article added that Russian government officials were also interested in the success of the Snake River boat. They too asked for the boat plans.[48]

The *Imnaha*'s success and fame continued. More than a year earlier, O. E. Guernsey had reminded President Miller, "I tell you Mr. Miller that you and I have got to see Eureka a success. Our whole future depends upon it." Now with the *Imnaha* on the river, it looked as if all their other plans would come to fruition. Guernsey could finally breathe easier.

Figure 11.12. Although Fargo Camp, pictured here, was only about ½ mile south of Eureka, the *Imnaha* continued on up the river from Eureka Bar and across the Imnaha Rapids to reach it. The frame of Eureka's boarding house is barely visible on the upper left. (Photo by Henry Fair, 1903, courtesy of the Nez Perce County Historical Society, Miller Collection.)

"I Knew the Boat Was Lost"

The steamboat *Imnaha*'s successful mid-1903 maiden voyage amounted to a shot in the arm for the Eureka Mining, Smelting and Power Company. Company officers had built their business, in part, on the promise of providing reliable river transportation on the Snake River south of Lewiston, Idaho. Delay after delay, however, had caused some investors to question the company's dependability. Now, with steamboat transportation as far as the Imnaha River a reality, the company could return to the business of mining and smelting, although complications with boat travel lingered. Natural navigational barriers restricted the *Imnaha*'s usefulness. When the river dropped, Captain Baughman had to line the boat through the Wild Goose and Mountain Sheep Rapids. Gravel shoals, boulders, and protruding rocks also contributed to a risky and slow upriver trip. If the Snake River was ever to become the water highway the Eureka Company and many others along that river corridor eagerly anticipated, the federal government had to deepen the channel and remove navigational obstructions. The Corps of Engineers had to "improve" the river.

Troubled by the corps' delays, the Eureka Company officers pressured their congressional delegations in various states to speed up improvement of the middle Snake River. Board member O. E. Guernsey, for example, reminded his Iowa senator that much of the three hundred thousand dollars that the Eureka Company had already invested in their property was "very largely Iowa money" and that a fair amount of that money came from the senator's Dubuque friends. "We should dislike very much," Guernsey emphasized, "to lose our new boat simply for the lack of the removal of a few bowlders [sic] from that river."[49]

Although the 1902 River and Harbor Act had authorized money to build a dredge for the Snake River from Riparia to Pittsburg Landing, construction delays postponed the river work. Even after the *Imnaha*'s maiden voyage in the summer of 1903, the dredge remained unfinished. Instead of completing it, the government hired Baughman and chartered the *Imnaha* from the Eureka Company "specifically for the task" of channel clearing. That fall, Captain Baughman began the work, and in August 1903, the Corps of Engineers sent a surveyor to Mountain Sheep Rapids to make plans for removing that impediment.

Meanwhile, developers of Eureka Mining, Smelting and Power Company had every reason to be optimistic. The federal government appeared committed to opening and maintaining a navigational channel in the Snake above Lewiston. Although work at the mines had been "greatly delayed" by the *Imnaha*'s government service, the Eureka Company had weathered the delay. In fact, during that time, a Dr. Alyea, the proprietor of the general store in Eureka, announced that he would soon be the Eureka town postmaster, with mail delivery three times a week from Joseph, Oregon.

In mid-September 1903, with the river rising, the *Imnaha* finally ceased government work. "Hard usage" throughout the summer required a thorough reinforcement of the boat's hull, keeping her off the river an additional three weeks.[50] Then, on the tenth of October 1903, after being out of Eureka Company service for eleven weeks, the *Imnaha* headed south loaded with passengers, lumber, machinery, and camp supplies.

Among the passengers on that trip were Eureka Company officials bound for the mines to inspect the proposed dam site at the mouth of Imnaha River. On that first trip since "channel improvement," the *Imnaha* had an accident, giving the Eureka men a clearer picture of the problems their company faced on a daily basis. Neither the Corps of Engineers nor Captain Baughman had removed the two large rocks near the mouth of Salmon River. Now, at that stretch of the river, as Captain Baughman tried to avoid the rock on the port

Figure 11.13. A crew from the *Imnaha* is preparing to line the sternwheel riverboat through the treacherous Mountain Sheep Rapids, a short distance below the Eureka mining camp. (Photo by Henry Fair, 1903, courtesy of the Nez Perce County Historical Society, Miller Collection.)

side, the *Imnaha* struck a strong current that swept her starboard side against the second rock. For twenty-four hours the crew struggled to repair the damage and failed, forcing the *Imnaha* back downstream where she tied up for the night at Captain John Landing.[51]

Further investigation of the damage revealed a large hole in the boat's side. Although Baughman called the hole "of little consequence," the *Imnaha* would have to return downstream for repairs that included extra bulkheads.[52] This additional costly delay lasted most of the fall, and it prevented the company from delivering critical supplies to its properties, especially enough gasoline to keep the electric machinery running. Company projects now amounted only to smelter preparation, masonry work, and building construction.[53] The Eureka Mining, Smelting and Power Company was facing disaster.

On November 7, 1903, the newly repaired *Imnaha* returned to Lewiston. During her long period of inactivity, tons of accumulated freight had piled up at Lewiston and various upriver landings awaiting delivery up and down the river.[54] At six o'clock Sunday morning, November 8, when steady rain suggested a favorable upriver water level, the *Imnaha* left for Eureka on her fifteenth trip south, loaded only with critical supplies for the town and camps. At noon on Monday the boat inexplicably floundered and sank.

After following their wreckage downstream for two days in small boats, Captain Baughman, chief engineer L. H. Campbell, and fireman J. Carsell reached Lewiston on the afternoon of November 10, 1903, and explained what had happened to an anxious community. The machinery had worked perfectly and they had a clean crossing of every rapid, but a "mere mishap" above Mountain Sheep Rapids had sent the boat to its watery grave. The only way still to clear those rapids involved a cable and a winch. With one end of a hemp rope securely fastened to the deadman buried on shore above the rapids and the other end of the one-inch cable kept afloat by a barrel below the rapids, a crewman could grab the floating end and haul the line aboard. Someone then attached the line to the steam capstan and winched the boat safely through the turbulence to still water four hundred yards above before tossing the cable and barrel back into the river. "Everything worked admirably . . . [until] in some manner the wheel picked up a bite of the line."[55] The cable became wrapped around the left eccentric rod, "which bent the rods and rendered the engines helpless."[56]

Without engine power, the *Imnaha*'s stern drifted toward the sharp rock—the one still standing due to the corps' foot-dragging—and struck the wheel squarely against the rock. The big paddle wheel folded back up over the boat. Simultaneously, the bow swung toward the Oregon shore "where it remained but a moment" before the stern slipped from the rock on the Idaho side. The steamer then did a 180-degree sideways turn and stopped, completely filling the channel. The boat stayed in place long enough for the crew to attach two large manila lines to the bank. The two lines held the boat in that position until all the passengers and crew got safely ashore "without the least excitement." In fact, Captain Baughman remembered, "The last man was ashore before anyone seemed to realize the great danger."[57]

Engineer Campbell observed the accident from the engine room. He looked through the stern hole toward the drive shafts and saw bent and broken eccentric rods. As soon as the shaft collapsed, he knew they were "at the mercy of the treacherous . . . Mt. Sheep Rapids." Campbell immediately started the pumps and opened the siphons in case the pipes broke. He then evacuated the engine room where escaping steam was a great danger. Once certain that he had secured the pipes, Campbell returned only to find "the entire stern had been stove in." That left him with no choice but to abandon the boat.[58] He and Captain Baughman were the last to leave.

The bow dipped as the disabled craft slipped into the deep current. The eddy below grabbed the boat, twirled it around several times, and then slammed it downstream into the rushing water. For a moment the *Imnaha* listed. Her boilers rolled off. Her hull jammed against the steep banks, reducing the mighty ship to nothing more than a bottom and partial sides. The pilothouse, deck wheel, and most of the hull resurfaced as fragmented debris over the next twenty-five miles. As for her boilers, they sank straight into the center of the river at the foot of the big eddy.

Ten passengers and the fifteen-man crew were lucky to be alive. They saved very little freight. Eureka Company's loss, valued at fifteen hundred dollars, consisted primarily of twenty-five tons of camp supplies, lime, and cement. The *Imnaha* hauled no mining or smelting equipment that fateful day. An Oregon rancher had tethered on the deck a prize white stallion that he had recently purchased and shipped by boat to avoid a long, stressful overland trip. Engineer Campbell paused, momentarily, just long enough to consider untying the horse, then decided not to risk his own life. The horse was the only fatality.

Why, despite evidence to the contrary, did people assume that the Eureka Mining, Smelting and Power Company intentionally wrecked the *Imnaha*—an assumption that gave birth to the myth of a scam? Gerald Tucker, a mid-twentieth-century canyon ranger and historian, interviewed Billy Rankin, an elderly Hells Canyon miner. Tucker learned that during Eureka Company's founding months, Rankin had sold them some of his mineral claims valued at fourteen thousand dollars in exchange for the transportation services of the *Imnaha*. When the *Imnaha* crashed, one of Rankin's Copper Mountain mine employees witnessed the accident, or so the employee claimed.[59] What he reported to Rankin suggested sabotage, at least according to Rankin. He saw the *Imnaha* crewman make his way to the stern of the boat with the cable and barrel float in hand. About halfway to the stern he heard the captain order him to "cast the float." The crewman couldn't believe his ears.

"Cast the float now?" he yelled back.

"Captain's orders. Do as you're told."

"If you want this dammed ship sunk, here goes cable and all into the stern wheel."

According to the witness, the crewman followed the order and cast the float over the side, inviting disaster. Inevitably the current would send the float and line right into the paddle wheel or eccentric rods. That's exactly what happened. Rankin's employee had no doubt that the captain intentionally ordered the destruction of his own craft. Understandably upset at his financial loss, Rankin chose to believe his employee. The eyewitness account of an intentional disaster reinforced Rankin's suspicions that the mining company never intended to generate any income off the mines. Rankin said that George Nehrhood (he called him Nehrhouse), "bought a lot of machinery" that never reached its destination. He claimed that Nehrhood arranged to have heavy pieces of machinery "unloaded from the *Imnaha* at various places along the Snake River." Rankin believed the company did not want those pieces to reach Eureka Bar, for, once they installed the equipment, the mine would have to begin producing. In Rankin's mind, all that the Eureka Mining, Smelting and Power Company directors wanted from the get-go was to milk the investors and line their own pockets.[60]

Over time that version of the accident gained momentum. Shortly after the wreck, however, although people were quick to assign blame, no one besides Rankin appears to have accused either Captain Baughman or the Eureka Company of sabotage. Most people held the government engineers responsible for the accident. Perhaps rightfully so, since the Corps of Engineers continued making plans to remove the rocks at Mountain Sheep Rapids as late as January 1904. Within the week, however, word reached town that the government engineers had received six hundred dollars to blow out the Mountain Sheep rock and another impediment at Cottonwood Bar.

Hoping to recover at least a portion of their losses, a week after the wreck the Lewiston Southern Navigation Company sent some professional wreckers upriver to salvage *Imnaha*'s machinery. The wreckers joined four former *Imnaha* deckhands on a reconnaissance trip. They believed the ship's boiler and wheel shaft had sunk a short distance above Cottonwood Bar, where Baughman had tied up the boat's battered hull. The salvage party went up the river in two small boats with two tons of supplies for the Fargo and Eureka mines. On their return trip they began work at Cottonwood Bar, salvaging the donkey engine, steam steering gear, cable, and boat rigging—all to be used on the new boat at a one thousand dollars savings. They built a raft from remnants of the hull and cabin deck to transport the salvaged materials to Lewiston. On the way they collected bedding, chairs, life preservers, gasoline cans, and similar items scattered along the banks for miles, a total of seven hundred pounds of materials. Then tragedy struck again. An eddy at the mouth of the Salmon River caught the men and the raft. In an effort to save the lost cargo two *Imnaha* crewmen drowned. The fate of the boiler and wheel shaft remains a mystery to this day.[61]

"The Company Will Not Be Embarrassed"

Eureka Mining, Smelting and Power Company officials who were in Lewiston at the time of the *Imnaha* accident immediately telegraphed other trustees to join them in Clarkston for decision-making time. They assured the anxious townsfolk that they did not intend to accept defeat. Company president James T. Miller insisted that "we have not lost heart and I shall enjoy my accustomed night's sleep."[62] O. E. Guernsey, the new treasurer, acknowledged that the accident would delay work at the mines but promised that "the company will not be embarrassed." And Eureka Company secretary and president of the boat company, G. A. Nehrhood, said the accident "would not seriously retard our mining

Figure 11.14. After the loss of the *Imnaha*, the Eureka Mining, Smelting and Power Company commissioned the construction of a second steamboat, the *Mountain Gem*, docked here at Eureka Bar. (Photo courtesy of the Nez Perce County Historical Society, Miller Collection.)

operations." They had "considerable smelter machinery on the ground," Nehrhood added, and they intended to continue installing it. "As an individual, I will say I am in favor of building a new packet."[63]

Without the boat, the communities of Lewiston, Clarkston, and Asotin stood to lose most of the canyon trade unless they took immediate action. Within three days after the accident, the townsfolk, working with the Eureka Company, formed the Lewiston Navigation Company; they planned to build a new boat. The Eureka Company insisted that local people own the new boat company, in part to "avoid charges the boat favors one property over others." Also, they reasoned, had local people held a controlling interest in the earlier Lewiston Southern Navigation Company, they would have had a greater interest in the company and been more aggressive in convincing their congressional delegates to pressure government authorities for river improvement. In that case, the *Imnaha* might not have been wrecked.[64] The Eureka board authorized at least ten thousand dollars toward the construction of a new boat. Local investors later learned that the money amounted to a one-year chattel mortgage rather than a direct contribution.[65]

Captain Baughman made recommendations for the new boat, which he estimated would cost about twenty-five hundred dollars. The 150-foot, 469-ton *Mountain Gem* improved on the *Imnaha* in numerous ways, including enclosed eccentric rods, a longer and more rigid hull, a bottom twice as thick, and watertight bulkheads up to the deck. With heavier timbers for the bottom and frame and boiler keelsons that extended to the main deck, the hull became more rigid and seaworthy. Also, bulkheads filled the hull—making the boat less vulnerable in an accident—and the boat's extra 25 feet displaced 3 inches less water than the *Imnaha*. The new boat handled easier yet carried 25 more tons of freight. The larger engines used a valve motion instead of the "old time" eccentric rods, and the 16-by-18-foot wheel exceeded *Imnaha*'s wheel by 6 inches. Finally, the 3-foot-longer boiler generated 20 percent more power.

The *Mountain Gem* made regular upriver runs throughout 1904 and into 1905, moving freight, supplies, and passengers in and out of the canyon. Baughman was the boat's first master, but within a short time, Captain William P. Gray took command.[66] Unfortunately, prolonged low water levels kept the *Mountain Gem* from going as far as Eureka until the spring of 1905. To generate business in 1904, the Lewiston Navigation Company tried to diversify the *Mountain Gem*'s services. Late in the year, they began to "extensively advertise" the upper Snake River run as "an ideal tourist trip, with scenery not surpassed in any part of the world." They hired two Lewiston photographers to capture the scenery and advertise the route. To accommodate the tourists' comfort, the boat company built a new upper deck that extended from the dining salon to the wheel. It covered the full width of the boat, providing ample room for passengers to stroll the decks. Expansion included storehouses in front of the wheel and three new staterooms behind the dining room. Additionally, the width of the buckets on the wheel were increased, so the *Mountain Gem* made better time.[67]

An unusually light winter snowfall had shortened the season, but by March 1905, a favorable water level finally permitted the *Mountain Gem* to ascend the "extreme upper river," her first attempt since being placed in commission. Large shipments of freight awaited delivery. Later that spring, passengers on a trip to Eureka included tourists from Minnesota and North Dakota. One of the passengers described the canyon's "picturesque" nature. He thought the trip "should be made by every resident of the country" and that "if the people generally knew of the grandeur" every upriver trip would have a full passenger manifest. That day *Mountain Gem* reached Eureka in ten hours. Although encumbered with a large consignment of freight, she "successfully ascended every rapid without the aid of a line." On the return trip the boat hauled six tons of freight from the Eureka mine, thirty-three tons of wool from Corral Creek, and an engine and boiler from Salem Bar.[68]

The *Mountain Gem* continued upriver runs through July and August of 1905, hauling such diverse cargo as eight hundred mutton sheep from a Grande Ronde ranch and ten tons of granite from Corral Creek.[69] She also periodically worked for the government engineers to keep the channel clear. Interestingly, neither Gray nor his employers continued to view the Eureka Mining, Smelting and Power Company as their most important customer. In mid-August of 1905, the *Tribune* announced that the *Mountain Gem* would go downriver to haul fruit and other produce between Lewiston and Riparia while the Oregon Railroad and Navigation Company boats were "tied up" by low water. The *Mountain Gem* and her predecessor frequently filled in at busy times when the larger boats were incapacitated.[70] This time, however, the steamer stayed on the lower Snake.

Unfortunately, financial trouble haunted the Lewiston Navigation Company. Eureka Company officials sued their Lewiston partners in the spring of 1906 to foreclose on the unpaid ten thousand dollar mortgage.[71] The case moved through the district court into the Idaho state supreme court, which ruled that the *Mountain Gem* be sold by July 19, 1906. The affair culminated at the mouth of Snake River, where Captain Gray took a final stand on behalf of his beloved boat. When the sheriff of Franklin County, Washington, attempted to seize the steamer, Gray heatedly ordered the sheriff off the boat, turned the boat around, crossed the river, and landed on the opposite shore, out of Franklin County jurisdiction—a noble but ineffectual defiance.[72] Ultimately the courts took control of the *Mountain Gem*. In the fall of 1906 the Lewiston Navigation Company was out of business.

The next year, the *Mountain Gem* and her captain, William P. Gray, operated from Celilo to Pasco for the Open River Navigation Company. The *Mountain Gem* and her more famous predecessor, the *Imnaha*, both built in Lewiston and designed exclusively for the rigors of upper Snake navigation, were gone. Other steamboats made occasional wheat runs to Couse Creek and additional landings above Asotin. Indeed, paddle wheelers continued to be an important part of Lewiston's transportation network until the middle of the twentieth century, but the era of steamboats in Hells Canyon ended when Lewiston Navigation Company went under in 1906.

The Skeleton of Their Fraud

Back in the fall of 1903, organizers of the Eureka Mining, Smelting and Power Company fully intended to honor their promises to shareholders and themselves, but that goal eluded them. A serious boat accident, cutbacks in productivity, and problems with management and personnel all took their toll, intensifying doubts throughout the company and threatening an adverse trickle-down effect to the stockholders, suppliers, and creditors.

Although Eureka camp manager and trustee Dennis Guernsey was upbeat and optimistic in public after the *Imnaha* accident, his private correspondence with his brother and company treasurer O. E. (Ell) Guernsey, tells a different story. Ell wrote that without the *Imnaha*, the company had decided to reduce its workforce. He wanted Dennis to cut every possible expense, and then he gave his brother a stern warning: "you are *absolutely* in charge of everything pertaining to the camp, and this board will hold you *personally responsible*."[73] Also, George Nehrhood feared that unless stock buyers at Sterling, Illinois, heard good reports from the foreman, the company would be "*up against it hard.*" That statement was more prophetic than Nehrhood could have imagined.[74]

Company correspondence reveals troubles with suppliers as well. For example, late in 1903 the Eureka Company awaited the delivery of lumber for its smelter, bridge, and dam. Contention between the sawmill operator and the freighting company hired by Eureka officials to deliver the lumber eventually resulted in the sawmill operator's declaring bankruptcy. As a result, the Eureka Company sued the freighter for twenty thousand dollars in damages, charging the freighters with late delivery of poor quality timber.[75]

As frustrations mounted, Ell Guernsey left his Iowa banking job to give full attention to Eureka matters. "Do you think that we will be able to land Eureka upon its feet?" he asked his brother Dennis. "I am going to go up or down with the Company." Ell wrote frankly to his brother, and his letters provide evidence of internal disputes between Eureka Company officers. For example, Ell once advised Dennis not to fear Nehrhood. Another time he wrote that "nearly every director in the company seems bound that I shall take the presidency" (although Ell thought he would be more effective as treasurer if he could convince the majority to vote for someone other than James T. Miller, the current president). "I know it will not please your friend Miller, but unless he turns over a new leaf, he is of very little use to us." Clearly, changes loomed on the horizon for company control.

Animosity among the founders and between the founders and stockholders grew. Just why Dennis Guernsey should fear Nehrhood remains unclear. Miller might have been "useless" because of his preoccupation with his wife's health. Other references, equally vague, imply serious internal problems. Records from the Superior Court of the State of Washington for Asotin County spell out those problems. Before the ten founders created the Eureka Mining, Smelting and Power Company, they individually owned or intended to purchase Oregon mining claims at the Imnaha and Snake River confluence. They incorporated specifically for the purpose of raising money to develop the mines, which included extracting the ore as well as operating a smelter and a transportation service for their ore and the ore of neighboring canyon mines. At no time did shareholders expect to pay for the purchase price of those mining claims, but essentially that is exactly what they did. When problems surfaced and found their way to the courts, violation of that basic premise appeared to be at the root of all subsequent cases. Therein lay "the skeleton of their fraud," according to one plaintiff.

In a 1908 case between the new Eureka Company board of directors and the original promoters, superior court judge Chester Miller ruled that "all proceedings were regular until the secretary told the bookkeeper to apply the receipts from the sale of treasury stock to payment of the amount due C.O. Howard, trustee." The promoters' mistake came in not notifying the stock purchasers that they were buying capital stock for the purchase of mine claims rather than treasury stock. Had the stockholders been given the opportunity to vote on the company's purchase of additional shares used to raise that money, it might have been a different matter, but that did not happen. The promoters' behavior was "irregular" making them "liable to the corporation for the amount they thus diverted." The judge ruled that their actions amounted to fraud and ordered each of the promoters to sell any remaining stock and apply the proceeds to help discharge their $25,564.87 indebtedness.[76] They did; none "lined their pockets" as the myth charges (see app. B).

In the final analysis, was the Eureka Mining, Smelting and Power Company's venture in the heart of Hells Canyon simply a swindle to milk gullible investors of their hard-earned cash? No. Did the promoters intentionally commit fraud? Probably not. Then why did

Figure 11.15. During happier times, O.E. (Ell) Guernsey, in the straw hat, and another company official walk down the *Imnaha's* gangplank past building supplies that include precut lumber for building construction. (Photo by Henry Fair, 1903, courtesy of the Nez Perce County Historical Society, Miller Collection.)

Figure 11.16. Men working in the Eureka Company blacksmith shop, with an ore cart in the foreground. A large crew of men worked hard to make the company's dream a reality. Its failure meant loss of work for most of them, although a small crew was kept working for an unknown number of years after the *Imnaha's* wreck. (Photo courtesy of the Nez Perce County Historical Society, Miller Collection.)

they invest such a large amount of money and time into a mining venture of questionable worth? They genuinely believed they "had a fortune in those mines," that patient, persistent development of their dream would pay off not only for themselves but for all their investors—their families, friends, and acquaintances. Neither greedy nor malevolent, the promoters were simply negligent. They unwisely trusted one another's management decisions without having any checks and balances in place. They paid for that negligence long ago. That should suffice.[77]

What happened to the Eureka Mining, Smelting and Power Company? Remaining records give no indication how long the company lingered on the books. Work at their mining property in the canyon sputtered along for a few years, kept on life support by a few hard-core miners like Daniel Mote, who hung on as long as they could. The *Mountain Gem* belonged to the past; the town of Eureka dwindled to obscurity after the post office closed in 1906. Canyon ranchers methodically removed wood and metal from abandoned buildings and facilities to use on their own properties. The grandiose plans of developers, stockholders, adjacent communities, and other mining interests up and down the canyon quietly slipped from memory, to emerge a few years later as an oft-repeated canyon myth started by one of the earliest disgruntled local investors. Today only the stamp mill's stair-step rock foundation near the mouth of the Imnaha River and tunnel openings along steep canyon walls testify to that celebrated era of the Eureka Mining, Smelting and Power Company in Hells Canyon. If the Forest Service—the current land owner—decides to disguise or obliterate the tunnel openings, it will erase most remaining evidence of that heady time of dreams and schemes.

Chapter 12

The Daniel Webster Mote Interlude

"Go directly to the cave without stopping at the house you pass. Return to the cave Wednesday morning and fill your pockets. Then without delay begin your journey back to Lewiston." Thus directed Daniel Mote's "automatic writings" for February 9, 1903.

These writings, which differed in appearance from his normal handwriting, were methodically recorded in his diary, and they guided Mote's daily affairs throughout his sojourn in Hells Canyon.[1] What follows is not so much a biography of Daniel Mote, but a glimpse into daily life in Hells Canyon from 1903 through 1922. Seen through the pages of Mote's diary, his life embodied the transitional period from the era of prospectors and mining companies to that of homesteaders and ranchers: the last phase of residence in the canyon.[2]

Daniel Webster Mote was born to Dillman and Sarah (née Vandeveere) Mote on December 11, 1853, the seventh of their ten children. Dillman was a successful blacksmith and farmer in Darke County, Ohio. Daniel and his siblings received a good education, enabling Daniel to pursue a career as schoolteacher and county superintendent of schools in Ohio. Perhaps driven by a lure of the West, and inspired by his automatic writings, in midlife Daniel left that all behind to wander westward. The stiff, correctly yet shabbily dressed easterner began life in the West as a drummer, a traveling salesman. He canvassed Idaho, Nevada, and Washington, selling cheap jewelry and cigar vending machines. As a drummer, he was a failure. Broke, discouraged, and lonely, he flirted briefly with the idea of teaching again. Two job applications resulted in one offer in Nez Perce County, Idaho. Although the job offer brought him to Lewiston, he turned it down. Mote immediately became immersed in the Hells Canyon mining craze.

Mote arrived in Lewiston, Idaho, aboard the steamer *Spokane* on February 2, 1903. Five days later, he left Lewiston, bound for the mouth of the Salmon River, with $5.05 in his pocket. (Frugal Mote religiously reported his expenditures and income.) Like other would-be prospectors, Mote may have been swayed by the heady promises of companies like Eureka Mining, Smelting and Power Company. But he also had another reason for heading south: his automatic writings specifically directed him to go there. That mystical communicator promised that if he went to the mines on Snake River, he would find his "cave of riches." If he could not find the cave of riches before he starved, or found some sort of work, Mote planned to "bother no one" and use his revolver to commit suicide.

Like so many others, Mote walked to the mines. He covered the first thirty-nine miles to Chapman's ranch, his first stay, in one day. Mote was a tall, slender, natural walker, and the trail on the Washington and Oregon side of the river was relatively easy. Nevertheless, to traverse that distance in one day was impressive. He spent the first night at Chapman's, paying him fifty cents for supper, lunch, and breakfast. The next day he pushed on.

Finding meals and overnight accommodations along the way was not unusual. At any of the cabins a traveler passed, on either side of the river, he could count on "S.L.B."—supper, lunch, breakfast—and a place to sleep for a small fee.[3] (Mote got to the point that he was abbreviating everything he could, but S.L.B. showed up consistently throughout the diary.) What is surprising is that enough people lived along these rough trails to make accommodations so readily available. As evident in the course of Mote's story, a veritable parade of people traveled along the trails—to the point that a day without visitors merited special attention.

From Chapman's ranch, Mote continued his journey south along the river. After only a few miles, sheer basalt walls drove him away from the river. He turned west, following a trail up Cache Creek, topped out at Downey Saddle, then descended Downey Gulch to Deep Creek, stopping each night to stay with homesteaders and prospectors. After Chapman's, Mote took lodging with James Warrens, then Captain George Lewis, then he headed on to Yandell's sheep ranch—where he bought a pair of socks for fifteen cents and paid seventy-five cents for S.L.B. His next stop was Charley Christy's place on Cherry Creek. Mote—humorless, mystically religious, teetotaler—readily made and kept friends. Surprisingly, he fit in. Charley Christy became and remained a close friend, as did Christy's prospecting partner, Z. T. (Zack) Humphrey. While at Cherry Creek, Mote did some prospecting. His prior experience showed: he knew his business and he spoke the language of the prospector—traits that may have endeared him to the two gentlemen.

From his Cherry Creek stopover, Mote headed up the creek toward the road camp, hoping to find work. As a favor to his host, he carried the outgoing mail to Christy's mailbox. Each mining camp and individual homesteader paid a private carrier for mail service out of Joseph.[4] Postal recipients had a mailbox along a trail that, under the supervision of contractor George Wallace, was fast being converted into a road. At the time, the Eureka Mining, Smelting and Power Company was constructing its road from Dobbin's Cabin to the river mines. Wallace required a large work crew to carve a wagon road out of a narrow, rocky, steep trail. Mote learned about potential work there and hoped to find employment. There was none.

Mote needed to earn money to supplement his dwindling reserves. Yet his "automatic writings," which now guided him on a regular basis, constantly assured him of instant wealth with minimal work. After leaving Chapman's, and before he reached Yandell's ranch, the writings promised, "Reward enough awaits you tomorrow." He would find a cave and fill his pockets, then return "without delay" to Lewiston. The next day the writings told Mote to go "into the pit" where he would find "one little nugget [worth] $20."

Torn between fantasy and reality, Mote went down to the Eureka Company mines on the Snake River, hoping to find employment there. Again no work. The relentless promises continued. On February 16, 1903, the writings told him that just above the mouth of "this turbulent Imnaha lies the spot you have sought." Two days later he recorded his most bizarre writing: "This night you shall be with me in Paradise, if there is more of this struggle against error than you wish to see. Low, I am with you always. If you wish, the cave of riches shall open to you at once."

Was the cave of riches death? Followed by Paradise? Whatever the meaning, a subsequent entry denotes Mote's unsettled state of mind, his torment of soul. "[I] went up to [the] little grotto in the rocks, kneeled, prayed, pressed the pistol to [my] temple but could not pull the trigger. The thought of loved ones at home nerved me for another struggle." From then on, although the automatic writings continued for years, Mote's diary gradually turned from the unusual to a simple record of daily activities.

Daniel Mote was nearly fifty years old when he wrote about contemplating suicide. This turning point—the decision to live in the face of failure and despair because of his love for people back home—apparently gave him the resolve to push on another forty-four years. Although he never quit looking, Mote never found his "cave of riches." He found his wealth elsewhere: in friends, in his surroundings, and in his faith.

Failing to find work with the Eureka Company, Mote willed himself on. He retraced the trail. As he headed toward the road camp, he met a prospector who persuaded Mote to turn back to Eureka. Along the way, Mote lost the trail and ended up at Michael Toomey's camp and mining claims on the lower Imnaha River. Mote, Toomey, and Toomey's partner, Hamilton Vance, developed a friendship that lasted through Mote's remaining years in Hells Canyon. At Toomey's, Mote also met a fellow traveler Bartholomew Harrington. He too sought employment and together they returned to Eureka. Neither found work.

Mote, however, met George Perry at Eureka, who advised him to cross the river to Idaho and look for work in the mines there. Word got around in the old mining camps. Very likely, after quickly and accurately summing up this newcomer, Mote's earlier acquaintances had sent word to George Perry that Daniel Mote was worthy of help.[5]

Perry rowed Mote across the river "through ice bergs" to J. W. (Jess) Smith's camp on the Idaho side. Smith, a "speculator in mines," provided them free meals and "sobered Geo. Perry."[6] The next day, Perry and Smith sent Mote upriver to Charles Hept's "bungalow," where Mote stayed while prospecting up and down the Snake River. One time Mote crossed paths with George Nehrhood, an official of the Eureka Mining, Smelting and Power Company, and a Mr. Hughes of the Fargo Company. They were afoot, on their way to Lewiston after crossing the Snake River near Eureka Bar. That two such prominent businessmen would walk such a long, difficult trail impressed Mote.[7]

While prospecting the Idaho shores, Mote located the "Echo Placer and Lode Mineral Claim" just beyond Zig Zag Creek. There, two weeks and three days out of Lewiston, he wrote a description of the claim, enclosed the notice in a sun-bleached cow's horn, and strategically placed the horn where others could find it. That was the custom; others respected those notices and rarely infringed upon the claim. Two days later, Mote was back at Smith's camp opposite Eureka Bar. Using the Eureka Company rowboat, the two men crossed the river and hiked to George Camp's ranch on Cow Creek, just up from its confluence with the Imnaha River on the south side of Cactus Mountain. Mote agreed to help Camp with the cooking and ditch work in exchange for room and board. That decision became "the turning point in Mote's western odyssey."[8]

From Rambler to Resident: Mote's Mining Career

From March 1903 until the summer of 1922, Daniel Mote lived on the lower Imnaha River near the mouth of Cow Creek, within earshot of Eureka Camp. Five months after settling there, he wrote to the Grand Hotel in Lewiston asking them to send his baggage on the steamer *Imnaha*. Obviously, Mote intended to stay, at least for a while. His new employment with Camp hinted at a willingness to do a wide variety of mundane tasks to generate a modest income. Nonetheless, Mote stayed true to his dream and continued to obey his automatic writings' admonition to search for the "cave of riches."

Almost as soon as he settled in at Cow Creek, Mote formed a partnership with Z .B. Humphrey and M. V. Knight. Their first mining claims included American Jack, Alpine, and Cottonwood on Cherry Creek and the Imnaha River; later they added Cambridge

Map 12.1. The section of Hells Canyon where Daniel Mote made his home. His homestead was near the confluence of Cow Creek and the Imnaha River, a few miles from the Eureka Mining, Smelting and Power Company where Mote first sought employment.

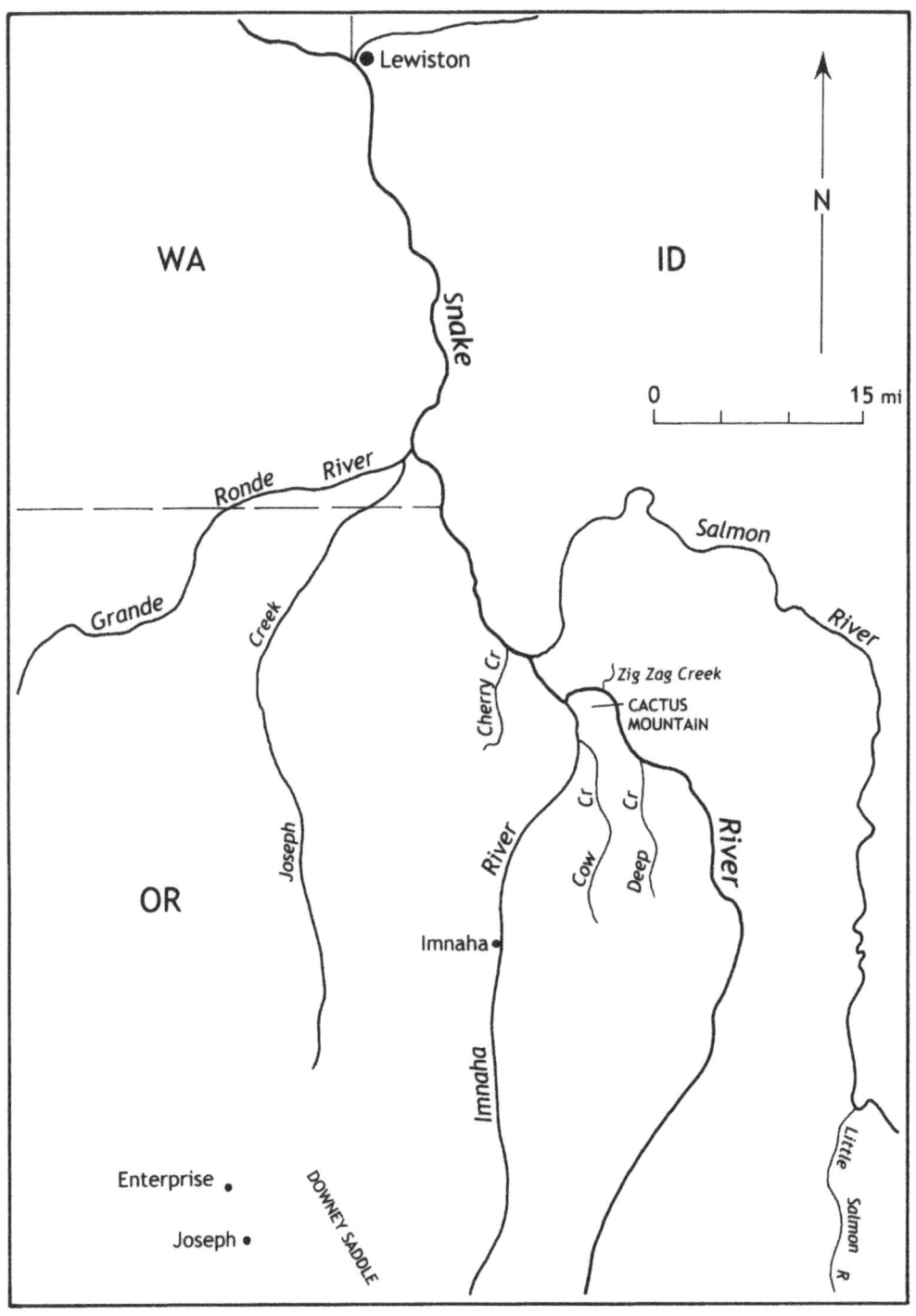

and Poker Pot claims. Poker Pot, Alpine, and American Jack commanded most of Mote's attention. (His initial claim, the Echo on the Idaho side of the river, must have been a bust.) Together the three men prospected, surveyed, built rock monuments to designate claims, recorded each, and performed backbreaking work to develop them.

Mote detailed the physically hard and dangerous work at the mines, which occupied his time and attention when not otherwise employed. One "exceedingly hot" July day in 1910, he complained of feeling sick. "Probably from carrying powder" on his back, he surmised, that caused him to absorb "enough nitroglycerin to affect the heart and nervous system." Another time—the weather was "clear and brilliant white cold" with snow "deep on the canyon trails"—Mote walked to his camp near the Poker Pot claim to muck out the tunnel, then, before nightfall, looked for firewood in "scarce and in dangerous places among the rocks covered with snow." That unnerved him. "For some reason and no reason I was glad to get away."

Mote faithfully worked on promising claims for the next fourteen years. None paid off. In spring 1916, his dismay rang poignant, but tinged with a hint of optimism. "There is practically no ore in the Poker Pot tunnel now! I have put in about all the time I have.... But if [the ore] does not come in the next 100 feet, I may never see it." Then his wry humor takes hold. "I might write a note to Germany about it." In the end, Mote admitted defeat and tried to sell his claims.[9]

Mote's frustration with exhaustingly hard work over so many years with nothing to show for it had taken its toll. On March 12, 1917, he wrote, "I am taking the long furlough. ... No one comes to buy the mines." Day after day his automatic writings perpetuated his gloom, telling Mote he could not develop the claims, he could not earn enough money "to buy grub-food and clothes," and he was "doomed to die alone and a beggar." Mote eventually snapped out of his funk, but never sold the mines. (The only canyon miners who made anything off their work and investment were the men who found a buyer during the boom years.)

Although Mote's revenue-generating work varied, he retained mining-related employment. Beginning in late 1903, the Eureka Mining, Smelting and Power Company periodically employed him. Reading between the lines of his diary, it appears the company used "locals" such as Mote to maintain the mining facilities between the time the *Imnaha* wrecked in November 1903 and the summer of 1904, when *Mountain Gem* went into service.

Late in November 1903, the Eureka Mining, Smelting and Power Company official O. E. Guernsey, hired Mote to perform unspecified work on company properties. The next month, Mote met Henry Huesby, also a company officer, handed him a "time certificate" for $18.75 and agreed to continue performing work that included shuttling company men back and forth across the river at Eureka Bar. Before Huesby left for Lewiston (by foot through Forest, Idaho), Mote spoke to him about a contract "to do assessment on eleven claims for $450" and the "use of the tent, supplies and the boat for taking care of the property." He and Huesby also discussed Mote's interest in three abandoned Eureka Company claims on the Idaho side of the river. In the years to come, Mote made occasional reference to other claims abandoned by the Eureka Company.

Mote's employment included work at the Eureka Company smelter. What seems to be the only documented proof that the smelter might have been in operation is itself vague. Was Mote working at a functioning smelter, or simply doing work preparatory to later installation of the machinery? (This section of the diary is difficult to read and sketchy.) "Filed a saw, 33 hours; at wood, 33½; 5¾ hours at the smelter. Smelter dirt and rock. Helped in the shop

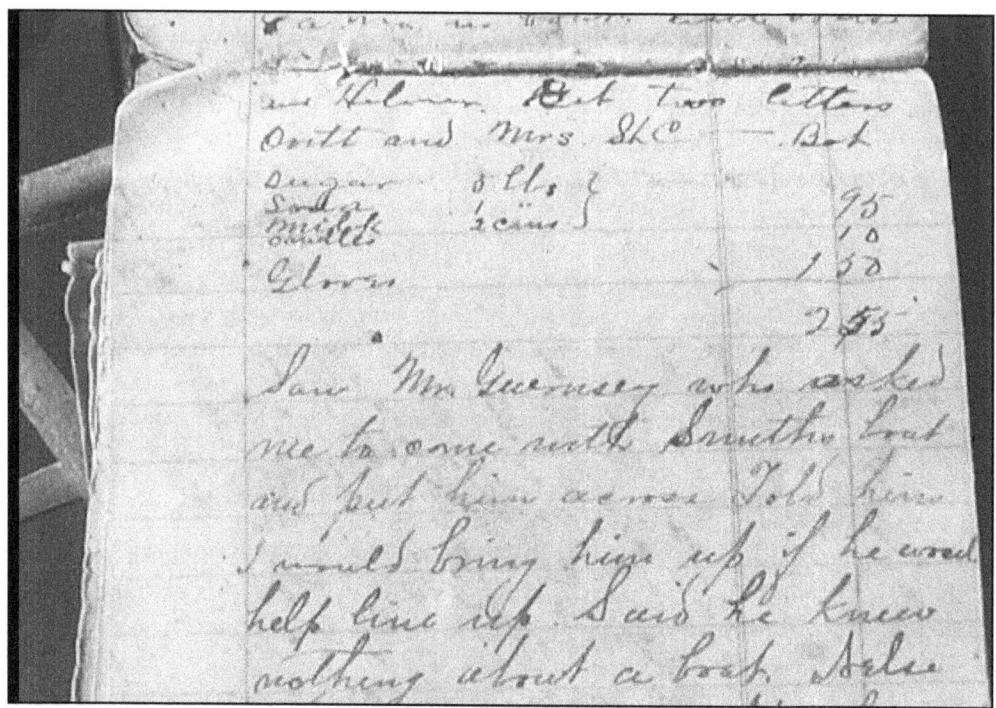

Figure 12.1. A page from Daniel Mote's diary showing how carefully he recorded his expenses. On this page he also notes seeing Mr. Guernsey, one of the Eureka Mining, Smelting and Power Company owners, who asked Mote to row him across the Snake River. Mote agreed, providing Guernsey would help him "line up." Guernsey responded that "he knew nothing about a boat." (The diary is archived at the Wallowa County Museum, Joseph, Oregon.)

one hour. Smelter, half a day. Smelter with rock gang. Lumber and clean . . . one half hour shoveling, 8½ hours packing buckets, cleaning and tearing up?" The exact nature of his work is vague. His financial report, only partially legible, suggests that he earned $73.35. If so, he was doing well by the end of the year, for a man who entered the canyon in February 1903 with $5.50.[10]

Mote maintained communication with Eureka officials as late as 1913, long after other sources implied that the Eureka Mining, Smelting and Power Company no longer retained their Oregon properties. On March 17, 1913, Daniel Mote wrote to the company president, C. O. Howard, to explain his delay in "mailing [the] affidavit." He also asked for something to do and "suggested the repair and installation of the Eureka dynamo at [his] camp as [next word illegible, perhaps "worthy"] of a $1,000,000 corporation." In a postscript Mote advised the president that Mote's friend Percifull had "disinfected and quarantined the Eureka boardinghouse" after a smallpox scare there. Clearly, for more than ten years Daniel Mote had some affiliation with the Eureka Mining, Smelting and Power Company.

Mote's January 1913 diary entry clarifies his reference to smallpox at the Eureka camp. "Palmer at Eureka has small pox." Mote was very sensitive to anything out of the ordinary in the affairs of his neighbors—near and far—and three days later wrote: "heard no shooting at Eureka. Wonder if Palmer is worse." Palmer should have been "shooting" dynamite at the mine. He was not. Ten days later, Mote's friend Percifull stopped by, had dinner, and told Mote that Palmer and Matheny both had smallpox and that he—Percifull—had "moved to his own house [from the boardinghouse], fumigated himself with sulfur, bathed and changed his clothes." Percifull then "wrote to [Wallowa County] Sheriff Marvin to notify the health office to clean and sterilize the building [boardinghouse] for the men and see that they are quarantined." The health office sent Percifull some disinfectant, which he eventually got around to using on the building, bedding, and clothing. By then the men were well.

Mote's self-education in mining, surveying, and assessing continued to benefit him. Beginning in 1909, he worked for the Rogers Mining, Milling and Smelter Company. The

Rogers brothers owned claims on lower Imnaha River and gradually absorbed many Eureka claims on the Snake River. Mote's first job for them was to survey and assess those new claims, which he did with surveyor W. E. (Ed) Adams. (Years earlier, when Adams worked for the Eureka Mining Company, he "refused" to hire Mote at the Eureka Fargo Camp.) Mote continued to work for the Rogers brothers on an irregular basis for a number of years.[11] Increasingly, however, Mote channeled his mining interests into his own claims on the lower Imnaha River.

Figure 12.2. The boarding house, which had dining facilities and would house 40 men, is shown here under construction in 1903. A few men lived in it for a number of years after the company's heyday. Daniel Mote mentioned the residents having to fumigate it after a smallpox scare. Gradually, homesteaders and miners removed the lumber for their own construction projects, but a depression visible today clearly outlines its location. (Photo courtesy of the Nez Perce County Historical Society, Miller Collection.)

By the Side of the Road

Although Daniel Mote went into the canyon as a miner and spent time working at mining claims, he spent most of his time, and earned most of his livelihood, working for his neighbors and canyon travelers. Mote, a multitalented man, willingly did any task, mundane or creative, for his neighbors and passersby. Generally, he either charged for the service or performed it as an in-kind task, trading his talents, services, food, or supplies for something of comparable value. Sometimes he simply performed a task out of kindness.

While taking care of Camp's place, Camp asked Mote to charge a dollar for each S.L.B. he served. One October day Mote came home to find a "Mr. Martin, sitting by a smoking fire in the cabin. He said he was a poor sheepherder." To come home and find someone making himself comfortable in one's cabin was not unusual for Mote or other canyon homesteaders. The next morning, while Mote was getting breakfast, the sheepherder "expressed the hope that I should not charge him for entertainment. I told him I should have to charge him one dollar by my arrangement with Mr. Camp. He said he had no money and went away about 8 a.m. to find a job. He was going [down] to the river to Fargo Camp."

A year later, when Mote moved into his own cabin, he considered his place a "hostelry" and continued to provide S.L.B. for friends and passersby. Sometimes he charged them for a meal or overnight stay; other times not, depending on his own financial needs at the time, his acquaintance with the person, or his assessment of their ability to pay.

Besides preparing meals and providing beds, Mote's services to others ranged from haircuts to blacksmithing. His skill as a blacksmith, no doubt learned from his father, met various needs. As a farrier, he designed and fabricated one unique product, a type of horseshoe used on the canyon's snow- and ice-encrusted rocky trails during harsh winters. He "toed" a regular horse shoe by welding to it three metal plates—one in the middle of the shoe and one on each end—that would grip the ice with each step. Mote usually went to the homestead to shoe the horses and provided the service year round. His other blacksmithing tasks included fabricating metalwork—"punching bridge irons"—for the nearby Imnaha bridge; repairing and designing various hand tools; and repairing plows and haying equipment.

Mote also picked up and delivered the mail—a task shared by all the canyon residents; sawed and hauled wood; cleared rocks from the road—"Strange how many bluffs are in my way here"—and other road maintenance; helped to build houses; repaired people's shoes; helped with harvest. Sometimes he house-sat, caring for the livestock, garden, and irrigation, when the owner was away. He also ran a pack string and periodically rented out the use of his horses. Neighbors like Tippett and Litch rented his pasture and water on a monthly basis, and other cattle and sheep men en route to grazing grounds pastured their animals briefly on his property.

Mote began his work as a farmer, another talent learned in Ohio, almost as soon as he settled in at Camp's place. He planted two acres of potatoes, half an acre of vegetables, and about two acres of hay and grain. "Have no team, no plow, no harrow, and no cultivators." Farming the rocky, sometimes steep benches of the canyon differed greatly from farming Ohio's fertile, level fields. Nevertheless, from his initial work running Camp's place to farming his own property, Daniel Mote joined a host of other early canyon homesteaders in transforming the barren land into a garden paradise.

The canyon has a long growing season, and the soil is fertile. So long as there is water, just about anything appropriate to a temperate climate will grow. Over the years Mote's garden included strawberries, onions, muskmelons, watermelons, squash, radishes, peas, wax beans, lima beans, lettuce, corn, and pie plant. He also cultivated, planted, and harvested wheat, barley, and rye hay for animal feed. Mote did not have his own orchard or vineyard, but his neighbors shared their orchards' produce, which always included apricots. He canned the fruit others gave him, his own produce, wild berries, and all the fish and meat he either caught or received as a gift or in-kind.

Nature provided huckleberries, blackberries, and gooseberries. Mote's observations about gathering huckleberries are amusing. "Huckleberry madness is a species of insanity affecting women and children." But for men, "when the wood and the water are out or the children's racket becomes unbearable," berry picking provided them a good excuse to get away. One Sunday in August, Mote fell into "a huckleberry trance wherein the gods condemned me to huckleberries for a thousand years for eating too much bear meat and venison. I woke when my bucket clattered to the ground and spilled half my pick. I quit. It's a business for birds and women."

Daniel Mote began his own homestead—near George Camp's place, across the Imnaha River from the Eureka Road and near the mouth of Cow Creek—a few months after he began working for Camp. Mote worked hard to acquire title to his place by "proving up" the claim and irrigating the land. He hoped the government would allocate him "twice the acreage" with irrigation, since that had been their practice thus far. Mote built his house between September and December 1904, when he could find the time. (Most of those four months he was in Lewiston working on a new railroad bridge.)[12] He moved into his new home—worth $300 by his estimation—Christmas Day, 1904. In the following years he "proved up" his homestead claim by building a cellar and shop (each worth one hundred dollars), digging a 752-foot ditch (he moved 225 feet of rock and 3,325 feet of dirt), and purchasing a half mile of finished fence. Mote first filed on his homestead in October 1914, then a second time nearly a year later.[13] No title. He continued to make adjustments on his claim, hoping to come up with the right combination of holdings and improvements, still to no avail.[14]

Mote explained why he was committed to securing title to his property. First, he acknowledged his advancing years—"the time I may work to create value is growing shorter." Second, he was acutely aware of national economic trends—"activity in homesteading may be even greater if there is a business depression, reduction of wages, labor trouble and consequently [a need for] homes by those driven from the cities." Third, he was taking advantage of the Homestead Act—"I'm entitled to it by law, and someone may try to crowd me out of my house." Finally, he wanted to leave a legacy—"I can now get water to irrigate it all, [I can] make it of use to the stockman and those coming after me."

During the hot summer months in the canyon's desert climate, without a reliable water source, the gardens, orchards, vineyards, and fields withered and died. Not that water was unavailable, it was in fact abundant in the numerous small creeks draining the canyon walls. The problem was getting the water from the streams to the crops. Only an irrigation ditch would work. Beginning high up the creek, so gravity would generate a regular flow down the main channel, the ditch required enough drop for the water to drain out onto the fields and gardens. Digging such a ditch, an exceptionally difficult, backbreaking, prolonged job, entailed blasting a path through solid rock, digging a gradual incline over rock-strewn slopes, and stretching the ditch over uneven ground to its destination, sometimes miles away. That was just the beginning. Keeping the headgate operational and the ditch clear of sediment, rocks, and vegetation constituted a year-round, time-consuming, frustrating chore. Mote detested that task.

One hot July day in 1909, Mote wrote, "Heat has been so intense and the torment from poison oak [which flourished in the ditches] so damned unbearable I've lost memory of each individual day's work." Another entry: "Too ill to work. Am I to be dragged to death by that Ditch?"

The ditch he referred to was the Lower Imnaha Irrigation and Power Ditch. Neighbor James Rice, whose property adjoined Mote's, hired Mote to engineer the ditch construction and help with the manual labor.[15] They agreed that for $320 Mote and Rice would share work on most of the ditch and that Rice would construct the remaining 160 rods himself.

Mote began the work in the spring of 1914. He was not a young man, and the work was hard. Most of the time, his daily diary notations simply indicated that he worked that day on the ditch—sometimes as long as ten hours—or that he hauled supplies back or forth to the ditch camp. However, if the work was unusual, excessively difficult, or frustrating, his comments went into more detail. August 1914: "Took off my shoes and socks and stood in the water while at work." December 11, 1914: "My Birthday! I worked until almost dusk and then went home." He turned sixty-one that day. The following May: "Ground drinks water so fast the ditches are not large enough to bring down all I can handle. Have spent 3 days at this and will require several more." Later he added, "As people pass by the trail across the river, they will see my work and say, 'poor old fella. He did a lot of work for nothing and other people.'"

When Mote learned that Rice planned to sell out and leave the area, the ditch took on a new meaning for Mote. "I am working now at the ditch, which will give me a home and the power of a hundred horses. More. It will give much more in satisfaction for the contribution to progress." He had earlier told his friend Percifull, "That ditch could be enlarged and improved to generate 3000 horse power, but . . . now I am making an irrigation ditch to irrigate my land." Rice paid Mote $263.57 for his work thus far and continued helping Mote until he finalized the sale.

Mote and a sheepman named Reed helped Rice build a rock wall to contain some of the water flow. They moved stone, some of which came from a cut they were making around Point Bluff, with a wheelbarrow. One cold February morning, "Rice and I worked on Point Bluff. Although it rained this morning and occasionally through the day, we drilled about 40 inches, shot two holes and two pockets." The two men mucked and drilled until noon. By the end of the day: "Point off." The seventy-foot rock cut around the point completed their project. Rice opened the headgate and turned in the water. Disaster. "Rice's wall leaked abominably so that the water did not reach the lower end of the completed ditch."

Frustrations mounted, best captured in Mote's April 1916 diary entry. After a heavy rain, enough to leak through Mote's roof, he went to the bluff to gather his tools, hoping to see a torrent of rainwater flowing down the ditch. "It made me just a little sick to look at that channel hewed out of the solid rock with almost 15 months of labor with not a drop of water in it and the possibility, even probability, of never having any run through it. A dream of years dashed by a rude awakening, to abject poverty and helpless old age!" The water would have supplemented Mote's existing water supply, but he could manage his homestead without it. Nevertheless, the tone of the journal entry is thoroughly painful. After months of persistent labor and so much optimism, there is not only present disappointment but also despair projecting itself into the future.

Mote lived at his place until 1922 when he moved to Joseph, Oregon. For nearly twenty years, he had devoted his life's work to developing his homestead—hoping to own title to the land—and his mining claims—hoping to find "pay dirt." The process became increasingly more important than the prize. Through those years, Mote's friends, surroundings, self-education, and goals blessed him richly. He was a well-informed man, always learning and sharing his knowledge with others. His self-education included a study of science, health, electricity, surveying, and trigonometry; in addition, he "amused" himself with geometry. He read the dictionary, and wrote his own; he read the Bible and memorized some passages; he read novels and all the newspapers and magazines he could get his hands on. What he "gave" to others was far more than the material. Indeed, the poem "The House by the Side of the Road" by Sam Walter Foss reads almost as if Foss were writing about Daniel Mote's years in Hells Canyon.

> Let me live in a house by the side of the road,
> Where the race of men go by—
> The men who are good and the men who are bad,
> As good and as bad as I.
> I would not sit in the scorner's seat,
> Or hurl the cynic's ban—
> Let me live in a house by the side of the road
> And be a friend to man.

Many of Daniel Mote's visitors were simply men trekking between the small settlement of Imnaha and the Snake River. Mote usually recorded their names, rarely mentioned their business, but if something about the visitor made him outstanding—which to Mote involved extensive travels, something the traveler had read and discussed with him, or the depth of his mind—then Mote's diary entry would be more detailed. He directed his hospitality, however, toward near and distant neighbors traveling between homesteads, work, or herding cattle and sheep from place to place. As the years advanced, those visitors included more married couples and their offspring.

Here are some typical days "in the house by the side of the road."

May 20, 1909: "Grace and Billy here. Grace remains for dinner. Took her home about 6 p.m. Walked, talked, fished, ran races, was quite a boy again for her sake and to her evident enjoyment." September 26, 1909. "Billy Lord comes. Rogers comes. Lord and Rogers stay for dinner. Rogers offered to bring in [my] supplies with his [own]. Lord and I went to Rice's but Rice had not returned. Indian came for 25 cents worth of potatoes."

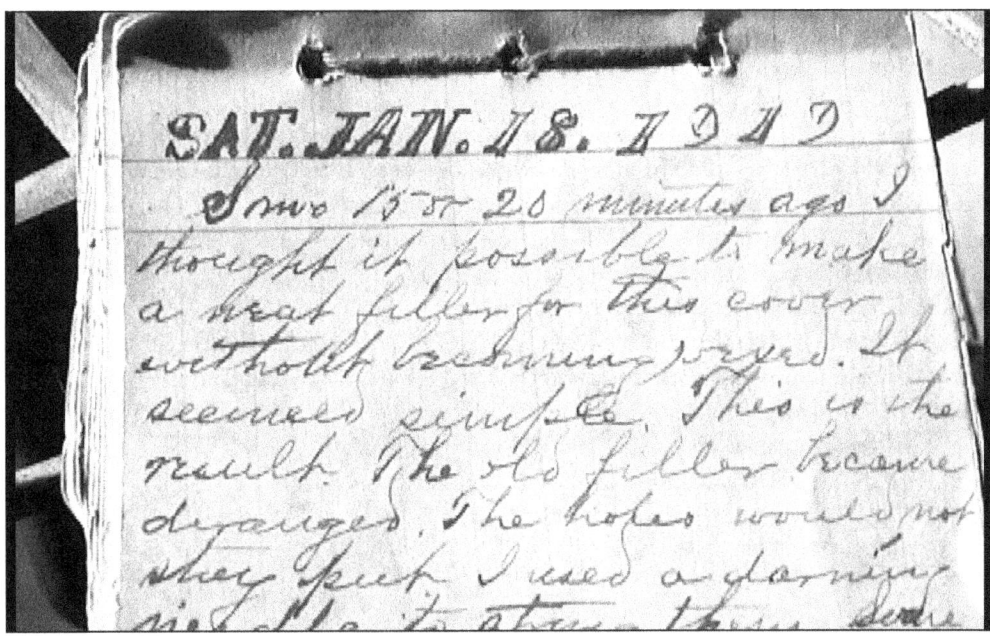

Figure 12.3. This page from Daniel Mote's diary, January 18, 1912, illustrates an ordinary task that merited his recording. "Some 15 or 20 minutes ago I thought it possible to make a great filler for this cover without becoming vexed. It seems simple. This is the result. The old filler became damaged. The holes would not stay put. I used a farming needle to string…" (The diary is archived at the Wallowa County Museum, Joseph, Oregon.)

Saturday, February 15, 1913: "Spent the day getting wood, visiting with Roy Tippett, George Greenwood, Mrs. Fish's boy, Henry Foster, etc. Am reading until midnight." The next day: "Vester Tippett and Roy stopped in and chatted for some time. Promised me a chance of work on the Buster claim. T. D. Percifull came for dinner and stayed all night."

Mote entertained his guests with more than food and conversation. On Saturday, May 3, 1913, he wrote, "Mr. Pratt drops in while waiting for Dan Throe's cattle. Plays `The Love Scene' and `Beautiful Blue Danube' waltz on the phonograph. Relate my ditch episode and agricultural history therewith associated. He seems appreciative, enjoyable and kindly. Tell him I have a backache." Two years later, also in May, "Raymond's boy was here at noon to notify me of the school meeting to decide the method of raising money for the schoolhouse."

Holidays were "normal" days. Guests were welcome but not always appreciated.

July 4, 1916: "Fancy! Expected to be alone the entire day." Two young men stopped by and Mote served them breakfast. After they ate and prepared to go, one of the youth "threw down a half a dollar to 'buy me gum and candy.'" That arrogant behavior of youth insulted Mote, and rightfully so. Christmas Eve, 1915, was not much better. When Mote returned home from work, he found George Camp in the house, reading. "He stayed all night. I packed four loads of wood. He did not offer to help at anything. Callahan came for supper and we three spent Christmas eve together. Not very merry nor entertaining in any respect." (Mote corresponded regularly with his family. He must have longed for a Christmas Eve with them, rather than with Callahan and Camp, but never mentioned it.)

The day of the week, the season, the year—it made no difference. The community was in constant contact, helping each other, visiting, sharing meals, spending the night. For a land usually considered remote, isolated, and distant, the interconnectedness of people in the canyon during those early years of the twentieth century would put any modern town or city neighborhood to shame. It was so unusual not to have a visitor or guest that Mote would mention their absence: "Ate a lonely supper of rice, milk, and beans." He spent his sixty-second birthday alone: "Today I am alone and intend to get wood up the river at the pine tree." He even missed company when communing with nature. Thursday, August 19, 1915: "Got up a bit earlier. Went to the isolated grove beyond the two saddles west and shot three grouse. Have lounged until about sundown. Think I'll take my gun and see the sun set. It is glorious. And just a cool breeze! And no people! But I'd love to have just one or two I know. I think I should."

People and their activities were important to Mote. Little things counted too—an aspect of his character that some visitors seemed to sense. One Thursday in February, Mote watched three people bound for Eureka, "two on horseback with 'chaps' and one—six-footer, huge—afoot. One man on horseback with two mules packed." Mote probably longed to cross the river to learn their identities and business. Later that day, after dragging some wood, he "rested, partly receptive, partly world-suggesting." Soon "Josephine, Mary, and Ruth Clemons [came] with coffee and the [Enterprise, Ore.,] Record C[hieftain]." Ruth brought a gift, a buttercup, for which Mote thanked her and "placed in my buttonhole." Was Ruth a child? I think that she was and that Daniel Mote enjoyed her visit, for he said that once he placed the flower in his buttonhole, "She jumped up and sang."

Broadcasting the News

Daniel Mote and his neighbors kept abreast of events within the region, the nation, and the world. When someone died, word spread fast. Help and support came from all directions. In the summer of 1908, Mote was near G. A. Miller when someone killed him. He did not elaborate, merely stated, "Stayed and attended him through the night on the bank of the Imnaha River at Rice's Ford. Miller died about 2:30 p.m." The next day Mote and some friends buried Miller.

The following summer, Mote's guest Aaron Wilson told him that three weeks earlier someone had found Charles Hept dead by a spring on his Idaho claim. That same man had befriended Mote years earlier, shortly after Mote considered suicide. Wilson also reported that the Ellis boys found Ike Baer's body. They supposed he died from snakebite, since they found him by his woodpile on his ranch with one shoe off. Two little boys were with him.

In May 1915, word spread throughout the canyon that Sylvia Steens had accidentally drowned in Joseph Creek. Mote learned about her death from Harry Vaughn, who was "irrigating in the rain." Sylvia was divorced from Charley McAnulty and had married Jidge Tippett only one year earlier. On May 4, 1916, Mote learned from mail carrier Lawrence Matheny that George Haas had died. Matheny was carrying the news to his uncle Sam Litch.

Then on July 19, 1917, word reached Mote of George Camp's death. He had hired Mote to care for his property, back when Mote was destitute and unable to get any other work. He had been Mote's neighbor for a number of years and therefore showed up on a regular basis in Mote's diary. At first Mote simply reported when Camp visited, what he wanted, or what he was doing. As time wore on, Camp became increasingly irritating to Mote—"Camp wears me out." Rarely did Daniel Mote write harshly about an individual; George Camp received that dubious honor—but Mote wrote nothing derogatory the day Camp died.[16]

Local news other than death notices also filtered through the canyon. On a daily basis, Mote learned of or shared a story about one person or another, their comings and goings. One riveting bit of news to cover the country in August 1915 was that "Mrs. Tippett and her sister were shocking in overalls." Most of the local gossip focused on the mundane, but people knew about significant events as well. "Women voted" at a 1915 school board meeting, where they discussed recalling the school board and levying a three-mill tax to support the school.

Did Mote approve of their vote? He did not say, but he frequently mentioned the school board's problems and decisions.

News reached Mote the spring of 1916 that the "Army Engineers for the Lock and Dam System" had proposed a survey of Snake River. Implied but not stated were the changes a lock and dam system through the canyon would bring. Mote rarely mentioned earlier activities on the Snake River, except mining. He made passing reference to the *Mountain Gem*, the last steamboat to serve the residents. However, in 1914, when Ed MacFarlane began his commercial boat service from Asotin, Mote's diary references to river travel increased.[17] MacFarlane's river service also increased the flow of road traffic on the other side of the Imnaha River from Mote's home. Mote regularly noted who was passing by and what their business was. Lower Imnaha residents had the choice of maintaining their regular mail service—they now had a paid carrier—or receiving their mail by boat. Mote never reported his choice. However, he endorsed the idea of putting in a warehouse on the Snake River at the mouth of Big Gulch—as a community service and revenue-generating scheme—and offered to help build the warehouse by donating a week's work.[18]

Daniel Mote, his friends, and visitors were also aware of events reaching well beyond their canyon borders. His diary disproves the assumption that Hells Canyon residents were isolated and ignorant of the world outside. They exchanged newspapers, books, and magazines on a regular basis. If they had no reading material to bring on a visit, they carried an accurate report of the news they had heard or read. Not surprisingly, by 1915 the war in Europe was in everyone's conversation. At first Mote's comments were merely in passing: May 22, 1915: "I saw in the *Oregonian* of May 18th the account of the *Lusitania* sinking off Queenstown by German submarine." However, as events in Europe deteriorated, the news pressed increasingly heavy on Daniel Mote. Thursday, May 30, 1916: "The German and French are making a killing at Verdun: the English, Russians and Turks in Mesopotamia. Shades of Nebuchadnezzar! What do things mean anyway?"

That same summer of 1916, Mote followed the presidential election closely. He had definite opinions about the Republican nomination. "The Republican Presidential Convention meets today [June 7] in Chicago. [Theodore] Roosevelt must NOT be nominated." On the other hand, "Wilson must be nominated" at the June 14 Democrat convention in St. Louis. Not surprisingly, on November 7, 1916, Mote wrote, "Went to Imnaha. Voted for WILSON. And MARSHALL. And state and county officers." The next day he killed the pack rat that had been tormenting him for weeks.

As the war progressed, Mote frequently made parallel inferences from events at home to events that divided humanity and drove people to war. In August 1917, he went to the mountains to hunt. It was also a time of reflection. "What are all the people doing in the great world? I cannot hear the booming of the greatest guns. The flyers do not come this way. No wail of sorrow nor shout of joy penetrates this vast silence." Nevertheless, the next evening, as he watched the sun set "in a sea of blood," he commented that "the suggestion let loose by that worn and overworked figure may resemble the poke of a curious boy with a hive of bees. But action must be started some way. The world is dying and needs 'first aid' now."

In the fall of 1917, Mote engaged in a minor dispute with Jack Tippett over a fence across Alpine Tunnel. Mote had built the fence and Tippett wanted it removed so his cattle could have access to the river. The parallel between their small dispute and world events struck Mote. He and Tippett reached an agreement, but the next day Mote wrote, "I must understand something, I suppose, of the Russian situation, of the Italian campaign, of the English and French and America's revolutionary laws and methods for creating an army and navy and making war as well as fighting it. I'm dissatisfied with fence lines." A few days later, Mote seemed to continue reflecting on the nature of fences and boundaries: "Have worked steadily about seven hours. Nobody! Silence! Isn't it fine! No roar of guns, no slaughter here, no fear and no fierce hate of men! Yet I am constructing barbed wire entanglements to guard my ground from thieves! Trouble could grow out of that."

As the war progressed, Mote's daily tasks seemed increasingly unimportant. December 2, 1917, what should have been an ordinary Sunday, the day he bathed, shaved, washed clothes, mended, wrote letters, and read—mundane but pleasurable, rewarding activities—was a troubling day: "I have no interest in anything except the war, and that is like a dull pain, a horror of woes to come."

As the war touched the canyon directly, Mote's self-reflections became ever more probing. In April 1917, Mote wrote, "What must be my part in the impending war? This question intrudes and may have to be answered. Sixty-three does not relieve one of responsibility." Then he added, "Morrison came by with the mail. . . . He said Kenneth Blevins, Bob Warnock, and Jesse Warnock, the latter Billy's boy, had enlisted. We are in the Great War, the Cruel War but for the freedom of all people, for human liberty and justice." The next year, in February, Billy Litch stopped by for magazines and dinner. He announced that "Punch Morrison will go out tomorrow for his examination. If accepted will quit work and go to San Francisco." Mote must have sensed what Kenneth, Bob, Jesse, and Punch faced. No doubt it troubled him. He just did not put it in words, though he continued to contemplate how he should respond to the distant war that had come so close to home. March 26, 1918: "It is raining and the thermometer is above 50 degrees. I have no rheumatic pain when quiet and only slight when active. Can this [be] sympathy with the pain and fear of the world at this moment? Has the Great Battle in France begun? If it has I should arise and gird myself. What!"

When Mote reflected upon the weather, his health, or present circumstances, he often recorded his thoughts in the context of a greater topic. He had "a toothache pointing to some deeper need of harmony in the great human organization." The weather often prompted his philosophizing. On July 3, 1913, he wrote, "A slow, cold, pitiless and persistent rain. It is a curious psychological phenomenon or spirit act that I associate this rain of 1913, a 20 year panic cycle, the Democratic reformation of commercial and financial conditions, the disastrous flood in the East and the severe winter here, the receivership of Frisco R.R. system and my own 'up against it.'" Events sometimes triggered positive responses. One Fourth of July, he examined his patriotism by saying, "So, 'I love my country,' but my love has hardly reached the state of infatuation, though I have never paid court to any other. I'll work cleaning stones from her road. . . . I will think. I will work. I will build a shrine to the silent wilderness." In response to his diminishing vision, May 5, 1917, Mote wrote, "My eyesight seems failing rapidly. Eyes do not accommodate themselves to long distances without long delay. Dreams of high achievement alternate with visions of a long rest in the closed Alpine Tunnel. Sometimes I vary this with a vision of my ashes in the ruins of my home."

Every now and then, Mote just complained: "Thermometer 38°. 6 a.m. There has been frost for several mornings. The poison oak is gay as a sugar maple and [has] been quite busy with my legs. There has been no time at all when I have not burned with the oak poison, ouched from dirt and gravel in my shoes or have not been extracting cactus spines. Even a yellow jacket stung me a day or two ago." The next day "a pest of flies gather in the house, suggesting rain."

Transitions

Mote's reflections tell much about the man. His story echoes countless other canyon homesteaders and ranchers. Who among them had not asked at sometime, "What prevented my staying where I was born, doing the things my father and mother taught and smoothing the last miles of their life trails and honoring their memory by doing in a quiet way, the things they hoped I would do?" (January 10, 1913). Or questioned a brother's wisdom when he asked if he could invest in Mote's mines? "Shall I permit Jesse to become involved in this blind struggle for the great wealth I faintly believe to be in this ground? Will it broaden and awaken him? Or will it paralyze him?"

What an interesting era Mote lived in, a time when some people used a telephone while others left messages in boxes or cans. He did not have a telephone and only mentioned one once, when the canyon residents needed a consensus on what to do with the school board members and clerk. He went into much more detail about a message he received mid-January 1917 at the Poker Pot camp. He found the message in a matchbox: "Mr. Mote, I stayed all night here. I have 5 head of cattle below here. Had to move them where they could get some feed. I built a brush fence across the trail; they wouldn't bother your camp. Will try to get them across the river as soon as it opens up. Ever so much obliged till better paid. C. S. Spain."

Technological progress to Daniel Mote meant his phonograph. Nevertheless, his physical isolation diminished as he more frequently left the canyon for Joseph or Enterprise. It was a two-day trip to town, and he often spent the first night at a hotel in the small town of Imnaha. The hotel presents another good picture of the blending of the old with the new. Although people may have reached town by car (though not Mote, certainly), they still bunked with strangers. "I bedded down with a horse buyer and slept almost none. He drove horses and crowded me to the rail."

Canyon residents rarely allowed the forces of nature to keep them from their travels or appointed tasks. One day in December 1915, with no snow on the ground at home, Mote prepared the horses to "pack Callahan's stuff" to Poker Pot. He had just got the horses saddled when a snow squall struck. That did not stop him. Then "a snowstorm struck me before reaching Dobbin's fence. At Toomey Saddle I turned back because the horses feet balled so badly. I feared they might go off the 'horseshoe.' I ordered the storm to stop and when I reached home it did. But my time was wasted just the same."

Despite such setbacks, Mote enjoyed the beauty of a winter day or any season when nature presented her best. January 21, 1913: "World glorious with brilliant sunshine on the beautiful new snow." May 1913: "The sun shining through the fog. Grand panorama of clouds, storms, fogs, mountains toward the sun rise." Four days later: "Seven Devils and Joseph mountains show their snowy peaks through the smoky haze." Passages of the awe-inspiring beauty that surrounded Mote filled his diary.

Even though good horses were indispensable to his work, as they were for all homesteaders, Mote also loved his animals and grieved when they died. His horses were free to roam the country in search of feed, so it could have been a few days after Bawley disappeared before Mote found him. January 1913: "Found Bawley dead at the foot of the cliff just above camp. Maybe he fell off the cliff." Mote scaled the four-foot rocky ledge to see if he could discern why the horse tried to climb it. "One hind shoe is gone. The kindest, gentlest horse I've ever had here."

Mote was always losing his horses. For example, on September 10, 1913, "I saw my horses last night." Neighbors kept him advised of their whereabouts. "Tippett told me the next Saturday he saw them as he went down [the road]." On the thirteenth, after working eight hours and eating dinner, Mote went after the horses. "Hunted until night, arriving at the house about 6 p.m. tired, tired! Where can they be?" For three more days, Mote searched everywhere for his horses, following leads from neighbors and passersby. His automatic writings even ventured an opinion. "You must not worry about the horses. They will be returned to you tomorrow." Mote finally found the horses at a neighbor's home. "They seemed as glad to see me as I to see them. I pat[ted] them and went on home." The next day Mote sent Joe Clemons after the horses and paid him $2.50 for one day on the trail.

Workhorses, though indispensable in the most rugged parts of the canyon, were destined for replacement by the truck in the more open sections of the canyon. Mote once commented that Rice was too busy with his automobile to work on the ditch. Another time, on a trip to Joseph, he saw three cars—unusual enough to merit a place in his diary. Then in December 1918, one day before his sixty-fourth birthday, Mote wrote, "The day before I was born—64 years after. I had a mind to make a 'roar' but I won't. My machine has lasted longer than a Ford, and the roads have been rough. The tremendous output of bodies may be some argument for standardization, yet it may signify something else." The "machine" he referred to was his own body, while the "standardization" alluded to Henry Ford's masterminding the assembly line. Mote's assessment of the benefits of automation compared to those of man and horse power appear to favor the latter.

Cars aside, change was coming to the canyon at an accelerated rate. Increasingly, Mote mentioned friends and neighbors who were moving from the canyon to nearby towns. Even Mote left the canyon more and more frequently to go to Joseph or Enterprise. In July 1916, his toothache drove him to a dentist in Joseph: "I wake with the firm conviction I shall have to have the tooth pulled. But that means a 50 mile ride and return." He left for town at 4:00 a.m. "Most delightful trip until rain, thunder, and hail came. Got in with Dan Throe. Arrived in Joseph about 4 p.m. Had Dr. Sturgis pull my tooth." (To make that kind of time, "got in with" meant he got in a car with Throe.) While in Joseph he saw many of his old neighbors—Camp, Percifull, Rice, Runnells.

He then went to Hillery Hunt's farm outside town and worked for him until September 23. Whether or not he planned that extended stay in advance, the time he spent there was profitable. He harvested, built fences, milked the cows, and performed other farm-related tasks while becoming good friends with Mr. and Mrs. Hunt. On November 3, 1918, he wrote, "I love those people and they love me. I tried to be good to them besides giving them their money's worth in labor." On another working trip to town, he did some plumbing and other odd jobs for the county school district. In Wallowa Valley the pay was better and the jobs more abundant. Possibly, without realizing it, Daniel Mote was laying the groundwork for an eventual move out of the canyon, even though a 1917 entry defiantly stated his resolve to stay there: "I am determined on keeping a hostelry, having some 10 cows, a pasture, 320 acres all fenced and $200 from Litch for grass, entertainment and service." But the defiance expressed in that passage also hints at the challenges of staying there. Ultimately, in 1922 he joined the parade of homesteaders exiting the canyon.

People simply could not make it as homesteaders or miners in the canyon. Adept ranchers expanded their holdings by gradually acquiring more and more homesteads and abandoned mineral claims. These ranchers, families like the Tippetts, transitioned into the final phase of residence in Hells Canyon. Their era, which began with Daniel Mote's, lasted into the 1970s and early 1980s, when ranchers relinquished their land to the federal government. Daniel Mote never found the cave of riches that initially drew him to Hells Canyon, but by keeping a diary of his many years "by the side of the road" where he was "a friend to man," Daniel Mote handed down an invaluable treasure that enriches us all.

Chapter 13

When the Roll Is Called

The year is 1887. You have been farming in the Midwest for several years. Although you are doing reasonably well, your county grows increasingly more crowded around you. You open the mail one day and see a clipping—"Information for Immigrants"—sent by your Idaho relative. According to that *Idaho County Free Press* article, you can buy a "well-improved ranch" in Idaho County for five dollars an acre, up to a total of a thousand dollars' worth. Now if you are someone from the "shiftless, lazy ne'er-do-well class" don't come, but if you are of the "enterprising class of people with a little money," you're welcome. Bring some stock cattle along, and you "will soon be on the high road to fortune." It's time to move west.[1]

Throughout the late 1800s, thousands of Americans left their shops and farms, joined European immigrants, and relocated on this most recent frontier—the ancient homeland of the Nez Perce people. Most, of course, lacked the money to buy a large, developed spread, but they had the resources to make the move and begin the homesteading process.

Within twenty years after that *Free Press* article appeared, farmers had claimed most of the tillable land within a one-hundred-mile radius of the middle Snake River. Soon, all that remained was the less-arable land in the neighboring canyons and forests. Determined to develop even that most unproductive land and provide homes and incomes for its expanding population, the federal government passed a series of amendments to the original Homestead Act of 1862. These acts were well suited to Hells Canyon settlement. Thus motivated, a flow of land-hungry agrarians moved to the draws and benches of Snake River, joining Daniel Mote and the other miners-turned-homesteaders already living there. They first staked off the better sections—benches where water was available or flat areas near the river—but soon every little creek up and down the river had someone living on it. During the first two decades of the twentieth century, the canyon hosted a comparatively large population. After the 1914 government survey of the Cave Gulch/Cottonwood Creek area on the Idaho side, "homesteaders invaded in numbers." Some twenty homesteaders filed for entry between 1908 and 1914.[2] Around the same time, Pittsburg Landing on the Oregon side had twenty-three different homesteads.[3]

Then the hard winter of 1918–19, followed by the livestock depression of the 1920s, forced numerous homesteaders out of the canyon. The Great Depression of the 1930s saw a small population increase as outsiders searched for a better life. By 1938 forty families and twenty single men, an estimated two hundred people, lived between the Grande Ronde River and Johnson Bar. They had about three thousand acres under cultivation and "considerable grazing land in the canyon slopes."[4] Another population estimate of that year showed more than fifty settlers on each side of the river between the mouth of the Imnaha River and Battle Creek, a few miles below the existing Hells Canyon Dam.[5] Then, outside job opportunities and military obligations of World War II, followed by market and lifestyle changes after the war, reduced the canyon population considerably. It never bounced back.

People moved to the canyon for different reasons. Si Bullock thought it would help his asthma.[6] An English nobleman known only as "Pap" came at his family's insistence. He was an embarrassment back home.[7] Some came because they heard it was a good place to live. Others, like a professor from back East, because it was a good place to escape to. "He'd just come in here and shut out the rest of the world."[8] Although most came as families, many single men and a few single women also made their homes in the canyon. Most single women owned their own claims adjacent to a relative's homestead. Some single men came just to claim a homestead, prove it up, and sell it to the adjacent landholder. "Then they could go to a more civilized area where there were more people and they might meet a gal."[9] Ralph Barton's explanation probably speaks best for homesteaders who stayed a while: "In the canyon you have everything necessary for life. A mild enough climate year round to raise anything you need. Water in the creeks. Plenty of wild game. The river brought wood. I could raise my cattle without having to put up much hay."[10] Those conditions kept body and soul together during times of a depressed economy. They also brought this era of homesteader and rancher back full circle to a way of life practiced for centuries by the canyon's Nez Perce residents, a life dictated by seasonal changes, a surprising variety of plants and animals, and shaped by extremes in elevation.

Players, Nonplayers, and Finaglers: Settlers, Squatters, and Shenanigans

By the early twentieth century, most of the canyon and adjacent country had been surveyed. In 1888 a government crew began at the base line, running from Cow Creek on the Imnaha River to Christmas Creek, and surveyed all the land north to the mouth of the Imnaha River. According to Doug Tippett, a rancher in that area, it was a rudimentary examination at best. "I don't know how they could ever run out those lines in seven days, especially in August," when canyon temperatures hover around 110 degrees for weeks at a time.[11] The survey on the Idaho side was probably equally imprecise. Nevertheless, once the land was charted, it could be claimed and sold as homesteads.

Settlers—the players—followed the government procedure established in the homestead acts for claiming property. Although the terms of each act varied slightly, the basic procedure was the same. An individual first applied for up to 640 acres of surveyed land, then resided on the claim for a set period while making "improvements"—anything from building a home and outbuildings, fencing in some of the property, or irrigating and cultivating a portion of the land. After paying $1.25 an acre for title to the property, the land was his or hers. Alternatively, applicants might list their claim with the proper authorities and sell it for a small fee to a potential homesteader, who would then add additional improvements to qualify the land for patent.

Daniel Mote was a squatter, a nonplayer. Squatters claimed up to 160 acres of unsurveyed land, lived on the place for a brief time, and made some improvements. Within six months, they could then pay $1.25 an acre, and once the place was surveyed, it was theirs. Squatters might also settle on surveyed land but decide not to go through the homestead application process right away. Under the homestead laws, after living there the required five-year period, a squatter had two years to "prove up" his land. That required a public description of the claim, generally posted in the post office or listed in the local newspaper, and the names of three or four witnesses who would vouch for him. The claimant then paid the final fees, usually $15, and received the title to the land. Daniel Mote belonged to that latter category of squatters but was never able to finalize his claim.

With shenanigans, common throughout the West, a person finagled his way into claiming property on which he never intended to live. He sidestepped the homestead laws altogether. Canyon rancher Ace Barton believed that claims to many of the Snake River benches involved shenanigans. He told of one "cattle baron" who arranged an "under the table" deal with some other men. The baron made "improvements" on land claims, such as putting up a pint-size shack or digging a hole and putting in a lilac bush. Then the other men witnessed his "good intentions," verifying that he met the requirements for a patent. When he got the patent, he sold the land to the witnesses. "The man got a nest egg and could go on his way."[12]

Whether in the canyon as squatters, settlers, or finaglers, people made their homes "along either side of the river, tucked in between rugged mountain vastnesses."[13] Some homestead cabins, perched on river benches near the shoreline, were visible from the river. Others hid in tributary canyons, which from the river looked too narrow for anything except the trail leading up to the home. A mile, sometimes two or three, above the river the narrow canyon opened to a bench large enough for a house, outbuildings, some pastureland, a garden, and often a small orchard. The variety of places in the canyon people found to make their homes was amazing, inspiring Edith Coleman in 1941 to describe the canyon as "looking like a whole notebook full of good stories."[14] Unfortunately, many of the good stories have been lost. Their absence makes a history of canyon ranchers less complete. But because some canyon families preserved and shared their memories, a general account of settlement patterns and daily life in the canyon emerges.

Settlement was usually a family affair. Family members often claimed adjacent tracts of land and shared the work. For example, at Cougar Bar, Frank Brown, the father, had a cabin at the lower northwest section of the basin; his daughter, Helen, claimed land above and adjoining his; brothers, Fred and Paul, had claims nearby.[15] In the Pittsburg Landing area Henry and Loula Curry each had a separate homestead of 160 acres. So did Henry's sister, Mary. After 1900, their sons, Albert, Henry Jr., and Ira, also took out claims.[16]

Even with numerous homesteads held by an extended family, homesteaders quickly learned that making a living remained difficult. Only by owning cattle or sheep, gradually increasing the herd size, acquiring adjacent homesteads to accommodate the growing herds, and expanding their government grazing permits for pastureland could a homesteading family succeed in the canyon. By the end of the 1920s, the families that succeeded in that harsh land were ranchers. Others left in defeat.

From the heady days of early homesteading the overall population of the canyon gradually declined, but the ranchers who stayed became increasingly more successful. Sons and daughters, sometimes even to the third generation, learned ranching from the first generation and stayed on to run the business after their elders were gone. As the business grew and family members shared in the work, ranching became much more than a business for them; it was a way of life they treasured. By the end of the twentieth century, outside forces had ended that way of life for even the most successful ranching families. What remained were sagging barns, tilting fence posts, and vivid memories—recounted by families in the next few chapters. A journey downriver from Hells Canyon Dam offers a glimpse of those families at their homes.

Deep in the Canyon: The Hibbses, Bartons, Wilsons, and McGaffees

Deepest in the canyon were the Bartons and Hibbses. In 1900 Martin and Ellen Hibbs bought squatters' rights to a homestead at Granite Creek from Dave Hiltsley. "Probably the most isolated and inaccessible ranch in all the Wallowa and Seven Devils Country," the log house and barns sat a mile up from the river in a broad opening, providing pasturage, garden, and orchard space, and a memorable view of the rugged, tree-dotted hills across the river.[17] Like many canyon couples, the Hibbses began with a single claim, but as their six children grew to adulthood, the family acquired additional land. Early on, Martin Hibbs added Frank Hiltsley's Three Creeks homestead less than a half mile away to his Granite Creek property.

The oldest Hibbs daughter, Lenora, became a prominent Hells Canyon figure. Her sister-in-law described her as "a woman who was tough and honest and told it like it is. She swore like a man, rode like a man, and behaved like a lady."[18] Before Ralph Barton married Lenora, his father-in-law-to-be told Ralph about Battle Creek, a place across the river from his Granite Creek home and about two miles deeper into the canyon. Ralph bought squatter's rights to the place in 1905.[19]

In 1911 Lenora and Ralph married and began their homestead at Battle Creek. Their house burned down two years later. The young Bartons lived briefly on the Imnaha River and then returned to homestead the "Hiltsley place" at Johnson Bar. A year later they sold out to Glenn Hibbs, Lenora's younger brother, and moved back to the Imnaha. After Ralph's death in 1934, Lenora and her son, Ace, traded their Imnaha ranch with the McGaffee brothers, who had Idaho homesteads at Bernard Creek and Sheep Creek. Billy and Mabel McGaffee

Figure 13.1. Ralph and Lenora Barton at Battle Creek. (Photo courtesy of Esther Hibbs.)

moved to the Barton's Imnaha ranch. Lenora and Ace moved first to Bernard Creek then to Sheep Creek, retaining the Bernard Creek place as a line cabin; then over the years they acquired a number of additional Snake River homesteads, many from the extended Hibbs family.[20]

One of Lenora's younger brothers, Earl Hibbs, continued cattle operations at Granite Creek with his bride, Esther Leonard, after Martin Hibbs died in 1934. They retained the place for a decade and then sold it to Lenora. A year later, Allen Wilson, son of canyon rancher Pete Wilson, and his wife, Hazel Barton (Lenora's daughter), owned the property. The Wilsons and their son, Kim, lived at Granite Creek another twelve years before selling out to Bud Wilson (not a relative).

Map 13.1. The ranch locations, as identified by the nearest creek, of the sheep and cattle ranchers discussed in chapters 13 through 20.

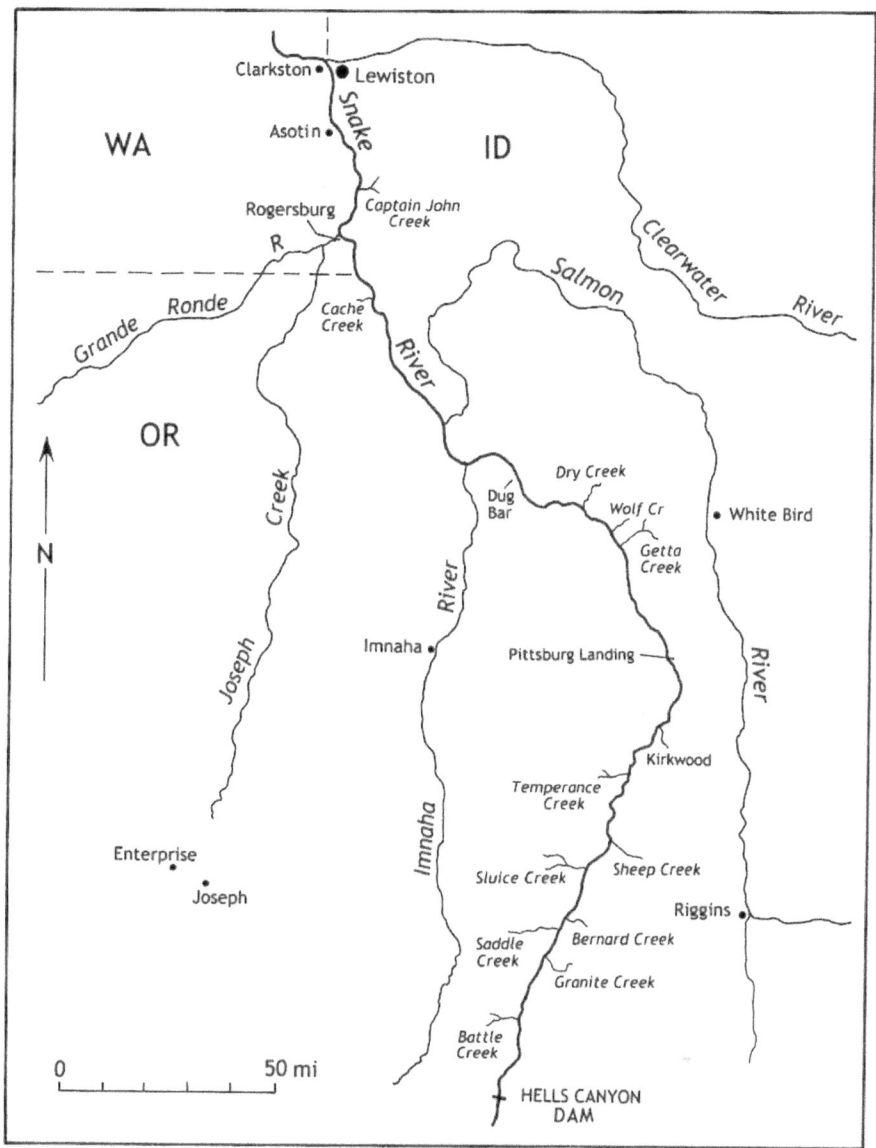

Figure 13.2. The Saddle Creek house, c. 1930. (Photo courtesy of William Wilson.)

Allen Wilson was brought up on the lower Snake; Hazel Barton, on the roaring Imnaha. They were both "from wilderness families" and shared the same values and ranching aspirations. Their marriage united the families and brought the Wilsons into the Barton and Hibbs fold. "The frontier Wilsons and Bartons were further united" when the Wilson family patriarch, Pete, married Lenora Barton.[21]

But long before that marriage, Leonard "Pete" Wilson and his first wife, Ethel, made their home at Saddle Creek. Their first move into the canyon was to the Imnaha River in 1915, where they settled on a place purchased from Pete's brother. Within a year they sold out and moved to the Saddle Creek area. The couple went into the cattle business with Fred Jensen, Pete's stepfather, who homesteaded at the mouth of Saddle Creek. In the years before the Depression, they bought out Fred's Saddle Creek place and "patched together seven homesteads."[22] There they raised their eight children—James (always known as Jimmy), Allen, Marjorie, Charles, Violet, twins Don and Dan, and Katherine (Kappy). The family was large and was dedicated to hard work. They all pitched in to make the cattle

Figure 13.3. James Wilson with his dog, Pug, when he was a Forest Service ranger. (Photo courtesy of William Wilson.)

operation a success, until the couple sold out in the late 1930s and divorced. Their daughter Violet and her husband, Buster Shirley, also from the canyon, lived at the family home at Saddle Creek until it burned in 1939. Shortly after that, Ken Johnson absorbed the ranch into his sheep operations. Pete married Lenora Barton, who at that time lived at Sheep Creek. In the early 1950s, she sold out to Bud Wilson.

The two McGaffee brothers worked cooperatively to establish a cattle ranch. In 1915, while Billy freighted and managed stores for various people in the Salmon River country—to "pay taxes and help build up the cattle herd"—his brother Alfred (Fred) and Fred's wife, Iphigenia (Gene), bought a homestead at Bernard Creek and moved into the canyon. Once they expanded the family holdings to include homesteads at Sheep Creek and Bill's Creek, Fred's brother Billy, his wife, Mabel, a Salmon River schoolteacher, and their daughter, Murrielle, joined Fred and Gene in the canyon.[23] Billy and Mabel lived at Sheep Creek for a brief period, then exchanged properties with Lenora Barton and moved to her Imnaha River ranch. "It was a pretty good ranch," but it was cold country and "required putting up lots of hay and feed."[24] The McGaffee family joined the Wilson family—and indirectly the Barton and Hibbs families—with the marriage of Pete and Ethel Wilson's oldest son, Jimmy, to Billy and Mabel's daughter, Murrielle. Murrielle was a canyon schoolteacher; Jimmy, a district Forest Service ranger. With that marriage, the ties that bind entwined ever closer in the upper reaches of Hells Canyon.

Sluice Creek, Pony Bar, and Temperance Creek: The Winnifords and Johnsons

When the three Winniford brothers and their families moved to the canyon from the Willamette Valley, they came with good educations and a willingness to work cooperatively together—characteristics that should have brought them success. Perhaps they lacked the inherited knowledge of canyon life shared by families like the Bartons and Wilsons. Perhaps they simply had poor timing. Whatever the reason, they failed.

Figure 13.4. Mina, Eileen on her lap, Walter, Wilma, and John Winniford. (Photo courtesy of HCNRA, Florence Winniford Smith Collection.)

The brothers settled near the Hibbses', Bartons', and McGaffees' places at the foot of Oregon's Hat Point. While working as a Forest Service ranger in Wallowa County, Frank Winniford, a 1910 graduate of Oregon Agricultural College, had learned of a couple of homestead opportunities in the Snake River Canyon. His two brothers, Walter and Willy, left their rainy Willamette Valley homes to pursue those dry homesteads. In September 1912 Walter moved to Pony Bar and Willy settled at the Hill homestead, two thousand feet above Pony Bar. The two men began canyon life baching it in a tent while beginning improvements and working for one of the Wisenors. In lieu of money, their employer paid them in cattle to build up their herd.

Their families—Walter's wife, Mina, their two toddler girls, and Stella, who traveled east to join her new husband, Willy—arrived months later. Walt and Mina's first cabin "did not meet the standards of the Homestead Act"—it was too small. Besides, sharing it with the rattlesnakes did not appeal to them. They built a new house. Willy and Stella lived on the Hill Homestead for two years. Then the family bought a homestead at Sluice Creek and moved there. Forest Service ranger Frank and his wife, Gertie, joined the family business and moved into the Hill Homestead. The three brothers and their wives made it through the disastrous winter of 1918, but at a cost. By 1924 none of the three families could afford to live there any longer. According to Walt and Mina's daughter Florence, they could never get out from under the debt incurred when they bought the Sluice Creek property. Also, the Forest Service required anyone running cattle on government land to put registered bulls in with the cattle. The Winnifords did—"they were the only ones in the canyon to do so"—but it put them even further in debt. When the bank at Joseph, Oregon, "got shaky," as did many regional banks at the time, and the three able Winniford men could not make any deals on their mortgages, their only recourse was to leave. The Winnifords left the canyon forever.[25]

Nearly seven miles down the river from Pony Bar, a large bench graces the shoreline near Temperance Creek on the Oregon side. There, more than three generations of canyon ranching knowledge brought success to the Johnson family sheep ranching business. While living on the Imnaha River, first generation Leonard Johnson started as a herder for an old-time sheep man and acquired sheep outfits as partial payment for his work. He expanded his operation to Dug Bar on the Oregon side of the Snake, then with his son Kenneth bought the Kirkwood place in Idaho, three miles north of Temperance Creek.

Kenneth ran the Idaho ranch while attending Washington State College. He attended classes during the fall term and worked on the ranch spring and summer terms. During that time he built the "Jordan house," now used as a Forest Service volunteer residence. Anna Maxwell, Kenneth's aunt, also lived there and helped with the work. Then, to bail out a relative downriver, Leonard and Kenneth sold their Idaho properties to Dick and Anna Maxwell and their partner, Len Jordan. Kenneth left the place "with his war bag, his bedroll, his saddle horse, and his dog," to relocate at family property on Temperance Creek.[26]

In 1935, a year after Kenneth moved to Temperance Creek, his Lewiston bride, Hazel Welch, joined him. Over the years, with the help of their two sons, the couple expanded the Temperance Creek Livestock Company to include eighteen homesteads—"small livestock operations" ranging from a hundred to four hundred acres each—that extended more than forty-six miles from Battle Creek to Dug Bar. Their son Greg and his wife, Gail, took over operations in the 1960s and ran the company until 1975, when the Forest Service bought them out. They continued operating the ranch under permit for a few years; ultimately, HCNRA policies forced them reluctantly to end the business.[27]

Kirkwood, Big Bar, and Pittsburg Landing: The Jordans and Wilsons

Len and Grace Jordan owned Kirkwood/Big Bar properties for eleven years, beginning in 1932. (Their partnership with the Maxwells was short-lived.) By canyon standards, they were something of an anomaly—latecomers, short-timers, and not related to other homesteaders, even though Len had worked for sheepman Jay Dobbin off and on since he was twelve years old. Grace, an educated woman from an educated family, recognized that their canyon experience was unique and merited recording. *Home Below Hells Canyon*, the story of their time there, remains one of the best books written about life in Hells Canyon. After leaving the canyon in 1943, Len went on to become governor of Idaho and a U.S. senator.[28]

Figure 13.5. Bud and Helen Wilson at Kirkwood in 1965. (Photo by Gunther Matschke, courtesy of the Bud Wilson Family.)

Brothers Lem and Bud Wilson of Nyssa, Oregon, were among the last families to go into ranching in the canyon. (They were not related to the Pete Wilsons.) In 1943 Bud and Helen Wilson purchased Big Bar and Kirkwood from Len and Grace Jordan and operated an extensive sheep ranch from there for the next thirty-two years. Their holdings included Idaho ranches from Pittsburg Landing to Granite Creek. Bud's improvements at Kirkwood included a road down Kirkwood Creek, lambing sheds, grain bins, new fencing, and a bunkhouse, now used as a museum. In 1976, under eminent domain proceedings, the Forest Service acquired the Wilsons' property as part of the HCNRA. Congressional legislation authorized HCNRA to set a purchase price for the Forest Service to buy canyon ranches. However, James Harvey, acting forest supervisor for the Nez Perce National Forest Service, determined the price was too high and initiated court proceedings to authorize condemnation of all ranch properties. Consequently some ranchers, like the Wilsons, who were initially willing sellers, decided to fight the condemnation in court. The Wilsons ended up selling—they had no choice—but at a favorable price.[29]

Lem and Doris Wilson bought their Pittsburg Landing, Oregon, property in 1951 from Jack and Celia Titus. For $150,000, they got the ranch, one band of sheep, and 150 head of Herefords.[30] Their ranch incorporated twenty-three different homestead claims, the earliest dating back to 1900. Lem and Doris Wilson remained at Pittsburg until 1975. It grew increasingly more difficult to make a living off ranching, so they diversified into tourism and subdivided their land along the river into vacation lots. They too reluctantly sold their property to the government as part of the HCNRA.[31]

Getta Creek, Ragtown, and Wolf Creek: The Arams, Johnsons, Hendersons, and Van Pools

Ten miles downriver from the Pittsburg area is Getta Creek, which drains Doumecq and Joseph Plains between the Salmon and Snake Rivers. In 1897 brothers Tom and James Aram, sons of Joseph Plains homesteaders John and Phoebe, sold their Grangeville, Idaho, implement dealership and started a cattle ranch on Getta Creek. They bought 4,000 acres that included top land and riverfront from Getta Creek south as far as High Range Creek and north almost to Wolf Creek. The ranch house was a mile from the river. Shortly after the purchase, Tom drowned while ferrying cattle across the Clearwater River at Lewiston. His father died a few years later, and his mother sold the upper homestead to the Spencers of Grangeville. James Aram continued to run the ranch out of Getta Creek and gradually added Joseph Plains homesteads to his operation. With the Depression came financial loss, forcing him to sell "the beloved Getta Creek ranch" to Slim and Mary Johnson (no relation to the Johnsons of Temperance Creek). Although James subsequently rebuilt his upper ranch "almost single handedly," in 1942 the family also sold that remaining property to the Johnsons.[32]

Slim and Mary Johnson owned more than 2,000 acres free and clear, and leased 1,600 acres including 600-plus acres of school section—public domain set aside to support the schools. There, they raised their four children and operated the cattle ranch. In 1961, Slim died in a farming accident; Mary and the children continued to run the ranch. "We kept doing it; that was all we knew," their daughter Polly explained. Polly and her husband, Lou Hollandsworth, continue to operate the upper ranch from their home six miles above the river.[33]

In 1908 Horace Henderson's father, Carl, took out a 160-acre homestead, covered with yellow pine, on Joseph Plains, Idaho. Carl sold it three years later, because "he didn't want those durn jack pines," and moved to the Snake River. The money from the sale was "the first one thousand dollars he ever had in his life." The family settled on High Range Basin, a couple of miles above the river and took over the homestead belonging to Carl's brother. (He was working on a Salmon River ranch and could not afford to live there.) For six months out of the year, Horace's parents stayed at the Brust place on Wolf Creek. Although they were working on the Salmon River at the time, they still managed to prove up on their High Range Basin homestead. Then they bought land on the Snake River about halfway between Getta Creek and Wolf Creek from a man known as Christianson, a big rancher "on top." The Hendersons put up four tents, where they lived for two years while building their house. One tent was the kitchen, one the dining room, and the other two bedrooms, all arranged with a courtyard in the middle. "Since each river boat landing had to have a name," a mailboat crew named their tent-home Ragtown.[34]

In 1914 David and Sarah Van Pool, who settled first on the Salmon River, bought a 320-acre "relinquishment" at Sulphur Creek on the Snake River three miles north of Wolf Creek. The Van Pools rebuilt the small house, added a barn, blacksmith shop, and some outbuildings. Five of their nine children who moved west with them—the other four were adults—each claimed adjoining land that had been "proved up and deeded to homesteaders." Their property extended up and down the river from Big Sulphur as far as Doug Creek. They summered at the "top ranch" and spent the winters at the River Ranch on Dry Creek. They also leased two sections of school land and small parcels of unclaimed government land. When it was Harold's turn to file on a homestead—he was the youngest—the only available land was a quarter-mile-wide strip about three miles in length along Snake River.

The government had been holding it for power sites. He and his wife, Tuppy, worked their small river homestead until 1940, when fire completely burned out his parents' ranch. After that Harold, his brother Heeman, and their wives ran the combined ranches. Harold and Tuppy sold their river home to Maurice Hitchcock in 1969.[35] "By then they held title to nearly 18,000 acres."[36]

At the Canyon's North Entrance: The Browns, Dobbins, Tippetts, and Earls

Birdie and Joseph Jay Brown originally settled Cache Creek around 1900. Three of their four children were born there. They built the house—minus the visitor's center added to the front—now used by the Forest Service as an entry to HCNRA. The Browns went into the canyon to prospect, but, as their grandson Dennis explained, "prospectors also had to make a living" so they raised sheep. In 1912 the couple filed on the 152-acre homestead, which extended south past Garden Creek.[37]

One of the canyon's earliest and largest sheep ranchers expanded his interests to include Cache Creek. Jay Dobbin began as a ranch hand for his uncle in the Wallowa Valley. He soon earned, saved, and invested enough money to buy two thousand ewes and lambs. That began his expansion from Wallowa Valley into the canyons, where he wintered his livestock in the mild climate on the "excellent grass." In 1896, he took out a 160-acre homestead on Eureka Creek near the mouth of the Imnaha River and an entitlement to graze sheep without charge on nearby government land. His sister, Etta, who also moved west from Illinois, claimed an adjacent homestead. Over the next few years, his ranch holdings increased as business prospered. By 1910 he was ready to bring his wife Mary Etta's youngest brother, Guy Huffman, into the partnership. Six years later, at the age of twenty-one, Guy bought a homestead at Cache Creek and supervised most of the Dobbin and Huffman interests on the Snake River until the 1930s.[38]

Another rancher established his cattle operation on Joseph Creek and the lower Grande Ronde, eight miles south of Cache Creek. James H. "Jidge" Tippett, once described as "a real-life counterpart to Zane Grey," began as a shepherd.[39] Ten years later, in 1903, he had earned enough money to buy a herd of cattle and prove up on his homestead in the Grande Ronde country. In 1919 Jidge bought 720 acres from Roy Lukes "deep in the canyon" at the lower end of Joseph Creek. On the original contract, "everything he bought was listed, right down to how many chickens there were." He continued building up his land holdings, his cattle herd, and a large family.[40] From that beginning the family corporation—the Tippett Land Company—consisting of Jidge, his sons, and sons-in-law—expanded to include more than 20,000 acres, including the Dobbin and Huffman sheep company and eight other ranches.[41] They held grazing privileges on 50,000 acres and owned 3,500 acres of irrigated land.[42] "Jidge owned the land; the second generation owned the cattle." Around 1954 the cattle partnership dissolved and "everyone went his own way." Jidge continued to own the land.[43]

Doug Tippett, Jidge and Jessie's youngest son, was too young to be part of the family partnership. After the partnership dissolved, he "stayed around by the folks" working for his father at their Dug Bar property. In 1957 Doug bought the place and ran a cattle operation with his wife, Janie, until they sold out to the Forest Service under the Hells Canyon National Recreation Act. After the sale they leased the place back with the understanding they could operate the ranch as they had "historically." That didn't work; government rules and regulations became too oppressive. "Finally I just said the heck with it. First chance I got to get out of there, why I did."[44] In 1974, Tippett Land Company sold their 6,400-acre lower Grande Ronde area home sites to the Washington Game Department to "preserve the ranch land in its present operating condition."[45]

Another long-standing family of early homesteaders in the lower canyon was the Earl family of the Captain John area. In 1889 Jasper Earl moved his family of three girls and two boys to the Idaho side of the Snake River across from Couse Creek. Six years later, they moved to the mouth of Captain John to put in a ferry. When they added a store and a post office, "a little community developed." Ten years later Jasper's business interests took him across the river to Couse Creek. There he "just squatted" and built a warehouse to receive grain from Martin Grade, making Couse Creek one of the most important steamboat stops on the upper river. In 1926 Earl family interests expanded to include Buffalo Eddy, "one of the last homesteads on the river [that] eventually filtered down through the family until it got around to me [Elmer Earl]." Elmer's parents and brother were then living two miles up the river at Captain John "in the old place." When Elmer's brother moved to Portland in the early 1970s, Elmer moved his family there and "abandoned the Buffalo place."[46]

All these family stories demonstrate settlement patterns along the Middle Snake River between the early 1900s to the mid 1970s. Furthermore, as later chapters reveal, those family stories highlight an extended family's cooperative work in forging a successful ranching operation and instilling in each family member a love of the land and of their ranching life.

Chapter 14

Stewards of the Land

Dictates of the clock prescribe the daily choices of twentieth-first-century Americans in such a way that most people cannot envision a life ordered by the rising and setting of the sun or the position of the snowline on the distant mountains. We move from climate-controlled buildings to climate-controlled transportation and endure adverse elements more when at leisure than at work. We decide where and how animals will fit into our lives according to our schedules, not theirs, and we rarely travel distances at their speeds. How different the rhythm of life was for the canyon ranchers, whose daily activities, like those of the Nez Perce, mirrored the natural order rather than the clock.

Both sheep and cattle ranchers moved at the animals' grazing speed and set up housekeeping near where the animals were feeding. All ranchers ranged their livestock over a vast tract of land comprised of private holdings and federal grazing permits from the river's edge to the canyon top and into the distant mountains. The Temperance Creek Sheep Ranch, for example for their four thousand sheep, had an estimated eight thousand acres in grazing permits alone, covering three separate grazing districts in Oregon.[1] Although grazing land was ample in the high plateau country, it was also fragile. Livestock had to stay on the move.

In the early years, there were many homesteaders "trying to build their cattle empire in this ideal environment." The ranchers were all competing for the range, and they "overstocked both the Oregon and Idaho sides." But as cattle rancher Ace Barton explained, "Most of the settlers went broke during the winter of 1918–19 and the livestock depression of the early 1920s."[2] Those who remained learned from their experiences. Most recognized the importance of being good stewards of the land for both economic and ecological reasons. Exceeding the land's carrying capacity by confining too many animals on too small a space, risked destroying its grazing potential. Overgrazing also damaged a landscape that meant much more to most of the ranchers than just a source of income. Some, in fact, argued that the animals themselves were beneficial to the land. Greg Johnson remembered when they first got the permit on the McGraw district, that a bare knob scarred the countryside. By the time they left the place in 1980, "there was grass growing all over that knoll because the sheep bedding there fertilized it, seeded it, and put [seed] in the ground. Sometimes what looks bad for one year ends up being a plus for the ground."[3]

Marjorie Chadwick described her father, Pete Wilson, as "an environmentalist before the word was even created." She said he rotated his land and his ranges and was "very protective of them," adding that he was typical of the people who were raised in the canyon. They all depended on the land and its resources, and "did not dare abuse them." At that time the Forest Service imposed few restrictions on land use; in fact, they "pretty much let you do what you wanted to, within reason," according to Doug Tippett, who saw common sense imposing its own restrictions. The Tippetts practiced good stewardship. In undated news clippings, one article called Jidge Tippett a "wise stockman" for recognizing that "forage must systematically be harvested for a durable, permanent operation." Jidge's sixteen hundred head of cattle was about 25 percent below the estimated carrying capacity of the range. He would not stock the range to its maximum capacity, for that range was "money in the bank."[4] Sharon and Bub Horrocks, who ran the Spencer Ranch on Joseph Plains during the 1970s, were "very careful not to overgraze." Sharon said that along the fence lines of bordering ranches, if their neighbors pastured too many cattle, "you could just tell the difference." Her husband kept a daily journal so the ranch hands who replaced them would know where to pasture each bunch and how many head each pasture could accommodate during the winter.[5]

The Forest Service allotted the McGaffee brothers grazing land for a specific number of cattle that could be kept on a given range. The allotment increased steadily by about twelve head a year for a number of years. Murrielle McGaffee Wilson explained that "when we got both ranches stocked to their limit, if we wanted to keep a young heifer we had to sell an old cow. So you just kept upgrading your stock that way."[6] Her father and uncle carefully monitored land use and kept the cattle moving. Both sheep and cattle ranchers had so much rangeland, if they saw a place that was overused, they simply did not graze it for a year.

Having adequate water was another reason to keep the animals moving. Polly and Lou Hollandsworth, who today run their operation much as her parents did, keep their three to five hundred head of cattle on the move with the help of their three dogs. "In this country, there isn't enough water. So you keep [the cattle] moving all the time."[7] To help spread out the animals, both cattle and sheep ranchers used fences and installed water tanks wherever they could find springs. By 1953 the Tippetts had dug out twenty-nine ponds near springs, for "if water holes are plentiful, cattle will eat available grass evenly. You cannot adequately distribute cattle with salt."[8]

The question of stewardship of the land often devolves into rancorous debate over which animals are better for the land, sheep or cattle? The age-old controversy has subscribers in both camps. Suffice it to say, one side will never convince the other. Listening to Max Walker, a longtime ranch hand for the Wilsons and Jordans, it sounds as if sheep are extremely intelligent in their choice of food while cattle are downright defiant.

> [The sheep] just went along, gosh darn, and . . . when it started raining [in the fall] and you had this bunch grass [all] growed up and real cured . . . the sheep would eat around the base and select the smaller leaves and the new green shoots that had come up in the old bunch grass—that's the spring growth of bunch grass. They'd eat the leaves and everything, but they wouldn't eat the coarse stands or the seed parts that come up, you see. On the cow range side, especially if it was on a ridge with heavy grass and there were too many animals concentrated on that ridge, well when an old cow starts feeding around the hill she'll just lop her old tongue around the whole bunch of bunchgrass and bite off the whole bunch, you see, and lop it up. . . . They'd just eat the whole thing.[9]

Winter in the Canyon

Ranchers knew they had to protect the grass on the lower ranges if they were to have enough winter feed. Pete Wilson could not raise enough hay for the number of cattle they ran, "so we had to take care of the rangeland to have enough winter grass," his daughter Marjorie said.

Figure 14.1. Bud Wilson delivers Christmas dinner to Snooks, one of his herders. (Photo by Gunther Matschke, courtesy of the Bud Wilson Family.)

"We would bring the cattle down from the top country in the fall, and he knew that he didn't dare overgraze that in the spring. . . . He was very, very careful."[10]

Most cattle and sheep ranchers "wintered"—usually from November to February—below the snowline near their main canyon homes. If the normal mild temperatures prevailed, the sheep bands and cattle herds grazed on surrounding blue, bunchgrass-covered benches and slopes, while herders kept them moving to prevent overgrazing. But if a "disaster winter" struck, they needed supplemental food. As sheep rancher Greg Johnson explained, "We almost never went down on the benches that were right above the river, because we considered that a haystack."[11] If the snow reached deep into the canyon, the temperatures dropped, and winter lingered, hay from those benches kept the livestock alive. Both cattle and sheep ranchers learned that valuable lesson during the winter of 1918–19, when heavy snow covered the land for so long the animals starved. From then on, canyon ranchers protected those critical "haystacks" and hoped they would never have to buy expensive supplemental feed.

Beginning in November, the Johnsons moved two bands of about two thousand sheep each to the lower bench pastures. They put the bucks in with the ewes, planning for lambing to begin in early April. After the ewes were "bucked out," the herder and his dogs spent the winter with the sheep on the benches, where there was usually enough feed to eat. To Hazel Johnson's way of thinking, "that's why that was known as the sheep country, you know."[12] The camp tender packed the mules with supplies for the sheepherder's camp. Besides bringing in food and other necessities, the camp tender was the herder's lifeline to the outside. Mail, newspapers, magazines, a few cans of tobacco, whatever he needed to make the lonely life more tolerable. When they had to relocate the flock, the camp tender helped the herder move his tent, supplies, dogs, and flock to a new location. That way of managing during the winter was consistent with time-honored sheep husbanding practices, except for the number of herders needed per band. Modern ranchers find it hard to believe, but Jay Dobbin, one of Hells Canyon's earliest sheep ranchers, apparently kept seven or eight men to a band of sheep because of coyote predators. After the government began paying bounty for coyotes, one herder was sufficient.[13]

Like the sheep ranchers, cattlemen also brought their winter stock down from the mountain ranges in late fall and pastured them on the low reaches through the winter, although the cows were kept in higher, more rugged terrain than their calves. Good bunchgrass along the river between Johnson Bar and Dry Gulch made that location one of McGaffee's favorite winter pastures for yearlings. They generally weaned the calves around the first of November and kept close watch through the winter. Murrielle McGaffee Wilson said that her dad would check "twice a day . . . to make sure that the calves were not in a bad place." If for some reason he couldn't check on them, "Daddy Pete [her father-in-law Pete Wilson] kept a lookout from the Oregon side and rowed across if necessary." A "bad place" usually meant steep, iced slopes where the cattle could easily lose their footing and slide off the hill to injury or death.[14]

Down the river, the Arams ran their cattle operation a little differently. They too drove the calves to lower elevations, down to nearby Getta Creek, "and left them on the gently sloping bench lands where they were protected from weather and could graze freely." However, if temperatures dropped and snow fell heavily in the mountains, the Arams moved the cows, pastured separately at Rice Creek Canyon, to the higher "home ranch" on Joseph Plains, where they fed the animals hay in the feedlots until the weather warmed.[15]

All the cattle ranchers "did a lot of riding" to keep the cattle moving and protect the winter range. Some days Jidge Tippett was in the saddle from five in the morning until nine at night.[16] Sharon Horrocks Wing said her son and husband both rode "pretty steadily" in the winter, keeping the water troughs chopped out and the cattle moving. They packed in and scattered mineral blocks (vitamin supplements) around "to make sure they were in areas where the cattle got enough to eat." Winter was not a time for the ranchers to hole up in their warm homes and wait out the season.

Lambing and Shearing

About February the pace quickened for both cattle and sheepmen, but in different ways. While their animals were still near winter pastures, the sheep ranchers began preparations

Figure 14.2. Livestock wintered near the Hibbses' Granite Creek ranch, about three miles above the river. The barn is in the right foreground; the house in the lower center. This picture was taken in 1940, the year Earl and Esther moved away. (Photo courtesy of Esther Hibbs.)

for their two cash crops—wool and lambs. Most of the earlier ranchers moved the flocks after the lambs were born, and then sheared them; later ranchers reversed the sequence.

Jay Dobbin first raised Spanish merino sheep with a fine, crinkly wool fleece that weighed about nine pounds; then after 1900, his band included Rambouillet sheep. He later crossbred his sheep with Hampshire, Shropshire, and Lincoln breeds.[17] Dobbin wintered his flocks on Snake and Imnaha River ranches and began lambing in late March. Lambing usually took twenty days. After the lambs dried off, the herders moved the ewes to larger enclosures and fed them a little hay and grain. They then moved "small bunches"—three or four hundred in a bunch—to a place where "a fella would go over there, stay with them, herd them, and take care of them." Ralph Beard, who worked a few years as shearer and camp tender for the elderly Jay Dobbin, described how the night crew took care of twins to ensure that the mother would accept both. "We'd have ropes, string, or cloth of some kind that we'd put on and tie two lambs together. Then the next morning, why, we'd just move the band out, and the ewes and lambs would stay there on the ground, and then the day crew would come in and take care of them. We'd bed them some place else the next night."[18]

Dobbin began shearing in late May or early June at shearing plants at the top of the canyon. His shearing crew of about ten to twelve local men per band met the animals and began work as soon as the weather was favorable. One man could clip about a hundred sheep per day. It was hard work for the men and hard on the sheep. Then, around 1901, the shearers switched to machine-powered clippers run first by waterpower, later by gasoline. With machine help, one man could shear half again as many animals per day. After shearing a ewe, they dunked her in a trough of sheep dip. James Brewrink described the ewe-lamb reunion: "As the ewes emerged into the pen with lambs, it was pitiful to see the confusion. The usual scent-matching between mother and lamb was gone due to the shearing and sheep dip."[19]

Once the shearers finished their work, they branded the stuffed woolsacks. Ralph Beard quoted Dobbin's explanation for his branding procedure. "'I've branded my woolsacks with a tomato can for fifty years and I don't want to change it now.' He'd just take a tomato can and put it down in a bucket of paint and then put it on his woolsacks. The brand on his sheep was an 'O' too." Evidently Jay liked canned tomatoes, always had some in camp, and found the cans convenient for branding.

Because Dobbin's shearing plants were not under cover, rain caused frequent—and expensive—delays. He had to feed the crew whether they were working or not. In 1923, for example, an outfit of twelve shearers expected to complete their work in one and a half days. Instead they sat around for eight days before the rain let up. Jay's wife, Etta, and their fourteen-year-old daughter had to provide three meals a day for ten days at Jay's expense.[20]

Ken Johnson of Temperance Creek was one of the first to change from May to February shearing. His son Greg continued the schedule, which all canyon sheep ranchers ultimately adopted. "I'd bring the sheep in [from pasture] normally the 10th of February and shear them. I would then keep them in the fields for an adjustment period because they have to adjust to not having their wool on. The weather normally breaks in the canyon by then and it's warm enough that the sheep tolerate it *really well*." It also helped to have the wool off before lambing season.[21]

In the early years of sheep ranching, when wool had to go out overland, it made sense to shear the animals near transportation. Wool sacks are heavy and cumbersome. Dobbin located his shearing plants at the top of the canyon to avoid that long and difficult uphill haul out to market. However, when mailboat service began on the Snake in the late 1910s, transporting the sacks was no longer a problem. Ranchers set up their shearing operation

Figure 14.3. The Brownlee Sheep Company shearing shed at the mouth of Zig Zag Creek, c. 1920. (Photo courtesy of HCNRA, George and Clarice Johnson Collection.)

on the river bars, where they could haul those three- to four-hundred-pound bags of wool by horse to the river and roll them onto the mailboat.

The Jordans sheared on Little Bar, four miles south of their Kirkwood home. Their shearing plant was about halfway between Meyers Creek and Hutton Gulch and close enough to the river to roll "the bags of wool down, [and stack] them next to the river waiting for the boat—high above the water." Their cookhouse was two hundred yards away from the shearing plant and adjacent to the stone cellar.[22] Like the Jordans, Bud Wilson set up the lambing and shearing sheds near the river. The sheds were wood frame structures with a canvas roof. When the operation was over, all they had to do was take down the canvas, roll it up, and haul it out for storage. The framing was permanent.[23] At Cache Creek, Dennis Brown's grandparents sheared the sheep at a shearing shed close to Garden Creek, south of the present Cache Creek home, and right above the steamer landing.[24] He described it as being quite a large shed that they and others used for many, many years. "A lot of sheep shearers would paint their names on the side of the building and the dates they were there."[25]

The Johnsons' shearing plant on Temperance Creek bar about a half mile above the boat landing was a completely enclosed, efficient facility with enough space for the entire shearing and sacking process, as well as a row of horse stalls to feed haying teams. Temperance Creek Sheep Ranch hired a crew of professional shearers, consisting of about ten shearers, a sack-tier, and a tromper.[26] They came into the canyon by mailboat specifically for that work and usually began at Temperance Creek, since the Johnsons sheared first. From there they moved on to adjacent ranches. Greg Johnson described the shearing process as being "quite an operation." It normally took four to five days and, in February, the weather rarely held up the work. The otherwise quiet canyon came alive with "the sounds of the clippers going, an engine running and sheep bawling. . . . . Any time you handle the animals they don't particularly care for it. But the shearers were always careful because by then they were [handling] pregnant ewes."[27]

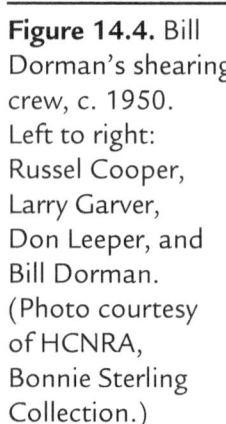

Figure 14.4. Bill Dorman's shearing crew, c. 1950. Left to right: Russel Cooper, Larry Garver, Don Leeper, and Bill Dorman. (Photo courtesy of HCNRA, Bonnie Sterling Collection.)

The crew began by putting ewes in the barn wrangling pens overnight so they would be dry the next day. When it came time to clip, the wranglers would move a ewe into a small pen where a shearer could grab her, shear her, and turn her loose in the pen right behind him. Shearers were paid per sheep, so someone kept count of how many sheep each man clipped. Next, wranglers moved the ewe into an alleyway where they vaccinated her and dusted her for ticks. The ewe was then moved to a sheltered area for a few days, where she could adjust to being without fleece.

Using methods perfected by Scotsmen years earlier, one man could shear twelve sheep in an hour. Thus, working an eight-hour day, each shearer could clip ninety-six animals a day. When shearing incorporated what is known in the trade as the "international pattern" of shearing, a man could clip twenty-four sheep in an hour, using only forty-six forward sweeps, or "blows," per animal. Australian and New Zealand shearing crews developed the method and rapidly exported it to sheep growers worldwide. Hells Canyon shearers often challenged each other—good competition put some sport in an otherwise dull task—and the shearers who used the new improved method always came out ahead in competition.[28]

As fleece fell from the animal's back, someone removed the animal tags and any undesirable wool, then threw the fleece into a huge seven-foot-long gunnysack suspended from a hole between the upper and lower levels of the barn. Inside that sack the tromper—usually a young man or sometimes a boy—used his own weight to tromp down the fleece. Not only did all the stomping tear up the fleece, but the job must have been thoroughly unpleasant. Greg Johnson described feeling claustrophobic when standing at the bottom of the sack with wool descending from above. Furthermore, "the wool stinks, and ticks and other disagreeable things are caught up in the wool." On most sheep ranches that disagreeable job ended sometime in the 1960s when mechanical trompers replaced the human. A big tube held the sacks while a hydraulic plunger shoved the fleece down into it. This put more fleece into the sack, "and it just worked a lot better."[29] An adept and speedy tier finished the job by closing the open end of each sack.

With the huge sacks stuffed and tied, it was time to ship them off to market. Initially, Jay Dobbin combined wagon train and rail transport, first hauling the sacks to the railhead at LaGrande, then Elgin, Oregon. The wagon trains, "a sheepman's pride"—sometimes a quarter mile long—were "fancy wagons pulled by fine teams." They moved from the top of the canyon—where the sheep had been sheared—on roads that were poor, narrow, and in places precipitous. At first, with no place to store the sacks while awaiting favorable market conditions, Dobbin and other Oregon sheepmen had no choice but to make an immediate sale. To create some degree of control over when they sold, Wallowa County sheepmen formed the Woolgrowers Warehouse Company in 1909, a year after the railroad reached Enterprise. They built a small warehouse in Enterprise where they could hold wool in storage until market prices became more favorable. Jay Dobbin was president a year after the company formed.[30]

A few years later, Dobbin used mailboat service to Lewiston to transport wool from the Imnaha sheep bands. Ralph Beard told about one time when Dobbin hauled all the wool to the mouth of Eureka Creek on the Snake River. His men piled the sacks on the riverbank for the next morning's boat. That night the river came up and washed every sack away. "I had that crop of wool all mortgaged to make a payment on my ranch in the valley," Dobbin told Beard. Beard marveled at his employer's ability to take everything in stride, even something as catastrophic as that. "I never had anything bother me so bad that I couldn't sleep in the night," Dobbin assured him.[31]

Ken Johnson made every effort to improve the quality of his wool. He began with two bands of poor sheep. "Ken worked over the years for fine wool sheep and bought the best bucks." Hazel Johnson said he bought Targhees; their wool was clean and fine. Over time that new breed so improved the wool quality that Pendleton Woolen Mills in Portland "always bought every bit" of Johnson's wool. Men's shirts, women's casual attire, and colorful blankets were made from their Hells Canyon wool. Over time, the couple increased the flock

Figure 14.5. A load of wool sacks on the *Idaho Queen*, docked at the Lewiston Snake River boat landing, c. 1960. Clarkston, Washington is in the background. (Photo courtesy of HCNRA, Hazel Johnson Collection.)

to three or four bands, "depending on the size [of the] lamb crop," and harvested well over one hundred sacks of wool a year. With each sheep bearing about ten pounds of wool, it took four or five mailboat trips to Lewiston to haul most of their crop. Ken also kept a truck at Pittsburg Landing and made several trips there hauling wool in his small boat to load on his truck bound for Lewiston.[32]

When their son Greg ran the business, he also used both the boat and truck to move wool to Lewiston, where they loaded the wool onto bigger trucks going to the Pendleton Woolen Mills in Portland. "A lot of years I'd ship the wool to them before it was even sold. It was just an understood thing that they would be getting it and it would be coming in March." The Portland company used Johnson's wool for white clothing and blankets because it was so clean, and they paid him a premium for keeping it that way. The wool market fluctuated considerably after World War II with the proliferation of synthetic fibers, but, as Greg said, "Pendleton always treated us well; whatever the market was, we'd do a little bit better."[33]

Wool sales provided one source of income. Lambs provided the second. "As the grass started to green up, normally it was two weeks to a month, we'd scatter the sheep out through all the canyon," Greg Johnson explained. They'd lamb on their own in little bunches and that was unique to the area." (Sheep tend to follow a pattern, returning to where they lambed the year before.) After giving birth, the ewe and her offspring then joined the flock also "pretty much on their own." Hazel Johnson remembered turning out

Figure 14.6. Bud Wilson's lambing sheds at Kirkwood. (Photo by Gunther Matschke, courtesy of the Bud Wilson Family.)

"all 3,600 or so" sheep to lamb. Herders were with them, "not to herd but to keep predators away and to [care for] the dogs." The herders camped "here and there—a homestead, a place of debt failure, maybe up at Pony Bar, maybe Sluice Creek. I know for sure at the Wisenor place." Some ranged as far south as Battle Creek. All the lambing took place on the open range. Unless someone was right there to help, the ewes that had trouble usually died. But, as Greg said, "I selected sheep that did not have lambing problems for that very reason." Hazel's job was to take care of the "bummers"—the ill, orphaned, or rejected lambs—by bottle-feeding them and watching over them until the animal gained strength enough to go out with the flock.[34]

Follow the Sunflowers

Around the middle of May, when lambing was over, the sheep growers rounded up the sheep, put the bands together on the higher benches, branded and earmarked them, docked their tails, and castrated the males. Sheep and herders alike then "followed the sunflowers" to higher elevations. Arrowleaf balsamroot, commonly known as sunflowers, blooms at ever higher elevations as spring turns to summer. Sheep love it, and do what their herders want—gradually graze their way up the rocky slopes toward summer pasture, eating sunflowers along the way. Every outfit followed a different route.

One of Bud Wilson's herders, Albert Crawford, was a World War II hero who earned a reputation in the canyon as being a "neat" camper and excellent herder. Each spring he and his two dogs would move a band south along the canyon face to Willow Creek, Sheep Creek, and Low Saddle. There he would stay until mid-June before gradually moving up through the Seven Devils on the Boise Trail to New Meadows. His friend Dick Sterling, who also had a reputation for neatness, and Sterling's wife, Bonnie, worked as Crawford's camp tenders. Each morning at daylight, Albert and the dogs left camp to begin their gradual upward trek. Dick and Bonnie packed camp, moved to the next site, and set up camp to await Albert's arrival. The process began along the river and continued from camp to camp all the way to New Meadows. Bonnie described their move downriver to Sheep Creek, which included passing through a place on the trail known as "Tight Squeeze," with the river straight below. "It wasn't easy pulling your feet out of the stirrups, laying down on your horse's neck and crowding the rock wall as close as possible to get through." Once at that same place, one of the packers was afraid to go through the squeeze. Bonnie grabbed the rope and led the pack mules to the other end. Her boss, Bud Wilson, took the packer to town and put her husband, Dick, back on the pack strings.[35]

Dobbin and Huffman wintered about fifty to sixty thousand sheep on the lower Imnaha and Snake River. After shearing, they made up summer bands of about ten thousand to a band and began the slow drive to the summer ranges. With five bands, there was not enough room to confine all the flocks to one side of the river. As a result, the Cache Creek bands

Figure 14.7. A flock of sheep docilely moves into a single file to cross a hazardous trail on their way to summer pasture. (Photo courtesy of the Bud Wilson Family.)

Figure 14.8. A Cache Creek crew directs a freshly shorn flock onto the ferry to move them to pasture across the river. (Photo courtesy of Robert McGrady.)

summered in the Idaho mountains. After rafting the sheep across the river, the herder moved the sheep about six or seven miles a day across Camas Prairie to the Clearwater or Nez Perce National Forests. The Imnaha bands summered in the Wallowa Mountains.[36]

Herders for Lem and Doris Wilson began their sheep drive to summer pasture at the end of June. They ascended five thousand feet, from a two-thousand-foot elevation at their Pittsburg Landing home to seven thousand feet at Hat Point. While the animals inched their way up, following the sunflowers and grazing the ever-greening grass in the higher elevations, back home Lem and Doris prepared camp supplies consisting of two camp boxes, a camp stove, a tent, ax, shovel, rifle, and sleeping bag. Food in each camp box included ham, beans, flour, sugar, coffee, canned milk, and canned fruit. Each box also held a water bucket, dish pan, soap, towels, and enough clothes for a month or two. Thus supplied, they ferried their summer supplies and gear to the Idaho side, loaded it in their pickup, drove to Whitebird, Grangeville, Cottonwood, and then crossed the river at Lewiston. Their route continued through southeast Washington to Enterprise and Imnaha, Oregon, then along the winding road to Hat Point and their Horse Creek supply cabin.

The cabin had a dirt floor, two bunks, a camp stove, a small table under a little window, and a storage bin in the corner for horse feed. There was a storage shed behind the cabin, a hitching post for the pack string, and a spring. From the cabin, Lem supplied the sheep camps; Doris stayed at the cabin with their two boys and made periodic trips back to their home at Pittsburg Landing.[37] Needing a better headquarters than Horse Creek, they relocated to Schaeffer Springs, down the ridge at the head of Cow Creek Canyon. Lem "managed to haul in lumber in order to frame up and build a small house," a place Doris considered "seventh heaven" after her prior accommodations.[38]

For Hazel Johnson, "everything happened" when they began moving the sheep bands to summer range. While the herders were still on the lower benches, their two camp tenders supplied them from the ranch. When it was time to move, it was also time to stock mountain supply camps. The Johnsons might still be haying at the ranch. If so, they "left the kids in charge" with a hired hand. Two pack strings moved into the mountains with the flocks, taking one band on through, and then coming back for another. In the meantime, Hazel and Ken "hightailed it by boat" to Pittsburg Landing, got in the truck and drove to Riggins,

Council, or Cambridge, Idaho, for groceries. From there they drove down Kleinschmidt Road, crossed the Snake River, and then if the road was not blocked by snow, went on to meet the band near McGraw Guard Station in Oregon's Wallowa Mountains. "The sheep would be coming from the Lookout area over Freezeout and right down the ridge." (That was the band going to the Sheep Creek country.) The couple met flocks bound for Lick Creek as they dropped down into the upper Imnaha River and headed around the bridge. The Johnsons' summer ranges included the McGraw area, the Big Sheep area, and the range on the Baker, Oregon, side of Eagle Cap Wilderness. One supply camp was located across the Upper Imnaha at Beaver Dam. Corrals were there, which they had built; Hazel's cook tent (an old Forest Service table they had been given); and a trailer where Hazel and Ken slept. Their second supply camp was on Lick Creek near the Forest Service's Lick Creek campgrounds. From the two camps they took supplies out to meet the pack strings, which in turn delivered supplies to the herders.

All the sheepmen kept their flocks in the high country until October. They then began moving the animals to lower elevations to separate the old ewes from the lambs. Buck lambs and most ewe lambs became the second marketable product from the flocks. Herders slowly trailed sheep bound for market to trucks in town, or the train. The other sheep—ewes held back for replacement breeding and some "bellwethers"—began their gradual move back to the lower elevations. A wether is a castrated male lamb kept to help lead the flock. He is gentle enough to be led across a bridge or over terrain most animals might resist. The flock follows. The bell around his neck makes it easy to locate him and his flock. Max Walker, who worked for the Jordans, said they usually kept ten "bells" with a band of 1,100 sheep. "When you get into camp at night and only have nine bells, you know a flock is missing."[39]

The Johnsons divided their bands at Lick Creek. From there they walked the lambs to Enterprise—a three-day trip—loaded them on to trucks, weighed the trucks, and sent them off to Superior Packing Company at Ellensburg, Washington. (Greg and his father both shipped lambs there "every year as long as I can remember." If some needed fattening, they first went to the feedlot at Hermiston, Oregon.) The Johnsons kept the white-faced ewe lambs so they could raise their own replacements for breeding and maintain their "closed herd." With a closed herd, if they lost an animal, they would know where to find it, since the animal was on home territory with established places to go. More importantly, the Johnsons had good, healthy animals and wanted to keep them that way. A newly purchased buck could potentially introduce disease into the band. To prevent that, Greg purchased bucks every year at the national ram sale in Utah from people who had raised them expressly for him.[40]

With the animals either off to market or returning to winter pastures, only the last step of the seasonal cycle remained—mating the bucks with the ewes. Hazel and Ken Johnson had their "bucking camp" at the Funk Place in Smooth Hollow, where they put up to one hundred bucks in with the ewes. They had gone to "great lengths" to keep the bucks away from the ewes throughout the rest of the year by pasturing them on their distant North-South Highway property in the Wallowa Valley.[41] With bucking complete, the seasonal cycle ended.

Calving and Branding

Spring introduced an equally demanding seasonal cycle to the cattlemen. Each rancher followed a slightly different schedule, but calving, branding, and moving the livestock dominated a rancher's day.

In order to protect the animals' health, the Arams wintered all the young cows about to bear their first calf at the Joseph Plains ranch, where they could watch the animals and feed them the best hay. In the spring, if a cow looked as if she were going to calve, a ranch hand moved her into the barn, checked her once during the middle of the night and again the first thing in the morning. The older cows, that had previously calved, bore their offspring on the winter range at Getta Creek and the river benches. Should any of those cow give birth in steep terrain where she could not get back, both the cow and her calf would die. Ranch hands had to make sure that did not happen. When the calves were three weeks old, the hands moved them with their mothers to steeper, greener areas on the south side of the creek, then, a few weeks later, to summer pasture on Joseph Plains.

During the June roundup, the ranchers separated the cattle bound for market—the beef cattle—from the rest of the herd. They then branded, earmarked, and, if necessary, castrated the calves. The branding process took three or four days. The hands next treated the animals for a disease called blackleg by putting a piece of smooth wire through the skin on the calf's shoulders and then fastening it in a loop—an old method "that seemed to work but they never knew why." Science later replaced that method with vaccinations. With all that finished, the time had come for the Arams to move the livestock not bound for market to their summer range.[42] In early July the ranchers turned the bulls in with the cows and heifers and left them there until mid-August, sometimes September. "The earlier the better for the calf health, for if they were born in June, the calf would not be old enough to wean before winter."[43]

By the 1970s, when the Horrocks were running cattle over land once used by the Arams, their cycle and method had changed very little. After calving in early April, neighbors came to help with calf roping and branding, "the old fashioned way" (like the Arams). Sharon Horrocks said they "liked the logic of the Old West." To them that meant "instead of slamming [the calves] around in a squeeze-shoot and banging and crashing and scaring the

Figure 14.9. An unidentified crew of men, a woman, and a dog round up cattle at Fly Blow corral on Joseph Plains. (Photo courtesy of Horace Henderson.)

heck out of them, we just roped 'em. It was a lot easier on the calves and the cow. [The mother] could go right along with her calf instead of being separated." At an early age, ranch youth learned to rope. From the time he was eight years old, Cole Horrocks got into the act, roping "about forty animals [his first year] before confessing he needed a break." The branding took about a month, and then the Horrocks could move the herd up on top. "We had everything kind of set right out. It just made it a lot easier if you had a good schedule." No doubt Sharon spoke for most of the ranchers.

Figure 14.10. Men, women, and children all helped round up and brand the calves. Here Ellen Lyda is holding down a calf for branding at the Aram's place on Joseph Plains, c. 1948. (Photo courtesy of Mary Johnson.)

When the grass greened and the snowline gradually receded, the McGaffees "started pokin' 'em up, depending on the season, in February or March." Their summer pasture at Dry Diggins on the Idaho side was a "good summer range" with ample springs and a few lakes. Near the Diggins, Fred McGaffee built a cabin and corrals. When the herds reached the cabin, the cowboys segregated the beef cattle destined for market from the calves and cows, and branded the calves. Then they moved the rest of the herd to Dry Diggins.

The Van Pools also began their cycle in February and March. "As the cows calved," they branded the calves "and put them at a slightly higher elevation called 'The Breaks.'" They also graded the yearling heifers and spayed those "not suitable for breeding . . . so they could run free." Harold Van Pool moved the few cows that had not yet calved to a small pasture around Sugar Loaf Knob and kept them there for branding. By early May, all the cows were in the Divide Creek area for summer pasture and breeding, while the steers were segregated in pastures around the Top Ranch on Joseph Plains.

The Beef Ride

Nearly all cattle ranchers summer-pastured their animals high in the mountains, often at great distances from their winter homes. Cattlemen worked with two herds, the beef cattle destined for fall market and the replacement cows and calves. Beef cattle usually included two-year-old stock, dry cows, and heifers undesirable for the breeding herd.

When Ralph Barton raised beef cattle on the Imnaha River, he delivered both cattle and hides to the railroad at Joseph. "If the prices were right my Dad would ride with them all the way to Omaha," Ace remembered. When Ace Barton and his mother, Lenora, were ranching on Snake River on the Oregon side, they ranged the non–beef cattle on Idaho's Seven Devils Mountains through the summer and drove the beef cattle to New Meadows, Idaho. In preparation for the drive, they packed up everything in boxes and took it along. Ace remembered their putting cream in a gallon jar. "Then when we'd get out to cow camp, we'd have butter." He and Lenora swam the cattle across the river, a time-consuming process that ended once they moved to their Idaho ranch. On the first day of their beef ride, Ace and Lenora, and sometimes a hand, moved the animals to either Bald Mountain or Old Timer. "You'd have to night herd them, of course," to cover that distance. The next day they drove them on down the east slope to a homestead on Shingle Creek, where they used the corrals,

Figure 14.11. Joseph Plains cattle ranchers Slim, Pete, and Tom Johnson are here preparing to go to cow camp, 1954. (Photo courtesy of Mary Johnson.)

with the owner's permission. From early the next morning through the night they continued on to the Little Salmon River, and then ascended it toward New Meadows, which they reached on the fourth day. From New Meadows the livestock went on to market by rail. In later years, the Bartons drove their beef cattle to the slaughterhouse at Cottonwood, bringing the herd down off the Seven Devils Mountains to Riggins and trucking the animals on to town.[44]

Esther and Earl Hibbs started moving the beef in late August from their Idaho summer pasture to Horse Heaven. "It was the best pasture, and we wanted the beef to get to it first so they could continue fattening up." After grazing the herd a while at Horse Heaven, they then trailed the herd on to Hass Flats close to Heavens Gate Lookout. There it took a while to round up the cattle, for the animals had scattered around through the rocks and canyons. "We would bring them up to the Lookout pasture and keep them in there for overnight. We planned to take out about thirty head including steers and culled cows . . . anything that didn't have a calf that year to raise." After collecting the herd and separating the beef cattle, Earl and Esther then trailed the animals over Pollock Mountain to the Little Salmon River and on up the river to New Meadows. Their beef ride took about a week, usually camping overnight at three camp sites along the trail—"no buildings, just under the trees."[45]

At one time Horace Henderson's parents ran 750 head of cattle. Summer range for them was in the high country on Joseph Plains. In August they drove the beef cattle to market. "Everybody would go together. They'd bunch all the beef cattle up and bring them very slowly and carefully out of there [off the Plains]." Since they were bound for Cottonwood, the livestock had to swim across the Salmon River. Young Horace yearned to go along, but he could only go so far. "I would get to stay out of school a couple days to go with the beef and I could come with the beef drive 'til they'd get to the top of the hill. They'd come right off where the road goes down now, right off that ridge and on down at the bridge on the [Salmon] river." That's when Horace's adventure would end. "I'd get off there and look out on the prairie. I could see all the warehouses out there. I'd hear old stories they'd tell about what was out there. Then my Dad would run me off and I'd have to go home. That'd make me fightin' mad, I'll tell you."[46]

Figure 14.12. Fall hunters prepare to ride to cow camp include, left to right, Earl Hibbs, Lenora Hibbs Barton, Lou Knapper, Mart Hibbs and Glenn Hibbs. (Photo courtesy of Esther Hibbs.)

The Van Pools also drove their beef cattle to Cottonwood, making two or three two-day drives from the ranch. Before Dave Spencer built the sales yard at Cottonwood, they loaded the cattle on the train in town and shipped them on to Portland. The Arams scheduled their fall activities to get the animals to Cottonwood a day before shipping date in order to ensure they reached Portland on a Saturday. That way the cattle could rest before Monday's auction. At daybreak on the first day of the drive, they herded the cattle onto the road as far as the fork to Boles, then down Hogback Ridge toward the Salmon River. Around noon, when they were two-thirds of the way down, the hands rested the animals a few hours before continuing on to the river. Before construction of the Salmon River bridge in the late 1920s, fifteen to twenty head of cattle swam across the river at a time. On the opposite shore, exhausted hands and belligerent cattle rested overnight before their second-day drive up Graves Creek to Cottonwood. There, on the third day, livestock were loaded on the train. By law, after seventy-two hours the cattle had to be unloaded and fed. If something delayed their departure at Cottonwood, the cattle sometimes had to be unloaded at The Dalles, Oregon. This meant the owner or a ranch representative was allowed to travel with the cattle at no charge.[47]

Figure 14.13. The Hibbses' "Old Timer" cow camp in the Seven Devils Mountains. (Photo courtesy of Esther Hibbs.)

Pete Wilson began his cattle drive in August or September. (Marjorie Wilson remembered it as August; Violet, as September.) He ran his two-year-old steers with the Marks brothers' cattle. The Marks did not have a very large herd but were a help when the drive began. "Some of us kids, the older ones, would make the cattle drive from our summer ranch to Enterprise, Oregon, which was about ninety miles at the time. It took us almost a week 'cause we took them real slow so we didn't run any weight off them." From the top of the mountain and Freezeout Creek, they drove the livestock down the Imnaha River and crossed the bridge at the little town of Imnaha. From there the cattle continued over the mountains to the Wallowa Valley railroad, then on to the slaughterhouse.

The herders stayed each night at one of the ranches along the way. About every fourth year, Pete Wilson would leave the rancher a two-year-old beef steer to pay for the overnight use of his pasture and a nice place to sleep. "Of course each of the ranchers was glad to have you visit and catch up on the news." Sometimes the Wilsons sold to a cattle buyer who received the animals at Enterprise and took them on to market. "But Dad soon stopped that." Livestock commissioners in Portland arranged with different meat companies to buy the livestock. To make sure the rancher got his fair share, Pete Wilson and most of the other Hells Canyon ranchers traveled to Portland with their investment (and always stayed at Portland's Imperial Hotel). "If you weren't there the commissioner might get quite a bit of money that you weren't aware of." Pete always knew what the beef sold for and how much the commissioner made "to do the paperwork."[48]

With the beef ride over, the ranchers and their remaining livestock returned to winter pastures. The cycle was the same, be it 1900 or 1980. All that changed were events from the outside world that intruded into ranch life. Even then, canyon dictates cast those events in a different light, as Bonnie Sterling related. In 1969 she and her husband were camped at Heavens Gate with Albert Crawford on the way to New Meadows. Bud Wilson's son-in-law came in that evening with a small television-radio combination; they "all took turns watching the first men land on the moon." The next morning, three men began their slow, time-honored beef-ride to New Meadows.[49] Undoubtedly that momentous event, so far removed by time and distance, left them awestruck each night as they gazed upon the far-off moon.

Year after year, Hells Canyon cattle and sheep growers lived by the same seasonal cycle. They lived with the animals and the land, bending to their needs and demands while reaping the rewards of that existence. It was hard but gratifying work on many levels. Greg Johnson possibly spoke for many fellow sheep and cattle ranchers when he described the life of working with livestock as "humbling."[50]

The Age-Old Controversy

So then, which is better, raising sheep or raising cattle? Everyone has an opinion, but the controversy is perhaps best summed up by this humorous story told in 1938.

The story begins in 1912. One day, while a sheepman trailed his sheep up the Imnaha/Snake River divide to summer range in High Mountains, he found a cow's skull. On it he wrote his personal ideas relative to cows and cowmen—"This is the best dam cow I ever saw. Wish all cows and their owners were as dead as this one." He then hung the skull on a limb beside the trail. A short time later a cowman came along and immediately penned an answer. "This skull is not a dam bit thicker than yours." The next year the sheepman again passed that way and spied the reply on the skull. He answered, "Speaking of thick skulls, yours is solid bone." A year later the cow man wrote his opinion of a sheepman who would "contaminate a decent cow's skull by writing on it." The next year (it's now 1915) the sheepman wrote an invitation to the cowman to meet him at that place and "they would find out about thick skulls, contamination, and other points of issue." The men continued similar correspondence for years, "but due to replies being written a year apart the sheep and cowman never arrived at a specific date to have their meeting." Finally the sheepman's route to his summer range changed. He could no longer make his annual replies so the matter dropped. "But the skull still hangs on the limb beside the trail with some of the writing still legible."[51]

Figure 14.14. It was Forest Service Ranger Grady Miller who found and recorded the cow shell correspondence in the "Age Old Controversy." (Photo Courtesy of Ace Barton.)

Chapter 15

Ranch Hands, Dogs, & Dadburn Predators

Ranch hands had many reasons to work in Hells Canyon. To some it offered an escape; to others an opportunity to start a new life—often in a new country; many enjoyed the freedom and isolation outdoor employment allowed; and some were canyon miners or homesteaders who needed to supplement their income. Unfortunately, few ranch hands left behind records of their work life. Even with information garnered from more recent employees and their employers, the picture remains incomplete. For example, in the early 1900s a few miners of Chinese heritage stayed in the canyon to work for others. Yet only one reference has surfaced to date. Frank O. Jacks returned to Cave Gulch with Pete Fountain after a forty-six-year absence. In recording his memories and reflections, he wrote, "I forgot to ask Pete about Hop Lou, who used to do all the farm work, that is putting in the hay crop, for the Fountain Brothers." Hop Lou must have worked a number of years for the Fountains.[1]

Help from Neighbors, Family, and Outsiders

Hop Lou may have been Jess Earl's and Billy Rankin's contemporary and acquaintance. Both men were miners and homesteaders who supplemented their income by working for others. Jess Earl made his home in Snake River country for most of the twentieth century, working for the Forest Service and river ranchers. His employment varied with the demands of the passing decades. Once he worked for sheep rancher Frank Wilson at Sommers Creek, living in the home Frank built during the 1920s. (Frank's family lived in Clarkston.) Jess built "a lot of buildings—chicken house, shop, corrals, etc." while working there. He knew carpentry but admitted, "I didn't know a thing about sheep . . . but I wasn't too dumb to learn."[2] He learned by observation and was especially aware of "other men's mistakes." During lambing, the older herders used too few corrals for too many nights. "It got dirty" and many lambs ended up as orphans. Jess just kept building corrals and would not corral sheep at one location for more than two nights. "My lambing record was tremendous."

Jess and his wife, Alice Madden of Orofino, married in 1932. He described life for them at Wilson's Sommers Creek Ranch as "just a matter of contenting yourself with a lot of hard work, lots of good horses to ride, and worlds of country to ride over." And his wife Alice? "My wife agreed to stay there nine months and never went out. She was plum happy with what she had."[3]

Billy Rankin also supplemented his mining income by working for others. Daniel Mote mentioned meeting Rankin on the Imnaha River. He did not particularly like Rankin; some of the other locals "viewed him as an eccentric because of the contradiction between his education and life style." The Arams, however, whose Getta Creek property was across the

Figure 15.1. A spectacular view from Bud Wilson's high mountain sheep camp. Bob Smith, the camp tender, barely visible on the lead horse, is bringing in supplies for herder Morris Kohlhepp. Three sheep dogs greet his arrival. (Photo by Gunther Matschke, courtesy of the Bud Wilson Family.)

river from Rankin's Oregon claim, spoke highly of him. The entire family liked his "cheerful presence" when he came to visit. In fact, he and James Aram were close enough friends that the Arams bought a quarter interest in Rankin's mine, and Billy in turn staked claims for James and Phoebe. (He was a "brilliant mathematician schooled as a surveyor.") Billy also helped James out on the ranch, working two seasons herding sheep for James during his short-lived experiment in sheep ranching.[4]

Help was scarce and the locals, no matter their age, pitched in to lend a hand. Horace Henderson's parents worked as ranch hands while establishing their own homestead. Horace didn't remember his mother receiving a salary, even though her work included preparing meals for the three or four hands who lived with them year-round. Horace's uncle, also a cowboy, could ride "outlaw horses." That was why, Horace explained, he got five dollars a month extra. The rest of the cowboys earned thirty dollars a month; the uncle's riding skill parlayed into thirty-five dollars a month.[5]

In most operations, ranch women cooked for the shearing crew. Often they needed to hire additional help and frequently turned to a neighbor. Lem and Doris Wilson hired Sevella Krebs, who lived about six miles upriver on the Idaho side, to help Doris. The two women began their day about 3:30 a.m., cooking breakfast. They nearly always prepared hotcakes, bacon, eggs, and lots of coffee, then served the meal in shifts, first to the shearing crew and then to the wranglers. The cooks and kids ate last. From breakfast cleanup they moved to baking two or three pies and light bread rolls for their biggest meal at night. Lunch was modest and usually cold. The evening meal was hot, filling, and appreciated. The men ended a hard workday with hot rolls, salad, vegetables, lots of meat, pies or cake, and fruit. Of course the cooks then had to clean up after that meal, which was usually long after dark, in preparation for the next day.[6]

Without her son Ace, Leona Barton could not have run her cattle operation. Ace said that sometimes they had a hired man help put in crops in the spring, but mother and son did the lion's share of the work. The same was true for Esther and Earl Hibbs. Earl usually hired

Figure 15.2. Jim Russel, ranch hand at Kirkwood, meets the *Wenaha* to pick up mail and supplies, c. 1950. (Photo courtesy of the *Lewiston Morning Tribune*.)

a "young kid" to work for him, and a man to help with the winter riding, but he never hired special crews. All the other work fell to Earl and his partner, Esther, a role she never questioned.[7] The Arams sometimes hired a man to help with the garden, orchards, hay, and cattle, but as the sons got older, those tasks fell to them, sometimes at the expense of their education. During the winters of John's fifth through seventh grades, his father took him out of school to help look after the cattle at Getta Creek. John always packed his schoolbooks, due to his mother's insistence, but never "cracked a book" while tending the cattle. His education did not suffer; they just rearranged his schedule.[8]

Jay Dobbin's hiring practices impressed Ralph Beard. Dobbin "gave more young people a chance to work" than any other man Beard knew. When Ralph applied for a job, Jay looked through his ledger book and "pretty soon came to my name." Ralph was pleased when Jay reported, "Well it looks to me like you're a canyon boy and you've worked with sheep before and I just believe I could use you." Ralph's primary job was camp tender for the bands along the Snake and Imnaha Rivers, although he often pitched in with lambing and shearing. Summers, when herders took sheep into the mountains, Ralph did the haying and worked on Jay's ranches in the Wallowa Valley. He received thirty to thirty-five dollars a month plus board. Dobbin always had one herder to a band, and one camp tender took care of two bands.

As camp tender, Ralph delivered provisions to one herder, returned to the ranch, rested up a day, then packed up and took off again. He supplied each herder about every two weeks with bacon, dry beans, flour (often mixed with salt and baking powder), rice, onions, coffee, dried fruit, potatoes, ham, and condensed milk. The flour was enhanced so the herder could prepare his "bannock," made by adding water and frying it in bacon fat in the camp skillet. Wild game, usually deer, grouse, and other birds, supplemented the herder's meals. Every herder had a rifle.[9]

Camp tenders sometimes delivered new clothing as well. Both cattle and sheepmen wore clothing designed to weather the elements. Many cowboys on the Idaho side bought clothing from the Salmon River Country Store at White Bird. For winter wear, that included several pairs of wool underwear, a woolen shirt, two pairs of Levis, heavy fleece-lined coat with fleece or wool collar, a dozen pair of woolen socks, two pair of work boots with six- or eight-inch tops, a pair of rubber overshoes, and a broad-brimmed hat. With so much time in the saddle, the cowboys' Levis lasted only three or four months, summer or winter. Summer wear amounted to Levis, work boots, cotton underwear, and a shirt. The ten-gallon hat was a year-round necessity.[10]

Figure 15.3. A sole rider, Bud Wilson, leads a string of mules laden with camp supplies along the ridgeline high above the Snake River. (Photo by Gunther Matschke, courtesy of the Bud Wilson Family.)

When Bud Wilson purchased Jordan's ranch, he "bought" herders Jim Russell, Morris Kohlhepp, and his wife, Dorothy.[11] Each had a separate camp. Bud's sister-in-law, Doris, described a typical camp. A nine-by-eleven-foot, heavy duty canvas tent opened at the front with overlapping flaps, top to bottom. Inside and to the right of the door was a wood-burning, shepherd camp stove, made by A. L. Dutcket of Imnaha. When in use, its telescoping stovepipe protruded through the ceiling of the tent. To the left of the tent door were the kitchen and "grub" boxes, specially designed to pack on a mule's back. A shelf at the front of the kitchen box converted into a small counter. Inside were cutlery, plates, and coffee cups on one side and salt, sugar, and other spices on the other. Food, of course, was in the grub boxes. Each camp had a one-gallon, gray-colored ceramic sourdough jug, and "usually a hand carved piece of wood . . . fit into the top of the jug" for use as a cooking stool. Rolled sleeping bags doubled as chairs. Outside the tent was a washbasin (filled with water carried by bucket from the nearest water source), soap, and a towel; nearby were the herd dogs' water and food pans.[12]

In 1954 Bonnie and Dick Sterling moved to the canyon from the Salmon River to work for Bud Wilson. Among a variety of other tasks, Bonnie cooked for twenty-seven men during shearing. She claimed to have "revolutionized traditional practice by setting a schedule," rather than feed the men when it suited their schedule. At 4:00 a.m., she and her husband Dick built a wood fire and put on two twenty-five-cup pots of coffee. She and Dick fixed breakfast and served the first ten men at 5:30. She cleaned up after them, served the next ten, and so on. Last to eat were the visitors and herders' wives. Once breakfast was over, Bonnie mixed sourdough biscuits for lunch—it took twenty-five pounds of flour each day. Lunch was at noon sharp, followed by cleanup and preparations for the 6:00 p.m. supper. Night men on lambing crews ate at 11:00 p.m. "I was turning out to be one heck of a good cook," she concluded.[13]

Sharon Horrocks worked right alongside her husband, Bub, at their Spencer Ranch employment. "I was pretty stout and pretty strong, always good with a hammer." So she helped build corrals "every place where we gathered and worked cattle." She also laid new linoleum, paneled walls, changed tires, ran the generators, and changed the oil. In her estimation, the only difference between her work and a man's work was the men "didn't cook or do dishes." One or two hands always wintered with the Horrocks and in the summer as many as six people. That meant lots of cooking and washing dishes. Sharon also kept track of all the cattle records and took care of any animal that needed doctoring. She bucked hundred-pound bales of hay just like any man and helped with the riding, branding, weaning, and vaccinations. Having grown up with horses, any time they required special attention, the task fell to Sharon. Summing up her work, she observed, "You don't want to sit there and wait for someone to come and do it for you." She was in every sense of the word a ranch hand.[14]

Good Help Grows Scarce

During the early years 1900s, most herders were men of Scottish origin from Appalachia. When they could not find work at home, they took their sheepherding heritage west. By midcentury, however, times had changed and the canyon no longer beckoned them. It became increasingly difficult for ranchers to find good ranch hands. Harold Van Pool had no farm machinery, and after two old hands died, he was unable to find help. Without help Van Pool simply could not keep up with the work. When his wife got cancer, he knew it was time to sell the ranch.[15] Ted Grote, an Enterprise pilot who made numerous trips into Hells Canyon on behalf of the ranchers, also commented on the difficulty of finding good hands. "Most herders today don't know how to herd sheep." Herders were supposed to let the sheep "just spread and go and then at night you start them back toward their holding pens." Flying out of the canyon in the evenings, Ted would often look down and see "the sheep were still all spread and not herded in, and you'd know that there was something wrong. So you'd have to go down and find somebody and take somebody else up to get the sheep straightened out. There was a lot of that."[16]

Hazel and Kenneth Johnson had some loyal and reliable hands. One camp tender stayed with them nineteen years, another eighteen. One began with Ken while he was still working the Kirkwood, Idaho, place and continued with him in Oregon—"a fine fellow." There was little difference between the quality of help they had during the 1930s and the 1950s, "as opposed to the help her son Greg had later." Hazel spoke frankly about their herders, saying although some of their help was worthless and some excellent, they found that many herders "often turned out to be the people that drank heavily." They only got alcohol when someone flew in and brought a bottle. Then "the whole outfit would get snockered to the gills." When intoxicated, the herders never caused the Johnsons any trouble; they just could not work. Usually they did their drinking in Lewiston, and it fell to Hazel to fetch them back. "I don't know how many times I have had to roust our hired help out of bars and [bawdy] houses in my day.... I had to get them back to work, you know."

Hazel described one herder who probably was anything but typical, but her story provides insight into some of the people working for them: "I know we had one, one herder—he was the meanest looking fellow you ever saw. He always wore a red bandanna around his neck. He always wore a hat. He had no teeth. And he was tough. He was an old navy man. And I remember one time we got him out of town. I don't know how we got him out, or if we did it by telephone, but he brought the madam up with him. She did have the good taste not to come to the house, but I went out and greeted her, which we should have, because she did take care of our men."

Hazel knew two bawdy houses well. "That's where our hired men stayed." From the herder's perspective, an occasional visit to "houses" in Lewiston—and other similar diversions—was probably a necessary escape from long, lonely months on the trail. Maybe they wished that their fortunes had taken them elsewhere. An ex-cowboy neighbor recently found a rusty old Prince Albert tobacco tin while riding the lower Imnaha trails. Inside was a neatly folded note with penciled writing on both sides. The spelling was poor, but the message was revealing. "Ellis. Kemp. West Jefferson, North Carolina. Ashe. Co. April 20/1939. Hurding sheep for Lou Warnock. $50 a month." On the reverse side, "Dry and hot as hell, not mutch water and no shade. Lonesome as hell and no place to go. Just one hill [torn piece of paper] shape and got a hard on and no money." The rest is illegible.[17]

Greg Johnson talked about the time a local man saw his father,

Figure 15.4. A sheep herder lived a solitary life and no doubt welcomed visitors. And here rancher Bud Wilson, shows his appreciation of good help by taking the time to give Raymond Blanco a haircut. (Photo by Gunther Matschke, courtesy of the Bud Wilson Family.)

Ken, put two herders in an airplane. They were both in the mountains, drunk, and in need of help. The man asked Ken what he did with those "disgusting old drunks." Ken replied that he sent them down to the river to his son. "He'll get 'em dried out and they'll take care of a band of sheep for a year and then probably go and do it again." The man made some derogatory comment. Ken replied, "My son's gonna give each one of those guys a band of sheep that's probably worth about $100,000. I wouldn't give you $100,000." Greg and his father both concerned themselves more with the quality of a man's work than his reputation. Greg said he hired one gentleman who beat a man to death—because the man had assaulted his daughter. That same employee was often the Johnson family babysitter. "We have had thieves, people who wrote bad checks. Except for alcohol and bad decisions, these were great people." In addition to hiring hands to herd the sheep and work as camp tenders, ranchers also sought someone reliable enough to monitor irrigation. If they found someone who was good, they tried to keep him as long as possible.[18]

Help Comes from Spain

When Ken Johnson was president of the Oregon Wool Growers, he was working to get foreign help, although they never hired any themselves. Like other ranchers, the Johnsons had trouble finding help during World War II. It was "awfully hard to get good help," Hazel remembered, "but we were fortunate that we did keep good help once we got them."[19] That help shortage during the war may have prompted the wool growers to look across the seas for herders. They found them in the Basques of Spain, people temporarily fleeing midcentury political and economic turmoil at home with hopes of improving themselves financially in North or South America. The Basque men had already established a reputation as good sheepherders in the mountainous West, even though most of them had had other occupations in Spain.

Seberno (Silver) Egana, was one of the first Basque men to venture into Hells Canyon for employment. He came to the Pacific Northwest sometime between 1910 and 1913 and began working for Dobbin and Huffman in 1914. Others followed—Gus Malaxa, Toney Martiartu, Jose Arriaga, Luciano "Lucy" Araigurana, Ramon Lauserica, a man known as Jess, and others. One source identifies Ramon Lauserica as the camp tender. Ralph Beard remembered that Silver Egana was "always" the camp tender. He said, "he couldn't read or write, but you could tell him a string of stuff that you needed in your camp and he'd go in and he'd come back and have everything you wanted." The ranchers provided food and shelter while the isolated herders saved their money. Their only expense was clothing, but every two or three years, when their visas expired, they were obligated to leave the country for a while. Most went to Canada; some returned home. After a short absence, they were back in the canyon.

During the 1920s three of the men decided to draw out their money and return to Spain, prompted in part by the frustration of dealing with language limitations. Back home they found disappointment. Many friends and relatives were dead or gone. (Poor economic and political conditions in the country made life difficult.) After returning to Oregon, the three asked for and got their old jobs back. Conventional wisdom, proved wrong by the facts, was that "few American workers could stand the lonely life of the shepherd," implying that the Basque herders relished it. However, that lonely life gave the hard-working herders an opportunity to build up a nest egg. During the difficult 1930s Jay Dobbin's Basque employees offered Jay their salaries to help keep his business going. It was a generous gesture but also a prudent business decision. Near the end of the decade, Dobbin helped set up Malaxa, Egana, and Martiartu in business at Cherry Creek ranch. After he retired in the late 1940s, Jay sold the rest of his canyon holdings to them but, at their request, continued to advise them in financial and legal matters.[20]

The Cherry Creek ranchers took Joe Onaidia, a fellow Basque, into partnership. Joe came to the United States in 1931 and worked as a sheepherder in Wyoming, Montana, and Utah before moving to Cherry Creek. Although he and Gus Malaxa had grown up five miles apart, they first met in 1949 aboard an airplane bound for Spain. Back home, the two men began courting the Ulasia sisters. Joe married Marjorie, Gus married Jana, and Cherry Creek Ranch in Oregon became their home. Try to imagine the women's first impression as they moved from the land of their family and ancestors, of their customs and language, to the barren, isolated reaches of Hells Canyon. They did not cross the continent with their travel-wise husbands—they traveled alone. They knew no English and met no one who knew their language. They had no inkling of the continent's enormity; they certainly had no idea what hard work awaited them once they reached their destination. At Cherry Creek they immediately began cooking meals for a shearing crew of twenty-five to thirty men, using a little wood stove, and hauled water to the kitchen in heavy wooden buckets.[21]

People of the canyon liked the Basque ranchers and respected them as honest, hard-working people. When he piloted the mailboat beginning in the 1950s, Dick Rivers often took Basque herders and ranchers in and out of the canyon. He said the men worked there for "good pay." Dick bought shoes, clothes, and anything else they requested in Lewiston and delivered the goods on the next mailboat. He said they "simplified the financial transactions with 'Dick pay.'"[22] They of course always reimbursed him. "Dick Rivers is a real friend to all us Basques," Marji Onaidia said.[23]

After the Onaidias and Malaxas sold the ranch, they moved to Enterprise. Pilot Ted Grote kept up a friendship with them that began at their Cherry Creek ranch. Sometimes when he delivered mail or supplies, he had to wait for them to return home. Inside the house, Jana and Marji always had some fresh-baked bread. "They kept it in a box underneath the floor. When I flew I never took a drink but Joe, Marji's husband, would say, 'well there's some wine and some bread there, you help yourself.' And they had homemade butter. I'd take some of that bread and oh, it had a hard crust. But you'd cut through it and it was just the softest, sweetest bread you ever ate. Put butter on it. That was better than dessert." After moving to Enterprise, Marji took Ted hot bread every year because he liked it so well.[24]

Canyon folk were inveterate storytellers. This included telling stories on one another in fun. James Brewrink told about the time a Basque herder came down the river in a large rowboat. He was trying to collect sheep "that had lost out when swimming a herd across the river." Brewrink watched from his mine. "[The herder] had collected five or six sheep and stopped at Wild Goose Landing to let them graze. The two camp dogs [Airedales named Rufus and Rastus] entered the picture and scattered the sheep across the river. To restore some order to the Basque's temperament, the whole mine crew was used in salvaging sheep and controlling dogs."[25] Bonnie Sterling described the time her husband packed supplies to Domingo Blanco's camp. Dick said as he started to ride off, Domingo announced, "I quit." He took off his hat, threw it on the ground, and stomped on it. "Two sheep go up one canyon, one sheep go up two canyon. I quit!" Dick laughed and left, hearing Domingo's complaints all the way down the trail. As it turned out, Domingo did quit. He put his personal belongings in his backpack and walked seventeen miles to the highway. The dogs had ransacked the grub box and the sheep were scattered everywhere when Dick returned.[26]

By the 1970s Basque immigrants had established themselves in other businesses outside the canyon. Their sheepherding days had ended. When the Cherry Creek ranchers sold out to Lem Wilson, Basque ownership of canyon property also ended. Some herders from Peru replaced the Basques, but the third wave of canyon herders were predominantly from the mountainous, nonmechanized country of Puruandiro, Mexico. They brought herding skills and a willingness to live and work in isolation; they also helped ranchers expand their workforce by hiring other family members. However, the times and circumstances did not permit their acquiring land and staying in the canyon. They arrived just as Hells Canyon ranching drew to a close.

The Indispensable Dog

Just as good hands were indispensable to the success of a rancher's operation, so too were the ranchers' dogs. These dogs were not the "friends" most people bring home and lavish attention on; these working dogs performed unique and valuable tasks. There are two kinds of working dogs: the drover's dog trained to drive livestock from behind, and the herd dog trained to bring animals to the herder. The Australian shepherd is a drover's dog that came to America through some Montana sheepmen. The men worked in Australia, got acquainted with the dogs there, and brought them home to their Montana ranches. Black-and-white border collies and various colored kelpies (Gaelic for "mate") are herd dogs descended from the Scot's collie, a herd dog in Scotland. Andy Dahlquist credits Bud Wilson with bringing the first good border collies into the canyon. Before their arrival, the top dogs were called "black and tans." Dahlquist first introduced kelpies into Idaho and Hells Canyon. They were bred in Australia through genetic selection to make the slick-haired animals better adapted to desert heat.[27]

Not one rancher who talked about his years in the canyon neglected to speak glowingly about his dog's faithful and amazing work. All the ranchers valued any good, reliable dog, whether it was a mutt or one bred for herding. Mixed or pure-bred Australian or American shepherds or border collies were the preferred breeds. Jay Dobbin favored the shepherds because the collies were "too much of a gentleman for the rocks of canyon country." Greg Johnson, on the other hand, described border collies as the "brightest and most ambitious. I don't think anyone even bothers to refute that." Greg's parents had Australian shepherds. His mother said they had sixteen to twenty-six dogs, all shepherds they had trained themselves.

Dobbin had at least two dogs to a band of about two thousand sheep. Their jobs were to keep the flock bunched together—darting first to the left, then to the right; round up the stragglers; and keep the sheep moving. Their second job was to provide companionship for the herders. Ranchers trained a dog when it was still a pup by putting it out with an experienced dog for about two years. Only about one pup in a litter became a good sheepdog. Greg Johnson started training the pups by making sure they knew their names and some of the basic commands. They learned the rest by observation. Lem and Doris Wilson had two favorites, Queenie, a border collie—"wonderful mother, raised quite a few good, smart dogs"—and Jack, an Australian shepherd, who sired many "very intelligent" offspring. Most dogs worked for eight years, then retired—hopefully to the well-earned leisure of eating, lounging, and sleeping.

"You can't do anything with sheep without a dog. Some of the things they do are just amazing."[28] Most sheepmen would probably agree. The sheep are not afraid of man; they are of the dog. He might just give a ewe a little nudge on the back of her legs to move her along, or he might have to be a little more aggressive or vocal. Whatever tactic the dog uses, the

Figure 15.5. Greg Johnson with his three dogs and a cougar carcass across the horse's back. (Photo courtesy of HCNRA, Hazel Johnson Collection.)

sheep obey. Some dogs respond to hand motions, others to verbal command, some to both.

A few dogs knew exactly what to do with no instructions. Greg Johnson's dog Freddie was a good example. "When we put the bands together in the spring, they were difficult to handle because they hadn't been handled for almost two months. We needed to bring the ewes and lambs down off this knob [where the sheep had bedded down] and put them across a creek." If the lambs ever got away, Freddie would "run back to that bed ground, two miles up on top of a ridge. We never went back. We just sent old Freddie and he'd go clear back up on top, round them up, and bring them back down." That evening, Greg or a herder would check to make sure that Freddie had gotten the lambs. "He always had."

Cattle ranchers depended as much on their dogs as the sheepmen did. Sharon and Bub Horrocks could not get along "without good stock dogs because of the steepness of the terrain. You'd kill a horse." They too used border collies, rotating five or six of the dogs so each could rest. They used the following commands: come by (left); way to me (right); take time (down); hold 'em (stop the cattle); and bring 'em (bring the cattle back). (The commands sound like Gaelic words originally used to train the animals.) "We handled our dogs soft. You don't have to yell and scream at a dog. They've got good hearing." Sharon described the payoff. "You can send a border collie plumb out of sight and just sit there and wait. Pretty soon they'll come back from up a draw with the cows." If the cows did not stay bunched, the dog would nip them into compliance. After a while the herd was "dog broke." Once they looked around and saw the dog, they'd "just line right out." But the rancher did not want the dog to bite the calves. The calf would bellow a protest and her mother would come back to see what was wrong. Then every other animal started to come back and pandemonium ensued. Sharon described one of their dogs that amazed everyone. "She'd run up [to the calf] and just punch it with her nose, then back out of sight. The calf would look around and kind of trot. We called it 'booping 'em.' She'd just walk up and go—BOOP."

Another time, Sharon was moving cattle with her husband's dog. She hoped to get out of sight before her husband got his cows, because the dog kept looking over at him. Sharon was too slow and the next thing she knew the dog was over helping her husband. She decided to act as if the dog was still with her. "I'm barking at [the cows] like there's still a dog there

Figure 15.6. Like many ranchers, Esther Hibbs developed a strong bond and mutual dependence with her horse. (Photo courtesy of Esther Hibbs.)

and they keep looking. Pretty soon they figure it out and I lost every one of them in the brush." The Horrocks' dogs worked for three or four years before retirement to the good life. "We took good care of them... because that's your old buddy that helped you out a lot of places."

Esther and Earl Hibbs had a shepherd named Rusty to help with the cattle. "Without Rusty we couldn't have herded the cattle," Esther fondly remembered. "He was the smartest dog you ever saw. He knew what the cattle were going to need before you did. He would go way wide and turn them back, turn them to the left, turn them to the right, go up on the mountain, bring them in. He was a wonderful dog." Earl trained Rusty to obey both verbal and hand commands.

One of the best examples of obeying hand commands comes from the story Murrielle McGaffee Wilson told about "Daddy Pete" and his well-trained dog. Pete's wife, Ethel, was left-handed. One winter, when illness confined Pete to the house, he asked Ethel to get on the mule and move the cows. He showed Ethel the hand commands to tell their dog what to do. She practiced the commands for a while then went out on the mule to collect the cows. But every time she gave the dog a command, he just sat there and looked at her. After many frustrated attempts to get him to comply, Ethel finally remembered Pete was right-handed. Once she used the correct hand, the dog willingly obeyed. "That's all he wanted."[29]

Dogs that belonged to the Basque herders did not always understand English. This frustrated many of the other herders. Jay Dobbin once had a dog at Eureka Creek, a red-haired pedigree, that he concluded was "just worthless." He gave it to a Basque and "by golly that dog was just a marvelous thing." It seems that once a dog worked for a Basque, it wouldn't work for anyone else. Is it perhaps because it did not understand English? All it takes to answer that question is a failed effort to befriend a "foreign" dog. It just sits there and looks at you. Just like Pete's dog, all it wants is to understand the command.[30]

Although everyone spoke of a favorite horse or maybe even a mule (those animals were just as critical to most ranching operations as dogs), few people spoke as if the animal's work was unique. That isn't surprising since horses and mules worked on farms and ranches in much of rural America, simply doing the work the ranchers expected of them. Horses and mules worked every bit as hard as dogs, so it was just as important not to overwork them. Sharon Horrocks explained that each cowboy working for the Horrocks had five or six horses in his string and he would rotate them—"one day on one horse, the next day on another." If they were starting a colt, one would be ridden the shortest distance until it was four or five years old. Then he could go on the longer rides. One day's worth of horse time when they were climbing steep hills amounted to twelve to fifteen hours in the saddle. If they had to move from riverbed to mountaintop, the cowboys "just [went] real slow and [would] stop and rest 'em up." If they overworked their horses, the animal would "trail founder." That meant "their heart was gone. They were tired and worn out. Just kind of slugging along." The rider had to take special care with younger horses because they often did not know how to pace themselves. If the cowboy was inattentive, he could "ruin the animal." It might get sick, "maybe come in that night, get colic, and you can lose them." Or they're so completely exhausted they "burn their lungs up"—called wind broke—and "can never breathe right again." When you hear a horse "kind of rattling all the time," that's what has happened.

Predators

Even with optimum market conditions, good help, and reliable transportation, ranchers were still held captive to nature's whims. Most did everything they could to protect themselves from livestock loss; they still expected to sacrifice some animals to foul weather and native predators.

Coyotes, cougars, bears, bobcats, and eagles frequently threatened the cattle and sheep herds of the canyon. The extent of the problem varied from year to year and place to place. Hazel Johnson said that during World War II predators, mostly coyotes, were so bad the Johnsons feared they might go out of business. The coyote, "a wily animal," tended to pick and choose its kill; cougar were like bear, they just slaughtered a bunch. For that reason, the Johnsons kept four "hounds" around all the time to scare off cougar. In spring, bald eagles that nested in the canyon would carry off young lambs to feed their young. During the summer, bears threatened the sheep. One time when the Johnsons were on top around Memaloose, a bear got into their flock during the night and killed some thirty animals. Ken and Hazel, sleeping in a tent nearby, didn't hear a sound.[31] When sheep are frightened, they are cowed into silence. Max Walker tells a similar story, but about a cougar kill. In the spring of 1934, they were trailing sheep to the summer range across the Pittsburg Saddle on their way to Camp Howard. Three men were with the front band, and Max and two others with the tail band. The sheep bedded down within fifty yards of the men's bedrolls. The next morning they awoke to find thirteen dead lambs. They never heard a sound and apparently their five dogs didn't either.[32]

Ace Barton remembered that although during the 1930s they lost quite a few horses "up in the hills" to cougars, bears caused more problems than the big cats. Bears frequented the creek bottoms, where the Bartons pastured the calves, and would always go after the calves. But bears caused an even bigger loss to Ace and Lenora when "they would just mutilate your orchards. The fruit would get ripe and the bears would move in. It was just a constant battle if you wanted to get any fruit. It was between you and the bear, the porcupine, and the raccoon." Considering ranchers' dependence on home-produced food, the loss was critical.[33]

The only time Esther Hibbs at Granite Creek had trouble with bears was when the animals raided the Hibbses' orchard. The bears wouldn't kill cattle as long as Esther or someone was at the place. And the Hibbses' dogs did a good job of keeping coyotes at bay. Although they saw signs of cougar, Esther never had an encounter with any of the illusive beasts. She did see a bobcat once.

Max Walker, who also worked in that area, said they did not have much trouble with cougar killing livestock. They considered "cats" (bobcats) and coyotes the worst predators;

Figure 15.7. Earl Hibbs is holding a bear pelt. Rather than threaten their livestock, bears caused more damage to the Hibbes' garden and orchard. (Photo courtesy of Esther Hibbs.)

eagles were the third biggest offender. Although there were many bobcats in the canyon, he "couldn't find their kills because they would kill an animal, drag it off, eat what they wanted, and bury the rest." He never had a bear problem in the winter or spring, except in 1933, when for some reason there were no huckleberries. "The boys [herders] killed twelve to fourteen bear that year." The next year, huckleberries grew in abundance. The herders took the sheep to the same place, but the bears presented no problem. "[The bears] won't bother sheep when natural food is available."

Pete and Ethel Wilson lost more cattle to bears than to cougar. It got so the bears killed the cows and ate what they wanted. "Then it got so they just killed them and played with them. They would eat their bag out for that milk and fat," Marjorie recalled. "Dad trapped bears all the time." He also trapped some coyotes during the winter, mostly to protect the calves, but occasionally to sell their fur. Ralph Beard also believed coyotes were the greater threat, but some bear killed a few sheep in the summertime. He added, "One or two years down there I remember some people said they had quite a problem with eagles getting their lambs," but added, " I never did see any eagles catch any lambs." Andrew Dahlquist recalled watching eagles jockeying even large deer into the rocks and knocking them off the cliffs. And he saw eagles peck a calf fetus as it emerged from its mother. He said the only way to protect the vulnerable newborn lambs from eagle attacks was to use lambing sheds.

Wolves and grizzly bears apparently lived in the canyon, but few people had any contact with either. Ralph Barton was losing calves up and down Granite Creek. He concluded the culprit was a lobo wolf. "They had their own means of taking care of predators," his grandson Ace remembered. [34] Lem Wilson thought he saw a grizzly bear near Hat Point; Ted Grote confirmed that he saw it while flying over the area. Surely others sighted the wolves and grizzlies, but the infrequent reports suggest no significant numbers.

Rattlesnakes count more as an irritation than a predator. When living in rattlesnake country, one reacts almost subconsciously to their probable locations. Parents cautioned children that they might be lurking under porches and around house foundations and other ranch structures, and to be careful in rocky areas and in high grass. And always, always watch where you stepped. The threat lessened when, on a cool day, the reptiles grew too lethargic to be dangerous and during the winter when they hibernated.

Doug Tippet's fourteen-year-old brother got careless. He was irrigating and rolled over a rock to use in a dam he was repairing. A rattlesnake struck him. "So he jumped on his horse and headed for the ranch." Only the hired man, Clarence Spangler, was there. Spangler immediately "filled the boy full of whiskey." They headed for a telephone at Rogersburg, six miles away, called Lewiston, and at Captain John—the end of the road at that time—met the "rig" coming to pick them up. They got the youngster to the hospital just in time. "I remember he was an awful sick kid. He just about didn't make it."[35]

Figure 15.8. Earl Hibbs (left) and Allen Wilson holding up a cougar pelt. For a time, ranchers controlled the predator population and supplemented their income with bounties collected on predator pelts. Allen was sometimes called "Cougar Allen" by visiting journalists due to his prolific hunting skill. (Photo courtesy of Esther Hibbs.)

Rattlers threatened humans more than dogs, horses, or livestock. Sheep were oblivious to them; cattle and horses wary and wise enough to avoid them. Dogs sometimes tangled with rattlesnakes and occasionally became quite ill as a result. One encounter usually taught them to avoid snakes.

Wild animals kill for food, that is part of the natural process. Ranchers knew that. They also realized that an abundance of docile, domesticated animals at a predator's "dining table" enabled the predator to kill frequently and eat selectively from its kill. When a ranch owner or hand found a mutilated animal dead or dying, he understandably retaliated. Conversely, when ranchers received bounties for animal pelts to reduce rampant predator populations, wanton killing of them often became excessive. Allen Wilson became so famous for his numerous cougar kills, he acquired the nickname "Cougar" Allen Wilson. Pictures of him posed with his many cougar hides proliferated in 1930- and 1940-era magazines about Hells Canyon, while pelt sales supplemented his income.

Doug Tippett has childhood memories of Washington paying a dollar for a pup coyote hide and five dollars for an adult. Oregon paid three dollars for any coyote hide. Ultimately, paying bounties proved ineffective. During the winter of 1947–48 Oregon Fish and Wildlife began periodically to "poison the whole country," scattering carcasses laced with a poison called 1080. "When they put it out, they got rid of any meat eaters, then the deer population just exploded." Even as late as the 1960s, when Doug worked as a guide, "we'd take out up to sixty-five buck deer in about twelve miles of the river and still not hurt the deer population." By the 1970s, the government had banned the use of 1080 poison and dropped the bounty on cougar pelts. With the resulting rise in cougar and coyote populations, Tippett observed, "there probably aren't that many deer in twenty miles of the Snake River." By then, however, sheep and cattle production in the canyon had ended. The predator's "dinner table" was once again set by nature.[36]

A Hard Place for Livestock

Hells Canyon was a hard place for livestock to live. The varied elevation and protected canyons that made it ideal country to raise livestock sometimes rendered man and beast helpless. An occasional drought sweeps the canyon, as it did during much of the 1940s. Hazel Johnson remembered, "The winds were horrible on Snake River, especially in the spring. It would dry out the area so badly." They had no rain and precious little feed. "Kenneth watched very carefully and when the time came, everything went up" to higher country and hopefully better pasture. Another time, while Kenneth attended a meeting at Salt Lake City, Hazel and the two boys had just finished putting up a second crop of hay when the Freezeout fire struck. Caused by lightning, it burned within a mile of their home and upper field. Hazel remembered it as "a nightmare—horrible." Fortunately, the sheep were on higher ground but so were all the hands. The fire stopped short of destroying the buildings and threatening their lives, but it took weeks to mop up from that fire.[37]

Dry conditions signaled the danger of grass or forest fire. Jay Dobbin remembered an especially bad grass fire one year. Another year, during a forest fire, an old bell goat saved his band of sheep from the flames. "He would run ahead, then stop and turn around every fifty feet or so and bleat loudly as if telling the sheep to hurry. He soon had them out of the trees into a big clearing where they were safe." Once, one of Dobbin's careless hands set a precious hay stack on fire. Dobbin and the men had just finished cutting and putting up hay at the Tulley Creek ranch. It was a hot day and they were happy to be finished and heading toward the cooler higher country. By chance, Dobbin looked back to see his field and haystack on fire. They rushed back, saved the building but lost most of the hay. Someone had flipped a cigarette into the field as he departed.

In droughts, anything can start a fire. Billy McGaffee was a heavy smoker. One day in the fall, during extremely dry conditions, he came to a place where wild animals had rolled. He dismounted and sat down for a smoke. He was careful to put the cigarette out in the dust before remounting. A few minutes later, his horse slipped and lurched forward. They continued along the trail, but for some reason McGaffee glanced back in time to see that the horseshoe striking the rock had caused a spark that ignited the dry cheat grass. Billy went back to put the fire out, relieved that he had seen it. He knew the Forest Service would blame him, the notorious smoker.[38]

Another time on Big Bar, Ken Johnson and his father were packing supplies in from White Bird around Suicide Point and down the river to the boat. While they were making a second river crossing, Anna Maxwell looked back to see a fire starting where they had been. She yelled to the hired man on shore. He fought the fire "like crazy" and extinguished it before it reached the hay fields. Anna "gave them what for, for tossing a cigarette down." The hands insisted they had not been smoking; Ken verified it. The sun had hit broken glass in the brush just right and ignited the dry grass.[39]

Hard winters caused the most hardship, for animals and humans alike. Carl Henderson "went broke and lost everything in 1918." That "cured" Horace, his son, of ever wanting to own a ranch. Two years of hard winter meant cattle either died or fell victim to rustlers. As he explained, "It was awful handy. All [the rustlers] had to do was just swim 'em across the river and they were in Oregon and gone." Horace did not explain the connection between rustling and bad winters (maybe they were low-principled ranchers who had lost their own herds), but he remembered as a young kid watching them steal twenty head of replacement heifers. He was too young to do anything about it. "Dad was gone to town and the guys knew it." Horace watched the rustlers go down the river about three miles to a good crossing and leave the state.⁴⁰ (The river would have been low and easily forded.) Jay Dobbin also lost livestock to rustlers that winter. He never caught them in the act, but as he said, "Cows don't fly."

The Van Pool operations suffered during the summer drought and hard winter of 1918. Having no available feed forced them to drive four hundred head of cattle across the ice-covered Salmon River to Cottonwood and on to feedlots at Grandview, Washington. The cost practically bankrupted them; Harold's working for the Forest Service for the next five or six years helped saved the ranch.

Bad winters hit the canyon in an interesting pattern beginning in 1918–19, recurring every decade thereafter on the eighth and ninth year, at least through the 1960s. The first decade caught Jidge Tippett with inadequate feed. Winter never caught him short again, including the "record-breaking" winter of 1948–49, when he had an eight-year accumulation of hay amounting to seven hundred tons. That hay carried his herds safely through the winter. The same year, with the river frozen over, the Johnsons were unable to get supplemental feed by boat. They had to hire Bert Zimmerly of Clarkston to fly in and drop hundred-pound sacks of cottonseed cake two or three times a week to feed their three bands of sheep. The cubed feed consisted of residue left over from milled cotton and other ingredients. It was high in protein and oil, and didn't take much to maintain an animal.⁴¹ They saved the sheep, but at a tremendous cost. Pete Wilson hired Zimmerly to drop cottonseed cakes and baled alfalfa for his cattle pastured up the river as far as Granite Creek. The snow was so deep all their supplies, including the feed, had to be flown in.⁴²

Unique to canyon country is the danger of livestock either getting stranded on a hillside rim (rimmed-up they called it) or "rolling" off the steep, rock-covered, frozen hill slopes. The Bartons lost a total of thirty-six horses when they slid off the north slopes, but no more than five or six cattle a year met the same fate.⁴³ Marjorie Wilson Chadwick said Ace's father had trouble with livestock sliding "because he didn't check on his cattle as often as Fred [McGaffee] and Dad did. Dad would, even if it was too slick to ride a horse. He'd check on his cattle and get them off those north slopes afoot. But you had to be with it about every day to make sure." If a cow did roll, it was generally a yearling. Her dad would find it and butcher it.⁴⁴ Marjorie's sister Violet hated to admit it, but she sometimes looked forward to a cow's losing its life to a winter slide. That way they could eat beef; their father never allowed them to slaughter cattle for home consumption.⁴⁵

While killing an injured animal was often the most humane thing to do, being a good rancher meant knowing how to care for sick or injured animals. Sharon Horrocks told about a horse that had gone off a cliff during the winter. He slid, jerked, and pulled the whole pack string over the cliff with him. Fortunately, he had a saddle on and fell upside down on his back. The incident occurred close enough to the ranch so they could bring him to the barn. She gave him a tranquilizer shot, knowing that the horse could easily die from the shock. The next day she gave him a liniment massage and put hot packs on him. Because his withers were "pushed down and mushy," he could not put his head down to eat or drink. Sharon held the water buckets up for him, fed him by hand, and doctored him every day for a month. Finally, he came out of it.⁴⁶

Another time she treated a bull that had rolled down the hill and broken his leg. He had not punctured the skin, avoiding possible infection, so they left him where he was, which luckily was by water. She and her son packed hay and pellets to the bull until he healed enough to walk to the barn. They continued to care for him. By the time the roads were open and they could haul him to town for slaughter, he "looked in show-shape."⁴⁷

Although veterinarians sometimes made visits into the canyon, most ranchers learned what they could about animal care. Bub Horrocks went to veterinary schools whenever he could, enabling him to do such things as operate on a cancerous eye or do cesareans. Marjorie Chadwick described her father as a "frustrated veterinarian" who learned animal medicine while working as a young man on a ranch in Harney County, Oregon. Greg Johnson outfitted with the basic medical supplies, but also worked with a veterinarian in Idaho on the experimental use of a selenium/vitamin E supplement, which was "pretty new and innovative."[48] Their best insurance for good animal health, however, was keeping their animals away from other, possibly diseased, sheep—"one thing Kenneth insisted on," his wife added.[49]

Lice and ticks, a constant problem, could seriously damage an animal's health. Pete Wilson believed magpies saved his cattle. His daughter Violet remembered magpies were always around the cattle. "Dad said they were a friend to the cattlemen because in the spring when the ticks were all over, the magpies would pick ticks [off the cattle's backs]." Even when the old cow lay down on her side, "why there'd be a magpie picking them off her stomach." In early spring, when the animals were their weakest, ticks proliferated. Without magpies, ticks got so heavy on an animal they literally drained its blood.[50]

Other ranchers used more scientific methods to control tick infestation. Jay Dobbin drove his sheep through vats of sheep dip. Jidge Tippett supposedly had one of the first dipping vats in the country. His cattle would "wallow through" a fifty-fifty mixture of DDT and alkaline mineral, a powder that causes the DDT to cling to the cattle for ninety days. He would also spray them if necessary for horn and heel flies.[51]

Keeping animals healthy and safe amounted to an endless, year-round duty that occupied the time and attention of ranchers, their families, and hired help. Those responsibilities—demanding enough for sheep and cattle ranchers in any environment—often seemed daunting in the hard land of Hells Canyon. It took tough people to stick it out, people imbued with an optimistic determination to persevere.

Chapter 16

Ties That Bind

"Did it take a special kind of person to live in Hells Canyon?" Granite Creek cattle rancher Esther Hibbs pondered the question. "I don't think it takes a special kind of person to live there," she said. "Maybe living there makes you into a special person."[1] Mailboat captain Dick Rivers described canyon residents as "good, honest people.... Their geography forced them to be that way."[2] Twenty-year canyon resident Gene McGaffee remembered, "Every day of life in that country meant facing danger in some form."[3] And Grace Jordan wrote, "A canyon is no place to nurture grievances. The walls never talk a man out of dissatisfaction."[4]

The natural environment of Hells Canyon and the Middle Snake River directed the flow of human history and molded the character of each person who passed through there. The dangers, challenges, and allure of the land either toughened or defeated the individual just as it inspired the beginning and forced the end of each historic period. Alternatively, the landscape and all that it embraced fostered a widespread allegiance to the canyon. Residents formed enduring physical, mental, and emotional ties. Those hardened by the land look back on the time they lived there with fond memories and a deep appreciation of that country's character-building qualities.

Marjorie Wilson Chadwick and her mother, Ethel Wilson, refused to fall victim to misfortune. When asked if their continuing in the face of adversity was part of life in the canyon, Marjorie thoughtfully answered, "I think it was. I really think it was." As Marjorie's elderly father reflected on his life, he confessed to his two daughters, "I've often wondered if your mother and I did right by keeping you children in the canyon." Their answers captured the essence of living there. Marjorie told him, "We learned to be independent and stand on our own two feet. We learned trustworthiness. It just taught us a lot that I know we would never have gotten any place else. And we learned to love nature." Violet Wilson Shirley added, "You gave us a way of life and you taught us things that most people never get ... to enjoy working and being honest; to always do a little more work than what you get paid for. That followed all of us through life. We learned all the good parts of being a human being, I think."[5]

Like other people, Hells Canyon residents went through peaks and valleys. So what made daily life along Snake River so memorable? What bound the people so tightly to that place? One thing was the powerful ties to the cycle of nature. Life there demanded hard work, disciplined patience, and self-sufficiency. At the same time, the canyon fostered both physical and emotional reliance upon one another. They were isolated—yet connected. Harold Van Pool captured that relationship: "Our neighbors were not close in distance but very close in friendship and assistance when called upon." An account of the daily life of twentieth-century Hells Canyon residents—should help explain what made their time there so unforgettable.

Figure 16.1. In this picturesque setting sits the Bernard Creek cabin a short distance above the Snake River. Note the irrigation pipe along the hill slope and the washing on the line. (Photo courtesy of William Wilson.)

No Place Like Home

Modest cabins, situated with a commanding view of the river and mountains or nestled snugly beside a picturesque stream, blended into the landscape. Nearby outbuildings surrounded each cabin: some type of cold storage cellar—often dug into a hillside—a chicken house, barn, storage shed, and corral. Every home had a garden; most had orchards; some, grape arbors. Over time, some cabins became larger and better furnished homes; others were abandoned and fell into disrepair.. A lilac bush, blue iris blooming along benches or creek beds, an ancient apricot tree, a rambling rosebush—that is all that remains of homes once bustling with activity.

The Carter mansion, the one home that merited the residents' special notice, is still known in Hells Canyon lore. Len and Grace Jordan lived a ways down Kirkwood Creek from Dick Carter, a colorful individual who at times manufactured and distributed moonshine. Carter built his mansion in 1920. He moved away while the Jordans still lived at Kirkwood.[6] Over the years, Carter's home evolved into a bunkhouse for Kirkwood ranch hands. While employed by Bud Wilson, Dick and Bonnie Sterling lived there briefly in the late 1950s. Bonnie remembered the mansion as "marvelous for its time and place . . . but a mansion only as it related to the wilds of Snake River." With hardwood floors throughout, numerous windows, a woodstove, big kitchen cupboards, a kitchen table and four chairs, a bedroom set that included a chest of drawers, and front and back cement porches, no wonder folks called it a mansion. After the Sterlings moved away, the 1920s-era home devolved into a derelict structure—filthy, decaying, and pack rat–infested. Still with a little imagination, its appeal remains vivid.[7]

What a contrast the Carter mansion made to the Granite Creek cabin that Esther Hibbs moved into as a bride. As soon as she started calling the one-room structure with an upstairs loft *home*, she "quickly" partitioned the single room into three areas—a bedroom, a kitchen, and a living/dining room. The kitchen and bedroom each measured about seven by eight feet. A five-foot-wide doorway divided the living room from the kitchen. In the kitchen, a small cookstove sat to the right of the door, a homemade cupboard to the left, with the sink between the cupboard and outside door. The "small hole" in the ceiling opened to the upstairs bedroom, reached by a ladder.

Esther immediately upgraded the cabin by covering the rough board walls and ceiling with blue building paper. Later she covered that with "regular wallpaper"—a blue-and-white flowered paper for the living room and bedroom, a small red-and-white printed oilcloth in the kitchen. Esther painted the plain board floors a pale green, along with the interior and exterior doors and windowsills. The remaining exterior went unpainted.

At first, the kitchen had no sink. The Hibbses carried in water by bucket. Esther soon changed that. "I built the sink and put water in it myself," she said with not a small amount of pride. Their irrigation ditch went right by the front door. First, Esther built a small reservoir up the ditch a short distance from the house and covered the outlet with a screen. From there she dug a ditch around all the embedded rocks and laid a "variety of sizes and shapes of pipes" brought from her Pullman home. "I could go around and back and under and so forth until I got to the house. Then I put a standpipe in under the house, up through the wall and into the kitchen. So I had cold water in the house. It was very crude, but it worked." Their bathroom? They had a privy out back. All the time she was there, they kept the privy in the same location, but did occasionally put lime down it and "of course" scrubbed it out. Esther jokingly added, "We had real toilet paper." The Hibbs cabin stood intact long after the last resident left. Then, in 2003, a mudslide rushed down the converging creeks, sweeping away the cabin and all surrounding buildings.

Figure 16.2. The modest Granite Creek cabin, where Esther Hibbs began her married life as a canyon rancher. (Photo courtesy of Esther Hibbs.)

The Arams considered their house on Getta Creek a "special haven" during the 1919 flu epidemic and a retreat during hard winters. "It was just like part of heaven to suddenly move out of all that cold to a place with warm days and nights," Jim remembered. The wooden house had one bedroom, a kitchen, a living area, and a stovepipe that went out the kitchen window. Each night the four children climbed a ladder to their mattresses in the attic. A small lean-to for storage or extra sleeping room hugged one side of the house.[8] When Slim and Mary Johnson acquired the Arams' place and moved into the "two old shacks," they remodeled it into a more spacious but still modest accommodation.[9]

Ralph and Lenora Barton and their three children lived in a small "one room affair" at Battle Creek. The only door opened into the one room—the kitchen, living room, and bedroom. Rough boards covered the floors; building paper covered the walls—a heavy paper with designs on it "so it sort of looked like wallpaper." Furnishings consisted of a cast-iron stove, a table, some straight-backed chairs, cupboards made from dynamite boxes, and a cast-iron bed in back.[10]

The Bartons built a slightly larger second cabin and covered the walls with old newspapers and magazines, characteristic of many Hells Cabin interiors. They brought down lumber for the frame from an old mill up Battle Creek at the Winchester mine, and packed shingle siding and "a lot of roofing" in from the Imnaha River. (Ranchers commonly engaged in the pragmatic practice of pirating lumber, metals, and any other usable material from abandoned mines and homes.) A pole-and-shake outhouse stood a short distance away. Digging a new hole to move the outhouse constituted such a difficult task, the Bartons only moved it once. "Always on Snake River," Ace explained, "when you wanted to dig a hole, before you got the pick and shovel you went and got the dynamite and some blasting caps, 'cause you were gonna need 'em.'" When Hazel Barton, Lenora's daughter, and her husband, Allen Wilson, moved into the Battle Creek cabin, they added a porch to the north side of the building and another room. The Forest Service preserved that remodeled cabin to give visitors some inkling of home life during the 1920s and 1930s.[11]

Hazel and Kenneth Johnson began married life in an interesting home at Temperance Creek. Twin cabins sat side by side with a roofed breezeway between them. Logs supported the rafters; short stakes protruding from each log provided a place to hang saddles. The Johnsons boarded up the breezeway, put in a floor, and converted the new area to a living room. They covered the walls with oilcloth and pulled the "big old chicken house" to one end of the living room, thereby adding a bedroom. There were no bathroom facilities, just a two-holer out back. Their son, Greg, thought the original log cabin ended up with six or seven different rooms. Nine years later, Ken and Hazel moved out of the twin cabins—"an ordeal in itself"—and into a new house. At the time, a big crew ran the sheep outfit. The Johnsons put the crew to work building the house. The mailboat hauled up lumber of "odd dimensions," forcing Ken to set up a sawmill to cut the appropriate sizes. The result was a three-story house.[12]

Log homes built in the "twin cabin" style like the Johnsons' first home appeared elsewhere in early canyon construction. Where logs were not available, stone and dugout structures sufficed. Frank O. Jacks described a one-room, stone-walled dugout home at Cottonwood Creek built by Henry Thiessen, "probably around 1890." It measured about ten by twelve feet, "a little smaller than usual," with the "usual fireplace," one window, and one door. The walls were "rubble stone with mud for mortar, and a sort of gable end at the chimney side." Square-cut nails anchored the heavy, hand-hewn frames, beams, and rafters.[13] When Jacks worked for Volney Fountain, he lived in a larger and more modern home nearby with five rooms, including a tack room. Once a cloudburst "deposited three feet of mud and rock against the back part of the house," blocking an outside door into the kitchen and a back room. Since they had not used the door "in five or six years," they just closed the door and did not use the back room. That was a simple solution.

Horace Henderson described another simple solution for constructing a unique, two-story cabin his father built on High Range. In the 1910s Carl Henderson built a house using lumber hauled up on Captain MacFarlane's *Prospector*. Henderson planned for a single-story structure, but MacFarlane delivered sixteen-foot lumber. Instead of sawing the boards in two, he built the two-story structure and "stuck it straight up in the dirt" against the hill. It had a post and rock foundation—the back corners, next to the hill, sat on rocks while the lower, front corners, "where the hill broke," sat on posts about three feet off the ground. "It wasn't very comfortable," for the wind blew up from underneath through the cracks in the floor. There was no siding, just batten over the cracks; the inside studding was uncovered. The structure needed no stairwell to the second story; the Hendersons just walked around to the back of the house, following the walkway up the bank to the upstairs opening.[14]

Figure 16.3. At Ken Johnson's place after the supply and mail drop. It appears the Johnsons also received a small load of lumber, possibly for their new house. (Photo courtesy of Robert McGrady.)

Keeping those rustic homes clean must have been a nightmare for the more fastidious homemaker, but most women probably developed a certain tolerance for the dirt. They didn't mention it, unless the dirt was someone else's. Some women talked about the extensive cleaning needed when moving into another person's house. And, of course, single men's habits received plenty of comment. After Janie Stone's "Grandpa Earl" had been living at her home for a while, bedbugs infested the place. "We had to set [the legs of] the bed in buckets of water so [the bugs] couldn't get to the bed. They'd eat you up alive. [Finally,] my husband took the beautiful bed—one of those high-topped ones that matched the dresser—out and burned it. We just couldn't get the bugs out." Her grandfather "just never paid any attention to them."

Putting up the Produce

"Make do," a popular term from the Depression, carried over to the rationing years of World War II. No matter where in the country they lived, everyone tried to make do with what they had. After the war, when rationing ended, freeing Americans to spend their wartime wages, Hells Canyon folk continued to make do. That way of life seemed best suited to their remote location and established lifestyle. Since they had to pack everything in on the backs of horses or mules, or shuttle it by mail boat and later airplane, it was just too expensive and inconvenient to do otherwise. From make-do came self-sufficiency and creativity.

Figure 16.4. Kirkwood when the Wilsons owned it, c.1960. Although not visible in this picture, the nearby creek and large river bar, as can be seen in Figure 16.5, provided ample room for the Jordan's orchard, vineyard, and garden. The white building was the house; today Forest Service volunteers stay there. The log structure was the bunkhouse; today it is a visitors' center. (Photo courtesy of the Bud Wilson Family.)

A long growing season and fertile soil made it possible to grow any plant adaptable to a temperate climate. Esther and Earl Hibbs always had a big garden, as did Earl's parents, Martin and Ellen. Both couples "lived from that garden," making the families "almost completely self-sufficient." Close to Granite Creek, Ellen planted two apple trees, two cherry trees, pear, plum, prune, and peach trees, and the first two walnut trees.[15] Magpies, raccoons, and bears turned her two walnut trees into a full-fledged walnut orchard "all up and down Granite Creek."[16]

Hazel Johnson described their garden: a strawberry patch, peas, corn, cucumbers, spinach, radishes, tomatoes, potatoes, squash, onions, and different kinds of lettuce—"you name it, we had it." When they first lived there, they were "very poor" and were forced to live on cured deer meat and whatever produce they grew. Hazel came down from one of the supply camps "a couple of times" a year to put up the produce. "I'd can fifteen hundred quarts of fruits and vegetables; that's all we had." Their lives depended on that produce. To keep from losing the garden and orchards to drought, fire, or predators, the Johnsons always hired someone to keep watch through the growing season, "even when we were very poor."[17]

The Jordans' place at Kirkwood must have been a veritable oasis—apple, apricot, and cherry trees next to the hill and irrigation ditch; walnut trees and apricot trees near the river; and raspberries and strawberries between the house and the hill. They kept a "tiny" yard around the house for coolness and trimmed the grape arbor into a trellis, so they could sit under it during the hot summers. Water from the creek irrigated their garden and potato patch.[18]

Ethel Wilson tended two big gardens. In the "upper garden," about halfway up Saddle Creek, she raised rutabagas, fall corn, horseradish, and potatoes. The lower garden was close to the ranch house. Orchards and berry patches grew at both locations. Although her husband helped put in the gardens, "it was always her and us kids' job to keep it up," Marjorie remembered. Ethel "didn't think she had done her summer canning unless she had at least a thousand quarts of fruit canned." She used an old wood stove. With summer temperatures outside hovering around 100 degrees, the heat she endured must have been intense. Yet, "she would just be singing and working" inside the house.[19]

One hot summer day, while her mother was in the middle of canning fruits and vegetables, Violet asked, "How can you stand it with that hot stove?" Her mother's answer: "I guess I got used to it growing up in Texas. It's just something you have to do." Violet remembered many mornings getting up to find "a whole lot of jars of fruit already canned, sitting on the table to cool." She figured her mother must have started at midnight. They also dried corn, stored in a big sack in the spacious cellar, and "made lots of pickles," stored in five-gallon crocks. Marjorie said her mother always made vinegar, which she used for pickling, vinegar pies, salad dressing, and cleaning. As she prepared fruit for canning, she set aside the peelings and cores to make the vinegar, to which she added sugar, or some other sweetener like juice, and water. The mix fermented a few days in a crock until a scum thickened on top that looked like "some kind of a slimy sheet of paper." That was "the start of mother." She bottled that vinegar and used a "little piece of the start of mother" to begin a fresh batch. That way the Wilsons had enough vinegar to use every day.

Figure 16.5. The northern end of Kirkwood Bar as it appeared in 2000. The boat landing is at the middle of the picture, where Kirkwood Creek enters the Snake River. The trail leads to the ranch house and visitor center, out of sight on the other side of the creek. (Photo by Sheri Worle.)

Canning was the best, usually the only, way to preserve enough produce, meat, and fish to last through the year. Hazel Johnson canned enough food for her family, their guests, and all their herders in winter camps. Along with her fifteen hundred jars of fruits and vegetables were around fifty quarts of beef, and varying amounts of jam and juice. She stored it all in an old, cool, dark snake-infested mining tunnel a few yards from the house.

Janie Stone, who lived below Rogersburg on the Idaho side, canned enough deer, sausage, and chicken to last through the summer. She first fried the venison a little "to kinda make it taste like it was fried meat." Then into the glass jars went the fried, thinly sliced meat, "juice and everything," which she sealed with lard and covered with a lid. Fresh eggs lasted a long time if placed in a water glass inside a stone jar and stored in a cold place.[20] Elmer Earl canned salmon in half pint jars "because it was so rich you didn't need a lot." The Earls liked salmon, and "the Finlanders around here ate a lot of fish stew."[21] For the Pete Wilson family, the main meat was fresh or canned sturgeon and jerked venison.[22] Esther and Earl Hibbs canned the fat of a bear that Earl killed every fall. They butchered the bear, reserved the meat for the dogs, and rendered out the fat. Sometimes one animal yielded five to ten gallons of fat, "enough for winter use." Esther used it for pie crusts and deep fat frying. She said it was sweeter, whiter, and not quite as heavy as pork lard.

Watering the Land

Although some of the ranchers had enough flat land in the upper benches to grow grain hay—oats, barley, or wheat—without irrigation, they all tried to cultivate small patches of alfalfa on the lower, gravel-deposit benches. The benches are greedy for water and alfalfa is a thirsty plant. Only by bringing water from the nearby creeks could the ranchers keep the alfalfa crops alive. The first yield came in June, when the canyon still had semifrequent rain. The second crop depended on "the quality of your irrigator and the amount of available water." Sometimes ranchers got a partial third crop of hay.[23]

Fortunately, almost all the irrigated land sloped toward the river, and the small streams that fed the ditches had a significant drop. It was not difficult to put gravity to work in the canyon irrigation systems. "You just turned it [on] and the water spread out, then you'd change it along," was Ace Barton's simple explanation of a task that was not always that easy. He said they harvested alfalfa and grass hay, and with four cuttings generally put up thirty-five tons a year. "We grew it all on little old pastures; postage stamp deals.... Anything you could get water on, you could grow hay."[24]

At Ragtown, a "beautiful garden, a huge watermelon patch," and an alfalfa field brought shades of green to a sun-bleached river bar. The Hendersons watered their crops from Getta Creek. A three-mile ditch skirted the field's upper side over to the garden at the far end. Using the field's natural slope, they flood-irrigated the land with small ditches that spread the water out from the main channel. The biggest problem was keeping the ditch cleared of rocks, leaves, grass, and any other debris that floated down. Poison oak lined the ditch, caught the debris, and made cleaning it an unbearable task. When the Arams bought the place, they gave up trying to keep the ditch clean and converted the hay field to grazing land.

The Johnsons at Temperance Creek used an irrigation ditch the previous owners built. Also a maintenance nuisance, it would wash out every other year. The only way to make repairs was by hand. Greg remembered his teenage summers "packing sacks of dirt from down on the bottom of the creek up the steep trails, pulling ourselves up with ropes, to seal the ditch up when it would wash out. It was a nightmare!" If a water spout filled the ditch full of gravel, someone had to shovel it out by hand. Without the ditch, they couldn't raise a hay crop.[25]

Using the same water they used on the garden and in the house, Pete and Ethel Wilson got four cuttings of alfalfa from Saddle Creek fields. Their domestic water came from a big ditch off the edge of the porch right outside the kitchen door; their drinking water, from a spring along the creek. The fields ran up and down the creek about a mile and a half; the trail to the fields followed the ditch. Like the Wilsons, everyone remembered their own irrigation ditch route. They could still visualize its every feature. But the ditch that captured most attention was the famous Meyers Creek tunnel ditch.

During the mining boom of the early 1900s, the Great Eastern Mine owners built a ditch from Meyers Creek to Big Bar, four miles south of Kirkwood. They cut timber higher in the mountains for wood flumes to move water around the hillside rims. When the mine closed and ranching dominated the area, Kirkwood ranch owners used water from that ditch to irrigate hay fields on Big Bar. Kenneth Johnson brought in some tinsmiths to improve the ditch, using pipe to replace the wood flume. The tinsmiths shot a ledge around the bluff and laid pipe on it. The trouble was, the rocks kept tumbling and mashing the pipes. Johnson then had to put in new sections. "But it worked very well."

Len Jordan, the next Kirkwood owner, used the same ditch. He just repaired "the thing every spring before we put water through it."[26] The next owner, Bud Wilson, decided to make some improvements. Instead of going around the hillside, his ditch would tunnel through it. Wilson hired Ace Duncan to dig the tunnel. Jordan described Duncan as a "tough little guy" who weighed about a hundred pounds. Ace Barton called him a "superb blacksmith." Since he owned mineral rights to the hill on High Bar and spent years digging tunnels in search of ore, Duncan was well acquainted with the area and knew how to accomplish his task. For two or three winters, he labored off and on at the Wilson tunnel. Duncan, who was eighty-one years old when he began that work, explained why it took so long: "It's slow going and the rock is awful hard. By the time I swing that eight-pound hammer seven or eight hours a day, I give out."[27] River travelers heading downstream can still see the ditch and tunnel on the Idaho side, a few hundred feet above the river: an amazing accomplishment, a testimony to perseverance and hard work.

Basic Equipment

With irrigation water available on most arable land, planting, watering, then harvesting the crops consumed spring, summer, and fall days. Seeding and cutting a hay crop in the canyon required only basic equipment—a plow and a mowing machine—and another full measure of self-sufficiency. Ace Barton said it was "no picnic" preparing the soil for a crop. The land at Sheep Creek was fertile but rocky. "If you dug all the rocks out of that field, the He Devil would've been lowered fourteen feet—*if* you got 'em all out of there." Barton used a "foot-burner plow" with a team. "There was just nothing but rocks. You'd just hit one and then the other. You'd get done and both of your sides would be black and blue with the plow handles banging you." The plowshare would last about a day, then it had to be removed and resharpened. It was "worn clear off in the rock pile and there was no way to get another one right away. So we'd have to take it to the forge and weld a point back on, using whatever you had."[28]

Esther and Earl Hibbs had hay fields at Three Creeks, a ways down the river from Granite Creek, and small patches of alfalfa at the mouth of Granite Creek. Their only mechanical equipment was a mowing machine. Such rough country made it impossible to haul the machine, intact, from one place to the other. From Three Creeks, "Earl would take the mower to pieces and pack it on two horses, put the tongue over his shoulder, and take the whole outfit to the mouth of Granite Creek." He reassembled it there to cut the alfalfa patches. Then he had to "repeat the process to get it on up the next mile to home," a mile, straight up the creek. "Part of the mower was so heavy, he had to lift it up by block and tackle, which he carried with him." Using the block and tackle and a tree, Earl was able to lift the mower onto the horse's back.

Ranchers at the other end of the canyon had the luxury of delivering their equipment by boat, like the Hendersons at Ragtown. "Of course, they had to take it apart—a hay rake and mowing machine, plows and everything," Horace Henderson said. They also had more land to cultivate than the upstream ranchers, even though it too was steep and usually rocky. Up the hill at High Range, Horace's dad used a reversible, hillside disk plow with a twenty-four-inch disk. "You would go around the hill, throwing the dirt down the hill . . . then you'd kick the catch loose and the team would just reverse and turn around and the disk would go the other way. It would turn either way and keep throwing the dirt downhill."

Runaways could be a problem when you worked with a team of horses. Frank Jacks remembered mowing hay the summer of 1926. The rake tossed a rock and spooked the team. Jacks could not stop or guide the team as they "headed down the hill toward the canyon." Just as he thought he "could pull the team around to the left to avoid a barbed wire fence, the line broke and the whole shebang tore through the fence onto the steep side of the canyon. Instead of continuing straight on down the slope, the team turned left and went around the hillside, scattering pieces of cast-iron mowing machine along the way." Somewhere along the way, Jacks bailed out. They found the horses standing on the hillside. They had small cuts and the harness was torn. But the hay was ready for cutting—now. Someone rode to a nearby telephone and ordered a new machine. A few days later, it arrived at the boat landing. "Volney [Fountain] and I put it together on the spot, wrapped the cast iron wheels with gunny sacks, hitched up a team, and drove the mower over and around the rocks and up Cave Gulch canyon to the ranch."

One Thousand Loaves a Month

Men needed haying equipment; their wives needed a good, big wood stove. Occasionally families acquired a stove from an abandoned homestead. It was there; they needed it; why not? Hazel Johnson loved her left-handed stove. "I had all the room in the world on that stove." She could bake six pies and twelve loaves of bread at one time, enough for a big work crew. How it ended up in her possession made a great story.

Apparently years earlier all of the neighbors went together and ordered the stove from a Montgomery Ward catalog and hauled it from Pittsburg Landing, over the benches, to Jim and Stella Wisenor at Salt Creek. The Wisenors had just built a new home. The stove was their housewarming gift. Years later, the Wisenors were gone and the cabin was empty, but the stove remained. Ken Johnson decided to haul it a mile upstream to Hazel. He took off the oven door, the warming door, the big water heater, and any other removable components and slung the frame on poles between two mules. "It was marvelous seeing what they [the mules] did. One mule would swing around the switchback (down Dry Gulch); the other stayed still. Then it would be his turn, you know, when they were coming around the switchbacks. It was marvelous." Hazel grew so attached to that stove, when the Johnsons finally left the canyon, her son Greg and a pilot, Ted Grote, flew to the old place to get it. They removed all detachable parts from the stove and loaded it on a wagon. The next morning

Figure 16.6. Daily life on the porch of the Mace Cabin on High Trail. Note how many domestic activities moved outside when the weather was nice. (Photo courtesy of HCNRA, Florence Winniford Smith Collection.)

another pilot, Bud Stengle, flew in to help them move the wagon to the airfield and load the plane. Hazel and her stove were reunited in Enterprise.[29]

Canyon women spent many hours canning, baking, and preparing meals in front of the hot woodstove. No wonder its importance lingered so long in their memories. It took a long time to heat those stoves, so they got up in the wee hours to start the fire. They kept the fire burning through the evening meal, even during the hottest days of summer. Most people worked around the heat if they possibly could. Pete Wilson let his haying crew rest during the afternoons. They returned to the fields as the day cooled. For the cooks, this schedule meant cooking late into the night, but it also gave them time away from the stove during the hottest part of the day.

Finding, cutting, and bringing in firewood were daily tasks, summer or winter, rain or shine, for everyone in the canyon. This practice continued right up until propane replaced wood for heating and cooking. In the higher country, finding wood was no problem. As Marjorie Chadwick explained, "Dad had a two-wheeled cart and he just hauled these big pines and travoised them down on this cart with the mules and then sawed them up at the house." But at the lower ranches "firewood—even driftwood—was hard to come by anywhere on Snake River."[30] At the Wilsons' main Saddle Creek ranch, Pete never let his family cut any trees around the place. They had to go up the creek, where "there would always be a dead alder tree or two." During the summer, between haying and irrigating, he sent a hired hand up the creek to saw up some limbs and snags "so there would be plenty of winter wood." Sometimes they used a mule to drag a log down, which Violet Shirley described as "quite an experience. The mule learned to go around [a bend] and watch in the back to see that it [the log] didn't catch on a rock. They got real smart that way." If someone brought a packhorse back to the ranch without a load and came upon a log close enough to haul, they would bring it on in.[31]

Everyone bought in bulk enough staples to see them through the winter and sometimes for a full year. Staples generally amounted to flour, sugar, and coffee. The Wilsons added raisins to their staples, which they bought in boxes about eighteen inches long, one inch wide, and six inches deep—"that's how they came," Violet remembered.[32] Every ranch had a milk cow. To make butter they separated the cream from the milk, then churned it. Just about everyone had chickens; some even experimented with turkeys. Almost all of them added wild game and fish, especially sturgeon, to their diets; they usually gathered native berries like huckleberries and serviceberries. And everyone had produce from the orchards and gardens.

A final necessity was yeast or sourdough starter. When Hazel Johnson moved into the canyon as a bride, she remembered her mother giving her a yeast starter, "because no matter what happened to me, I was going to have to bake bread." Dick Maxwell and Max Walker met the couple at the end of the road with a horse and mule; the mule was to "bring the bride into Snake River." Although Hazel was a city girl, unprepared for either horse travel or ranching life, she knew she had to guard that quart jar of starter. "I slept with that confounded starter," she recalled.

Baking large amounts of bread every day was a responsibility no canyon women could avoid. Marjorie Wilson remembered that her mother, Ethel, "seldom made less than a thousand loaves of bread a month." They ate bread at every meal. To feed a large family and the Saddle Creek hired hands, Ethel baked sixteen loaves every day. She mixed bread dough in a big dishpan. Ingredients included, among other things, white store-bought flour or their hand-ground wheat flour, "everlasting yeast," and water from the boiled potatoes. As Violet explained, when boiling potatoes, "you never salted the water, because you drained it off and kept that to put into the yeast. That fed it [the yeast], you know." Years later, as she talked about her mother "taking hot loaves of bread out of the oven," letting one cool a few minutes, then "slicing it, putting a little butter on it, maybe a sprinkle of sugar and cinnamon," she could recall the taste of that bread.

Scrubbing Up

About once a week, the old family cookstove did double duty. It cooked the evening meal and then heated a pot of water for the weekly bath. The Wilsons, a family of ten, and just about every other canyon family, used a middle-of-the-room tub arrangement until modern conveniences caught up with them. The Wilsons had two round tubs, a large and a small one. (Violet usually preferred the bigger one.) One of the kids hauled in water from the ditch to the house and heated it in a pot on the stove while supper cooked. After the meal came time for the weekly bath. "Usually about three of us had a bath in the same water, the younger ones before me," Violet said. "I always felt like that water was pretty dirty by the time it got to me, so I'd always have to add another gallon or two so it wouldn't seem quite so thick. I did lots of scrubbing off afterward." She preferred a summer bath in the ditch. "Mother would take us out to the ditch and scrub us out there in cool water. It felt pretty good."[33]

Esther Hibbs matter-of-factly said she bathed in a tub in the middle of the living room. Janie Stone vividly remembered a relative who bathed in the river—once a year. "If he went to a dance, he put clean clothes on top the others. He just kept wearing those clothes until summer when he took his bath."

Over time, the metal tub gave way to the bathtub or shower, usually at the woman's insistence. Grace Jordan refused to bathe in the conventional canyon method. She demanded a tub similar to what she had enjoyed in their Willamette Valley home. But with space at a premium, there was no room in the house for a regular tub. So Len improvised by building a concrete tub, half of which stuck out one side of a partition, where the bather got in. The other half, under the sink on the other side of the partition, was where the feet went and the faucet was located. Today Forest Service volunteers staying at Kirkwood use that most unusual tub. Violet Shirley, who volunteered her summers at Kirkwood for many

Figure 16.7. Domestic life also moved outside at the Wilsons' Saddle Creek ranch house, pictured here, possibly with Ethel Wilson standing beside the porch. (Photo courtesy of William Wilson.)

years, used the tub while caretaking there. "How could you not? All the work they did there and everything. It sure beats that old round tub I grew up with."[34]

When the Wilson family first lived at Saddle Creek, they did their laundry on a washboard. Then "Dad found a hand machine. It was us kids' job to pump the old hand-washing machine for mother, while she did the washing."[35] The hand-powered machine "had a round tub, a hand wringer, and there was a ratchet on the side of the handle. You stood there, [pumping] back and forth, to make the gyrator turn. We'd take turns at it 'cause anything was better than scrubbing on that board." The last three years they lived in the canyon, they had a Maytag washing machine packed in on horseback. It was an old gasoline-powered machine "with a ringer and everything. . . . Boy, we thought we had the world by the tail."

Fond memories of canyon life lingered long after people moved away. Bonnie Sterling "loved the solitude of the canyon." Sheep rancher Greg Johnson said, "Probably not a day goes by that I don't miss some part of being down there. I thoroughly loved it. . . . It was just a *neat* life." Violet Shirley echoed almost the same words. Cattle rancher Harold Van Pool said his years on the ranch will "always be a cherished memory." And Esther Hibbs remembered her ten years in the canyon as being "the best years of my life."[36]

For Ace Barton, who spent a memorable childhood and a challenging later life in the canyon, the canyon offered solace and healing. After being stationed in the South Pacific for three years during World War II, Ace returned to his Hells Canyon home. As he walked down toward the Snake River from Hat Point, Oregon, Ace remembered feeling "shook up. I had seen some pretty bad things, being in the infantry and being shot up myself. I didn't know whether I wanted to go back, then I got to thinking maybe isolation might be the best therapy. . . . I would spend hours just sitting on the riverbank throwing rocks at the river, just aimlessly. Finally it all began to gel a little bit."[37]

To look into the eyes of people who have such deep feelings about that special place is to know their souls are still connected to the canyon.

Chapter 17

Rubbering, Neighboring, & Tolerating

Ethel Wilson and Gene McGaffee visited across the river by hollering. "One winter when the passes were snowed in and they didn't see anybody else, they decided that once a week at a certain time of day" they would meet on opposite sides of the river, get down next to the water, and talk to one another. "Their voices carried well. They'd visit about all the housewifely duties that you didn't talk to the men about." Violet Shirley said she thought that saved her mother's sanity that winter.

Ethel Wilson loved the canyon but "craved the companionship of other women."[1] The men not only sympathized with the women's plight but also understood the women's significant contribution to the success of their ranches. Pete Wilson and Fred McGaffee rigged up a private telephone line across the river from Idaho to Oregon between the two homes. Laying that line across the river was "something to watch." From Violet's perspective downstream on the Oregon side, she could see the two men trying to tie together all the ropes they could find. "They had to have it long enough to stretch across the river, so it took every rope on both ranches to do it." They fastened the telephone wire on one end of the rope and loaded the rope coil in a rowboat. "I remember watching from the bank how they rowed so hard and it seemed like the boat was hardly moving. But it was pulling that [rope] across." They fastened the rope on the Oregon side, where Pete had a team of mules tied and ready. The mules "began pulling it and pulled it back [from the river] as far as they could. Then he fastened that to a post he had there, brought the mules back," and hooked them on again. The two men "kept pulling until they got the wire clear across [the river] and fastened to a big alder tree to hold it." Pete put up poles to take the line on up to the house.[2] Ethel and Gene no longer had to holler across the river. Then, around 1932, Pete let the Forest Service hook onto their phone line and later "the Forest Service brought in a line from Riggins all through the Dry Diggins Lookout and on down" to Saddle Creek. The Wilsons could call to Riggins. "But that was the only phone." The Wilsons never did have a connection the other way to Enterprise.[3]

Ranch women used telephones for socializing, but more importantly to conduct ranch business. However, because no phone company was willing to invest the time, labor, and money required to wire the canyon for so few customers, the only way to get a phone system was for neighbors to make the investment and do the work, like Pete Wilson and Fred McGaffee had done. Janie Stone lived only twenty-five miles above Lewiston, but there was no phone company connection between her place and town. They had a telephone from her home to her uncle Emmett Earl's, "then you could talk to anybody you wanted to from there. It was a line [around the immediate region,] not hooked into a Lewiston phone company." Elmer Earl said they used "two wire lines strung on poles from Waha as far up as Billy Creek." Without the cooperation of their neighbors, they would not have had a line at all.

Figure 17.1. The latch string was always out to visitors, like Silas "Si" Bullock, Winniford family friend and long-time canyon resident, pictured here with a young Winniford girl and her pup. (Photo courtesy of HCNRA, Florence Winniford Smith Collection.)

Residents of the canyon and Joseph Plains also volunteered money and labor to build a telephone line connecting White Bird to the little community of Joseph on the Idaho breaks. The line crossed Rice Creek, where the Arams had one of their homes. By tying into that White Bird connection, they could run a line on down to their second place at Getta Creek. They used a battery-operated crank phone at each place. Years later the line to White Bird was in such disrepair, the Joseph Plains people connected across the Salmon River to Cottonwood.[4]

Horace Henderson talked about his parents' phone connection from High Range to Getta Creek. There was no operator. Each ranch had its own individual ring. "If you couldn't ring them, why somebody else would answer, and they'd try to ring them. After a while, you'd get who you were after."[5] The situation had not changed five decades later when the Horrocks lived on Joseph Plains. Sharon said they "had a telephone that was run on just a little old cable out through the trees. Most of the time it didn't work or you couldn't really hear, so we only used it for emergencies."[6]

Hazel Johnson and Grace Jordan visited daily on the phone, "checking in and talking about what could be happening on the river between our outfits." They used a "single line and old fashioned telephones that you rang."[7] Their "central" was in White Bird, but never available at night. The phone line ran from Temperance Creek across the river to the Jordans' at Kirkwood, on to the Circle C at Pittsburg Landing, and then across the mountains to White Bird. When people along the river or in the nearby mountains called one another, they called direct. "They would know our ring" and answer the call. "Those were what we called local calls."[8] But if someone was calling from outside the canyon or vice-versa, they had to talk to the operator (or central) first.[9]

By the time Lem and Doris Wilson moved to Pittsburg Landing in 1951, the telephone company maintained about six miles of line from White Bird to the Salmon River side of the divide. From there to the Snake River, four ranchers maintained the party line. "One would hear all along the line as people picked up their phone to listen in." Though everyone commented on that rural habit of "rubbering," they all seemed to take it in stride. But some were more guarded in their conversations than others. Doris Wilson remembered that Hazel Johnson always spoke "very diplomatically."[10]

All phone service was unreliable, especially during winter when heavy snow in the mountains and frequent storms downed the lines. After ranchers made the initial installations, the Forest Service built and maintained the phone lines to wire the fire lookouts. One of Jess Earl's many jobs while working for the Forest Service was to maintain a phone line on the Oregon side. At Memaloose one line branched south to guard stations at Lookout Mountain and the McGraw. "That was as far as we had to go, that way. The other way it branched at what we called the Elbow on top. One line went down a ways and across the canyon to Mormon, then to the Cow Camp where it dead-ended. The other branch went on down the ridge to the Kneland place and on to Pittsburg." The line hooked on to a line from Granite Creek Lookout in Idaho. Jess always carried extra wire and all the necessary tools on a "good gentle mule." If a line was broken, he would have to "run back both ways for a mile, take a saddle horse, and pull it together to get the come-alongs on it so we could take the slack out."[11]

Neighboring Came in Many Forms

"Eat some, take some, leave some." So read a sign at an old cabin at Dry Diggins.[12] People never locked their doors; if no one was home, stop in anyway. Guests, expected or unexpected, were welcome. "The first thing you'd ask a person when they'd come through the door was if they were hungry or thirsty or needed anything," Sharon Horrocks remembered.[13] Erma Van Pool described the "closeness that people had from working together. They felt insulted if people did not stay for dinner." Erma married Harold after he left the canyon, but shared his canyon values. "Even at our home in Lewiston, we expected people to visit and stay the night."[14]

Neighboring also meant helping with barn or house raising, or with building a corral. "If you needed help you just called on your neighbors. If you were, say, putting up a building, why everyone would just gather on a certain day and up it would go. The women would get together and they'd have a big feast and that's the way they did it." Carl Henderson demonstrated that community commitment by building and maintaining a community corral at the Fly Blow on Joseph Plains, Idaho, which everyone used for branding "or whatever." He never received any compensation for his work.[15]

Hazel Johnson described Celia Titus as "one of the best neighbors we could have had. She was always there for you.... She would saddle up her horse and be on her way to come help." Celia was strong both physically and mentally—"She had to be, she was raised in the country"—and she lived the values of sociability that were consistent with her upbringing. However, as Hazel noted, even though the Titus and Jordan families were the Johnsons' close neighbors, always "there for each other when necessary, we were all very busy, so there wasn't any coming and going and visiting like one would expect people to do in an area like that."

Neighboring manifested itself in unexpected ways. For Hazel Johnson it launched a brief career. When she first arrived at her new home, Guy Huffman sent her a tom turkey. Once she learned Hazel had a tom, neighbor Celia

Figure 17.2. When the weather was pleasant, family, friends, and ranch hands often ate outdoors. Ralph and Lenora Barton are pictured here with unidentified guests. (Photo courtesy of Esther Hibbs.)

Figure 17.3. Earl Hibbs and Esther Leonard stand in front of his Granite Creek home. Earl is cleaning sourdough off his fingers after preparing a meal for Esther and her mother. (Photo courtesy of Esther Hibbs.)

Titus sent her a hen. "I was in the turkey business," Hazel chuckled. Her flock, sometimes as large as one hundred, enjoyed scattering about the countryside. "In addition to other chores, I had to hunt for turkey eggs." They were all up and down the creek. Sometimes the turkeys would fly from the high bank behind the house to the roof of the shearing plant; sometimes they even flew across the river. "But they'd come back, then they'd wander up in the field and the dog and I would get them in at evening time." Every fall, Hazel killed and plucked the turkeys. She watched prices in the paper. When they were favorable, she sold her turkeys to her husband "because I wanted my money for Christmas." Ken, in turn, hired Bert Zimmerly to fly the turkeys to Lewiston to sell. Zimmerly "got a lot of publicity in the *Tribune* over it," Hazel remembered. But one time, Kenneth paid Hazel more money for the turkeys than he received back from their sale. "He put me out of the turkey business in a hurry."[16]

Deep in the canyon at Bernard Creek, the Bartons did not "neighbor" very much. The terrain restricted access south toward Homestead and made downstream travel difficult. Below them were the Johnsons and Jordans, their closest neighbors. "The Jordans were never sociable so we never neighbored with them much, except Len. He'd come by and stay once in a while," since he ran his sheep toward Bernard Creek. When the Bartons moved downstream to Sheep Creek, they would row across to visit the Pete Wilsons "except when the river was too high and dangerous." Ace remembered neighboring with them "quite a bit" and with Kenneth Johnson, "a good neighbor. You couldn't beat him for a neighbor." But because there were "no boats down that way," they could visit only by yelling back and forth across the river. Consequently, the Bartons "did not have much association with Kenneth and his family."[17]

Esther Hibbs went into the canyon in search of solitude—not companionship—and lived out her dream there. When she first went into Hells Canyon aboard the mailboat, on a Washington State College science fieldtrip, her love of the outdoors led to a yearning to live there in the wilderness. From the Johnson Bar boat landing, as she and her friends hiked on up the river, she was sure she had found her ideal wilderness home. Then down the trail rode a handsome cowboy. Surprised and somewhat disappointed to see anyone there, she asked where he came from. "From my place up the river at Granite Creek," he told her. That handsome cowboy became her husband. They shared her wilderness dream for the next ten years, living in the wilds of Granite Creek.

Esther did not mind their lack of company at Granite Creek. Very few strangers passed by; a neighbor's rare visit they long remembered. Once, neighbors Clyde and Alberta Morrow stayed overnight, but getting there was "quite a little jaunt." However, the Hibbses occasionally visited Earl's two sisters. Mary Stickney lived at Johnson Bar, the navigation terminal for the mailboats. So when Esther made her weekly trek downriver to pick up the mail, she usually stayed overnight with Mary. She also stayed frequently with Earl's other sister, Lenora, at Sheep Creek.[18]

Figure 17.4. Stella Winniford and Mamie Hyatt enjoy each other's company while in camp. (Photo courtesy of HCNRA, Florence Winniford Smith Collection.)

Some ranches, like the Stickneys' at Johnson Bar and the Wilsons at Saddle Creek, sat along well-traveled routes. "I think we knew everybody on the river. . . . Our place on the Oregon side was the first night's stop," Marjorie Chadwick remembered. "If you were coming from the Imnaha and going downriver, you could just about make it to our place for the night and our home was always open to travelers for food and lodging." From the Wilsons' place, the traveler would generally "make it the next day to Pittsburg to the Tituses or to Temperance Creek" if they were going on over the saddle to Grangeville. Some of the Wilsons' regular visitors were "old bachelors, kinda skinned up" who panned for gold. They were "real congenial and nice to have around."[19]

At the other end of the canyon, Janie Stone said, "I don't think a week ever went by that we didn't have some kind of company. It was amazing. . . . I used to keep a kettle of beans back on the stove all the time." Many of her visitors were "cowboys looking for cows," but they also had many neighbors. In fact, there were so many, some had to move out, "because it got so crowded they couldn't make a living down there. They had to do something; they all had big families."[20]

To Marjorie Chadwick, the story that epitomized canyon neighboring in the early 1900s was Minnie Marks Shevlin's account of an outing to Fred Jensen's place. Fred Jensen lived at Saddle Creek. He had a huge orchard and garden and always invited his neighbors to take some fruit, even can it on the spot if they wished. In August 1907 he invited Minnie to come for a load of peaches. She, her husband, Frank, and friends from Enterprise "put saddles, pack pockets, and peach boxes into our friend's buggy and took off." They got as far as her parents' home at Freezeout. Fred Jensen was there to get his mail and help with haying. Minnie's party left the buggy and continued on saddle horses; Fred picked up his mail, a jar of butter, and a box of eggs from Minnie's mother and joined them. The small group proceeded on a quarter mile to her Aunt Eliza Wilson's home at the mouth of Freezeout. Minnie dropped off her young son with them; her cousins, Pete and Buck Wilson, joined the travelers. The party en route to the Snake River now numbered ten.

When they reached the mouth of Saddle Creek, she "never saw so much stuff growing in such a small place in [her] life." Bill and Agnes Hiltsley heard they had arrived and crossed over from Idaho to join them. Minnie gathered vegetables from the garden while the others picked peaches. "Fred started a fire and washed his largest cooking utensil" while Minnie prepared a stew of bacon and vegetables. Fred, who only had enough sourdough for himself, "got three or four cans of cream, poured it into the starter, added some vinegar to sour it, and some flour" then whipped the dough until it was bubbling and light. He mixed enough biscuits to fill an oven-size bread pan. For dessert, they each peeled and sliced their own tomatoes and peaches.

Fred had twin cabins—one was his living quarters, the other his bedroom. He put out clean bedding for the women and then began tuning up his five-string banjo. Frank pulled out his violin and they played "some old-time dance music. The echo in the big cliffs just across the river was beautiful." Minnie's brother, Alfred, "would start up and do the calling when they played a quadrille." The music lasted until 1:30 in the morning. Then the men bedded down with a quilt or tarp on an alfalfa shock near the cabin while the three women slept on Fred's clean sheets.

Coffee, bacon, eggs, and sourdough hot cakes made "another nice meal" the next morning. After breakfast, the Hiltsleys turned back home. Pete Wilson and Evan Stephen stayed to help Fred with the haying, and Buck Wilson started up the trail with his .22 rifle, ahead of the others. When the main party reached the Marks' and Wilsons' cow camp, they found Buck with a fire burning, coffee brewing, and four "nice young grouse" ready for the women to prepare. "Clem opened the almost airtight lumber grocery box in the tent and started to mix up a batch of baking powder bannocks. Alfred had sliced potatoes frying. When the grouse browned just right, Buck put them all in a pan, added a small amount of water and set them back to steam while he added flour to the grease and stirred up a nice batch of grouse gravy." After eating lunch, they continued on to Freezeout. The men removed the horses' saddles, unpacked the peach boxes, and loaded them into the buggy. Minnie and Frank picked up their son and headed up the road to their ranch; Alvin and Gertie went down the road toward Enterprise.[21]

Women, who might have been most susceptible to feeling isolated, discovered ingenious ways to compensate and recognized even the smallest encounters; other women just plain relished the isolation. "They say four walls get the best of you," Janie Stone said, "but I never let it get the best of me. All the women I knew seemed to like living there." In reading his mother's diary, Doug Tippett realized that at times she felt left out. "She would say that all the men rode off [and the older children] for their daily work and she'd be left out on the porch just looking out. They'd be gone until late at night, and she was expected to have this big meal." She had a large family of boys but only two daughters. However, after Jidge, her husband, died, "she looked back on those times as the happiest times of her life. Then she missed it, but I think that is typical."[22]

Canyon Visitors

Neighboring extended to canyon visitors. Some of the ranchers' favorite visitors were descendants of people who originally lived there. Nez Perce people came to the canyon to fish and hunt, passed through on their way from the Lapwai reservation to the Wallowa Valley, or lived in the area with a non-Indian. For them, "neighboring" was a two-way arrangement. Their reciprocal relationship always involved sharing gifts, food, favors, and hospitality.

The Pete Wilsons looked forward to visits from Mrs. Hill and her grandson. They lived on the Imnaha and once a year drove a team of horses and buggy, with "her camp outfit and everything," past the Wilson home at Saddle Creek on their way up the river to fish salmon. "She always made it a point to stay all night with my mother. They enjoyed each other. She was always bringing us kids moccasins." Marjorie remembered "one time she brought a pair of buckskin gloves with a big gauntlet that was all beadwork with roses on it. I had those for years. We always loved to see her."[23]

Dennis Brown's grandparents lived along a "favorite Nez Perce river crossing" from Cave Gulch to Cache Creek. For a number of years they watched Nez Perce men in hunting parties cross the river by holding on to the horses' manes and tails. When his grandfather bought a rowboat, "they never got wet again." If he was busy haying, "they'd holler and holler, and finally Grandpa would come down with his boat, and he'd row them all across." When they finished hunting, he rowed them back. Dennis added, "They were always good about leaving venison and fish and also supplied the family with moccasins and other items of clothing."[24]

The Earls' place at Captain John was a traditional Nez Perce fishing site, where they built stone walls out into the water and used a dip net to catch the salmon, or they "would build scaffolds out [from a basalt wall at Captain John Rapids] and dip along the wall. They caught lots of fish there." Sometimes as many as a hundred people would come to fish in the spring, with "scads of horses." From there they continued on their way to open range in the mountains to fatten up the animals. When they got through fishing, they would have a rodeo. The horses were all "full of bunch grass, spirited and needed to get broken in a little."[25]

Elmer Earl remembered visiting with many Nez Perce people as a boy. They were "great to visit with" and would trade if they wanted something. Their trade stock might be a manufactured or homemade blanket, but "they always made us kids moccasins and gloves." Joe Albert, an elderly and generous Nez Perce man, regularly brought gifts for Elmer and his brother. Elmer explained how Joe sized the gifts: "He would count the wrinkles [on the foot or hand], and come back and have moccasins and gloves that fit."[26]

Elmer's parents had a small flourmill and reciprocated by giving Nez Perce visitors some flour. One time they borrowed his dad's boat and accidentally broke the oar. They brought it back, showed his dad the broken oar, and said, "tomorrow." The next day "there was a new oar in the boat. They sent somebody clear to town and bought an oar. That was about twenty-five miles, one day's trip."

The salmon run usually began mid-May and lasted fifteen or twenty days. Afterward "the river was plumb full of eels, which they'd catch by the hundreds of pounds." The Nez Perce cleaned the eel, spread them out, and dried them. "Then they used huts made of willows and blankets, six to eight feet high and six foot square on the inside. They put sticks across to lay the fish on," built a small fire underneath, and by placing leaves on the fire "made smoke with a sage flavored, fuzzy-leafed willow." Elmer said they sat in the tent, "fiddling with that fire and would come out with their eyes watering."[27] Janie Stone, who lived nearby, said her husband, Ralph, had often stayed with Joe Green of Lapwai when he was a kid. As an adult he always looked forward to Joe's visits. "They'd fry those eels and cook them on a stick over the bonfire." Her husband loved to eat with Joe and his family.[28]

Slim Southwick was half Nez Perce and known locally as "Indian Slim." Over the years, he had worked on different ranches as a packer and herder. After Jim and Dick Blankenship at Rolling Bar left the canyon, they told Slim he could stay in the house if he would feed the cattle. He put in a big garden and canned the produce, so he had ample food. But his clothing was inadequate for the harsh winter ahead. Ted Grote had been flying groceries into the Blankenships' and stopped by when Indian Slim was there alone. "He had been down there all winter. His hair was long and all, and all he had was just a little coat with no lining—a denim jacket. And it was cold, I mean twenty below zero. He asked me if I'd give him a haircut." Ted had nothing to cut with but promised to bring something the next day.

"So when I went to town I bought a down coat because the old guy was just feeding the cows for nothing, just to have a place to live." He also brought his wife's hand clippers, a pair of scissors, and a comb. "I think he looked like he was butchered, but anyway I got that hair off. When I got ready to leave, I gave him the coat. He just stood there and cried. It was cold and I remember him standing there crying. He brought a couple cans of pickles or beans that he canned and gave them to us."

A Bunch of Misfits

"People from the outside, even practical-minded ones, sometimes spoke of an ominous air hanging over the silences of the deeper gorge between the end of the boat run and Hells Canyon proper."[29] Esther Hibbs lived in that section of the canyon and did not remember any "ominous air." She and Earl, however, were conscious of their isolation and wary of strangers. They relied on their sixth sense in judging them. Once when they were home at Granite Creek, a man by the name of Marshall stopped at their place. With a life goal of climbing every mountain in the United States, the Seven Devils were next on his list. The Hibbses invited him to stay in their tent near the orchard as long as he wished. Marshall accepted their hospitality, but the offer surprised him. "You people haven't even asked me my name." Esther explained that "in this country, you don't ask too many people about their background."

Marshall was a good man, but the Hibbses and most other canyon residents also crossed paths with objectionable people. Not everyone was sociable, helpful, and congenial. To ignore those undesirable people paints an imperfect image of life in the canyon. Some genial but eccentric individuals and some out-and-out despicable people lived there. Fellow residents knew what kind of people they were and generally tolerated their presence. But strangers stood out, "especially if they came in on foot."[30]

Since suspicious-looking characters showed up at Saddle Creek from time to time, Pete Wilson made sure his children carried pistols with them. He admonished the children, "If you ever have to shoot, shoot to kill, 'cause you may not have a second chance." Once, while Marjorie was dressing, she looked up and saw a stranger at her window. She screamed and ran into the living room. Her mother and her brother Allen were alone in the house with her. Allen took his gun, crossed the ditch, and found the stranger chopping wood at their woodpile. When Allen asked him what he was doing, he said he hoped to get something to eat and was chopping their wood to pay for it. So he came into the house and Mrs. Wilson fed him breakfast. Marjorie remembered him wearing "a pair of old overalls and shirt, but where those overalls gapped we saw a pair of dress pants."

After breakfast, Allen rowed the stranger across the river. He asked for instructions to "the nearest settlement." Allen told him how to reach White Bird, but as he rowed back across, he noticed that the man had turned right; to reach White Bird, he should have gone left down the trail. The Wilsons later learned that the same man had been at Fred and Gene McGaffee's, chopping wood. "Fred put him on the run." That fall, while riding up Rough Creek, Pete Wilson came to a cave where he had once stored his dynamite. He saw that someone had made a bed of hay, using hay from the Wilson haystack nearly a mile away. Upon further investigation he found thirty to fifty empty food jars and realized that man had been living off the Wilsons—for how long, he had no idea.

Another time Ethel Wilson was gathering winter squash when an old man came by with his nine-year-old "daughter." They stayed the night. That evening Pete asked the man his name. Pete had heard of him but did not know anything about him. When the two left the next morning, Pete called someone in Enterprise. He learned that a poor family was camping with "a whole litter of children" on the upper Imnaha River. That old man had bought one of the girls from her parents and was taking her out of state to Idaho County. "Dad told the sheriff, and the Idaho authorities came and picked him up. He admitted he was using her." The old guy ended up in an Idaho prison.[31]

Not all questionable characters came in from the outside; some were homegrown. Max Walker described the head of one prominent canyon family as a man who "really lacked the Lord." Did the canyon make him mean? "No, he was a mean person to start with." He occasionally "slapped" his wife around and "caused her a lot of discomfort." He even beat a young woman boarding with them. The man "took an instant dislike" to his stepson, who lived with them a short time, and "ended up running him off." The young man moved into an old cabin on the south fork of Rush Creek and tried to trap and live off the land. The winter of 1918 he disappeared. "Word passed up and down the river. . . . Pete Wilson, Billy Winniford, and Jack Titus, formed a search party but did not find him."[32]

That spring a second search party found the young man's remains near the cabin, leaning against a tree with a gun across his knees and the hindquarters of a deer hanging in the tree. No one knows exactly when they last saw him, but they concluded he had died sometime that December or January. Forest Service ranger Gerald Tucker supposed his death was related to the 1918 flu epidemic.[33] Ace Barton had another theory. The old man "kicked him out in the middle of the winter; he went up there to live and trap; and the kid starved to death. That's what it boiled down to."[34]

Unknown locals killed a man near Divide Creek, apparently because he was secretive. "When he came to the region, he wouldn't divulge what he was up to," Jim Chapman explained. "The people thought something was wrong with him. They knew what caliber gun he had. One day, some of the men found his gun on a trail. Legend goes that someone picked up his gun and shot the man with his own gun. The man got to his cabin before he died." The two suspects "pulled their freight before anything could be done to arrest them."[35]

It Takes All Kinds

Not all eccentric canyon behavior was illegal—it was just, well, different. People in the Lewiston Valley like to tell the story of George Ackerman. He came to the country in 1879 and proved up his homestead ten miles above Asotin. He was "gregarious, convivial, and loved to attend the local 'dos,'" but he was a lonely bachelor. So, twelve years after moving there, at the age of forty-four, Ackerman decided to respond to a Chicago matrimonial brochure featuring a raven-haired, German beauty. She agreed to marry him under the following conditions: he would provide a good well or nice spring so she would not have to drink from a dirty river called Snake; he would build her a comfortable rock house along the lines of an Alpine chalet—one with humans above and animals below; and she would have a nice orchard. (The list continued but those were the main requirements.) George agreed and began the house-building project, hauling rock "to the point of becoming obsessed."[36]

One day he got a letter from her: "I cannot accept your proposal," it read. George stopped going to Asotin, he never again opened his mailbox, and never spoke to another woman. He even stopped raising stock because "it involved females. But his building became a mania." Over the next thirty years he moved an estimated twenty-five thousand tons of rocks to build two fine rock houses and a two-mile fence around his orchard.

Local lore claims that George Ackerman wore women's clothing whenever he went to town. Dick Rivers, who as a child often visited Ackerman with his grandmother, said that "simply was not true." He concluded that somewhere in the telling, Ackerman's story became confused with that of another man who lived alone on the Grande Ronde River, although Dick didn't recall that man ever going to town. That man made his own clothes, including dresses. "Once a rancher rode by and saw this man sitting down near his garden, reclining against the tree, with a dress on. He rode by a few days later and the man was still there." When the traveler stopped to check, he found the man dead. Ackerman's only family was a sister in Germany. Dick wanted to set the record straight, because there was "no one here to stand up for him."[37]

No one considered "Dirty Dick" (not Rivers) a nice man, not because he was a bootlegger but because people suspected him of cattle rustling and having incestuous relations with his older daughter. Canyon residents shunned men like him; conversely, most residents welcomed a moonshiner. Producing moonshine was common practice in the canyon, generally done for individual consumption but sometimes for profit. When Dirty Dick lived on Sluice Creek, he sold his "five gallon crops" on the Imnaha. By braiding rawhide around the jugs, he "could take them on a sawbuck saddle, put canvas on the top to keep yellow jackets out, and haul it over to Imnaha to peddle it." Did people ignore his other, suspected, behavior? Apparently so.[38]

Fred Reed and his father, George, took up a homestead at Kirby Creek after their Percheron business folded. Fred had some cattle but also "went to moonshinin' and made more money off that than off his cattle."[39] Press Brewrink hauled freight up the river to the mouth of Indian Gulch, between Rogersburg and a mining camp on the Idaho side. Someone always paid him in advance for "chicken feed" (cracked corn which they bought by the ton), burners, and fuel oil for "incubators." Brewrink sometimes hauled copper pipe and barrels. "Dad delivered several loads at the requested site, and by the next weekly trip it would be gone into the hills," his son James recalled. Carrying a heavy load up the gulch weekly should leave some visible trail, yet Press saw none. "This was no small trick." Someone up there had a large moonshine operation going, but Press never knew who it was.[40]

Some of the Earls made moonshine for sale, when they weren't panning for gold. They had to have enough money "for things that were necessary." The reason their cabins had a front and back door, Janie Stone explained, was so when someone looked out the front window and saw a "revenuer" come up the hill, they could "skedaddle out the back door and out of sight."[41] Elmer Earl said "practically everybody did it. It was a way to avoid starvation and pay your taxes." Whenever it looked like they might lose their place, "they'd go out and make ten gallons of booze. It was haphazardly done." Elmer remembered Roy McCoy, who made moonshine in an old tunnel toward the mouth of Cottonwood Creek. The remains of a little rock cabin sit right on top of the bank above the tunnel. McCoy "just squatted there" so he could make his moonshine. "Making moonshine is a hell of a job. Most people wouldn't do that much work." Elmer thought, however, that the superior moonshine came from red-headed Cora Fountain's still up Cave Gulch. "That old gal made whiskey that was out of this world. Nobody ever did find out just how she made it." Cora was a "little bit of a woman," who along with her brother, Chet Coburn, ran the outfit up Cottonwood Creek. They never made very much, but it had a grand reputation, "far better than Dick Carter's product."[42]

Dick Carter (not to be confused with "Dirty Dick") was the canyon's most famous bootlegger, perhaps because of Grace Jordan's story about him. By the time Max Walker met him, Carter's notorious career had ended. He had sold the Carter mansion and was living at the head of Kirby Creek in the "old C. J. Hall place." Max said he was "kind of an old Dutchman, hot-tempered but kind of likable."[43] With the exception of Billy McGaffee, no one knew anything about Carter's background. One time, however, when Carter was drunk, he told Billy that he had been a doctor, had a beautiful wife, and had shot a man whom he suspected of having an affair with her. The court exonerated him, but his children turned against him. Embittered, he changed his last name to Carter—his mother's maiden name—and headed west.[44]

Carter was an intelligent businessman. He had stills inside what looked like rock shelters at several locations on Kirkwood Creek, up Sheep Creek in the Clark's Fork area, and other places. Max Walker described two of them on Clark's Fork. Dug into the hillside and laid up with logs, they measured about ten feet by twelve feet. Carter made tin roofs from aviation gas cans—the gas he used for his burner under the still—and covered them with moss. "Unless you stumbled right on 'em, you couldn't see 'em." A small, V-shaped trough flume, elevated on little stilts ran out of the creek and around some trees to one of the "cabins" where he set his mash barrels. "Inside that cabin there was a platform on each side. You could walk in the middle. There was room for four fifty-gallon wooden barrels on each side.... That was where he set his mash." Carter used cracked corn, but Max did not know where he got it.[45] The neighbors remembered Carter hiring various men to pack in ten horse loads of sugar (about two hundred pounds to the horse) and the equivalent amount of cracked corn. "They'd go up into Lost Valley over various trails that were more or less hidden and camouflaged with stock pastured in there. And when they'd come out, they'd have a ten-gallon keg of whiskey on each side."[46]

Carter's product was top quality. He "polished that old still until it shined like a moon, and he washed it out with soda and scoured it." He would also double-run all of the whiskey. After he ran it through the first time with the mash and distilled it, "why he started the old still up and ran the raw whiskey back through it again so it was actually real pure." To color it, he ran it through charcoaled oak kegs. Max Walker estimated that Carter sold it for five to six dollars per gallon jug—the going rate at the time—but did not sell much locally because everyone else made moonshine for local consumption.[47] When Murrielle McGaffee taught the Jordan children, she became well acquainted with Dick. She liked him and respected him as an educated man. "He told me himself" he was selling his whiskey to the Lewiston Elks Club.[48]

Dick Carter was clever, not easily caught. Jess Earl, who worked for a probation agency for eighteen months, said he knew Carter (although he called him Clarence Carter) "who used to make moonshine at Kirkwood Creek. He shot at me a time or two." Carter was not the only one to shoot at Jess. "Finally it got to the point that we were spotted and it really can get dangerous. So I made up my mind that I had enough of it and quit."[49] It took the patience of an undercover agent to finally put Carter in jail. Max Walker recalled seeing "some guy" hanging around Riggins, befriending the locals, going to the local dances—just fitting in. "After a couple of three years, everybody figured he was a fixture around the community, a regular Joe." Dick and the other local bootleggers often took a little product to the dances for their friends, so when the man asked Dick to sell him a ten-gallon keg of whiskey, Dick agreed. They met at an old sawmill on Cow Creek, and "Dick took him over across the creek to where he had the keg buried." The man paid him, and then asked Dick to pack it to his car for him. "Dick said he knew he was had right there, so he just balked on that." The agent got him for selling whiskey but could not hang a charge of transporting whiskey on him. Dick served nine months of a year's sentence in the Boise penitentiary, then returned to the canyon.[50]

Figure 17.5. One opportunity to socialize with neighbors and canyon visitors was when fishing for sturgeon. Here James Wilson (left) and Max Walker show off their sturgeon caught near Saddle Creek the winter of 1938-39. (Photo courtesy of William Wilson.)

That's when Max Walker met Dick Carter. One day in 1933, a year after the repeal of Prohibition, Max made his regular weekly mail run to Lucille for his neighbors.[51] He took Dick's mail back to him. Dick opened it and discovered a bill for $12.50—tax on the ten-gallon keg of whiskey he sold to the agent. "Dick hit the ceiling…stomped on his hat…and everything else when he got that thing."[52] A short time later he showed up "all in a sweat" at the Jordans to ask Len Jordan what he should do. "I'd send them a money order for $10 or $11," Len advised. "Well they might come right back and tax me for another 1,000 gallons," replied Dick. Len assured him the judge had not convicted him for making more than ten gallons. "They couldn't do that."[53] Apparently Carter paid, closing the door on his illegal operations.

An interesting postscript to Carter's life provides another glimpse into the lives of some canyon bachelors. Like George Ackerman in the late 1800s, Carter also "ordered" a bride. Mae was a nurse in Baltimore. After getting acquainted through correspondence, they decided to marry. Carter sent Mae some money to come out west, got arrested for moonshining, telegraphed her what happened, and suggested she postpone the trip. She came anyway. "She evidently burned her bridges behind her," Murrielle Wilson surmised. "He had a bunch of horses and she was a good rider, so she helped him get his horses out on pasture and get ready to go to jail." During Carter's incarceration, Mae stayed with Mr. and Mrs. Clay Davis and voluntarily packed the mail around the canyon, just for something to do. Every week she went to Lucille, picked up everyone's mail, and then rode the trails delivering it. "She also helped the Davises and rode down to look after the Carter place." When Dick got out of jail, she met him with his horse in tow, all shod and ready to ride. Murrielle McGaffee thought they were married when Mae first came west and were still married after Carter's release. Max Walker was sure they were divorced before Carter went to jail. At any rate, at some point, Mae and Dick divorced, and she married Fred Ballard, a canyon resident and one of her mail recipients.[54]

Martin's Murder

A rancher lies dead outside his burned cabin. Alongside his head lies his brown Stetson. A bullet hole above the headband is testimonial to a killer's sharp aim. In the ashes of the cabin a spent revolver and the charred bones of another person rest inexplicably together in a crumpled heap. The rumble of a now distant thunderstorm echoes the violence of hours before. Patrick McCarthy, who spent four years researching the murder, called the crime an "anachronism" that belonged in the nineteenth century yet was "symbolic of the inhospitable nature of the canyon."[55]

Esther Hibbs remembered Earl's telling her about three men who were spending the winter at a deserted cabin on Sheep Creek, a few miles downriver from their Granite Creek place. Occasionally one of them would go to Johnson Bar to pick up supplies from the boat, but every time one man left camp, another remained behind and the third always watched the man meeting the boat. "We had a good idea they were hiding out. We never knew why. We just always suspected it." Earl Hibbs had good reason to be suspicious of unknown neighbors and unusual behavior after the murder of his seventy-two year old father, Martin.

It was late June 1934. Martin's wife had died eight years earlier, leaving Martin and his youngest son, Earl, to run their Granite Creek ranch. The two men went to a Forest Service meeting in Riggins, Idaho, but first asked Joe Anderson and another man, who were prospecting at Warm Springs, to keep an eye on the place and tend to the irrigating. After the Riggins meeting, Earl went on to Pullman, Washington, to see his fiancée, Esther, and Martin headed home. He got home the next evening, "unpacked the mule, unsaddled his horse, took his spurs off, and put them by the cabin." His grandson, Ace Barton, speculates that Martin then "started to walk away from the cabin to turn out the mule and horse when somebody shot him from behind."[55]

Ace and his widowed mother, Lenora, were living on the Imnaha River at the time. Lenora had not heard from her father and decided to ride over for a visit. Pete Wilson helped her cross the river to Idaho. She rode up Granite Creek. When she reached the homestead, she found her father dead under the cherry tree and the two-story log cabin burned to the ground. "It about done her in, because she had just lost her husband a few months earlier and her brother the year before."[56] Lenora's mettle held; she went back down to the river and called over to the Wilsons for help. Pete rode downstream to the McGaffees to use their phone. He called Idaho County sheriff Walter Altman and the county coroner George Trenary. Max Walker was twenty-five miles downriver picking raspberries with Len Jordan and John "Posey" Bouguet when Clay Davis, a rancher who lived on the upper reaches of Kirkwood Creek, arrived with news of the murder. They saddled their horses and a mule and rode to the murder scene. When they reached Granite Creek that evening, Pete Wilson, Billy McGaffee, and Clive Lloyd were already there. Later that night Coroner Trenary and Sheriff Altman arrived. They impaneled a coroner's jury at the crime scene.

Figure 16.3. Although all canyon ranch homes were remote by today's standards, this Idaho cabin at Granite Creek, three miles above the river and well beyond the head of navigation, was especially remote. It was here that Martin Hibbs died at the hands of an unknown assailant. (Photo courtesy of Esther Hibbs.)

Hibbs's body faced west, lying under a huge cherry tree about thirty-five feet from the cabin. His head, with a bullet hole in the back, rested partially on his saddle.[58] What brought Martin's life to such a grisly end generated wide speculation. Max Walker surmised that seventy-two-year-old Hibbs topped out around the north end of Seven Devils and went to his summer cow range at the head of Sheep Creek. There Martin spent the night. The next morning he left one horse and a load of salt and rode on down to his home with groceries, horseshoes, and the remaining supplies. He unpacked the groceries from the packhorse, carried one load into the cabin, and set it against the wall next to the staircase. Max saw the remainder of the second load leaning against the rock foundation on the west side of the house.[59] Martin must have placed it there temporarily and returned for the saddle.

Did the unidentified man in the cabin think he was shooting an intruder and fire his weapon before realizing it was Martin? Did he intentionally kill him? Or was a third party involved, someone who was gunning for one man and killed the other to cover his tracks? The official ruling was murder/suicide. Joe Anderson was named as the guilty party. Patrick McCarthy and Ace Barton agreed. Esther and Earl Hibbs, however, concluded a third person down the hill shot up toward the house. "It couldn't have come from the guy in the house," because of the way the bullet entered Martin's head. Max Walker concluded that if the unidentified dead man was Joe Anderson, and if he killed Martin, it was probably no accident. Martin was "moving around" too much for Anderson not to know who he was. He believed Hibbs was the target, but not necessarily targeted by the man in the cabin. Walker suspected longtime canyon residents. According to Walker, Martin Hibbs had some enemies. "He was quarrelsome and cantankerous, quick-tempered. He'd fight a buzz saw if he had to, but he was tougher than an old boiled owl's hoot." Bickering among landowners, confrontational and ill-tempered personalities, and old hostilities were "characteristic of the canyon." Authorities tracked Anderson's partner to Boise and proved he had been out of the canyon before the murder happened, thus dashing suspicions that he was the killer. The body in the cabin was never identified and the murder remained unsolved. "It's a mystery and probably the truth will never be uncovered," Max Walker concluded. "It's one of the mysteries of the canyon here."[60]

The wild and isolated topography of Hells Canyon facilitated the escape of Martin Hibbs's killer; it enabled most Prohibition-era moonshiners to conduct business. For a few people, the topography encouraged a penchant to break or push the limits of the law. The natural landscape also determined how and when the residents communicated with one another, the frequency and circumstances of neighboring, even their willingness to turn a blind eye to eccentric behavior. It fostered acts of friendship, hospitality, reciprocity, and helpfulness. People relied on common sense to know when to be neighborly and when to be wary, but for most of the people living in and traveling through Hells Canyon and the Middle Snake River country, the latchstring was always out.

Chapter 18

Events Memorable & Heartbreaking

Canyon hospitality grew partially from necessity, partially from desire, and partially from a sense of responsibility. Children learned that responsibility from their chores, listening to their parents, observing their surroundings, and through their education. Everyone learned to be reliable; others depended upon them in numerous ways. "When you'd tell them that you'd be at such and such a place at a certain time, if you weren't, they'd come lookin' for you. There were so many mishaps," Ace Barton explained. "People really observed that."[1] If someone needed help, another would be there if possible. But if there was no way of reaching help during an emergency, then resilience and resourcefulness were ones only recourse. Although accidents and medical emergencies were not strangers to canyon life, folks used a measure of common sense, reason, and frequently their faith to see them through. The people knew how to make the good times memorable and the difficult times bearable.

"There Were So Many Mishaps"

Snake River is dangerous. Rapids, whirlpools, and unexpected water fluctuations can seize even the most cautious person; carelessness often proves fatal. A treacherous whirlpool can arise unexpectedly. Ralph Beard described this phenomenon before the Hells Canyon dam went in. Smooth water would all at once start whirling and open up into a big thirty- or forty-foot pool. "Water would just be pouring down in that [pool] just like water pouring down a stovepipe." Jay Dobbin told Beard about watching a big fir tree come down the river. Suddenly "it just started whirling and this tree finally stood on end. It went right down in one of them holes." Dobbin watched for quite a while. "Pretty soon the tree came up again down the river two or three hundred yards. It just shot straight up clear out of the water. There wasn't a limb on that tree." If a whirlpool can do that to a tree, think what it could do to humans. Al Victor's two boys were fortunate.[2] During spring when the river was high, the boys went fishing in their boat. One time after going through a rapid, they immediately came upon a whirlpool. They couldn't avoid it. "The boys were thrown out of their boat down into it." Al, their father, who was watching from an elevated position on shore, said he saw them "standing down on the bottom and all they could do was just look straight up, clinching each other's arms, and just a sayin' their prayers. Pretty soon the water started filling up from the bottom and they washed right back up to the top. That was the last time they ever played in the river."[3]

More often than not, the river was not so forgiving. In 1911 Frank and Alberta Hiltsley started upriver from Sheep Creek headed to Saddle Creek. Alberta was afraid of boats and refused to board, so while she walked along shore, Frank took the boat. She started first.

Figure 18.1. Wilma and Florence Winniford, playing in Rush Creek under the watchful eye of the photographer, would have already been warned about the dangers of the river and creeks. (Photo courtesy of HCNRA, Florence Winniford Smith Collection.)

After waiting and waiting for him at Saddle Creek, Alberta called across the river to the Wilsons for their help. From both shores they searched and searched before accepting that Frank had probably had an accident and drowned. Hoping to raise the body to give it a proper burial, Pete dynamited the Saddle Creek eddy. Up came a twelve-foot sturgeon but no body. They later found Frank's body at the mouth of Hutton Gulch, where Pete and Jack Titus buried him. Alberta moved from their Three Creeks homestead right after the accident but did not leave the canyon. She just relocated to another homestead between Race Creek and Bernard Creek.[4]

Over a half century later, in 1972, tragedy struck Lem and Doris Wilson. Their twenty-three-year-old son, Gary, died in a boating accident. He and his brother, Ray, had just left the boat dock at Pittsburg Landing. The motor quit. The boat drifted, began to sink, and then capsized. Lem witnessed the accident. He boarded his nearby plane and began an aerial search. Two outfitters arrived by boat and found Ray hanging onto a gas can, but they did not see Gary. The Idaho County sheriff, friends, and neighbors helped Lem search for his son. Ultimately, accepting the worse, Lem hired someone to keep watch at the mouth of Somers Creek. About three weeks later Gary's body appeared.[5]

Hazel and Saxby Boles had a ranch near the mouth of Wolf Creek. One spring day in 1924 they rowed their three children across the river to a sandbar to play. While the children played, Hazel and Saxby ventured into the river. The current caught Hazel and pulled her down. Saxby tried to reach her, but the current caught him too. Finally Hazel surfaced and made it to shore, but the river swept Saxby away. The children watched from shore.[6]

Parents always cautioned their children to be careful around the river. But from the child's perspective, witnessing something tragic like the Boles children did, permanently etched that warning in their minds. Marjorie Chadwick remembered watching her father and uncle using grappling hooks in big eddies near their home, looking for the bodies of three drowning victims. Less tragic but equally memorable was watching animal corpses float by, victims of an upriver flood. Marjorie was only five or six years old, but remembers "standing up on this little plank by our Saddle Creek house watching the river." A team of buff-colored Clydesdales, still harnessed together, floated down the river, dead. "I can remember seeing pigs, chickens, cows come down. You see something like that and you never forget it. You know enough to watch that river."[7]

Canyon inhabitants' lives were fraught with danger. Even when others were close enough to help, an accident might have a tragic ending. Young Donald Johnson received help, but too late. John and Jennie Johnson had a sheep ranch near the mouth of the Imnaha River. One day two of their six sons—Donald and Murland—were hunting along Snake River when Donald "had the misfortune of accidentally shooting himself." His ten-year-old brother ran to the ranch for his mother, took her to Donald, and then went to their neighbors' ranches looking for help. It was roundup time, and he could only find two men. They reached Donald and his mother at dark. Jennie Johnson had torn up most of her clothing for bandages and tourniquets. The men gave her their coats and improvised a stretcher. Using a lantern the men had brought, Jennie led the way as they began to climb the steep mountainside. By daylight the exhausted party had only reached the ridge at the head of Schuler Canyon. Jennie returned to her home to take care of her younger sons and then rode downriver to her neighbors' house. Fortunately both women were home. They saddled up, rode to a telephone at the Joe Clemmens' place near Buckhorn Springs, and reached Dr. Hockett at Enterprise. Word spread to John Johnson and other ranchers at the Tippett ranch roundup headquarters. Sixteen men helped the two stretcher bearers, taking turns as they climbed the mountain to the nearest road. From there Donald rode to Enterprise by car, reaching the hospital forty hours after the shooting. "The wound and shock proved to be too great an ordeal for him. He passed on the next Monday morning. He was only thirteen at the time of his death."[8]

One winter Sharon and Buster Horrocks were riding down to the Salmon River to get cattle that had been "rimmed in" and were starving. In order to reach them, Sharon had to leave her horse and move out onto a "straight, steep mountain side" that was sloughing off. "I was moving along a bluff, using my hands and moving sideways with my feet." Buster's old dog got spooked and tried to run between Sharon and the mountain. She lost her footing. "I shot my feet out and started down the hill, digging in with my fingernails. I felt a hand grab the back of my collar." Buster told her to hold still for a while until he could get his footing. "My fingers were just gripping into the mountain. I was very strong, but he was very, very strong." Buster pulled Sharon up to safety.[9]

Ellen Hibbs became seriously ill at the Hibbses' cow camp. Her husband, Martin, and son Earl had gone back to the ranch; only Edna, their young daughter, was there to care for Ellen. Fred McGaffee, who was at his nearby camp, learned she was ill and rode to Granite Creek to tell Martin and Earl, then home to tell his wife, Gene, who was Ellen's dear friend. They rode back to Ellen with their nine-year-old son, Everett, and joined Martin and Earl. Ellen was so sick, the only way to move her the twenty-five miles to the nearest road was on a stretcher. The men lashed lodgepole pines together for her bed and then proceeded to "accustom" two mules to hauling the bed by having young Everett ride in it.

When the mules were ready to make the long and dangerous trip, Fred and Martin took turns leading the front mule while Earl rode the back mule. Edna, Everett, and Gene followed behind, leading a couple of packhorses. "Most of those trails are steep inclines," Gene wrote "When we were going up the hill, her pillow faced the lead mule. Then going down the other side, we reversed her position. . . . She always greeted us with a smile and some witty remark about the elegance of her equipage, or how extraordinary such a procession would surely look to an observer." From an Oregon lookout tower, an "observer" was indeed watching. The ranger on duty saw they were headed to Horse Heaven Lookout in Idaho and called to tell the ranger there. "When we appeared at that station late that afternoon, we were greeted with an unexpectedly cordial welcome." They spent the night at the lookout. The next day, around three o'clock, they reached the home of a friend, where the McGaffees kept their car. Help was now only fifteen miles away.[10]

Ellen was fortunate to have competent help. Max Walker had to rely on his own resources. He was alone on a ridge somewhere between Brownlee Saddle and Kirby Creek. Reaching to catch an unmarked lamb, he stepped on a rock and broke his ankle. "I looked down at my ankle and it was just turned up the side of my leg on the outside. So I shoved it back in place, pushed on it with my other foot, jumped up and it just popped out again." He crawled to his tent and got his new Hanley catalog. (Len Jordan had stopped by a bit earlier and brought it along with some handkerchiefs and short-sleeve shirts. Hanley's was a department store in Pendleton.) "I folded it real stiff and bound it on the inside of my ankle with four bandana handkerchiefs." Max spent the night on the ridge.

The next morning, after getting the sheep headed up the ridge, he crawled about three-quarters of a mile down to the bottom of the canyon, where he had his horse staked by the tent. He dragged the saddle out of the tent, got onto a big rock, saddled the horse, then pulled himself up on it. Max rode down Myers Creek to the shearing plant at Little Bar. He used the phone in the cook tent to call Dick Maxwell and Len Jordan, asking that Dick stay with the sheep while Len took him home. At Kirkwood, Max soaked his ankle in hot water, taped it with two-inch tape, and made a crutch. Grace Jordan's parents from Enterprise met them at Imnaha and drove Max back to town. By now four days had passed since the accident. The doctor at Enterprise told Max he had "done a good job setting" the break, so back to work he went. Max said he wore that tape for more than a year.[11]

Folks sometimes avoided a serious accident because they just got lucky. During the middle of the night, a room-size boulder crashed down to the Barton place. It missed the chicken coop and stopped between the blacksmith shop and barn. It could just as easily have rolled right over the house, with the family inside.[12] Another time, Ralph Beard was taking a string of about twenty mules to the shearing plant when a heavy rainstorm began. "I stopped in a swale of green pines," dismounted, rolled a cigarette, and smoked until the rain let up. He continued on to about sixty feet past the trees when a "heck of a thunder and bolt of lightning hit all at the same time." It shook Ralph and frightened the mules, which all ran up beside him. Then Ralph saw, about a hundred yards around the point, lightning had struck "a big pine tree about three feet through" and reached all the way down the road toward the shearing plant. "If I hadn't stopped, rolled my cigarette and smoked it, I'd have probably been right there when it happened. It would have killed the whole bunch of us."

Pete Wilson was a cowboy of rodeo fame. He knew how to break horses and was an expert horseman. However, even the best horsemen can have an accident. Pete got lucky. While he was breaking a horse in the Black Butte country, the colt slipped and went down on Pete's leg. "There was kind of a limb, or a root, where the cattle had dug it out. [The colt's] forefeet went under the root and through it." Pete tried "every way in the world to break loose." Finally he managed to get his knife out of his pocket, hoping to dig his way out. He scratched futilely at the ground, but "the horse would struggle on him and he just couldn't get out." Finally the horse lay still. Pete resumed his digging. Then, when he "was almost ready to put the horse to sleep," suddenly "the horse started struggling." The horse pulled out his leg from under the snare and got up on one leg. Pete eased out his own leg, worked the horse loose, and made it back home about ten o'clock that night.[13]

Young Kappy Wilson "rode her horse into the sickle bar on the mowing machine." Her sister, Marjorie, was sure "the old mare was trying to scrape her off." Kappy cut her leg around the knee. "Well, the folks knew they didn't have time to go to the Imnaha for a car" and take her on to Enterprise. So Pete got out his suturing outfit and Ethel, who had been a trained nurse, helped hold Kappy down. They gave her a shot of Novocain, which they kept on hand for the livestock, and sewed her up. "She healed beautifully. The Lord was really good to us. Really good," her sister Marjorie affirmed.[14]

The Lord may also have intervened in a Tippett near tragedy. Don Tippett's wife gashed her hand while cutting wood. Don applied a tourniquet, then ran to the phone to call for help. The phone hadn't worked for a month, despite his tinkering with it off and on by the hour. "Now in a matter of minutes, he had it going." Don called for a plane and his wife got the needed help.[15]

Women about to give birth tried to be in a town when their time came. However, Hazel Johnson's first three children died at childbirth. "So, with Duane, I was told to be very careful. I spent a good share of that time in bed." When he and, later, Greg were born, Hazel stayed on the river until just a few weeks before each birth, then went to Lewiston where Ken's parents and her widowed mother lived.[16] Jessie Tippett usually went to Spokane, probably alone, to deliver her babies. When her third child was due, she was en route to Spokane but only got as far as Rogersburg. "The baby wasn't going to wait any longer. So the fella that ran the store there, he delivered the baby for her."[17]

Ethel Wilson gave birth to eight children, her last one in a hospital. For the other births she went to her grandmother's place on the Imnaha and got help from two midwives.[18] At age five or six, Marjorie was with her mother, Ethel, when she had a miscarriage. But Marjorie did not understand what had happened until years later. It was summer; the family was living at the upper ranch. "Mother took me and the packhorse and went down [to the main ranch] to can peaches. Then she loaded up a load of peaches for us to eat." Ethel wanted to take a mattress back with them to the upper ranch, "so we loaded that on top the peach boxes on the little horse that I had been on. It was about seven miles to the upper ranch, but it was a switchback trail, real steep." Usually when packing the horse, they didn't hook the ropes over the saddle horn in case the packhorse pulled back. "But she dropped the loop over her horn and was doing something when that darned old horse reared back and pulled her saddle horse over on her. She lay there and said, 'Honey, can you get that mattress off the diamond [hitch] for me?'"

Marjorie got the mattress and helped her mother lie down. "Of course I was scared. She kept trying to reassure me, and said, 'Honey, get on your horse—hurry—go get your dad and tell him to bring Nan [her grandmother].... Tell them to hurry." Marjorie did as she was told; she brought back Pete and Nan. "That must have been terrible for her to get on a horse and ride. The next morning, I remember Dad riding up through the field. He had a little box on the front of the saddle." When Marjorie was a young woman, her mother told her that her father made the box, lined it with towels, and buried the babies up "under the big tree in the middle of the field by the corn patch." Ethel Wilson had lost twins that day.[19]

Illness, accidents, drowning, miscarriages—anything could happen to anyone at any time. March 1953 *Popular Mechanics* ran an article on the Tippett family. When the author asked, "What happens when sickness or injury strikes," Jidge Tippett answered, "Well, God and the neighbors have looked after quite a bit of that." He added, "You'd be surprised how much you can do without a doctor if you have to. You take care of a lot of things yourself, like the time I cut my hand with an axe. Lard and carbolic acid repaired the damage." That pretty well sums up how canyon residents faced their emergencies.

Faith and Fun

Not everyone, of course, turned to lard, carbolic acid, or even God for help. But for those who believed in Him, they were comforted in times of need just knowing He was there. The natural environment also testified to His presence. Ethel Wilson, a "dyed-in-the-wool Southern Baptist," told her daughter Marjorie, "Honey, how could you not believe in God when you look and see this beautiful country, the sky, and the sunsets?" Her other daughter, Violet, asked how they could be believers "when we're not out there going to church." Her mother looked across the creek from the kitchen to where the rims went straight up. "See that over there, Violet? I always think of that as being the altar of a church. I can look

Figure 18.2. Ethel Wilson, a woman of strong faith, each day saw the hand of God reflected in her surroundings. (Photo courtesy of William Wilson.)

over there and do my praying and I know that God hears me just as well as He does in church. If you believe in God, He'll hear you no matter where you are." Violet said that "really stayed with me and got me through hard times."

The Wilsons honored their faith every Sunday with an hour of Sunday school instruction. Although Pete was not affiliated with a specific denomination, "he was a Christian too." When they lived on the Imnaha River while the children attended school there, "all the people got together and had church in the Freezeout School." Elsewhere in the canyon, schools doubled as churches if the population of churchgoers was large enough to support it.

Each family celebrated holidays in different ways. Easter was "very, very special" for the Wilsons. They also made a "big to-do" of Christmas. Pete made sure Santa Claus remembered the children and Ethel helped by making Santa's suit. One year Shorty Wolper, who worked for the Wilsons, said he was going to spend Christmas Eve on the Imnaha but would join them the next day. "He disappeared. We assumed he got on his horse and left." After supper the children heard a racket outside, then in came Santa Claus with gifts for the kids. "That was really quite exciting until he turned to leave." Violet looked down, then over to her sister Marjorie. "Then I looked back down and saw he was still wearing his spurs. We knew Shorty's spurs." The two girls did not tell the other children.[20]

The Wilson's Christmas presents were mostly homemade, maybe a new dress or spurs for the boys. One year when it was "really tight" the children received only a baseball. Violet remembered Topsy, a doll made from an old gray sock with a white heel and toe. "Mother made clothes for it—a couple of dresses, little panties, and she had yarn for the hair. I was so thrilled over that doll." Her dad once made the twin boys a white wooden wagon with wooden wheels. Ethel always ordered something special for the occasion. Their Royal Club coffee came in five-gallon cans. Attached to each can was a large Pepper Creek peppermint stick wrapped in cellophane. "Mother would take those off as she opened one of the cans and saved them for Christmas." When the holiday arrived, "we always had a big peppermint stick, and Dad always had oranges for us."[21]

Just about every family celebrated the Fourth of July, either individually or as an extended community. Families living on the Oregon side, from the canyon to the Wallowa Valley, packed up their "camp outfit" and gathered at Imnaha Park. They danced for a couple of nights, had a big potluck dinner and barbeque, maybe a gymkhana, and then returned to their everyday chores. The Wilson family usually celebrated at home; they could not afford to take the time off from haying and canning. Pete took a couple packhorses or mules into the mountains on the north side, where big snowdrifts lingered in the heavy timber. He collected lots of snow, put it on clean burlap sacks, wrapped them in a blanket and tarp, and brought the snow home. "For two days we had homemade ice cream. To this day, it's not the Fourth of July unless I have ice cream."[22]

Get-togethers other than holiday gatherings helped everyone socialize and keep in touch. Elmer Earl said that living on a ranch meant "long, hard days. Then on the weekends, it was great to have community gatherings." His grandfather built a "real nice park up the creek" where they would have picnics. He jury-rigged a swing powered by the flume that ran their waterwheel. Sometimes they made ice cream. Someone from town would bring a three-hundred-pound hunk of ice, wrapped in blankets and put it in a box packed with sawdust. From thirty to sixty people might show up for a weekend picnic. They ate, played cards, rode the swing, pitched horseshoes, had foot and horse races, and played baseball and other games.

Everyone loved an all-night community dance. The men "always wore overalls; they'd get a new pair." The women, because they rode to the dances, "put their dresses in a box and tied them on the back of the horse. Maybe set a kid or two on them." They had a fire and made coffee in a big copper boiler; the women brought sandwiches and cakes for their midnight supper. Someone in the crowd always played a musical instrument. Many of the dances were circle dances, so "everyone danced with everyone whether you had a date or not." They also two-stepped to songs like "The Yellow Rose of Texas," waltzed to "Over the Seas Waltz," and do-si-doed in lots of square dances—"just regular, old-fashioned dances."[23] The children nodded off as the evening progressed and slept where they could find an out-of-the-way place to lie down. By three in the morning, or thereabouts, the teens and adults were usually ready to call it quits. When dawn broke, they all headed back home.

When Violet Shirley was fifteen, she convinced her two older brothers that she was old enough to attend the community dance. Reluctantly they agreed to take her. It was winter, and the only way to reach the Imnaha Park schoolhouse, where they held dances, was by

Figure 18.3. Neighbors and friends gather at Sheep Creek to celebrate Christmas. In the back row are Jimmie the cook, Dick Maxwell, Billy McGaffee, Murrielle McGaffee, Mabel McGaffee, and Mrs. Tripper. Kneeling in the front are Len Jordan, George McGaffee, Fred McGaffee, and Mr. Tripper. (Photo courtesy of William Wilson.)

horseback up and over the Freezeout Saddle. When they got to the party, Violet changed from riding clothes into her good clothes and danced all night long, pausing at midnight to have "lunch." After the dance, they mounted their horses and rode back home. Violet was so tired she fell asleep on the horse, lost her balance, and dropped off into a snowbank. Within a short time her brothers discovered she was no longer riding behind them and rode back in search of her. There they found her, still sound asleep, with Old Molly waiting patiently. Her angry brothers swore not to take her to another dance until she was old enough to stay awake on the horse.

Murrielle McGaffee was teaching at Kirkwood when Louise, a friend from California, was visiting. Louise stayed with Murielle's parents. They were going to go to a dance at Riggins with their dates, Jimmy Wilson—Murrielle's fiancé—and Jordan's "young camp tender," Max Walker. Jimmy picked up Louise at the McGaffees; the two rode down to the Jordans to join Murrielle and Max. Early Saturday morning, they rode across the divide toward Lucille, left their horses with friends outside of town, hiked into Lucille, and caught a ride to Riggins. They danced until four o'clock in the morning. Sunday morning they hired someone to take them to Lucille, rode back to Kirkwood, and spent the night. The next morning Jimmy took Louise back to the McGaffees and rode on home. The dance highlighted Louise's already memorable Hells Canyon adventure. "Never [had I taken] four days to go to a dance."[24]

Leisure time at home was rare and precious. Family members relaxed by listening to the phonograph or radio, or by reading a book or magazine article. "You did a lot of reading," Ace Barton fondly recalled. His favorite magazines were *Colliers*, *Liberty American*, *Cosmopolitan*, and the *Saturday Evening Post*. When Jay Dobbin lived in Enterprise, he had his *Saturday Evening Post* sent to Les Oliver, his foreman at Cache Creek, "so the boys in the bunkhouse could read it." Magazines passed from place to place, and then papered cabin walls.

Although Harold Van Pool's formal education didn't go beyond the eighth grade, he was an avid reader of mysteries and detective stories. But when it rained, he pulled out the *National Geographic*, and dreamed of the day he could visit those far-off places. Finally he did. Before his wife, Tuppy, died of cancer, they took a world cruise. After her death, he continued to travel. On one of his cruises he met his second wife, Erma. Together they continued to see the world he had dreamed about from his Hells Canyon home. Much later, in 1980, the Horrocks were helping with branding when their son Cole met a *National Geographic* photographer. The photographer was their guest for a few days while taking pictures for a story about ranching in Idaho. "That guy took 600 pictures of me on my paint horse," Cole told his mother. After leaving Joseph Plains, the photographer traveled to Mount Saint Helens to shoot the erupting volcano. The eruption caught him and he died. The magazine never released the ranching article.

Hazel and Kenneth Johnson were both "avid readers." They subscribed to the *Enterprise Chieftain*, the *Lewiston Morning Tribune*, and the *Idaho County Free Press*, along with news magazines like *U.S. News & World Report* and *Time*. When they considered purchases, they studied mail order catalogs. They also loved to play cards. Whether they were "squabbling or not," they would sit down and play a game of cribbage, "maybe every night." In the evenings they also listened faithfully to programs on the radio.

During the 1920s, when the radio was a "big source of private entertainment" elsewhere, few canyon homes had radios—except Paul Brown and Jim Madden "down the river a couple of miles," Frank Jacks recalled. Even as late as 1926, when Jacks considered buying a phonograph, "the radio was just beginning to be mentioned around Lewiston." By the 1930s that had changed; radios filled the canyon with the sounds of music, news, comedy, and suspense. At Granite Creek, as a Christmas present Esther and Earl Hibbs received their first battery-operated radio with an outside antenna. They could usually pick up a station from Lewiston and one from Boise, but to save battery power, they restricted their listening to the news and one "fun program." Their favorite—*Durable Mike Malloy*. Greg Johnson remembered "everybody" having a Halicrafter radio—"those great big enormous radios that were multiwave. All of the sheepherders had those and they all listened to them forever."

The adults who remembered growing up in Hells Canyon obviously cherished their time spent there. Children had fun. Nature provided the resources; their individual creativity gave them ideas for turning the mundane into a game or toy. Ace Barton told about a game he and his sister invented. "There was a big rock down below the cabin. We'd catch snails and put them on the rock, take our pocket knives, and scratch a brand on them. They were our cattle." Sometimes their game was interrupted and the two "herds" would be mixed together. Usually a dispute over ownership ensued and perhaps some wrestling around. "We'd get in a big row and have to take it to a higher court—my mother." If the children had siblings near their age, they had playmates. If not, then, like Doug Tippett, they "made [their] own fun." However they adapted, canyon children learned dependability and self-sufficiency at an early age—traits that served them well throughout their lives.

Graduating to the Next Higher Chore

The children also learned how to work—hard by today's standards—at a very early age. Horsemanship played a role in that work. Ace Barton rode after cattle when he was about five. "Then I drove derrick horses puttin' up hay when I was six." Horace Henderson "always had a saddle horse. The walkin' wasn't too good. There was some of those old wild cows that would run you up a tree. They didn't take to a person on foot." Like Ace, he began riding after cattle at a very young age. When he was ten, his parents let him ride trails alone. Marjorie Chadwick could not remember "when I couldn't ride a horse; I can't remember when I couldn't milk a cow. Really, I can't." Her sister Violet said their parents taught them to do everything. "We were very self-sufficient, and the girls had to learn to do everything that the boys did. I built fences, roped and castrated calves, pitched hay—I did it all."

Everyday chores—sometimes fun, sometimes profitable, sometimes baffling—taught responsibility. Mothers expected their daughters to help in the kitchen. And, as Ethel Wilson knew all too well, the learning process sometimes took time. One morning, young Violet decided to bake some bread. She had watched her mother work and knead the bread. However, when Violet began kneading down the dough, "it didn't raise, and it didn't raise and I thought, well, I didn't make it right." Since Violet did not want her mother to see how much flour she had wasted, she dug a hole near the garden, put the dough in it and "covered it up with dirt good." Toward evening, Ethel returned from the upper place and wanted Violet to help her gather vegetables in the garden. The day

Figure 18.4. Billy Wilson helps his father James build a doghouse while getting an early introduction to chores and hard work. (Photo courtesy of William Wilson.)

had been warm and the dough had risen in the hole. "There was this big mushroom puffed up there with the dirt on top of it." Violet thought she had covered it well. All her mother said was, "Oh, you must have had trouble making bread today, huh Violet?" Ethel asked Violet to tell her the next time she wanted to make bread, "and I'll see to it that you get it right."

In time Violet did "get it right" and helping in the kitchen became her daily chore. As children got older, Violet explained, they "graduated to the next higher chore." Another of her "higher chores" was to shut the doors in the chicken house in the evenings so raccoons and skunks couldn't get in. To get there she had to cross the creek. If it was already dark, that was a "dreaded chore." She was afraid of the dark. During the summer, when the Wilsons lived at cow camp, she packed chopped wood to the house and filled the wood box. One time, after dark, she squatted down to pick up a load, looked up and "right there in front of me sat a bear—right there, eye to eye. I just screamed, threw the lantern, and ran to the house." Her dad was playing a trick on her. He shot a bear that had been killing their cattle, realized she had a cub in the tree, killed it, and put the body where Violet would see it. (Sometimes the ranchers made a pet from an orphaned cub; Pete probably thought that killing one was more humane.)

Parents or grandparents often made children responsible for caring for their own animals. That chore had the potential of turning a profit. Pete and Ethel Wilson always gave their children a colt. Over the years, Marjorie's "Bess kept having colts." By the time Marjorie got married, she had amassed a small herd of horses. Her cow also produced offspring, twelve by the time Marjorie married. She sold her cattle and horse herds to her brother Allen.

Greg Johnson's grandfather gave him and his brother Duane each a milk cow when the boys were four or five. "Dad loaned us the money to buy a bull. It took two years to get the bull into the ranch." Apparently the animal was broken to lead, but the sheepherder bringing him in got drunk and turned him loose. The next year the Johnsons found their bull and finally got him to the ranch. Their two milk cows "stayed at the bottom of creeks and grazed on burdock." Over the years the herd multiplied, until it had increased enough to "cause problems." When it came time to take them to market, catching the animals "was like rounding up deer." It took the boys two years, but they finally rounded up two hundred head of what had become wild animals. On the way to market, "they tore down most of the fences on the Imnaha River. They jumped seven- to eight-foot-high corrals at the sales yard. They even jumped from one pen to the next." Finally, after removing all the people, horses, and everything from the sales ring, the auctioneer sold the wild cattle. Greg knew they didn't have them all, "because we were missing the infamous bull." When they finally captured him, that put an end to their cattle business. Nevertheless, it had put money in the pocket for Greg and Duane.

Play kept canyon children outdoors, and work sent them all over the country, often alone and at very young ages. Their parents prepared them well for that freedom. "Watch out for rattlers and don't go near the river." "If you find a gun, knife or matches, don't touch it, then go tell an adult." Cautions and warnings were part of life. "We were perfectly safe because this was drilled into us."[25] Still, parents worried, like Doug Tippett's mother. "She talked about that many times. The [big] kids would take off, and they might be gone all day." Jessie Tippett had no idea where her children were. "There were all kinds of places that they could get hurt—fall off a rim or out of a tree. In the winter Joseph Creek would freeze over, and you always had to test the ice, you know. If you'd ever fall in through one of those deep holes in the ice, that'd be the end of it. No one would ever know where you were." One of the reasons the older kids—and Doug when he was old enough—"took off" was to get "predator points." Each year the county held a "predatory animal contest. Each entrant got prizes for a magpie wing, a rattler, or a coyote foot, or whatever." One of the top prizes was a .22 rifle. "All three of my brothers won the rifles." Doug helped his next oldest brother win his rifle. "The next year he was going to help me, but they discontinued the contest." Boys and girls grew up around firearms; they were an important tool for life in the canyon. Parents taught children to respect guns and, when they were old enough, how to use them.

Despite their seemingly isolated home life, canyon children "weren't complete hillbillies," as Marjorie Chadwick pointed out. "We got out a lot." She particularly enjoyed going to a rodeo with her father and brother Allen. In his younger years, Pete Wilson won regional fame on the rodeo circuit. He even rode with the famous Nez Perce horseman Jackson Sundown. Later, "to supplement the family income," Pete provided the rodeo with strings of bucking horses.

When six-year-old Carmen Winniford Yokum stayed at her grandparents' Clarkston home, she found herself comparing their home to her own place at Sluice Creek. She concluded that electricity acted "like coal oil and it came through a hole in the middle of the wire. The 'click' when the switch was turned was a match striking inside . . . that lighted the light." She made a reasonable comparison to the lamps and lanterns they used at home; figuring out indoor plumbing proved more difficult. Their Sluice Creek privy emptied into a small stream. But "what was happening with the toilet inside the house at Grandpa's and Grandma's? A careful tour around the outside confirmed my suspicions. Nothing was coming out anywhere. Grandma McGee took considerable pride in her housekeeping, and I didn't want to hurt her feelings by suggesting she was doing something dirty." Although certain that waste was building under their home, Carmen kept her silence.[26]

Ellen and Alex Warnock made their four girls wear split skirts even when working at the homestead. After one of the girls had observed White Bird girls wearing jeans, she returned home to announce, "I'm not going to help you any more with the outside work . . . until you make some changes." She demanded that her father get her and her sisters some jeans. He did. A generation later, Violet Shirley and her mother had differences over a similar issue. Violet wore jeans during a hard day of work with her brothers. But at day's end, her mother would say, "Now get your clothes changed, Violet. You are a girl and someday you'll realize that you are a girl and need to know how to act properly in a dress."[27]

The Three Rs

Nearly all parents on Snake River recognized the importance of educating their children. Most parents who grew up in Hells Canyon had not received the education they wanted their children to have. Parents with good educations who moved into the canyon expected the same for their children. Whatever their own background, the adults did everything possible to ensure their children got an education. Early in the century, enough homesteaders lived in the canyon to form school districts, build a schoolhouse, and support a teacher. As the population declined, some mothers educated their children at home through correspondence courses. Some families hired a teacher to live with them. Most of the families, however, either bought or rented a home in a nearby town and the mother stayed with the kids while they went to school. Or they boarded the child with family members or friends in town.

In the early 1900s most canyon children attended rural schools. Rufe Wisenor described those early schools. Enrollment was small, "never more than seven children," but

Figure 18.5. A typical rural schoolhouse of the early 1900s. Here some of the children at Joseph Plains school are playing "London Bridge Is Falling Down." (Photo courtesy of Horace Henderson.)

those "children" might be as young as four or as old as twenty. Many schools operated only during the summer months. If the children rode to school from home, they spent hours a day on horseback. Most often, teachers and students camped along with the teacher near the schoolhouse. Students shared the few schoolbooks they were able to obtain; they rarely had the luxury of a school desk or a personal writing slate. It was hard to find and keep teachers.[28] Most were fresh out of teacher training, often the same age as or even younger than their oldest students.

Two schools halfway up the Idaho slope above the Snake and Salmon river confluence testified to the population fluctuation before and after the severe winter and livestock depression of the early 1900s.[29] As a youngster, Horace Henderson would have attended one of those two schools. He rode about four miles with his older sister, Claire, to summer school at Spring Camp's river breaks. "A lot of kids lived farther than that." One of his photos showed at least a dozen horses "parked back here in the back—everyday. We'd pile our saddles under the old schoolhouse." He attended school there from first through eighth grade—seven months each year—then went to Cottonwood for high school.[30] By 1938 only about thirty residents remained in that once heavily populated region.

Another example of an early—and Wallowa County's most remote—school was Snake River School (also known as Pittsburg School) located on the Oregon side seven miles above Pittsburg Landing. School records show students there as early as 1908, continuing up until 1928. The first time the Wallowa County superintendent evaluated the school, as the state required, he hired a horse and rode all the way there from Enterprise. Seven days later he reached the school.[31] The county superintendent visited a school once a year and observed an activity like a spelling bee. He also tested students on their "history and stuff like that."[32] At the end of the eighth grade, each child had to pass a state test.

The first Snake River (Pittsburg) School was a log cabin "on the bench near the high trail, just north of Two Corral Creek." Within a few years, a frame building replaced the log structure.[33] School enrollment was high because of the number of people homesteading on both sides of the river. A family from the Salmon River side of the mountains, the Rogers, had a ten-year-old son attending the log school; their daughter Patty taught there. The teacher and her brother went home to Idaho every two weeks. "They would go get their horses at Two Corral, a couple of miles from the school, ride seven miles to Pittsburg ferry, cross the river, ride over Pittsburg Saddle, and down to their parents' ranch on the Salmon River." Patty Rogers's students ranged from six to eighteen years of age. They all camped near the school during the week; on weekends the children went home.[34] Among her students were the Stockdale and Wisenor children from Idaho, who also had to catch the Pittsburg ferry to attend school.[35]

When Florence Winniford attended school, in 1918 and 1919, her mother, Mina, taught the first year and her aunt Mary Hyatt the second year. Florence had sixteen classmates, including her three siblings. She described getting to school from home as "quite an excursion for the whole family." They took milk cows and saddle horses, and set up camp with a "floored and walled tent" near the old log school. Mina planted a garden; she and the older girls prepared meals. On weekends the Winnifords went to the mountain top "where father would be caring for cattle."[36] Florence's younger sister, Carmen, liked it when the family set up housekeeping near the school. It's not often that a four-year-old gets to go to school with the big kids.[37]

Walter and Mina Winniford dismantled and moved their Pony Bar log cabin a mile up the river to Rush Creek. Between 1920 and 1924 it was a school. Mina taught during the spring and fall; Walt, who had been a teacher in the Willamette Valley, in the winter. Their students included their own children—Wilma, John, Eileen, and Florence—along with their cousin Maxine Winniford; Jimmy and Allen Wilson; and Earl Hibbs. Jimmy and Allen rode down from Saddle Creek by mule, stayed at the school during the week, and returned home for the weekends. Earl "would go down on Monday" from Granite Creek: "they'd take him across the river to Rush Creek and he would go to the school." Most of the time, he also went home for the weekends.[38]

Ethel Wilson was responsible for reactivating the Saddle Creek school district in 1933–34 so they could hire teachers in their home. Their first teacher was Murrielle McGaffee, who had just completed studies at Lewiston Normal School. Before she could take the job, she had to pass a test to prove her knowledge of Oregon history and civics. She passed and began her new career by helping fifteen-year-old Marjorie move school supplies over the ridge from the old Pittsburg School, Oregon, to Saddle Creek.

They packed up a globe, an unabridged dictionary, a cloth blackboard, chalk, library books, and textbooks, then proceeded to retie the load six times in eight miles before they reached Temperance Creek. "The next day we made it back to Saddle Creek with our loot, and both of us promptly learned to throw a diamond hitch." Murrielle's students that year were the Wilson children—twins Don and Dan, Charlie, Violet, and Marjorie, whom Murrielle was helping with tenth-grade subjects. For "entertainment that winter the older children and I would ride out over the Saddle to Imnaha to go to the Grange dances," Murrielle fondly recalled. Perhaps she was most interested in "entertaining" Jim Wilson, her student's oldest—and very handsome—brother. They became engaged at the end of that school year. The next year she worked for the Jordans, tutoring their two children at Kirkwood.[39]

During the school year many canyon parents boarded their children in town—both near and distant. Ace Barton spent his first seven years at Parks School on the upper Imnaha, then attended his eighth grade in the village of Imnaha. His family paid five to ten dollars a month to board him, "a pretty good sum for those days." He kept his horse where he boarded "so when I got a chance, I'd ride back to Snake River." It was a full day's ride, followed by a boat trip across to the Idaho side. When Ace reached high school age, he spent the first two years at Enterprise, and the third in Pullman, Washington, with Esther and Earl Hibbs, who had moved out of Granite Creek by then. In his senior year, Ace worked at a Forest Service lookout while putting himself through school at Riggins.[40]

Oliver McNabb, who ran the mailboat on the Snake River, recalled very few children

Figure 18.6. The enrollment in this school was high for a rural school. Included in this picture are Ruth Barton and her sister Hazel, front row, second and fourth from left; Earl Hibbs and perhaps a sister; and some of the Marks children. All of these families lived deep in the canyon. (Photo courtesy of Ace Barton.)

on his mail runs during the 1950s. Most were going to school in town.[41] Duane and Greg Johnson, whom Oliver would have known, went to school in Enterprise. Their mother taught Duane his first year, then "we were getting quite a little assistance from the sheepherders, so she thought maybe it would be a good thing if they got us around other children. Maybe our vocabulary would improve a bit." So Hazel moved to Enterprise with the boys to complete their education.

When Doug Tippett was a first grader at Joseph Creek School, about eight children attended school there, including his older siblings and two or three other kids. One student, about eighteen years old, was "still in the eighth grade." Doug received a multifaceted education. "The older kids put me up to a lot of things, including kicking the teacher in the shins. I knew how to get out through the woodshed and leave school. And I'd come back if I felt like it. . . . So it was quite a school year." The teacher "didn't teach me very much. But my mother, being a teacher, knew that I wasn't ready for second grade. So I started over in Clarkston." After a brief interruption, the Rogersburg school was reopened in 1938, so Doug's parents rented a house in Rogersburg and he went to school there. By the time Doug reached high school, his parents were traveling quite extensively. Doug stayed alone in Clarkston his last two years, writing his own excuses for any absences, "always to go home to do ranch work."

During the early 1900s there was a "winter schoolroom" in the attic of the Grande Ronde Mercantile Company building in Rogersburg. Store owner Charlie Nyberg "put some smooth boards on the ceiling, painted them black, gave us each a piece of chalk, and we learned our phonics on the ceiling." Helen Brown Nyberg, his daughter, remembers how they "lay on those beds and looked at the ceiling. That's where we learned our sounds and learned to read. I had *Black Beauty* and all of those books before I was out of the first grade."

Then, in 1913, the Asotin School District granted Rogersburg-area parents permission to establish a school. At the time the AAI Mine at Wild Goose employed some families who lived close enough to help the district comply with a state regulation requiring at least seven students within a certain radius of the proposed school. James Brewrink's father was working at the AAI, and "at Mr. Decker's request to meet the required number," enrolled James in school. Since daily trips from the mine to the Rogersburg school were "impossible," James boarded with the Deckers, who operated the Rogersburg store. James, as the oldest student, was charged with "stove tender" duties. The teacher (Mrs. Decker perhaps) spent time at the supper table using James "as her practice student." During school she usually had him reading or doing book problems. "I was poorly adjusted to group classwork and playground, but must have had the required 3 R's, as shown by my report cards."[42] In the school's early days, the school's furnishings were rustic at best: students sat on nail kegs; planks on saw horses served as their desks; the teacher sat on a box, and a woodstove heated the building.[43]

When declining populations could no longer support rural schools, rather than board their children or move the family, some parents chose to teach their children at home. In 1947 the *Saturday Evening Post* featured the lives of Allen and Hazel (Barton) Wilson when they were living at Granite Creek. Richard Neuberger, the author, found their method of educating their son, Kim, most interesting. "From a school in far-off Baltimore, the Wilsons buy detailed correspondence courses for a child the age of Kimmy. The cost is $100 a year. The school even sends Kimmy's pencils, textbooks, crayons, and tablets." Hazel and Kimmy observed "regular school hours," with good results. Kimmy "reads more than the average eight-year-old."[44] When Kim was in eighth grade, he lived in Riggins with

Allen's brother and sister-in-law, Jim and Murrielle McGaffee Wilson. "He was far ahead of the rest [of the other students]," Ace Barton remembered.

Kim's parents used a correspondence course from Calvert School in Baltimore, an educational program used extensively for decades by homeschoolers up and down the canyon. Even as late as the 1970s, some Snake River families still used Calvert School homeschooling materials. Although most children in the Joseph Plains region lived in town during their school months, Sharon Horrocks wanted to educate her son, Cole, at home. She didn't have a degree in teaching and the "Idaho Department of Education was very skeptical." However, because Calvert was one of the schools they approved of, the Idaho officials agreed to let Sharon teach Cole so long as he went to Grangeville on a regular basis to be tested.

Each month during the school year, Sharon and Cole bundled up his month's assignments and sent them out on the mail plane. The Calvert School teacher sent the graded papers back with comments in the columns and corrections. "She would write a letter with it, the things she thought we should do or the things that we were doing fine. It was really very complete." Cole had a different teacher at Calvert every year, and received the same assignments as the students in Baltimore. "[The teacher would] write and say that they [his classmates] really enjoyed Cole's compositions because they were about the area where he was growing up and knew about. When Cole's envelopes would come, the kids would be so excited." Sharon and Cole had class every weekday, but if something was "really boring" off they would go— fishing, hunting, riding, anything for a break. Then back to the books.

When Cole was a high school freshman, they moved to Grangeville. "The teachers commented that he must have never had a television, because he could read so well and retain what he read." Cole received a good education. What about Sharon? She probably learned a lot too. Because of those eight years spent learning together, "my son and I have a tremendous relationship." She added that "Grace Jordan tells the same thing in *Home below Hells Canyon*. We went through the same things she did. Things didn't change."[45]

Map 20.1. River route from Lewiston to Johnson Bar. This was the weekly route of Hells Canyon mailboats throughout the twentieth century.

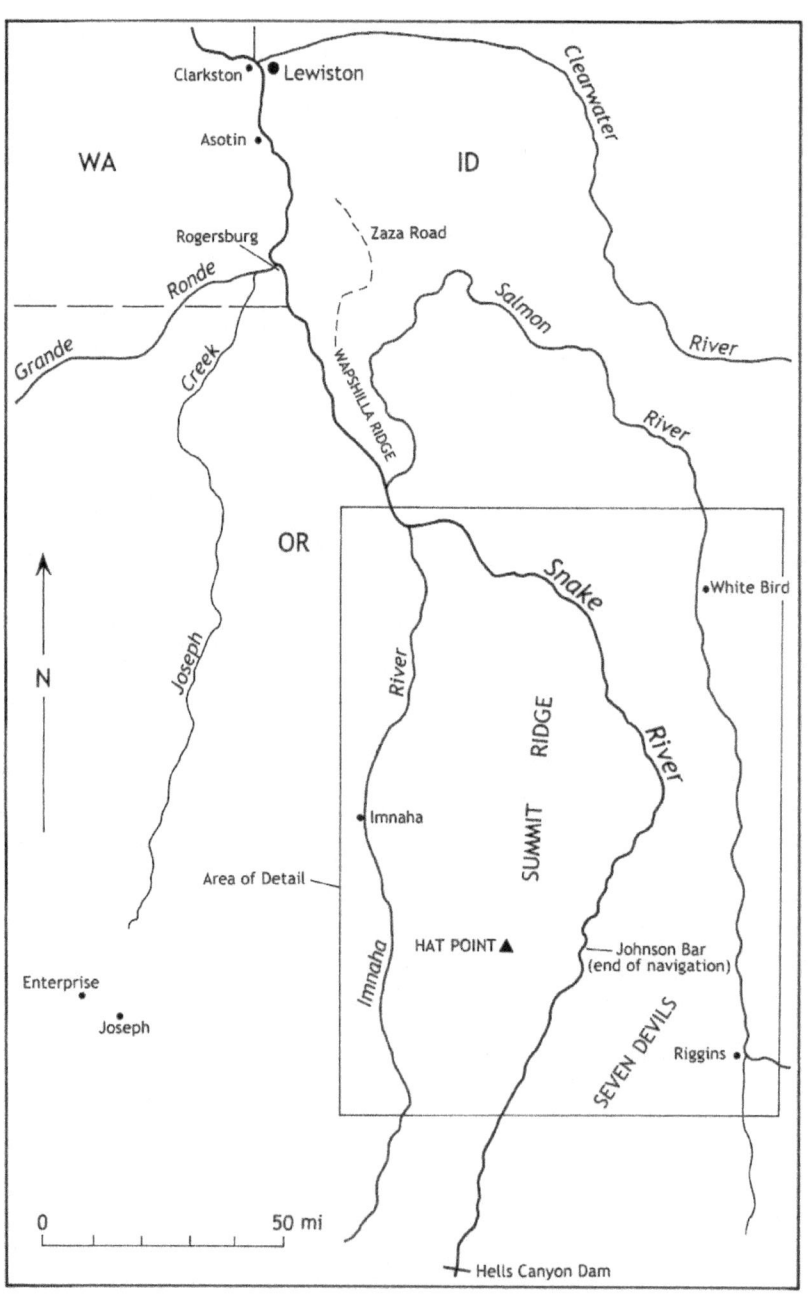

Chapter 19

Up, Down, Out, & Across

Carmen Winniford Yokum remembered children's vocabularies always including "up and down long before they had any real notion of sideways." From her Sluice Creek cabin nearly one hundred miles above Lewiston, Carmen's "perimeter of the canyon was more often defined by out and in," although she sometimes heard people speaking about "going down to Lewiston."[1] Throughout most of the twentieth century, that perception rang true. Leaving the canyon or traveling through the canyon always meant going up, down, out, or across. Whether in the deepest sections of Hells Canyon or more open areas far to the north, people traveled *down* the river and *out* to Lewiston. *Up* came their supplies and mail. They rode *up* a steep trail from the shoreline to ridge or mountain tops, usually with many ups and downs along the way, and *out* to a neighboring town. Sometimes they went *across* the river, then *up* and *out*.

Following nearly the same roads or trails, and encountering comparable degrees of difficulty, ranchers moved with their livestock up and down the trails; they went up, out, and sometimes across for mail and supplies, to go to school, or attend community functions. Most early trails followed ancient routes long used by Nez Perce travelers. Homesteaders and miners added trails to that network. After 1906 when the Forest Service came on the scene, they expanded the existing mountain trail network by adding their own trails, and maintaining them all. Although their trails were for fire prevention and control, the ranchers were the main beneficiaries.

In those early years, delivering mail to distant mines and ranches involved riding the trails up, down, in, and out. When the mines at Battle Creek were operating, Everett Barton packed in the mail from Imnaha on a regular basis.[2] Every time the mail arrived, someone would set off a blast up in a mine so everyone knew the mail was there. Ellen Hibbs, living across the river at Granite Creek, was expecting some trees from a mail order company. When she heard the blast announcing the mail, she knew her trees had arrived. "So she saddled her mule, crossed the river, and probably went fifteen to twenty miles over the mountains to pick up her trees." Across, up, and down—Ellen wanted her trees and that was the only way to collect them.[3]

Men and women made difficult rides over long distances, frequently alone. If they needed something or had made a commitment to

Figure 19.1. Grandmother Winniford, astride her horse Skeet, on her way to Hill Homestead. (Photo courtesy of HCNRA, Florence Winniford Smith Collection.)

Figure 19.2. Parents adopted innovative ways to move children and supplies from place to place. Here two Winniford girls found comfortable accommodations in some old gasoline cans on the family mule. (Photo courtesy of HCNRA, Florence Winniford Smith Collection.)

do something, they had no other options. Esther Bly grew up far to the north on Joseph Creek near the confluence of the Grande Ronde and Snake Rivers. Her father operated a post office out of their home. In 1902 he hired his twelve-year-old daughter, Esther, to deliver mail once a week to the Wild Goose Mines across the breaks in the Snake River canyon. "Every Saturday I made a dollar," she proudly recalled. At sixteen, Esther married her neighbor, Walter Day. She then found herself often making another mail ride the opposite direction—a rugged, twelve-hour ride to Anatone, Washington, and back. Walter had the contract to carry mail from the Anatone post office to Bly (her father's post office). If Walter was too busy farming, Esther made the mail run. The Asotin County deputy sheriff gave her a pistol—just in case—because there had been "several recent shootings." She never used it.[4]

About the same time, the three Winniford families of Oregon owned homesteads much farther to the south, just below High Trail and at Pony Bar on the river. Because their hay and cattle were in the lower part of the canyon, they made frequent trips between the two places. High Trail was the better route, but snow closed it in during the winter, forcing them to use the treacherous River Trail. "Bad places" along that route included Devil's Ladder, another nearby ledge that had no name, and Needle's Eye. Devil's Ladder was about a mile and a half from their Pony Bar cabin. What initially appeared to be a not-too-steep approach became "unbelievable in roughness and steepness." Rock configurations in the cliff provided what seemed to be steps, very steep and dangerous to be sure, but still steps the horse could climb up on. Women and children always led their horses across that stretch of the trail. Men did too if they doubted their horse's surefootedness. The unnamed bad place near Devil's Ladder was a narrow ledge on a three-foot-wide rim with a cliff straight up on one side and straight down on the other. People walked horses over that section too. Slick rock provided perilous footing for the horses. If the animal slipped, it would go into the river. Old Buck, Winniford's packhorse, once started to slip, but the "wise old boy sat down and turned in such a way that his front feet came in contact with the only solid ground between him and the brink." At Needle's Eye riders had to unpack every pack animal, lead it through, and then repack the load at the other end.[5]

For Ethel Wilson, a Texas girl who lived in Burns, Oregon, before moving to the canyon in 1914, her first view of Wallowa County was a shock. Shock turned to fear when she and her husband, Pete, started to go up over the mountain from the Imnaha River and down the other side into Hells Canyon. "She hung onto the saddle horn so tight that by the time they got down to Saddle Creek, she had big water blisters on both of her hands." Her oldest son was riding behind her and Pete carried the baby. Though the trip "just seemed like it was really hell," Ethel grew to love the canyon.[6]

Jimmy and Allen Wilson (the two children who rode in on that first trip with Ethel) grew up in the canyon. Later, when they were in their teens, they drove a wild range bull from Waterspout Canyon up the trail to their Saddle Creek ranch. Allen led his horse behind the bull, swatting at the stubborn beast to keep him going. Jimmy rode behind. As

Figure 19.3. Another unique method of transportation for the Winniford children was this device holding the girls suspended between two horses. (Photo courtesy of HCNRA, Florence Winniford Smith Collection.)

they approached a narrow rock shelf with a fifty-foot drop, the bull refused to continue. He suddenly stopped, turned, and charged down the narrow trail. There was enough room for him to get past Allen and his horse, but not enough room to pass Jimmy mounted on his horse. "The bull lowered his head and continued down the trail at full speed.... Certain death seemed inevitable for both Jimmy and the horse. Then the horse ... reared up and jumped, allowing the bull to pass under the horse and rider. There was somewhat of a collision, but horse and rider came down in the trail right side up and very little the worse for the experience."[7]

Jimmy and Allen's sister Marjorie often rode to the Imnaha for the mail. She was about nine years old, and her younger sister Violet usually rode along. Like most of the residents living above Sheep Creek on both sides of the river, the Wilson's mail came in from Enterprise by stage (later by truck) to the town of Imnaha. Families living close by picked up and held mail and parcels for the people living in the canyon. The Joe Marks family got the Wilsons' mail. When it was time to ride out for it, the two Wilson girls usually left early in the morning and got back by dark. Sometimes they left late in the afternoon and stayed with their grandmother, who lived near the Markses, and returned early the next day. If their dad had a special supply order, they picked it up too. "It took two of us to get on a box and lift a hundred-pound sack of sugar up, tie one on each side of the mule."

Years after leaving the canyon, Marjorie Chadwick said she would now be "scared to death to ride over those trails." But while growing up at Saddle Creek "us kids used to gallop our horses over them every place we could. Dad would have killed us if he'd seen us." On one trail — the Buck trail — they were supposed to get off and walk. But if the children trusted the horse, they disobeyed. "I think I'd crawl around it now," she added.[8]

Everybody talked about the dangerous trail from Sheep Creek to Kirkwood that climbed through Half Moon Saddle and around Kirkwood Creek. It was especially dangerous in the winter when the "sliding ground" guaranteed no safe footing.[9] In 1926 the Forest Service replaced that route with Suicide Point trail, a safer yet more frightening trail across the face of a "single portentous rock" two to four hundred feet straight above the turbulent Snake River.

Figure 19.4. Bud Wilson, with a packer and packstring, climb the trail above Snake River on their approach to Bernard Creek. (Photo by Gunther Matschke, courtesy of the Bud Wilson Family.)

Grace Jordan described her first trip across the new trail. "As our trail ascended without switchbacks, edging near the drop, it also narrowed. We made a bend and were suddenly out on the face of the cliff." Far below boiled a turbulent Snake River. "Presently the trail became a virtual stairway, one rock above another, each one sloping out, with a flimsy coping of small stones to mark the edge." Dick Maxwell rode behind Grace on that first trip, calling out, "Don't lean toward the wall that way! If you can't ride straight, lean out."[10] Murrielle McGaffee Wilson also had vivid memories of the Suicide Point trail. It came "right around the lip of the bluff on the point and you could spit right in the river. It was plenty wide enough, so your packs didn't scrape, but if you went off, there was no place to catch hold."[11] The Forest Service has widened the trail, but hikers may sympathize with the Oregon state cattle inspector whom Grace Jordan watched get off his horse and crawl along the trail.

When Murrielle Wilson rode the trails, Needle's Eye scared her more than Suicide Point. The trail crossed rocks that were like plates, one going one direction, the second another direction. Often the horse would refuse to cross. If he slipped between the rock plates, he was stuck until he could work himself loose. Murrielle always dismounted and walked. The Forest Service finally blasted out the rocks, removing that section altogether.[12] Eagle's Nest, a narrow Forest Service trail carved through solid cliffs between Yreka Creek and Sand Creek, was "fit only for an eagle's nest." It involved a steep climb, straight up and straight down, over a cliff and under a cliff. If the river was high "the rider had to ride around a cliff edge right over the water and back to the trail."[13] In 1950, four years after building Eagle's Nest, the Forest Service added a rock guard along the edge of the most dangerous section.[14]

Even for the best riders, their first exposure to canyon trails could be terrifying. Esther Hibbs, a seasoned equestrian in her Palouse Hills home, admitted her first Hells Canyon trail was "rather formidable looking." Looking down "spooked" her. But she knew two things: the horse could negotiate the trail and she could stay in the saddle. "He isn't going to want to fall off, so I'll be all right," she reasoned—a logic that probably sustained many other canyon riders. She also knew she must lean out over the trail instead of back towards the bluff, which would throw the horse's balance off. What for any frightened or unseasoned rider would have been an unnatural response was for Esther "the best way because it was kind of a bend and that would be the normal way you would ride."[15]

Riding those trails became an even greater challenge when pack strings were involved. In the fall and spring, families from the upper canyon ranches on both sides of the Snake usually ordered supplies from Enterprise. The mail stage or truck delivered the supplies to Imnaha, where a family member picked them up and packed them on home. The Wilsons rented a shed by the road at the mouth of Freezeout Creek. Once Pete knew the supplies were coming, he would start a pack string going over the mountain. "You prayed there wouldn't be much rain while that was going on. Made it a lot more difficult to put tarps on everything."[16] It took seven or eight days to go out, load supplies, and return to the river ranch—fourteen miles and "quite a haul."[17]

Once the mailboat became dependable and trails improved, many upper canyon ranchers rode down to Johnson Bar for their mail and supplies. The Wilsons, however, continued going to Imnaha since the trail on the Oregon side to Johnson Bar was far too dangerous. One section along that trail, called "the Bluff," was blasted out of solid rimrock. The overlap was so low that at times they had to take the saddle off, pack it up, and lead the horse through the rock cut. "You didn't carry any freight or anything like that because it was about a forty-five degree angle." To avoid that impossible stretch, packers *could* go halfway up the mountain, around, and back down to the river. It was easier to go to Imnaha.

Figure 19.5. Riders and pack mules cross narrow and precipitous Eagle's Nest Trail. (Photo courtesy of Violet Wilson Shirley.)

Initially there were few places to travel for any distance along the riverbank, with the exception of a lower Snake River section in Washington. Over time, ranchers cut passable saddle horse trails along the river to avoid that perpetual climb up and around tributary canyons, and back down to the river. Then, beginning in the 1920s, the Forest Service began cutting river trails through Hells Canyon. By the late 1940s "a single trail along the east bank of the river" ran "through the seventy-five mile length of the deepest part of the canyon."[18]

River Crossings and Landings

Ranchers crossed the river for many reasons—to move livestock, get supplies, visit cross-river neighbors, or simply "go out." They first used rowboats and then motorized boats. If they could find a long quiet stretch with sandy beaches on both sides, rowing across the river was no problem. However, since such places were rare, "most of the crossing places used by the old-time residents . . . were in the quiet stretches above the rapids [although] some were quite marginal as far as safety was concerned." Ideally, the old-time residents used a back current close to shore, rowed upstream, then out into the main current to drift with the flow and row across. Most accidents happened when there was not enough room to cross before coming to the head of some rapids.[19]

Cattle and horses swam across. The Wilsons kept halters on the horses and led them behind the boat. If the horse had never been in the river, "at first it would be kind of panicky, but then [it would] soon settle down." Whoever was rowing the boat talked to the horses, and soon they would start swimming.[20] Jim Chapman fastened his horses to the boat and they swam behind. "They would puff like thunder to get in and out of the current," he added.[21] Many ranchers let the horses swim untethered.

A few hearty souls tried to run ferries—for personal use and as a service to neighbors. At Pittsburg Landing, a ferry linked Oregon and Idaho, replicating an ancient Nez Perce crossing. Mike Thomason, who lived on the Oregon side, started a ferry there in 1891. He hired his neighbors to run it. Albert Kurry operated it around 1910, then Jack Titus operated and eventually owned it. Over time, the ferry became more of an inconvenience than an

Figure 19.6. The Snake River road south of Asotin, Washington, completed in the late 1930s, ended here at the mouth of the Grande Ronde River (center right). The town of Rogersburg, out of sight on the south (opposite) side of the Grande Ronde, was accessed by a ferry a couple of miles above the confluence. (Photo courtesy of the Asotin County Historical Society.)

asset for Jack, since he had to drop whatever else he was doing when someone wanted to cross the river. "One night he was so irritated he cut the ferry loose and let it float down the river."[22] By then the mailboat was in business, providing cross-river ferry service as well as transportation in and out of the canyon.[23]

Fifty-two miles downriver, Jasper Earl received a license in 1903 to operate a cable ferry at Captain John. Travelers could then head upstream from Lewiston on the Washington side, cross the river at Captain John, continue along a six-mile, homestead trail on the Idaho side to a natural river crossing at the Grande Ronde. Like all ferries in the region, a cable spanning the river guided the Captain John ferry across while the current propelled it. By 1925, frustrated from contending with nature's many moods, Jasper quit operations. Around 1930, the Earls operated a second ferry at the same location. It was about twelve feet wide, forty feet long, and powered by an old car engine still attached to its Model A frame. Their third ferry, operating in 1950, was twice as wide and fifteen feet longer. It could carry fifty thousand pounds, had a V-8 Ford engine for power, and used outboard motors "for the auxiliary." The Earls also rigged up "two car rear ends . . . and a propeller to turn it all the way around and power it both directions."[24]

Investing in a grain warehouse and river landing proved far more lucrative than ferry service, but only where steamboats could navigate the river. For decades, farmers and shippers demanded an "open river" that would allow passage of a single boat from Astoria, Oregon, at the mouth of the Columbia River, to the head of navigation. Finally, in the spring of 1915, the dream came true. Celilo Canal was completed, bypassing the slow and expensive portage around Celilo Falls near The Dalles, Oregon. To celebrate, a flotilla of riverboats steamed upriver to Lewiston. Celebrants from throughout the region welcomed them with parades, picnics, dances, speeches, and more speeches and an excursion on Portland's *J. N. Teal* to the mouth of the Grande Ronde River. The excursion was in part to show off the country; it was also to demonstrate that the head of navigation could easily extend that far when the river conditions were right. Once celebrations in Lewiston ended, the flotilla descended the river to join in festivities all the way to Astoria, leaving the local folks with a sense of mission accomplished.[25]

During those early years, ranchers who saw the benefits of using the river for profit were looking beyond just simply providing local conveniences. To ship wheat and farm produce by boat—either all the way to Portland or merely as far as the railhead at Lewiston—inspired ranchers south of Asotin to build landings, warehouses, and access roads. On the Idaho side at Waha Landing, Jim Chapman built a road down the slope to a warehouse and steamboat landing. The river there was so shallow Chapman had to build rock piers into the river "a hundred feet or more to get where the water was deep enough to float the steamboats when loaded." He ran a cable tramway from the warehouse—located back against the hill—to the river dock. Chapman operated the business until the late 1920s.[26]

On the Washington side, area farmers maintained three steamboat landings. Couse Creek (Graham's) Landing, north of the mouth of Couse Creek, was the site of the Dodd post office and an outlet for sacked grain brought down the grade from Montgomery Ridge. Jim and Bert Roupe and their brother-in-law Emmett Earl built and ran one grain warehouse there; Alec Martin, another.[27] Two roads led to the Couse Creek warehouses—one down the creek, a second two and a half miles on downriver from Martin Grade. Roupe's 450-foot-long warehouse could store forty thousand wheat sacks.[28] In 1917, a few miles farther south, Fred, Frank, and Dolph Boozer built a grain chute from a midpoint on Weissenfels Ridge down to the river. The plan was to feed loose grain in at the top of the four-inch metal pipe and let gravity pull it down to the warehouse, where someone probably sacked the grain, since steamboats at the time could not accommodate loose grain. Unfortunately for the Boozers, friction scorched much of the grain during the drop, forcing the brothers, as well as later owners, to experiment with ways to improve the means of delivering the grain to the bottom of the chute. The solution was to keep the chute full, adding at the top the same amount released at the bottom. The Boozer brothers operated the chute and warehouse for a few years before selling the business. Some time in the mid 1920s a grass fire burned the wooden supports and, since the chute was less than efficient, the venture ended with the fire.

The Ausmans, who operated a large farm on Weissenfels Ridge, extended a road on down the ridge to just below the mouth of Ten Mile Creek, where they had a boat landing and warehouse.[29] During high water in the spring and fall, steamboats picked up grain and other farm produce at each landing. Even as late as 1938, when the valley's last steamboat, the *Lewiston*, retired, Captain John Akins still made regular stops at Couse Creek and occasional stops at Ten Mile and Waha to pick up sacked grain.[30]

Rogersburg and the River

Early in the twentieth century a small community evolved at the mouth of the Grande Ronde River in Washington, reached from the south by a Forest Service and Wallowa County road through Cold Springs and Road Gulch. From the north, wagon roads dropped from Anatone Flat to the Washington Snake River shores at the mouth of Ten Mile Creek, Couse Creek, and the Grande Ronde River, with trails leading to Rogersburg. Eventually a road from Asotin inched its way up the river to a point across from Captain John until it was extended to Rogersburg in 1938. That remains the farthest upriver access point by car and the only place north of Hells Canyon dam where one can drive along the river in any of the three states.

Figure 19.7. Although in this photo, c. 1900, the steamboat *Lewiston* is on an excursion trip, steamboats made infrequent upriver trips as far as Wild Goose Rapids to carry passengers, deliver supplies, and pick up sacks of grain. This steamboat's replacement, also the *Lewiston*, continued the runs until 1938. (Photo courtesy of the Nez Perce County Historical Society.)

For a time the fledgling community of Rogersburg promised to become the gateway and supply center to the middle Snake River country. George Rogers of Asotin believed the land at the mouth of Grande Ronde was "a natural trading point for many small ranchers that lived up the Grande Ronde and Joseph Creek nearly to Enterprise." He envisioned it as "the closest trading point for many ranchers along Snake River, whose only outlet was by boat."[31] In the 1890s Al Rogers had a gold mine at Lime Point on the Idaho side. He did not make enough money mining so he "came down and built a store and post office and established a trading post" at the mouth of Grande Ronde River.[32] That early business venture must have been the spark that inspired the Rogers brothers to plat a town site on both the north and south sides of the two rivers in 1904 and name it Rogersburg. A few years later, they joined a group of Asotin residents in forming a corporation to mine the lime deposits a short distance above the Grande Ronde. They began building a cement plant on the Snake River near Asotin and planned to barge the lime twenty-seven miles downstream to the new plant. Shareholders believed the proposed Union Pacific water-grade railroad from Weiser to Lewiston would soon become a reality—the survey that year looked promising, they thought—and in the meantime they would rely on the *Mountain Gem* for upriver transportation.[33]

Charles Brown of Asotin was enthusiastic about buying stock and "getting in on the ground floor" of the cement business. His wife, Nellie, "was more cautious and dissuaded him." Instead, in June 1912 they paid George Rogers one hundred dollars for two, fifty-by-one-hundred-foot lots at Rogersburg and agreed "before delivery of the deed" to build a "cement block, brick or stone" store—not less than twenty five by eighty feet and two stories high—and a temporary frame building for immediate use." Rogers's insistence that they build a store suggests his desire to either continue or reestablish his earlier efforts to make Rogersburg a trading center, although the Browns did not mention either of the brothers having had an earlier store there.

The Browns moved to their new property right away. They lived in two large tents on the south side of the confluence while constructing a frame building. The front of the building housed a temporary store, and the back provided living quarters to supplement the tents. By late summer, they had the Grande Ronde Mercantile Company stocked with supplies delivered by steamboat or packhorses. The Browns' business grew slowly but steadily, enough so that by the following year they began construction on the concrete store. By the end of the second year they had finished the permanent, two-story store and made the original frame building their home.

Figure 19.8. Farm country towers above the boat landings on the Snake River. This picture of Montgomery Ridge on the Washington side a few miles above Asotin, shows the Hendrickson ranch, which was moved down to the river from the ridge in 1947. (Photo by author, 1981.)

Unfortunately for the Browns, the cement venture folded in less than a year. Construction on the Asotin plant ended; stock sales closed; and the Union Pacific Railroad announced the water-grade railroad was not feasible.[34] The expected trade with the lime pit miners and their families would not materialize nor did the anticipated business from Joseph Creek and the Grand Ronde. Nevertheless, after considerable effort soliciting business from ranchers up the Snake River, the Browns generated large orders. Charles Brown filled the orders directly from Lewiston wholesale houses and delivered them personally on the weekly mailboat.

The Browns had enough neighbors to begin a school, but foot traffic in the store remained light. Elmer Earl described the place as "the supply point and gathering place for all the homesteaders and ranchers for twenty-five miles or more back up in the hills,"[35] but Nellie Brown remembered store customers as "few and far between," although sometimes "a man would come with one or more packhorses and get quite a bill of goods."[36] James Brewrink said he remembered customers reaching the store by horse and pack train, but his family arrived by foot and rowboat from their mine, a one-mile walk to the boat landing and a couple of miles by boat to the store.[37] If customers were coming from the north or east, Brown often ferried them across the Snake or Grande Ronde Rivers. Usually they stayed the night or at least enjoyed a good meal with the Browns before heading out.[38]

Despite the potential for customers at the Grande Ronde Mercantile Company, the Browns had to supplement their store income with a ranch. So in 1912 they bought the 195-acre Zindell place about two miles up the Grande Ronde River. Martin Zindell, the original owner, had maintained a post office out of his home since early 1901, and operated a ferry across the Grande Ronde. Brown immediately moved the ferry downriver near his mercantile store, closed the Zindell post office, and opened another one at Rogersburg. Zindell's mail had arrived over a twenty-mile mountain trail from Anatone; Brown's mail came up by boat from Asotin. His Grande Ronde ferry business ended when a spring flood broke the ferry loose and sent it into Snake River. Others attempted to operate ferries at the mouth of the Grande Ronde. Then after World War II, Roy McCoy and others moved the ferry three miles up the Grande Ronde River to deeper water. They operated it for a couple of years until the county built a bridge.[39]

Nellie Brown recalled that after Dobbin and Huffman bought the Cache Creek ranch, "we could see that they would have their own commissary and buy their supplies wholesale. So we thought it best to sell the store." In the summer of 1915, the Browns inventoried the store merchandise and sold the stock, the store, all equipment, the lots, and the buildings to E. S. Decker. Four years later, Len Jordan witnessed the sale of the Browns' remaining

Figure 19.9. Barely visible near the center of the picture is all that remained in 1981 of the Rogersburg store and post office, 1912-1939. The Grande Ronde and Snake River confluence is out of sight to the right. Recently, the Rogersburg area has taken on new life as more and more people move there. (Photo by author.)

four hundred acres to Jay H. Dobbin, thus ending the Brown family's involvement in Rogersburg development.

Decker continued to run the post office and operate a store in Rogersburg. He conducted postal business from a small, ornate metal cage labeled "Post Office" in the corner of the store. James Brewrink remembered Mrs. Decker, who usually ran the store, as "a stately lady who dressed and behaved in a manner that had to have been taught in more civilized surroundings." On the second floor were bunks for the children and storage for supplies. While the Deckers lived there, Rogersburg's permanent population included them and a "transient or two as their hired help." They had a shed at the boat landing, their home, and the two-story store, which Brewrink said was "completed in town." The Decker home was large enough to take in boarders, and "when a dozen people who lived back in the hills somewhere could be arranged to respond to the fiddle playing 'Holly Sloan,'" they had a dance in their home.[40] After the Deckers left, a number of other people operated the post office. Postal service ended when the store closed in 1938. The Browns' and Deckers' gave Rogersburg an identity as a supply center for the region and gateway to the canyon. Once the river road from Asotin reached Rogersburg, the tiny community lost its position as supply center. But its identity as gateway to the canyon persisted.

Mail to the Citified Folk

The steamboats *Imnaha* and *Mountain Gem* had confirmed the need for upriver boat service to supply a growing population of ranchers and miners. They also proved that a steamboat was unable to meet that demand. By 1906, when the *Mountain Gem* left upper river service, rivermen had been experimenting with alternatively powered freight and passenger boats for a number of years. From their experiments evolved gasoline launches, the type of boat used to carry supplies, mail, and passengers into the canyon for the next five decades.

In 1900 George Kruger launched his little gasoline-powered, screw-wheeled cargo boat, the *Wild Goose*. During its maiden voyage to Asotin, Kruger realized the boat's screw wheel was not suited to the rocky river, so he replaced it with a stern-wheel. He then loaded a ton of cargo for the Rogers brothers and set off the next day on a three-day trip to their Imnaha mines.[41] That same day, the Lewiston paper announced that B. C. Church, "the Asotin flouring man," was building a naphtha-fueled yacht capable of hauling three thousand pounds of freight. Church planned to use the boat to deliver flour and other supplies to the mining camps. A Portland boat builder provided the plans and supplied the machinery "on a guarantee that the boat will carry the cargo to Pittsburg landing at any stage of water."[42]

At about that same time, Jim Chapman and Roy Favor ran a freight boat up the river, hauling grain and feed every other day. They used two poles to ride through eddies and pull through rapids; sometimes a horseback rider on shore had to pull them through the rapids;

and many times they wore blisters on the palms of their hands rowing across the rapids in low water. They cooked and lived on the boat.[43] In 1915 Chapman built the *Billy Bryan*, named after the three-time Democratic presidential nominee William Jennings Bryan, "who was 'always running but never got there.'"[44] Other rivermen, including Joe Hart, Lawrence Sitkus, and Roy McCoy, experimented with various river craft.

Figure 19.10. This 1938 picture shows a section of the new Snake River road from Asotin to Rogersburg, built by Depression-era Works Progress Administration workers. The federal work program not only put unemployed men to work, it also enabled motorized access to remote sections of the country. (Picture source unknown.)

Boats smaller, tougher, and faster than steamboats were on the Snake River to stay. The captains just needed a way to transform them into a paying business. Roy McCoy, who briefly ran the Rogersburg store and post office, had the right combination of owning a boat and general store. He just didn't run deep enough into the canyon. Charles Brown of Rogersburg realized the business potential upriver but didn't have his own boat to deliver the merchandise. Finally, an entrepreneurial Asotin, Washington, hardware merchant by the name of Ed MacFarlane arrived at the winning combination.

In partnership with his uncle, Richard Glover, the two men provided equipment for Snake River miners and upland farmers from their Asotin store. In the summer of 1909, they finagled a deal with one of their customers: in exchange for a half interest in the man's mining claim, they would order and deliver his requested cargo. Once the equipment arrived in Asotin, the two merchants wondered how they were going to get it to the mouth of the Grande Ronde River. Their only solution was to build a boat, which they began to do late that fall.[45]

In early February 1910 MacFarlane's steel-hulled, thirty-six-foot *Flyer* was ready to launch. Its two-cycle, three-cylinder Fario engine was temperamental at first, but after "snorting and sputtering at intervals for about two days, it decided to go."[46] For backup, he and Glover carried a fourteen-foot oar and oarlock on the stern. They delivered the first load, fifteen hundred pounds of mining machinery, to the Grande Ronde miner by 1:30 p.m., the same day they took off from Asotin, and were back in town by 4:00—impressive timing for that period. A few more successful trips convinced "everyone" they "were getting through all right," so other miners and ranchers asked MacFarlane to

Figure 19.11. Ed MacFarlane (left) and passenger Dr. Clements of Washington State College (University) during a 1931 WSC field trip to Hells Canyon. MacFarlane made a living on the Snake River delivering mail and supplies from 1910 until 1939. He was in partnership with Press Brewrink between 1926 and 1935. (Photo courtesy of Irene Markx.)

Map 20.2. Frequently used trails following mountain ridges on both sides of the Snake River. Numerous side trails intersected from the canyon to the Salmon and Imnaha Rivers.

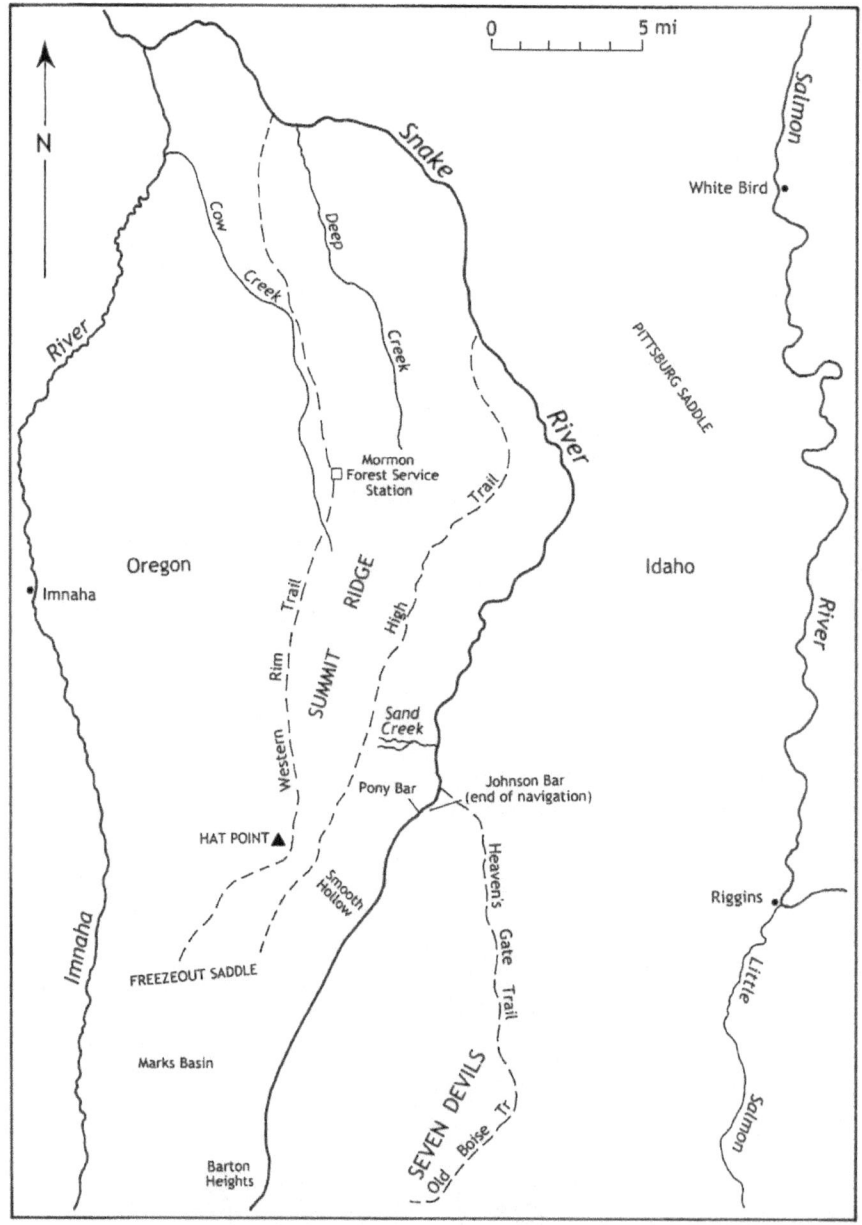

haul their freight. Soon, the two hardware merchants expanded their delivery service into a once-a-week upriver trip, with MacFarlane putting his past navigation experience to work on the river while Glover attended the store.[47]

So long as river conditions remained favorable, the *Flyer* maintained regular mail runs, as well as additional services. S. C. Martin, assistant engineer of Oregon Short Line (Union Pacific), had a survey crew on the river from Homestead to Lewiston. The *Flyer* reached their camp near Deep Creek about eleven o'clock on December 3, 1911, stopped for a brief period, then continued on upriver. Returning the next day, MacFarlane reported they had gone four miles above Pittsburg Landing to Defiance Eddy, without having to line through any rapids. On December 15, the *Flyer* returned and helped the survey crew move their camp from Dug Creek to Cache Creek, passing "a box canyon gorge below the mouth of the Imnaha River for a distance of some four or five miles. A wild ride in a motor boat." Four days later, the *Flyer* returned with mail and supplies for the camp—and November paychecks for the crew. The day after Christmas, with more than four inches of snow on the ground, the *Flyer* dropped more supplies and mail at camp and returned three days later with another survey party bound for Lewiston. By January 3 the *Flyer* was off the river. While the survey crew was still camped at Anaconda Gulch below Cache Creek, Martin wrote that the engineer in charge of surveys, a Mr. Stacey, "came in from Lewiston afoot. The motor boat [*Flyer*] was unable to navigate." By the time the rest of the survey party reached Lewiston, "the river was a flowing stream of cake ice."[48]

The *Flyer* was too small to satisfy the growing demand for freight transportation, so in the spring of 1912, MacFarlane launched the sixty-five-foot *Prospector* "with its twin 100 horsepower Scrips engines and twice the carrying capacity" of the *Flyer*.[49] Five years earlier Congress had authorized money for open river work from the mouth of Snake River to Pittsburg Landing but regular service remained problematic until 1914, when MacFarlane received federal funds to blast obstructing rocks out of the channel. By 1918 the Portland District of the Corps of Engineers had spent $426,527 on that work. MacFarlane's funding

Figure 19.12. The *Clipper*, possibly with Captain Ed MacFarlane bending over the bow. (Photo courtesy of Irene Markx.)

probably was part of that expenditure, supplementing work done around 1910 south of Lewiston by the corps' dredge the *Umatilla*.⁵⁰

Once MacFarlane finished his work, and was satisfied that he could push farther upriver, he and nineteen passengers decided to see how far the *Flyer* could go during high water. "His friend, Stewart Winslow, a steamboat captain on the lower Snake, accompanied him with his fast little launch, the *Tillicum*." They left the *Tillicum* at Johnson Bar, put the passengers to work helping line the *Flyer* through Rush Creek rapids, and headed on to the hundred-foot long, eleven-foot drop of Granite Creek Rapids, known by river runners today as the infamous "green room." The *Flyer* lacked power to climb the rapids and lining through was impossible. All they could do was turn back. Nevertheless, the channel was now open and navigation possible the entire ninety-one miles from Lewiston to Johnson Bar.⁵¹

In 1919 MacFarlane built the *Clipper* in partnership with A. M. Peterson, and for a brief time, the two men operated it, the *Flyer*, and the *Prospector* under the name Snake River Boat Company. Although no formal government Snake River mail contract yet existed, their company continued mail delivery services. MacFarlane proved his navigation skills time and again. A much later river pilot, Dick Rivers, said of MacFarlane, "It took guts to defy the Snake." He described one trip when MacFarlane operated in three states to climb one rapid. At Madden Bar the main channel churned with debris from a flash flood down Garden Creek. With the *Clipper* on the Idaho side, the crew began lining through the rapids. "Resourceful Captain MacFarlane cut a section from a stranded log, converted it into a capstan, made a block fast on the Washington shore and hauled the boat around part of the jam. He then moved the line upstream into Oregon and repeated [the process]," successfully clearing the rapids.⁵²

Another pilot on the river during MacFarlane's time, William Pressly "Press" Brewrink, was piloting the sluggish *Swastika* to supply his mining interests at Wild Goose and Imnaha. In 1915 he bought Jim Chapman's speedy *Billy Bryan*, and four years later his good business sense landed him the first Snake River mail contract. Each week at Lewiston, Brewrink picked up mail addressed to "River Route, Lewiston, Idaho," and delivered it to eager ranchers and miners all the way to Pittsburg Landing. He held that contract for two years, running the *Let's Go* and the *Clipper*, which he bought from MacFarlane and Peterson.⁵³

In December 1921 the government granted the mail contract to Ed MacFarlane's Snake River Transportation Company and extended the route beyond Pittsburg Landing to Johnson Bar.⁵⁴ In 1924 the contract went to Johnny Ames and Archie Rowland, who in turn subcontracted it back to Press Brewrink. Two years later, MacFarlane hired Press Brewrink as an engineer and supercargo and within a short time brought him into the business. The two men stayed in business and held the mail contract together for the next twelve years. In 1935 MacFarlane turned the business over to Brewrink and retired to his Lewiston home.

After taking over the Snake River Transportation Company, Press Brewrink stayed with the freight, passenger, and mail business until mid-1938, when he lost the mail contract to Kyle McGrady. Since Brewrink no longer had that annual twenty-five hundred to three thousand dollars from the U.S. Postal Service to keep his freight and passenger services afloat, he left the river for a few months. (Maybe that was when Press "tinkered with his Stanley Steamer, until one day when it quit in the middle of the Lewiston-Clarkston bridge.")⁵⁵ Then in early 1939, he resumed boat services in competition with McGrady, but without a mail contract. Press Brewrink's river career came to an abrupt end on October 31, 1940, when he died from complications during surgery.

Between 1928 and 1935, when MacFarlane and Brewrink together ran the Snake River Transportation Company, they operated the *Flyer, Prospector, Clipper,* and *Idaho*—a fifty-eight-foot boat, capable of hauling eight tons, that had been built in 1922. MacFarlane used boat plans from a magazine to build all four boats. However, for the sixty-five-foot long, shallow-draft *Chief Joseph*, which he and Brewrink built in 1935, "Press insisted on using a marine architect. Ironically, she was a failure—a fuel hog, too slow and clumsy for river use."[56] The *Chief Joseph* did not stay long on Snake River.

Their mailboat run averaged forty-six different landings in three states between Lewiston and Johnson Bar. Ranchers living beyond the mailboat's reach continued to haul their own mail and supplies overland. Violet Wilson Shirley voiced the opinion of those upriver ranchers when she said, "We thought the people downriver from Sheep Creek or even Rush Creek who got their mail and supplies on the mailboat were pretty citified. They didn't have to pack all their supplies over the mountains."[57] For the ranchers living below Johnson Bar, however, going *in* and *out* of Hells Canyon became ever more a matter of going *up* and *down* the river.

On their weekly run to those "citified" ranchers, MacFarlane and Brewrink left Lewiston early in the morning and reached Pittsburg Landing by evening, where they spent the night. The next morning the mailboat continued on to Johnson Bar, arriving around midmorning and returning to Lewiston the same day. In addition to delivering mail and supplies, MacFarlane and Brewrink conducted all regular post office business out of the boat, picked up and dropped off passengers, and ferried scows loaded with sheep, horses, or pack strings across the river.[58] They moved lumber from Pittsburg Landing and copper ore from some of the remaining mines. Freight charges per hundredweight varied from twenty-five cents when delivered at Asotin to two dollars for delivery at Johnson Bar. Stock salt had special rates; ore ranged from fifty-two to sixty-three dollars a ton. Passengers paid between fifty cents to go to Asotin and six dollars to Johnson Bar. They could take fifty pounds of baggage and carried their own bedroll and food.[59]

Anyone who wanted to board the boat along the route simply waited by a landing. Carmen Winniford Yokum, whose family lived at Sluice Creek, said she and her mother once waited all day at the landing. No boat. They went back down the next day and waited

Figure 19.13. Ed MacFarlane and Press Brewrink established Johnson Bar as the end of their mail deliveries, and it remained head of navigation for subsequent mailboat captains. This aerial picture, looking north about seven miles below Johnson Bar, provides a sense of the river and canyon through which they passed. Suicide Point, and the rugged trail scraped around it, is on the right (Idaho side) with Hominy Creek in the foreground and Salt Creek further down river, both on the Oregon side. (Photo courtesy of Robert Hoyle.)

Figure 19.14. In 1931 a Washington State College (University) botany class took a field trip aboard the *Clipper*. Professor Clements stands on shore taking a head count. (Photo courtesy of Irene Markx.)

Figure 19.15. WSC botany student Irene Markx at the wheel of the *Clipper*, with some of her classmates in the foreground. (Photo courtesy of Irene Markx.)

some more. Finally the boat came.[60] On another trip, Carmen and her mother were the only passengers. Mr. Brewrink was the captain ("we were never allowed to call grown-ups by their first names") and Mr. Leonard Sitkus the engineer. Mr. Brewrink, she remembered, was "always friendly," but tall, dark, young Mr. Sitkus scared her. The *Idaho* "had a long bench built along each side, otherwise the cabin was bare. Sometimes excess cargo was piled in the middle." When Mr. Sitkus finished his duties, he stretched out on the bench opposite Carmen and her mother and fell asleep. A big rapid rolled the boat to port, flinging young Carmen off her seat and "propelling" her "mightily" across the cabin. She caught herself by hitting Mr. Sitkus hard with the heels of her hands in his "unsuspecting mid-section." Expecting a big hand to reach out, grab her neck, and toss her overboard, Carmen scurried back to the protective arm of her mother on their side of the boat. She bravely apologized to Mr. Sitkus, who "with a grunt…turned over, settled down and went back to sleep, not caring that he had just become a small girl's own, personal bogeyman."[61]

During those early years, few people probably foresaw the permanent changes MacFarlane and Brewrink were introducing to the canyon, for it took nearly three decades before the importance of tourism became evident. Two or three times while aboard the *Imnaha* or *Mountain Gem*, Eureka Company officers had commented casually on how the canyon's unique beauty might attract sightseers. But their minds were focused on mining, not tourism. MacFarlane also saw that potential. For a short time, he "solicited parties within a radius of fifty miles of Lewiston to make excursions up the Snake."[62] Mostly fishermen and hunters responded, although a growing number of students, scientists, and adventurers scheduled river excursions.[63] In time, it became too difficult for MacFarlane to advertise and organize the trips, so he simply responded if a group requested an outing. Soon "student classes from the colleges at Pullman and Moscow made annual trips" and kept the boats "in constant service."[64] One consequence of the college excursions was an expanding national awareness of a place soon to be known as Hells Canyon.

Professor L. F. Pickett of the Washington State College Botany Department must have been a regular visitor there, for over time he identified more than a hundred varieties of wildflowers in the canyon. Was it Captain MacFarlane who showed Pickett a favorite canyon flower, a deep rose beauty that only opened to full bloom on afternoons in May? Was Pickett responsible when in 1936 the Biological Society of Washington named the flower MacFarlane's four-o'clock (*Mirabilis macfarlanei*), consequently directing the botanical world's attention to that region?

Figure 19.16. Lewiston photographer and theater director A. H. (Al) Hilton taking a 16 mm movie of the *Clipper* in 1921. (Photo courtesy of Nez Perce County Historical Society.)

Fox Film Corporation cinematographer Eric Meyell, a MacFarlane passenger, was one of the first photographers to use motion pictures to show the canyon's unique potential for sturgeon fishing. A short time later, in 1921, Lewiston theater director A. H. (Al) Hilton boarded the *Clipper* with his cumbersome 16-mm movie camera and a desire to portray the astounding beauty of his region. He came home with a thousand feet of motion film, which Paramount Pictures executive Al Lewis said showed "the most wonderful scenery in the United States, equaling if not surpassing anything in the Rockies." Otis W. Freeman of the College of Education in Cheney (now Eastern Washington State University) traveled on one of MacFarlane's last trips, and in 1938 the American Geographical Society published his article detailing characteristics of the landscape and canyon life.[65] What those scholars, writers, and photographers initiated under MacFarlane's and Brewrink's watch, others repeated.

"This Worldly Strife"

Ed MacFarlane died in October 1949, nine years after Press Brewrink's unexpected death. Hells Canyon lost two pioneer rivermen that decade; more importantly, the canyon ranchers lost two good friends remembered for far more than their navigation skills. Carmen Winniford Yokum fondly remembered Press and Edna Brewrink, who befriended many Hells Canyon people, even loaning money to a number of families, "to help them in different situations." With their Fifth Street home only a few blocks from the Lewiston hospital, the Brewrinks often housed people from the river when they had family in the hospital or were themselves recuperating. Edna visited the sick and gave people used clothing. In order to get wool for the rugs she enjoyed braiding and hooking, she bought "everything left after a rummage sale," then gave away everything except wool clothing. Carmen's family "was one of the recipients. We had one of the most fabulous collections of 'dress-up' clothes children ever had."[66]

Alfreda Elsensohn and Robert G. Bailey, both authors of mid-twentieth-century regional history and MacFarlane's and Brewrink's contemporaries, remembered MacFarlane as a poetic man moved to write about the river and canyon he loved. Bailey published his "May on Snake River," inspired by the canyon's green-swathed hill slopes and spectacular array of wildflowers.[67]

> Glorious breeze from the hills so green—
> Breathe deep, take in the scenery serene.
> In yonder dell and woodland glade
> Where flowers bloom of every shade.
> All go to make this worldly strife
> Somewhat easier in this life.
>   —Mac, 1933

Chapter 20

Flirting with Angels

Kyle McGrady has emerged as the most famous of the Snake River mailboat pilots, primarily because earlier Hells Canyon publicity sparked by Ed MacFarlane and Press Brewrink spread to a growing audience ever more eager to learn about this "last frontier." In the telling and retelling of McGrady's story, however, some of the facts got muddled along the way. Either thirty-year-old Kyle McGrady, a Lewiston garage mechanic, "overheard a rancher telling another that he couldn't continue operating without reliable riverboat service and on a whim decided to get into the business,"[1] or McGrady was an unemployed garage mechanic, who, while "loafing around home," read that the post office department was seeking bidders on a contract to carry mail.[2] Both versions are plausible. What is certain is in 1938 farmer-turned-mechanic Kyle McGrady, who knew nothing about piloting a boat on the treacherous Snake River, made a huge gamble and, over time, won. But initially, "McGrady got the bid with dire prophecies of failure."[3]

Kyle's Fleet

Kyle and his wife, Florence, dug deep in their pockets and bought a six-year-old, secondhand outboard motorboat, the *Dawn*, from Carl Gustin of Clarkston. Only a few weeks before the mail contract began, either he hired Press Brewrink and Ed MacFarlane or they volunteered to help him. In any case, each went up the Snake River a few times with Kyle to teach him where the rocks were and how to work through the rapids. Years later, Jess Earl described Kyle as "kinda wild and [a man who] liked a lot of fun, but he was a boatman and a real one. He had more guts than any one man ever had, or ever will have on that river again."[4] Guts he may have had, but his skill as a boatman faltered even before his job began.

Kyle himself confessed that he and Tom Tumelson of Lewiston were checking sturgeon traps and going over the mail route when he picked the wrong channel at Horse Tail Rapid, fifty miles above Clarkston, and plunged the boat onto the rocks lining the shore. As soon as they hit, the two men worked the boat toward the shore and got close enough to jump out with the tie line in tow. They tied up the boat, which rapidly filled with water and broke loose. The two watched the twenty-seven-foot *Dawn* breaking

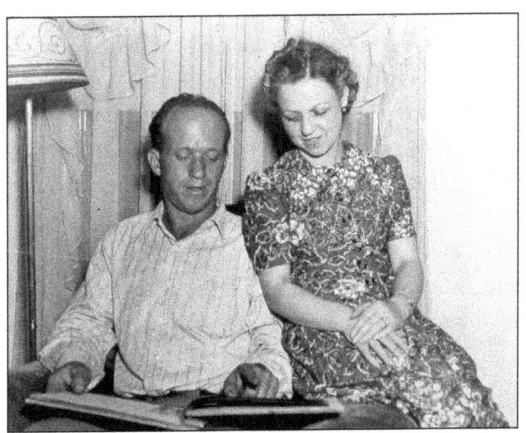

Figure 20.1. Kyle and Florence McGrady looking at one of Florence's many scrapbooks about Kyle's mail and delivery services into Hells Canyon between 1938 and 1950. (Photo courtesy of Robert McGrady.)

into pieces under the water, taking all their fishing equipment, camp materials, and guns down with it. (Some say the boat exploded and burned, but there is no proof of that.) Wreckage floated downriver, alerting people below to what might have been a fatal accident. Frank Hastings, whom McGrady and Tumelson had visited just the night before, discovered some of their wreckage near the Madden Ranch and initiated a search. He found the two men hiking overland to the mouth of the Salmon River and took them to Cache Creek, where they phoned home to relieved families. Back in Clarkston, Kyle told Florence, "That river hasn't got me licked yet."[5] He wanted another boat, although they had no idea how they would afford one.

Stories handed down say rancher Joe McClaren collected money from other ranchers to help McGrady buy another boat and the McGradys used it plus money they raised by mortgaging their home to buy the *Idaho*. However, weekly newspaper reports indicate that McGrady did not purchase the *Idaho* for another two and a half years. He hired an unnamed boat for his first mail run, scheduled for Friday, July 1, 1938. On that initial trip, a few miles above Pittsburg Landing, the engine quit and the craft turned over. Once Kyle got the boat righted, he discovered the engine had fallen into the river. These two accidents seemed to prove the "dire prophecy of failure." But Kyle was a determined man, one not easily beaten. Brewrink filled in for him while he searched for another boat.

Maybe it was the *Wauna* that Kyle and Florence bought with help from canyon ranchers and a mortgaged home, maybe not. At any rate, that was the boat they purchased after the unnamed boat capsized. The old *Wauna* had been out of service several years, so they probably got it at a good price. McGrady installed two, 90-hp motors, made the launch "shipshape," hired Archie Rowland as pilot, and began the mail runs. Soon the local newspaper proclaimed that the "hard-luck navigator of the Snake" had overcome his "jinx with the third boat" by making the weekly upriver run without incident.[6]

In September 1938 the water was so low the *Wauna* could go only to the mouth of the Salmon River. Undaunted, McGrady transferred undelivered cargo and mail to his fourteen-foot outboard motor boat, the *Pumpkin Seed*, which he transported on the *Wauna* for such an emergency. The smaller craft continued making deliveries for the next forty-three miles, to Johnson Bar. Then in November, hard luck hit again. The *Wauna* left Lewiston Friday morning as usual, but could go no farther than the Salmon. There McGrady beached for the night and returned to Rogersburg the next morning, without transferring the cargo to the *Pumpkin Seed*. He intended to go on to Lewiston early Sunday morning. As he prepared breakfast for himself and deckhand Frank Hastings, the small gasoline stove in the pilothouse exploded. He and Hastings escaped with their lives—and the mail. Most of the cargo, primarily groceries, and a portion of the boat went up in flames. It was a two thousand dollar–loss and the *Wauna* had no insurance.

Kyle immediately began repairs while using the *Pumpkin Seed* on the weekly mail run, trucking mail and cargo to Rogersburg and launching the *Pumpkin Seed* from there. Christmas was only a month away. Knowing the smaller craft could not carry the heavy holiday loads, Kyle admonished his five workers to make the repairs as fast as they could, "so as not to disappoint the people." On Christmas Day 1938 the *Wauna*, the "aquatic sleigh," left Lewiston with ten sacks of parcel post, mostly presents, a bag of Christmas greetings, and three tons of freight. Despite "fog, low water and the difficulties that may develop from a long trip with new motors," Kyle played Santa Claus all the way to Johnson Bar.

Kyle's hard luck and his on-again, off-again service might have been the incentive Press Brewrink needed to put his eighteen-year-old craft the *Idaho* back on the river. He had not run the boat since McGrady got the mail contract in July, but that fall he began to overhaul the motors, repair the deck, and replace all the woodwork in preparation for renewed river transportation service. Late in February 1939, he announced that the *Idaho* would be making regular weekly cargo and passenger runs, departing Fridays. For most of that year, both boats provided commercial service to canyon residents.

Perhaps Press Brewrink took too much of McGrady's business. Something motivated McGrady to build a new boat that October. The forty-five-foot launch had a triple-welded hull and a twenty-two inch draw. Berg Shipyards of Seattle cut and shaped the metal for the hull, and Andrew Berg himself came to Clarkston to supervise the electric welders. McGrady used the *Wauna*'s two motors on the new boat and added a reduction gear, making it possible to increase the power of the propellers to 140 hp each. The ten-ton capacity boat would go upstream 18 mph under normal circumstances and could carry thirty-five to fifty passengers. The new boat was indeed an improvement over the *Wauna* and nearly as good a boat as Brewrink's *Idaho*.

McGrady named his steel gray, black-trimmed launch *Florence*. He built a pilothouse, roofed over the cargo-carrying part of the hull, and put a catwalk around the boat. Later he installed a passenger cabin at the stern and rigging over the entire structure. Kyle and Florence launched the *Florence* on November 24, 1939. Her maiden run was successful as were all subsequent trips. Two months later Kyle replaced the two old *Wauna* motors with two new 100-hp motors.

After Press Brewrink's sudden death late in 1940, his *Idaho* stayed in river service. McGrady bought the boat and used both it and the *Florence* to serve his growing business. He replaced the *Idaho*'s motors with two new 82-hp diesel motors with a three-to-one reduction gear. They were the first diesel motors used on the Snake. McGrady had to get a priority from the War Productions Board for the new motors. Idaho senator D. Worth Clark helped him secure that priority by arguing that McGrady's boat "makes possible the grazing of thousands of sheep on slopes and hillsides which otherwise might be useless." Mail service must continue and the "area's production of wool and mutton" must be ensured. Later, while aboard one of Kyle's motor craft, an insurance appraiser said to him, "Young man, you certainly believe in flirting with angels. You're about as safe a risk as a submarine." Kyle had been flirting with angels for some time. The appraiser recommended coverage and his company allowed four thousand dollars on the boat, even though the motors alone cost five thousand dollars.[7]

In July 1940 McGrady replaced the *Pumpkin Seed* with a new all-steel, eighteen-foot long, inboard motor boat. The *Pumpkin Seed* made the round trip from Rogersburg to Johnson's Bar in one day; the new boat could run the 186-mile round trip from Lewiston to Johnson Bar in thirteen hours, putting it back at the Lewiston dock the same evening. Even with the river low and the rapids studded with rocks, the new boat's hull held up under the Snake's "buffeting wild waters" and proved more reliable than any other craft.

The *Florence*, the *Idaho*, and the unnamed new boat teamed up to serve the canyon residents until September 1941. Then in smooth water at the foot of a rapid near Cache Creek, the rudder dropped off the *Florence*. McGrady safely maneuvered the boat to shore and once again searched for transportation home. He planned to order parts from Spokane, make repairs, and have the boat back in service for Friday's mail run. Apparently that did not happen, for that *Florence* disappeared from the weekly *Lewiston Morning Tribune* reports. Another *Florence* appeared two and a half years later, July 1944, to join the *Idaho*. McGrady's new specially designed, flat-bottomed *Florence* was forty-five feet long with a twelve-and-a-half-foot beam. (The *Idaho* was fifty-three feet long with an eleven-foot beam.) It had a lighter draft, was more maneuverable, and traveled at twelve to 15 mph upstream and 25 down, as compared to the *Idaho*'s 7 mph up and 15 down. Kyle's tourist business had grown considerably. His two big reliable boats met local and tourist demands for his remaining years on the river. He put the *Idaho* under skipper John Olney's command and piloted the new *Florence* himself.[8]

Until the winter of 1941, Kyle failed to fully appreciate how important his business was to Hells Canyon residents. That winter, pasture was "as worthless as straw," and Ivan Simmons of Dug Bar was caught without feed for his thousand head of sheep. He contacted Kyle, who agreed to bring up a load of grain on his next trip. Knowing Simmons would lose his flock without that food, McGrady loaded the *Idaho* with barley and oats and headed upriver into "one of the fiercest storms in the history of the Pacific Northwest." Snow coated the pilothouse, forcing Kyle to open the window to see. Soon his gloved hand stuck to the wheel, snow covered his upper body, and ice floes bumped against the sides of the boat. "At Wild Goose the jam in the river towered high above the pilothouse. For seven hours, the diesels hammered stubbornly" as McGrady "pushed and heaved the boat against the frozen mass. He locked the wheel and attacked the jam with a shovel; his pocketknife would have served as well." He could go no farther. Safely home, he went to bed with a fever "produced both by grippe and bitter disappointment." The freeze closed the river for three weeks. There was no way even to pack feed into Simmons' flock; they all perished. The experience sobered Kyle, who later said, "You know, I started this thing as sort of a lark, but I just couldn't stop now. These people count on me. If I stopped taking this boat up the river, I don't know what they'd do, I really don't. The women and old men could never climb out over the mountains, I'm sure of that." He fully appreciated what that boat meant to the canyon people.[9]

River Route, Lewiston, Idaho

By the time Kyle added the last *Florence* to his fleet, he had proved himself the "real boatman" Jess Earl remembered, dedicated to his business and willing to serve his customers of "River Route, Lewiston, Idaho" in a wide variety of nonconventional ways for a postal service mail carrier. Each week, the *Lewiston Morning Tribune* ran an update of McGrady's river business, enabling valley residents, who had always had a marginal interest in the Snake River, to keep up on canyon affairs. The articles listed the names and destinations of the passengers going upriver, the returning passengers and where they boarded, even the passengers who traveled from place to place within the canyon. Anyone in the Lewiston-Clarkston valley who cared to could know the comings and goings of cattle and sheep ranchers and their children. They knew who the ranch hands were and where they worked, who the commercial fishermen were, who was sluicing which gravel bars for gold, and who the trappers were. They got a sense of sheep ranch operations by reading about the movement of the lambing, shearing, and haying crews. They even knew who the tourists were, where they were from, and what their business in the canyon was. The articles described some of Kyle's regular upriver cargo, the cargo he hauled from landing to landing, and the cargo he brought back to Lewiston, as well as the various

Figure 20.2. The mailboat at the Lewiston, Idaho, Snake River Avenue boat landing during the 1930s. Wool sacks were unloaded to rail cars at the landing for shipment to Portland; cumbersome cargo often shipped to Lewiston by rail was transferred directly to the boat for upriver destinations. (Photo courtesy of Robert McGrady.)

additional services McGrady provided. Florence clipped all the *Tribune* articles and kept them in family albums along with pictures, business brochures, and articles that appeared in other publications. The scrapbooks, some with their handmade wooden covers, provide a valuable picture of weekly river traffic from the late 1930s through the 1940s.

Figure 20.3. Kyle McGrady supervises as crew and ranch hands coax a reluctant horse aboard the *Florence* to be ferried across the river. (Photo courtesy of Robert McGrady.)

During his first year on the river, "rough, tough, and bald" Kyle McGrady "who swore like a sailor" made forty regular landings between Lewiston and Johnson Bar.[10] A year and a half later the number was down to twenty, and by mid-1944, with so many changes going on in the outside world, McGrady was making only fifteen regular mail landings.[11] However, the type of upriver cargo he carried remained the same, averaging from 3 to 5 tons and always including mail sacks and parcel post. His grocery load, which sometimes figured in the tons, was especially large during lambing and shearing seasons. A single order might include a ton of apples or potatoes, or 110 pounds of cherries. During the holidays, turkeys roasted and dressed at a valley restaurant might supplement the large, special grocery orders. Late fall and winter he hauled 20 tons or more of livestock feed, usually consisting of oats or cottonseed cake. Stock salt went upriver by the ton throughout the year. Dobbin once placed an order for a ton of borax, and one year before shearing, McGrady's load included 3,000 pounds of wool tags. He frequently carried equipment and bait for sturgeon anglers, as well as motors and other mining equipment for the miners. He filled one order from Kirkwood and Johnson Bar for irrigation pipe and numerous orders for lumber to build lambing sheds and corrals. Ranchers needed seed and farm equipment, and someone ordered 1,900 pounds of cement. Incidentals always filled the cargo bay—boots for Ace Duncan, a Bible to Christmas Creek, a bear trap for Jack Titus, a new dress for Darlene Wilson, or a complete set of bathroom fixtures for the Johnson Ranch. And people didn't forget the day their prized home or farm appliance arrived on the boat.

One of McGrady's most valuable services was shuttling people, animals, and goods from landing to landing. He regularly ferried seasonal work crews from ranch to ranch, as well as heavy and cumbersome equipment. Miners, always in search of better digs, had him haul hydraulic equipment from bar to bar; sturgeon fishermen used him to help set their traps at various places along the river. He ferried 10 tons of hay across the river at Couse Creek, and moved a half ton of flour—a year's supply—and ton of salt from Pittsburg Landing to Summers Creek. He once picked up two hundred fence posts at Rogersburg to deliver to the Dobbin ranch at Cache Creek.

Frequently when the river was

Figure 20.4. McGrady's *Idaho* ferrying a pack string across the river. Note the U.S. Yacht Ensigns flag with 13 stripes and a circle of stars around an anchor. (Photo courtesy of Robert McGrady.)

Figure 20.5. During the winter of 1942, while three people look on, Kyle McGrady (right front) and three other men begin to load a wrecked airplane onto the *Idaho*. The wings are already on the cargo hold. (Photo courtesy of Robert McGrady.)

low, ranchers trucked supplies and equipment normally sent all the way by boat over the saddle to Pittsburg Landing, where McGrady picked them up with one of his smaller boats and moved them on to their final destination. Many miners, who worked both Snake and Salmon river bars, moved supplies and equipment across the saddle to Pittsburg Landing for Kyle to deliver elsewhere on the Snake River. Over a single four-week period, McGrady made a number of trips from Pittsburg Landing to the Johnson's Temperance Creek ranch, hauling loads of lumber for their new ranch house. McGrady could ferry eight hundred to a thousand head of sheep at a time, and he often ferried accompanying large pack strings. Sheep ranchers at Rogersburg and Couse Creek also periodically moved sheep bands between Washington and Idaho via Kyle's ferry service. So did Dobbin and Huffman. In fact, they used McGrady's ferry service so often he kept a specially designed livestock scow at Cache Creek. And he hauled Frank Wilson's new Hereford bull, plus five wranglers to keep the animal under control, nine miles from Pittsburg Landing to Sommers Creek.

Kyle's boats rarely returned to Lewiston empty, especially during spring shearing. Piled high in the center of the boat were bloated, six-hundred-pound, smelly, tick-filled sacks of wool. One load of wool from the Johnson Ranch was 34 sacks, or eight tons, destined for the Pendleton Woolen Mills. Another from the Jordans consisted of 25 sacks bound for Nezperce Roller Mills in Lewiston. Jack Goldsmith sent down 22 sacks from Couse Creek. Kyle's cargo might also include trappers' pelts bound for Pacific Hide and Fur in Lewiston. Or it might be small pokes or tins of gold dust destined for deposit at Sapp's Grocery Store. When commercial fishing was legal, Kyle sometimes hauled 700 to 800 pounds of sturgeon. Miner James Clark, who was working Johnson Bar, once peeled chittum bark from the trees and sent it down with Kyle. The bark, used in "certain medicines," was destined for Lewiston stores; the rest was shipped on to other markets.

An even more unusual cargo was a small airplane with its wings

Figure 20.6. The airplane is nearly loaded, with possible last minute instructions from Kyle McGrady standing on top of the pilot house. (Photo courtesy of Robert McGrady.)

clipped and propeller splintered. Bob Titus, son of Jack and Celia Titus, was flying into his parents' Snake River ranch, when the pilot, his University of Idaho chum, attempted to land on an alfalfa field airstrip at Pittsburg Landing covered with a foot of wet, heavy snow. The snow sucked the nose down as soon as the wheels hit the field. The two passengers emerged unscathed but at a loss as to how to return the plane to Moscow. McGrady's boat seemed the only answer, so they removed the wings and hauled the plane to the river. They then mounted horses and rode over the mountains to White Bird. From there they made it back to their university classes, and Kyle hauled their airplane to Lewiston.[12]

Help Comes in Many Forms

Kyle moved things upriver, downriver, and in the case of fishing, up and down. McGrady used his boats and regular canyon runs to feed the nation's hunger for sturgeon and caviar. Despite the economic depression, there was good money in both the fish and its roe. Sturgeon shipped to Lewiston went to Portland until a full railroad car was accumulated, then to New York City, where sturgeon meat was "considered a delicacy." Many men made a living or supplemented their income by fishing for sturgeon. Each day before his weekly mail run, McGrady drew a bucket full of eels from the Clearwater River at the Washington Water Power dam near Lewiston. Then at each landing along the mail run, "his customers got the mail with one hand and a writhing eel with the other."[13] McGrady helped them set lines and collect their catch at different landings. Until the mid 1940s, when it became illegal to catch the giant fish for commercial purposes, McGrady even supplemented his own income by sturgeon fishing, bringing in an extra seventy-five dollars a week with each catch.

Kyle sometimes earned money in unlikely ways. For example, when "burly miner" John Oscar Potter was floating his scow, engine, and pump to an unworked placer field, "he ran afoul of rocks in the swift rapids." Thinking the scow was inextricably stuck, he left it, and began to row to Lewiston when he met McGrady. "She's yours for a cigarette," the frustrated miner told McGrady, so they made the sale. McGrady salvaged the equipment, "rigged up sluice boxes and a connecting hose to the water pump and began mining." By afternoon, he netted four dollars worth of gold dust and ended up with equipment worth seventy-five dollars, all for one cigarette. But Potter didn't mind the exchange. He was now "foot loose and fancy free," content to be out of the mining business.[14]

Miners like the Onley brothers lived year round in wooden scows

Figure 20.7. Not only did Kyle McGrady provide bait for Snake River sturgeon fishermen, he also set out his own lines along his Snake River mail run. Here he proudly shows off a recent catch. (Photo courtesy of Robert McGrady.)

that doubled as equipment transports. However, whenever McGrady showed up, if the miner was ready to relocate, McGrady's boat provided a much easier move. Kyle frequently picked up John, Lawrence, or Joe Onley at one landing and dropped them off near another claim and brought John's wife and five children into the canyon for visits. Kyle hauled other permanent miners from claim to claim, like Duncan Conrad, Oakey Grogg, William Mitchell, Francis Smith, and John Nelson (plus many more), and temporary workers from Spokane, Pullman, and Lewiston who were drawn to the canyon to work at the Pullman mine near the Salmon and Snake river confluence. During the Depression, it was normal to read in the *Tribune* about gold prospectors and their families in the canyon. Men and their families were trying to keep body and soul together with a little gold dust, and if Lewiston residents thought the canyon was strictly a man's world, the frequency of women's names in McGrady's weekly passenger report should have changed that perception. For example, Clara Ilyer, who cooked for the lambing crew at Cougar Bar, was a regular spring passenger as were other women working as ranch cooks.

When Ava Simmons found a man ill at the long-abandoned Homestake Mine, McGrady was also, literally, a lifesaver. One bleak November day Mrs. Simmons hiked to the man's isolated cabin for newspapers and found him helpless, stricken with a prostrate gland ailment. She stopped McGrady about twenty-nine miles below Johnson Bar on his return run. He did not want to carry an injured passenger over the rapids in the dark, so he and his passenger, Carl Sigler, a Summers Creek miner, bunked at the Homestake cabin for the night. The next morning they improvised a stretcher, carried the sick man one mile over a trail to the boat, and rigged up an army cot in the launch for a more comfortable ride. They reached Lewiston at 10:30 Sunday morning.[15]

Another time, in the middle of the night, Kyle responded to a call for help from Rogersburg. Fourteen-year-old Bob Gill at Divide Creek had appendicitis and a man walked from there to Rogersburg to call for help. Kyle navigated through the dark with the aid of his big searchlight. The *Florence* occasionally grazed boulders but reached Divide Creek safely by dawn, in time to deliver the boy to the operating table in Lewiston. Twice in one week McGrady hauled poison ivy victims to Lewiston for treatment. Jack Wilson of Deep Creek, hoping to cure himself, made and drank a brew of poison ivy leaves. The doctor who finally saw him claimed it was "the worse case of poison ivy I have ever seen." That same week, McGrady made an emergency return trip from Cherry Creek to get Leslie Triplett to Lewiston. He was covered with poison ivy skin eruptions, but at least had not drunk a concoction to cure himself. Henry Newton broke his collarbone and three ribs when his horse pitched him. He had ridden through treacherous Salmon River rapids for eight miles before encountering Finnish miners Ed and Eino Luoto at Wapshilla Creek. They rowed Newton downstream to the Salmon/Snake confluence and waited with him for several hours until McGrady's launch arrived. When a runaway team of horses pulling a wagon loaded with eight hundred pounds of hay ran over a ranch hand at Dry Creek, his mates carried him to the landing and waited with him for McGrady's return to Lewiston.[16]

Weekly riverboat reports reminded *Tribune* readers that the effects of World War II had reached the canyon. McGrady helped Oregon mining engineers establish a base camp at Jim Creek and kept the camp supplied while they looked for minerals essential to the war effort. He bought monthly War Bonds for his customers and helped them with their rationing books. As notary public, one of his postal duties in 1941 was to register all men between twenty and forty-four for the draft.[17] In early 1942 McGrady returned with forty-eight more registration cards—for men from forty-five to sixty-five. "Several men had to walk many miles to fill out the registration cards."

The war did indeed reach the canyon, and the canyon reached out to soldiers stationed worldwide. How many of McGrady's outbound passengers were going off to war? At the time, probably everyone knew the answer, for regional newspapers regularly listed the names of those joining the military. Men were streaming out of the canyon, joining the larger flow from nearby towns and cities, connecting the people on the home front to each other and giving them common hopes, concerns, sorrows. But despite this common bond, canyon life, epitomized by Kyle McGrady and his boats, was unique. When the entertainment world turned its attention to the canyon and its people, the message it recorded spread round the world.

In June 1944 *Tribune* readers learned that men stationed at a Seabee training center in Rhode Island viewed a film about McGrady and Hells Canyon. Local man Don Fouste, who was stationed there, wrote, "The eastern boys were amazed at the ruggedness of the country and all expressed a desire to make the trip there sometime." Philip Dresser, who once worked for the *Tribune*, was stationed in the South Pacific. He had not been home for four years, but one day his ship repair unit enjoyed 20th Century Fox's travelogue *Mail Man of the Snake*. Home had come to him. "Kyle McGrady catching sturgeon was a sight that few have seen," he wrote. "Many now believe the stories I have told about my home area."

Florence McGrady and Ruth Sapp

Hundreds of articles about Kyle McGrady's doings appeared in the *Lewiston Morning Tribune* during his tenure as mailboat pilot—some only a few sentences, others full-length feature articles. Florence McGrady probably wrote news releases for the *Tribune*, helping bridge the distance between canyon and valley while keeping the public apprised of her husband's business. That, in turn, helped his business grow. She helped in many other ways, too. When Kyle needed someone to drive to Rogersburg to meet him, she did it. When he began serving food on the boat, she either prepared it or arranged for it. If a bachelor needed his clothes mended or some other domestic task done, she did it. She probably even looked in on sick and injured passengers Kyle brought to town for hospitalization and acted as their message courier to and from the canyon.

But mostly, Florence partnered with Ruth Sapp, a valuable ally in Lewiston. In 1915 Ruth and George Sapp opened a grocery business in Lewiston. Two years later J. Ray Johnson of Clarkston took their first order up the Snake River by boat. George Sapp began to take a special interest in canyon residents and decided to offer them "unusual" services through the mail boats. In time, Sapp's Grocery became the only Lewiston business some ranchers and miners knew. When George died in 1932, Ruth briefly closed the business, then reopened it nearby on Lewiston's Main Street, where she operated the store until her death in 1956. Mrs. Sapp (never Ruth) provided valuable customer service to canyon residents throughout that entire period, collaborating with Ed MacFarlane, Press Brewrink,

Figure 20.8. Kyle McGrady gives his wife Florence a kiss before departing the Lewiston dock. (Photo courtesy of Robert McGrady.)

Kyle McGrady, and his successor, Oliver McNabb. By 1940 a *Tribune* article claimed she had become so indispensable to canyon residents, some of whom she never met, that "see Mrs. Sapp" was a byword in the canyon.[18]

When Florence or Kyle brought in a prospector's gold dust, Mrs. Sapp, who had a license to handle gold, weighed it and credited it at thirty-five dollars per ounce. Then she and Florence filled the prospector's order for grub, tobacco, clothing, and other essentials. Prospectors, even if they never met Mrs. Sapp, would sometimes ask her to write a letter to a relative and send them the remainder of the money, or deposit it in the bank, or send money left over from his supplies back upriver. A wartime article reported that, "Kyle, Florence, and Mrs. Sapp conspired to cut down enough on the frontiersmen's rations, both liquid and substantial, to purchase each of them a War Bond a month." Before commercial sturgeon fishing ended, Mrs. Sapp arranged to market the sturgeon and caviar at Portland and Seattle. She might also sell a rancher's turkeys, bail a herder out of jail—if he "celebrated too unwisely"—or loan someone money who was in town and down on his luck.

She filled every order sent to town from her inventory, or from another store if she didn't have the requested item. It might be a cookstove or mowing machine, a pair of nylons or some yard goods. In 1940 she sold enough barbed wire to build four miles of fence. If the item wasn't in stock in one of the valley stores, she had the store owner order it. Every item the customer ordered went on their grocery bill and sometimes a single grocery order was as much as a thousand dollars. There were no credit checks, no signed agreements. People trusted Mrs. Sapp and she trusted them. Both parties respected a code of trust and honesty that extended to the other businesses with whom Mrs. Sapp dealt. In essence, she was indebted to those stores and could pay them only when she received payment. She said she might not even recognize the customer on the street, but she knew he would pay the bill. She once described her customers as "the best people in the world," and stood by that assertion with each order she sent upriver.

The ranchers loved and trusted Mrs. Sapp too. Esther Hibbs remembered Mrs. Sapp as "wonderful. You could order anything at all from her. You could send your hat down to be cleaned. She would take care of it and pay the bill. You would pay her. She would also shop for the size jeans you wanted and make a good selection. It was wonderful!" Janie Stone "just loved her. We'd order all that stuff through her. Every time we sent in an order to her, she'd always stick in a little bag of candy for the kids. They looked forward to that order coming." Ace Barton called her a "grand old lady."[19] When she died at the age of eighty-one, Sapp's Grocery Store closed its doors forever.

Exposing Hells Canyon to the Nation

Throughout the 1940s a national audience came to know the details of McGrady's mailboat activities and Mrs. Sapp's store. Some early magazine articles reached a specialized audience, like John Parker's "Fast Lady from the Upper Snake" in the December 1940 *Pacific Motor Boat*. But it was Richard Neuberger, an Oregonian, whose nationally known feature articles introduced the entire nation to Hells Canyon. One of his first articles, "Nations Deepest Chasm," appeared in the *New York Times* in July 1940. Then in May 1941, he; Robert Mansfield, a journalism professor from the University of Washington; S. Eugene Allen, editor of the *Oregon Labor Press*; and George Godfrey, director of publicity for the University of Oregon, joined McGrady on a trip into the canyon. When the *Tribune* interviewed them, Godfrey, who hoped to feature the canyon and mailboat trip in *Life*

Figure 20.9. An empty pack string approaches the boat landing as Kyle McGrady heads to shore. Often a number of people rode along in anticipation of their mail, their order that Ruth Sapp filled, and news from town. (Photo courtesy of Robert McGrady.)

Magazine, predicted, "If properly exploited, the trip could become as popular as jaunts to and around the Grand Canyon." Not only the spectacular scenery but also the people living there intrigued Neuberger. He judged that most Americans thought such individuals and the lives they led existed "only in novels and other fiction." Over the next few years, Neuberger developed that theme in numerous publications, before moving into the world of politics, where he continued his interest in both publicizing and protecting the canyon.

In June 1941 Neuberger's article "How to Visit the Snake Canyon," appeared in the *Sunday Oregonian*, with photographs by George Godfrey. The next May Neuberger returned to the canyon with an assignment from *Saturday Evening Post*, accompanied by photographer Victor H. Jorgenson Jr. Later that month *Harper's Magazine* featured a Neuberger article called "Seeing the Northwest." On July 10, 1942, Vic Jorgenson returned to the canyon with local camera buffs Ira S. Dole and Norman M. Purviance. McGrady took them as far as Johnson Bar. Jorgenson stayed on the boat, while a pack string met Dole and Purviance and took them another seventeen miles up the canyon. For two weeks the local photographers filmed the canyon's beauty and rhythm of life, providing, more than sixty years later, an exceptional visual record of that era in the canyon.

Neuberger's "Deepest Canyon on the Continent," appeared in *Travel Magazine* in September 1942, and his *Saturday Evening Post* article "The Mail Carrier of Hell's Canyon" appeared a month later with Jorgenson's photographs. The two articles were very similar, depicting by word and image a compelling blend of human interest stories and a traveler's account of the mailboat trip. Neuberger obviously came away from his canyon experience enthralled with the beauty of the countryside, exhilarated by the ride, and with a profound respect for the river pilot, Kyle McGrady. His writing was colorful, somewhat overdramatic in the style of the 1940s, and tended to exaggerate the rural aspects of living there, but his word picture introduced the audience to the unusual Snake River mail run. Here are some excerpts from the article.

Friday morning, "just as dawn [lit] the skies" Neuberger boarded the *Idaho* at the Lewiston wharf "to begin its spectacular run" up the river. Gradually they left behind signs of civilization

Figure 20.10. A view from the back of Kyle McGrady's mailboat. At first passenger accommodations were rustic at best. As the mail run became a more popular tourist attraction, he significantly improved the accommodations. (Photo courtesy of Robert McGrady.)

until "the wilderness [enclosed] the scene." The gentle chug of the diesel engines, "echoing through the twisting lava corridor," signaled the "people of the wilderness that neither white water nor gorge a mile deep halts the United States mail. They come down out of draws and ravines in the rugged abyss and wait for the boat. . . . A little boy holding the reins of a frisky cowpony had ridden nine miles over narrow sheep paths to get his father's supplies and newspapers." The boy "shifted his holstered six-shooter to the side of his leg" and commenced to load the packhorse. Upriver, "a burly sheepherder named Jack Davis" climbed aboard for Kyle to notarize his Selective Service questionnaire. Next, Doc Abbott, needed a dozen postage stamps. "While a deckhand looped the painter around a hackberry bush, McGrady brought out a battered cigar box that served as post office" and sold Doc his thirty-six-cents worth of postage. Observing miners sluicing the gravel bars, Neuberger noted that "a skilled miner willing to work hard can sift out as much as $7.00 worth of gold a day. Most of them make closer to $2.00." Half a mile below the Salmon River, the *Idaho* stopped "to pick up two husky lads from Spokane who had been hired to do the preliminary work on a gold strike. A week in the canyon, hemmed in by gaunt cliffs, had been enough for them. They could not stand it any longer." But one passenger—"curly-haired, lantern-jawed" thirty-year-old Bill Mitchell—loved the canyon. He disembarked at Temperance Creek in a pelting rainstorm with his heavy hydraulic mining equipment. McGrady told Neuberger, "Bill came up this way from California four years ago. He got the canyon in his blood and can't get it out."

That night, the "*Idaho* snubbed gently against the shore" below a grassy slope, seventy-five miles above Lewiston. The rain stopped and "stars began to wink through the veil of clouds." High above, the distant rims looked like the "ruins of a Grecian temple." As the campfire dimmed only the "ceaseless murmur of the river broke the silence." Next morning, *Idaho*'s diesel engines awoke the camp with an "early reveille." After breakfast, they boarded and continued up the river. "At times the craft, with propellers thrashing furiously, seemed to be on a treadmill. Then inch by inch the *Idaho* gained headway and surmounted the crest of the rapids. Heavy waves slapped and slammed against the boat's riveted sides. Every so often a big boomer broke over the prow and drenched the passengers." The intrepid pilot gripped the mahogany wheel "like a mariner rounding the Horn" as the "*Idaho* brushed within a few feet of saber-toothed rocks that could rip its hull to shreds."

At Johnson Bar, "where [the] *Idaho* ends its bold journey, two trails twist up the wall of the abyss." One was long and easy, winding up the rocky bed of Saddle Creek to Freezeout Saddle. The other was short and precipitous, ascending the cliffs to Hat Point. Occasionally, the author demonstrated his ignorance of the people of Hells Canyon: "Only in summer can the cliff trails be traversed, and then rarely by the wives and daughters." But he can be forgiven, for that misconception of the abilities of the wives and daughters came from Kyle himself. When Kyle and Tom Tumelson had to abandon the *Dawn* and began hiking out of the canyon, Kyle learned firsthand how difficult it was to travel on land. Afterward he said, "the women and old men could never climb out over the mountains, I am sure of that."

Article after article picked up versions of that assumption, until probably everyone but the women and old men themselves believed they were incapable of riding the trails.

After Richard Neuberger's *Saturday Evening Post* article appeared, the local folk took issue with the tone of his message. Grangeville's *Idaho County Free Press* claimed it was "Just Too Nice." They charged that Neuberger had "prettified the pretty, romanticized the ordinary, and emboldened the bold." They did not appreciate his picturing "old coots" coming for their mail and were especially incensed with Neuberger's insinuations that the canyon people had to be told there was a war on, when "nearly everybody in the canyon has a radio and listens to the news so diligently that when they come out to civilization they know more about what is going on than those who have dailies that they are able to read." The *Free Press* added that Kyle McGrady was "disturbed by the brightness of the light thrown upon him." Nevertheless, that bright light continued to illuminate him in a variety of subsequent articles and motion pictures. Throughout the rest of the decade, illustrated magazine and newspaper articles about McGrady and his Snake River mail run written by Neuberger and many others appeared in such publications as *Diesel Progress*, the *Seattle Sunday Times*, the *Oregonian*, the *Statesman*, the *Spokane Daily Chronicle*, *Pacific Pathways*, the *Postal Record*, *Scenic Idaho*, and *Popular Mechanics*.

And those in the print media weren't the only ones fascinated by the canyon and its inhabitants. The combination of the nation's most unusual mail carrier, the spectacular and relatively undiscovered landscape of Hells Canyon, and people who seemed to step from the pages of fiction was also too compelling for movie producers, amateur or professional, to ignore. Men like Purviance, Dole, even McGrady himself, showed their amateur footage to appreciative local audiences. In November 1942 Mr. and Mrs. C. S. Van Eaton of Sioux City, Iowa, boarded McGrady's boat and headed upriver with two and a half tons of cattle feed.[20] The first night the Van Eatons camped at a river bar seventy miles above Lewiston, their second night at Johnson Bar, and their third night at Bush Creek. Van Eaton described the experience as "the most thrilling trip in North America," one "full of surprises," like when he spoke with Jim McGovern, a sheep herder of thirty-seven years who "talked with a college

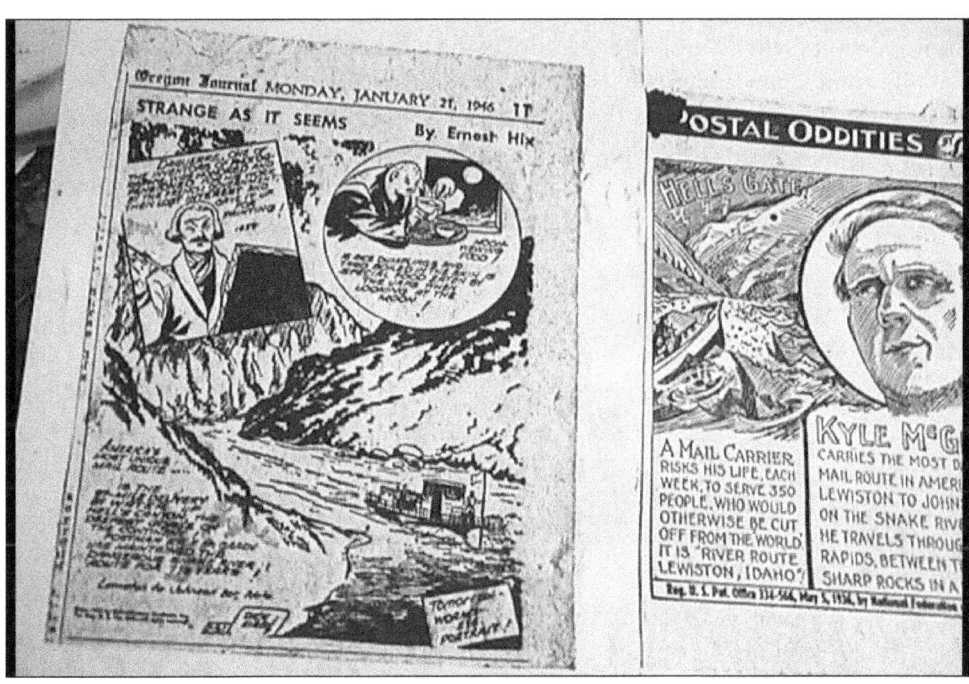

Figure 20.11. Kyle McGrady "risks his life each week to serve 350 people who would otherwise be cut of from the world," or so claims this page from a U.S. Postal Service publication, right. The 1946 *Oregon Journal*, left, highlights "America's most unique mail route." (Article courtesy of Robert McGrady.)

accent." Convinced that "no place in America . . . can offer the primitive mix that Hells Canyon does," Van Eaton imagined a couple of lodges. "You could run boats up there, charge $10 a night, have your big game hunts and nice lodging and the canyon will be famous." Was Kyle McGrady listening?

During the 1940s a theater ticket bought much more than just the featured film. Moviegoers first enjoyed a travelogue or other high interest piece along with short news updates and a cartoon. In June 1943 Twentieth Century Fox sent Seattle cameraman Chalmers D. Sinke into the canyon to film a travelogue, narrated by the famous newsman Lowell Thomas. Sinke, his wife, and their nine-year-old son boarded the *Idaho* with fifty other passengers heading for Johnson Bar, where the Sinkes stayed a week. The next month they returned for a second filming. In the spring of 1944, while in Seattle on a business trip, McGrady walked past a large theater whose marquee advertised "Mail Man of the Snake." McGrady later told the local paper, "It is quite unusual for a man who is not an actor to find accidentally a large theater which is playing a motion picture starring himself." He went into the theater to watch the Sinke travelogue and admitted later that it was "quite a good picture."[21]

Having a Heck of a Good Time

Kyle McGrady saw the tourism potential of his business early on and over the years worked to "properly exploit" the growing national interest in sightseeing, hunting, and fishing in the canyon. In May 1940 he introduced "one-day Sunday excursions" to Getta Creek, available for four dollars a person through the spring months. The boat left early in the morning and returned late at night. Community organizations from throughout the Inland Northwest chartered boats for two-day excursions, then wrote about the trip for their local papers. Students from Washington State College, the University of Idaho, and Lewiston Normal School continued the canyon excursions introduced by MacFarlane, and occasionally high schools held their senior picnic in the canyon. Word spread about the wonders of Hells Canyon and the thrill of the mailboat ride. Then in June 1941, when a family from Connecticut booked passage and made the headlines—"Easterners on a Trip up the Snake"—others in the valley began to realize the tourism potential in their own backyard. On the fifth of July a *Tribune* article, "Canyon Attracts Many Tourists," suggested that publicity of the mailboat trip and McGrady's Sunday excursions had played a role in attracting thirty-one people from seven states for a Fourth of July canyon trip. The highlight of the trip was when the boat stopped "miles from civilization to hear President Roosevelt's 4th of July speech over three portable radios." McGrady recalled that his "easterners, as well as his western passengers reported having 'a heck of a good time.'"

McGrady promoted his growing business with a 1943 brochure advertising the "Grand Canyon of the Snake River:

Figure 20.12. Kyle McGrady often put his passengers to work helping him and a crewman unload equipment and supplies at a canyon ranch, as one passenger is doing here. (Photo courtesy of Robert McGrady.)

Known as Hell's Canyon." For six dollars, a passenger could take a "185 mile trip on the Scenic Snake River," and have "an opportunity to see the deepest canyon on the North American continent . . . in ease, comfort and safety." (That was on his regular weekly mail trips.) A party of up to fifty people could charter the boat any time except Friday or Saturday. The Sunday excursions were available to anyone, if enough passengers signed up. The brochure added that "a stove and cooking utensils are available for free use"—implying they better bring their own food—and "plans are under way to provide tents, cabins, and sleeping accommodations"—bring sleeping bags as well. Tourists, fishermen, and hunters responded in increasing numbers. In 1944 the following ad appeared in regional newspapers:

> Get Your Group Together and Take the
> Overnight Excursion Up the
> Beautiful Snake River
> Travel in Comfort
> See Nature at Her Roughest
> You've read about it in the Saturday Evening
> Post and it will soon be seen in the movies
> NOW GET THE THRILL FIRSTHAND
> Must Call Kyle McGrady for
> Reservation and Prices
> Phone 1084

The flow of sportsmen increased considerably over the next few years. McGrady dropped them off at places like the mouth of the Imnaha River or Wolf Creek and picked them up the next day. On one trip, five fishermen went down the gangplank at Wolf Creek with beds, grub, and tackle, and then called back to McGrady, "Where the heck is the creek? I can't catch anything in them cliffs." McGrady told them the creek was "upcountry a quarter mile" and reminded them to be back at the landing at 10:30 the next morning "unless you want to make a raft of those posts."[22] If it the primitive mix was what they were after, McGrady surely catered to their wishes.

His "sightseers" were also pretty much on their own. Leone Von Cadow described a trip into the canyon in her local newspaper, the *Dayton (Wash.) Chronicle-Dispatch*. At the beginning of the trip, "you settle yourself on some sacks of coal, oil drums, bedding or stuff, and wonder what's in store for you." But you quickly get acquainted with the crew and fellow passengers and "soon you're one big happy family." In the evening, you prepare your own supper. "There is a 3-burner gasoline stove at your disposal and in the course of time you manage to feel well fed. The nice part is: no garbage to carry out, just a toss and she's overboard, likewise paper plates and cups." (McGrady admonished passengers not to swim in the river; it was too dirty. Clearly, people then viewed the river as a giant disposal unit. He didn't help the situation. Esther Hibbs remembered a privy in the back of McGrady's boat "that was flushed all the time.")[23] Von Cadow continued, describing the night's accommodations. "After supper you proceed to the gentle art of making your bed in the hard sand or on top of the boat—the boat is well anchored. A rope is laid all around the sleeping area as some one said that snakes wouldn't crawl over a rope." For that reason, women generally slept on the boat while men laid out their bedrolls on the more comfortable sandy beach.

Sand Creek Lodge

McGrady knew he had to provide better accommodations. In July 1944 he announced plans to build a tourist lodge at Johnson Bar. As head of navigation, that was the logical place for his lodge. What's more, the extensive flat along the river had half an acre of sand at the lower end. The place cried out for development and recreation. The Forest Service approved a special use permit for the project that he was to begin "as soon as lumber and other materials become available." (Due to the war, building materials were in short supply.) Starting with thirty-five cabins and a dining lodge, the place would house hunters during the fall and "excursionists" other times of the year. There would be pack and saddle horses available "for the convenience of guests." After the war was over, he would reoutfit the river packet *Florence* into a luxury craft with refrigeration on board for lunches and drinks, and "comfortable seats, making it possible for visitors to travel into the nation's deepest canyon with comfort."[24]

In the meantime, that September 1944, McGrady announced plans to add "a most unique hunting service" to accommodate his growing hunter clientele. He was "acclimating" the burros to boat travel so he could ship them to Johnson Bar and solve the "packing out" problem in the rough terrain. After taking the sportsmen to "choice" deer hunting sections along the river, he would double back to Johnson Bar, pick up the required number of burros, and drop them off wherever the hunters needed to pack out their trophy.

Kyle McGrady was not the only one to envision a future of canyon tourism and try to capitalize on it. In the spring of 1945 Alice and Henry Petri (she from Canada, he from Tacoma) took a "spectacular honeymoon trip" from Lewiston to Sand Creek aboard the *Florence*. (In her reminiscence, Alice Petri always referred to the place as Sand Bar.)[25] Kyle McGrady was at the helm on his first trip of the season, and they were his only passengers. They sat on the plain old hard benches, held onto the ropes, and got the "full benefit" of sprays and splashes from the open sides. But the country overwhelmed them. The beautiful shiny boulders intrigued Alice—Kyle told her "God polishes them all by hand." Trying to see the top of the canyon, she almost fell over backward. Alice also observed the "goodly variety of smells" on the boat, speculating that sometimes Kyle forgot to deodorize after "his regular passengers," the sheep, were aboard. But "that was part of our adventure."

That night, while camped out at Sand Bar, they enjoyed the "thousand sights of the river and wildlife," and on the return trip talked about how nice it would have been to have had more comfortable accommodations there. The conversation turned from casual speculation to "wouldn't it be exciting to build a lodge." Back in town they talked to a few of the local people, visited the Lewiston Chamber of Commerce, and tried to measure local opinion about building a lodge in the canyon. "Everyone including McGrady said it was needed." (The Petris seemed to be unaware of McGrady's plans to build a lodge there.) Alice and Henri bought six "very large" army surplus tents, beds with real bedsteads, white sheets, pillows, and army surplus blankets, then hired Kyle to take them and their equipment back to Sand Bar.

Five of the tents would provide temporary sleeping accommodations; the sixth would be a cooking and dining hall until they built a wood lodge. Alice wrote that within a short time "the lodge was shaping up, but we still had to put the electricity in and install a walk-in freezer." Their finished Hells Canyon Lodge sat near a cluster of tents with a large covered porch around at least two sides and a steep-pitched roof. All the building materials came in by boat with regular boatloads of guests.

Alice said at first, she was "terrified of the night's darkness" each time their guests left. There were no sounds of other humans, wildlife, birds, not even a breeze stirred. The dark was like pitch; on cloudy and moonless nights she felt hemmed in by the canyon walls, and she was lonely. Then, one day McGrady brought them a baby fawn whose mother had been shot. "That was one of the highlights of our life at Sand Bar." On his next trip, McGrady brought a baby bottle and before long, "Joey" had pushed loneliness from the canyon. He met every boat arriving at the landing. Butch the dog—a favorite of the guests—three cats and two pack mules joined their family.

Gradually, and with Kyle's help, Alice and Henri were learning canyon life. The first few months bustled with visitors. Kyle brought in extra boatloads of guests; the Petris never knew in advance how many to expect. Some guests even arrived by air, like Don Bonomi, who flew in from Clarkston with Jack Houston of Zimmerly Air Transport. Bonomi met a friend, Thomas W. Campbell of the *Lewiston Morning Tribune*, and together they rode two "Rocky mountain canaries"—burros—from the landing field to the "lodge construction site." At the lodge "genial Henri Petri, pipe in mouth" greeted them "while industriously at work with a hammer and power saw." Even though the lodge was incomplete, the facilities were "even now strained by the flood of persons waiting to spend a weekend or more in the great outdoors."[26] Business looked promising indeed.

Then the river level lowered. Petris got news that the *Florence* had hit a rock and sprung a leak. The Petris were marooned. Food and water started to run low. Henri laid a fifteen-hundred-foot wooden trough to the nearest spring, providing water until the spring dried up. The nearest potable water was four miles away "at a small farm," where the generous family gave them necessities "to keep alive." Soon the farmer too "dried up. . . . We decided to risk our lives and row our leaky rowboat across the river with whatever personal belongings we could carry." Turning their backs on everything they had accumulated for their Sand Bar dream, Alice bailed out the water as Henri rowed across to the Idaho side.

Safely on the opposite shore they hiked up the He Devil and fortuitously "found Mrs. Wilson, a good packer with a good string of mules." She gave Alice a high-spirited horse trained to take the lead and instructed her "never try to hold the horse back." "Riding that horse up the tremendous narrow trail," Alice was terrified beyond describing, but "by the grace of God" they arrived at the Wilson home. Alice, who never called their guardian angel anything but "Mrs. Wilson," described her as "108 pounds of true grit, who shoed all her own horses and played nursemaid to every mean and sick bull."[27] Except for her twelve cats and four dogs, Mrs. Wilson lived alone on the high mountain. She decorated her home with moose heads and deer horns, with cougar, bear, and bobcat, all of which she had killed. When asked about her husband, she told Alice she had no time for anyone who was good for nothing "and that meant most men."

The Petris "could not get Hells Canyon out of [their] blood." Within a few months, they learned they could see the canyon from Horse Mountain Lookout, "the only place where the top of the canyon can be reached by car." Six miles from the lookout sat the tiny town of Cuprum, Idaho—population 5. They booked a room at the rustic Darland Inn. The proprietors, Mr. and Mrs. Darland, were ready to retire and the inn was for sale. Alice and Henri immediately seized the opportunity, gave the place a new face and a new name, Copper Lodge, and followed their honeymoon dream. For the next four years, they enjoyed the canyon from above while catering to tourists—including luminaries like actor Gary Cooper. Forty years later Alice Petri wrote, "Copper Lodge, Cuprum, felt like 'Heaven' after Hell's Canyon on the Snake River. This was indeed God's country,

Figure 20.13. Kyle McGrady's Sand Creek Lodge, with either the *Florence* or *Idaho* docked in the foreground. (Photo courtesy of Robert McGrady.)

and we'll always love it because we were once part of it."[28]

In her brief memoir, Alice did not write about their business dealings nor did she mention what became of the family pets or the tents and other equipment at Sand Bar. Apparently they simply rowed away, leaving everything behind for whoever wished to claim it. That person must have been Kyle McGrady. As soon as the water level rose and he could again navigate the upper reaches of his run, Kyle was no doubt surprised to find the Petris' place abandoned. Maybe they later contacted him and sold him their building, tents, and equipment, or perhaps the three had made prior arrangements in the event the Petris' venture failed. Maybe Kyle had even hired them to build his lodge. At any rate, a picture of their lodge beside a picture of McGrady's completed lodge at Sand Creek, Oregon suggests that he used their facilities. By spring of 1947 he had proper accommodations for his excursionists and hunters.

A two-day, round-trip on Kyle's mailboat, with overnight accommodations at Hells Canyon Lodge, cost $8.50. Customers were still "given number two priority" to the mail and cargo on the boat, although they usually rode the *Florence*, taking advantage of her more comfortable leather seats. The passengers reached the lodge in the evening, in time for a meal served "American style" from "lockers full of elk and other foods that abound in the wilds of the area." Tents provided sleeping quarters.[29] When Jess Earl stayed at the lodge, he remembered McGrady having a "night club" there. "He had dollar slot machines, also nickel and dime machines. He never kept women there, but there were women [who] came on the boat all the time, you know of course." Earl described the lodge as a large building with a walk-in freezer. "They furnished a lot of good food on a big, long table family style." There were also "about" five, sixteen-by-sixteen-foot square sleeping tents. Unlike at Petri's, where an inadequate water supply helped drive them out, the Sand Creek lodge had water piped down: "all the water you wanted, and a shower out there.... It was really quite a nice place."[30]

By 1948 the cost of McGrady's round-trip and lodge package had nearly doubled, to $17.50. His total passenger-per-year count was approximately two thousand—most were tourists. Traffic was heaviest in spring. He usually did not make the run in low water during August and part of September; he resumed in time for the fall hunting season. McGrady announced in 1949 that he planned to put a fifteen-passenger boat in operation so he could make the run year round. He also hoped the Corps of Engineers

Figure 20.14. A closer view of McGrady's lodge. (Photo courtesy of Robert McGrady.)

would have the five worst parts of the river blown out and wing dams constructed to make upstream travel easier. But Kyle McGrady's time on the river was short, not long enough for him to see either dream materialize.

Bitter Years

Kyle McGrady began his Snake River career under the specter of defeat, and in truth failure always dogged him. Events of the memorable winter of 1948–49, although by no means constituting a defeat, nevertheless led to financial loss and frustration. Large sections of the river froze solid. At Buffalo Eddy, ice trapped and held the *Florence* for thirty-three days. Kyle tried every way he could to break her loose, including setting off blasts of dynamite. Hazel Johnson's mother was on her way back home to Clarkston aboard the boat when it got stuck. She said the ice just froze up around them. She was taking home some baked chicken and a couple of loaves of bread. Mr. Van Pool was on his way to town with a crate of eggs, so her chicken and bread and his eggs were dinner for everyone on board that night. "And here was my dear mother cooking them," Hazel added. Van Pool reluctantly sacrificed his eggs ("he was tighter than Old Billy") and her mother sacrificed a couple weeks' supply of food. By the time warmer weather of February released the ice's grip, Kyle McGrady had sacrificed thirty-three days of service and income. He and the passengers made it safely back on foot to Clarkston, where he waited for spring thaws so he could get back to work.[31]

Real tragedy and a profound personal loss struck Kyle in the spring of 1949. Kyle was on one of his Sunday cruises with a number of passengers. The water was high and the river full of debris. When he started to climb Wild Goose Rapids, the boat hit a sunken log, disabling both propellers. Kyle's eighteen-year-old son Kenneth and deck hand Bill DeVault grabbed one of the tie lines and went overboard, hoping to snub the rope around a hackberry tree and move the boat into calm water. But they couldn't. DeVault hung on

Figure 20.15. Ice on the Snake River during the winter of 1938-39. A similar ice jam a decade later entrapped the *Florence* for thirty-three days. (Photo courtesy of Robert McGrady.)

to the line and passengers pulled him aboard. Kenny stayed on the island, waving as the boat drifted helplessly downriver with Kyle yelling back, "Stay there. We'll come back for you."

Finally, at Rogersburg, McGrady got the boat to shore and phoned home to tell Florence about the accident. She called Zimmerly Air Transport in Clarkston asking for someone to take the floatplane to Wild Goose and pick up Kenny. Word didn't reach pilot Bert Zimmerly until McGrady was back in Clarkston. McGrady boarded the plane as it was about to take off, and into the darkness of the canyon they went. They circled above Wild Goose, tossing out flares for clearer vision while Zimmerly set the plane down on a dangerous river. Kenny was not on the island. He was a "powerful" swimmer. Most everyone assumed he tried to swim the short distance to shore and walk out of the canyon rather than spend the night on the island. Several months later his body surfaced at White Salmon on the Columbia River.[32]

Today people who remember riding with Kyle describe him as being friendly—he always had a smile on his face—and very accommodating, a man who obviously loved his work. But "after the boy drowned in Snake River, [Kyle] gave up."[33] He left River Route, Lewiston, Idaho, in 1950. The family moved to Pasco, Washington. Four years later Kyle, Florence, and their youngest son, Bob, moved to Colfax, Washington, where Kyle returned to his earlier work, operating a service station. Kyle McGrady died in 1970.

Chapter 21

Into the Modern Era

The Inland Navigation Company of The Dalles, Oregon, took over Kyle McGrady's government mail contract in 1950. Their business was to move cargo, deliver mail, and transport passengers, not cater to tourists. Consequently, the company chose not to use Kyle McGrady's lodge. For the next twelve years, the lodge became an overnight stop for a variety of canyon travelers, who "cluttered the place [up] so bad" that the Forest Service finally burned it to the ground in 1962.[1] With the smoke went the last evidence of the Petris' and McGradys' dreams of transforming Hells Canyon into a tourist getaway. Inland Navigation otherwise continued McGrady's business as usual. The mailboat made its weekly run; ranchers continued their annual migratory cycle. Tourists ventured up the river and floated down in greater numbers, but without the convenience of lodges and special services. Whispers of dam building from distant meeting halls periodically funneled into the canyon and brought in a few power company officials but stirred up limited reaction from ranchers, tourists, or the new mail carrier, Oliver McNabb.

The McNabb Years

In June 1950 Oliver McNabb, "an interesting gentleman who always had a big smile on his face," came to Hells Canyon and the Middle Snake River in the employ of the Inland Navigation Company.[2] Like McGrady, Oliver McNabb's unique employment attracted national media attention. Unlike McGrady, McNabb came to that job as an employee of a large Columbia and Snake River shipping company. He was not a novice drawn to the Snake River by the challenge of a new adventure but an experienced river pilot who accepted Snake River employment at his company's behest, approaching his work with the confidence and dedication of a professional. He came with numerous navigational challenges and adventures already under his belt, having piloted commercial boats on the Columbia River between Portland, Oregon, and Pasco, Washington. Although Oliver McNabb viewed his eight years on Snake River as "just a job," he retained a love of the canyon and fond memories of his canyon acquaintances for years after leaving Hells Canyon.

During McNabb's first two years in the canyon, he operated the *Imnaha*, a twenty-four-foot Chris-Craft runabout. For his remaining six years on the Snake River, he operated the *Wenaha*, a fifty-two-foot passenger and freight packet with a fourteen-foot beam. McNabb described the white, green-trimmed boat—with "Inland Navigation Co." boldly displayed on both sides—as "very similar" to McGrady's Snake River boats. It had an aluminum wheelhouse at the bow. The back section opened to the stern for cargo and passengers and the middle section of the upper deck was removable to house anything from a sheep

Figure 21.1. Oliver McNabb is pictured here at the wheel of Inland Navigation Company's mailboat, the *Wenaha*. He piloted the company mailboats on the Snake River from 1950 until 1958. (Photo courtesy of Oliver McNabb and used with the permission of photographer Don Rains, Maritime Museum, Astoria, Oregon.)

to an airplane body. The flat-bottomed steel hull had a tunnel stern for a shallow draft of fourteen inches when light and two feet when loaded. "Twin Jimmies," two 165-hp General Motors engines, powered the *Wenaha*.[4]

McNabb described a typical trip. Promptly at six o'clock every Wednesday morning, McNabb, deckhand Bill DeVault, and pilot Jim Redmond left their Lewiston port near Nezperce Roller Mills to begin the weekly mail run. They passed the mouth of the Grande Ronde at 11:00 a.m. and made the first stop nine miles later at Wendel Mathison's Garden Creek landing.[5] The *Wenaha*'s next stops were Cache Creek, to deliver Les Oliver's mail, and Cherry Creek. (McNabb never knew the names of the Cherry Creek Sheep Company owners.) Around noon they reached the mouth of the Salmon River, where the crew and passengers ate lunch on board. One of McNabb's passengers described a typical lunch of cold meat sandwiches, deviled eggs, potato salad, and baked beans, "served by the Captain's first mate, steward, chef, and deckhand, not to mention mail carrier up the beaches, Bill DeVault." (At any time throughout the day coffee, milk, Cokes, and pastries were available in the galley—a "very popular service.")[6]

While passengers ate lunch, the *Wenaha* continued upriver to the next stop—first to "one of the Tippett brothers" at Dug Bar. From there they went on to Biden Tippett's mail drop at Deep Creek; Harold Van Pool's at Dry Creek; Christmas Creek where one of the canyon Johnson's lived; on to Mrs. Morrow's place at Wolf Creek, and then to the last delivery that day, the Blankenships at Roland Bar. Around 5:30 in the evening, the *Wenaha* reached Camp Creek on the Oregon side, where the passengers and crew spent the night.

When they beached at Camp Creek, DeVault immediately began preparing supper while everyone else set to work pitching the three tents, setting up cots, and rolling out bedrolls. They unfolded the dinner table and chairs while passengers lined up cafeteria style and passed through the galley, filling their plates with a satisfying meal. After supper, when the dishes had been washed and the dining table and chairs put away, the crew put out more cots and bedrolls on the boat's floors. "There were even sleepers on the top deck."

The next morning everyone had an hour to eat a sumptuous breakfast and break camp. By seven, the *Wenaha* was off to Jack Titus's place on the Oregon side of Pittsburg Landing (where McNabb later delivered mail to Lem Wilson). At Pittsburg Landing, they crossed over to Circle C and left the mail—McNabb never met the hands working there—then on to Bud Wilson's at Kirkwood, Ken Johnson's at Temperance Creek, and before noon their last stop, Sheep Creek. As he did at most places, McNabb stopped for a brief visit (in this case with Lenora Barton and her son Ace) before heading back home, traveling much faster so he could "keep control of the rudder" while spinning "the steering wheel with the dexterity of a gymnast." *Wenaha* pulled into the Lewiston port promptly at five o'clock Thursday evening.

Figure 21.2. *Wenaha* passengers appear to be enjoying Oliver McNabb's chicken dinner, and he seems to be enjoying their company. (Photo courtesy of Oliver McNabb.)

Someone came down at nearly every stop to pick up the mail and visit. "After the first couple trips, they knew the time we would be there," McNabb explained. Although McGrady had been a hard worker—which McNabb himself testified to—he did not approach the job with the professionalism that a company man and experienced riverboat pilot did. There were many times when McGrady failed to reach a landing at the expected time and sometimes did not even make it that day. People would often walk to the mail drop, wait around for a few hours, then go home and return the next day. That rarely happened on McNabb's watch.

Ace Barton remembered McNabb as "the only one who made it a practice of getting there." When McNabb was just getting started in the business, his boat broke down at Temperance Creek. "We just figured it was business as usual and you couldn't depend on Inland Navigation," Ace recalled. "Then that night the dogs all went out and barked and we went out and there was old [he was only thirty] Oliver McNabb. He'd borrowed a horse from Bud Wilson and brought the mail up that night." Ace and Lenora invited him to spend the night, since it was so late. "But he had to get back and wouldn't stay all night. He rode back over those trails without any light or nothing all the way to Temperance Creek." That impressed Ace.[7]

McNabb described Ace Barton and all his canyon customers as interesting people with interesting stories to tell, but wanted to make it clear: "They were just ordinary people." Possibly, he was reacting to the exaggerated pictures of canyon residents and mailboat pilots that still appeared in print, for although McNabb obviously enjoyed the work, it was, after all, "just a job."

Piloting a riverboat was not a new experience for Oliver McNabb. The only thing different was the location of his work. The changing seasons, especially the autumns, and the canyon wildlife engaged him, but the river was not especially challenging. Wild Goose Rapids and Mountain Sheep Rapids, two places that foiled riverboat travel from its inception, to McNabb were now inconsequential, probably cleared by the Corps of Engineers. Shortly before McNabb began his run, the corps had improved the channel at Temperance Creek and just below Camp Creek. During his stint on the river, McNabb helped the corps put in navigation markers, which guided him and all boat pilots for nearly four decades, until they were no longer necessary. (Now jetboats have such a light draft "they can go anywhere," and do not require an identified channel.)

McNabb was a good pilot, and a modest one. A woman once said, "They tell me you know where every rock in the river is." McNabb replied, "I sure don't, but I sure damn well know where there ain't any."[8] In the boating business, he explained, "you just take everything as it comes along. Sure, we pulled in tows on a boat run aground; it's all in a day's work." If a rock "poked a hole in the bottom of the boat," McNabb simply placed a piece of wood over it, put a jack on it, pumped out the water, and made permanent repairs back in Lewiston. All in a day's work.[9]

McNabb's service to canyon ranchers varied little from McGrady's; he just had fewer customers and patrons. Most important, he was their mailman. If no one was at a landing to hand over or receive the mail, he delivered and picked up mail in anything from a regulation RFD mailbox stuck in the sand a few feet from the water's edge to a dynamite box or drained gasoline can parked beside a fencepost. His customers transacted all business normally done in a post office just as they always had. McNabb also carried the same types of cargo: cattle feed, baled hay, salt, cottonseed cake, household goods, and groceries.

Mrs. Sapp was still at her Lewiston grocery store to fill customers' orders. Oliver thought she was "real nice" but "quite old," maybe in her seventies. (She died two years before his mail run ended.) He remembered a man working in the store with her, but she still took care of orders for her canyon customers, as she always had. Since there were no phone lines from the canyon into the Lewiston-Clarkston valley, either the people mailed in their grocery order or, more often, McNabb dropped it off when he was in town. The following Tuesday he would pick up the order at Mrs. Sapp's store and deliver it to the ranchers on Wednesday or Thursday.

In addition to grocery, clothing, ranch and home supplies, the *Wenaha* delivered or picked up more cumbersome and unusual cargo. McNabb remembered hauling cars, jeeps, Caterpillars, and airplanes—"anything needed on the ranch." In McNabb's day, since the only roads in were at Dug Bar, Pittsburg Landing, and Kirkwood, once a rancher got a jeep or truck to his place, he usually confined its use to his canyon property. Sometimes a person might foolishly attempt to drive in a car, which usually had to be hauled out by boat. Many ranchers had airplanes. They landed on rough strips that often damaged the landing gear. The solution? Remove the wings and send the fuselage downriver for repair. Around 1956, McNabb carried drilling equipment for the Bureau of Reclamation and Nickols and Thompson, a company hired by Washington Water Power, to drill test holes at proposed dam sites in Pleasant Valley, High Mountain Sheep, and Mountain Sheep.

McNabb continued to carry three-hundred-pound sacks of wool to Lewiston, usually forty-five to sixty-five per trip. To load the sacks, he landed the boat along the bank, set out two, eighteen-foot planks, rolled the heavy sacks down to the boat and up the planks into the hold. McNabb also ferried sheep across the river, but

Figure 21.3. Oliver McNabb delivered mail into all sorts of mailboxes along the river banks. This one looks portable enough to move when the river rises. (Photo courtesy of Oliver McNabb.)

in his boat rather than a scow. He laid out the planks, then walked a sheep up the plank and "helped" it jump down into the cargo hold. Once the first, reluctant animal walked the gangplank, the others followed. McNabb usually did not charge for ferrying services nor did he charge when shuttling regular, resident passengers or work crews from one landing to the next. Bonnie Sterling frequently took advantage of his generosity. She was cooking at Kirkwood and, "when no one was around to cook for," she would call Hazel Johnson at Temperance Creek to tell her she would be on the boat. Hazel would come down to the landing, and she and Bonnie visited while the men transferred cargo.[10]

Figure 21.4. Passengers boarding the *Wenaha* stabilize themselves by using a guide rope. (Photo courtesy of Oliver McNabb.)

McNabb's paying customers were regular passengers and an increasing number of tourists—mostly "elderly" from all over the country. He charged forty dollars for a round-trip from Lewiston, with everything furnished. Oliver's wife, Marge, prepared the meals at home, and he served them out of the boat's galley on board the *Wenaha*. The evening meal was good, hot, and filling; one tourist recalled eating fried chicken, tossed salad, green beans, bread, coffee, cake, and peaches. If a group of up to fifty-two people—the boat's passenger capacity—arranged a tour, he accommodated them but did not actively solicit their business.

How did canyon life during McNabb's 1950s era compare to earlier decades? First, "there were no children. They lived in town and maybe went to the canyon in the summer." He rarely saw people walking along the river and always stopped if he thought someone wanted a ride. Doors remained unlocked and canyon hospitality was still a viable part of life there, even though there were increasingly fewer and fewer people to share that hospitality. Most all of the ranchers were college educated—"they had to be to run the operation as a successful business"—and they expected their children to have a college education as well. McNabb took a number of hunters into the canyon, but very few fishermen. Around 1994 he returned to the canyon and was sad to see that without domestic animals grazing the hill slopes, weeds and thistles were growing where he remembered "a nice looking canyon." He was also surprised to learn that "hundreds" of people were hiking the trails.

In 1958 Inland Navigation decided not to bid again on the mail contract, and Oliver McNabb left the Snake River. The contract went to Dick Rivers. McNabb went first to Alaska, then operated seagoing tugs along the Pacific Coast from Washington to California, and river towboats on the Columbia River. In 1967 Inland Navigation named him port captain in charge of its river operations, and he and Marge moved to Vancouver, Washington. Two years later, he began working for Tidewater Barge Lines, which after 1974 brought the McNabbs back to the Lewiston-Clarkston valley. With the lower Snake River dams completed, tugs and barges could navigate the Snake River as far as Lewiston and Clarkston. Tidewater Barge Lines made him company operations supervisor at the ports of Wilma, Clarkston, and Lewiston. There he worked until his retirement in the late 1980s, doing work he enjoyed at a place he loved.

Rivers on the River

As a boy, Dick Rivers of Asotin sailed a dinghy and paddled a canoe on the Snake. When he was about sixteen years old he went up the river with Kyle McGrady. He liked McGrady and enjoyed the "experience of being on the river," but admitted years later that he "really didn't like the canyon . . . well yes in February it was pretty, but in the summer it was too damned hot."[11] Dick worked for a while as a deckhand on the valley's last steamboat, the *Lewiston*, and then began his own business cutting and towing logs from upper Corral Creek on the Idaho side. "As far as I know, I'm the only one who ever towed logs down this river," he said. "Everyone else had better sense."[12]

After fifteen years, when Rivers decided the logging business was "way too much work for the return," he decided to make a different type of living off the river and, in 1958, "bought the mail contract from Oliver McNabb," inaugurating the longest mail run of any Snake River carrier. In most respects, Rivers was the antithesis of Oliver McNabb. He was a "good old boy"; McNabb, an outside professional. Rivers was a rough and burley man; McNabb a quiet gentleman. McNabb approached his work as a professional; Dick gave the appearance of being casual, almost flip, about his work. The appearance, however, proved deceptive. Like Oliver McNabb, Dick Rivers was an excellent pilot whose skill behind the wheel earned the respect of his regular customers as well as tourists.

Although some of Rivers's predecessors were more outgoing than others, each was congenial and enjoyed his work and his customers. That wasn't always true of Dick Rivers. Elmer Earl, who began working "for his childhood chum" in 1961 and stayed with him twenty years, described Rivers as "a very coarse type of person. He could be plumb rude, but sometimes it was necessary. He was operating a boat." When passengers boarded the boat, the deckhand handed them a small piece of paper—"Notice to Passengers of This Boat." Here is a sampling of their instructions: "No. 1. Keep your damn feet off the seats!" "No. 2. Don't get snotty with the crew—remember, your pilot is still learning to steer and he is more scared than you." "No. 7. If you don't like the food and drinks, you can go plumb to hell . . ." "No. 16. If the motor falls off, don't show any fear; it might frighten the crew." And on it goes through number 20. Interspersed throughout is the admonition "Keep your damn feet off the seats."

That was Dick Rivers, rough around the edges, a subtle humor, but a darn good pilot. Dick laughed about his shortcomings, announcing that he was "already a son-of-a-bitch" before he began the mail runs. "The canyon had nothing to do with that unless it reinforced it." For twenty-four years, Dick Rivers was the "mailman of Hells Canyon," and though he served a declining number of ranchers and miners, the number of tourists, hunters, anglers, politicians, power company officials, and media representatives grew. He packaged his Rivers Navigation Company excursions with overnight accommodations at his Copper Creek, Oregon, property and enjoyed the excuse to do what he loved—build and operate riverboats.

His first six years in business, Dick piloted the *Idaho Queen I*, a thirty-foot-long, steel-hulled, prop-driven craft.[13] Then, in 1964 the Lewiston Fairgrounds hummed with the sounds of light manufacturing as retired marine expert Wayne Backus from Portland began work on *Idaho Queen II*, a forty-eight-foot, twenty-three-ton boat equipped to carry six tons. It drew twenty-two inches of water with an additional inch for every ton. Twin, 260-hp diesel engines equipped with twin propellers housed in tunnels powered the boat.[14]

He once explained to a passenger, "You've got to know what you are going to do before you get into the rapids." When a boat starts to slide, "like a car on ice, it can't be stopped.

Before you know it, you're in the rocks or on the bank." The captain also has to know when not to push his luck. He described a thunderstorm, with lightning hitting the rich vein of copper on one side of the river and jumping clear across the river to the other side. It just bounced back and forth like a ball. "It scares the hell out of you," he admitted. "When that happens, we stop till it blows over." Once they waited three hours until it was safe to continue.

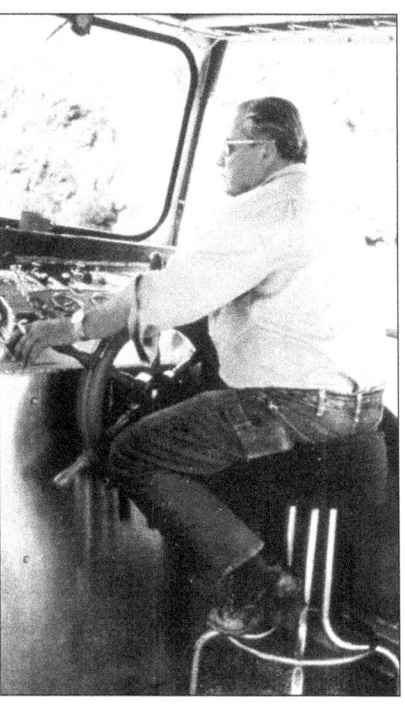

Figure 21.5. Dick Rivers is pictured here behind the wheel of one of his *Idaho Queens*. (Photo courtesy of Dick Rivers.)

From 1964 to 1974, Rivers used both boats, but during that time the river changed, making their safe operation increasingly more problematic. Dams in upper Hells Canyon caused the water level to fluctuate without warning, sometimes lowering the river flow so much that at places where Dick would normally glide over, he would hit a boulder or run aground on a gravel bar. Dick got on the phone once a week with Idaho Power Company for a "brief, barely polite phone conversation" to learn how many hours of navigation they would allow him before "pulling the plug."[15] The problems became so serious Dick finally opted for a different type of boat—a jetboat.

The boat steers better with props, he explained, "but this river eats up wheels and struts, so I decided to try jets." In 1973 Dick and Bruce Oakes of Moscow, Idaho, designed *Idaho Queen III*, a forty-one-foot aluminum jetboat with a fifteen-foot beam and a twenty-four passenger capacity—"light enough to get by with Detroit 6-53 [motors]." It was a good boat, but Rivers needed a bigger boat. Therefore, he sold the first two *Idaho Queens*, used boat number three for one-day trips, and added *Idaho Queen IV* to the fleet. He designed and built the fifty-foot aluminum boat. It weighed nine tons and was powered by twin diesel, V-8 engines with fourteen-inch Jacuzzi jet pumps.[16]

Each of his last three boats made 12 to 14 mph upriver with a flat-water speed of 25 mph; each ran about one thousand hours a year, reflecting the increasing demands of tourism.[17] That was where the money was. Rivers transformed his Copper Creek holdings seventy miles above Lewiston from a logging operation headquarters to tourist facilities with a lodge, cookhouse, twelve cabins, and outbuildings. He and longtime friend Elmer Earl, plus other pilots and deckhands, catered to a growing number of sportsmen and tourists on the river while Ralph and Helen Beard, among others, managed the Copper Creek facilities. By 1966 Rivers's tourist business, plus that of three other charter boat companies based in Lewiston, boasted four thousand visitor-days on the middle Snake—up 300 percent from only four years earlier.[18]

One of Rivers many tourists was the German author A. E. Johann, who made two trips into the canyon with Dick. He was writing a book about the Pacific Northwest, *Westwärts nach Oregon*, with numerous references to Dick Rivers in the Snake River chapter. Other writers continued the tradition of writing about the mailman of Hells Canyon, and persisted in romanticizing the isolation of the ranchers and dangers of the river. "Captain Rivers pits his skill against the vagaries and treacherous cunning of the tawny, fanged serpent that is the Snake," one author wrote.[19] Such writing, often repeated, helped Rivers's tourist business, and he still had responsibilities to his canyon customers.

Although the routine was the same as his predecessors', Rivers's postal patronage had declined. In 1966, for example, Rivers made thirteen mail drops, down three from Oliver McNabb's count. The numbers continued to drop over ensuing years. Each Wednesday morning at 6:30, Rivers left port in Lewiston to begin his ninety-two-mile stretch to Johnson Bar, with overnight stops at Copper Creek. He was back in Lewiston on Thursday evening. As the boat approached the first stop, thirty-six miles upriver on the Idaho side, Dick blasted his horn. "A lone woman at the beach" met them. "Before we pulled away a man on horseback arrived. As we left the woman was riding and the man walking. The tip of the house roof peaked over a hill at the end of the trail."[20] At their next stop on the Oregon side, the entire family was waiting. Dick said almost everyone met him at the boat, visited with him, and extended him their hospitality.[21]

As had his predecessors, Rivers hauled such things as hay bales, barbed wire, cedar posts, block salt, boxes of groceries, and once a blue-speckled mule. The animal refused to go up the gangplank. Dick's son Swede, who worked for his dad, had to go around that mule and move each foot forward, one at a time, to get him aboard. "That mule sure didn't want to ride this river," Dick said. "Don't ever say a mule doesn't have common sense." One time, Antonio and Jess Arrospide pursued a sheep among the steep hillside rocks twelve feet above the river. Dick backwatered his boat and angled it between the sharp shore rocks just below a jutting ledge. Above, on the precipice edge, Jess wrestled the ewe, grabbing her foreleg and dangling her down to the waiting hands of the deck passengers. Ten miles later, she was back with her fold. When Dick wasn't saving sheep, coaxing mules aboard, or delivering mail and catering to passengers, he worked with the Corps of Engineers to blast out rocks and install channel markers. He also helped them build a wing dam at upper Cottonwood Creek to direct the channel flow.

Dick shared the river with a growing number of commercial rafters. One famous rafter, Georgia Mae White, began commercial rafting on the Snake during McNabb's period and always timed her trips when the mailboat was not running, assuring her passengers that no motorized boats ran the river. However, when Dick took over the mail run, he changed the schedule somewhat, and her rafters and the mailboat ended up at Pittsburg Landing at the same time. "She had two badly sunburned women with her and told them it would be five days before they could get out. I told them I could have them in Lewiston in two hours, so they went with me. Georgia was quite angry." During Dick Rivers's twenty-four years on the river, an increasing number of rafters—private and commercial—shared the river, along with many commercial and private jetboats. The Snake River had become an aquatic playground as ranchers and miners had all but vanished from the canyon.

Airplanes to the Rescue

When Kyle McGrady needed help finding his son, he called on Bert Zimmerly of Clarkston. Albert L. "Bert" Zimmerly was an innovator and daredevil, an adept businessman, a skilled pilot, and an angel of mercy. During World War II he trained pilots at his Clarkston airfield. After the war, he sponsored acrobatic shows and organized an aviation operation that grew from Zimmerly Airlines to Empire Airlines, Idaho's first commercial airline. Bert built a seaplane hangar on the Snake River near Lewiston to train pilots to land on water, a skill McGrady was counting on one spring night in 1949 when Bert Zimmerly successfully landed in the turbulent river but failed to find Kyle's son Ken.

For the people of Hells Canyon country, Zimmerly, or one of his pilots—Don Wolfe, Jack

Houston, and Clyde Martin—had been a lifesaver numerous times. Zimmerly once flew a forest ranger stricken with Rocky Mountain fever from high in the Seven Devils Mountains to Grangeville, saving his life. During the fall of 1948 the river was so low McGrady's boat couldn't run for most of the season. Then a record-breaking winter swept through the country, freezing the Snake solid for a month, drifting the roads closed, and stranding ranchers like Ace Barton without fall supplies and without enough feed for the livestock. They relied on Bert Zimmerly for everything from range checkers (sacked pelletlike animal feed) to domestic supplies.[22] The only way to get people, supplies, and feed into the canyon was by parachute. Clyde F. Martin said he and Zimmerly flew "about 50 tons of sheep feed up the river that winter."[23] A short time later Zimmerly died in a sudden snowstorm in the gentle hills of the Palouse north of Lewiston.

Frank Hill of Grangeville, Ted Grote of Joseph, and Bud Stangle of Enterprise continued the air service, which became increasingly important to the ranchers. From the 1960s through the 1980s there was "a great deal of plane activity from Enterprise and Lewiston" to Temperance Creek, "bringing in hired help or getting someone out."[24] Temperance Creek had several advantages for pilots and ranchers. There were three different places to land a plane. And the forty-five-minute flight to Enterprise was across Freezeout Saddle, where the pilot didn't need much elevation to get out of the canyon. This was certainly preferable to the half-hour trip downriver to the closest usable road then an hour-plus ride to the nearest town. Some ranchers, like Ken and Greg Johnson and Bud and Lem Wilson, learned to fly and kept their own planes at the ranch. Nonetheless, ranchers also continued to use commercial pilots.

Ted Grote, who taught many of the ranchers how to fly, flew into Hells Canyon for about thirty years, beginning in 1950, when he bought a cattle ranch and "ran the airplane business to keep my ranch." At that time, the ranches on Snake River had a radio system connecting to Billie Overbiling in Boise. She maintained the radio seven days a week, twenty-four hours a day. In an emergency, people would call Billie, who relayed the message to pilots like Ted Grote in Joseph. "She'd tell me what they wanted, and I would either pick people up and

Figure 21.6. Pictured here at the Lewiston boat landing is an airplane from the 1930s or 1940s. This might have been one of Bert Zimmerly's airplanes. (Photo courtesy of Robert McGrady.)

take them in to the ranch or go down, pick them up, and take them out." They even called in grocery orders to Boise, and Billie conveyed the order to Grote, who had an Enterprise store fill the order, which he then delivered, usually to sheepmen when they moved to summer range or were getting ready to shear.

Grote also flew the sheepmen around their ranges, looking for pockets of sheep. When the animals moved to summer range, he flew overhead in search of lost sheep and cattle. In July 1960 lightning struck all the way down through the canyon country, igniting the whole canyon. Grote "flew with the Cub and . . . dropped everything you could think of" for the firefighters. He flew in mail only when Dick River's boats were iced up.[25]

Grote's Super Cub "would land very short, get in very short, and out very short," all necessary characteristics for canyon flying. Heading downriver on a regular run, he provided service first for Bud Wilson at his places from Granite Creek to Kirkwood on the Idaho side, then to Ken Johnson's places at Sluice Creek (where the strip was "plenty long at 1,000 feet") Battle Creek, and the Funk Place, "straight on top underneath Memaloose Forest Service tower." On down the river were the Blankenship brothers at Tyron Creek at their short Roland Bar strip, and in the summer at one of their cabins "on top." He flew in to the shortest airstrip of all at Ralph Longfellow's at Christmas Creek. "You could just touch and get on the brakes and when you came out, you came right to the edge of the river and pulled back not over 280 to 300 feet, from the water to the house." From Christmas Creek, Grote flew to Clay Van Pools on the Idaho side, to Dick Rivers's operation at Copper Creek, then to Gus Malaxa and Joe Onaidia at Cherry Creek, and the Tippets' places at Dug Bar, Jim Creek, and Rogersburg.

Weather determined Grote's flight plans, but sometimes it caught him by surprise. Snow might get so heavy he couldn't see. "I'd just find a little spot and hunker down." Using rope and stakes that he always carried, Ted tied down the plane. "You'd darn near freeze some times, but you had to do it. Lots of times you'd have to sit and wait." When he decided to take a chance and fly out, he would go through Freezeout Saddle, "and then you'd have to go clear down and crawl around up the Imnaha to get back in." He once spent two or three nights "sitting on a ridge in Snake River. Just me and the airplane." He never had any serious accidents.

Hazel Johnson's mother seemed to attract accidents. One time she was bound for Clarkston from Temperance Creek with potted tomato plants. Either Bert Zimmerly or one of his employees was probably at the controls when the plane wrecked at Dug Bar. Everyone went down with the plane, and everyone turned over with it. But no one was hurt, and "her tomatoes weren't damaged one whit." Another time, the pilot nearly wrecked the plane taking off from Temperance Creek. Watching from the house, Hazel was sure the plane was going down, but the pilot recovered control and delivered her mother safely out of the canyon. After that, her mother announced, "never again would she ever get in a plane."

At the Spencer Ranch on Joseph Plains, where Sharon and Bub Horrocks worked, a small landing strip on the ridge top ran up and down. Frank Hill of Grangeville flew in on the uphill side and out on the downhill side. At the end of the runway was a straight drop about three to four thousand feet into the river. Sharon remembered how people responded to the arrival of a plane at their Joseph Plains home. Before her family went to the ranch for the winter, they trucked in supplies in bulk. Hill flew in fresh produce once a week, weather permitting, along with any forgotten necessities and winter supplies. "When the plane was coming in everyone would be real happy in the morning. If it got later in the day and the plane still wasn't there, the mood changed." Then in flew Frank Hill "and it was like Christmas. Everybody would run out there to meet the plane."[26]

Bud Stangle of Enterprise began commercial service in 1962, delivering groceries, supplies, and mail, and shuttling people and animals at Dug Bar, Christmas Creek, Pittsburg Landing on the Oregon side, Johnson Bar, and Kirkwood. His one or two trips a week were "kinda fun," but always required keeping "pretty close" watch on the weather. If it was foggy, snowing, freezing rain—"you just don't go, that's all." If fog trapped him in the canyon, he used nature's roadmap and flew down to the mouth of the Imnaha River, then up the Imnaha, and out the highway. In winter, he "used heating lamps and everything else to get them engines warmed up," but once in the air, it was nice flying weather in the "heavy, still and smooth air."

Canyon pilots knew the many navigational challenges they faced—traveling from high to low altitudes, snaking low along the river gorge, and reading a potential landing site. The sites were few and, to a novice, impossible to land on. But pilots like Stangle mastered landing sites: "You'd fly over it back and forth and look it over real good. Sometimes you'd kind of roll your wheels along to see how rough it was." If he had to land on an untested spot, he "just stopped as quick as [he] could, then [got] out to see what kind of a place" it was. Bud Stangle's few mishaps occurred when a tail wheel came off "a time or two," nothing serious. One night Bud "tore an airplane up down at Tyron Creek." He made frequent landings at Christmas Creek (until someone built a shed on his landing field) and across the river in Longfellow's field at Roland Bar. In the fall and summer he landed at Dug Bar and Pittsburg Landing until the Forest Service took it over, touched down at a cabin in the trees "underneath Hat Point," flew groceries to the Funk Place, and hauled sheepherders back and forth.

Ranchers often asked Stangle to look for lost sheep or cattle, especially in the fall when they were moving the livestock. If snow was on the ground, he tried to spot fresh tracks. Once, when Stangle spotted Greg Johnson's three missing bucks, he and Greg, "hog-tied… and put them in the 206. Greg sat on one of their heads that had horns so it wouldn't flop around and I flew them down to Temperance Creek ranch and let them out. I've hauled just about everything you can put in an airplane." Indeed he has. A caretaker at a horse ranch had a few rabbits that by spring had multiplied into "a load of them. They were in the manger and everywhere." Bud hauled all fifty-two rabbits out to Enterprise.

Every trip into the canyon turned into a story for the pilot, but by 1989 when Bud Stangle sold his business to Joe Spence, the sheep and cattle ranches were all but gone. Instead of flying to serve the ranchers' needs, in the end he flew to take in government employees or tourists. His stories no longer revolved around the people who lived in the canyon.

Twenty-two years earlier an article for the *Saturday Evening Post* foretold this time—"Farewell to Hells Canyon." Writing about the upper end of the canyon, the original Hells Canyon, John Skow predicted its death "by drowning" behind Hells Canyon Dam. He also anticipated that not many years later the proposed High Mountain Sheep Dam would drown most of the remaining Hells Canyon. The first dam became a reality; a federally mandated protected status prevented the second, but in doing so helped usher in a different loss, the end of generations of cattle and sheep ranchers who lived and worked in the canyon, building their dreams in that hard yet beckoning land. Their departure was less brutal but just as final as the Nez Perce exodus from Hells Canyon one hundred years earlier.

Epilogue

When I was a child, stories and images of Hells Canyon frightened me. As a young adult with no prospect of leaving my Clarkston, Washington, home to venture south into the canyon, I simply ignored the place. Then, after a twenty-year absence, I returned to the Lewiston/Clarkston valley with an urge to learn about the region's history. My new interests led me back to Hells Canyon.

Enticed by my first trip into Hells Canyon, and intrigued by stories of steamboats plying its turbulent waters and ambitious mining ventures in such an inaccessible place, I began what became an on-again, off-again twenty-year quest to learn first about the navigation and mining stories and then about all other human activities in Hells Canyon and along the middle Snake River. My quest began as an intellectual venture probing the archives of regional repositories. At that stage, I saw the canyon setting as less important than the human history that unfolded there—a history applicable to any western setting, I thought. The more I learned, the more I yearned to physically experience the canyon. Each visit taught me a lesson, bringing me ever closer to the realization that I must understand the land before I could fully know its history. I visited the canyon at every opportunity.

Gradually Hells Canyon and the middle Snake River evolved into a dynamic, vibrant place in my mind. Hells Canyon taught me that the land shaped the course of human history as surely as the people—something I had understood intellectually but not viscerally. As I was boating on the river, sleeping on its banks, walking the canyon shores and trails, experiencing its seasons, or examining its finer points while staring awestruck at its splendor, I began to put Hells Canyon history in proper perspective. But I needed one last element to complete that understanding—I needed to meet the people who had lived and worked there.

The many genial canyon residents who shared their experiences and memories helped complete the picture of interaction between people and land. I first sensed vitality in the people with whom I spoke. Next I found it in their books and memoirs, then in their photographs. The people imprinted that vitality on the land; the land imprinted its strength on them. What was true for those most recent residents, I came to realize, was true for everyone who had ever lived and worked in Hells Canyon. The land molded them all while each gave something of themselves back to that land. To appreciate the place—Hells Canyon and the middle Snake River—you cannot remove the people. To appreciate their history, you cannot divorce them from the land. They belong together.

I love the river and the canyon—its natural beauty, its geographical and historic ties to my home. But I also love it because when I am there, I hear trapped in the canyon walls and whispered by the river and creeks the voices of the people who once called the canyon home. Their stories—real and imagined—add a unique dimension to the canyon. Through their stories comes a picture of mettle and lessons learned. Honor the Creator. When times grow difficult, learn to keep a cool head, be creative, and self-reliant. Others need you. Be there for them; keep the latchstring out and the door always open. Learn to share the good times but also to make your own fun. Your word must be rock solid. To survive and succeed in that hard land, each person must be reliable, responsible, and willing to work—hard. The surroundings demand one's respect; their beauty solicits one's enjoyment. That is the reality of canyon life.

But as stories filtered to the outside, a romanticized version of canyon life emerged, a hyperbole that sometimes evolved into myth. The land molded that image and the image lingers, often confusing history with fiction. It is the historian's task to ferret out the difference, but not ignore it. Those imagined stories become as much a part of Hells Canyon history as its historical facts, and make it equally endearing.

To me the canyon of today is not the place it once was. Today we enter it as visitors—or administrators—and take from it different kinds of stories. An ability to live in harmony with the canyon environment and its seasonal change is no longer needed. Few face the challenges of the changing seasons, of the work, of the isolation. Nor will we know the camaraderie of sharing that way of life with canyon neighbors. With the absence of permanent residents, whether they are Nez Perce, miners, or ranchers, that ingredient of life that makes the canyon special will, I fear, slip away.

I want the canyon the way it was. But when? When the Nez Perce lived there? Yes, it would have been beautiful, unsullied, and peaceful and I wish those Nez Perce who so choose could return to the life their ancestors once knew in the canyon. But because I have no way of identifying with life at that time, that is not the period for which I long. Nor can I identify with the explorers, fur trappers, or miners who briefly passed through the canyon on their way to riches and fame. No, the only time with which I can identify is the time of the ranchers, whose time overlapped with my own. To me their life came close to idyllic, even though the historian in me knows that is not the whole truth. Nonetheless, because that is the time most vivid to me, I close with the words of some of the people I came to know while writing these pages. What did the canyon mean to them? What do they see today when they go back?

Sweet Memories

Marjorie Wilson Chadwick, who died a few years after I interviewed her, remembered returning to the canyon years after she left. "It isn't near the same. I've been back to Saddle Creek. Of course, the house has burned, and it's slowly going back to nature. It just makes me sad. All those beautiful fields that people had worked so hard for, and the water is still there. You'd ride those little hot trails, and you'd come up on these ranches, and it was beautiful. Even a little patch of alfalfa was so green and cool looking. And you'd be so hot and tired, and you'd have shade and water and greenery around you. To me it was so beautiful. The people that stayed in there loved the canyon. They didn't last very long if they didn't. You had to love it."[1]

Violet Wilson Shirley would "go to sleep listening to the different birds and all. And the creek, you could hear that. And the crickets, in the nighttime in the summer, always chirping. That was such a wonderful sound. It was just the best sleep therapy one could ever have."[2]

Ace Barton "could hear every little sound. The river and creeks are sort of a lullaby to me. Most of the time it was pretty quiet, just the natural sounds—a few hawks, an eagle or two, a coyote."[3]

Esther Hibbs also remembered the sounds. There was the roar of the two branches of Granite Creek, "one on the right and the other on the left of the house. The rocks would turn over in high water; we could hear them rolling. We would hear someone coming, could hear the horses on the bottom of the rocky creek." And the smells? "They varied from day to day. . . . The spring was wonderful. Everything was fresh and green. Cherries and lilacs were in bloom. It was gorgeous."[4]

Even someone who lived there as recently as Sharon Wing had vivid memories reminiscent of a much earlier time. It was "the most fabulous cattle country I ever saw. There used to be the most beautiful bunches of grass on the hills I've ever seen in my life. It's gone."[5]

Greg Johnson "loved the mornings because it was always exciting. [You] didn't always know what was going to happen every day down there. I enjoyed all the seasons." But Greg was at the age where he bridged the old and the new generations. He grew up in the canyon and saw the changes by living through them. "Some time in the 1950s, the whole era just kind of changed. All those little homesteads went away. They went broke and became part of the bigger ranches. That eliminated a bunch of people every time it happened." By the time he took over the ranch as an adult, the canyon Greg knew as a child had already changed.[6]

Dennis Brown only saw the land through his parents' and grandparents' eyes, and as a Forest Service volunteer at Cache Creek Interpretive Center. He remembered that his father was "always impressed with the awesome beauty of the canyon, and the tremendous power of the river." His father told Dennis about seeing the huge whirlpools that would form and then disappear. Dennis added his own impressions: "The beauty and grandeur, especially at sunrise and sunset, are just almost impossible to describe either in words or pictures. Absolutely gorgeous."[7]

Frank Jacks, who returned to his Cave Gulch home many years later with friend and fellow resident Pete Fountain, best captured the nostalgia of the ranching era.[8] "Together we surveyed the scene of decay and ruin and a time now gone forever. Pete was saying something of the people who had lived here and I think we both were thinking the same thing. We could see one or two riders coming in, tired and weary, maybe someone saddling up the night horse to go out and bring in the rest of the horses. Maybe you could smell a whiff of wood smoke and the hungry smell of potatoes and bacon frying; maybe someone was chopping wood or the dog was barking. There were a thousand and more sights and activities of a time and kind of people who are not with us anymore."

That is the canyon I would like to have known. Just as each fleeting era momentarily filled the canyon with hardships and laughter—with people as real as the rocks of their canyon, only to fade into the next era—so too did the ranchers' era. Had there been no dam controversy, had there been no conservation and ecological movement to protect the canyon from development and dams, the ranching era would still have ended, ultimately. That is what this book is about—human change through the passage of time, in a place that, from our perspective, seems constant and enduring. The mesmerizing Snake River and its boundless tangle of canyon walls; the distant, lofty purple mountains skirted by a mosaic of earthly hues; the minutiae of plant and animal life—all testify to those passages and direct the unfolding of canyon history. "You had to love it."

Photo courtesy of Sheri Worle.

Appendix A

Clearing the Channel

In the fall of 1902 the canyon south of Lewiston hummed with activity. Whenever the river rose high enough, the OR&N steamboats *Lewiston, Spokane,* and *Norma*—each approximately 160 feet long with a maximum light draft of 2 feet—regularly traveled to river landings as far as Wild Goose Rapids. Pack animals on both sides of the river and small boats moved supplies for mines and quarries up and down the canyon, and the Eureka Mining, Smelting and Power Company began establishing camps and developing their properties. Company officers hoped that by the time the steamboat *Imnaha* was completed the river channel would be cleared of obstructions.

The River and Harbor Act of 1902 included twenty-five thousand dollars to fund a survey from Lewiston to Pittsburg Landing. There were no plans to deepen the river channel above Lewiston.[1] The survey was finally begun in September 1902, too late in the season to start at Pittsburg Landing as planned. The surveying engineer received orders to begin at the Imnaha River and to take dynamite along to blow out some of the worst boulders. That should have satisfied local developers. Instead they were livid. To delay the survey until after the river started to rise and then fail to survey the entire stretch of river that Congress had authorized, was "useless and wicked neglect," claimed W. M. Libby, a Clarkston founder and an officer in the Lewiston Navigation Company. Libby and other founders of Clarkston, Wash., hoped to make the new town a railroad center, connecting a rail line east up Snake River and another line north through the canyon. Until the railroad was finished, and as incentive to see it finished, river transportation and canyon development were important to Clarkston's development scheme.[2]

Nonetheless, engineer F. C. Schubert, along with a transit man, a leveler, and nine other men, left Lewiston on September 20, 1902, to begin their eighteen-day survey of the Snake River from the mouth of the Imnaha River to Lewiston. Traveling in three or four bateaux, they fought the current by rowing and cordelling to the mouth of the Imnaha. There they began the survey, running a transit and level line down the river to its junction with the Clearwater at Lewiston and documenting the topography and location of the rapids, rocks, and navigational obstructions along the way. At the time, the river level was optimum for the survey. After he finished, engineer Schubert recommended that steamboats use the line at Cochran Islands, which had gravel bars on both shores; at Shovel Creek Rapids; and at Wild Goose Rapids. He explained that it was not the depth of the channel but the "excessive slope of the stream with its consequent rapids and many dangerous rocky points and bowlders [sic]" that made navigation difficult. By removing those reefs and boulders "light draft steamboats can use the river at average stages as far up as Douglas, four miles above the mouth of the Imnaha." Schubert apparently failed to complete the recommended blasting during the survey, but he intended to send a small crew upriver to take out the most serious obstructions, specifically at Mountain Sheep Rapids, as soon as possible.[3]

The *Lewiston (Idaho) Morning Tribune,* May 19, 1903, reported that the dredge, also authorized in the 1902 River and Harbor Act, was delayed because the original plans did not call for heavy enough equipment. A June 23, 1903, *Tribune* article gave the final plans for the dredge. It was to be a minimum of ninety feet long, have a twenty-six-foot beam, and a speed of at least nine mph in still water. The hull would be of wood. Facilities included a cabin, pilothouse, bulkheads, storerooms, and bunks; equipment included a steam capstan, steering gear, and machinery. In the lower story were the engine and two small staterooms, forward and after cabins, bathrooms, and a dining room. The engines would work under 165 pounds of pressure. The boat was designed mainly for shallow digging in compacted gravel, swift water, and depths varying from three to twelve feet. The machinery would be powerful enough to operate a one-cubic-yard dipper in the compacted gravel.

Ultimately, each of the dredges *Wallowa*, *Norma*, *Umatilla*, and *Asotin* worked on the Snake River channel, but primarily below Lewiston and after 1903. The steamer *Asotin*, built around 1904, worked the Snake under the command of Drew Lanker and R. L. Baughman. Like its sister ship, the *Umatilla*, it met its fate on the Columbia. In 1918, an ice jam caught it below Pasco, crushing its hull to pieces.

Instead of waiting for a dredge, the Corps of Engineers hired Captain Harry Baughman to clear the river channel. He began work the fall of 1903. First he identified and designated the navigational impediments. Then he equipped the *Imnaha* for removing the boulders by fitting a crane at the steamer's bow on a movable platform capable of swinging to different positions. Next, the crew installed on the platform a drill powered by the boat's steam boiler to make holes in the rocks for blasting powder.[4] They removed a large rock and reef that extended nearly to the surface at Buffalo Rock, several rocks below the water surface at Captain Lewis Rapids, and a reef at the Grande Ronde River that extended across the channel. Additional impediments included three jagged rocks at Shovel Creek; reefs at China Gardens, Cache Creek, and Cottonwood Creek; a large reef near the mouth of the Salmon River; and a large rock in the middle of the river at the mouth of Deep Creek. A Corps of Engineers report later described Baughman's "imminently successful" operation. While the captain moored the *Imnaha* at the obstruction, the men drilled and charged the rock from the bow. Then the boat dropped back down the river, and someone set off the blast with an electrical device from shore.[5] Baughman and his *Imnaha* unquestionably made the river safer.

In the meantime, the corps sent in a surveyor to determine how best to clear Mountain Sheep Rapids. At first the surveyor planned to send in a four-man crew to blast the offending rock out of the water with five hundred pounds of powder. (The two hundred pounds they had used the previous fall had merely blown the top off the rock.)[6] However, once he saw two more rocks of the same size "hanging as if by a thread" from the mountain side, Captain Baughman suggested using a series of smaller blasts on the river rocks and securing each of the two overhanging rocks in place with ring bolts and cables. Unfortunately, no one implemented this or any other suggestion that year. January 1904 found the corps still making plans for the removal of that Mountain Sheep rock. A spokesman explained that they needed "the most experienced rock men"—many of whom were available at the mines a few miles away—and "the best equipment" to meet the challenge. Ironically, "best equipment" had crashed a few months earlier at that same Mountain Sheep Rapids obstruction.

Nearly two years later, in 1905, the Corps of Engineers surveyed the last stretch of the middle Snake from Pittsburg Landing to the mouth of the Imnaha River. The surveyor, F. C. Schubert, and his party of eleven men "hauled" their three, twenty-five-foot boats about a hundred miles overland to Pittsburg Landing, where they began the survey. They documented forty-three rapids in that twenty-six-mile stretch and speculated that if a boat could make it to the Imnaha/Snake confluence, it could probably travel all the way to Pittsburg Landing. Echoing the dream shared by steamboat pioneers for the past forty years, the *Lewiston Morning Tribune* excitedly announced, "This proves the view so often expressed that the upper Snake river during a long period each year can be safely navigated to Pittsburg." The editor reminded his readers that a large part of the Salmon River country and the isolated copper properties in the Pittsburg Landing area would benefit from steamer transportation. Even then, one of those properties, the Great Eastern mine, had "a large quantity of high grade ore" awaiting shipment.[7]

The potential for upriver steamboat navigation continued to attract regional developers as late as 1935. Throughout that period—from 1902 to 1935—Congress passed a series of acts to maintain an open Columbia/Snake navigational channel deep into Hells Canyon, five feet deep at low water, at Lewiston, with widths varying from 60 to 150 feet.[8] Although work above Lewiston remained sporadic, crews removed numerous boulders and rocky points. Some time after 1903 at the Mountain Sheep and Wild Goose Rapids work crews also replaced the temporary deadman with an iron ring anchored in a boulder above each rapid. These embedded rings helped the steamers line through those obstacles. Ultimately, Johnson Bar on the Snake River, fourteen miles above Pittsburg Landing, became the head of navigation. By then, however, an entirely different economic base dominated the canyon and a different type of boat served its needs.

Appendix B

Fraud or Just Poor Business Practices?

On November 5, 1901, midwestern investors had agreed to purchase the Delta Group mining claims, located near the mouth of the Imnaha River, for the initial sum of $18,000, later reduced to $15,000. On January 15, 1902, the company incorporated as Eureka Mining, Smelting and Power Company with a fixed capital stock of 2 million shares set at the arbitrary value of $2 million, "according to the customs of mining operations." The promoters then subscribed for the entire capital stock and in exchange transferred all rights and interests in their mining claims to the corporation, "without regard to the actual value of the locations." Each promoter next received credit for 200,000 shares, or one-tenth of the total capital stock. After deciding how much money it would take to operate the mines, each promoter donated 60,000 shares back to the company to raise that sum. This sum they called treasury stock and put on the market for 50 cents a share, with assurances that proceeds would be used exclusively for property development as outlined in the company prospectus. When Eureka Company set the capital stock value at $2 million, it was based on stock prices of $1 a share. The prospectus said they were selling shares at that price; court records claim stock initially sold at 50 cents a share.

On March 22, 1902, the company treasurer, C. O. Howard, advanced the purchase price of $15,000 to the original owners of the Delta Group claims. Eureka Company owned many claims besides the Delta Group in the area, but later litigation only involved their handling of the purchase and payment of those Delta Group claims. Howard also advanced an additional $10,500 to perfect and patent those claims and to cover his expenses. A month later each of the ten promoters, including Howard, transferred a total of 40,000 shares of their personal stock to Howard and called those shares "trustee stock." They put that stock on the market with the proceeds to be applied for payment of the advanced $25,500. The money for the sale of those additional shares did not go into the company treasury but remained in trust to perfect and patent the Delta Group claims.

After that separate fund was created, the treasury stock price rose from 50 to 75 cents a share. The promoters continued to sell exclusively to friends, family, and acquaintances, assuring all the buyers that the proceeds would only be used for property development, not for the purchase of mining claims. George Nehrhood, C. O. Howard, Levy Hubbel, H. G. Johnson, and M. S. Howard sold stock in Waukon, Iowa; O. E. Guernsey in Dubuque, Iowa; Joseph T. Miller and William J. Wilkerson in Sterling, Ill.; and E. O. Guernsey at Dell Rapids, S.D., and Janesville, Wis. In the fall of 1902, however, Secretary Nehrhood instructed the bookkeeper to credit the sales of treasury stock toward payment for the advanced $25,500. From January through September 1903, that is exactly what the bookkeeper did. He entered the treasury stock sale in a separate registry, calling it trustee stock, and never considered it to be treasury stock. In May 1903, when the treasurer completed payment for patenting and perfecting the Delta Group claims, he had a balance in the trustee account of $529.55.

In other words, before the ten founders created the Eureka Mining, Smelting and Power Company, they individually owned or intended to purchase Oregon mining claims at the Imnaha and Snake River confluence. They incorporated specifically for the purpose of raising money to develop the mines, which included extracting the ore as well as operating a smelter and a transportation service for their ore and the ore of neighboring canyon mines. At no time did shareholders expect to pay for the purchase price of those mining claims, but essentially that is exactly what they did. When problems surfaced and found their way to the courts, violation of that basic premise appeared to be at the root of all subsequent cases.

Litigation started within the circle of the founding ten when Lorenzo D. Lively, one of the original shareholders, filed a complaint in January 1903 against the "Eureka Mining, Smelting and Power Company, G. A. Nehrhood, and Henry Huesby" to recover losses for stock he claimed he bought but never received. He accused the company of fraudulently transferring capital stock to the treasury to avoid issuing it because the company lacked the necessary finances to purchase mining claims. With the primary parties residing in different states, Lively named Henry Huesby of Clarkston, Wash., and the Eureka Company, incorporated in Washington, to keep the case out of the U.S. circuit court. (Surviving court records are limited and some barely legible. Little additional information about these court cases exists. Consequently the information here is sketchy, intended only to shed some insight into company operations and problems at the time.)

Lively claimed that G. A. Nehrhood sold him 136,000 shares of Eureka stock, which Lively never received, and demanded either the 136,000 shares or their capital value of $102,000—an arbitrary figure that was never market tested. The treasury stock never had any market value. In fact, the sale of treasury stock never extended beyond the family and personal acquaintances of the original promoters, despite efforts to the contrary. Between the first of December 1904 and the end of January 1905, most of the promoters had transferred 780,777 shares of their remaining stock to the company "without consideration." That included the 90,000 shares of original treasury stock that remained unsold when court proceedings began in 1908.[1]

Despite ample records to the contrary, which surfaced in subsequent court cases, Lively insisted he had been neither a trustee nor one of the original founders, only a company representative doing the bidding of the corporate officers and the board of directors. The case ultimately settled out of court on June 20, 1904, with the Eureka Company issuing Lively 136,000 shares of "nontransferable" capital stock. Lively accepted the stock without objections. Twice later his fraud charges reappeared, first in 1908, and again in 1911. In 1911, the court ruled in favor of Lively and against the original Eureka Company trustees. It found the trustees guilty of wrongfully diverting $24,970.00 from the treasury and fraudulently allocating it to themselves by applying the money to the purchase of mining claims.[2]

The judge's ruling excluded motive. It made no mention of intent to commit a crime. Had the judge done so, he might have provided the definitive answer to the question of whether company founders intentionally committed fraud or were simply guilty of sloppy bookkeeping and poor business practices. Claiming that they were following standard business procedures of the day may have been the founders' best defense. These events occurred before the infamous stock market crash of 1929. In the early 1900s, few if any guidelines directed company organization, the distribution of shares, or the sale of stock. A review of the company's testimony, prepared by vice president C. O. Howard with company president James T. Miller's approval, indicates that apparently the founders of Eureka Mining, Smelting and Power Company believed they had properly organized the company, properly distributed the stock, and kept proper and accurate records. They did not foresee the potential problems that became increasingly evident when treasury stockholders formed a new board of directors and took control of the company in August of 1904. Many of those new directors had had first-hand acquaintance with the day-to-day operations of the mines; and others were now in positions to more closely examine company records.

Late in 1904, the new board's first act was to discontinue work at the Eureka mine and restructure the corporation. The following July they unanimously voted to hire Jellum and Jones, a Lewiston assaying firm, as mining engineers and placed the mines under the management of John Baker (the same man who earlier worked as Dennis Guernsey's foreman). Work at the mines resumed, which included sinking a 100-foot tunnel to "tap the Mother Lode" and determine the vein's extent. With a positive report in hand, board members planned for future property development. In July, 1905, some of the new directors filed a claim against the Eureka Company, alleging that the founders had misrepresented the facts to investors. The plaintiffs requested that the Eureka Mining, Smelting and Power Company be placed in receivership.[3] John Bender of Lewiston, the attorney representing the original founders, could not understand why Facey and others wanted to take such action. He said quite a number of the other plaintiffs visited the mine some time ago; some even worked there before buying stock. Those stockholders voted unanimously to hire Jellum and Jones as the mining engineers, were aware that the engineers made a thorough examination of the properties, and reported "that the company had an excellent prospect." Bender believed the company was in good financial shape and the operations carried on "to the satisfaction of the management of stockholders of the company."

He was confident that "when the time comes the company will be able to show a complete defense to any cause of action that these plaintiffs may allege." The court agreed, ruling that "there seemed no sufficient reason for asking that a receiver be appointed to serve the company's affairs.[4]

Shortly after taking control of the Eureka Company, the new board also rewrote the bylaws to prohibit the transfer of stock until the owner paid any debts owed on that stock. The by-law stated: "The stock of this corporation shall be held for the indebtedness of the owner thereof to this company and no transfer of the same shall be made on the books of the company until said indebtedness shall be paid." The stockholders, including the original holders, voted for the by-law, either in person or by proxy. Then, in 1908, based on that bylaw, the new board of directors brought charges against all ten of the original shareholders, H. G. Johnson, G. A. Nehrhood, C. O. Howard, M. S. Howard, William J. Wilkinson, J. T. Miller, H. M. Peterson, L. D. Lively, J. E. Hubbell, and O. E. Guernsey, charging them with fraud and nonpayment of debts owed the company. The debts amounted to a total of nearly $34,000. The plaintiff—the new board of directors of the Eureka Mining, Smelting and Power Company—claimed that the ten defendants wrongfully directed 40,000 shares to the company treasurer, C. O. Howard, who took the receipts totaling $21,564.87 and applied them toward the purchase of the Delta Group. The plaintiff called that a fraudulent transaction. Conversely, with that transaction the defendants—who referred to themselves as promoters—claimed that they had merely discharged their indebtedness to the Eureka Company.[5]

Throughout 1902 and 1903, most of those original ten promoters had left their own businesses in the Midwest to devote full attention to the development of company properties. Their only compensation amounted to 15 percent of each share they sold, which most did not collect. James T. Miller, company president, claimed that he never received any money from the company. From the beginning each promoter recognized the huge gamble he was taking. Their correspondence underscores that time and again. Nothing in the correspondence hints at intentional fraud or even a recognition that their bookkeeping might be irregular. In a long article published in the *Sterling Evening Gazette* in response to an earlier article entitled "Devious Ways of Copper Barons," former company president James T. Miller explained what happened. His account corresponded with court records, except that he made it very clear that he did indeed pay for his share of the Delta Group claims.[6]

According to Miller, in December 1901, the Imnaha Mining Company had recently organized to purchase the Delta Group claims at the Imnaha-Snake River confluence. One of the investors had a one-tenth interest in the new company but refused to pay. In a search to find his replacement, the Imnaha Mining Company came to James T. Miller, who already owned some claims in the Imnaha District. The Imnaha Mining Company members invited Miller to a reorganization meeting in Waukon, Iowa, and asked him to consider buying that man's share of the Delta Group and one-eighth interest in an adjacent claim. The total cost, in cash, would be under $2,000. The company would then reorganize under the name Eureka Mining, Smelting and Power Company. Miller agreed, expecting to receive 200,000 shares in payment, with 60,000 of those shares transferred to treasury stock. Immediately upon joining the original investors, Miller sent the Eureka Mining company a draft for $1,843.75 for his shares in the Delta Group claims, and on March 26, 1902 he transferred his interest in those claims to the company. Two days later he signed the agreement to have 60,000 of his shares put in the treasury. There is no reason for James T. Miller to have lied about paying for his share of the Delta Group—it could be easily disproved. This statement, as far as Miller was concerned, clearly contradicted the plaintiff's charges.[7]

Miller continued to explain his role in the Eureka Mining, Smelting and Power Company as he faced charges of fraudulent appropriation of funds. "I was always asked to donate to the Eureka company, or the boat company or something else about the company. I donated it." He claimed that he never received a nickel back in the way of salary for two and a half years "of the hardest work that I ever did." Miller claimed that it was he who obtained the Eureka town and smelter sites from the Rogers brothers of Asotin, Washington, something "others could not do." The company paid only for the survey.

He asserted that other promoters acted equally selflessly. They donated their time to the company. "Let me ask how many in the company today would leave their stores and occupations and do what those first stockholders did?" C. O. Howard, "an old man" now deceased, spent three years in Oregon working hard for the company. "He left his own large business to hired help and received no pay for his time doing this work." Levy Hubbel, also an old man, "spent time and money working for this company without pay. Do these things count for nothing?" Of C. O. Howard and Ell Guernsey, company treasurers, Miller asked, "Can anyone say that they did not account for every dollar? How could any money be taken out of the treasury? They gave $50,000 bonds." Miller concluded his and his colleague's defense by reminding the reader that the Eureka Company had not failed as had other mining companies. "It stands high with all of those who have examined it and have known of its qualities."

Under Washington law, no actual subscription is necessary to form a mining operation, but the promoters themselves agreed to the purchase price of the claims and the expenses of perfecting them. Miller explained that sometime in 1902, he transferred 4,000 shares of his stock to trustee C. O. Howard, "for work he was doing or had done in obtaining the properties." Miller admitted that he did not know where the money went. He said that the Imnaha Mining Company had negotiated the purchase price for the Delta Group at $15,000 and set the payment deadline for Apr. 1, 1902. As the deadline approached, the Eureka Company officers wanted to be sure that they had the money on hand because the parties in Lewiston, claiming that the property was worth $100,000, wanted to "back out of the agreement." Miller said he knew nothing about the purchase arrangements—he joined the company later—but assumed that the original trustees must have used the money to buy the Delta Group or he would never have received the deeds.[8]

Superior Judge Chester Miller saw the promoters' actions differently than Miller remembered. According to him, "all proceedings were regular until the secretary told the bookkeeper to apply the receipts from the sale of treasury stock to payment of the amount due C.O. Howard, trustee." That was the $25,500 Howard used to purchase and perfect the Delta Group. The promoters' mistake came in not notifying the stock purchasers that they were buying capital stock rather than treasury stock. Had the stockholders been given the opportunity to vote on the company's purchase of the 40,000 shares used to raise that money, it might have been a different matter, but that did not happen. The promoters' behavior was "irregular" making them "liable to the corporation for the amount they thus diverted." The judge ruled that their actions amounted to fraud and ordered each of the promoters to sell any remaining stock and apply the proceeds to help discharge their $25,564.87 indebtedness. They did.

Map C.1. Dams and proposed dam sites, from the first proposal in 1902 to the creation of Hells Canyon National Recreation Area in 1975.

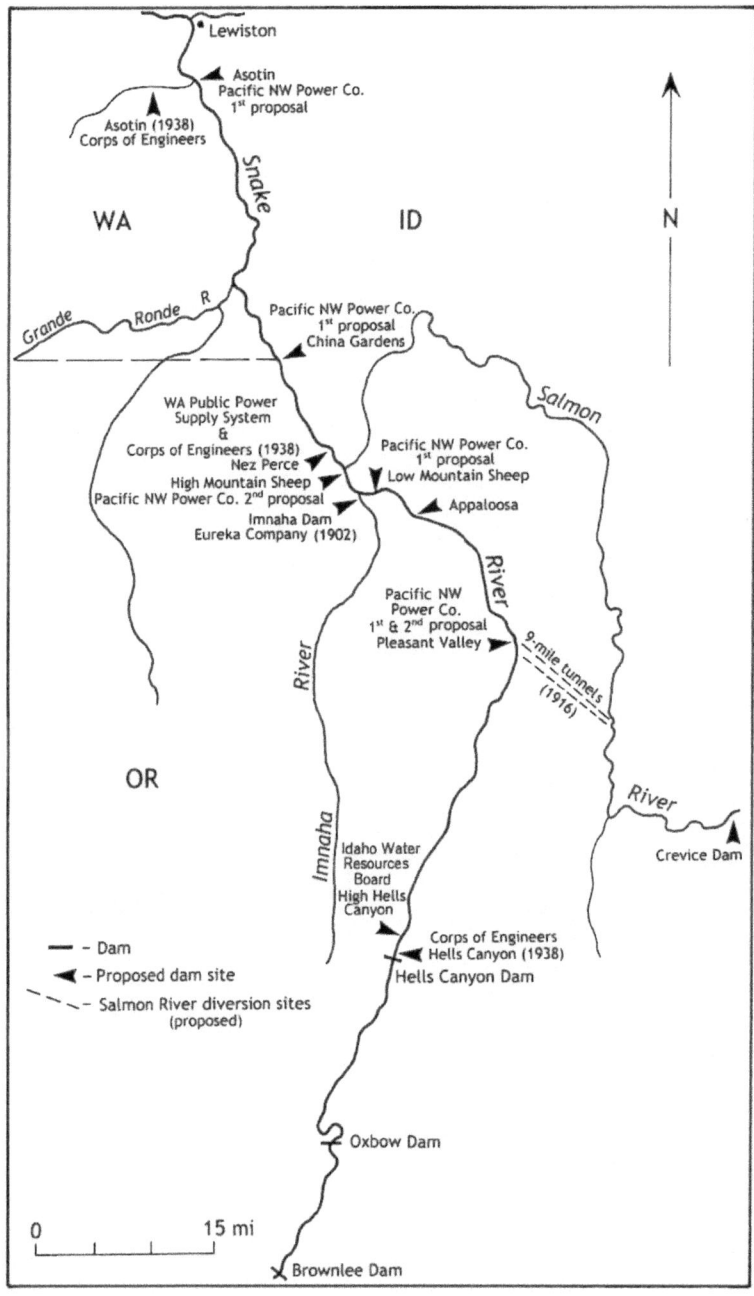

Appendix C

The End of an Era

Controversy over the so-called Snake River question—who should build the dams, where should they be located, indeed, should they be built at all—ran through the administration of six presidents, was debated and studied by at least five federal agencies, moved in and out of congressional committees for more than thirty years, and even made it through the judicial system to the Supreme Court. Between 1947, when Idaho Power Company submitted its first application to build a dam at the upper end of Hells Canyon, and 1980, when Congress deauthorized the last dam, the middle Snake River served as a battleground and focal point of conflicting national values.

After World War II, increasing demands on dwindling resources forced the nation to reconsider long-held ideas and values. How should we use our natural resources? If our waterways were to be dammed, who should build them—the federal government, public utilities, or private companies? Should we consider alternative energy sources? Would science and technology ultimately find ways to protect fisheries if dams were built? Should wild lands and wildlife habitats be protected. If so, using what criteria?

Each chapter of the controversy took a slightly different turn and with each turn the nation gradually redefined its values and priorities. The discussion began quietly among federal agencies, in the halls of Congress, and among a few Pacific Northwest utility companies. Most Americans initially assumed that the rivers would be, indeed must be, dammed. As the question of who should build the dams stirred public interest, a debate ensued, and gradually people began to question whether dams *should* be built. Citizen organizations, Indian tribes, businesses, federal and state agencies, and individuals entered the dialogue, turning the once remote and unknown section of Idaho, Oregon, and Washington into a nationally recognized battleground for conflicting ideologies.[1] Ultimately, the dams introduced a new era in Hells Canyon.

Dam Talk—and Plans

Early canyon residents knew about future hydroelectric plans for the Snake River as early as 1902, when the Eureka Mining, Smelting and Power Company announced its intention to dam the mouth of the Imnaha River to power the machines and light the town. Within two decades, Oregon state engineers had "identified six major dam sites in a hundred mile stretch" between Oxbow and the state's northern border.[2] Idaho set aside six, forty-acre power sites along the Salmon and Snake Rivers.[3] One site, a quarter mile stretch along the river near Dry Creek, became part of the Van Pool homestead acquisitions. Another site attracted a controversial but marginally popular proposal known as the Salmon River Diversion Project. A portal cut just below the small town of Lucille would divert the Salmon River into a nine-mile tunnel through the mountains and drop 400 hundred feet into the Snake River just above Pittsburg Landing. (It would also uncover "fabulous riches in gold" in the drained area of the Salmon.)[4] A 125-foot-high dam just below the Salmon River portal would force the water through the tunnel; a 500-foot-high dam thirty-nine miles below the Snake River portal would complete the project.[5] In 1928 German financiers backed the project, hoping to establish a $20 million nitrate plant in the Northwest wilderness. Their German-American representative, A. G. Liebmann, spent six months trying to obtain flow and storage permits for the site from the Idaho Department of Reclamation.[6] A lone rancher from Stanfield, Oregon, blocked the scheme by refusing to grant the Germans an option on land that he owned there.[7]

Eleven years later, the Idaho State Planning Board was still considering the project, envisioning a seven-mile tunnel through the mountains from the mouth of Poodle Dog Creek on the Salmon to Corral Creek on the Snake with a 450-foot elevation difference between the two tunnel openings. The completed project would dry up more than sixty miles of the Lower Salmon River, "even then recognized as the richest producer of anadromous fish in the nation."[8] International events intervened to end that diversion project.

Federal involvement after World War II broadened the Snake River drama in both scope and duration.[9] In 1947 Idaho Power Company submitted its first application to build a dam south of Hells Canyon at the old Brownlee's ferry site. The FPC (Federal Power Commission, now the Federal Energy Regulatory Commission) took no action because Secretary of the Interior Oscar Chapman and Idaho senator Glenn Taylor objected, wanting instead a single, larger, federally constructed dam farther north and deeper into the canyon. Thus began a prolonged aspect of the controversy—who should build the dams?

In that same year, the Corps of Engineers fine-tuned plans for multiple use of the Columbia/Snake waterways, following guidelines known as the 308 Review Report.[10] The report envisioned the entire Columbia/Snake system as a single, multifaceted project that included the construction of four Snake River dams below and three dams above Lewiston. The proposed dams south of town were Asotin, five miles above the small town of the same name; Nez Perce, near the mouth of Cherry Creek and about three miles below the Salmon River confluence; and Hells Canyon, near the mouth of Hells Canyon Creek in the deepest section of the canyon. Asotin and the four dams below Lewiston were to improve navigation and support "electro-metallurgical and electro-chemical industries in the lower Columbia River." The lime deposits near the mouth of the Grande Ronde River could be tapped and transported if a dam at Asotin, with navigation locks, were built.[11] The two dams deeper in the canyon would provide a reserve water supply for consistent hydroelectric power and help control downstream floods.

The corps, however, anticipated one serious problem should a high dam be built below the mouth of the Salmon River—degradation of an important fish-spawning ground in the Salmon River watershed. Few people, even then, wanted to sacrifice this valuable resource. The corps' recommended alternative was a series of low dams between Lewiston and the Salmon River and two high dams, one at Mountain Sheep just above the mouth of the Imnaha River, and one in the heart of the canyon at the base of the Seven Devil Mountains. People knew that dams and migrating salmon were not compatible. By choosing the corps' proposed alternative, they would sacrifice the smaller run up the Snake River.[12]

In 1949, two years after the corps's initial report, Senator Warren Magnuson of Washington introduced Senate Bill 2180 to authorize $3 billion to build the dams outlined in the 308 Review Report. Herbert G. West, managing secretary of the Inland Empire Waterways Association, promised "100 percent approval of the people of the Pacific Northwest." It had been more than a decade since the corps's 308 Report appeared, a decade of nothing but "squabbling and inaction." West demanded a vote one way or the other on Senate Bill 2180.[13]

To say that Senate Bill 2180 had 100 percent approval was pure hyperbole. Widespread dissatisfaction with the federal government's earlier Grand Coulee and Bonneville dams on the Columbia River and the organizational structure of the Tennessee Valley Authority polarized discussion of who would build the dam. President Harry S. Truman envisioned a Columbia Valley Authority akin to his predecessor's TVA—thus opening the door for federally constructed dams rather than the private dams outlined in Report 308—and asked the army engineers and Bureau of Reclamation to provide for "an orderly development of the Columbia Basin." The ensuing debate delayed congressional authorization of the 308 dams. Truman's critics charged "dictatorial powers."[14] A water conservation organization in south Idaho claimed that Senate Bill 2180 had "no legislative provision for Idaho's future irrigation."[15] The Idaho state legislature also got into the fray, suggesting that private companies would be more responsive to Idaho's irrigation needs.

Despite the nation's concern about declining energy resources during the Korean War, efforts to construct dams in Hells Canyon were undermined by the contentious question of who would build them.[16] The cry for increased production of hydroelectric energy, added to already loud demands for flood control, helped sway opinion in favor of building dams on the middle Snake River. Idaho Power Company again applied for a license from the FPC, but this time the Interior Department filed a protest, blocked action, then submitted its own Hells Canyon dam bill before the House Interior and Insular Affairs committee. It included a request for an expensive Mountain Home, Idaho, reclamation project. The wording and expense of the Mountain Home project killed the bill.

Public, Private, or Partners?

In 1952 President Dwight D. Eisenhower brought to the executive branch a different philosophy on resource development and dam construction: Wherever possible, private enterprise should take charge of development projects. "The responsibility for resource development and its cost should be borne by those who receive its benefits."[17] However, if private companies complied with all the criteria, the company could not make a profit on Snake River dams without government help. Eisenhower therefore proposed a "partnership concept" whereby the private utility company would install the electrical generating equipment and market the electricity, while the federal government would finance the unprofitable flood control, navigation, and fish conservation features.[18] In 1953 Eisenhower's secretary of interior Douglas McKay, the former governor of Oregon who "always enthusiastically supported the maximum development of the water resources as proposed in the 308 Review Report," withdrew his department's earlier objections to Idaho Power's application.[19] The Idaho company resubmitted an application to the FPC and a yearlong hearing began in July 1953.

In 1955 the controversy again found its way to the Senate floor. Democrat Wayne Morse of Oregon and twenty-nine cosponsors introduced Senate Bill 1333, requesting congressional authorization to construct, operate, and maintain a federal, multipurpose dam—Hells Canyon dam—on the Snake River between Idaho and Oregon at the mouth of Hells Canyon Creek. The "towering wall of concrete" would reach more than seven hundred feet above bedrock "in a gorge so tight that the reservoir thus created would be scarcely wider than the river it replaced."[20] Democratic senator Richard Neuberger of Oregon, who had visited Hells Canyon as a journalist numerous times with Kyle McGrady, argued that "the high [federal] dam would be dollar for dollar the better investment . . . a nearly ideal development of the Middle Snake."[21]

In May of that year, FPC examiner William J. Costello issued his report on the Idaho Power Company application, recommending a license to the Idaho company for three small dams at the upper end of the canyon—Oxbow, Brownlee, and later Hells Canyon. The power capacity would be the same as one, high dam but "construction costs would be $404 million for the federal dam compared to $195 million for the three dams."[22] Based on the examiner's recommendation, the FPC unanimously voted to license all three dams.

A High Dam Somewhere

Costello's report shocked Neuberger, who called it a "strange decision" based on political climate. He claimed that Costello had admitted that the federal project would be a better choice, but made his recommendation because three small dams were better than no dam at all. (Congress still had not yet authorized *any* dam on that stretch of the river.) Neuberger didn't agree, arguing that without adequate reservoir storage on the Snake River, "pressure would increase to find upstream power and flood control elsewhere in the Columbia Basin." Secretary of Interior McKay and Oregon's governor Paul Patterson had already mentioned damming the Salmon and Clearwater Rivers in Idaho as substitutes, even though both rivers were important salmon spawning grounds. Other proposed dam locations also presented problems—Glacier View would invade Glacier National Park, and Libby, Montana, would require paying Canada for flooding some of their land. Nevertheless, in order to get maximum benefits from the authorized lower Snake River dams, there had to be *some* high dam *some* place.

Neuberger, the man who made a name for himself a decade earlier writing about the beauty and wonder of Hells Canyon, joined others in advocating a high dam at Hells Canyon, where it would do the least damage to wildlife and to fish migrations. Hells Canyon, he argued, was barren and unattractive, sparsely populated, and prohibitively inaccessible. The National Park Service had advocated the Hells Canyon dam to make the area more accessible to visitors as early as 1939 and had shown interest in setting Hells Canyon aside as a national park.[23] The service estimated that the high dam project, "with its access roads, facilities and structures, would attract 50,000 to 65,000 visitors a year." Idaho Power Company development "would attract about half that many."[24]

However, a canyon dam, all parties agreed, should be built for its hydroelectric, not recreational, potential. Senator Wayne Morse voiced regional concerns that the Pacific Northwest's economy would stagnate without sufficient cheap electric power to attract industrial development. Smaller, privately built dams, he believed, could not meet that need. Public power utilities concurred. Gus Norwood, executive secretary of the Northwest Public Power Association, best summarized the argument, "The real question is one of full development versus a 60% development."[25]

In the spring of 1955, public hearings of Senate Bill 1333—authorizing federal construction of Hells Canyon dam—held at Boise, Lewiston, and Portland demonstrated popular sentiment supporting a watershed dam to provide water storage built *somewhere* in the Columbia/Snake River system, just not the Clearwater or Salmon Rivers.[26] North Central Idaho Wildlife Federation members spoke about the danger to grazing and traveling routes of the "finest herd of wild elk in the US" should anyone build the proposed Bruce's Eddy and Penny Cliffs dams on the Clearwater River. That organization favored a high, federal dam in Hells Canyon.[27] N. Ira Gabrielson of the Wildlife Management Institute concurred: "The national conservation organizations are opposed to any dams on the Salmon and Clearwater for the reasons which you advance." Those two rivers were "the two most important spring Chinook salmon spawning streams still available in the Columbia River system, and should be kept clear of dams at all cost."[28] With the Sierra Club's argument that defeating the federal Hells Canyon dam "poses a dangerous threat to conservation in the Columbia River basin," Senator Neuberger asked their California representative, David Brower, to support the federal Hells Canyon dam. He feared that current efforts in the Senate to save Dinosaur National Monument would "be a Sunday school picnic" compared to the impending battle should a federal Hells Canyon dam *not* be built "and the way cleared for an assault on the Salmon, Clearwater, and Glacier."[29]

In 1956 the Wilderness Society voiced the same concerns. Society president Olaus Murie wrote to Frank Church, assuring him that although they took no position on federal versus private dams, they "concluded that the Hells Canyon dam, which would not interfere with the fish migration and other wildlife values in the Clearwater area, would meet various kinds of water storage needs and make the Clearwater dams unnecessary."[30] The California Farm Research and Legislative Committee viewed the controversy from the perspective of irrigation farmers who need cheap fertilizer. Only with low-cost electricity from a high dam, they believed, could the vast phosphate deposits in southeast Idaho be mined and converted into cheap fertilizer.[31]

In the meantime, on August 4, 1955, the Federal Power Commission voted unanimously to license the construction of the 205-foot-high Oxbow, 395-foot-high Brownlee, and 320-foot-high Hells Canyon dams. The Office of Defense Mobilization backed that decision and endorsed the dams. Protests from Oregon senators Wayne Morse and Richard Neuberger; Washington senators Warren Magnuson and Henry Jackson; James Murray and Mike Mansfield of Montana; and Representatives Edith Green of Oregon, Gracie Pfost of Idaho, and Lee Metcalf of Montana, all elected officials supposedly acting on behalf of their constituents in the Pacific Northwest, had no effect on the decision.[32]

That did not stop debate on a federal Hells Canyon dam outlined in Senate Bill 1333. In September 1955 opponents of the FPC's decision to grant the license to Idaho Power, spearheaded by the National Hells Canyon Association, filed a petition with the FPC for a rehearing. When the FPC denied the petition, the association petitioned the U.S. Court of Appeals in November 1955 for review of the commission orders. So long as Senate Bill 1333 was pending and the FPC decision remained in court, nothing was final.[33]

Idaho Power had already begun construction on Brownlee dam.

More Players Enter the Fracas

Idaho Power was not the only company coveting the middle Snake. In 1955 the Pacific Northwest Power Company (PNPC), a coalition of private power companies that included Pacific Power and Light, Portland General Electric, Washington Water Power, and Montana Power, filed a petition with the FPC to build low dams at Mountain Sheep, just above the Imnaha River (an alternate 308 Report dam), and Pleasant Valley at Pittsburg Landing. Both sites were downstream from the proposed federal Hells Canyon dam. PNPC also planned for regulating dams at China Gardens, above the mouth of the Grande Ronde River, and at Asotin. At the same time, the Nez Perce dam site below the mouth of the Salmon River (one of the original sites proposed in the 308 Report) emerged as PNPC's alternative to the Mountain Sheep/Pleasant Valley proposal. Ultimately, the FPC concluded that PNPC's Mountain Sheep/Pleasant Valley project did not suit the Corps of Engineers' comprehensive 308 plan and denied their application. The Mountain Sheep/Pleasant Valley Project—that would store only five hundred thousand acre feet of water—"would not realize the storage possibilities and needs" and it would jeopardize the fish runs. The FPC ruled that the Nez Perce dam project was better adapted "for the purpose of developing the rivers."[34]

Even though Idaho Power had begun construction on the smaller dams, the high Hells Canyon dam question did not go away. Most Republican politicians favored private or partnership construction. Democrats wanted federal construction, as reflected in comments made at the 1957 Democratic National Convention in San Francisco. Wayne Morse of Oregon believed a high, federally built dam was a vital link to the full development of the Columbia River Basin. Republican president Dwight Eisenhower, he argued, "is the stumbling block . . . a betrayer of public trust." Joseph O'Mahoney of Wyoming backed the high federal dam on the assumption that "we should use all of our natural resources so that the country is not dependent on foreign sources."[35]

At that time, Idaho's freshman senator, Frank Church, favored construction of the federal dam. In 1957 he assured fellow senators that concerns in south Idaho about losing water rights should a high dam be built were nothing but a "cleverly planted scare" intended to produce "an artifice that may well impede the whole progress of the development of the West." If the concern had validity, he argued, it would be applicable to the construction of any government dam anywhere.[36] Nevertheless, Morse and Neuberger included a statement of water rights in their Senate Bill 555, a revamped version of defeated bill S. 1333. When the Senate approved Bill 555, Church claimed that the dam would be "a tremendous stimulant to free enterprise." For the first time, Idaho would have "an abundance of cheap power" that would attract "the kind of new private investment we so badly need." In his early years in the Senate, Frank Church favored dam construction over preservation.[37]

Pacific Northwest Power Company did not receive a license for the Pleasant Valley/Low Mountain Sheep proposal but they did not give up. In 1958 the company again filed for a license to build a dam that better conformed to the corps' 308 requirements—High Mountain Sheep situated just above the mouth of the Salmon River. It too generated much opposition. Oregon Fish and Wildlife argued that "two distinct sets of fishery problems are involved in this project." First, the proposed Salmon River diversion dam would jeopardize the Salmon River fish migrations unless it was no higher than fifty feet, with fishways designed by the Fish and Wildlife Service and Idaho Fish and Game. Second, Mountain Sheep dam would be a 560-foot obstruction and "absolute block" to the fish migration on up the Snake River and into the Imnaha River. However, because "some solution to the problem may be forthcoming," Fish and Wildlife added recommendations to the proposal that, if met, might mitigate the problem.[38] Evidently protecting the Snake River fish runs was a consideration at that time, but not one enthusiastically supported.

Most Mountain Sheep dam opponents still wanted a dam some place in the canyon, but one built by the government, not a private power consortium. The National Hells Canyon Association favored congressional authorization of a federal dam at the Nez Perce site near the mouth of Cherry Creek, but Congress should defer construction until the fish passage problem could be solved. In 1959 Senate and House concurrent resolutions addressed that problem. Thus far, Idaho Power Company had a "terrible record" complying with directives to protect or assist fish migration.[39] Skimmer devices and facilities that they used at Brownlee and Oxbow were "a fiasco . . . ill conceived and impractical" that would eventually lead to the "complete destruction of all the salmon" with spawning grounds above the dams. T. F. Sandoza, president of the Columbia River Packers Association, asserted that Idaho

Power Company's failure was "an outstanding example of why we don't want to build any more high dams on the Middle Snake with experimental fish passage facilities."[40] His was a voice crying in the wilderness. Most people placed an inordinate confidence in science and technology. They believed fish experts were "making great strides" in solving both the upstream and downstream migration problems and would ultimately find the answer.

Pacific Northwest Power Company continued to propose various dam options. In 1960, after they applied for a license to begin immediate construction of Mountain Sheep and Pleasant Valley dams—with later construction of Crevice and Lower Canyon dams on the lower Salmon—the FPC again identified the Nez Perce site as "the superior project." Adding to the confusion, Washington Public Power Supply System, a conglomeration of sixteen Washington public utility districts, filed suit in the U.S. District Court of Oregon asking judgment on authorization to construct either Nez Perce or High Mountain Sheep dams. The public power consortium and the private companies were at war. In March 1962 Secretary of Interior Stewart Udall recommended waiting for a preliminary, detailed study, then having the Bureau of Reclamation build the dam. Udall asked the FPC to make that recommendation to Congress.

Both PNPC and WPPSS objected. The FPC refused Udall's request and instead recommended PNPC build High Mountain Sheep dam and denied the WPPSS application for Nez Perce and High Mountain Sheep. In the meantime, Idaho Power Company finished construction on Brownlee and Oxbow dams. Hells Canyon was their next and last project. If a high, midcanyon dam were built, it would destroy Idaho Power Company's last dam.

Should Any Dams Be Built?

In 1964 PNPC received a fifty-year license to construct and operate High Mountain Sheep dam with a reservoir of fifty-eight and a half miles to Hells Canyon dam, prompting an immediate response from WPPSS and the Department of Conservation of Washington state, which petitioned the court of appeals to set aside the FPC license. Secretary Udall did likewise. Extensive court proceedings dominated the next year and a half. Finally, in a three-to-zero decision, the court of appeals affirmed the FPC license to PNPC for High Mountain Sheep dam. The case then moved to the Supreme Court, which remanded the case back to the FPC, ordering them to rehear the entire proceedings with appropriate consideration given to the possibility "that the best dam for Hells Canyon might be *no dam at all*."[41]

That decision, written by Chief Justice William O. Douglas, changed the tone of the entire debate: "It is not our task to determine whether any dam at all should be built or whether if one is authorized it should be private or public.... The test is whether the project will be in the public interest. And that determination can be made only after an exploration of all issues relevant to the 'public interest' including future power demand and supply, alternate sources of power, the public interest in preserving reaches of wild rivers and wilderness areas, the preservation of anadromous fish for commercial and recreational purposes, and the protection of wildlife."[42]

By 1967, with passage of the Wilderness Act three years earlier, views about natural resource use gradually shifted toward conservation and preservation. Nuclear energy—the cleanest, least expensive, and most beneficial of all energy sources—was the preferred alternate energy source. Commercial and recreational fishing activists demanded that waterways and spawning grounds be protected. Indian tribes opposed the destruction of sacred grounds and resources. Consequently, just as competition between potential dam builders intensified, the future of dams became problematic; dam opposition became better organized and broader based. The Hells Canyon Preservation Council—incorporated at Idaho Falls in August 1967—effectively solidified national support for preservation. When, in 1968, Idaho Power Company's last dam, Hells Canyon, inundated the upper canyon, groups like the Preservation Council needed only to point to the transformed river to expand that support.

The entire middle Snake River, however, could still become a series of lakes. Through the remaining 1960s and into the 1970s, old and new contenders continued to propose dam projects. Pacific Northwest Power Company and Washington Public Power Supply System joined forces to apply for a license to build the High Mountain Sheep and requested a six-month postponement for their earlier joint request to build there. (This was designed to stall High Mountain Sheep while maneuvering a compromise through Congress.) The Idaho Water Resources Board filed for preliminary permits on the Appaloosa and Mountain Sheep sites, both above the mouth of the Imnaha River, and applied for congressional authorization to construct and operate a $400 million facility at the Appaloosa site.

Secretary of Interior Stewart Udall appeared determined to find a compromise. In 1968 he proposed a three-way agreement between Pacific Northwest Power, Washington Public Power Supply System, and the Department of Interior whereby the federal government "would build and operate the dam, and the other two would finance the building of the electrical generating facilities."[43] Udall willingly compromised, so long as the federal government was involved to ensure maximize power output of nine federally owned downstream Snake and Columbia River dams."[44]

Senator Len Jordan of Idaho—who thirty years earlier had operated a sheep ranch at Kirkwood—immediately registered his "vigorous opposition," arguing that "under our Idaho Constitution, water for irrigation has higher priority than water for power purposes."[45] Senator Frank Church joined Jordan in opposing the plan; together they introduced a bill in the Senate to put a ten-year moratorium on any dam construction in the canyon. Neither the Appaloosa project nor the moratorium passed Congress that year.

Moratoriums

With Richard Nixon in office in 1969, the new secretary of interior, Walter Hickle, pulled the Interior Department out of the three-way bid for a dam and recommended a three-to-five year moratorium on any development. Church and Jordan reintroduced their ten-year moratorium bill. The Hells Canyon Preservation Council wanted legislation to protect the region "from the canyon floor to its alpine peaks," not a moratorium. They proposed a Hells Canyon–Snake River National River. Senator Church twice refused their overtures, claiming that to do so would violate his agreement with Jordan.[46]

The council turned to Congressman John Saylor of Pennsylvania, who introduced a House bill to create the Hells Canyon–Snake National River, and Senator Bob Packwood of Oregon, who introduced an identical bill in the Senate. Both bills remained in limbo throughout that session of Congress. In the spring of 1970, the Senate passed the Church-Jordan moratorium bill, taking pressure off Congress to rule on the Packwood-Saylor national river bill and allowing preservation groups time to strengthen their support. With funding from the American Heritage Society, plus help from dedicated, highly visible celebrities like Arthur Godfrey and Burl Ives, local grass-roots activists, and a cadre of other concerned citizens, the Hells Canyon Preservation Council increased its membership, funded its lobbying efforts, and publicized its cause.[47]

In the fall of 1970 secretaries of the Interior and Agriculture Departments recommended portions of the middle Snake River be included in the National Wild and Scenic Rivers system. Throughout the rest of the year, environmental groups and wildlife federations filed briefs opposing any further dam construction. Even the FPC staff attorneys advised against licensing any dams. FPC examiner William Levy ignored them and recommended early in 1971 a license to Pacific Northwest Power Company for High Mountain Sheep.

The controversy was far from over, and conflicting actions in Congress did not facilitate a solution. In 1971 Senator Packwood reintroduced his national river bill in the Senate, as did Saylor in the House.[48] Church and Jordan also reintroduced a modified moratorium bill, extending the moratorium to 1978. (The previous bill had died in the 91st Congress because of inaction in the House.) Representative Orval Hansen of Idaho introduced the same seven-year moratorium in the House.[49] Idaho had recently established a water resources board; Senator Jordan asked for more time to make possible their study.[50] Senator Church no longer argued for a federal dam, since nuclear energy would "continue to advance at such a pace as to outmode such high hydroelectric dams." He wanted to preserve "the unique scenic and recreational values of the Middle Snake and its critical importance to the anadromous fish and wildlife resources of the Columbia River."[51] The two Idaho senators agreed on the necessity of postponing dam construction, but from opposing positions. Jordan wanted a storage dam to impound irrigation water; Church wanted a free-flowing river.

The Jordan-Church moratorium bill received a favorable report in the Senate Interior Committee, again postponing the Senate's decision on Packwood's bill. Jordan criticized Packwood for turning the controversy into an emotional issue, fearing that Packwood's bill would foreclose the state of Idaho's options. Church thought the moratorium presented the best way, ultimately, to preserve the natural canyon.

In 1970 Idaho gubernatorial candidate Cecil Andrus campaigned on a platform of a free-flowing Snake River. Once elected, he urged the FPC to deny all license applicants and joined Governors Dan Evans (Washington) and Tom McCall (Oregon) in calling for the protection of the Pacific Northwest's "national treasure." They argued that "if all the dams proposed on Snake River were built" they would not help "the impending power shortage." Nuclear energy was their preferred power source.[52]

While Hells Canyon Preservation Council members traveled throughout the Northwest "gathering together under one banner the old warriors of former conservation campaigns as well as a host of new volunteers," the bill to save Hells Canyon wound its tortuous course through the legislative maze.[53] Opposing factions formed as words flew. In 1970 Hugh Smith, a Pacific Northwest Power Company representative, speaking in Coeur d'Alene, Idaho, to the Outdoor Writers Association of America, captured one side of the argument. While referring to recent articles in four national magazines, Smith requested that reporters leave their "lyricism outside the door, and provide us with some honest reporting" when "controversial matters in which public support is being wooed." He objected to their use of emotion-generating terms—"deepest canyon in the North American Continent," "the last remaining stretch of free flowing river," "great white water experience," and "our children should have some place to go where they can see nature as it was before man intruded." With the exception of the deepest canyon, Smith contended, such phraseology was applicable to any stream or creek in the country. One article, he suggested, even doctored the photography to make the canyon country more appealing.[54]

Smith set himself up for harsh rebuttal. "At least twelve national magazines have [featured] stories about the Middle Snake; so too have scores of secondary and regional magazines, and numerous national, regional, and state newspapers," environmental activist Ferris Weddle noted. "They have all opposed dams on the Middle Snake with explicit and legitimate reasons why." As far as doctored pictures—"I doubt it. The Middle Snake is spectacular, so spectacular in fact it's difficult to photograph. Therefore, picture-faking doesn't appear necessary." Other reasons to halt the canyon dams included numerous archeological and historical sites; the canyon's esthetic, botanical, geological, and wildlife values; steelhead and salmon runs. "A great many people," Weddle concluded, "are already finding quality recreation in the Middle Snake without a reservoir," and he quoted 1969 studies by the Idaho Fish and Game and the Oregon Game Commission documenting more than two thousand upriver boat trips made annually with 69 percent of them anglers.[55]

Similar arguments ultimately paid off, but it still took time. The National River Bill passed the Senate in 1974 but, despite support from Oregon's influential congressman Al Ulmann, it failed in the House. In 1975 the Sierra Club proposed a new bill with cosponsorship from a majority of the House Interior Committee. Washington congressman Lloyd Meeds guided the bill to its final passage, and President Gerald Ford, after rejecting the utility companies' last-ditch efforts, signed the bill December 31, 1975, "as a New Year's Eve present." Hells Canyon National Recreation Area (HCNRA) became a reality. There would be no dams between Hells Canyon dam and the Grande Ronde River.

Throughout that entire struggle, the only dam authorized by Congress—in 1962—was the Asotin dam, designated for electricity and commercial Snake River navigation to the mouth of the Grand Ronde River. With all other dam sites eliminated and cement companies prepared to invest in the Grande Ronde River lime deposit sites and nearby processing plants, pressure mounted to build a dam five miles south of Asotin. In 1977 Washington governor Dixie Lee Ray asked that it be reconsidered; seventeen Pacific Northwest electric co-operatives sought permits to reinvestigate the project; and Pacific Northwest Waterways Association lobbied in Washington, D.C., for its construction. The Bureau of Outdoor Recreation, however, requested that the Corps of Engineers participate in a study to add the thirty-five-mile stretch of Snake River—from Asotin to the boundary of the

National Recreation Area—to the National Wild and Scenic Rivers system. Although Congress did not approve that addition, it did deauthorize the Asotin dam in 1980.[56]

The Ranchers

Throughout that thirty-year struggle over how to "use" Snake River, what were the ranchers saying? Many testified at the various hearings, concerned about how the dams would affect their ranch business. Their reactions varied with the location and type of the dam under consideration at the time. Sharon Wing, for example, said High Mountain Sheep dam would have been bad for the Spencer Ranch on Joseph Plains, for they would have lost all their summer range.[57] Horace Henderson was opposed to that dam for the same reasons. He also objected to any dams on the Salmon.[58] During the debates, Ace Barton mediated a seminar in Riggins, Idaho, with people from the Enterprise country and Idaho Power Company. "When it was over, the people . . . were pretty anti-dams," he remembered. "Different ones that worked over there for sheep outfits were pretty vocal." An Idaho Power representative later told Ace, "Well, I'm glad they didn't bring it to a vote tonight or we'd have lost out."[59]

However, the few ranchers I interviewed years after the establishment of HCNRA had a different outlook. Perhaps their changed circumstances altered their response: they no longer looked at the subject as a threatened rancher but as a rancher put out of business by the HCNRA. When dams were under consideration, most ranchers knew they would lose winter range, and many would have to relocate their homes to higher ground. Nevertheless, they expected adequate compensation and did not anticipate losing Forest Service grazing permits critical to their operations. They would have to make adjustments, to be sure, but each rancher could still operate. Some even expected the dams to benefit the region. "It was going to be a higher and better use of the country and they would certainly have compensated everyone," Doug Tippett believed. "This would have been a negotiated thing, not government confiscation." He admitted, however, that since the question "never got to the stage of talking cost and sales," he was guessing. "Back then the thinking was far different than it is now, you know. People hadn't seen how a big government project coming into an area changes everything." He was comparing what he thought it would have been like had the dams gone in with what happened after the creation of HCNRA.[60]

Though most of the ranchers expected to stay in business, that was not possible under a federally protected recreation area. Commercial pilot Ted Grote, while not a rancher, owned canyon property. He and his wife, Opal, had bought 160 acres on top of the ridge near Saw Creek from Lem Wilson to use "to take hunters in." When change came, the Grotes were the last ones to leave: "[the government] just sent us a check for what they figured it was worth."[61] When Lem Wilson started selling sections of his property, the government initiated a process of property acquisition. Their thinking was that Wilsons' subdivision threatened the upper canyon just as subdivision and development had already invaded the lower canyon on the Idaho side near Wild Goose Rapids.

Greg Johnson, who had just taken over his parents' sheep business at Temperance Creek, requested a scenic easement from the Forest Service. That way he would keep title to his property and pay taxes, yet relinquish control of the property to the Wallowa Whitman National Forest Service that managed HCNRA. It "probably would have been an idiotic thing to do," he said with hindsight. "They wouldn't do that." To continue working the land of his parents and grandparents, he leased the property back from the government until 1980. "Then it finally got more than I was willing to handle."[62] One of the canyon's last ranches ceased operations when Greg Johnson left.

Whatever the outdoor enthusiasts, sportsmen, or tourists may today think about a federally protected recreation area, most of the families still in the ranching business and dependent on federal grazing land and unrestricted use of their private property found that under the new Forest Service guidelines, they could no longer stay in business. It was more than they were "willing to handle." Ace Barton, however, said he was glad they stopped the dams. "I will always credit Floyd Harvey as one of the instigators that stopped them." Floyd Harvey, an outfitter who had a camp at Pine Bar, must have known that, should dams be built, he would lose money as an outfitter. But his love of the free-running river dominated his drive to protect it. Harvey worked closely with regional and national conservation and environmental groups and, by bringing Secretary of Interior Walter Hickle, Burl Ives, Arthur Godfrey, and other big names to Hells Canyon, helped generate national publicity for his cause. He and the others saved the river, but neither Harvey nor anyone else knew what changes would follow—good or bad.

Barton said that there was indeed "absolute change" during the dam controversy and afterward. "After it became a more notorious canyon, a different element started to use it—boaters and floaters. You'd have to have a fellow on every one of those homesteads with a shotgun because they'd pack everything off."[63] In fairness to the "different element," that was a time when interior design dictated things rustic. Old buildings and antiques disappeared throughout rural areas, not just in the canyon. Nevertheless, such behavior was alien to people who lived and worked there. Sharon and Bub Horrocks once found a man loading up their anvil. "I found this old antique anvil," he proudly told them. Bub told him he used it all the time to shoe horses. Antique indeed. Dick Rivers also saw a profound change in the character of the canyon and the people frequenting it. "The river is now a playground [thus] altered as surely as if a dam had been built."[64] Most of the people I interviewed agreed.

The River Today

Today, although Snake River flows freely from Hells Canyon dam to Lewiston, Idaho, it is a different river from the one the ranchers knew. Jetboats and water level fluctuations from Hells Canyon dam have obliterated the once beautiful, sandy beaches that lined the Snake above the Salmon River confluence. Some sediment from the Salmon River still replenishes sandy bars below the confluence, but they too are diminished. Alfalfa fields that once made green the bars and benches are gone. Livestock no longer dot the hillsides. The mailboat serves a few places, but is not the lifeline to a vibrant, scattered community of ranches it once was. Ranch houses have been destroyed, or turned into interpretive sites or Forest Service facilities, and mine entrances are blocked. And always, seemingly everywhere, some type of watercraft is on the river.

Controversy continues to engulf the middle Snake. Will the Wallowa-Whitman National Forest Service continue to administer Hells Canyon National Recreation Area, or will the National Park Service take over? What role will the Nez Perce tribe—and other tribes whose water and fishing rights are protected by treaty—play in current and future discussions regarding the administration and use of the middle Snake? How will the HCNRA administrative agency deal with the growing recreational demands on the river? Will they have to resort to permit use to keep both jetboaters and floaters happy? How will we protect the fish runs? Or will we? Most of the current debate centers around breaching the lower Snake River dams, but some groups advocate removing or at least breaching Idaho Power Company's three Hells Canyon dams as well. Are we ready to take such extreme measures?

Managing Hells Canyon and the middle Snake River as a national recreation area presents numerous challenges. Private and collective opinions abound concerning how Wallowa-Whitman National Forest should carry out its management responsibilities. But weren't rigid assumptions as prevalent in earlier decades? In the early stages of the dam controversy, the general consensus was that river resources should be used to best serve the needs of the majority—and those needs were identified as providing hydroelectric energy, flood control, irrigation, recreation, and maybe even navigation. From both sides of the debate came an assumption that science would find a way to save the fish and that nuclear energy would replace hydroelectric power. Most canyon visitors now agree that Hells Canyon National Recreation Area and Wild and Scenic Rivers protection is best for the river, canyon, and surrounding country. Some would like to see the river run free throughout the entire canyon, at the expense of Idaho Power Company's three dams. Will Snake River run free in the twenty-first century, or will a new set of national and regional concerns demand some type of nullification of the river's protected status? Will tomorrow's priorities replace today's? The tortuous history of Hells Canyon clearly demonstrates that ideals, philosophies, and assumptions change.

Notes

All quotations within notes are from the source cited for the text unless otherwise noted.

CHAPTER 1. FROWNING PRECIPICES, MAD RIVER, AND THE SIDEHILL GOUGER

1. Almost everyone agrees that the lower Snake River runs from Lewiston, Idaho, to the Columbia River confluence. Fewer agree about the middle and upper Snake River. I identify the river from Farewell Bend to Lewiston as the middle Snake River; the upper Snake River is from Farewell Bend east to Yellowstone National Park.

2. Irving, *Astoria*, 267, 277.

3. Irving, *Complete Works*, 167–68.

4. *Lewiston (Idaho) Morning Tribune*, Nov. 11, 1903; Ashworth, *Hells Canyon*, 66.

5. Wiggins, interview. Wiggins used the pseudonym "Clem Stretchett" when writing tongue-in-cheek as a Wallowa County historian in numerous local publications.

6. W. Wilson, interview.

7. Carrey, Conley, and Barton, *Snake River*, 2.

8. Ashworth, *Hells Canyon*, 66; Elsensohn, *Pioneer Days*, 2:163. Albert Kleinschmidt, a miner who developed the Seven Devils mining region, hired Haller to test Snake River navigation feasibility between Weiser and Lewiston, no doubt to see if that was a viable way to export ore.

9. Bailey, *Hells Canyon*, 35; Jordan, *Home Below Hells Canyon*; Vallier, *Islands and Rapids*, 6–7.

CHAPTER 2. ACCORDING TO THE ROCKS

1. Vallier, *Islands and Rapids*. Unless otherwise noted, the information for this chapter comes from that source, Vallier's lecture notes, and his much-appreciated editorial contributions to this chapter.

2. The term "exotic terrane" refers to terrane moved from its original position and distinctly different from surrounding terrane.

3. Vallier, *Islands and Rapids*, 15.

4. From a vantage point on the Oregon side of the river between Halfway and Joseph, the Hells Canyon National Recreation Area interpretive signs describe the limestone deposit and the region's geology. At the USFS visitor center at Enterprise, Oregon, additional interpretive signs explain this complex puzzle.

5. The Columbia River Basalt Group includes the Saddle Mountains basalt (beginning approximately 6 million years ago [Ma]), Wanapum Basalt (13.5 Ma), Grande Ronde Basalt (16.5 Ma), and Imnaha Basalt (17.5 Ma). See Vallier, *Islands and Rapids*, 34–35.

6. Hooper, "The Columbia River Basalts."

7. Vallier, *Islands and Rapids*, 102–3.

8. Ashworth, *Hells Canyon*, 5.

9. John E. Allen, in Hells Canyon Series, "Early Wanderings," claimed that the depth of Snake River cut through the carving and eroding processes reached 6,000 feet.

10. Ibid.

11. "Valley Firm Owes Debt to Prehistoric Flooding," *Lewiston (Idaho) Morning Tribune*, Aug. 15, 1995, 3A.

12. . What the miners either did not know then or did not choose to know was that due to nature's capricious way of forming canyon walls, the veins were choppy, unpredictable, and never extensive. See chapters 9 through 11 for a history of the mining era in the canyon.

13. Vallier, *Islands and Rapids*, 42.

CHAPTER 3. A LAND DIVERSE & BEAUTIFUL

1. One of the canyon's few primitive roads is at Dug Bar. When we dropped him off, other people were there

to help him.

2. Contact Hells Canyon National Recreation Area, Clarkston, Wash., for information about the plants and wildlife native to Hells Canyon, including plant species unique to Hells Canyon and plant and animal species listed as threatened or endangered.

3. Bruce Womack, lecture and interview. All archeological information in this chapter comes from this source unless otherwise noted.

4. The Bernard Creek Rock Shelter, dated by the radiocarbon as about 7,100 years old, is the oldest site yet discovered in Hells Canyon. It and numerous other shelters throughout the middle Snake River country were home to the aboriginal people.

5. Reddy, "Empty Land," 8.

6. Gurcke et al., "Archeological Reconnaissance," 13.

7. Arrowheads found at a particular stratum helped date human activity there, as did differences in shape, design, and rock types of the arrowhead. Other items, such as mortars and pestles, bone awls, needles, perforated elk teeth, gaming pieces, and the bones of dogs, identify the site as having been occupied in more recent times. Gurcke et al., "Archeological Reconnaissance," 13.

8. Womack, lecture and interview.

9. Reddy, "Empty Land."

10. During the Nez Perce War of 1877, James Reuben told General Oliver O. Howard how his people used the rafts to ferry supplies across the river. They loaded the rafts, tied four horses abreast to the rafts with small ropes, put four naked men on the horses, and swam across (Howard, *Nez Perce Joseph*).

11. Womack, lecture and interview.

12. According to a rock art survey of Hells Canyon, there are more than 175 sites between Hells Canyon Dam and Buffalo Eddy, with motifs that include human and animal figures, tally marks, and geometric forms (Keyser, *Indian Rock Art*, 103–4).

13. Ibid., 114.

14. Boreson, lecture and interview. At Pittsburg Landing, nearly 30 boulders are covered with art at two separate locations.

15. Keyser, *Indian Rock Art*, 104.

16. A significant petroglyph image in the upper reaches of the canyon depicts Great Basin influence. It is a "shield figure" that shows a human in front of a large, round shield. Ethnographers place the epicenter of that design in Utah. From there, they believe, it traveled north into Hells Canyon and Salmon River (Keyser, *Indian Rock Art*, 104).

17. Buffalo Eddy, Idaho, covers an area about 200 by 300 yards wide and shows sporadic occupation for 6,000 years or more (Historic Site Inventory, Idaho State Historic Preservation Office, Feb. 1979).

18. *Lewiston (Idaho) Morning Tribune*, Apr. 20, 1941.

19. Ibid., Aug. 13, 1961.

20. Womack, lecture and interview. Only 200 of the 900 archeological sites within the HCNRA are from the historic period.

21. Reid, "A Working Draft."

22. Josephy, *Nez Perce Indians*, 28. Horses, introduced to the Americas by the Spaniards in the 1500s, gradually spread north and west over the next 200 years

23. Each year the women cut from 25 to 35 lodgepole pines for tepee poles.

24. James, *Nez Perce Women*, 11.

25. Ibid., 21, and McFarland, "Flora."

26. The berries they consumed included serviceberries, rose hips, wax and sticky currants, globe and fools huckleberries, hawthorne berries, and chokecherries.

27. McFarland, "Flora."

28. Idaho State Historic Preservation Office, Historic Site Inventory. During low water you can still see some

of the 10 fishwalls scattered for nearly 300 yards along the steeply sloping beach

29. Landeen and Pinkham, *Salmon and his People*, 92: "Whitefish, trout and pikeminnows were considered supplementary foods rather than staples and were caught for immediate consumption." See also James, *Nez Perce Women*, 26.

30. National Register of Historic Places, Anthropology Department, University of Idaho. Moscow.

31. Cochnauer, Lukens, and Partridge, "Status of White Sturgeon." Today, sturgeon sizes range from 3 to 6 feet (91.5 to 183cm).

32. Shawley, "Nez Perce Trails," 101.

33. Ibid., 102.

34. Carrey, Conley, and Barton, *Snake River*, 367. The scout, A. C. Smith, was en route to the 1876 Lapwai council when he found Indian caches on the bar near the stream and named the creek.

35. James, *Nez Perce Women*, 69.

36. See chapter 7 for a more complete account of the Nez Perce War of 1877.

37. Marshall, "Nimiipu Social Groups," 143–44.

38. During the Nez Perce War of 1877, Chief Joseph was credited by the army and newspaper reports as the war chief when, in fact, the other band chiefs had placed him in charge of the women and children.

39. Quoting an elderly Nez Perce woman, James wrote: "A few Down-river Indians went [to buffalo country]; for example, Looking Glass came from Asotin, but he married an Up-river Indian woman, so they were familiar with going to the buffalo country" (James, *Nez Perce Women*, 9–10).

40. Ashworth, *Hells Canyon*, 6. Battle Creek on the Oregon side of the river was named after one lopsided skirmish in which a group of Nez Perce warriors "obliterated" a Shoshone village located there.

41. The National Register of Historic Places shows habitation sites on the Idaho side from Tammany Creek near Lewiston to China Garden Creek, upstream approximately 40 miles. There are 58 seasonal campsites, 25 burial sites, 21 pithouse sites, 8 storage shelter sites, plus pictographs, storage pits, fishwalls, and sweathouses. Most of those sites were used extensively during late prehistoric and early historic periods. For village site locations, see also Shawley, "Nez Perce Trails," and Josephy, *Nez Perce Indians*, map 162.

42. U.S. Department of Agriculture, Hells Canyon Management Plan.

43. Shawley, "Nez Perce Trails."

CHAPTER 4. THE WINDS OF CHANGE

1. *Journals of the Lewis and Clark Expedition*, vol. 7:293, 327–30, 9:315–18, 10:235. For this segment of the Lewis and Clark travels, Moulton relied on personal communication with Merle Wells of the Idaho State Historical Society and John J. Peebles, author of "The Return of Lewis and Clark." All direct quotes in text and notes are in the expedition members' original spelling.

2. The village belonged to "the chief that took care of our horses." That would have been Twisted Hair, whose main village was near Canoe Camp on the Clearwater River, where the expedition members built their five canoes the previous fall. Ordway, however, never gave his name, nor did he identify the "old chief" with whom they later traveled. He probably was not Twisted Hair, however, or Ordway would have mentioned that.

3. *Journals of the Lewis and Clark Expedition*, 9:315. Ordway noted: "The Indians grass houses leak."

4. They were possibly traveling due west along an established Nez Perce trail between Mason Butte and Cottonwood Butte. The unlevel timbered country was west of present-day Cottonwood.

5. University of Idaho anthropologist Stephen D. Shawley collected data from members of the Nez Perce tribe for his 1977 report "Nimiipu Trails" that also shed light on their possible travel route. Most scholars believe they descended Deer Creek or a ridge to the west of the creek. Shawley's research supported that assumption, for he showed the Deer Creek area as a main thoroughfare from the west side of Camas Prairie to Salmon River (Shawley, "Nez Perce Trails").

6. *Journals of the Lewis and Clark Expedition*, 9:316. Patrick Gass elaborated on that exchange in his June 2, 1806, journal entry: "One of the men got two Spanish dollars from an Indian for an old razor. They [the natives]

said they got the dollars from about a Snake Indian's neck, they had killed some time ago. There are several dollars among these people which they get in some way." He assumed the Snake Indians, "some of whom do not live very far from New Mexico," got the dollars from the nearby Spanish (10:235).

7. *Journals of the Lewis and Clark Expedition*, 7:327. "About 20 miles above it's junction with the South branch [Snake]." The captains summarized Ordway's journey, estimating the total travel distance from their Kamiah camp to the Salmon River to be about 50 miles.

8. Ibid., 329.

9. Ordway said they followed the Salmon "down some distance" before they left it to ascend a creek. That creek could have been China Creek, about two miles down the Salmon from Deer Creek, as Idaho historians John Peebles and Merle Wells believed, or it could have been Wapshilla Creek, an additional three miles down river. According to Shawley's research, a Nez Perce trail ascended both creeks. The trail up Wapshilla Creek continued on to the ridge of the same name and then followed the ridge north and south. Shawley did not indicate that the China Creek trail reached very far up the creek (Shawley, "Nez Perce Trails").

10. Historian Steven Evans, Connie Evans, Nez Perce tribal elder Allen Pinkham, and I surveyed possible travel routes across remote Wapshilla Ridge. We concluded that their trail went up the east slope of Wapshilla Creek from the Salmon to the ridge, then descended the upper section of Cottonwood Creek drainage, following a northwest direction. A trail depression is plainly visible and there is a spring close by, always an indication of where a Nez Perce trail might have been. Because the lower section of Cottonwood Creek is too steep a drop into the Snake River for horse travel, the three 1806 explorers and their guides probably cut northwest to Cougar Creek drainage and followed the breaks to the Snake, nine miles below its confluence with the Salmon. The lower stretch of that route definitely qualifies as "the worst hills."

11. *Journals of the Lewis and Clark Expedition*, 9:316. Peebles believed they went down China Gardens Creek, and Wells believed they followed a ridge further south between China Gardens Creek and Cave Gulch. Shawley's maps show no trails descending the west slope of the Craigs to the Snake River (Shawley, "Nez Perce Trails"). Ordway's wording implies that they traveled down a ridge, as Wells suggested, rather than along a creek.

12. *Journals of the Lewis and Clark Expedition*, 7:330. There "the river was nearly 200 yeards wide."

13. If they descended China Gardens Creek and the fishery was located at Wild Goose Rapids, as Peebles believes, the men rode an additional two and a half or three miles along the banks of the Snake to reach it. Wells believed the fishery was located at McDuff Rapids south of Wild Goose Rapids. However, those rapids are covered by high water in June.

14. *Journals of the Lewis and Clark Expedition*, 9:316. Ordway said it was 100 feet by 20 feet.

15. U.S. Congress, Senate, "Examination of Snake River." Symons's description of Cochran's Islands does not match our image of Celilo Falls (U.S. Congress, House, Captain Thomas W. Symons, Corps of Engineers, letter, Dec. 21, 1891).

16. *Journals of the Lewis and Clark Expedition*, 9:316. Moulton noted this was not a word used by Lewis and Clark. He added, "It may represent the Nimiipu term *a'a*, 'couse cake'" (9:317n.6).

17. On the opposite shore, Ordway saw "only" three dip nets at three different fishing places.

18. Clark reported the men had some difficulty buying the fish but did not elaborate. Probably the fishermen were negotiating for higher payment than Ordway wanted to meet, since the Nez Perce were shrewd traders and the expedition men beggarly poor.

19. That route probably took them back across Wapshilla Ridge, down Wapshilla Creek to the Salmon, then back up Deer Creek.

20. Possibly they went on down Deer Creek to the river, up across Hoover Point, and back down to the Oxbow of the Salmon near Maloney Creek, then up Maloney Creek to the large village. The village may have been near the present town of Keuterville (*Journals of the Lewis and Clark Expedition*, vol. 9).

21. The first village was probably near today's town of Stites; the second, near Kooskia.

22. All the journals are brief in their descriptions of Hells Canyon. Lewis and Clark noted only that "both forks above the junction of Lewis's river appear to enter a high Mountainious Country" (*Journals of the Lewis and Clark*

Expedition, 7:327, 330). Ordway failed to describe the wild rivers and hostile terrain. Ordway, Frazer, or Weiser, however, must have conveyed a negative account to Patrick Gass, who wrote: "The men had a very disagreeable trip as the roads were mountainous and slippery" (10:235). Maybe by then they were so hardened to difficult travel and so accustomed to seeing spectacular landscapes that neither particularly impressed them.

23. Ronda, *Astoria and Empire*, 25. Canadian visionaries and North West Company partners including Alexander Henry had spent the previous 14 years exploring the possibilities of expanding trade along the navigable waters from Montreal to the Pacific Ocean with trading posts along the route to discourage American and Russian fur trade ventures, and ultimately break the British East India Company's trade monopoly in China. It was Alexander Henry, Astor's business partner from about 1790, who, as Ronda noted, became "the personal and intellectual connection between the world of Canadian exploration and John Jacob Astor" (*Astoria and Empire*, 29).

24. Ibid., 180.

25. Stratton, "Hells Canyon," 5.

26. Barry, "Trail of the Astorians."

27. Irving, *Astoria*, 262.

28. Carrey, Conley, and Barton, *Snake River*, 11. They traveled up Mann Creek to the headwaters of Monroe Creek, and crossed the hills to the head of Wolf Creek.

29. Ronda, *Astoria and Empire*, 189.

30. Ibid.

31. Carrey, Conley, and Barton, *Snake River*, 12, quoting from Hunt's journal. Washington Irving described how they made the canoe "Indian fashion." They drew up the "edges of the skin with thongs, and [kept] them distended by sticks or thwart pieces" (Irving, *Astoria*, 266).

32. Carrey, Conley, and Barton, *Snake River*, 12. Geologist Tracy Vallier, who read a draft of this chapter, believes they were probably at the narrows just south of Eagle Bar.

33. J. Neilson Barry, who retraced their route in 1903, believed that from Huntington, Hunt's men followed "along the present line of Northwestern railroad to probably a short distance beyond Homestead where they were forced to turn back and retrace their steps" (Barry, "Trail of the Astorians").

34. Vallier, "Probably they were at Squaw Creek/Bull Creek rapids," personal communication with the author.

35. Irving, *Astoria*, 267.

36. Ronda, *Astoria and Empire*, 190.

37. Ibid.

38. This happened near Raft Creek, hence its name.

39. Corless, *Weiser Indians*, 17–18. The Shoshone urged the strangers to spend the winter in their village. Hunt charged them with "talking with a 'forked tongue,' and challenged their courage by calling them women" (Irving *Astoria*, 275).

40. Ronda, *Astoria and Empire*, 192. The three men were J. B. Turcotte, A. LaChapelle, and Francois Landry.

41. Irving *Astoria*, 280.

42. Ronda, *Astoria and Empire*, 192–93.

43. Irving, *Astoria*, 282.

44. Ronda, *Astoria and Empire*, 193.

45. Miles Cannon believed that after leaving Hunt at Caldron Linn, Mackenzie's party stayed along the north bank of Snake River to the mouth of the Weiser River, then proceeded along an Indian trail north up Monroe Creek, crossed to Mann Creek, then east back to the Weiser River, which they followed north to its source. From there they descended the Little Salmon River and followed it to its junction with the main Salmon River near present-day Riggins, Idaho. At the mouth of Whitebird Creek they climbed to Camas Prairie, then dropped to the Clearwater River near present-day Stites and proceeded downstream to the Snake River (Cannon, "Snake River in History," 1–23). Carrey, Conley, and Barton, also believed the 11 men followed that general route as they

"struggled northeasterly through Six Lake Basin, or Rapid River, and down to the Salmon River by way of the Little Salmon" (*Snake River*, 11). J. Neilson Barry implied they were either on or near Snake River the entire route before they ascended Captain John Creek to the headwaters of Sweetwater Creek, dropped down to the Clearwater near Lapwai, and reached Snake River near Lewiston, Idaho" (Barry, "Trail of the Astorians").

    46. Irving, *Astoria*, 292.

    47. Ross, *Adventures of the First Settlers*, 185.

    48. Irving, *Astoria*, 292–93. The full quote is, "At length after twenty-one days of toil and suffering they got through these mountains and arrived at a tributary stream of that branch of the Columbia called Lewis River of which Snake River forms the southern fork."

    49. Ross, *Adventures of the First Settlers*, 185.

CHAPTER 5. MACKENZIE AND THE CAPTAIN

    1. Seton, *Astorian Adventure*, 100.

    2. Ibid., 103. Although Seton described the location as the head of navigable waters, he noted in an 1835 letter published in *American Monthly Magazine* that they ascended the Clearwater River "as far as it was practicable to drag the canoes" (Seton, *Astorian Adventure*, app. A, 191; from letter published in *American Monthly Magazine* 5, no. 5 [July 1835]: 368–75).

    3. According to A. W. Thompson, "New Light on Donald Mackenzie's Post," 26, they probably traveled up the Clearwater River at least as far as Kamiah.

    4. Irving, *Astoria*, 393. He described those people as being from "the neighborhood of the Falls of the Columbia [Celilo Falls]."

    5. Seton, *Astorian Adventure*, 104. "About 5 miles above the Forks, on a Prairie" is a few miles west of Hatwai Creek. The prairie reference is confusing in today's context, but a Clearwater River site that could fit that description is about four miles east of the Highway 12/Highway 95 interchange. There is a large, level area near the river.

    6. Ibid., 105. Seton noted that those people were "at present gone to war against the Blackfeet and to hunt the Buffaloe and will not return before the next spring."

    7. Ibid., 191. The reference to horses implies the Nez Perce living farther up the river had much smaller horse herds, a fact verified by the Astorians' earlier decision to move downriver. The Courteois are the Kootenai of north Idaho, eastern Washington, and western Montana.

    8. When Seton wrote his journal, only Patrick Gass's journal had been published. Men of the Lewis and Clark expedition also used the word "Kamoenum," with various spellings, for the Snake River but never used the word Tashepas in reference to the Nez Perce. In "New Light on Donald Mackenzie's Post," A. W. Thompson suggests Seton might have been referring to Shoshone, Bannocks, or Flathead, but rules out each group and concludes that the reference was to the Nez Perce who lived on the Snake in the vicinity of Hells Canyon. At the time of his writing, Thompson did not have access to Seton's full journal, but in the published journal is Seton's 1835 letter that verifies Thompson's assumption. The Nez Perce who wintered along Snake River and its tributaries had slight cultural and linguistic differences from their Clearwater river drainage cousins (see chap. 3). Seton obviously picked up on those differences but failed to note their many similarities.

    9. Ibid., 105. The exact wording in Seton's journal was: "They go to war against the Tuelicums or Snakes who inhabit fur[ther] . . . [the r]iver and are seperated from the[m] . . . ridge of mountains." The editor, Robert Jones, added the bracketed letters.

    10. Ibid., 105–6.

    11. Ibid., 105.

    12. Due to the poor beaver population and expensive horses, Mackenzie traveled north to discuss options with John Clarke, who had built his post near the North West Company's post, Spokane House. There the Astorians learned from their British competitors that the two nations were in a state of war.

    13. Alexander Ross provided the popular misconception that the Astorians first relocated and ultimately left the Clearwater country because the Nez Perce men were "accustomed to an indolent and roving life" and would

not "submit to the drudgery of killing beavers." He continued: "They spurned the idea of crawling about in search of furs; 'Such a life,' they said, 'was only fit for women and slaves'" (Ross, *Adventures of the First Settlers*, 218).

14. A. W. Thompson explained the name "Perpetual Motion" Mackenzie: He explored the Clearwater River to Kamiah before deciding on a location. He rushed to Spokane House, back to the Clearwater River, then to Astoria. From there he was again on the Clearwater River, at three different locations, and finally back at Astoria. All that within a little more than one year.

15. He was a "free trader" and under no contractual obligation to the company. He may also have had a child, for when Seton later conducted a head count, he included a woman and child among the 20 men.

16. Ronda, *Astoria and Empire*, 265.

17. Seton, *Astorian Adventure*, 113.

18. Ibid., app. A, 189, from letter published in *American Monthly Magazine* 5, No. 5 (July 1835): 368–75.

19. Ibid., 192.

20. Ibid., 194. Seton's original diary account and his later 1835 recollections exhibit slight variations on the story, with more elaboration included in the later account. This is a compilation of the two.

21. This point is confusing. In the diary Seton said they moved 2 miles away. He later said they moved only 400 to 500 yards above the Nez Perce camp on the same side of the river, on the banks of a Clearwater River tributary. Thompson believes they relocated at what is now Cherry Lane, about 20 miles above Lewiston on the south side of the Clearwater River. As he notes, Clark's map indicates that was a large village site.

22. They had come upon Seton by chance when he was some distance from camp, "building chateaux en Espagne [daydreaming]." Le Grand Coquin demanded to know where camp was located. Seton said he would show them, mounted the horse behind Le Grand Coquin, and into camp they rode.

23. Seton, *Astorian Adventure*, 194. Their "war costume" consisted of "deer skin leggins and moccasins, buffalo robes wrapped around their loins and resting on the saddles in front; their faces and bodies painted in various colors; their heads fantastically adorned with feathers; a round shield made of buffalo bulls hide . . . hung on their bridle-arm; and immediately in front of it rested their guns" (195).

24. In the original account, Seton said that after the Cayuse refused to partake in the scheme, Mackenzie told Le Grand Coquin that he intended to recover the goods by any means necessary. The Nez Perce agreed, smoked with them, and left.

25. Seton, *Astorian Adventure*, 197. The location was "where the bank was precipitous and lofty" and the area "enclosed by a semicircular line of earth" about three and one-half feet high. It "appeared as if regularly constructed by men similarly situated to ourselves." Thompson suggested the spot was on the south bank of the Snake River about three miles below Clarkston, where the columnar basalt cliffs have that appearance. However if he is correct about their prior location being at Cherry Lane, on the opposite side of the river, the location should be on the north bank near the confluence. Lower Granite Dam has raised the water level so no comparable site can be identified today.

26. See Ronda, *Astoria and Empire*, for a complete account of the decision to sell, Mackenzie's influence in coming to that decision, and the efforts by Astor in New York to retain and then regain the company.

27. Ross, *Fur Hunters of the Far West*, 167. The "Snake Indians," a term used extensively by the fur traders, were people of the Shoshone, Bannock, and Northern Paiute nations. Alexander Ross described the "Snake Country" as an area bounded on the east by the Rocky Mountains and on the south by the "Spanish waters" or Colorado River drainage. To the west it extended from a northwest spur of the Blue Mountains to the "height of land beyond the Umpqua River." The north boundary abutted Nez Perce country, from the "said spur of the Blue Mountains and crossing the great south branch or Lewis River [Snake] at the narrows [Hells Canyon]." He added: "For an Indian country it may be called thickly inhabited, and may contain 36,000 souls or nearly one person to every four miles square."

28. Atkin, "Snake River Fur Trade," 295–312.

29. Letter to Cox, Feb 12, 1817, from Spokane House, in Cox, *Adventures on the Columbia River*, 249.

30. Ross, *Fur Hunters of the Far West*, 136. In the vicinity of "River Skam-am-naugh" (identified by Ross's

editors as Indian Creek) Mackenzie "acquiesced" to the Iroquois' wishes (they were "plotting mischief") and left them there to work the beaver-rich creek.

31. Point Successful was probably someplace between what is now Hells Canyon Dam and Oxbow Dam.

32. Irving, *Adventures of Captain Bonneville*, xx.

33. Carrey, Conley, and Barton, *Snake River*, 19.

34. Irving, *Adventures of Captain Bonneville*, 55.

35. From Portneuf, the small party departed Christmas morning, 1833, heading out along the south side of the river in what is now south Idaho. They traveled for several days before reaching American Falls, and then continued to parallel the river's northern bend along the south, then west, side, but several miles back from the river for easier crossing of the deep tributary canyons. By this time, the Hudson's Bay Company had acquired all North West Company facilities.

36. There were at least 100 families of "Digger" Indians encamped, who showed great curiosity in the new arrivals. In order to escape their "inquisitive neighbors" Bonneville traveled on a considerable distance before camping for the night. Bonneville inserts a description of the Shoshone people. Their poverty and discomfort struck Bonneville, but their ingenuity impressed him. For one thing—something the Americans learned and quickly adapted—they always carried a "slow match," made with long ropes twisted from the bark of the wormwood (sagebrush) and always kept lighted. With that they could gather some dry wood, apply the match, and have an instant cheering blaze (Irving, *Adventures of Captain Bonneville*, 163).

37. Irving, *Adventures of Captain Bonneville*, 165.

38. William Ashworth believed they were on a "platform halfway up McGraw Creek Divide . . . on the south end of a great bench or terrace nearly a mile wide which, though broken by numerous tributary canyons, is traceable northward for some thirteen miles along the canyon face" (Ashworth,. *Hells Canyon*, 23). Tracy Vallier thought they may have been on the ridge just south of Pine Creek above the Oxbow. But, as he added, "Who really knows?" (Vallier, personal correspondence with the author, 1999).

39. Irving, *Adventures of Captain Bonneville*, 167.

40. Ibid.

41. According to Carrey, Conley, and Barton, from their Kirby Creek camp the next day they "climbed a small ridge and moved north along the Squaw Creek benches as far as the divide between Thirty-two Point Creek and Steamboat Canyon" (*Snake River*, 20). Kirby Creek is the upper of the two canyon Kirby Creeks. Hells Canyon Dam reservoir now floods the site.

42. Ashworth believed the scout "reached and scaled Barton Heights. From this point it is possible to get a long look forward down the deepest part of the gorge" (Ashworth, *Hells Canyon*, 23).

43. From the summit they descended the opposite ridge into the saddle, and then traveled north along the divide near the head of Smith Canyon to Summit Creek, then descended Summit Creek to its confluence with the Imnaha (Carrey, Conley, and Barton, *Snake River*, 20).

44. Irving, *Adventures of Captain Bonneville*, 170.

45. Bonneville had earlier distinguished between the Upper Nez Perce, whom they met along the Salmon and Lemhi Rivers, and the Lower Nez Perce whom they would soon meet. Using Seton's distinction of the two groups of Nez Perce, the upper people would have been the Sahaptians and the lower people the Tashpas.

46. Members of the Nez Perce tribe say that was a term used to describe some of the Lewis and Clark expedition members.

47. Irving, *Adventures of Captain Bonneville*, 174–75.

48. Carrey, Conley, and Barton, *Snake River*, 21. The village was under the headmanship of Yo-mus-ro-y-e-cut. Bonneville met the upper Nez Perce the year before on the upper Salmon River.

49. It is at this point in their journey that historians disagree on their route. Elgin Victor Kuykendall wrote: "Upon the identity of the river depends the key to the mystery of Bonneville's route through Northeast Oregon and Southeast Washington." He explained that although many believe the Way-lee-way River is the present Wallowa River because of the name similarity, he claimed the Nez Perce called the Grande Ronde River by that name.

Kuykendall believed the explorers left the Imnaha Valley and headed to the upper country, still traveling parallel to the Snake. They followed Cold Springs Ridge, dropped down Horse Creek to Joseph Creek, then on to the lower Grande Ronde River valley (Kuykendall, *History of Garfield County*, 21).

50. Irving, *Adventures of Captain Bonneville*, 179. These people were members of the Chief Joseph band of Nez Perce whose winter quarters were at this location.

51. Ibid., 180.

52. Ibid., 182–83. Irving quoted Bonneville directly.

53. Ibid., 184.

54. Kuykendall identified O-push-y-e-cut, the name Irving used, as Looking Glass. He quoted one of the early settlers of the region, Robert Bracken, who wrote in the *Asotin County Sentinel* of 1894: "Among the Indians on the Grande Ronde River are four aged members of the tribe who distinctly remember the time and the great reception the [Bonneville] party received on reaching this place, then an Indian village [Asotin]. Three of these Indians at the time were about fourteen yeas of age. The fourth was born near the stream of the Imnaha, and is now over eighty years old, and shook hands with the bald white chief and his men" (Kuykendall, *History of Garfield County*, 22).

55. Irving, *Adventures of Captain Bonneville*, 188.

CHAPTER 6. STEAMBOAT PIONEERS

1. Each boat delivered about 800 tons of merchandise monthly. That together with the 200 tons delivered overland by freighters ran the town's sales from $15,000 to $20,000 a week (Stewart, "Steamboats on the Columbia," Oregon Historical Society).

2. *Golden Age*, Mar. 22, 1864.

3. There are three conflicting accounts of this expedition. The earliest comes from Lewiston's *Golden Age*, "Snake River Route to Boise Mines." Feb. 5, 1863. Edmund Pearcy's biography in *Illustrated History of North Idaho* includes his brief version of the trip. A third account comes from a 1939 *Lewiston (Idaho) Morning Tribune* article that includes an undated letter Allen wrote.

4. Lindsay identifies them as Allen, Edmond Pearcy, James D. Agnew, William Simpson, and "one other." The Snake and Salmon Rivers run parallel at this point, separated by Joseph and Doumecq Plains at the north end of the Seven Devils range (Lindsay, "Seven Devils," 12–15).

5. *Golden Age*, Feb. 5, 1863. Carrey, Conley, and Barton use as their source a 1939 *Lewiston (Idaho) Morning Tribune* article reprint of a letter by Levi Allen, written an unknown number of years later. The letter contradicts Allen's 1863 *Golden Age* account. He wrote that their explorations took them back and forth across the mountains separating the Snake and Salmon Rivers, from the rivers confluence to the Oxbow, 140 miles, by Allen's reckoning. Thirty days later they reached Lewiston, reporting that "no paying gold mines were found during the prospecting trip." He added, "an account of the turbulent Snake river canyon was brought back by the members." According to estimates by Carrey, Conley, and Barton, Allen's party ended up on the main Salmon River near the present-day town of Riggins, Idaho, and then continued up the Little Salmon River past Payette Lake, and on to Horseshoe Bend on the Payette River (Carrey, Conley, and Barton *Snake River*, 23–24). Edmund Pearcy remembered, years later, that they took the bateau south to the Salmon, possibly the same distance Allen reported. From there, encumbered with heavy backpacks, they prospected the Salmon River country by foot before crossing the mountains to Pittsburg Landing. There they hired Indian horses and recrossed the Seven Devils to the Little Salmon and ascended it to what we now call New Meadows before returning to Snake River. He claimed that on their return trip across the mountains they discovered copper and gold in the Seven Devils (*Illustrated History of North Idaho*).

6. *Golden Age*, Feb. 5, 1863.

7. Interior development by 1867 included 19 ferries, 4 toll bridges, and 14 main roads. Eight pack trains, 8 express and stage lines, and 8 stage stations accommodated land travel east and south of Lewiston to the neighboring mining regions (W. Brown, *Appraisal of Nez Perce Reservation Land*).

8. See chapter 9.

9. *Golden Age*, Oct. 24, 1862. An 1863 map of Oregon shows a trail from Walla Walla to the Grande Ronde

Valley and "Harney's Cut Off" from Umatilla to the Grande Ronde. The trails intersect just south of the Powder River.

10. *Golden Age*, Oct. 24, 1862. General George Wright, Fort Vancouver, to Brigadier General L. Thomas, Adjutant-General of the U.S. Army, Washington, D.C.

11. "The Glamour Never Lost Its Shine," *Lewiston (Idaho) Morning Tribune*, May 14, 1961.

12. Elsensohn, *Pioneer Days*, 2:155.

13. *Illustrated History of North Idaho*, 108. Although no records track how many individuals or small parties used the river as a transportation corridor, sources indicate more use than previously thought. Noyes Holbrook of Lewiston stated that in 1863 he "journeyed by boat up the Snake River." The Sept. 5, 1863, *Golden Age* noted, "there will probably be between 2,000 and 3,000 men winter[ing] on the bars of Salmon and Snake rivers." Most prospectors would have been on the Salmon; yet some were on the Snake and used boats to access their camps.

14. Portland merchants maintained some of their market by shipping up the Columbia to Umatilla and then sending freight cargo overland across the Blue Mountains to the Idaho and Oregon goldfields. The OSN thus retained a small portion of its river business but lost its edge to overland freight competition.

15. *Golden Age*, Mar. 22, 1864. The account of the Molthrop and Collins trip comes from an earlier issue of the *Mountaineer* and was reprinted in the *Golden Age*. Their full names are not given. At the time, two similar portages bridged navigational impediments on the Columbia River—one at the Cascades, the second at Celilo Falls/the Narrows—although neither was as long as the proposed Snake River canyon portage.

16. Ibid.

17. See Simon-Smolinski, *Journal, 1862*, for a full account of this first steamboat trip to the Clearwater.

18. Carrey, Conley, and Barton, *Snake River*, 30, quoting from William Gray's account of the venture. William P. Gray began his river career seven years earlier at age 13 under the tutelage of his father.

19. Lockley, *History of the Columbia River Valley*.

20. U.S. Army Corps of Engineers, "Improvement of the Upper Columbia and Snake Rivers." Michler claimed that it took the *Colonel Wright* 14 days to ascend the river, rather than Gray's much more probable 4½ days, and that they made the first 45 miles on the first day. Their return trip took 1 day. Twin Rock, by Michler's reckoning, was 30 miles above the Salmon River.

21. *Lewiston (Idaho) Morning Tribune*, "Early Days," Feb. 22, 1903. Stump claimed the trip had "no particular value" but the 1903 article added that "he had taken a steamer farther into the heart of a region lying to the east [of the Pacific Ocean] than any craft had ever gone before." According to that article, it took Stump eight days to maneuver the *Colonel Wright* upstream "about 100 miles" and he returned in less than five hours.

22. Additional confirmation includes the following: D. E. Buchanan, engineer on the *Shoshone* wrote about the *Colonel Wright*, "The highest a boat ever ascended from below was a little above the mouth of the Salmon River" (Buchanan Papers, "Description of the River above Lewiston," Oregon State Historical Society Library). The *Lewiston (Idaho) Morning Tribune*, June 27, 1901, raises the question, did the *Colonel Wright* make an earlier, successful trip into the canyon? The article appeared when valley people were excited about the prospects of having a stern-wheeler built specifically for canyon use. Lewiston pioneer Ezra Baird claimed that the *Colonel Wright* made a trip to Elbow Rapids some nine miles above Pittsburg Landing in 1863 and carried about 60 miners and 60 tons of freight.

23. Reed, report, quoted in "Steamboat Down the Snake," 25.

24. Ibid., J. C. Ainsworth to S. G. Reed, Mar. 27, 1866.

25. The Oregon Steam Navigation Company freight transfers included two on the Columbia—the Cascades and the Dalles—where cargo had to be unloaded and reloaded to bypass the navigation impediments, transfer to wagons at Umatilla, to the *Shoshone* on the Snake, and from the boat to wagons headed south to Ruby City or north to Boise City.

26. Lindsay, "Seven Devils," 12, quoting from *Owyhee Semi-Weekly Tidal Wave*, Silver City, Idaho. May 25, 1869.

27. U.S. Army Corps of Engineers, "Improvement of the Upper Columbia and Snake Rivers."

28. Ibid.

29. Ashworth, *Hells Canyon*, 30–31. The falls were located just above present-day Hells Canyon Dam.

30. Reed, report, quoted in "Steamboat Down the Snake," and a *Lewiston (Idaho) Teller* article of May 23, 1895. In his 1875 government report, chief of engineers Maj. Nathaniel Michler explained: "The pilot had announced the impossibility of proceeding farther down with the steamer, at least without wraping [sic] her by the aid of heavy hawsers around the sharp, abrupt, rocky projections of the perpendicular banks of the river" (U.S. Army Corps of Engineers, "Improvement of the Upper Columbia and Snake Rivers").

31. *Lewis and Dryden's Marine History*, 181.

32. U.S. Army Corps of Engineers, "Improvement of the Upper Columbia and Snake Rivers," 763.

33. *Lewiston (Idaho) Teller*, May 23, 1895. According to Lewis and Dryden, Smith reconsidered the matter and it was he who hired Miller and Buchanan, "owing to the heavy expense incurred in her construction and the utter worthlessness in that inhospitable region" (*Lewis and Dryden's Marine History*, 181).

34. Captain Michler based his account on a later interview with Buchanan. Deep mud on the usual Pine Creek Valley trail altered their travel route (U.S. Army Corps of Engineers, "Improvement of the Upper Columbia and Snake Rivers").

35. U.S. Army Corps of Engineers, "Improvement of the Upper Columbia and Snake Rivers" 763. Michler described "Indian Cave" as a "place well known as the spot where many whites were massacred. . . . The natives have painted in their own style the atrocious manner in which they killed their captives." He may have referred to pictographs in that area.

36. Ibid. They recrossed the Snake River to Snow's Shanty and "arrived at Chaflin's or Miner's Camp." Michler was unclear where they made the initial Snake River crossing.

37. Ibid.

38. Buchanan Papers, "Description of the River above Lewiston," Oregon State Historical Society Library.

39. U.S. Army Corps of Engineers, "Improvement of the Upper Columbia and Snake Rivers," 232.

40. Mills, *Stern-Wheelers*, 132.

41. U.S. Army Corps of Engineers, "Improvement of the Upper Columbia and Snake Rivers."

42. Mills, *Stern-Wheelers*, 132. They landed for the night at the foot of "Seventy Mile Great Canyon," as Major Michler identified it (U.S. Army Corps of Engineers, "Improvement of the Upper Columbia and Snake Rivers").

43. Mills, *Stern-Wheelers*, 132.

44. Michler located Pine Flat as 10 miles "beyond the foot of the Great Cañon."

45. *Lewiston (Idaho) Teller*, May 23, 1895.

46. *Lewis and Dryden's Marine History*, 182.

47. The *Shoshone* was later taken across the falls at Celilo, used on the middle Columbia as a cattle boat, and then sent on through the Cascades to Portland. There the OSN sold it to the Willamette Transportation Company, who hauled it on skids around the falls at Oregon City to run on the upper stretches of the Willamette River. A year later it hit a rock opposite Salem and sank. The next year the hull floated free and landed on the riverbank. An enterprising farmer converted it to a hen house.

48. Willingham, *Army Engineers*, 20.

49. U.S. Army Corps of Engineers, "Improvement of the Upper Columbia and Snake Rivers."

50. Ibid., 782.

51. *Lewiston (Idaho) Teller*, July 18, 1874.

52. Ibid., Mar. 23, 1878. The only other river commerce that decade was a log boom at the mouth of the Grande Ronde River. At least 19 men worked there under the direction of Thomas Wright, supplying timber-starved Lewiston with lumber. There had been an unknown number of prior log drives from that location (*Lewiston [Idaho] Teller*, July 4, 1878).

53. Lower canyon commerce improved with a road from Lewiston to Enterprise and the Wallowa country. In 1878 Edmund Pearcy, who operated a ferry across the Snake at Lewiston, built a wagon road from the ferry landing to the mouth of "Assotin" Creek and up the bluff across Anatone Flat toward the Grande Ronde River.

Pearcy then laid out a route into Wallowa County where the citizens were "deeply anxious to open the [trade] route to Lewiston." Pearcy's road, well to the west of the Snake, furnished a commercial link for the two regions. Over time the middle Snake River commerce helped regional development (*Lewiston[(Idaho) Teller*, Sept. 13, 1878).

CHAPTER 7. WAR THREATENS HELLS CANYON

1. Lewiston did not have boat service during the fall months, when the Oregon Steam Navigation Company insisted that low water kept steamboats off the river. Captain Thomas Stump challenged that assumption and the OSN's monopoly with his privately owned stern-wheeler, the *Northwest*. The *Lewiston (Idaho) Teller* reported Nov. 1, 1878, that the captain successfully carried 70 tons of freight "up the most difficult portions . . . with perfect ease . . . [demonstrating] that the river can be navigated by steamers to this point at any stage." His success inspired the OSN to serve Lewiston on a more regular basis.

2. For an excellent account of the events leading up to and surrounding the Nez Perce War, see Josephy, *Nez Perce Indians*, 509. For Nez Perce perspective of the war, see L. V. McWhorter's *Yellow Wolf: His Own Story*, or Nez Perce Tribe, *Treaties Nez Perce Perspectives*.

3. Tucker Papers, file no. 6, "Wallowa County History," quoting "Memoirs of the American Anthropological Association 'Tribal Distribution in Oregon,'" by Joel V. Berreman, 1937.

4. Bartlett, *Wallowa Country*, 44.

5. Ibid., 48.

6. Ibid.

7. Ibid., 54.

8. Josephy, *Nez Perce Indians*, 509.

9. Tucker, *The Story of Hells Canyon*. Tucker was a ranger in Wallowa National Forest during the early to mid-1900s.

10. Josephy, *Nez Perce Indians*, 511.

11. Ibid., 513.

12. *Lewiston (Idaho) Teller*, June 14, July 21, July 28, and Aug. 4, 1877.

13. Lyman, *History of Old Walla Walla County*, 401.

14. In Lewiston's Pioneer Park, near the main entrance of what was once Carnegie Library, a remaining rifle pit is still plainly visible.

15. *Lewiston (Idaho) Teller*, June 30, 1877.

16. McWhorter, *Yellow Wolf*, 68.

17. Elsensohn, *Pioneer Days*, 1:285. Regional and national newspapers, and many later historians, falsely credit Chief Joseph as the only war chief of the nontreaty bands. Yellow Wolf explained that Joseph was in charge of the women and children while chiefs like Looking Glass, White Bird, Toohoolzote, and Ollokut planned war and retreat strategy.

18. Greene's scouts did not arrive until July 28, 1877, while Greene and two companies of infantry were still in the mountains near Florence (Josephy, *Nez Perce Indians*, 501). They were obviously not using the Old Boise Trail and were consequently on the wrong side of the Salmon to be much help anyway.

19. Josephy, *Nez Perce Indians*, 532.

20. McWhorter, *Yellow Wolf*, 68.

21. Josephy, *Nez Perce Indians*, 535.

22. McWhorter, *Yellow Wolf*. "Pottoosway" branches were used for perfuming tepee homes to keep bugs from furs and robes.

23. Elsensohn, *Pioneer Days*, 1:292.

24. Ibid. Carrey, Conley, and Barton observed that the Indians often called Pittsburg Landing Canoe Camp (Snake River). That may have been Hunter's reference, but he uses both place-names. If both refer to the same place, his travel descriptions are imprecise.

25. Elsensohn, *Pioneer Days*, 1:293.

26. Bartlett, *Wallowa Country*.

27. *Lewiston (Idaho) Teller*, May 26, 1877.

28. Bartlett, *Wallowa Country*.

29. The letter is from the *Mountain Sentinel*, July 21, 1877, and quoted in Bartlett's *Wallowa Country*, 75. Using Tucker as her source, Bartlett identified Cullen's landmarks and ranch sites with contemporary place-names.

30. Most returning Nez Perce were given the choice of where they would live. Chief Joseph was not; he had no option but to live out the rest of his life on the Colville Reservation.

31. Arnold, *Indian Wars*, 172. The treaty's wording identified the lands included in the reservation as "sections of the Portneuf [later Fort Hall] and Kansas Prairie countries." Everyone interpreted Kansas Prairie, which does not exist in Idaho, as meaning Camas Prairie. Idaho has two regions known by that name: the Camas Prairie of southeast Idaho and the Camas Prairie of north central Idaho, the heart of Nez Perce country.

32. Ibid., 181. The two Bannock men were identified only as Charley and Jim.

33. Glassley, *Pacific Northwest Indian Wars*, 227. There were two reservations for the Paiutes: Winnemucca Reservation in Nevada and Malheur Reservation in southeast Oregon. Chief Winnemucca, after whom his reservation was named, did not join the warriors. His daughter Sarah served as adviser and interpreter for Howard throughout most of the campaign.

34. Howard, "Outbreak of the Paiute and Bannock War," 587–92.

35. Ibid., 589. Howard quoted from General McDowell's orders from San Francisco: "If our people have done wrong, for which settlers have been shot, endeavor if possible to do justice in the case, by securing the offenders on both sides, and delivering them to the civil authorities, before resorting to so expensive a proceeding as war." Howard added: "How thoroughly his instructions accorded with my own judgment!"

36. Arnold, *Indian Wars*, 173.

37. The *Lewiston (Idaho) Teller*, quoting the *Oregonian*, wrote that the Bannocks under Buffalo Horn planned to enlist the Paiutes and then proceed north to Salmon River. The article also mentioned that "Egan[,] a Paiute chief[,] is on the warpath with a force of 400" (*Lewiston [Idaho] Teller*, June 21, 1878).

38. Ruby and Brown, *Indians of the Pacific Northwest*, 251.

39. Ibid.

40. Howard ordered steamboat captains on the Columbia to prepare for their crossing. "Patrolling gunboats, the *Spokane* and the *Northwest*, quickly detected them [groups of Bannock-Paiutes] and poured fire into their canoes, killing several and destroying the craft." Those Indians were trying to avoid the war by crossing to the north side of the Columbia River (Ruby and Brown, *Indians of the Pacific Northwest*, 252).

41. *Lewiston (Idaho) Teller*, July 12, 1878. Leland was in Walla Walla as representative of north Idaho at Washington's constitutional convention, lobbying for north Idaho Territory's admission to the proposed new state of Washington.

42. *Lewiston (Idaho) Teller*, July 19, 1878. In a letter to his wife, Emily, dated July 13, 1878, and posted at Fort Walla Walla, Jenkins A. FitzGerald, army surgeon under Colonel Bernard's command, wrote: "Yesterday through a blinding dust more difficult to bear than any other feature of the campaign . . . we arrived at Fort Walla Walla. General Forsyth takes command of this outfit and we move for Lewiston and Mount Idaho at 1 PM. General Howard has preceded us." Bernard's men never made it to the Salmon River country. Instead they were ordered south to the headwaters of the Grande Ronde River. From there FitzGerald wrote a long, sad letter home about a Umatilla Indian attack upon the "Snakes," as he called the band they were tracking (Fitzgerald, *Army Doctor's Wife*, 344–46).

43. *Lewiston (Idaho) Teller*, Aug. 2, 1878. Penseroso's letter was dated July 16, 1878; his first name is unknown.

44. Ibid. Penseroso described a plant (the name of which is illegible, possibly "secu"; it may have been a *Calochortus elegans*, also known as elegant cat's ear or mariposa lily) "which abounds in the hard, rocky soil. . . . The root is greatly esteemed by the Indians as a delicacy. It is white, shaped like a small onion and has a sweet nutty flavor. The flower is shaped like a tulip, creamy white spotted with purple tint."

45. Sis A Nim-Max Howit was an old Nez Perce camp, which translated meant Thornbark Ridge.
46. *Lewiston (Idaho) Teller*, Aug. 2, 1878.
47. Ibid., Aug. 16, 1878. Up to 400 Bannocks were crossing the Snake at Brownlee's ferry at the time of publication.

CHAPTER 8. GOLD, GREED, AND MURDER
1. Elsensohn, *Idaho Chinese Lore*, 14. During the 1860s the "upper Country" referred to the mining camps of Idaho Territory or Eastern Oregon. The Chinese population so increased that the 1870 census showed Idaho Territory with the largest percentage of Chinese per capita in the nation, listing 71 Chinese in Lewiston and 675 in nearby mines.
2. Ibid., 70.
3. Wegars, "Rice Bowls." The Granite Creek site was about 50 miles from Baker City in the Wallowa Whitman National Forest but not in Hells Canyon.
4. Carrey, Conley, and Barton, *Snake River*, 304.
5. U.S. Congress, House, "Examination of Snake River."
6. Idaho State Historic Preservation Office, Historic Site Inventory.
7. Elsensohn, *Idaho Chinese Lore*, 15.
8. *Idaho County Free Press*, Grangeville, Idaho, Aug. 6, 1886.
9. Stories handed down by later Snake River settlers testify to Chinese miners' presence on the middle Snake. In the mid-1930s Stephen Cook, while working on a government survey of the Snake River, described the Chinese miners' boats as remembered by river residents. "Some of the old settlers said the boat had long banks of oars and a man would sit at one end setting the rhythm with the Chinese sing-song" (Stephen Cook, Asotin, Wash., personal diary for June 25, 1934, to April 4, 1935, loaned to the author).
10. Zhu, "No Need to Rush," 43–57.
11. According to Gerald Tucker, Forest Service ranger in Hells Canyon during the 1940s and canyon historian, some Chinese miners diverted Salt Creek, 90 miles above Lewiston, in order to sluice the sand and gravel along the Snake (Tucker, "Massacre for Gold," 26–48).
12. Zhu, "No Need to Rush," 51.
13. Ibid.
14. Ibid., 55.
15. Ibid., 49.
16. Ibid., 50.
17. Ibid., 57.
18. Bailey, *Hells Canyon*, 401–2. Bailey quoted from a 1902 *Lewiston (Idaho) Morning Tribune* article. The second figure comes from the *Lewiston (Idaho) Teller*, Apr. 26, 1888, and the last from Ashworth, *Hells Canyon*, 42.
19. Ashworth, *Hells Canyon*, 41. Gold enticed a second wave of miners to the canyon a decade later and a third wave during the Great Depression. During both periods many of those miners found pay dirt.
20. Rautenstrauch, "A Skeleton in the Closet." See R. Gregory Nokes, "A Most Daring Outrage: Murders at Chinese Massacre Cove, 1887". *Oregon Historical Quarterly*, Fall 2006, for an account of the massacre published after this chapter was written.
21. Stratton, "Snake River Massacre," 109–29.
22. Ashworth, *Hells Canyon*, 41. The nearest town was Joseph, Oreg.
23. Stratton, "Snake River Massacre," 115. Bill Rautenstrauch wrote that Stratton was stymied by a local "conspiracy of silence" and therefore concentrated his research on federal records, newspapers from throughout the region, and records of interviews with area rancher George Craig (Rautenstrauch, "A Skeleton in the Closet"). Gerald Tucker believed that four boatloads of miners left Lewiston in the fall of 1886. Once they reached the mouth of the Salmon River, they scattered. One crew of 10 continued deep into the canyon to Salt Creek. The

other 31 men eventually congregated around Deep Creek, 25 miles closer to Lewiston, where they "worked the gravel of a cove with shovel, pan and fluvial ore rockers" (Tucker, "Massacre for Gold," 27).

24. Stratton, "Snake River Massacre," 115, quoting from *Origin of Wallowa County Place-Names* by J. H. Horner. Dug Bar was the Nez Perce river crossing site used in 1877 when the Wallowa band moved to the Lapwai reservation (see chap. 7).

25. Stratton, "Snake River Massacre," 117. The *Lewiston (Idaho) Teller*, May 3, 1888, confirmed those names. Ashworth stated there were eight men in the original gang, but did not give their names. He and the *Teller* article claimed that Carl Hughes had second thoughts and begged to be left out of the planned attack on the Chinese miners (Ashworth, *Hells Canyon*, 42). Hughes is spelled Hughs in numerous accounts.

26. Stratton, "Snake River Massacre," 117, quoting from the *Lewiston (Idaho) Teller*.

27. Ibid. Stratton believed that the camp and murder site was not Deep Creek but a quarter mile downriver at Robinson Gulch. Both sites fit his description.

28. Ashworth, *Hells Canyon*, 43. Ashworth based his account in part on a 1902 *Lewiston (Idaho) Morning Tribune* article. He contended that 32 miners met their death at Deep Creek in one brutal attack. It was hot; the miners were resting in their cool dugouts when 7 murderers rode directly into camp and opened fire at close range. They shot some of the miners; others died as they attempted to flee. One man ran to the river and nearly escaped. Then, as he swam for safety, "the grinning cowhands took turns firing at his bobbing head." Silence fell over the canyon after the last brutal act. For some unexplained reason, Ashworth believed the 3 murderers decided to "tidy up the place a bit." They carried all the victims down the steep bank to the water and then piled them in the Chinese's boat. "The pile in the boat grew until there were 29 bodies in it. The men 'became fatigued'" before loading the remaining 3 bodies and they left the victims where they died—2 on the Deep Creek bar and the third across the river. The killers then knocked out a hole in the side of the boat and set it adrift. Once they disposed of the bodies, they buried 17 flasks of gold dust at the murder scene with the intention of returning to retrieve it later. One of those 3 thugs soon disappeared; many suggest he, too, fell victim to the insatiable greed of the others.

29. Brewrink, "Chronicles," in author's possession. Years later, Brewrink's mother insisted they had been at Upper Deep Creek. "But in my memory," Brewrink added, "Lower Deep Creek seems to fit best the rough nature of the site" and it was within "the usual scope of my travels at that age."

30. Carrey, Conley, and Barton, *Snake River*, 304–8.

31. *Lewiston (Idaho) Teller*, June 16, 1887. The news that 34 Chinese miners had been murdered just above the mouth of the Imnaha River for their $30,000 in gold dust first appeared in the *Teller*, Apr. 26, 1888, reprinted from a Wallowa County newspaper. The *Teller* added that the news reached Wallowa County when some white men chanced upon the bodies of two Chinese miners. "Their tents were blown down" and the "large amount of provisions and mining utensils" appeared "used but very little." Small piles of cartridge shells were scattered about near the river. In the next week's *Teller* issue, May 3, 1888, the death count was reduced to 10 and the monetary loss to $4,000 to $5,000.

32. Ibid., June 30, 1887.

33. Ashworth, *Hells Canyon*, 44. He wrote: "Local newspapers called it 'the crime of the century'; abbreviated accounts appeared as far away as the East Coast."

34. *Lewiston (Idaho) Teller*, June 23, 1887.

35. Tucker, "Massacre for Gold," 27.

36. Ibid. The three bodies must have been those found in the Snake River before Lee She reached Lewiston.

37. Stratton, "Snake River Massacre," 119. Joseph K. Vincent, originally of Salem, Mass., was a forty-niner in California and "not easily shocked by man's depravity." He moved from California to Hawaii in 1855, then to southwest Oregon with the gold rush where he fought as a volunteer in the Rogue River War, was captured and held for five days before being rescued—his legs and feet nearly frozen. During the Civil War he enlisted in the army and received an assignment to Idaho's Fort Lapwai. There he served for three years. While at Fort Lapwai, in the winter of 1864–65, Lewistonians were in a quandary over what to do about Boise City's "stealing the capital." Territorial judge John G. Berry appointed Vincent as a special deputy marshal and charged him with enforcing an

injunction forbidding the removal of the territorial seal and archives from Lewiston (*Illustrated History of North Idaho*, 570–71). Vincent's name first appeared in a Lewiston newspaper in an 1863 advertisement as an auctioneer, work he did for at least the next 15 years. He also sold lime. He fought as a volunteer in the Nez Perce War and later served as provost judge under one of his commanders. He was also the son-in-law of Alonzo Leland, owner of the *Lewiston (Idaho) Teller*. Vincent moved to Cottonwood the year after the Chinese massacre investigation, where he ran a hotel, and five years later moved to Mount Idaho. He was elected probate judge and served one term. Joseph K. Vincent died in 1909 (*Lewiston [Idaho] Teller*, Aug. 30, 1878, and *Grangeville [Idaho] Globe*, Mar. 24, 1909).

38. *Lewiston (Idaho) Teller*, June 30, 1887.
39. Carrey, Conley, and Barton, *Snake River*, 305–6.
40. Tucker, "Massacre for Gold," 27.
41. Stratton, "Snake River Massacre," 119–20.
42. *Lewiston (Idaho) Teller*, July 14, 1887.
43. Tucker, "Massacre for Gold," 28.
44. Carrey, Conley, and Barton, *Snake River*, 306–7.
45. Stratton, "Snake River Massacre," 120. In 1882 the United States had enacted a piece of legislation now known as the Chinese Exclusion Act. It denied Chinese the right to immigrate to this country. Under the guise of protecting American jobs, it became a green light for anti-Chinese actions. Chang Yin-huan was at the time negotiating with the Americans for monetary compensation to the families of Chinese who had already fallen victim to the hate and bigotry of some Americans. The negotiations involved payment of $276,619.75 "'for all losses and injuries' suffered by specified groups of Chinese nationals in this country." That figure did not include the Hells Canyon "injuries" since no one knew the full extent of the crimes. Unfortunately, despite Chang Yin-huan's appeal, when China did eventually receive the money, it included nothing for the families of the Hells Canyon victims.
46. Ibid.
47. According to both Gerald Tucker, in "Massacre for Gold," and Carrey, Conley, and Barton in *Snake River*.
48. Stratton, "Snake River Massacre," 122–23. Why six rather than seven were under indictment is not clear.
49. Ibid., 123, quoting from G. L. Rives, Acting Secretary of State, to I. I. McArthur, May 10, 1888, Miscellaneous Letters of State Department, RG 59, National Archives and Records Service.
50. Carrey, Conley, and Barton, *Snake River*, 308.
51. The indictment read: "The State of Oregon *vs.* T. J. [listed elsewhere as J. T.] Canfield, Bruce Evans, C. O. Larue, Heyram [*sic*] Maynard, Carl Hughes, and Robert McMillan, accused by the Grand Jury of the county of Wallowa . . . of the crime of murder committed as follows. Acting together on the first day of May, A.D. 1887 in the County and State aforesaid, purposely, felonious and of deliberate and premeditated malice, killed. . . . Ah Jim, Ye Lee, Wy Lee, Hop Sing, Hee Lee, La Bate, Kim Linn, Wee Gee, Song Kim and Hop Gee [following each victim's name was the comment "whose real name to the grand jury is unknown"]." Trial information from court records, Wallowa County Courthouse, and Rautenstrauch, "A Skeleton in the Closet." All subsequent references to the trial, unless otherwise noted, are from these sources. In the injunction the massacre date is "the first day of May"; throughout the questioning the date used is the last day of May.
52. Stratton, "Snake River Massacre," 123. Rumor had it that LaRue died in a poker game in California. Stratton also noted that Canfield served a term in the Kansas state penitentiary and then operated a blacksmith shop at Glenns Ferry, Idaho. Evans "lost himself" in the Big Hole country of Montana.
53. In February 1995, while searching through an old safe for unrelated material, the Wallowa County Clerk came across the court records of the trial—information that would finally supplement the otherwise sketchy material available to historians of the crime.
54. Wallowa County court records, and Rautenstrauch, "A Skeleton in the Closet."
55. Further inquiries about Maynard's knowledge of the geography of the region reveal that Hughes believed it was about five miles from the Deadline (Deep) Creek/Snake River confluence to where the trail left Dead Eddy

to go up the draw to the Douglas cabin. Therefore he had never been any closer than five miles to the murder scene and had never been in a position to see the Chinese camp.

56. Besides Vaughn, the other witnesses included George Kernan, A. Z. Palmer, J. W. Beals, J. S. Hosnes, Luke Booth, E. W. Rmbole, and K. J. Martin. Additional witnesses included Geo. Branscom, Della Horn, William Caldwell, Sara Potter, Luisa Render, E. A. Clampett, William Gimmel, John Martin, George Craig, and Charles E. Vest.

57. *Wallowa County (Oreg.) Chieftain*, Feb. 16, 1999.

58. Tucker, "Massacre for Gold," 48. Craig specifically claims that 31 Chinese miners died that fateful day. An 1888 article from Wallowa County claims that 34 died. The next week the newspaper had reduced the number to 10 (see n31 this chapter). Craig may have heard the correct number from his Wallowa County acquaintances, or he may have exaggerated it for reasons known only to him. He or others from Wallowa County clearly appear to be the source of the larger numbers and most historians accept those figures. I am not so sure.

59. Nelson, "Final Journey Home," 70–76.

CHAPTER 9. BULL-HEADED FOOLS

1. See chapter 6 for a more detailed account of Allen's ventures.

2. Reddy, "Reluctant Fortune." Reddy quoted from an 1877 *Idaho Statesman* article reprinted in the *Statesman*, Oct. 30, 1927. Professor Lewis concluded that the "chunks of boulders of ore" would yield 35 percent of the copper alone, and "500 tons of pure copper" would yield 50 percent "without any labor in extracting the ore."

3. Lindsay, "Seven Devils," 12–15, and ISHS, Reference Series.

4. Reddy, "Reluctant Fortune," 9. J. H. (Johnny) Rodgers was the manager.

5. "The Union Pacific and Overland Route," *Historical Early Oregon*. Corvallis, Oreg.: Western Guide Publisher, 1972. On the map: "A company is organized to build a railroad from Baker City through the Eagle and Pine Valleys. This will touch en route several mining camps and terminate at Seven Devils, Idaho, said to be the richest copper discovery in the United States."

6. *Nez Perce News*, Lewiston, Idaho, Apr. 3, 1883. "Oregon Short line surveyors still maintained at an expense of $500 per day. This is proof positive that the Oregon Short Line means business, and confirms my former opinion that there is nothing . . . to prevent the OSL from building to Puget Sound by way of the Snake River."

7. Elsensohn, *Pioneer Days*, 1:157.

8. Reddy, "Reluctant Fortune," quoting the *Weiser (Idaho) Leader*, July 26, 1889. A few months later the manager again told the editor about the "healthy condition of mining matters in this district," and that in 15 mining locations and groups "the amount of copper to be seen above the ground" amounted to 91,500 tons (Reddy, "Reluctant Fortune," 9, quoting the *Weiser (Idaho) Leader*, Sept. 13, 1998).

9. ISHS, Reference Series, 5, and Reddy, "Reluctant Fortune," 10–11, quoting a *Rathdrum Courier* article reprinted in the *Weiser (Idaho) Leader*, Dec. 12, 1890, which identifies Albert Kleinschmidt and Samuel Hauser, of Helena, Montana, as the incorporators.

10. For 30 years Jacob Kamm had been master steamboat builder and one of the principal partners in the highly successful Oregon Steam Navigation Company.

11. Miller, "Early Oregon Scenes," 275–84. The watchman was C. H. Kent.

12. "Steamboat Opposition," *Lewiston (Idaho) Teller*, May 23, 1895. "The navigation of the Snake in that region being impracticable eleven months of the year," *Teller* editor Alonzo Leland explained.

13. Ashworth, *Hells Canyon*, 45.

14. U.S. Congress, House, "Examination and Survey of Snake River."

15. Carrey, Conley, and Barton, *Snake River*, 43–44.

16. *Lewiston (Idaho) Teller*, May 23, 1895. Years earlier, this same William Gray, assistant pilot to Captain Len White, tackled the turbulent Snake above Lewiston in the steamer *Colonel Wright*.

17. Captain Gray, Pasco, Wash., Dec. 2, 1920 to Director, U.S. Geological Survey, Washington D.C., letter reported verbatim in Carrey, Conley, and Barton, *Snake River*, 50–55.

18. "The Steamer *Norma*," *Lewiston (Idaho) Teller*, May 30, 1895.
19. Gray thought the starting date was May 17, 1895 (letter in Carrey, Conley, and Barton, *Snake River*, 50–55).
20. Gray remembered the hole in the hull being "forty feet long and four feet wide" (ibid.)
21. From the 21st of May on, both sources agree on the dates.
22. This account of Calamity Bill appeared in "The Steamer *Norma*," *Lewiston (Idaho) Teller*, May 30, 1895. Gray did not mention him.
23. See chapter 6 for a full account of the *Shoshone*'s run through Hells Canyon.
24. Although no source mentioned Farwell's newspaper affiliation, he may have been the *Lewiston (Idaho) Teller* reporter. However there was also an "enterprising correspondent" who from the Oregon shore scrutinized the *Norma* going through Copper Creek Rapids.
25. Reddy, "Reluctant Fortune," 12. Allen's tax bill for one year alone was $600.
26. ISHS, Reference Series, 5.
27. Lindsay, "Seven Devils," 14.
28. *Idaho County Free Press*, Grangeville, Idaho, Oct. 15, 1897. According to this article, the investors bought the "Peacock mines" (Old Peacock and South Peacock) as well as the Helena and White Monument mines. Those properties remained in litigation for 20 years after the sale.
29. Lindsay, "Seven Devils."
30. Reddy, "Reluctant Fortune," 14, quoting the *Weiser (Idaho) Signal*, Aug. 11, 1898.
31. ISHS, Reference Series, 6.
32. Ibid.
33. Carrey, Conley, and Barton, *Snake River*, 139. The smelter was located four miles down Indian Creek from the mine.
34. "River Improvements," *Lewiston (Idaho) Teller*, Mar. 2, 1897.
35. Dudgeon, *John Flynn's Stories*, 35. A Huntington man by the name of Mills built the steamboat at his hometown and named it after his daughter. The *Mable* weighed only 59 tons and was 70 feet long.
36. Reddy, "Reluctant Fortune," quoting the *Weiser (Idaho) Signal*, Nov. 18, 1897.
37. Carrey, Conley, and Barton, *Snake River*, 140.
38. Reddy, "Reluctant Fortune," 15–16, quoting the *Weiser (Idaho) Signal*, Dec. 1, 1898, and Mar. 9, 1899. The company spokesman was F. J. French, who elaborated on additional work done in the district.
39. Lindsay, "Seven Devils," and ISHS, Reference Series, 7.
40. Reddy, "Reluctant Fortune," 16–17.
41. ISHS, Reference Series, 8.
42. Carrey, Conley, and Barton, *Snake River*, 132.
43. Allen, Hells Canyon Series, "Hells Canyon Lays Bare Rocky History; "Early Wanderings"; and "Snake River Follows Fault Lines." "The Iron Dyke . . . had several tunnels. The lower tunnel was 1,300 feet long and rich copper ore was mined there from a body 140 feet wide and 210 feet long, which was encountered at 800 feet" ("Snake River Follows Fault Lines").
44. Grunig, interview.
45. A turntable is a rotating platform used to turn railroad cars and locomotives around. Homestead was the end of the line.
46. Carrey, Conley, and Barton, *Snake River*, 133.
47. Grunig, interview.
48. Production records "for the period of 1910 to 1934 show 34,000 ounces of gold, 256,000 ounces of silver and fourteen million pounds of copper realized from the operation" (Carrey, Conley, and Barton, *Snake River*, 135).
49. "An example of untapped potential rests on the Idaho side at the forks of Deep Creek, five miles above Eagle Bar, where Hells Canyon Dam now looms. It's called Red Ledge, where Tom Heady staked out the first

copper claim in 1894" (Carrey, Conley, and Barton, *Snake River*, 149). In 1906 the Kleinschmidt interests took an option on the Red Ledge mine, "described that year as being a mile long, 2,000 feet wide, and 'as red as a freshly painted barn' because of oxidized iron that colored the copper ore" (ISHS, Reference Series, 8–9). At one time the Butler Ore Company of Boston operated there at what Gerald Tucker calls "one of the largest high grade copper ore deposits in the United States" (Tucker, *Story of Hells Canyon*, 49). In the 1920s a bridge across the Snake from the base of Kleinschmidt Grade, which by then extended down river to Eagle Bar, should have facilitated development of the mine. However, "a fraudulent promotion of the Red Ledge, along with properties at Landore," led to the suspension of all major Seven Devils mines for a year. As late as the 1970s, Red Ledge, covering 1,500 acres with 23 patented claims and numerous unpatented lode and mill site claims, had not produced anything at all (Carrey, Conley, and Barton, *Snake River*, 149, and ISHS, Reference Series, 9).

CHAPTER 10. SUCCESS TO THE ENTERPRISE!

1. Although many people believed the Clearwater and Snake river corridors provided an easy water grade for a transcontinental line through Lewiston, one was never built.

2. The reservation included some excellent farmland desired by outsiders. When the federal government passed the Dawes Severalty Act of 1887—proposed to introduce the Indians to individual land ownership and agriculture by allotting them farming acreages—and applied it to the Nez Perce Reservation a short time later, regional farmers and developers demanded that allotting agent Alice Fletcher complete her work so the reservation could be "opened." See E. Jane Gay, *With the Nez Perces*, for an excellent account of that chapter in Nez Perce history.

3. Fahey, *Ballyhoo Bonanza*, 96.

4. Leopold, "Land Ethic."

5. *Lewiston (Idaho) Teller*, Jan. 23, 1880. Simpson arrived in Lewiston—presumably with a load of lime—"by way of the Snake river in a flat bottom sail boat," designed to carry 20 passengers up the river, under sail, "with considerable speed." An 1882 government survey report described his boat and operation. "Near the mouth of the Grande Ronde a limestone ledge appears on both sides of the Snake." On the Washington side, the ledge emerged above the mouth of the Grande Ronde. The ledge on the Idaho bank lay a short distance north of the river junction, below a series of minor rapids that Symons called Lime Kiln Rapids. There, a small crew of men burned the lime in a nearby limekiln. Symons estimated production at around 600 barrels that year (U.S. Congress, House, "Examination of Snake River from Lewiston to Mouth of Salmon River," and Captain Thomas W. Symons, Corps of Engineers, letter, Dec. 21, 1891). See also, U.S. Senate, "Examination of Snake River," and accompanying copies of reports from Captain C. F. Powell, Corps of Engineers.

6. *Lewiston (Idaho) Teller*, Nov. 16, 1884.

7. Earl, *Hells Canyon*, 230. Earl referred to him as Cap Louis. Either he or the *Teller* misspelled the last name.

8. Ibid., 256–57. Elmer Earl, lifelong canyon resident at Captain John, described the kilns. "When these furnaces, or kilns, were fired, they were filled with layers of wood and lime rock. First, a wood layer about two feet deep, then a foot of rock, then more wood, then more rock until they reached the top." A damper controlled the fire at the bottom, and it had a lid on the top. The furnaces consumed voracious quantities of wood. Each time the burning material settled, in went more wood. After the furnaces had cooled down a few days, the work crew removed the marketable lime and disposed of the slag at the bottom. "This live lime was nasty stuff to handle, as it is very caustic and will explode if dumped into water."

9. At Lime Point, in about 1910, "promoters of a cement plant in Asotin" dug the 110-foot long tunnel that is still prominently visible from the river (Earl, *Hells Canyon*, 257). West Coast Portland Cement Company cut a tunnel and had several buildings at Lime Point. The company installed the first plant unit for an intended production capacity of a million barrels a day. Lime Point "contains over 500 acres of cement materials. A USGS analysis of an average sample shows it [to be] of exceptional purity" (cited in Carrey, Conley, and Barton, *Snake River*, 375).

10. The surveyors built a raft "of all the driftwood we could find in the vicinity" and floated seven miles to

Cochran Island. There they built a larger raft "of sufficient size to go safely over the rapids below." Symons referred to the Salmon-to-Lewiston reach of the river as "the middle Snake" and described it as flowing "between rugged, barren bluffs, only less steep and high than those of the Cañon of the Snake," the section of Hells Canyon now inundated by Hells Canyon Dam and perhaps north to Granite Creek. The riverbed was "rocky and irregular throughout" and alternated between short navigable pools and rapids "where the current flows in chutes between walls of rock or dashes and swirls, on an elevated bed, against sharp knolls and large bowlders [sic]." Symons thought the best time to navigate the river was between late summer and early fall. Thirteen obstructions inhibited navigation; six were so serious they required removal before boats could navigate even at favorable stages. It would take an estimated $32,604 to "improve" the river, excluding work at Grande Ronde, Wild Goose, and Grotto Falls impediments, which required more extensive surveys. (U.S. Congress, House, Captain Thomas W. Symons, Corps of Engineers, letter, Dec. 21, 1891).

11. *Lewiston (Idaho) Teller*, Apr. 26, 1888. The men were S. C. Hale, Chas. Baker, H. T. Madgwick, T. H. Worden, A. Anderson, and L. Schutz. The article does not indicate on which side of the river the ledge was located. Three of the original prospectors sold their Grande Ronde district interests to Captain Ephraim Baughman and J. Q. Moxley of Lewiston, who believed that they had "secured an interest in a very valuable mine" and that it would "induce further prospecting in the canyon."

12. Ibid.

13. Ibid., Dec. 21, 1900.

14. Ibid., Sept. 18, 1890. George Morrison and a Mr. White discovered the quarries in the fall of 1890.

15. Ibid., Feb 12, 1891. Harry Madgwick, a well-known Lewiston contractor and builder, visited the stone quarry and "returned enthusiastic," claiming that it would make "beautiful buildings" and be in "great demand for finishing work." The stone was located near the surface "in such an advantageous position" that it would require little work to remove. Magnesia Stone Company planned to send a traveling salesman throughout the inland Northwest to market the rock and expected an immediate return on its investment. When river conditions permitted, OR&N stern-wheelers, the *Annie Faxon, Lewiston,* and *Spokane,* regularly picked up and delivered cargo south of Lewiston. The only other reference to the Billy Creek area was a brief article in the April 16, 1902, *Lewiston Morning Tribune.* A placer miner "cleaned up $15,000" in gold with a rocker during six weeks' work. In a subsequent article his Lewiston friends set the record straight. The "amount was $1500 and the gold came from a rich pocket" (*Lewiston [Idaho] Morning Tribune,* Apr. 23, 1902).

16. *Lewiston (Idaho) Teller,* April 23, 1891.

17. Ibid., Jan. 28, 1900. The investors were Scott Wilcox of Birch Creek, W. J. Clemans of Anatone, Newton Hibbs and mining associates of Lewiston. They kept the discovery secret until they filed their claims on the coalfields and adjacent lands at the Walla Walla land office, then planned for immediate development. This field was within easy road access; the domestic market for coal was growing; and, since in timber-barren regions such as this one, steamboats supplemented scarce cordwood fuel with coal, the OR&N expressed an interest.

18. "Extend Grand Ronde Survey," *Lewiston (Idaho) Morning Tribune,* Dec. 14, 1905.

19. Ibid. Most of what is known about Perry Mallory comes from a flurry of news reports the year before. He had been a shareholder in the Big Buffalo group, a promising gold dig in the Buffalo Hump district. Questionable business practices by primary investor Charles Sweeny prompted Mallory and about three dozen additional plaintiffs to sue. Mallory received $7,500 (Fahey, *Ballyhoo Bonanza,* 102–6).

20. Interestingly, Elmer Earl, whose parents were homesteaders at Captain John, writes nothing in his memoirs about either rumors or evidence of Mallory's or Wild Goose Company work on the creek, nor does he mention the Hether brothers' 1904 mining venture there.

21. "Out from the Mines," *Lewiston (Idaho) Morning Tribune,* Jan. 5, 1905. Daniel Hether had earlier located on the "old Salmon bar" between Captain Lewis Rapids and the Grande Ronde River. Leaning more toward farming than mining, he built a "substantial and commodious house" with the intention of converting the bar to "one of the finest fruit ranches along the river." His brothers stayed with him and from there ran their various mining operations, including the Captain John strike.

22. W. W. Saunders was superintendent of a mining company of "Lewiston parties" that included H. B. Street and Ben Mallory. The only other reference to Salmon Bar mining appeared five years earlier, in 1900, in what must have been a sizable hydraulic mining operation of 120 acres. The miners had just put in $7,000 to $8,000 worth of hydraulic machinery and were operating with a "fine head of water . . . handling about 1800 yards each 10 hour shift." They claimed that they made $630 per ten-hour shift and cleared $450 (*Lewiston [Idaho] Morning Tribune*, June 18, 1900).

23. *Lewiston (Idaho) Teller*, June 20, 1889, reprinting an undated *Oregonian* article. The *Oregonian* correspondent hoped someone in Portland would be inspired to build a copper smelter. He claimed, "The only disadvantage holding this district back from immediate development is the crying want of a copper smelter in Portland. There is plenty of copper ore in this region alone to supply such a smelter with all the ore needed." The Idaho copper belt extended for 30 miles on both sides of the Snake River, with innumerable ledges comprised of "from thirty to seventy percent copper" and paying quantities of silver and gold. At that time, only the Butcher Boy was capitalizing on the district's potential. Its ore runs were 65 percent copper, worth $160 per ton; silver, valued at $23 per ton; and gold at $7.

24. *Lewiston (Idaho) Teller*, June 18, 1896.

25. Ibid. An old prospector by the name of Canter discovered the promising ledge of copper. Soon two men, J. B. Perkins and E. C. Strong, were "on the ground and lost no time securing a bond upon the property." Prominent Lewiston businessman W. F. Kettenbach and Lewiston pioneer Ezra Baird were behind-the-scenes co-owners.

26. Ibid., July 25, 1896.

27. *Lewiston (Idaho) Morning Tribune*, Jan. 24, 1900. By the time they incorporated, the investors had completed a 400-foot tunnel and considerable crosscut work, revealing the Anaconda ledge. It was a 72-foot-wide deposit of copper, gold, and silver with average values of $28.51 to the ton. One "rich pay strike" showed copper at $50.91 a ton, silver at $42.95, and gold at $5.37. The Craig properties included 24 claims. The company also had work crews on claims 12 miles upstream at Deep Creek, 12 miles downriver at Captain John, and at the Craig properties just below Wild Goose Rapids on the Idaho side. A group of claims at Birch Creek, under bond to the Idaho Investment Banking Company in 1900, may also have been associated with the Wild Goose company.

28. Ibid., Oct. 18, 1900. George S. Bailey was the manager and superintendent of the mines. The Anaconda group of claims was the most active, with values ranging from "$85 to $200 in gold, silver and copper." E. D. Potvin, in charge of the packing, on one trip left Lewiston with two men and 10 pack animals. They went to Buffalo Rock (Big Eddy) where they picked up 4,000 pounds of supplies for the mine, supplies freighted by wagon up the Washington side, shuttled across the river to Buffalo Rock, and then transported on to the mine by pack string.

29. Ibid., Nov. 2, 1900.

30. Ibid., July 16, 1913.

31. Brewrink, "Chronicles," in author's possession. James never gave the AAI mine's full name. He said only that his father worked on Snake River during the winter months for Pullman Mining and Milling Company and that the AAI mine was one of their many holdings. The "Chronicles" includes a map showing Pullman Mining and Milling Company mines at the mouth of the Salmon, Deep Creek, and Wild Goose Rapids.

32. *Lewiston (Idaho) Morning Tribune*, Mar. 27, 1903.

33. Ibid., Mar. 14, 1903. The claims were the Treasury, Gold Bug, and Yellow Boy. Wundrum acquired abandoned property—known as the Yellow Boy—at Cave Gulch. After a little surface work he "went down the hill 50 feet, made an opening," then continued 50 feet farther, near the base of the hill. At the lower opening, after digging through 20 feet of loose rock and dirt, Wundrum exposed the "five foot lead" that had generated all the excitement. The ore body contained "large silver values" as well as gold.

34. Ibid., Mar. 15, 1903. The gold "showed streaks of free gold remarkably similar to the Wild Rose ore of Pierce, a rich district currently in production."

35. Ibid., Apr. 8, 1903. Since the new steamer was still four months away from completion, the shipment was most likely in Lewiston awaiting the arrival of one of the regular lower Snake River steamers. They would have hauled the ore to Riparia, Wash., transferred it to the train, and shipped it on to the Tacoma refinery.

36. Ibid., Apr. 4, 1903. The New York expert located four claims next to the Wundrum strike and eight claims on the Cotton (Cottonwood) Creek section. He also offered the owners of the Wundrum strike "$100,000 for the purchase of the claims or $200 a day to work the mine for a period of one year." They refused both offers. Instead, claimants took steps to organize the Craig Mountain Mining District, with Cave Gulch at its center. Within a short time, they changed the name to the Wundrum District in honor of Herman Wundrum.

37. Through 1903, other names became associated with Cave Gulch. Andy Kavanaugh, of Buffalo Hump and Warrens districts, owned "very promising property" at the Fairview claim on Garden Creek Slope (*Lewiston [Idaho] Morning Tribune*, June 17, 1903). The Ohadi Mining and Milling Company was working two ledges, one an extension of the Wundrum strike, with plans to "soon" build a mill. Work on the Cave Gulch properties could "easily be seen from the steamboat" and as late as September, Wundrum properties were still being worked with a full crew (*Lewiston [Idaho] Morning Tribune*, Sept. 10, 1903). By November, their tunnel was 135 feet long and 80 feet deep on the lead. The average width of the lead was 3½ feet but at points as wide as 7 feet.

38. In January 1905, the *Lewiston (Idaho) Morning Tribune* ran a comprehensive update on mining operations in Snake River. There was still considerable activity in the Cave Gulch district, with the focus on China Garden Creek. C. A. Sherlin, manager of the Golconda Mining Company, had just opened "an exceptionally good lead" adjoining the Ohadi. Ole Hether owned water rights on China Garden Creek. Along with Sherlin, he straightened and bridged the creek channel and made plans to build a mill somewhere on the creek bottoms in the spring. Hether and Sherlin expected China Garden Creek to furnish "power to the extent of 500 horse power" and transmit it to both Cave Gulch and Corral Creek (*Lewiston [Idaho] Morning Tribune*, Jan. 5, 1905).

39. *Lewiston (Idaho) Morning Tribune*, May 5, 1906. The Yellow Boy tunnel was at that time about 350 feet long with a number of shafts driven on the property. The ledge of galena ore had an average width of 3 feet, and assayed at 60 percent lead, 100 ounces in silver, and $79 in gold per ton. Herman Wundrum remained actively involved in the mines. During May 1906, he extracted "some excellent samples of galena" from the Yellow Boy Mine and was arranging for the Clarkston Reduction Company to handle some of his ore. By summertime, Wundrum hoped to install ore bins along the river to streamline the process. The wagons would haul the galena extracted from the tunnels and haul it to the ore bins. Then, when the river rose and the boat was ready to run, there would be no delay preparing the ore for shipment. Other mining operations in the canyon were planning to do the same thing.

40. Ibid., Feb. 16, 1900.

41. Ibid.

42. Ibid., June 4, 1900.

43. Ibid., Feb. 16, 1900.

44. Ibid., Jan. 27, 1903.

45. Ibid. Twenty-four hundred feet of the Eureka Mining, Smelting and Power Company's granite holdings were along the riverfront.

46. Ibid. See Chapter 11 for a complete account of the Eureka Mining, Smelting and Power Company operations.

47. Ibid.

48. Ibid., July 16, 1903. Niles and Vinson had not relocated to Lewiston before they sold out. The Garlinghouse/Nixon reduction and finishing plant was on Main Street opposite the courthouse.

49. Carrey, Conley, and Barton, *Snake River*, 370. The authors believed that piles of those window ledges still sat on the riverbank near Corral Creek. A 1905 newspaper notice, however, stated that equipment had arrived in Lewiston to "handle the large blocks" of granite as they are "channeled out of the ledge." The equipment included derricks and tools and was to be sent up river by boat within the week (*Lewiston [Idaho] Morning Tribune*, Jan. 25, 1905).

50. Carrey, Conley, and Barton, *Snake River*, 370. In 1925 Arza's son, Arthur, and his grandson Richard, "after several ventures," opened a quarry at Corral Creek. If not the same quarry that Niles and Vinson had begun so many years earlier, it lay adjacent to that one. The Garlinghouse family worked that quarry until 1930.

51. Both Alfreda Elsensohn and Otis W. Freeman described the junction of the Snake and Salmon Rivers as

being "one of the chief copper developments" in the region (Elsensohn, *Pioneer Days*, vol. 2; Freeman, "Snake River Canyon above Lewiston").

52. *Lewiston (Idaho) Morning Tribune*, July 16, 1913.

53. Ibid., May 15, 1938.

54. Freeman, "Snake River Canyon."

55. Carrey, Conley, and Barton, *Snake River*, 360.

56. Freeman, "Snake River Canyon."

57. *Lewiston (Idaho) Morning Tribune*, July 4 and July 28, 1903. The three Minnesota investors were J. F. Sperry, H. C. Tracy, and G. A. Madison. Lewiston investors were William Campbell, C. S. Van Brundt, and Nez Perce country attorney B. S. Crow.

58. Ibid., July 28, 1903. The river mileage is about 15½ miles, but land travel along the Snake usually involves considerably longer distances.

59. Ibid., July 6, 1903.

60. Carrey, Conley, and Barton, *Snake River*, 294. Jim Dorrance claimed that he moved the rails to a site above Bar Creek.

61. *Lewiston (Idaho) Morning Tribune*, Jan. 21 and Jan. 23, 1903. One cold January, Tuttle returned to the mine after picking up supplies in Lewiston. The difficulty of his return route illustrates the early miners' resolve. From Lewiston he traveled roads on the Idaho side through a series of steep climbs and deep drops to Grangeville, then down the precipitous White Bird Hill to the small isolated community of White Bird. From there, Tuttle climbed to Joseph Plains—the northern extension of the Seven Devil Mountains—crossed Pittsburg Saddle, and dropped down Kurry Creek to Pittsburg Landing. At the landing, he transferred supplies from muleback to small boats that he sent downriver to the Oregon mine. Tuttle's arduous route using a variety of conveyances was a commonly used method for traveling to and from the mines above the Salmon on both sides of the river.

62. Ibid., July 22, 1903. The town site was in the vicinity of Robinson Gulch, about seven to eight miles below Copper Mountain and Copper Creek, with Copper Creek the more likely location.

63. Carrey, Conley, and Barton, *Snake River*, 296.

64. *Idaho County Free Press*, Grangeville, Idaho, July 23, 1897. One mine was the Pacific, about a half mile from the Snake and 500 feet above river level. Others included the Ollie, El Dorado, El Captain, El Moro, St. Elmo, and Silver King. The Silver King was two miles from the Snake. A crew was at work at the Ollie in the summer of 1897, working on a ledge that showed up "a very strong and massive vein fully six feet wide between walls." The best way to reach the property was "by way of the Salmon river, cross Remington's ferry, the Deer Creek wagon road over the saddle and down onto Pittsburg creek."

65. *Lewiston (Idaho) Morning Tribune*, June 10, 1903.

66. Carrey, Conley, and Barton, *Snake River*, 276, 283.

67. Ibid., 278.

68. *Lewiston (Idaho) Morning Tribune*, Sept. 9, 1903.

69. "Bring Ore on Rafts," *Lewiston (Idaho) Morning Tribune*, Apr. 13, 1900. Captain Baughman claimed that by simply improving the slough at Wild Goose channel, which he estimated would cost $5,000, the river could be navigated during "the ordinary stage of water." Sheepman J. D. Thiessen, who also would benefit from steamer service above Wild Goose, said he would contribute $1,000 toward a fund to make those channel alterations. Ezra Baird, J. L. Eckert, and George Reed were listed as Great Eastern owners. Baird hoped to sell his property, but was well aware that the mine's location encumbered the sale. He had received a letter from his Chicago agent advising him of a potential sale. When the interested party had visited the Great Eastern property a few months earlier, however, the first thing he saw was "great quantities" of sacked ore on the shore ready for shipment. Baird had counted on OR&N boats reaching Pittsburg Landing during high water that spring, but when the boats did not arrive, the company could not "make the showing they otherwise could have done." Either Baird retained an interest in Great Eastern after the sale or his sale fell through (*Lewiston [Idaho] Morning Tribune*, Mar. 18, 1903).

70. Carrey, Conley, and Barton, *Snake River*, 234.

71. *Lewiston (Idaho) Morning Tribune*, July 16, 1913.
72. Battle Creek is about seven miles north of present-day Hells Canyon Dam.
73. Himmelwright, interview. The description of packing comes from his interview.
74. Barton, interview by Bruce Womack.
75. Himmelwright, interview.
76. Barton, interview by Bruce Womack.

CHAPTER 11. EUREKA!

1. Ashworth, *Hells Canyon*, 52.
2. For an interesting examination of the power of the myth in American history, see Robertson, *American Myth, American Reality*.
3. Ashworth, *Hells Canyon*, 50.
4. Bartlett, *From the Wallowas*, 102, and Carrey, Conley, and Barton, *Snake River*, 342–44. After working through a ledge of iron down to the water line, "miners struck a large body of red oxide copper ore." Immediately, R. B. Hibbs rode to Joseph to telegraph the news to New York. The same article observed that this strike "sustains Professor Lingren's [sic] opinion of the district." He believed "the original formation was copper and . . . iron was a later surface composition."

World-renowned mining geologist Waldemar Lindgren had been in the district and, apparently, viewed its copper content favorably. The Swedish-born geologist was a member of the U.S. Geological Survey. He received his training in "Europe's foremost mining school, the Königliche Bergakademie at Frieberg, Germany" before coming to the United States in 1883. He was with the U.S. Geological Survey for nine years and in 1911 was appointed chief geologist. He also was a professor at MIT and became head of the Department of Geology in 1912 ("Waldemar Lindgren"). Lindgren filed a mining report in 1900 on his earlier fieldwork in the gold camps of eastern Oregon, including the Bonanza District, 10 miles west of Sumpter, Ore. (B. Smith, "Celebrated Geologist"). Could he have been the curious engineer with impressive credentials who visited Hibbs and Barton? (*Lewiston [Idaho] Morning Tribune*, Jan. 13, 1900).

5. Ashworth, *Hells Canyon*, 50. Hibbs and Barton "bonded their claims to the Idaho Exploration and Copper Company for a sum reputed to be in the neighborhood of $100,000 and retired from the scene." Lucien Evans and brothers Sam and Frank E. Johnasse were prominent in reports of the Idaho Exploration and Copper Company. Evans was examining engineer for the company; Frank Johnasse superintended the development of the properties; and his brother Sam filled in when Frank was in the East. Their home was in Keokuk, Iowa. The company board of directors met in New York (*Lewiston [Idaho] Morning Tribune*, Jan. 13, 1900).
6. *Lewiston (Idaho) Morning Tribune*, Jan. 23, 1900.
7. Reputedly, valuable ore samples also came from the Idaho side. T. R. Frye and his son James owned 17 claims on Divide Creek, a little more than two miles above the mouth of the Imnaha. They had an "excellent specimen of peacock copper taken from the Last Chance." Their claims were also under bond to the "eastern company" (*Lewiston [Idaho] Morning Tribune*, Mar. 20, 1900).
8. J. F. Tuttle, who made the report, had had mining experience in Butte, Mont., and Roslyn and Washougal districts in Washington. At the time, he was superintending five claims in the Imnaha District for the Jonathan Bourne Company of Portland. He also said a Portland expert by the name of Brareton had examined the district and given it "flattering" reports (*Lewiston [Idaho] Morning Tribune*, June 21, 1901).
9. Ben Thresher and his partner, Julius Steiner, owned eight claims near the Imnaha group (*Lewiston [Idaho] Morning Tribune*, Feb. 7, 1900). Like most original claimants, Thresher and Steiner transferred their properties to Portland-Imnaha Copper Mining Company, under the management of J. A. Hilliker of Minneapolis. Thresher stayed involved, using reports from "well-known experts" who thoroughly examined the properties "to generate investor interest" in Spokane and Minneapolis. The experts believed they had "one of the finest leads they [had] ever seen." In addition to the tunnel and shaft work required for development, the Portland Company planned to use the Imnaha River for power to run the equipment and to build a tramway. Thresher, in the meantime, was

in Lewiston "superintending the building of a new boat that will have the carrying capacity of 30,000 pounds" (*Lewiston [Idaho] Morning Tribune*, Sept. 5, 1900).

10. Men from Fargo, N.Dak., backed the Fargo Gold and Copper Mining Company. In addition, Portland-backed Western Union Mining and Developing Company and the Oregon Copper Company were operating at the Imnaha/Snake confluence (Bartlett, *From the Wallowas*, 104).

11. The sale was for $15,000; they received $2,500 in cash.

12. O. E. Guensey to James T. Miller, President, Lewiston, Idaho, Sept. 8, 1902, Miller Papers, Nez Perce County Historical Society.

13. Board members and officers were from Sterling, Ill.; Dubuque, Iowa; and Waukon, Iowa. Two men, Henry Husebye and L. D. Lively, listed their residence as Clarkston, Wash., and Lewiston, Idaho, respectively.

14. Murdoch, *Boom Copper*, 182.

15. "1902 Eureka Mining, Smelting and Power Company Prospectus," Miller Papers, Nez Perce County Historical Society. Beginning with a capital stock value arbitrarily set at $2 million, the officials set aside 600,000 shares of the capital stock as a treasury fund to "finance the necessary equipment and start running the business, with no unsold portion dividend bearing."

16. Murdoch, *Boom Copper*, 183.

17. "1902 Eureka Mining, Smelting and Power Company Prospectus," Miller Papers, Nez Perce County Historical Society. Potential investors need a bottom line, and the 1902 prospectus provided it. The company projected a net daily earning capacity of $6,430. That included $500 from the custom smelter (100 tons at $5 profit per ton); $650 from the concentrating plant; $230 per year from the sale of electrical power at $50 per horsepower per year; and $5,000 from their own ore. "That would give us a net annual earning capacity of $2,057,600 or over 100% on an annual dividend upon the par value of our stock. Stock capable of earning the above dividends is easily worth ten times its par value." That stock first sold for $1.00 per share and "last year" (1901) paid dividends of 220 percent on its stock. The company later reduced the per share selling price to 50 cents.

18. *Lewiston (Idaho) Morning Tribune*, Feb. 7, 1902. Two weeks later, the *Wallowa County (Oreg.) Chieftain* perpetuated the confusion about the smelter's location. It was to be somewhere between the Grande Ronde and Imnaha Rivers and was "directly the result of the operations of the Fargo Company." (The article never explained that vague reference to Fargo Company, which was, in fact, a subsidiary of the Eureka Company.) The *Chieftain* described the founders as eastern capitalists and "well known smelter men." They were H. G. Johnson and G. A. Nehrhood of Waukon, Iowa; C. O. Howard and M. S. Howard of Omaha, Neb.; Wm. J. Wilkinson of Sterling, Ill.; James T. Miller of Chicago; O. E. Guernsey of Dubuque, Iowa; J. E. Hubbell of Lansing, Mich.; H. M. Peterson of Fargo, N.Dak.; and L. D. Lively of Lewiston. Most had personally visited the "copper belt" the previous November before announcing their interest in putting in a smelter. The company intended to have a boat on the river within three months, by June 1, 1902, at the latest (Carrey, Conley, and Barton, *Snake River*, quoting the *Wallowa County [Oregon] Chieftain*, Feb. 22, 1902).

19. Hazel to Wallace, Feb. 22, 1902, Miller Papers, Nez Perce County Historical Society. W. H. Hazel of Baker City, Oregon, who had just completed his assessment of the mines, estimated the copper value average at 12½ cents per pound. No other assay from that early date has surfaced. The complete report was as follows: Legal Tender, surface $5.46; Mt. Lion, $5.46, vein sample $30.77; Little Giant or Mammoth (Iron), $6.76; No. 2 vein, Mt. Chief, $5.52; Mountain Chief ore $55.18; Mountain Chief Gauge 82; Delta Ore, $32.27, vein sample $9.78; Mother Lode Iron Cap, $20.00 gold; Mt. Lion ore, $103.22; and the average values of ores $39.44. Later in the year, some irregularities appear in subsequent assays. According to letters Miller received in October, F. Vanderwater of Janesville, Wis., wrote that the Mountain Lion Mine showed 14 85/100 percent copper, $2.06 worth of gold, and $1.27 in silver (F. Vanderwater, Janesville, Wis., to James T. Miller, Sterling, Ill., Oct. 14, 1902, Miller Papers, Nez Perce County Historical Society).Two evaluations showed "great divergence," but, Andrew Prater, the assayer did not go into detail. He did, however, conclude that someone must have mixed up the sample numbers. The estimates from the W. H. Stowell Company of Spokane were what Prater expected the ore to carry (Andrew Prater, Spokane, Wash., to James T. Miller, Lewiston, Idaho, Oct. 20, 1902, Miller Papers, Nez Perce County

Historical Society).

20. Dennis Guernsey of Dubuque, Iowa, brother of company trustee O. E. (Ell) Guernsey, was possibly mine superintendent as early as that summer and oversaw most of the work. In September, his brother wrote to him, "I hope the trustees are now on the ground and have great faith, for you have everything in your power to place this company on its feet." In the meantime, although individual Eureka Company officers went west to check on progress at the mine, they spent most of their time traveling throughout the nation in search of equipment for the smelter, mines, and boat (Bartlett Papers, Joseph, Oreg.).

21. At Riparia, Guernsey met with "the chief engineer" who "knew the river well." He had a sketch of the kind of a boat they needed. Guernsey told Miller it was important to begin construction on the boat immediately. In the meantime, they had to take advantage of the high October river to get the small, 50-ton smelter on the ground and running. With it operational, they would "have a good idea of the quality of their ore." They could then bring in three or more 50-ton smelters during high water next spring. The *Prospectus* had called for two additional 100-ton smelters (O. E. Guernsey to James T. Miller, Sept. 8, 1902, Miller Papers, Nez Perce County Historical Society).

22. After visiting a machine shop in Portland, and another earlier in Lake City, Minn., Nehrhood decided to contract with the Portland shop, urging them to begin with the boilers, since that would take the longest. The engines were under construction elsewhere. Company trustee C. O. Howard of Omaha, Neb., had already hired Joseph Supple, boat builder on the Yukon, to build the hull. Nehrhood expected to have the boat delivered by Jan. 15, 1903 (G. A. Nehrhood to James T. Miller, Sept. 26, 1902, Miller Papers, Nez Perce County Historical Society).

23. Nehrhood to Miller, Sept. 30, 1903, Miller Papers, Nez Perce County Historical Society. The Fargo people would hold only one of the four offices; a Lewiston attorney would serve as the fifth director. Nehrhood told company president Miller, "I have worked out a scheme . . . with the unknowing full consent of Fargo which will give Eureka full control of the Lewiston [Southern] Navigation Company." We do not know Miller's reaction to this news, but Nehrhood reported that the company treasurer, C. O. Howard, thought the scheme was "a dandy."

24. Nehrhood to Miller, Sept. 30, 1903, Miller Papers, Nez Perce County Historical Society. Nehrhood estimated it would take the Rogers men four days to build the boat, four to get it to Eureka, and two more to reach Pittsburg Landing. Unexpectedly high costs ran $300–$400 to freight from Elgin on down to the mine (Nehrhood to Miller, Oct. 23, 1903, Miller Papers, Nez Perce County Historical Society).

25. Nehrhood seemed to have problems with company treasurer C. O. Howard for failing to get adequate money in the local bank to cover their daily operating expenses. Those expenses in late October included two ore cars, two tons of steel rail with spikes and splicers, 2,000 pounds of dynamite, and some gasoline, which accounted for almost all the $2,000 cash Howard sent him (Nehrhood to Miller, Oct. 23, 1903, Miller Papers, Nez Perce County Historical Society).

26. Nehrhood to Miller, Oct. 14, 1902, Miller Papers, Nez Perce County Historical Society. Pacific Telephone Company of Spokane would not run a line in without a guarantee of $5,500 worth of business.

27. Nehrhood to Miller, Oct. 14, 1902, and Guernsey to Miller, Oct. 15, 1902, both in Miller Papers, Nez Perce County Historical Society. O. E. Guernsey's son-in-law Fred Vandervater wrote to Miller asking for clarification of conflicting reports. He had sold nearly 20,000 shares of stock in his hometown of Janesville, Wisc., to folks who were "very enthusiastic about everything they read about Eureka" but were concerned that the smelter had not been delivered. His father-in-law had told the stockholders at their last meeting that the manufacturer would ship the smelter to Lewiston immediately and it would go on to the mine as soon as the river was high enough. Now a circular from Miller claimed that a strike at the shop had delayed the manufacturing of the smelter. Which story was true? The contradiction placed Vandervater in an embarrassing position with the shareholders, who were "red hot" to learn the truth.

28. It took until October before Nehrhood and Howard agreed upon boat specifications and let contracts for the construction. At that date, the total estimated cost was $17,000 (letter to Joseph T. Miller, Sterling, Ill., Oct. 10, 1902, unsigned but probably from Nehrhood, since he was in charge of the boat committee, Miller Papers, Nez Perce County Historical Society).

29. *Lewiston (Idaho) Morning Tribune*, Jan. 23, 1903. Charles Wallace was the road contractor. The road cost the company $10,000; Wallowa County pledged $2,000 toward what the *Joseph (Oreg.) Herald* called "the most perfect mountain road imaginable" (*Lewiston [Idaho] Morning Tribune*, Feb. 3, 1903, and Bartlett, *From the Wallowas*, 108).

30. Carrey, Conley, and Barton, *Snake River*, 350. The mill reportedly produced 350,000 feet of lumber for the mines, smelter, and other camp buildings as well as cordwood to fuel the smelter.

31. They used Durkee power drills with a 500-strokes-per-minute capacity and a gasoline engine to power the drills until they installed the power plant (*Lewiston [Idaho] Morning Tribune*, Nov. 22, 1902).

32. In January 1903, the *Tribune* announced that machinery for the smelter was on the way. At the end of the month, the first shipment still had not arrived. Some was "en route . . . [and] expected early next week," while some was still being manufactured in Denver (*Lewiston [Idaho] Morning Tribune*, Jan. 24, 1903). That next week, however, only the electrical equipment reached Lewiston. It came by boat "all the way from Schenectady, New York" (*Lewiston [Idaho] Morning Tribune*, Feb. 3, 1903).

33. *Lewiston (Idaho) Morning Tribune*, Feb. 27, 1903. It is always "the" smelter, not "a" smelter. Mining engineer C. S. VanBrundt of Boulder, Colo., set up an office in Lewiston and made frequent visits into the canyon. Convinced that the people of Lewiston did not appreciate the region's potential, he told the locals that it took eastern capital "to push this country to the front" because local capital was "too timid" (*Lewiston [Idaho] Morning Tribune*, May 6, 1903).

34. *Lewiston (Idaho) Morning Tribune*, Feb. 27, 1903. In 1903 Deer Creek was known as Eureka Creek.

35. Company correspondence does not describe the boardinghouse. However, the remaining stone foundation clearly shows a large, L-shaped structure with what appears to be a cooking area in the smaller section.

36. *Lewiston (Idaho) Morning Tribune*, June 20, 1903.

37. Ibid., July 4, 1903.

38. Ibid., Nov. 18, 1902.

39. Ibid., Jan. 7, 1903. Lewiston did not have rail service from the west along the Snake River until 1908. Dignitaries who helped make *Imnaha* a reality were present. John Olson, mining expert of the smelter company, was joined by J. A. Huesby, director of the Lewiston Southern Navigation Company and secretary of Fargo Gold and Copper Mining Company. W. J. Wilkinson, treasurer of the boat company, was not able to be there but his son filled in on his behalf. J. Merrill, superintendent of the Miners' Telephone Company, and J. F. Sperry, general agent of the phone company, represented additional Eureka subsidiary companies.

40. *Lewiston (Idaho) Morning Tribune*, Jan. 24, 1903. *Imnaha*'s nickel steel shaft was 21¼ feet long and 7¼ inches in diameter.

41. Also on board were *Tribune* editor W. B. Stainton and Baughman's crew: chief engineer L. H. Campbell; assistant engineer A. J. Walker; second assistant engineer A. P. Brown; firemen Eph McFarland and John Oure; mate G. H. Bluhn; watchman Fred Schwartz; steward Ambrose McDonald; cabin boy C. A. Dunstrude; and deckhands H. McFarland, Lewis Hansen, Olof Rosbold, J. A. Wolf, C. L. King, and Claude Wilkerson.

42. The account of *Imnaha*'s first trip is from the *Lewiston (Idaho) Morning Tribune*, July 4, 1903.

43. *Lewiston (Idaho) Morning Tribune*, Mar. 1, 1903. W. J. Clemans, of the Grande Ronde coalfields, delivered coal to the warehouse to test it on the *Imnaha*'s maiden run. Clemans was sure "its steaming qualities will show up to splendid advantage." However, Baughman later said, "a few more pounds of steam would have run the main channel. In fact, the *Imnaha* can climb a tree. The coal is inferior and the boiler fouled."

44. Many years later, another steamboat captain, John Akins, described the relationship between a river craft and its master. It might well apply to Captain Baughman as he faced Wild Goose that July morning. "They were as one. The master knew the sympathetic feel of his craft and the craft knew the master's hand. Each was alert, understanding. . . . They teamed together, these river pioneers, each exalted in a mutual triumph, and in adversity they mediated in sympathy" (ibid., July 9, 1933).

45. Ibid. July 9, 1903. One of the passengers was the freight agent of the Northern Pacific, who planned to "take a private conveyance" from Eureka through the section of Oregon that would be "served by the boat line."

Northern Pacific Railroad might have been considering building their own boat for the upper Snake or had plans to use their *Hannaford*, built on the Clearwater to help lay the rails up that stream, for there was some talk of putting in an NP landing in the canyon.

46. Today a ring embedded in a large boulder on the shore remains as a reminder of this early period of river navigation. A cable from the boat, threaded through the ring and back to the boat's capstan, enabled the crew to winch through the rapids. Exactly when and who installed the iron rings at Wild Goose and Mountain Sheep Rapids is unclear. Folklore insists they were installed for the *Imnaha*'s use, but evidence suggests they were installed later during *Mountain Gem*'s time on the river. Until then, boats used a deadman to secure a line on shore. It could have been a tree or a large boulder.

47. *Lewiston (Idaho) Morning Tribune*, July 15, 1903.

48. Ibid., July 21, 1903.

49. Guernsey to Allison, Penrose Memorial Library, Whitman College.

50. *Lewiston (Idaho) Morning Tribune*, Sept. 12, 1903. Boat officials believed with river improvements that the upper river would "permit uninterrupted service several months." Proposed roads to river landings included one down the Grande Ronde and a second to the mouth of Cave Gulch, demonstrating people's eagerness to make the river a transportation corridor.

51. Ibid., Oct. 13, 1903. The two rocks normally presented no threat unless the Salmon River was running faster and higher than the Snake River.

52. Ibid., Oct. 15, 1903. Baughman explained that "had the steamer been fitted with a sufficient number of bulkheads," they could have continued to Eureka. However, water flooded in and made it impossible to proceed without a false (temporary) bulkhead.

53. Ibid., Nov. 2, 1903.

54. Ibid., Nov. 8, 1903. A full crew at Idaho Granite Company had prepared rock to send downstream; supplies for the upriver run piled up in the Eureka Company warehouse in Lewiston.

55. Ibid., Nov. 11, 1903.

56. "Special Report of the Eureka Mining, Smelting and Power Company," submitted by G. A. Nehrhood, Secretary, n.d. (Miller Papers, Nez Perce County Historical Society). The remaining account of the accident comes from both Nehrhood's report and the Nov. 11, 1903, *Lewiston (Idaho) Morning Tribune*.

57. This version is the Eureka Company's version. Captain Baughman did not mention their ever putting out lines to hold the boat, even briefly, but said the passengers and crew got ashore. It all happened so quickly and the landing was made in so short a time . . . that the best of order prevailed" ("Special Report of the Eureka Mining, Smelting and Power Company," Miller Papers, Nez Perce County Historical Society).

58. Later Baughman explained that when the engines were designed, "I urged manufacturers to build boilers with the valve motion enclosed in the hull and without the eccentrics on the outside" But because the contract required the boat company to keep the engines in repair for a period of years, they ignored his advice. The manufacturers' ignorance of rough western rivers and the types of engines those rivers required cost the Eureka Mining, Smelting and Power Company its most valuable asset. (*Lewiston (Idaho) Morning Tribune*, Nov. 11, 1903).

59. The employee was Aaron Wilson.

60. Tucker Papers, file no. 6, "Wallowa County History."

61. Salvage plans were reported in Nov. 17, 1903, and Apr. 20, 1941, issues of the *Lewiston (Idaho) Morning Tribune*. The four deckhands were Bert McFarland, Ephraim McFarland, J. Carslay, and M. Carslay. The two McFarland men died in the accident.

62. Miller's troubles mounted. He got word shortly after the accident that his wife in Illinois was dangerously ill. He hurried home to be with her. Miller's wife was Eva Cool from Peru, Ind. (Joe Miller to author, Feb. 1, 2000, personal communication).

63. *Lewiston (Idaho) Morning Tribune*, Nov. 11, 1903. According to Nehrhood, the company could send heavy machinery down the wagon road from Elgin, but not for six weeks because the ground was too soft. They needed a good freeze.

64. Ibid., Nov. 13, 1903.

65. Ibid., Nov. 29, 1903. The company incorporated under the directorship of William F. Kettenbach, O. A. Kjos, J. B. Morris, G. A. Nehrhood, C. F. Allen, E. H. Libby, and H. M. Peterson. During construction, Baughman supervised the main construction and Campbell supervised the boiler and engine work

66. This was the same W. P. Gray who had successfully guided the steamer *Norma* north through Hells Canyon nine years earlier and piloted for Thomas Stump, reputedly the only captain to successfully navigate a steamer into the canyon beyond Pittsburg Landing. John F. Stump, Gray's pilot on the *Mountain Gem*, was the son of Thomas Stump.

67. *Lewiston (Idaho) Morning Tribune*, Nov. 2, 1904. The photographers were Henry Fair and S. Leslie Thompson.

68. Ibid., June 15, 1905. Mr. Lundquist of Idaho Granite Company was the passenger who commented on the scenery. He counted on the regularity of the *Mountain Gem* to move new equipment to his quarry where he planned to renew operations "on an extensive scale." At the time, he had granite scheduled for Lewiston and Clarkston delivery. The outlook for his company was "very bright and already large contracts have been secured in Spokane and Portland."

69. The granite was to be used on the new Lewiston normal school, now Lewis-Clark State College's Centennial Reed Hall. The ranch was owned by a Mr. DeBeaumont.

70. *Lewiston (Idaho) Morning Tribune*, Aug. 12, 1905.

71. Ibid., May 30, 1906.

72. Ibid., July 8, 1906.

73. Ell Guernsey to his brother D. C. Guernsey, Manager, Eureka, Oregon, Dec. 10, 1903, (Bartlett Papers, Joseph, Oreg.).

74. Nehrhood to D. Guernsey, Dec. 12, 1903, Bartlett papers (Bartlett Papers, Joseph, Oreg.). Nehrhood wrote: "Have it understood that he [John Baker] is foreman under you with power to act and discharge, and you will get along. You may depend upon it. He will not allow anyone to speak in a derogatory manner of you." Baker's predecessor "made a specialty of that."

75. Ell wrote to Dennis about the freighters McCully and Company. They "have been down to Lewiston trying to scare our people into paying Bixby's bills [Bixby was the sawmill operator], threatening to throw him into bankruptcy and tie up all our lumber"(Ell Guernsey to his brother D. C. Guernsey, Feb. 4, 1904, Bartlett Papers, Joseph, Oreg.). McCully and Company also accused the Eureka Company of cutting timber on government land. Eureka Company officials continued to have troubles with suppliers into 1905. That year the Eureka Company entered into a lawsuit with an Ohio company and named the Lewiston National Bank, custodians of a sum of money in an escrow agreement between the two parties, in the lawsuit. The charge: failure to supply satisfactory drills. The supplier guaranteed that the drills would work for eight hours; they could barely work six hours.

76. Under the new board of directors, the company voluntarily took assignments of large portions of the stock held by the majority of the promoters and issued certificates for nearly all of the remainder of their stock. There was little stock left belonging to the promoters upon which a lien could be attached.

77. Joe Miller to author, Feb. 1, 2000, personal communication. Joe Miller, James T. Miller's grandson, believed that neither his grandfather nor any of the other founders had much mining experience, and he thought that someone had misrepresented the mining claims in the Imnaha District when his grandfather purchased them. Although his grandfather owned some stock in other mining companies, he was a salesman for the Troy Stove Company of Chicago and St. Louis with a sales district of 11 western states. He had a good income and, with many business contacts through his work, was ideally situated to be used by the "Eureka mine group."

CHAPTER 12. THE DANIEL WEBSTER MOTE INTERLUDE

1. Since the early days of spiritualism, automatic writings have been one way a medium can receive communications from the spirit world. The practice began in America in the mid-1800s. Beginning around 1900 and continuing through the 1920s the practice became increasingly popular. For many it was just another parlor

game; Daniel Mote, however, took the practice and resulting communications very seriously.

2. I am indebted to the work of Wallowa County historian Grace Bartlett, who transcribed the Oregon period of Daniel Mote's small, sometimes barely legible diaries, which covered the years from 1903, when he first reached Oregon, to 1941, when Mote's eyesight failed. Grace interviewed Mote in his later years and arranged to have the diaries deposited at the Wallowa County Museum, along with her transcriptions and brief summary of his first few months in the canyon.

3. Bartlett, introduction to Mote diary, 4–5, Wallowa County Historical Museum.

4. Ibid.

5. Ibid., 10.

6. Mote, a nondrinker, frequently wrote that someone needed sobering up. However, he never judged that individual. Many years later, he told Bartlett about the kindness George Perry showed him then and later, and spoke with sadness about Perry's suicide.

7. Nehrhood and Hept came from Vaughn's Ranch south of Eureka on the Oregon side and were going to Lewiston through Forest, Idaho.

8. Bartlett, introduction to Mote diary, 11.

9. The following spring, 1917, Mote offered some of his claims to "the McCully people" for $15,000 and a third interest in some of his other claims. No deal.

10. Unfortunately, because the diaries for most of 1904 and all of 1905 are missing, we cannot benefit from Mote's firsthand account of company activities, or his work for the company, during that time. If they were located, that might set the smelter question to rest (see chap. 11).

11. One job was to locate and prepare a site for the Rogers brothers' proposed smelter, an idea the brothers ultimately abandoned on the advice of a mining expert.

12. The bridge was the Oregon Washington Railroad and Navigation bridge. Mote worked two months for Mark Nader and two months for Emerson and Peterson.

13. Mote described his homesteading process to friend and neighbor Winniford (first name omitted) in March 1916. Winniford was there to take his "affidavit to settlement, improvements, and residence on the place," as the process required.

14. June 1916, Mote wrote, "I think I'll straighten out my land papers, for I'll have to make affidavits, relinquishments, etc, before a notary." He would relinquish Silver Bell Mill site as mining property "so as to amend the original entry to include the said Millsite [in his homestead claim]. Then if proof suffices, the patent [should] issue one entire 100 acres. Also the fees paid on 5 acres are to be returned to me." The next month he received a registered letter from the land commissioner at La Grande, Oregon, "directing the republication in connection with my homestead entry #013999 under the act of June 11th, 1906."

15. Rockwork, Mote informed Rice, generally cost $20 per foot. That would make the job worth $10,000. "He was silent."

16. Mote often got irritated with people, but his irritation usually passed quickly. The only man Mote judged harshly for no apparent reason was Billy Rankin, an infrequent visitor, whom Mote called a "liar and a hypocrite." That same Rankin initiated the rumor that Eureka Mining, Smelting and Power Company intentionally sabotaged the steamer *Imnaha*.

17. See chapter 19.

18. Jack Tippett must have headed the project. The proposed structure was 8 x 10 feet.

CHAPTER 13. WHEN THE ROLL IS CALLED

1. *Idaho County Free Press*, Grangeville, Idaho, Aug. 12, 1887.

2. The Desert Land Act of 1877 allowed the purchase of up to 640 acres at 25 cents an acre. Under that act, the applicant had to live on the land for three years and irrigate at least one-quarter of the property. Then, after paying an additional $1.25 per acre, he or she received the patent—title—to the land. Under the Timber and Stone Act of 1878 a person could pay $2.50 per acre for up to 160 acres of land "unfit for cultivation" and "valuable chiefly for

timber." Finally, the Forest Reserve Acts of 1906 and 1909 enabled a man or woman to apply for up to 320 acres of land listed through the Forest Service. Once the applicant complied with the various rules and regulations, the Forest Service ranger evaluated the homestead and its improvements. If the claimant adhered to the "spirit and letter of the Homestead law," he or she then paid a few fees and received a patent. Information and quote about homesteaders, from Elsensohn, *Pioneer Days*, 2:184.

   3. D. Wilson, *Life in Hells Canyon*, 53.

   4. *Lewiston (Idaho) Morning Tribune*, Oct. 23, 1938, and Elsensohn, *Pioneer Days*, 2:175.

   5. Tucker Papers, file no. 6, "Wallowa County History."

   6. Barton, interview by Bruce Womack.

   7. Rivers, interview. Unless otherwise noted, all information about Dick Rivers is from notes made in a personal interview or private papers he shared with the author.

   8. Barton, interview by Bruce Womack.

   9. Shirley, interview.

   10. Barton, interview by Bruce Womack.

   11. Tippett, interview.

   12. Barton, interview by Bruce Womack.

   13. Edith Coleman, "River Route," *Idaho Farmer*, July 17, 1941, quoted by Elsensohn, *Pioneer Days*, 2:176.

   14. Ibid.

   15. Jacks, typescript, author's personal papers.

   16. Barton, interview by Bruce Womack.

   17. Tucker Papers, file no. 476.

   18. Hibbs, interview.

   19. Barton, interview by author.

   20. Martin Hibbs's second daughter, Mary, married Ralph Stickney. When Martin died, Mary and Ralph received the Johnson Bar property. In the 1940s Lenora and Ace bought the Johnson Bar property.

   21. Neuberger, "They've Gone Wild," 79.

   22. Shirley, interview.

   23. M. and J. Wilson, interview. Also Murielle's personal papers, loaned to author by her son Bill Wilson, Boise, Idaho.

   24. M. and J. Wilson, interview. See also M. Wilson, *Hells Canyon Romance*, for Murielle's biography, published by her son Bill Wilson after this chapter was written.

   25. F. Smith, *Snake River Daze*, and Yokum, interview.

   26. H. Johnson, interview.

   27. Ibid., and G. Johnson, interview.

   28. Jordan, interview. Because Grace Jordan's book *Home Below Hells Canyon* is readily available and so richly details their life at Kirkwood, I chose not to duplicate that material in this book. Unless otherwise noted, material about the Jordans comes from their interview.

   29. Although the federal government legally owned the land, by leasing back what was once their property and its material improvements from the Forest Service, the Wilsons could have continued to operate the ranch and retain their grazing permits. Instead, they sold their herd and permits to Bill Walters, owner of Big Canyon Ranch. A year later Walters sold his 2,400 head of sheep and grazing permits to Andrew and Neola Dahlquist of Buhl, Idaho. Their grazing rights extended from Kirkwood to Three Creeks, all on the Idaho side, and they leased the property from the Forest Service, which included the "Jordan house" and all the outbuildings, but ran the ranch from their home at Birch Creek on the Salmon River. In 1978 Dahlquist sold sheep he bought from Walters, paid Bud Wilson, bought a ranch in White Bird, and restocked both ranches, before selling to Frank Fulford of Brewster, Wash. (Dahlquist, interview).

   30. D. Wilson, *Life in Hells Canyon*, 12.

   31. One homestead claim that made up Lem and Doris's property belonged to Jess Earl, who bought the

property in 1944. He paid $5,500 for a $30,000 outfit that included 1,500 head of ewes and 1,060 deeded acres. The range that went with the deeded land amounted to 24,000 acres. Jess ran the place for five years then sold out to Jack and Celia Titus (J. Earl, interview by unidentified interviewer). Celia Wisenor Titus's family owned the smallest Pittsburg claim, 28½ acres on Salt Creek, which her parents, James and Estelle Wisenor, acquired in 1926 (D. Wilson, *Life in Hells Canyon*, 179). Over the years the Wisenors and their sons, Rufus and Wes, expanded the sheep ranch. When James died, his daughter, Celia, and her husband, Jack, received one of the homesteads. Jack Titus was also a longtime resident of the canyon. He and his brother Vern each had a homestead at Temperance Creek. Celia's brother Wes Wisenor lived nearby at the mouth of Salt Creek.

32. Youngdahl, *Arams of Idaho*, 158.
33. Hollandsworth, interview.
34. Henderson, interview. The Brust family was one of the earliest families in the canyon. They had a place on Wolf Creek and another on Doumecq Plains.
35. Van Pool, interview. Harold married Erma after his first wife died; she never lived on the ranch. Unless otherwise indicated, information about the Van Pools comes from the Van Pool interview, or Van Pool, "Harold Van Pool Ranch History," which Erma gave to the author.
36. Carrey, Conley, and Barton, *Snake River*, 302.
37. Brown, interview.
38. Evenson, "Jay H. Dobbin," Wallowa County Museum, and *Illustrated History of Union and Wallowa Counties Region*, s.v. "Jay Dobbin," 649–50.
39. Gibbs, "Cattle Ranching in a Canyon," 125.
40. Tippett, interview. Doug gave the author undated newspaper and magazine clippings about the Tippett family.
41. Tippett, interview. Jidge's wife died shortly after their marriage in an accident. His second wife, Jessie Wilson, was his lifelong partner.
42. Gibbs, "Cattle Ranching in a Canyon."
43. Tippett, interview.
44. Ibid.
45. Weatherly, "Jidge Tippett."
46. E. Earl, interview. See also Earl, *Hells Canyon*.

CHAPTER 14. STEWARDS OF THE LAND
1. G. Johnson, interview.
2. Barton, interview by Bruce Womack.
3. G. Johnson, interview.
4. Tippett, interview, and family newspaper clippings loaned to the author.
5. Wing, interview.
6. M. and J. Wilson, interview.
7. Hollandsworth, interview.
8. Gibbs, "Cattle Ranching in a Canyon," 276. Ranchers put out blocks of salt that animals cluster around as they do around water. But using blocks of salt in an effort to distribute cattle across the range would be prohibitively expensive.
9. Walker, interview.
10. Chadwick, interview.
11. G. Johnson, interview.
12. H. Johnson, interview.
13. Dobbin files, Wallowa County Museum.
14. M. and J. Wilson, interview.
15. Youngdahl, *Arams of Idaho*, 130.

16. Gibbs, "Cattle Ranching in a Canyon," 124.
17. Evenson, "Jay H. Dobbin," Wallowa County Museum.
18. Beard, interview.
19. Brewrink, "Chronicles," in author's possession.
20. Dobbin files, Wallowa County Museum. The first two years they were in business, Lem and Doris Wilson at Pittsburg sheared during May. They changed to February because "it was easier on the sheep and the men" (D. Wilson, *Life in Hells Canyon*, 33).
21. G. Johnson, interview.
22. Jordan, interview.
23. Sterling, *Sterling Years*, 127.
24. Because steamboats could reach those lower river stretches on a more regular basis, the Cache Creek ranchers had the benefit of river transportation much earlier than upriver ranchers.
25. Brown, interview.
26. The wool went into large, burlap sacks. In order to maximize the amount of wool in each sack, a man or boy would get into the sack and tromp the wool down as it descended upon him. Once filled, the top of the sacks were tied by a sack-tier.
27. G. Johnson, interview.
28. Dahlquist, interview.
29. G. Johnson, interview.
30. Evenson, "Jay H. Dobbin," Wallowa County Museum.
31. Beard, interview. He also quoted Dobbin as saying, "One time the bank went busted out in Enterprise, and I lost $150,000. And another time it went busted and I lost $75,000."
32. H. Johnson, interview.
33. G. Johnson, interview.
34. Ibid.
35. Sterling, *Sterling Years*, 160–61.
36. Beard, interview, and Evenson, "Jay H. Dobbin," Wallowa County Museum.
37. D. Wilson, *Life in Hells Canyon*, 27
38. Ibid., 65.
39. Walker, interview.
40. G. Johnson, interview.
41. H. Johnson, interview.
42. Youngdahl, *Arams of Idaho*, 97.
43. Ibid.
44. Barton, interview by author.
45. Hibbs, interview.
46. Henderson, interview.
47. Youngdahl, *Arams of Idaho*, 99.
48. Chadwick, interview, and Shirley, interview.
49. Sterling, *Sterling Years*, 226.
50. G. Johnson, interview.
51. Tucker Papers. "Feudin' Days" was told to Gerald Tucker by District Forest Ranger W. G. (Grady) Miller in 1938.

CHAPTER 15. RANCH HANDS, DOGS, AND DADBURN PREDATORS

1. Jacks, typescript, author's personal papers.
2. J. Earl, interview by unidentified interviewer, and J. Earl, interview by author.
3. J. Earl, interview by unidentified interviewer, and J. Earl, interview by author.

4. Youngdahl, *Arams of Idaho*, 74–75.
5. Henderson, interview.
6. D. Wilson, *Life in Hells Canyon*, 21.
7. Hibbs, interview.
8. Youngdahl, *Arams of Idaho*, 79.
9. Beard, interview.
10. Youngdahl, *Arams of Idaho*, 93
11. Other herders who worked for Bud Wilson included Henry Bowen at Granite Creek; Del Catron at Lightening Creek; Bill and Irene Winters; Raymond Blanco; Albert Crawford; and Henry and Jay Jones.
12. D. Wilson, *Life in Hells Canyon*, 87–88.
13. Sterling, *Sterling Years*, 117.
14. Wing, interview. Did she receive a salary? I forgot to ask.
15. Van Pool, interview, and Van Pool, "Harold Van Pool Ranch History."
16. Grote, interview.
17. H. Johnson, interview.
18. G. Johnson, interview.
19. H. Johnson, interview.
20. Beard, interview, and Dobbin files, Wallowa County Museum.
21. *History of Wallowa County*, 288.
22. Rivers, interview.
23. Tussing, "Queen of the Canyon."
24. Grote, interview.
25. Ibid.
26. Sterling, *Sterling Years*, 157.
27. Dahlquist, interview.
28. G. Johnson, interview.
29. M. and J. Wilson, interview.
30. Beard, interview.
31. H. Johnson, interview.
32. Walker, interview.
33. Barton, interview by Bruce Womack.
34. Ibid.
35. Tippett, interview, and Gibbs, "Cattle Ranching in a Canyon." That snakebite victims should drink whiskey is a longstanding and persistent myth. In fact, whiskey is not an effective snakebite remedy and may actually be harmful.
36. Tippett, interview.
37. H. Johnson, interview.
38. M. and J. Wilson, interview.
39. Ibid.
40. Henderson, interview.
41. H. Johnson, interview.
42. Chadwick, interview.
43. Barton, interview by Bruce Womack.
44. Chadwick, interview.
45. Shirley, interview.
46. Wing, interview. Sharon never said what happened to the other animals in the pack string, but if they had also been injured, she would surely have mentioned it.
47. Ibid.

48. G. Johnson, interview.
49. H. Johnson, interview.
50. Shirley, interview.
51. Gibbs, "Cattle Ranching in a Canyon."

CHAPTER 16. TIES THAT BIND

1. Hibbs, interview.
2. Rivers, interview.
3. Carrey, Conley and Barton, *Snake River*, 172, reprinted in full from an account written by Gene McGaffee of an incident in the life of her friend Ellen Hibbs.
4. Jordan, *Home Below Hells Canyon*.
5. Chadwick, interview, and Shirley, interview.
6. Dick Carter's story continues in chapter 18. Grace Jordan's book *Home Below Hells Canyon* has helped the place retain a degree of fame to this day.
7. Sterling, *Sterling Years*, 175.
8. Youngdahl, *Arams of Idaho*, 78.
9. Hollandsworth, interview.
10. Barton, interview by author.
11. Ibid.
12. G. Johnson, interview, and H. Johnson, interview.
13. Jacks, typescript, author's personal papers.
14. Henderson, interview.
15. Hibbs, interview.
16. Barton, interview by author.
17. H. Johnson, interview.
18. Jordan, interview.
19. Chadwick, interview.
20. Stone, interview.
21. E. Earl, interview.
22. Chadwick, interview.
23. G. Johnson, interview.
24. Barton, interview by Bruce Womack.
25. G. Johnson, interview.
26. Jordan, interview.
27. Barton, interview by author.
28. Barton, interview by Bruce Womack.
29. H. Johnson, interview. Horace Henderson said his mother had a big Home Comfort Range that came up on the boat. They had to haul it to High Range, which was no problem for his father, who could "pack just about anything that could be moved." They took it apart, removing the heavy oven, firebox, and grates, and packed it on two packhorses. "The frame went on one side and all the heavy stuff on the other side" (Henderson, interview).
30. Henderson, interview.
31. Chadwick, interview, and Shirley, interview.
32. Shirley, interview.
33. Ibid.
34. Jordan, interview. See also Jordan, *Home Below Hells Canyon*, for Grace's story of their bathtub.
35. Chadwick, interview.
36. Sterling, *Sterling Years*; G. Johnson, interview; Van Pool, interview; Hibbs, interview.
37. Barton, interview by author.

CHAPTER 17. RUBBERING, NEIGHBORING, AND TOLERATING

1. Shirley, interview.
2. Ibid.
3. Chadwick, interview.
4. Youngdahl, *Arams of Idaho*, 51–52. I remember my father, Bill Simon, telling about his father and many other Cottonwood residents stringing a line from Cottonwood to the Van Pool place a short distance above Big Sulphur Creek. My grandfather had a hardware and implement dealership in Cottonwood; many of his customers lived in that area.
5. Henderson, interview.
6. Wing, interview.
7. Jordan, interview.
8. H. Johnson, interview.
9. When Jess Earl was working for Frank Wilson at Somers Creek, they ran a phone line from there to Pittsburg, about eight miles, where Frank and Minnie Wilson were living (J. Earl, interview by unidentified interviewer).
10. D. Wilson, *Life in Hells Canyon*, 91. The ranchers who maintained that party line were Bud Wilson at Kirkwood and the Circle C ranchers at Pittsburg on the Idaho side; Kenneth Johnson at Temperance Creek and Lem Wilson at Pittsburg on the Oregon side.
11. J. Earl, interview by unidentified interviewer.
12. Barton, interview by author.
13. Wing, interview.
14. Van Pool, interview, and Van Pool, "Harold Van Pool Ranch History."
15. Henderson, interview.
16. H. Johnson, interview.
17. Barton, interview by author, and Barton, interview by Bruce Womack.
18. Hibbs, interview.
19. Chadwick, interview. During these years, Jack and Celia Titus lived at both Temperance Creek and Pittsburg Landing, Oreg.
20. Stone, interview.
21. Shevlin, "Eighty Years."
22. Tippett, interview.
23. Chadwick, interview.
24. Brown, interview.
25. E. Earl, interview.
26. Earl, *Hells Canyon*, 224. By counting the wrinkles on the foot or hand, Joe Albert had a fairly accurate measure for sizing the moccasin or glove.
27. E. Earl, interview.
28. Stone, interview.
29. Jordan, *Home Below Hells Canyon*, 76.
30. Hibbs, interview. It's likely her guest was the Wilderness Society founder Bob Marshall, after whom a wilderness in Montana was named.
31. Chadwick, interview.
32. Tucker, *Story of Hells Canyon*, 63.
33. Ibid.
34. Barton, interview by Bruce Womack.
35. Swank, "Reflections." Gladys Swank wrote for the *Lewiston (Idaho) Morning Tribune* during the 1960s. This typescript is probably a copy of one of her articles.

36. Clough, "No Mail-Order Bride."
37. Rivers, interview.
38. Barton, interview by author.
39. Personal files of the Murrielle McGaffee Wilson family.
40. Brewrink, "Chronicles," in author's possession.
41. Stone, interview.
42. E. Earl, interview.
43. Walker, interview.
44. M. and J. Wilson, interview.
45. Walker, interview.
46. E. Earl, interview.
47. Walker, interview.
48. M. and J. Wilson, interview.
49. J. Earl, interview by unidentified interviewer.
50. Walker, interview.
51. In 1917 Idaho passed a law prohibiting the manufacture, distribution, and sales of alcohol. Federal prohibition began in January 1920 and ended December 1933 with ratification of the 21st Amendment.
52. Walker, interview. Max was not sure what the tax was; the Jordans said it was $1.25 a gallon.
53. Jordan, interview.
54. M. and J. Wilson, interview.
55. Barton, interview by author.
56. Ibid.
57. McCarthy, "Martin Hibbs Murder," from notes taken by author.
58. Ibid. The local newspaper stated 14 people signed a statement claiming Hibbs had been shot in the back.
59. Walker, interview.
60. Ibid.

CHAPTER 18. EVENTS MEMORABLE AND HEARTBREAKING

1. Barton, interview by author.
2. Beard, interview.
3. Ibid.
4. Barton, interview by Bruce Womack.
5. D. Wilson, *Life in Hells Canyon*, 180–81, quoting from *Lewiston (Idaho) Morning Tribune*, June 1972. The outfitters were Floyd Harvey and Earl Pea.
6. Youngdahl, *Arams of Idaho*, 159–60.
7. Chadwick, interview.
8. Memories of Alexander B. and Sarah Jane Findley, *Wallowa County (Oreg.) Chieftain*, Sept. 17, 1959, part of a series from Mar. 12, 1959 through Jan. 6, 1960. The neighbor women who helped were Mrs. Chenoweth and Mrs. Berland.
9. Wing, interview.
10. For a complete account of this event, see Gene McGaffee's version in Carrey, Conley, and Barton, *Snake River*, 171–76. The source gives no date, however Ellen Hibbs died in 1926.
11. Walker, interview.
12. Barton, interview by author.
13. Chadwick, interview.
14. Ibid.
15. Gibbs, "Cattle Ranching in a Canyon."
16. H. Johnson, interview.

17. Tippett, interview.
18. Lottie Shields and Rachel Thompson were the midwives.
19. Chadwick, interview.
20. Shirley, interview.
21. Chadwick, interview.
22. Shirley, interview.
23. E. Earl, interview.
24. Walker, interview. Also Murrielle McGaffee Wilson personal papers loaned to author by her son Bill Wilson, Boise, Idaho.
25. M. and J. Wilson, interview.
26. Yokum, interview.
27. Shirley, interview. Violet's husband, Buster, was the grandson of Ellen and Alex Warnock.
28. D. Wilson. *Life in Hells Canyon*, 96.
29. Elsensohn, *Pioneer Days*, 2:181.
30. Henderson, interview.
31. Barklow, *School Days*, 451. From then on, the county superintendent took the stage to the town of Imnaha the first day, rented a horse and rode to Pittsburg Landing the second day, and reached the school the third day.
32. Chadwick, interview.
33. D. Wilson, *Life in Hells Canyon*, 97. The school was located about three-quarters of a mile to the southwest and "approximately five and a half miles from the river at Two Corral Creek."
34. Barklow, *School Days*, 452.
35. Barton, interview by Bruce Womack.
36. Barklow, *School Days*, 451–55, quoting "District 69, Snake River or Pittsburg, 1918–1924," by Florence Winniford Smith.
37. Yokum, interview.
38. Hibbs, interview, and Barklow, *School Days*, 451. Esther Hibbs thought Earl's school only lasted "about three or four months in the winter," but Florence Winniford Smith implied it lasted longer (quoted in Barklow, *School Days*).
39. Barklow, *School Days*, 451. Violet Shirley remembered home teachers as being "right out of the Normal School in Oregon. We always enjoyed these new teachers 'cause we thought they were so dumb." Her parents, however, usually became good friends with the teachers and kept in touch with them the rest of their lives (Shirley, interview). Marjorie said her mother helped the children with their schoolwork, even though she "could only do math problems in her head." She made the kids figure out the process. So if the teacher was "dumb," their mother compensated for that deficiency. Ethel only had an eighth-grade education, but "by-heck, she was smarter than most high schoolers" (Chadwick, interview).
40. Barton, interview by author. Generally someone at the Wilson place at Saddle Creek would put Ace across the river in a boat and care for his horse.
41. McNabb, interview by author, tape recording.
42. Brewrink, "Chronicles," in author's possession.
43. Nyberg, interview.
44. Neuberger, "They've Gone Wild," 79.
45. Wing, interview.

CHAPTER 19. UP, DOWN, OUT, AND ACROSS
1. Yokum, "A Child's Trip."
2. Barton, interview by Bruce Womack.
3. Hibbs, interview.
4. Day, "Postwoman Packed a Pistol."

5. F. Smith, *Snake River Daze*, 22–23.

6. Shirley, interview. Jess Earl, who worked for Forest Service ranger Gerald Tucker on the Wallowa National Forest, helped maintain the 600 miles of mountain and canyon trails. About opening a nine-mile trail from Saddle Creek to Battle Creek, he said, "You couldn't even lead a jack rabbit through it to start." He surveyed much of the trail himself "with my eye" and since it was "travelable—you could pull a pack string through"—he "didn't think it was a failure." His hardest job in trail maintenance was keeping the Saddle Creek trail clear over the top. "It finally grew up in thorns and we had to crawl clear back under and cut the thorns and drag 'em out with a horse" (J. Earl, interview by author).

7. Tucker Papers, file no. 6, "Wallowa County History," as told to him by Ethel Wilson and family.

8. Chadwick, interview.

9. M. and J. Wilson, interview.

10. Jordan, *Home Below Hells Canyon*, 60.

11. M. and J. Wilson, interview.

12. Ibid.

13. F. Smith, *Snake River Daze*, 22–23. The prior route across Eagle's Nest ascended high into the rims to pass above the vertical rock bluffs.

14. Tucker, *Story of Hells Canyon*, 67.

15. Hibbs, interview.

16. Shirley, interview.

17. Chadwick, interview. Marjorie explained that they first used alforjas—big heavy canvas, leather-reinforced sacks with flaps that buttoned—and loaded them on sawbuck saddletrees. Later they changed the saddletree to the Robinette ("a fellow on the Clearwater, Robinette, perfected it"), wrapped supplies in big canvasses, and tied them on the tree using a diamond hitch.

18. Elsensohn. *Pioneer Days*, 2:162.

19. E. Gray, "Yesterday and the Day Before."

20. Shirley, interview.

21. Swank, "Reflections."

22. D. Wilson. *Life in Hells Canyon*, 103.

23. Two other ferries licensed in 1861 and 1862 to operate on the middle Snake are something of a mystery. W. W. DeLacy and Jerad S. Hurd received a license to operate a ferry some place on the Snake between the Grande Ronde and Powder Rivers—that's as specific as it got. Most likely, hoping to capitalize on an anticipated gold rush into the canyon, they expected Snake River to become a thoroughfare between Lewiston and Boise. Probably they never actually operated the ferry. The second license was to D. R. Griggs and Green White to run a ferry near the mouth of the Grande Ronde (Lockley, *Voices of the Oregon Territory*).).

24. E. Earl, interview. See also Earl, *Hells Canyon*, 166–72. After 1958, with Brownlee Dam operational, the river fluctuated too much to run the ferry, and the business ended.

25. Simon-Smolinski, "Lewiston's Greatest Day," 8–15. As long as steamboats plied the Columbia and Snake waterways, Celio Falls near the Dalles, Oreg., presented a major navigational obstruction. All cargo had to be off-loaded, transported by rail around the falls, and reloaded on a second boat. It was a slow procedure and so expensive that the boat companies could not compete with railroads in moving natural resources to Portland and the ocean. Shippers were therefore at the mercy of questionable railroad pricing policies. What Open River schemers did not realize was the rapid transformation in shipping that trucks and improved roads would soon bring to the interior. The Celilo Canal was almost a relic on the day it opened.

26. Earl, *Hells Canyon*, 42–43. Earl uses the name Chatman rather than Chapman, which was the spelling used in other written sources.

27. Weatherly, *Best of Jawbone Flat Gazette*, 2:19–22.

28. E. Earl, interview.

29. Weatherly, *Best of Jawbone Flat Gazette*, 2:79–82.

30. Akins, personal log, Steamer *Lewiston,* Nez Perce County Historical Society.
31. H. Brown, "Genealogy and Family History."
32. E. Earl, interview, and Earl, *Hells Canyon,* 237–48.
33. H. Brown, "Genealogy and Family History." The railroad was supposed to involve several bridges across the Snake with tunnels through various rock points. But it would eliminate the costly haul over the Blue Mountains of Oregon. See also Kuykendall, *Historic Glimpses,* and Simon-Smolinski, "Of Dreams and Schemes," for a brief history of Charles Francis Adams and others who envisioned the Union Pacific line down the canyon in conjunction with the founding of Clarkston as a planned, irrigated garden community and railroad center.
34. According to Gerald Tucker, "Billy Rankin did a considerable amount of work for the engineers in charge of the survey." He never gave up his dreams of developing his mining claims once the railroad came through the canyon. "Therefore it was a great disappointment when estimates for the costs of construction were too high to be considered practical by officers and directors of the Union Pacific Company" (Rankin, "Some Notes," in Tucker Papers).
35. Earl, *Hells Canyon,* 238.
36. H. Brown, "Genealogy and Family History."
37. Brewrink, "Chronicles," in author's possession.
38. H. Brown, "Genealogy and Family History."
39. Earl, *Hells Canyon,* 241.
40. Brewrink, "Chronicles," in author's possession.
41. *Lewiston (Idaho) Teller,* Dec. 15, 1900. A news article in the *Lewiston (Idaho) Morning Tribune* the day before claims that two men identified only as Crugal and Greer had just built a 4-hp gasoline sailboat called the *U&I.* After its first run they replaced the original screw with a stern-wheel, which was better suited to the rocky river. They were leaving the next day for Imnaha with 10 miners and a cargo of 1,000 pounds of powder and tent outfits for the Rogers Brothers. Obviously, it was the same boat, with a different name, and cargo, and the same owner with his name spelled differently. *Wild Goose* is the name of a boat used nearly a decade later by MacFarlane between Lewiston and Asotin, according to Carrey, Conley, and Barton (*Snake River*). It may have been the same boat.
42. *Lewiston (Idaho) Teller,* Dec. 15, 1900. The fate of both the *Wild Goose* and Church's yacht escaped later news reports.
43. Swank, "Reflections."
44. Carrey, Conley, and Barton, *Snake River,* 70.
45. Ibid., 60, quoting MacFarlane's account of the beginning of his boat career, no source. His cargo included a St. Clair air drill, Fairbank engine, compressor and air tank, water tank, pipe, hose, and tools to drive a tunnel.
46. Ibid.
47. Bailey, *Hell's Canyon,* 255. MacFarlane spent five years in Alaska on the Skeena, Stikine, and Yukon Rivers and operated boats in Puget Sound and the Kootenai Lakes of British Columbia.
48. Ibid., 91. During these years, they were delivering mail without a formal government contract.
49. Carrey, Conley, and Barton, *Snake River,* 62. Bailey claimed *Prospector* was not built until after the successful trip to Granite Rapids in 1914, but the quoted newspaper article proves it was 1912. That summer the Lewiston paper reported that Mr. and Mrs. Albert Kurry, "who own and operate the ferry at Pittsburg Landing," were in town. They came on the *Prospector* and Mrs. Kurry "claimed the distinction of being the first woman . . . [to enjoy] that privilege since the establishment of the service" (Elsensohn, *Pioneer Days,* 2:167, quoting from unidentified newspaper of July 11, 1912).
50. Willingham, *Army Engineers,* 51. See also Elsensohn, *Pioneer Days,* 2:168.
51. Carrey, Conley, and Barton, *Snake River,* 62–63.
52. Pacific Northwest Power Company, "General Historical Information."
53. Bailey, *Hell's Canyon,* 255.
54. Ibid. Carrey, Conley, and Barton, in *Snake River,* said he got the contract to Pittsburg Landing in 1926.

55. Carmen Yokum to author, Mar. 3, 2004, personal communication.
56. Carrey, Conley, and Barton, *Snake River*, 66.
57. Shirley, interview.
58. A scow was a wooden, rectangular, box-shaped boat with wood sweep oars out each end and a tent for shelter on the deck. The remaining mines were Ezra Baird's and Jack Eckert's Great Eastern Mine and the Blue Jacket mine between Pittsburg and Sheep Creek.
59. Elsensohn, *Pioneer Days*, 2:168.
60. Yokum, "A Child's Trip."
61. Ibid.
62. Elsensohn, *Pioneer Days*, 2:168–69.
63. Bailey, *Hell's Canyon*, 258
64. Ibid.
65. Freeman, "Snake River Canyon."
66. Ibid.
67. Bailey, *Hell's Canyon*, 262.

CHAPTER 20. FLIRTING WITH ANGELS

1. Carrey, Conley, and Barton, *Snake River*, 78, and "Mail Carrier," *Seattle Post*, 1942, McGrady Family Papers. I am grateful to Bob McGrady, Kyle and Florence's son, for sharing the family scrapbooks with the author. Some of the material has no documentation. Unless otherwise noted, all newspaper and magazine articles cited in this chapter are from the McGrady Family Papers.
2. Parker, "A Fast Lady," 63.
3. Ibid.
4. J. Earl, interview by unidentified interviewer.
5. "Mail Carrier," *Seattle Post*, 1942.
6. *Lewiston (Idaho) Morning Tribune*, July 17, 1938.
7. Ibid., and *Travel Magazine*, Sept. 1942.
8. *Lewiston (Idaho) Morning Tribune*, July 7, 1944, and *Popular Mechanics*, Feb. 1949 (author and title missing). There is some discrepancy in boat length. *Popular Mechanics* has the boat 60 feet long. The article adds that it is powered by two 165-hp diesels, a statistic not mentioned in the *Tribune*.
9. "Mail Carrier," *Seattle Post*, 1942.
10. Petri, *Copper Lodge*, 10.
11. *Lewiston (Idaho) Morning Tribune*, Dec. 25, 1944.
12. Ibid., Jan. 25, 1942.
13. Ibid., Apr., 14, 1939.
14. Ibid., Aug. 26, 1939.
15. *Wallowa County (Oreg.) Chieftain*, Sept. 11, 1939.
16. *Lewiston (Idaho) Morning Tribune*, June 16, 1940.
17. In February 1942 McGrady registered Jess Earl (Sommers Creek); Fred Jorgenson (Getta Creek); Harold Van Pool, Ralph Hunter, and William DeVault (Dry Creek); Joseph Shannon and John Logan (Dug Creek); Ed Luoto (Deep Creek); Frank Pine (Pittsburg Landing); Albert Paul (Divide Creek); Gus Malaxa (Salmon River); Luciano Aranguena and Lester Oliver (Cache Creek); and Edwin Gonia (Temperance Creek). DeVault and Hunter of Dry Creek were his only 20-year-olds.
18. *Lewiston (Idaho) Morning Tribune*, Dec. 22, 1940.
19. Stone, interview; Barton, interview by author.
20. *Lewiston (Idaho) Morning Tribune*, Nov. 6, 1942. For eight years the Van Eatons had been producing "motion picture travelogues for distribution to service clubs, schools, and parent teacher associations" in the Sioux City area with "one of the largest private collections in the nation."

21. Ibid., May 31, 1944.
22. Dick d'Easum, "Idaho Out-of-Doors" *Boise Statesman*, June 19, 1944.
23. Hibbs, interview.
24. *Lewiston (Idaho) Morning Tribune*, July 4, 1944. According to the article, Wallowa national forest issued the special use permit.
25. Ace Barton confirms through correspondence with Alice Petri that Sand Creek and Sand Bar were the same locations on the Oregon side.
26. "Hands and River Help Pluck Canyon's Golden Fleece," *Lewiston (Idaho) Morning Tribune*, May 19, 1946.
27. Ace Barton said "Mrs. Wilson" was his mother, Lenora Hibbs Barton Wilson, conversation with author.
28. Petri, *Copper Lodge*.
29. Advent, *Pacific Pathways*, 29–33.
30. J. Earl, interview by unidentified interviewer.
31. H. Johnson, interview.
32. Don Thomas, *Lewiston (Idaho) Morning Tribune*, n.d.
33. H. Johnson, interview.

CHAPTER 21. INTO THE MODERN ERA

1. J. Earl, interview by unidentified interviewer.
2. G. Johnson, interview.
3. McNabb, interview, tape recording. Unless otherwise indicated, all the information about McNabb's period on the river comes from his interviews or from his personal papers.
4. Ibid.
5. Although the trip from Clarkston to the Grande Ronde River seems quite long, that is how McNabb remembered it.
6. A. N. Thorndike, "That Controversial Snake," typescript, 8 pages, from Oliver McNabb personal papers, loaned to author.
7. Barton, interview by author.
8. Ibid.
9. Although Inland Navigation Company remained McNabb's employer throughout his eight years on the river, at their request he formed the Snake River Transportation Company to pay the bills, keep the books and bank account, and take care of all of the business.
10. Sterling, *Sterling Years*, 123.
11. Rivers, interview.
12. Dick Rivers bound the logs together in a raft and pulled them at the end of a 125-foot rope through the canyon to Asotin. His rafts held 100,000 to 120,000 board feet and were about 100 feet long by 32 feet wide. The only other people to try rafting logs on the middle Snake were William P. Gray and his son, who in 1858 built a raft of logs from timber cut on the Grande Ronde and attempted to send it down river to wood-hungry steamboats on the Columbia. The log raft broke apart before reaching the Clearwater confluence.
13. Although Rivers claimed to have designed and built both *Idaho Queen I* and *II*, a Pacific Northwest Power Company document stated that Wayne Backus of Portland designed and built both boats ("General Historical Information").
14. Pacific Northwest Power Company, "General Historical Information."
15. Skow, "Farewell to Hells Canyon."
16. Sharp, "Charming the Snake," 65, and Rivers, interview.
17. Rivers, interview.
18. Tussing, "Queen of the Canyon."
19. Rivers personal papers, author and title unknown.

20. Orchard, "Just Rambling."
21. Rivers had special friends there who continued to mean much to him years after he left the Snake. In fact, the Rivers and Van Pools retired to Lewiston and settled down across the street from each other.
22. Barton, interview by author.
23. Shreve, "Remember That Daring Bert Zimmerly."
24. H. Johnson, interview.
25. Grote, interview.
26. Wing, interview.

CHAPTER 22. EPILOGUE
1. Chadwick, interview.
2. Shirley, interview.
3. Barton, interview by author.
4. Hibbs, interview.
5. Wing, interview.
6. G. Johnson, interview.
7. Brown, interview.
8. Jacks, typescript, author's personal papers.

APPENDIX A. CLEARING THE CHANNEL
1. U.S. Congress, House, War Department. No. 2. Engineers.
2. Libby to Turner, Penrose Memorial Library, Whitman College.
3. U.S. Congress, House, "Report of Major W. C. Langfitt."
4. *Lewiston (Idaho) Morning Tribune*, Aug. 15, 1903, and Miller Papers, Nez Perce County Historical Society.
5. *Lewiston (Idaho) Morning Tribune*, Aug. 29, 1903.
6. Ibid., July 15, 1903.
7. Ibid., Aug. 22, 1905.
8. U.S. Army Corps of Engineers, *History of the Walla Walla District*, 1:22–30.

APPENDIX B. FRAUD OR JUST POOR BUSINESS PRACTICES?
1. *Lewiston (Idaho) Morning Tribune*, July 29, 1905.
2. Ibid., July 17, 1905.
3. Ibid., July 29, 1905.
4. Ibid.
5. Superior Court for the State of Washington, Asotin County, Case 423. The history of litigation involving Eureka Mining, Smelting and Power Company and its founders comes from this case, plus cases 692, 701, and 923.
6. *Sterling (Ill.) Evening Gazette*, Mar. 17, 1908, Miller Papers, Nez Perce County Historical Society.
7. Ibid.
8. Ibid.

APPENDIX C. THE END OF AN ERA
1. For a thorough study of the history of dams in Hells Canyon up to 1977, see Ashworth, *Hells Canyon*.
2. Ashworth, *Hells Canyon*, 64–65.
3. Elsensohn, *Pioneer Days*, 2:144.
4. Ibid., 2:192–93, quoting Tish Erb, *Lewiston (Idaho) Morning Tribune*, May 9, 1943.
5. Ashworth, *Hells Canyon*, 64–65.

6. Ibid.

7. Elsensohn, *Pioneer Days*.

8. Ashworth, *Hells Canyon*.

9. Congress authorized the formation of the Federal Power Commission in 1920, assigning the bipartisan regulatory agency to review proposals from private companies to build hydroelectric dams, making sure their proposals provided for navigation, flood control, irrigation, and recreational use. Wildlife habitat and fishery protection was not a consideration at that time.

10. "308 Report," authorized by Congress under the River and Harbor Act of 1927 was published in 1934.

11. Inland Empire Waterways Association, "Henry M. Jackson File." Inland Empire Waterways Association was formed in 1934 by chambers of commerce of several Snake River towns to promote river development, including navigation locks and slack water navigation.

12. U.S. Army Corps of Engineers, "Columbia River and Tributaries Review Report, Interim." See also Willingham, *Army Engineers*, 94.

13. Herbert G. West to A. L. "Bud" Alford of the *Tribune*, July 20, 1949, Inland Empire Waterways Association, "Henry M. Jackson File."

14. Ganham, "New Frontiers of the West."

15. "SWIWCP Explains Further Its Stand on Hells Canyon," *Idaho Daily Statesman*, July 9, 1951.

16. Staff Paper, Idaho Power Company Hydroelectric Projects on the Snake at Oxbow and Brownlee, Oregon, and Idaho, n.d., Neuberger Papers, "Power Hells Canyon," Knight Library. In 1950 the Department of the Interior established the Defense Electric Power Administration to assess the situation. The following year, when rapid increase in power consumption had lowered the industry's margin of reserve to 6 percent, the agency announced its power expansion program.

17. "Federal Spending Facts," Council of State Chambers of Commerce Bulletin, no. 133, May 30, 1955, Neuberger Papers, AX78, "Hells Canyon General," Knight Library.

18. Federal Spending Facts, Bulletin No. 133, May 30, 1955 by Council of Chambers, Neuberger Papers, "Hells Canyon General," Knight Library.

19. Herbert G. West to Irvin A. Hoff, Administrative Assistant to Warren Magnuson, Jan. 6, 1953, Inland Empire Waterways Association, "Warren G. Magnuson File." To Democratic senator Warren Magnuson of Washington, the Idaho Power Company was nothing more than an eastern-owned power company bearing the name Idaho for regional acceptance. When the company filed their annual report to the Oregon Public Utilities Commissioner in 1953, Magnuson noted, all but 2 of the 30 largest stockholders listed came from New England states. Surely, such a company did not meet Eisenhower's criterion as a "regional private utility company."

20. Ashworth, *Hells Canyon*, 72.

21. Neuberger to Oakes, July 13, 1955, Neuberger Papers, "Hells Canyon General," Knight Library. Senator Richard Neuberger in a letter to John B. Oakes of the *New York Times*, Costello was the "only person who heard all of the 150 days of testimony [on SB 1333] and received nearly 400 documents."

22. Neuberger to Oakes, July 13, 1955, Neuberger Papers, "Hells Canyon General," Knight Library.

23. Elsensohn, *Pioneer Days*, 2:160. In 1939 the proposed Hells Canyon National Park "met with disapproval from State mine inspector, who said that it should not be made into a park until its resources had been exploited, including the mineral, hydroelectric, and scenic attributes."

24. Lloyd Tupling to Eric Lindroth, M.D., of Long Beach, Calif., n.d., Neuberger Papers, "Hells Canyon General," Knight Library.

25. Gus Norwood, Executive Secretary of Northwest Public Power Association address to International Mine, Mill and Smelter Workers at Spokane, Wash., Mar. 16, 1955, Neuberger Papers, ibid.

26. In 1973 the Corps of Engineers built Dworshak Dam on the North Fork of the Clearwater River, a few miles above the confluence with the main Clearwater River to provide the reservoir for downriver dams' hydroelectric production.

27. Orton R. Brigham, Secretary of District Two Wildlife Federation to Richard Neuberger, June 9, 1955.

Neuberger Papers, "Hells Canyon General," Knight Library.

28. Gabrielson to Neuberger, July 1, 1955, Neuberger Papers, ibid.

29. Neuberger to David R. Browner, Sierra Club of California, June 11, 1955, Neuberger Papers, ibid.

30. Mire to Church, Nov. 10, 1956, Church Papers, ser. 1.1, box 68. f. 3, Albertsons Library.

31. California Farm Research letter to California Delegation in Congress, Apr. 4, 1955, Neuberger Papers, "Hells Canyon General," Knight Library.

32. February 1956, National Hells Canyon Association issues of discussion, Neuberger Papers, ibid.

33. "Summary of Federal Power Commission Decision Regarding Snake River Development Program," IPC, Nov. 30, 1955, Neuberger Papers, "Power Hells Canyon," Knight Library.

34. Nez Perce Project Report, Federal Power Commission, Project No. 2173, Neuberger Papers, "Power Middle Snake," Knight Library.

35. "Excerpts from the Remarks of Senator Church Submitted before the Water, Power, and Conservation Panel of the Democratic National Conference in San Francisco, Feb. 16, 1957," Section 3-6, Water Rights Protection in S. 555, *Congressional Record*, Thursday, May 16, 1957, Frank Church Papers, ser. 1.1., box 68, f.1, Albertsons Library.

36. "Excerpts from the Water Rights Section of the Speech in Support of the Hells Canyon Bill, Delivered on the Floor of the Senator by Senator Frank Church on June 19, 1957," *Congressional Record*, Church Papers, ser. 1.1., box 68, f.1, Albertsons Library.

37. Church to Leo R. Hawkes, Preston, Idaho, July 13, 1957, Church Papers, ser. 1.1., box 68, f.1, Albertsons Library.

38. From Fish and Wildlife Service Report, n.d., Neuberger Papers, "Power Middle Snake," Knight Library.

39. See Ashworth, *Hells Canyon*, for a thorough discussion of Idaho Power Company's fish protection record.

40. Sandoz to Neuberger, May 22, 1959, Neuberger Papers, "Power Middle Snake," Knight Library.

41. Ashworth, *Hells Canyon*, 139.

42. Holm, "Shortage of Water," quoting Douglas in June 1967 Supreme Court decision.

43. "Power Groups Back Appaloosa Dam," *Idaho Daily Statesman*, Nov. 9, 1968, Inland Empire Waterways Association, "Appaloosa Dam File," VII no. 3.

44. "Udall Acts to Short Circuit Utilities Plan, Urges Government Build Snake River Dam," *Wall Street Journal*, May 20, 1968, Inland Empire Waterways Association, ibid.

45. "Senator Jordan Lambasts Udall for Backing Appaloosa Dam," *Idaho Daily Statesman*, May 17, 1968, Inland Empire Waterways Association, ibid.

46. Hells Canyon Preservation Council, Inc. Newsletter, n.d. [ca. 1969], Church Papers, ser. 1.1., box 68, f.15, Albertsons Library. To the Preservation Council, Church "seemed to underestimate the tremendous national support that has been rising in hopes of enacting our bill . . . but seems very much impressed by the apparent strength of those few interests lobbying for a dam."

47. Snake River outfitter Floyd Harvey, Lewis-Clark State College professor and Snake River outfitter John A. K. Barker, and journalist/author Annette Tussing of Lewiston and Clarkston each fought to stop dams in the canyon.

48. To solicit top-level support, Packwood met with President Nixon; William Ruckelshaus, administrator of the EPA; Russell Train, scientific assistant to the president; and Secretary of Interior Morton. Senators Birch Bayh, Jacob Javits, Walter Mondale, Ted Kennedy, and George McGovern joined Packwood, making it a bipartisan issue. Packwood anticipated problems in the House from James McClure of Idaho, a "friend of dam builders," (according to the Hells Canyon Preservation Council) and an influential member of the House Interior Committee.

49. Jordan argued that, "the belated recognition of Idaho's interest in the energy potential of a river rising largely from the State's own watersheds appears to have come about largely because of the introduction of our moratorium bill last session and not out of the corporate generosity of the downstream utilities" ("Jordan-Church Moratorium," Hells Canyon Dam, vertical file, Idaho State Historical Society Library).

50. "Jordan-Church Moratorium," Hells Canyon Dam, vertical file, Idaho State Historical Society Library.

51. "Jordan-Church Moratorium," Hells Canyon Dam, vertical file, Idaho State Historical Society Library.

52. Andrus, McCall, and Evans to John Nassikes, Chair, FRC, June 15, 1971, Church Papers, ser. 1.1., box 68, f.17, Albertsons Library f. 17.

53. Sierra Club, Brock Evans, "Success at Hells Canyon," Apr. 6, 1976, Neuberger Papers, AX78, "Hells Canyon General," Knight Library.

54. *Lewiston (Idaho) Morning Tribune*, July 5, 1970.

55. Ibid. Ferris Weddle quoted Conrad L. Wirth, former director of the National Park Service, and F. D. Voorhees, recreational consultant of Seattle: "The trouble with looking at Snake River canyon, without placing it in the country in which it belongs, was like looking through the wrong end of the telescope. The narrow view is likely to be the small view and the wrong view. If you move up and out of the canyon and look around to the east, the west, the north, and the south, what is borne on you is that there is a great mountainous country with deep gorges, virgin wilderness, alpine valleys, and breathtaking beauty completely surrounding the Snake River Canyon, of which the Snake River canyon is only a part."

56. Petersen, *River of Life*, 149. See Petersen's book for an in-depth look at the proposed Asotin dam as well as the other Snake River dams below Lewiston. See also U.S. Army Corps of Engineers, *History of the Walla Walla District*, 1:89.

57. Wing, interview.

58. Henderson, interview.

59. Barton, interview by author.

60. Tippett, interview.

61. Grote, interview.

62. G. Johnson, interview.

63. Barton, interview by author.

64. Rivers, interview.

Bibliography

Primary Sources, Archives, and Personal Documents

Akins, John E. Personal log. Steamer *Lewiston*. Chronological entries 1925–35. MS box no. 29, folders 36 and 37. Nez Perce County Historical Society, Lewiston, Idaho.

Bartlett, Grace. Personal papers. Used by permission of Ann Hayes and Tom Butterfield, Joseph, Oreg.

———. Introduction. In Daniel Webster Mote (Canyon resident/miner), personal diary 1903–41. Transcribed by Grace Bartlett. Wallowa County Historical Society Museum, Joseph, Oreg.

Brewrink, James. "The Chronicles of James Brewrink." Typescript, 17 pages, undated photocopy, with pictures. Author's personal papers.

Brown, Harold F. "Genealogy and Family History of Charles B. Brown and Wife, Nellie May (Forbes) Brown, 1976–1979." Asotin County Historical Society Museum, Asotin, Wash.

Brown, William. C. *Appraisal of Nez Perce Reservation Land Ceded to United States of a Treaty Cession, 1863–1867*. Valuation report. Vol. 1. Nez Perce County Historical Society Museum, Lewiston, Idaho.

Buchanan, D. E. Papers. "Description of the River above Lewiston. Descent of Steamer Sho-sho-nee. 1870," Portland, July 31, 1881, to Captain C. F. Powell, [Army] Corps of Engineers, U.S.A. MSS. 553. Oregon State Historical Society Library, Portland.

Church, Frank. Papers. Ser. 1.1, box 68, f.3, f.11, f.15, and f. 17. Albertsons Library, Boise State University, Boise, Idaho.

Dobbin, Jay. Rancher. Files. Wallowa County Museum, Joseph, Oreg.

Evenson, Catherine Dobbin. "Jay H. Dobbin: Livestock Rancher of Wallowa County, Oregon." American Sheep Producers Council. Denver, 1981. Wallowa County Museum, Joseph, Oreg.

Gray, Elliott. "Yesterday and the Day Before." Pioneer Reminiscences file. Carnegie Library, Lewiston, Idaho.

Guernsey, O. E. Guernsey, Dubuque, Iowa, to Senator William B. Allison, Dec. 10, 1902, no. 103, box 1044, 44294/10. Penrose Library, Whitman College, Walla Walla, Washington.

Harts, William H. Corps of Engineers, Portland, to Brig. Gen. John M. Wilson, Chief of Engineers, Washington D.C., Aug. 1, 1899. no. 103, file 3041013. Penrose Library, Whitman College, Walla Walla, Wash.

Hosford, Leonard. "History of Stern and Sidewheel Steamboats on the Columbia, Snake, and Willamette Rivers in Oregon, Washington, Idaho, and Montana in the United States and British Columbia Canada from 1835 through 1947." MSS 2195B, V. 5. Oregon Historical Society, Portland.

ISHS (Idaho State Historical Society). Reference series, no. 116. Site report: Seven Devils. Revised Dec. 1981.

Idaho State Historic Preservation Office. Historic Site Inventory, Feb. 1979.

Inland Empire Waterways Association. Penrose Library, Whitman College, Walla Walla, Wash. "Appaloosa Dam File," VI no. 3, VII no. 3, VIII no. 3.

———. Columbia Snake River Report, Working Papers, 1936.

———. "Freight Rate Reduction, 1961–1965" and "Navigation," VF=VI, drawer no. 3.

———. "Henry M. Jackson File," VF=V, drawer no. 4.

———. "Navigation Hearings, 1944," VF=VI, drawer no. 2.

———. "Warren G. Magnuson File," VF=V, drawer no. 4.

Inland Navigation Company. "Application for Certificate of Public Convenience and Necessity for Operation of the Willamette, Columbia and Snake Rivers." Dec. 1935. VF=I, drawer no. 4. Penrose Library, Whitman College, Walla Walla, Wash.

Jacks, Frank O. Typescript, 13 pages. "Special to Pete, Frank Jacks, 16 Sept., 1973. Clarkston, Wash." Author's personal papers.

"Jordan-Church Moratorium. The Future of Idaho's Water." Hells Canyon Dam, vertical file, Idaho State Historical Society Library, Boise, Idaho.

Libby, W. M. To George Turner, U.S. Senator from Spokane, Washington. File no. 44292, entry 103. Penrose Library, Whitman College, Walla Walla Wash.

McFarland, Sandi. "Flora Found in the Hells Canyon National Recreation Area: Prepared for Hells Canyon Interpretive Workshop, April 1999." Lewis-Clark State College Library, Lewiston, Idaho.

McGrady Family. Papers. Scrapbooks with newspaper clippings, magazine articles, and other miscellaneous information. Author's personal papers.

Miller, James T. Papers. President Eureka Mining Company. Nez Perce County Historical Society, Lewiston, Idaho.

Mote, Daniel Webster. Canyon resident/miner. Personal diary, 1903–41. Transcribed by Grace Bartlett. Wallowa County Historical Society Museum, Joseph, Oreg.

Neuberger, Richard. Papers. AX78. Folders: "Hells Canyon General," box 23; "Power Middle Snake" and "Power Hells Canyon," box 24. Knight Library, University of Oregon, Eugene.

Rankin, William F. Canyon resident/miner. "Some Notes on the Life of 'Billy' Rankin ... Including an Interview by Bob Wiggins at Grangeville, Idaho, 1967." In Gerald Tucker, personal papers, Tucker file, no. 6, "Wallowa County History," U.S. Forest Service, Baker, Oreg.

Sharp, Don. "Charming the Snake." *Motorboat*, Apr. 1979.

Shevlin, Minnie. "Eighty Years in Wallowa County." *Wallowa County (Oreg.) Chieftain*, n.d. Wallowa County Museum, Joseph, Oreg.

Stewart, Earl King. "Steamboats on the Columbia—The Pioneer Period, 1850–1869." Ph.D. diss., Willamette University, 1948. MSS. 1590. Oregon Historical Society, Portland.

Swank, Gladys. "Reflections of Jim Chapman and Roy Favor along the Snake River." Typescript, 18 pages, ca. 1938. Snake River files, Carnegie Library, Lewiston, Idaho.

Tucker, Gerald. Forest Service ranger. Personal papers. Tucker file, no. 60. "Wallowa County History." U.S. Forest Service, Baker, Oreg.

———. File no. 476. U.S. Forest Service, Baker, Oreg.

Van Pool, Harold. "Harold Van Pool Ranch History—Quarter Circle V." Typescript, 7 pages, undated (ca. late 1980s). In the author's possession.

Yokum, Carmen. "A Child's Trip Out of Snake River Canyon, 1922." MS for a talk given May 1983 at Enterprise, Oreg. In Grace Bartlett papers. Used by permission of Ann Hayes and Tom Butterfield, Joseph, Oreg.

Interviews and Lectures

Allen, George. Grandson of canyon miner and explorer. Interview by author, tape recording and transcription, Lewiston, Idaho, Feb. 22, 1996. Idaho Oral History Center, Boise.

Barker, John A. K. Snake River outfitter. Interview by author, tape recording, Lewiston, Idaho, Sept. 14, 1995. Idaho Oral History Center, Boise.

Barton, Ace. Canyon resident. Interview by author, video recording and transcription, Riggins, Idaho, spring 2003. Wallowa Whitman National Forest, Enterprise, Oreg., and Idaho Oral History Center, Boise.

———. Interview by Bruce Womack, tape recording and transcription, Pittsburg Landing, Idaho, Apr. 1, 1982.

Wallowa Whitman National Forest, Enterprise, Oreg., and Idaho Oral History Center, Boise.

Beard, Ralph. Ranch hand. Interview by author, tape recording and transcription, Asotin, Wash., June 26, 1996. Wallowa Whitman National Forest, Enterprise, Oreg., and Idaho Oral History Center, Boise.

Bingham, Richard T. Botanist. "Plant Communities of Snake and Salmon River Country." Lecture, Hells Canyon National Recreation Area, Lewiston, Idaho, Sept. 2, 1987.

Boreson, Keo. Archeologist. "Rock Art of Hells Canyon." Lecture and interview, Hells Canyon National Recreation Area, Lewiston, Idaho, summer 1989. In the author's possession.

Brown, Dennis. Grandson of canyon rancher/miner. Interview by author, video recording and transcription, Asotin, Wash., Apr. 23, 2003. Wallowa Whitman National Forest, Enterprise, Oreg., and Idaho Oral History Center, Boise.

Chadwick, Marjorie Wilson. Canyon resident. Interview by author, tape recording and transcription, Boise, Idaho, June 13, 1995. Idaho Oral History Center, Boise.

Dahlquist, Andrew. Sheep rancher. Interview by author, transcription, Lewiston, Idaho, Aug. 2004. In author's possession.

Earl, Elmer. Resident/river pilot. Interview by Bruce Womack, tape recording and transcription, Snake River, June 7, 1981. Wallowa Whitman National Forest, Enterprise, Oreg.

Earl, Jess. Ranch hand/ranger. Interview by author, tape recording, Clarkston, Wash., Feb. 3, 1995. In the author's possession.

———. Interviewer not identified, handwritten transcript, Apr. 10, 1982, Imnaha, Oreg. Wallowa Whitman National Forest, Enterprise, Oreg.

Elson, Arvid. Forest Service employee. Interview by author, tape recording, Snake River Road, Washington, Sept. 14, 1995. Wallowa Whitman National Forest, Enterprise, Oreg., and Idaho Oral History Center, Boise.

Grote, Theo "Ted." Canyon pilot. Interview by Christi Shaw for the author, tape recording and transcription, Enterprise, Oreg. July 12, 1995. Idaho Oral History Center, Boise.

Grunig, Catherine "Kitty." Mining community resident. Interview by author, tape recording and transcription, Boise, Idaho, June 14, 1995. Idaho Oral History Center, Boise.

Harris, Katherine Wonn. Canyon teacher. Interview by Aldyth Logan, tape recording and transcription, Lebanon, Oreg., ca. 1975. Wallowa Whitman National Forest, Enterprise, Oreg., and Idaho Oral History Center, Boise.

Henderson, Horace. Rancher. Interview by author, tape recording and transcription, Grangeville, Idaho, Jan. 16, 1995. Idaho Oral History Center, Boise.

Hibbs, Esther. Canyon rancher/resident. Interview by author, video recording and transcription, Hermiston, Oreg., autumn 2003, Wallowa Whitman National Forest, Enterprise, Oreg., and Idaho Oral History Center, Boise.

Himmelwright, Fred. Canyon miner. Interview by Grace Bartlett, transcription, Joseph, Oreg., Dec. 5, 1975. Grace Bartlett personal papers. Used by permission of Ann Hayes and Tom Butterfield, Joseph, Oreg.

Hollandsworth, Polly. Rancher. Interview by author, tape recording and transcription, Hollandsworth Ranch, Joseph Plains, Idaho, Aug. 2, 1995. Idaho Oral History Center, Boise.

Horrocks, Sharon. *See* Wing, Sharon Horrocks.

Johnson, Greg. Canyon rancher/resident. Interview by author, video recording and transcription, Enterprise, Oreg., Oct. 23, 2003. In the author's possession.

Johnson, Hazel. Canyon rancher/resident. Interview by Bruce Womack, tape recording and transcription, Enterprise, Oreg., Mar. 8, 1992. Wallowa Whitman National Forest, Enterprise, Oreg.

Jordan, Len, and Grace Jordan. Canyon ranchers/residents. Interview by Bob Nisbet, tape recording and transcription, Boise, Idaho, July 1, 1980. W15.1 File=SnakeRR3.doc, SO Office, Wallowa Whitman National Forest, Baker, Oreg., and Idaho Oral History Center, Boise.

McCarthy, Patrick. "Martin Hibbs Murder." Lecture, Idaho History Conference, Lewis-Clark State College, Lewiston, Idaho, Apr. 11, 1981.

McGrady, Bob. Son of mailboat captain. Interview by Patricia Keith, video recording, Spokane, Wash. Apr. 2005. In the author's possession.

McNabb, Oliver. Mailboat captain. Interview by author, tape recording, Clarkston, Wash., May 16, 1985. In author's possession.

———. Interview by author, video recording, Clarkston, Wash., July 18, 2003. Wallowa Whitman National Forest, Enterprise, Oreg., and Idaho Oral History Center, Boise.

Nyberg, Helen Brown. Rogersburg resident. Interview by Dorothy Cook, tape recording and transcription, ca. 1990, Asotin, Wash. Asotin County Historical Society Museum, Asotin, Wash.

Rivers, Dick. Canyon mailboat captain. Interview by author, transcription, Lewiston, Idaho, Sept. 8, 1995. In author's possession.

Seibly, Walter W. Canyon doctor. Interview by author, video recording, Clarkston, Wash., summer 2004. Idaho Oral History Center, Boise.

Shirley, Violet. Canyon resident. Interview by Patricia Keith, video recording and transcription, Salem, Oreg., Nov. 6, 2003. Wallowa Whitman National Forest, Enterprise, Oreg., and Idaho Oral History Center, Boise.

Stangle, Bud. Canyon pilot. Interview by Christi Shaw for the author, tape recording and transcription, Enterprise, Oreg., Oct. 13, 1995. Idaho Oral History Center, Boise.

Stone, Winifred "Janie." Interview by author, tape recording and transcription, Lewiston, Idaho, July 26, 1995. Idaho Oral History Center, Boise.

Tippett, Doug. Canyon rancher. Interview by author, tape recording and transcription, Tippett Ranch, Joseph, Oreg., June 21, 1996. Idaho Oral History Center, Boise.

Vallier, Tracy. Geologist. "Geology of Hells Canyon." Lecture and interview, transcription, Hells Canyon National Recreation Area, Lewiston, Idaho, summer 1989. In author's possession.

Van Pool, Erma. Wife of canyon rancher. Interview by the author, transcription, Lewiston, Idaho, summer 1995. In author's possession.

Walker, Max. Canyon ranch hand. Interview by Bruce Womack, tape recording and transcription, Oct. 1980. Wallowa Whitman National Forest, Enterprise, Oreg., and Idaho Oral History Center, Boise.

Wiggins, Robert. Amateur historian and teller of tall tales. Interview by author, Clarkston, Wash., July 1995. In author's possession.

Wilson, Murrielle McGaffee, and Jimmy Wilson. Canyon residents. Interview by Joyce Houssden and Sue Von Allen, tape recording, Aug. 1981. Wallowa Whitman National Forest, Enterprise, Oreg., and Idaho Oral History Center, Boise.

Wilson, William. Son of Murrielle. Interview by author, Boise, Idaho, June 1995. In author's possession.

Wing, Sharon Horrocks. Ranch hand. Interview by author, tape recording and transcription, Clarkston, Wash., Jan. 4, 1995. Idaho Oral History Center, Boise.

Womack, Bruce. HCNRA archeologist. "Archeology of Hells Canyon." Lecture and interview, Hells Canyon National Recreation Area, Lewiston, Idaho, summer 1989. In author's possession.

Yokum, Carmen. Canyon resident. Interview by author, video recording, Eugene, Oreg., May 6, 2004. In author's possession.

Secondary Sources

Advent, John. "North America's Deepest Gorge." *Pacific Pathways*, Feb. 1947.

Allen, John. Hells Canyon Series. "Hells Canyon Lays Bare Rocky History of Region," Sept. 1, 1984, and Sept. 13, 1984; "Early Wanderings of Snake River Lost amid Basalt Floods," Sept. 20, 1984; "Snake River Follows Fault Lines along Part of Course," Sept. 9, 1984. *Portland Oregonian*.

Arnold, R. Ross. *Indian Wars of Idaho*. Caldwell, Idaho: Caxton Printers, 1932.

Ashworth, William. *Hells Canyon: The Deepest Gorge on Earth*. New York: Hawthorne Books, 1977.

Atkin, W. T. "Snake River Fur Trade, 1816–1824." *Oregon Historical Quarterly* 35, no. 4 (Dec. 1934): 295–312.
Bailey, Robert G. *Hells Canyon: Seeing Idaho through a Scrap Book.* Lewiston, Idaho: Privately published, 1943.
Barklow, Irene Locke. *School Days in the Wallowas: A History of the 91 Schools and Communities, Past and Present, of Wallowa County, Oregon.* N.p.: Privately published, 1992.
Barry, J. Neilson. "The First Born on the Oregon Trail." *Oregon Historical Quarterly* 12, no. 2 (June 1911): 164–70.
———. "The First Explorers of the Columbia and Snake Rivers." *Geographical Review* 22 (1932).
———. "The Trail of the Astorians." *Oregon Historical Quarterly* 13, no. 3 (Sept. 1912): 227–39.
Bartlett, Grace. *From the Wallowas.* Enterprise, Oreg.: Pika Press, 1992.
———. *The Wallowa Country, 1867–1877.* Fairfield, Wash.: Ye Galleon Press, 1984.
Beal, Merrill, and Merle Wells. *History of Idaho.* Vol. 1. New York: Lewis Publishing, 1959.
Bingham, Richard T., and Douglas M. Henderson. *Guide to the Common Plants of Hells Canyon.* U.S. Forest Service, Northern Region, Hells Canyon National Recreation Area: U.S. Department of Agriculture, n. d.
Bishop, Ellen Morris. *In Search of Ancient Oregon: A Geological and Natural History.* Portland, Oreg.: Timber Press, 2003.
Cannon, Miles. "The Snake River in History." *Oregon Historical Quarterly,* Mar. 1919.
Carrey, Johnny, Cort Conley, and Ace Barton. *Snake River of Hells Canyon.* Cambridge, Idaho: Backeddy Books, 1979.
Clegg, Edith. *Against the Current in 1939.* Cambridge, Idaho: Cambridge Museum, 1995.
———. "Rattlesnakes and Rapids: A Woman's Journey against the Currents in 1939." Ed. Cort Conley. *Idaho Yesterdays* 28, no. 3 (Fall 1984): 10–28. http://www.idahoptv.org/outdoors/shows/recollection/Rattlesnakes.html.
Clough, Bob. "No Mail-Order Bride for the Snake River Hermit." *Good Old Days* 20, no. 5 (November 1983): 7–9.
Cochnauer, Timothy G., James R. Lukens, and Fred E. Partridge. "Status of White Sturgeon, *Acipenser trasmontanus,* in Idaho." Lewiston: Idaho Department of Fish and Game, 1985.
Cole, Heidi Bigler. *A Wild Cowboy.* Cambridge, Idaho: Rocky Comfort Press, 1992.
Coleman, Edith. "River Route." *Idaho Farmer,* July 17, 1941.
Corless, Hank. *The Weiser Indians: Shoshoni Peacemakers.* Salt Lake City: University of Utah Press, 1990.
Cox, Ross. *Adventures on the Columbia River.* Ed. Edgar Stewart and Jane R. Stewart. Norman: University of Oklahoma Press, 1957.
Day, Terence. "A Postwoman Packed a Pistol as She Carried Mail to Mines." *Lewiston (Idaho) Morning Tribune,* May 30, 1973.
d'Easum, Dick. "Idaho Out-of-Doors." *Boise Statesman,* June 19, 1944.
Densley, Lillian Cummings. *Saints, Sinners, and Snake River Secrets.* Baker City, Oreg.: Privately published, 1987.
Douglas, Jesse S. "Matthews' Adventures on the Columbia." *Oregon Historical Quarterly* 40 (Mar.–Dec. 1939): 105–48.
Dudgeon, Muriel. *John Flynn's Stories of Mineral.* Fruitland, Idaho: Strange Printing Svc., 1966.
Earl, Elmer. *Hells Canyon: A River Trip.* Lewiston, Idaho: Privately published, 1990.
Elliott, T. C., ed. "Journal of Alexander Ross' Snake Country Expedition, 1824." *Oregon Historical Quarterly* 14, no. 4 (Dec. 1913): 366–88.
Elsensohn, M. Alfreda. *Idaho Chinese Lore.* Cottonwood, Idaho: Corporation of Benedictine Sisters, 1970.
———. *Pioneer Days in Idaho County.* Vol. 1. Caldwell, Idaho: Caxton Printers, 1947.
———. *Pioneer Days in Idaho County.* Vol. 2. Caldwell, Idaho: Caxton Printers, 1951.
Eureka Mining, Smelting and Power Company v. H. G. Johnson, G. A. Nehrhood, C. O. Howard, M. S. Howard, William J. Wilkinson, J. T. Miller, H. M. Peterson, L. D. Lively, J. E. Hubbell, and O. E. Guernsey. Case no. 701. Washington. Superior Court for Asotin County, 1909.
Eureka Mining, Smelting and Power Company v. Lewiston Navigation Company. Idaho, District Court for Nez Perce County, 1907.

Eureka Mining, Smelting and Power Company v. L. D. Lively. Case no. 692. Washington. Superior Court for Asotin County, 1908.

Fahey, John. *The Ballyhoo Bonanza: Charles Sweeny and the Idaho Mines.* Seattle: University of Washington Press, 1971.

Findley, Alexander B., and Sarah Jane Findley. "Memories of . . ." Series. *Wallowa County (Oreg.) Chieftain,* Mar. 12, 1959–Jan. 28, 1960.

Fitzgerald, Emily McCorkle. *An Army Doctor's Wife on the Frontier: The Letters of Emily McCorkle.* Ed. Abe Laufe. Pittsburg: University of Pittsburg Press, 1962.

Foss, Sam Walter. "The House by the Side of the Road." *One Hundred and One Famous Poems.* Ed. Roy C. Cook. Chicago: Cable, 1928.

Freeman, Otis. W. "The Snake River Canyon." *Geographical Review,* Oct. 1938.

———. "Snake River Canyon above Lewiston Is Narrowest and Deepest Gash in Continent." *Lewiston (Idaho) Morning Tribune,* Oct. 23, 1938.

Ganham, Erwin D. "New Frontiers of the West." *Christian Science Monitor,* Sept. 8, 1949.

Gay, E. Jane Gay. *With the Nez Perces: Alice Fletcher in the Field, 1889–92.* Lincoln: University of Nebraska Press, 1981.

Gibbs, Rafe. "Cattle Ranching in a Canyon." *Popular Mechanics,* Mar. 1953.

Glassley, Ray Hoard. *The Pacific Northwest Indian Wars.* Portland Oreg.: Binfords and Mort, 1953

Golden Age: Journal of the Nez Perce County Historical Society. Lewiston, Idaho, 1862–64.

Gurcke, Karl, Robert Lee Sappington, Diana Rigg, and Ruthann Knudson. "Archeological Reconnaissance of the Shoreline of the Lower Granite Dam Reservoir, Washington and Idaho." University of Idaho Anthropological Research Manuscript Series, no. 55. University of Idaho: Laboratory of Anthropology, 1979.

Haines, F. D. "McKenzie's Winter Camp, 1812–1813." *Oregon Historical Quarterly* 37 (Mar.–Dec. 1936): 329–33.

Harris, Katherine Wonn. *Topping Out.* Boise, Idaho: Aldyth H. Logan, 1972.

History of Idaho Territory Showing Its Resources and Advantages. San Francisco: W. W. Elliott, 1884.

History of Wallowa County, Oregon. Joseph, Oreg.: Wallowa County Museum Board, 1983.

Holm, Don. "Shortage of Water Delays Excursion Trip up Grand Canyon of Snake." *Portland Oregonian,* May 21, 1968.

Hooper, Peter R. "The Columbia River Basalts." *Science* 215 (Mar. 19, 1982): 4539.

Hooper, Peter R. ,W. D. Kleck, C. R. Knowles, S. P. Reidel, R. L. Thiessen. "Imnaha Basalt, Columbia River Basalt Group." *Journal of Petrology* 25, no. 2 (1984): 473–500.

Howard, Oliver O. *Nez Perce Joseph, An Account of His Ancestors.* New York: Da Capo Press, 1972.

———. "Outbreak of the Paiute and Bannock War." *Overland Monthly* 5, no. 9 (1887).

Idaho Lore, prepared by Federal Writers Project of the WPA. Vardis Fisher, state director. Caldwell, Idaho: Caxton Printers, 1939.

Illustrated History of North Idaho. N.p: Western Historical Publishing, 1903.

Illustrated History of Union and Wallowa Counties. N.p., 1902.

Irving, Washington. *Astoria.* 1911. Portland, Oreg.: Binfords and Mort, 1967.

———. *The Complete Works of Washington Irving: The Adventures of Captain Bonneville.* Vol. 16. Ed. Robert A. Rees and Alan Sandy. Boston: Twayne, 1977.

James, Caroline. *Nez Perce Women in Transition, 1877–1990.* Moscow: University of Idaho Press, 1996.

Jordan, Grace. *Home Below Hells Canyon.* Lincoln: University of Nebraska Press, 1957.

Josephy, Alvin P, Jr. *The Nez Perce Indians and the Opening of the Northwest.* New Haven: Yale University Press, 1965.

The Journals of the Lewis and Clark Expedition. Vol. 7, *March 23 to June 9, 1806.* Ed. Gary Moulton. Lincoln: University of Nebraska Press, 1991.

———. Vol. 9, *The Journals of John Ordway, May 14, 1804–September 23, 1806, and Charles Floyd, May 14–August 18, 1804.* Ed. Gary Moulton. Lincoln: University of Nebraska Press, 1995.

---. Vol. 10, *The Journal of Patrick Gass, May 14, 1804–September 23, 1806*. Ed. Gary Moulton. Lincoln: University of Nebraska Press, 1996.

Leopold, Aldo. "The Land Ethic." In *A Sand Country Almanac*. New York: Oxford University Press, 1968.

Keyser, James D. *Indian Rock Art of the Columbia Plateau*. Seattle: University of Washington Press, 1992.

Kuykendall, Elgin Victor. *Historic Glimpses of Asotin County, Washington*. Clarkston, Wash.: Clarkston *Herald*, 1954.

---. *History of Garfield County*. 1947; Fairfield, Wash.: Ye Galleon Press, 1984.

Landeen, Dan, and Allen Pinkham. *Salmon and His People: Fish and Fishing in Nez Perce Culture*. Lewiston, Idaho: Confluence Press, 1999.

Lewis and Dryden's Marine History of the Pacific Northwest. Ed. E. W. Wright. Portland, Oreg.: Lewis and Dryden Printing, 1895.

Libbey, F. W. "Snake River Passage." State Department of Geology and Mineral Industries. *Ore.-Bin* 10, no. 1 (Jan. 1948).

---. "Some Mineral Deposits in the Area Surrounding the Junction of the Snake and Imnaha Rivers in Oregon." GMI Short Paper, no. 11. State of Oregon Department of Geology and Mineral Industries, Portland, 1943.

Lindsay, Winifred. "The Seven Devils." *Idaho Yesterdays* 14, no. 2 (Summer 1970): 12–15.

L. D. Lively v. Eureka Mining, Smelting and Power Company. Case no. 923. Washington. Superior Court for Asotin County, 1911.

Lorenzo D. Lively v. Eureka Mining, Smelting and Power Co. et al. Case no. 432. Washington. Superior Court for Asotin County, 1904.

Lockley, Fred. *History of the Columbia River Valley*. Chicago: S. J. Clarke, 1928.

---. "Reminiscences of Captain William P. Gray." *Oregon Historical Quarterly* 14, no. 4 (Dec. 1913): 321–54.

---. *Voices of the Oregon Territory: Conversations with Bullwhackers . . . and Near-Poets, and All Sorts of Conditions of Men*. Eugene, Oreg.: Rainy Day Press, 1983.

Lyman, W. D. *History of Old Walla Walla County: Walla Walla, Columbia, Garfield, and Asotin Counties*. Vol. 1. Chicago: S. J. Clarke, 1918.

McCurdy, H. W. *Marine History of the Pacific Northwest*. Seattle: Superior, 1966.

McWhorter, Lucullus Virgil. *Yellow Wolf: His Own Story*. 1940; Caldwell, Idaho: Caxton Printers, 1986.

Marshall, Alan G. "Nez Perce Social Groups: An Ecological Perspective." Ph.D. diss., Washington State University, Pullman, 1979.

Miller, James D. "Early Oregon Scenes: A Pioneer Narrative." Pt. 3, "River Navigation: 1861–1881." *Oregon Historical Quarterly* 31, no. 3 (1930): 275–84.

Mills, Randall. *Stern-Wheelers Up the Columbia*. Lincoln: University of Nebraska Press, 1947.

Murdoch, Angus. *Boom Copper: The Story of the First U.S. Mining Boom*. Calumet, Mich.: Drier and Koepel, 1964.

Nelson, Judy. "The Final Journey Home: Chinese Burial in Spokane." *Pacific Northwest Forum* 6 (Winter–Spring 1993): 30–76. http://www.narhist.ewu.edu/pnf/articles/nelson.html.

Neuberger, Richard. "Nation's Deepest Chasm." *New York Times*, July 1940.

---. "How to Visit the Snake Canyon." *Sunday Oregonian*, June 1941.

---. "Seeing the Northwest." *Harper's Magazine*, May 1942.

---. "The Deepest Canyon on the Continent." *Travel Magazine*, Sept. 1942.

---. "The Mail Carrier of Hells Canyon." *Saturday Evening Post*, Oct. 1942.

---. "They've Gone Wild—and Love It." *Saturday Evening Post*, July 19, 1947.

Nez Perce Tribe. *Treaties: Nez Perce Perspectives*. Lapwai, Idaho: Nez Perce Tribe, 2003.

Orchard, Vance. "Just Rambling." *Walla Walla (Wash.) Union Bulletin*, Apr. 4, 1965.

Pacific Northwest Power Company. "General Historical Information of the Snake River Country." July 1966. Typescript, 5 pages, loaned to the author by Dick Rivers.

Parker, John. "A Fast Lady from the Upper Snake." *Pacific Motor Boat*, Dec. 1940.

Peebles, John J. "The Return of Lewis and Clark." *Idaho Yesterdays* (Summer 1966): 10.

Petersen, Keith. *River of Life, Channel of Death: Fish and Dams on the Lower Snake*. Lewiston, Idaho: Confluence Press, 1995.

Petri, Alice. *Copper Lodge in Hells Canyon: A Memoir*. Idaho City, Idaho: Cold Hill Press, 1991.

Platt, John. *Whispers of Old Genesee and Echoes of the Salmon River*. N.p.: Privately published, 1959.

Platt, Kenneth B. *Salmon River Saga*. Fairfield, Wash.: Ye Galleon Press, 1978.

Powell, Barbara. *Citizens of North Idaho: Newspaper Abstracts, 1862–1875*. Medical Lake, Wash.: Privately published, 1986.

"Power Groups Back Appaloosa Dam." *Boise Idaho Daily Statesman*, Nov. 9, 1968.

Rautenstrauch, Bill. "A Skeleton in the Closet." *Wallowa County (Oreg.) Chieftain*, Feb. 16, 1995.

Reddy, Sheila D. "The Empty Land: The Search for the Nez Perce on the Payette National Forest." Heritage Program, Payette National Forest. U.S. Department of Agriculture, Intermountain Region, 1993.

———. "Reluctant Fortune: The Story of the Seven Devils." Heritage Program, Payette National Forest, U.S. Department of Agriculture, Intermountain Region, Apr. 1996.

Reed, Simeon G. Report, Oregon Steam Navigation Company, Sept. 4, 1866. Quoted in "Steamboat Down the Snake." *Idaho Yesterdays* 5 (1961–62): 5.

Reid, Ken. State Archeologist, Idaho State Historical Society Preservation Office. "A Working Draft of a Timeline for the Hells Canyon Education Tour," 2004. In the author's possession.

Richie, Deborah Waite. "Troubled Waters, Threatened Forests: Hells Canyon National Recreation Area." Master's thesis, University of Montana, 1988.

Robertson, James. *American Myth, American Reality*. New York: Hill and Wang, 1980.

Ronda, James P. *Astoria and Empire*. Lincoln: University of Nebraska Press, 1990.

———. *Lewis and Clark among the Indians*. Lincoln: University of Nebraska Press, 1984.

Ross, Alexander. *The Fur Hunters of the Far West*. Ed. Kenneth A. Spaulding. Norman: University of Oklahoma Press, 1956.

———. *Adventures of the First Settlers on the Oregon or Columbia River, 1810–1813*. Lincoln: University of Nebraska Press, 1986.

Ruby, Robert H., and John A. Brown. *Indians of the Pacific Northwest*. Norman: University of Oklahoma Press, 1956.

Schwantes, Carlos A. *In Mountain Shadows: A History of Idaho*. Lincoln: University of Nebraska Press, 1991.

———. *A Long Day's Journey: The Steamboat and Stagecoach Era in the Northern West*. Seattle: University of Washington Press, 1999.

———. *The Pacific Northwest: An Interpretive History*. Lincoln: University of Nebraska Press, 1989.

Seton, Alfred. *Astorian Adventure: The Journal of Alfred Seton, 1811–1815*. Ed. Robert R. Jones. New York: Fordham University Press, 1993.

Shawley, Steve. "Nez Perce Trails." University of Idaho Anthropological Research Manuscript Series, no. 44. Moscow: University of Idaho, 1977.

Shreve, George. "Remember That Daring Bert Zimmerly." *Lewiston (Idaho) Morning Tribune*, Dec. 26, 1979.

Simon-Smolinski, Carole. *Journal, 1862: Timothy Nolan's 1862 Account of His Riverboat and Overland Journey to the Salmon River Mines, Washington Territory*. Clarkston, Wash.: Northwest Historical Consultants, 1983.

———. "Lewiston's Greatest Day—Or Was It?" *Golden Age: Journal of the Nez Perce County Historical Society* 12, no. 1 (Spring–Summer 1992): 8–15.

———. "Of Dreams and Schemes." *Lewiston (Idaho) Morning Tribune*, Oct. 31, 1999.

Simon-Smolinski, Carole, and Patricia Keith. *Journey to Eureka: A Hells Canyon Story*. VHS and DVD. Lewiston, Idaho: Lithophragma Production, 2000.

Skow, John. "Farewell to Hells Canyon." *Saturday Evening Post*, July 1, 1967, 76–83.

Smith, Bridget F. "Celebrated Geologist Visits Blue Mountains." *Historical Gazette* 1, no. 1 (1900). http://www.aracnet.com/~histgaz/hgv1n1.htm.

Smith, Florence Winniford. *Snake River Daze.* N.p.: Privately published, 1985.

Smith, O. J. "Hells Canyon, One of the World's Deepest Gorges, Has Face Lifted." *Twin Falls (Idaho) Times News,* July 2, 1967.

Stacy, Susan M. *Legacy of Light: A History of the Idaho Power Company.* Boise, Idaho: Idaho Power, 1991.

Sterling, Bonnie. *The Sterling Years.* Halfway, Oreg.: Hells Canyon, 1995.

Stratton, David H. "Hells Canyon: The Missing Link in Pacific Northwest Regionalism." *Idaho Yesterdays* 28 (Fall 1984): 3.

———. "The Snake River Massacre of Chinese Miners, 1887." In *A Taste of the West: Essays in Honor of Robert G. Athearn,* ed. Duane A. Smith. Boulder, Colo.: Pruett, 1983.

Thompson, A. W. "New Light on Donald Mackenzie's Post on the Clearwater, 1812–1813." *Idaho Yesterdays* 26, no. 18 (Winter 1974): 3.

Tucker, Gerald. "Massacre for Gold." *Old West* (Fall 1967): 26–48.

———. *The Story of Hells Canyon.* N.p.: Privately published, 1977.

Tussing, Annette. "Queen of the Canyon." *Spokesman Review Sunday Magazine,* June 9, 1968.

U.S. Army Corps of Engineers. "Columbia River and Tributaries Review Report." Interim report no. 3, Hells Canyon Dam Snake River, app. F. Portland, Oreg., Dec. 22, 1947.

———. *History of the Walla Walla District.* Vol. 1. Washington, D.C.: GPO, 1948.

———. "Improvement of the Upper Columbia and Snake Rivers, Oregon, and the Territories of Washington and Idaho," by Nathaniel Michler. Report of the Chief of Engineers. Y1676 44-1 ARCE, 1875, Pt. 2. GG3.

———. "Snake River Oregon, Washington, and Idaho." Report of the Chief of Engineers, 1931, pp. 1892–93.

U.S. Congress. House. "Improvements on Upper Columbia and Snake Rivers, Oregon and Washington Territories." House Executive Documents. Vol. 4, serial no. 1905. Engineers Report, app. KK. 46th Cong., 2nd sess., 1879–80.

———. "Examination of Snake River from Lewiston to Mouth of Salmon River." Report of Secretary of War. House Executive Document. Vol. 2, pt. 3, serial no. 2097. 47th Cong., 2nd sess.

———. Captain Thomas W. Symons, Corps of Engineers, letter, Dec. 21, 1891. Executive Documents. Serial no. 2953. 52nd Cong., 1st sess.

———. "Examination and Survey of Snake River, Idaho and Washington." House Documents, Document no. 127. Vol. 64. 56th Cong., 2nd sess.

———. "Report of Major W. C. Langfitt: Improvements of Rivers and Harbors in Western Oregon of Columbia River above Mouth of Willamette River, Including Snake River, Oregon and Washington." Includes letter to Brig. Gen. G. L. Gillespie, Sept. 9, 1902. House Documents. Vol. 12. War Department Reports. Vol. 11, serial no. 4638, 1903–4. 58th Cong., 2nd sess.

———. War Department. Engineers. No. 2, pt. 1. Report, "Upper Columbia and Snake Rivers, Oregon and Washington." House Document no. 4636. 58th Cong., ///2nd sess. Washington: GPO, 1904, 603.

———. Hearings before the Subcommittee on Irrigation and Reclamation of the Committee on Interior and Insular Affairs. H.R. 4719, H.R. 4730, H.R. 4739, and H.R. 4740 "To Authorize the Construction, Operation, and Maintenance of the Hells Canyon Dam on the Snake River between Idaho and Oregon, and for Related Purposes." July 11, 12, 13, and 15, 1955. Serial no. 14. 84th Cong., 1st sess. Washington: GPO, 1956.

U.S. Congress. Senate. Hearings. Senate Bill 2670. "To Authorize Channel Improvements on the Columbia and Snake Rivers between Celilo Falls, Oregon, and Pittsburg Landing, Idaho." Senate Committee on Irrigation and Reclamation. Congress 1932. VF6; Drawer no. 2. "Snake River Improvement Hearings." Penrose Library, Whitman College, Walla Walla, Wash.

———. "Examination of Snake River from Lewiston to the mouth of Salmon River, Idaho." Letter from Chief of Engineers of Feb. 16, 1882, and accompanying reports from Captain C. F. Powell, Corps of Engineers. Reports. Senate Executive Documents, no. 112. 1882. 47th Cong., 1st sess.

———. "Water Rights and Power Sites in Idaho." Senate Document no. 3370. Serial no. 5657. 61st Cong., 2nd sess.

———. Subcommittee on Irrigation and Reclamation of the Committee on Interior and Insular Affairs. Hearings on Senate Bill 1333. 84th Cong., 1st sess.

———. Hearings before the Subcommittee on Parks and Recreation of the Committee on Interior and Insular Affairs. S. 657, "A Bill to Designate the Hells Canyon National Forest Parklands Area, and for Other Purposes," and S. 2233, "A Bill to Establish the Hells Canyon National Recreation Area in the States of Idaho, Oregon, and Washington, and for Other purposes." Dec. 6, 1973, LaGrande, Oreg.; Dec. 14 and 15, Lewiston, Idaho. 93rd Cong., 1st sess. Washington: GPO, 1974.

———. Hearings before the Subcommittee on Public Lands, Reserved Water and Resource Conservation of the Committee on Energy and Natural Resources. S. B. 1803, "A Bill to Designate Certain Lands in and Near the Hells Canyon National Recreation Area as Additions to the Hells Canyon Wilderness, Oregon, and for Other Purposes." 99th Congress, 2nd sess. Washington: GPO, 1987.

U.S. Department of Agriculture. Hells Canyon Management Plan, 1989, app. B, "History."

———. *Final Environmental Impact Statement: Wild and Scenic Snake River Recreation Management Plan.* Forest Service, Pacific Northwest Region, Wallowa-Whitman National Forest, Oreg. 1994.

———. *Recreation Management Plan for the Wild and Scenic Snake River: County of Baker in Oregon, Counties of Nez Perce, Idaho, and Adams in Idaho.* Forest Service, Wallowa-Whitman National Forest, Oreg., Nez Perce and Payette National Forests, Idaho. Hells Canyon National Recreation Area. Oct. 1994.

———. *Wild and Scenic Snake River: Recreation Management Plan.* Forest Service., Jan. 1999.

Vallier, Tracy. *Exotic Terrane.* VHS. Oley, Pa. Bullfrog Films, 1991.

———. *Islands and Rapids: A Geologic Story of Hells Canyon.* Lewiston, Idaho: Confluence Press, 1998.

"Waldemar Lindgren of the U.S. Geological Survey." Ed. Keith Whittle. *Historical Gazette.* http://www.aracnet.com/~histgaz/lindgn.htm.

Walker, Dan. *River and Rock.* VHS and DVD. Lewiston, Idaho: Dan Walker Productions, 2004.

Weatherly, Robert P. *The Best of Jawbone Flat Gazette.* Vol. 1. Clarkston, Wash.: Valley American, 1984.

———. *The Best of Jawbone Flat Gazette.* Vol. 2. Asotin, Wash.: Privately published, 1986.

———. *The Best of Jawbone Flat Gazette.* Vol. 3. Asotin, Wash.: Privately published, 1987.

———. "The Jidge Tippett." *Washington Cattleman's Association,* Nov. 1975.

Wegars, Priscilla. "Rice Bowls in the Diggings: Chinese Miners Near Granite, Oregon." Joint Western Conference of the Association of Asian Studies, Lewis-Clark State College, Lewiston, Idaho. Sept. 1996.

Willingham, William F. *Army Engineers and the Development of Oregon: A History of the Portland District U.S. Army Corps of Engineers.* Washington, D.C.: GPO, 1983.

Wilson, Doris. *Life in Hells Canyon: A Private View.* Middleton, Idaho: CHJ, 2002.

Wilson, Murrielle McGaffee. *A Hells Canyon Romance.* Ed. Bill Wilson. Boise, Idaho: Crzma Press, 2004.

Wunder, John. "The Courts and the Chinese in Frontier Idaho." *Idaho Yesterdays* 25, no. 1 (Spring 1981): 23–32.

Youngdahl, Kristi M. *The Arams of Idaho: Pioneers of Camas Prairie and Joseph Plains.* Moscow: University of Idaho Press, 1995.

Zhu, Liping. *A Chinaman's Chance: The Chinese on the Rocky Mountain Mining Frontier.* Boulder: University Press of Colorado, 1997.

———. "No Need to Rush: The Chinese, Placer Mining, and the Western Environment." *Montana: The Magazine of Western History* 49, no. 3 (Autumn 1999): 43–57.

Index

Page numbers in italics refer to illustrations.

~: A :~

AAI mines, 108, 242, 339n31
Abbott, Bert, 113
Ackerman, George, 223–24
Adams, Charles Francis, 358n33
Adams, W. E. (Ed), 127, 131, 149
Agnew, James D., 327n4
Ainsworth, J. C., 54–55
Akins, John, 345n44
Alaska Legal Tender Mine, 90
Albert, Joe, 221, 354n26
Allen, C. F., 347n65
Allen, John E., 319n9
Allen, Levi, 50–51, 90–91, 97, 327n4–327n5
Allen, S. Eugene, 272
Almota, 66
Altman, Walter, 227
alum deposits, 10
American Falls, Idaho, 10, 326n35
American Mining Company, 91, 97
Ames, Johnny, 258
Amrich, Theresa, 100
Anaconda ledge, 107, 339n27–339n28
Anatone Flat, 329n53
Anderson, A., 104, 338n11
Anderson, Joe, 228
Anderson, John, 53, 55
Anderson, Peter, 53
Andrus, Cecil, 316
Ankeny, A. P., 51–52
Annie Faxon, 338n15
Appaloosa Dam, 315
Araigurana, Luciano "Lucy," 192, 359n17
Aram, James, 168, 188, 205
Aram, John, 188–89
Aram, Phoebe, 188
Aram, Tom, 168
Aram family, 187–88, 205; as ranchers, 168, 174, 182, *183*, 188–89
Arriaga, Jose, 192
Arrospide, Antonio, 290
Arrospide, Jess, 290

Ashworth, William, 3–4; on Bonneville, 326n38, 326n42; on mining, 80, 119–20, 333n28, 333n33
Asotin, 300
Asotin, Wash., 1, 2, 8–9, 48, 73, 242, 327n54, 337n9, 360n12; and boats, 129, 138, 155, 254–55, 259, 358n41; and rock art, 18–19; and Rogersburg, 251–54, 255
Asotin Creek, 22, 48, 66, 329n53
Asotin Dam, 310, 313, 316
Astor, John Jacob, 40, 325n26; expeditions of, 32–39, 323n28, 323n32–323n34, 323n39, 323n45, 324n2–324n3, 324n5, 324n13, 325n24–325n25; Irving Washington on, 32–34, 37, 323n31, 324n48
automatic writings, 143–45, 147, 347n1

~: B :~

Backus, Wayne, 288, 360n13
Bailey, George S., 339n28
Bailey, Robert G., 262; *Hells Canyon*, 1–2, 4
Baird, Ezra, 116, 328n22, 339n25, 341n69, 359n58
Baker, Chas., 104, 338n11
Baker, Dorsey S., 52
Baker, John, 304
Baker, John A. K., 363n47
Baker City, Ore., 92, 181, 335n5; and mining, 76, 79, 113
Baker Valley, 54
Bald Mountain, 183
Ballard, Fred, 226
Ballard's Landing, 92, 95, 98, 100
Bannock, 22, 24, 38, 43, 61, 325n27, 331n35; at Fort Hall reservation, 71, 74, 332n47; as scouts in Nez Perce War, 66, 330n18; and War of 1878, 61, 71–74, 331n37, 331n40
Barry, J. Neilson, 323n33, 323n45
Bartlett, Grace, 348n2
Barton, Ace, 162, 205, 291, 356n40; on dams, 317–18; on homesteading, 161; on irrigation, 209–10; on life in Hells Canyon, 214, 218, 223, 229, 236–37, 297; and mail service, 285; on mining, 116–18; on murder of Martin Hibbs, 227–28; on ranching, 171, 183, 188, 197–98; on Ruth Sapp, 272; on school, 241–43
Barton, Everett, 245
Barton, Guy, 116
Barton, Hazel. *See* Wilson, Hazel Barton
Barton, Lenora Hibbs, *117*, 162, *162*, 164–65, *184*, 205, 219, 227, 285; as rancher, 183, 188
Barton, M. E. (Elmer), 120, 342n5
Barton, Ralph, 116, *117*, 160, 162, *162*, 205, *217*; as rancher, 183–84
Barton, Ruth, *241*
Barton family, *118*, 232
Barton Heights, 326n42
Battle Creek, Ore., 103, 166, 321n40, 342n72; Bartons at, 116, *118*, 162, 205
Baughman, Ephraim, 52, 129, 131, 338n11
Baughman, Harry, 100, *130*, 300; and *Imnaha*, 128–37, 346n52, 346n57; and *Mountain Gem*, 138–39, 347n65; and navigability of Snake River, 98, 341n69
Baughman, R. L., 300
Bayard, Thomas F., 84

Bayh, Birch, 363n48
Bay Horse Rapids, 94
Beals, J. W., 335n56
Beamer, Wally, 8
Beard, Helen, 289
Beard, Ralph, 229, 232, 289; on ranching, 175, 177, 189, 192, 198
Bear Paw Mountains, 68
Beaver Dam, 181
Bee, F. A., 83
Bender, John, 304–5
Berg, Andrew, 265
Bernard, R. F., 71
Bernard Creek, 162, 165, *204*
Bernard Creek Rockshelter, 17, 320n4
Berry, John G., 333n37
Big Bar, 167, 210
Big Buffalo group, 338n19
Big Sheep area, 181
Bill's Creek, 165
Billy Bryan, 255, 258
Billy Creek, 50, 63, 105, 130, 338n14
Birch Creek, 339n27
Bitterroot Mountains, 8, 27, 30, 68–69
Blackfoot, 38, 324n6
Black Lake, 98–99
Blake, Isaac, 97–98
Blanco, Domingo, 193
Blue Jacket mine, 90, 97, 99
Blue Mountain Island Arc, 5, 7
Blue Mountains, 5, 9, 41, 54, 73, 328n14
Bluhn, G. H., 132, 345n41
Bly, Esther, 246
Boise Basin, 49, 52
Boise City, Idaho, 54, 328n25
Boise River, 32
Boise/Ruby City road, 54
Boles, Hazel, 230
Boles, Saxby, 230
Bonneville, Benjamin Louis Eulalie de: William Ashworth on, 326n38, 326n42; expedition of, 2–3, 43, 45–48, 326n35, 326n38, 326n41–326n43, 326n49; and Indians, 43, 45–48, 326n36, 326n45, 327n50, 327n54
Bonneville Dam, 22
Bonneville Flood, 10
Bonomi, Don, 279
Booke, Alphonso, 53
Boom Copper (Murdoch), 122
Booth, Luke, 335n56
Booth, W. R., 68–69

Boozer, Dolph, 251
Boozer, Frank, 251
Boozer, Fred, 251
Boston and Seven Devils Copper Company, 98–99
Bouguet, John "Posey," 227
Bowen, Henry, 352n11
Box Canyon, 3, 96
Bracken, Robert, 327n54
Branscom, Geo., 335n56
Brecky, A. R., 127
Brewrink, Edna, 261–62
Brewrink, James, 108, 224, 242, 253–54, 339n31; on Chinese miners, 81, 333n29; on ranching, 175, 193
Brewrink, William Pressly "Press," 108, 224, 258–65, 271–72
brigade system, 40–41
Brower, David, 312
Brown, A. P., 345n41
Brown, Birdie, 169
Brown, Charles, 252–55
Brown, Dennis, 169, 176, 221, 297
Brown, Frank, 161
Brown, Fred, 161
Brown, Helen, 161
Brown, Joseph Jay, 169
Brown, L. P., 66
Brown, Nellie, 252–54
Brown, Paul, 161, 236
Brownlee Dam, 8, 12, 50, 311–14, 357n24
Brownlee ferry, 332n47
Brownlee Sheep Company, *176*
Buchanan, Daniel E., 55, 57–58, 328n22, 329n33
Buckhorn Springs, *124–25*
Buffalo Eddy, Idaho, 17–18, *18–19*, 170, 320n17
Buffalo Horn, 71–72, 331n37
Buffalo Hump district, 103, 338n19
Buffalo Rock, 130, 300, 339n28
Bull Creek, 323n34
Bullock, Silas "Si," 160, *216*
Burst family, 168, 350n34
Butcher Boy mines, 107, 339n23
Butler Ore Company, 336n49

~: C :~

Cache Creek, 22, 144, 169, 300, 321n34; and ranchers, 176, 179, *180*, 351n24
Cactus Mountain, *123*, 127
Caldron Linn, 32, 35, 323n45
Caldwell, William, 335n56
California Steam Navigation Company (CSN), 54–55
Calvert School, 243

Camas Prairie, 105, 179; and Astor's expedition, 36, 323n45; and Indians, 63, 68, 71, 331n31; and Lewis and Clark expedition, 28, 30
Camp, George, 145, 149–50, 154
Campbell, L. H., 135–36, 345n41, 347n65
Campbell, Thomas W., 279
Campbell, William, 341n57
Canfield, J. T. (Tigh), 80–81, 84–86, 334n52
cannibal, 3
Cannon, Miles, 323n45
Canoe Camp, 330n24
"Canoe Encampment," 67
canyon lore, 3
canyon trails, 245–49
Captain John Creek, 170, 250, 339n27; and Astor's expedition, 36, 323n45; rock quarries at, 105, 338n14
Captain John Landing, 130, 135
Captain Lewis Rapids, 130, 300, 338n21
Carsell, J., 135
Carslay, J., 346n61
Carslay, M., 346n61
Carter, Dick, 204, 224–26
Carter, Mae, 226
Cascade Mountains, 8, 10, 328n25
Cascades, 328n15
Catron, Del, 352n11
cattle ranchers, *184*; Arams as, 168, 174, 182, *183*, 185, 188–89; Bartons as, 183–84, 188; and beef cattle rides, 183–85; and branding, 181–83; and calving, 181–83; Hendersons as, 184, 188, 200; Hibbses as, *174*, 184, 188; Horrocks as, 172, 174, 182–83, 190; Johnsons as, 168; McGaffees as, 172; and railroad, 184–85; and salt blocks, 172, 350n8; Sterlings as, 185–86; and summering, 182–83; Tippetts as, 169, 172, 174, 199; Van Pools as, 168–69, 183–85, 190–91, 201; Wilsons as, 164–65, 172–74, 185; and wintering, 173–74, 185–86
Cave Gulch, 110–12, 159, 322n11; mining at, 110–11, 339n33, 340n37–340n38; and transportation, 110, 346n50
Cayuse, 34–35, 39–40, 71, 325n24
Celilo Canal, 250
Celilo Falls, 250, 328n15, 357n25
Chadwick, Marjorie Wilson, 164, 202, 232–33, 238–39, 296; on environmentalism, 171; on horses, 232, 237; on life in Hells Canyon, 203, 208–9, 212–13, 230, 247; on ranching, 172–73, 185, 198, 201; and school, 241, 356n39; on visitors, 219–22
Chang Yin-huan, 84, 334n45
Chapman, Jim, 81, 223, 249, 251, 254–55
Chapman, Oscar, 310
Chea Po, 80
Cherry Creek, 144, 193
Cherry Lane, 325n21
Chief Joseph, 259
China Bar, 46
China Creek, 322n9

China Garden Creek, 50, 77, 300, 322n11, 322n13, 340n38
Chinese Exclusion Act, 334n45
Chinese Massacre Cove, 79
Chinese miners, 75–77, 79, 187, 332n1, 332n9, 332n11; murder of, 80–87, 333n28, 333n31, 333n33
Christmas Creek, 24
Christy, Charley, 144
Church, B. C., 254, 358n42
Church, Frank, 312–13, 315–16, 363n46
Clampett, E. A., 335n56
Clark, D. Worth, 265
Clark, William, 27, 48. *See also* Lewis and Clark expedition
Clarke, John, 37–39, 324n12
Clarkston, Wash., 1–2, *2*, 14, 127, 138, *178*, 299, 347n68, 358n33; and boat service, 287; and Bonneville, 48; founded, 299, 358n33; and *Imnaha*, 138; and mailboat service, 265, 271; and mining, 105; and Nez Perce War, 66; and plane service, 290
Clarkston Heights, Wash., 48
Clearwater National Forest, 180
Clearwater River, 1, *2*, 7, 28, 49, 68, 76; and Astor's expedition, 36–39, 323n45, 324n2–324n3, 324n5; and Lewis and Clark expedition, 27, 30; and Mackenzie, 38–39, 42, 325n14
Clemans, W. J., 338n17, 345n43
Clemmons, Joe, 231
Clifford, Charles, 51
climate, 13–14
Clipper, 257, 258, *260*, 261, *261*
coal, 103, *105*, 130, 338n17, 345n43
Coburn, Chet, 224
Cochran Island Rapids, *29*
Cochran Islands, 30, 299
Coleman, Edith, 161
Colonel Wright, 49, 53–54, 131, 328n20–328n22, 335n16
Columbia Plateau, 8, 19
Columbia River, 7, 29, 49, 319n1, 328n14–328n15, 331n40; Basalt Group, 8, 319n5; and fur-trading business, 37, 40, 42
Colville Reservation, 69, 331n30
Conrad, Duncan, 270
Cook, Stephen, 332n9
Coon Hollow Creek, 7
Coon Hollow Rapids, 130
Cooper, Gary, 279
Cooper, Russel, *176*
copper, 11, 89, 91, 101, 103, 319n12, 336n49, 339n23; at Anaconda ledge, 339n27–339n28; belt in Idaho, 105, 107, 119–20; at Cottonwood Creek, 107, 339n25; at Divide Creek, 342n7; in Imnaha district, 105, 120, 342n4; in Oregon, 99–100; at Peacock mine, 90, 335n2; at Salmon River, 112, 340n51; at Seven Devils Mountains, 51, 90, 327n5; at Snake River, 112, 340n51; and Union Pacific Railroad survey, 104–5; at White Monument, 90, 335n2; at Wild Goose Rapids, 105, 107
Copper Creek, 92, 114; Falls, 95–96
Copper Ledge Falls, 55, 57–58

Copper Lodge, 279–80
Copper Mountain, 114
Copper Mountain Mining and Milling Company, 114, *115*
Corbett, W. H., 52
Corps of Discovery, 27
Corps of Engineers: on *Colonel Wright*, 53–54; and dams, 316, 362n26; removing obstructions from Snake River, 124, 128, 133–34, 137, 257, 280–81, 285, 290, 300; survey of Snake River by, 30, 59, 76, 104; and 308 Report, 310, 313
Costello, William J., 311, 362n21
Cottonwood, Idaho, 184–85
Cottonwood Bar, 137
Cottonwood Creek, 29, 159, 206, 300, 322n10; copper at, 107, 339n25
Cougar Bar, 24, 161
Cougar Creek, 29, *110*, 322n10
Cougar Rapids, 130
Council, Idaho, 99
Courteois, 324n7
Couse Creek, 48; Landing, 129, 251
Cow Creek, 145; Canyon, 180
Cox's rapids, 129
Craig, George, 80, 86–87, 332n23, 335n56, 335n58
Craig Billy Crossing, 67
Craig Mountain Mining District, 340n36
Craig Mountains, 28–29, 105, 130
Crater Lake, 10
Crawford, Albert, 179, 185, 352n11
Crooks, Ramsay, 33–34
Crow, B. S., 341n57
Cullen, John W., 68–69
Culver, Andy, 60
Cuprum, Idaho, 97–100, 279
Curry family, 161

~: D :~

Dahlquist, Andrew, 194, 198, 349n29
Dahlquist, Neola, 349n29
Daly, Marcus, 90
dams, 4, 24, 309–16
dance, 100, 235–36
Davis, Clay, 226–27
Dawes Severalty Act of 1887, 337n2
Dawn, 263–64
Day, John, 34
Day, Walter, 246
Deborah, Idaho, 99
Decker, E. S., 253–54
Deep Creek, 79, 144, 300; mining at, 79–80, 336n49, 339n27, 339n31
Deer Creek, 30, 66–67, 127, 169, 321n5, 345n34

Defense Electric Power Administration, 362n16
DeLacy, W. W., 357n23
Delaunay, Joseph, 34
Delta Group, 303, 305–6
Denver, Joseph, 51
Desert Land Act (1877), 348n2
DeVault, William, 281–82, 284, 359n17
Devil's Ladder, 246
Devils Thorne, 2
Divide Creek, 63, 183, 342n7
Dobbin, Etta, 169, 175
Dobbin, Jay, 200, 229, 236, 253–54, 267–68, 351n31; and dogs, 194, 196; as rancher, *125*, 167, 169, 173, 175, 177, 179–80, 189, 192–93, 201–2
Dobbin, Mary Etta, 169
dogs: and ranchers, 194–96
Dole, Ira S., 273
Dorion, Marie, 32, 34–35
Dorion, Pierre, Jr., 32
Dorman, Bill, *176*
Dorrance, Jim, 341n60
Doug Creek, 168
Douglas, Thomas J., 80
Douglas, William O., 314
Doumecq Plains, 350n34
Downey Gulch, 144
Downey Saddle, 144
dredge, 299–300
Dresser, Philip, 271
Dry Creek, 168
Dry Diggins, 183
Dry Gulch, 174
Dubreuil, J. B., 34
Dug Bar, 18, 23, 80, 166, 333n24; and Nez Perce, 24, 63, 69
Duncan, Ace, 210, 267
Dunstrude, C. A., 345n41
Dworshak Dam, 362n26

~: E :~

Eagle Bar, 323n32, 336n49
Eagle Cap Wilderness, 181
Eagle's Nest, 248, 249, 357n13
Earl, Alice Madden, 187
Earl, Elmer, 170, 221, 224, 337n8, 338n20; on life in Hells Canyon, 209, 215, 235, 253; and Dick Rivers, 288–89
Earl, Emmett, 251
Earl, Jasper, 170, 250
Earl, Jess, 187, 225, 349n31, 357n6, 359n17; on Kyle McGrady, 263, 266, 280; on telephone lines, 216–17, 354n9

Eckert, J. L., 341n69, 359n58
education, 239–43
Egan, 72
Egana, Seberno, 192–93
Eisenhower, Dwight D., 311, 313
Electrolytic Company, 114
Elk City, Idaho, 103
Ellensburg, Wash., 181
Elsensohn, Alfreda, 4, 262, 340n51
Enterprise, Ore., 177, 181, 185, 319n4, 329n53
Eureka, Idaho, 127–28, 132, 142, 345n35
Eureka Bar, *124*
Eureka Creek. *See* Deer Creek
Eureka Mining, Smelting and Power Company, 113–14, *123*, *125*, 141–42, 299, 303–6, 340n45, 344n20, 347n76, 361n5; assessment of mines of, 123–24, 343n19; blacksmith shop of, *141*; boardinghouse of, *133*, *149*; boat for, 124–25, 344n22; and canyon myth, 119; and dam at Imnaha River, 309; drills at, 127, 345n31; and *Imnaha*, 112, 128, 137–38, 300, 346n57; and mining claims, 120, 140–41; and *Mountain Gem*, 138–39; power generating tent, *126*; and problems with suppliers, 140, 347n75; and river transportation, 123, 134, 343n18, 344n21; road built by, 126, 144, 345n29; sawmill at, 345n30; and smelter, 123–27, 147–48, 343n18, 344n21, 344n27, 345n32; stamp mill of, *126*; start up of, 122–24, 343n15; stock prices of, 343n17; telephone service for, 125, 344n26
Evans, Bruce, 80–81, 84–86, 334n52
Evans, Connie, 322n10
Evans, Dan, 316
Evans, Lucien, 342n5
Evans, Steven, 322n10
exotic terrane, 5, 7, 319n2

~: F :~

Fair, Henry, 133, 347n67
Farewell Bend, 54, 319n1
Fargo Gold and Copper Mining Company, 120, 125, 343n10; camp of, 127, *133*; and Eureka Mining, Smelting and Power Company, 123, 343n18
Farwell, F. D., 94
Favor, Roy, 254–55
Federal Power Commission, 310–12, 362n9
Fenn, Frank, 66
ferry, 357n23; at Ballard's Landing, 100; at Cache Creek, *180*; at Captain John Creek, 250; at Grande Ronde River, 253; and Lewiston, Idaho, 250, 329n53, 357n23; at Pittsburg Landing, 115, 240, 249–50, 358n49; at Snake River, 329n53
fires, 200
Fisher, Ed, *117*
FitzGerald, Jenkins A., 331n42
Florence, 265–66, *267*, 270, 278–79, 281, 359n8
Florence, Idaho, 103
Fly Blow corral, *182*
Flyer, 116, 255, 257–58, 358n48

Flynn, John, 98
Ford brothers, 98–99
Forest, Idaho, 147, 348n7
Forest Reserve Acts, 348n2
Forest Service, 142, 319n4; and Battle Creek cabin, 205; and Hells Canyon Lodge, 278, 283; and homesteading, 348n2; and Kirkwood, 213; Lick Creek campgrounds of, 181; maintaining canyon trails, 245, 247–49, 357n6; and ranchers, 166–67, 169, 171–72, 317, 349n29; and telephone service, 215–16
Fort Astoria, 35–40, 325n14
Fort Boise, 51
Fort George, 40–41
Fort Hall Reservation, 71, 74
Fort Nez Perces, 40–41, 43, 50
Fort Okanogan, 40–41
Fort Spokane, 38, 40–41
Fort Walla Walla. *See* Fort Nez Perces
Foss, Sam Walter: "The House by the Side of the Road," 152
Fountain, Cora, 224
Fountain, Pete, 187, 297
Fouste, Don, 271
Frazer, Robert, 28–30
Freeman, Otis W., 113, 261, 340n51
Freezeout Creek, 185
French, F. J., 336n38
Frye, James, 342n7
Frye, T. R., 342n7
Fulford, Frank, 349n29
Funk Place, 181, 292–93

~: G :~

Gabrielson, N. Ira, 312
Garlinghouse, Arthur, 340n50
Garlinghouse, G. A. (Arza), 112, 340n48
Garlinghouse, Richard, 340n50
Garnet Creek, 99
Garver, Larry, *176*
Gass, Patrick, 321n6, 322n22, 324n8
Gates, John, 54
Gerbert, John, 108
Getta Creek, 168, 209; Arams at, 168, 174, 182, 187–89, 205
Gill, Bob, 270
Gimmel, William, 335n56
Glenns Ferry, 71
Glover, Richard, 255, 257
Goblin, 2
Godfrey, Arthur, 315, 317
Godfrey, George, 272–73
Going, S. G., 68

Golconda Mining Company, 340n38
gold, 25, 80, 89, 101, 103, 113, 332n19; at Anaconda ledge, 339n27–339n28; at Battle Creek, 116; in Buffalo Hump district, 338n19; at Captain John Creek, 105; at Cave Gulch, 110–11, 339n33; and gossans, 11, 319n12; and Nez Perce Reservation, 25, 49; at Seven Devils Mountains, 51, 90, 327n5
Gold Bug mine, 339n33
Goldsmith, Jack, 268
Gonia, Edwin, 359n17
gossans, 10–11, 319n12
Graham's Landing. *See* Couse Creek: Landing
Grand Canyon of Snake River, 3
Grande Ronde Basalt, 8, 319n5
Grande Ronde Mercantile Company, 242, 252–54
Grande Ronde River, 4, 27, 51, 62, 73, 169, 300; boats on, 58, 130, 133; and Bonneville, 47, 326n49; coalfield at, *105*, 130, 338n17, 345n43; and copper, 104, 338n11; and ferry, 253; and Lime Point, 104, 337n8–337n9; and limestone, 7, 104, 337n5, 337n7–337n9; log boom on, 329n52; and mining, 104–5, 338n21; and road, 346n50
Grande Ronde Valley, 34, 45, 51, 73, 104, 327n9
Grangeville, Idaho, 341n61
granite, 103, 111–12
Granite Creek, 76, 167, 332n3; Hibbses at, 162, 204–5, *205*, 207, 210–11; Rapids, 11, 258
Granite Rapids, 58
Grant, U. S., 62
Graves Creek, 185
Gray, A. W., 94
Gray, Robert, 27
Gray, W. H., 53
Gray, William Polk, 53, 139, 328n18, 335n16, 360n12; and *Norma*, 94–97, 336n19–336n20, 347n66
Gray's Landing, 94
Great Eastern mine, 116, 210, 300, 341n69
Green, Edith, 312
Greene, John, 66, 330n18
Griggs, D. R., 357n23
Grogg, Oakey, 270
Grote, Opal, 317
Grote, Ted, 198, 211–12, 221–22, 291–92, 317; on ranching, 191, 193
Grunig, Kitty, 100
Guernsey, Dennis, 140, 344n20
Guernsey, O. E. (Ell), 122, 134, 137, *141*, 147, 303, 305–6; and smelter, 126, 343n18, 344n27; on success, 133, 140; on transportation, 124–25, 344n21
Gustin, Carl, 263

~: H :~

Hailey, John, 59
Hale, S. C., 104, 338n11
Half Moon Saddle, 247
Hall, Lewis, 99
Haller, 319n8

Haller's Canyon, 4
Hannaford, 345n45
Hansen, Lewis, 345n41
Hansen, Orval, 315
"Harney's Cut Off," 327n9
Harper, J. B., 71
Harper's Magazine, 273
Hart, Joe, 255
Harvey, Floyd, 317, 355n5, 363n47
Hass Flats, 184
Hastings, Frank, 264
Hat Point, 13, 166, 180
Hatwai Creek, 324n5
Hauser, Samuel, 335n9
Hazel, W. H., 343n19
Heady, Tom, 336n49
Heaven's Gate, 2, 185
He Devil, 4, 13
Hedges, W. F., 57
Helena, Idaho, 91–92, 97, 336n28
Heller's Canyon, 3–4
Helles Bell, 97
Hells Canyon, 1–5, 8, 13–14; aboriginal people of, 16–17; and dam controversy, 4, 24, 309–16; and Lewis and Clark expedition, 27–30; river highway through, 49–50
Hells Canyon (Bailey), 1–2, 4
Hells Canyon Dam, 4, 7, 12, 24, 57, 92, 159, 161, 251, 293, 320n12, 326n31, 329n29, 336n49, 342n72; and area before, 101, 229, 318, 326n41, 337n10; and controversy, 311–14, 316
Hells Canyon Lodge, 278–80
Hells Canyon National Park, 362n23
Hells Canyon National Recreation Area (HCNRA), 4, 169, 316–18, 319n4, 320n20; and ranchers, 166–67, 169–70
Henderson, Carl, 168, 200, 206, 217
Henderson, Claire, 240
Henderson, Horace, 168, 206, 211, 216, 237, 240, 317, 353n29; on ranching, 184, 188, 200–201
Henderson family, 209, 211
Henry, Alexander, 323n23
Hermiston, Ore., 181
Hether, Daniel, 105, 338n21
Hether, Nels, 105
Hether, Ole, 105, 340n38
Hibbs, Earl, 162, *184*, *198–99*, *218*, 226–28, 231, 241, *241*; and dogs, 196; garden of, 207, 210–11; and radio, 236–37; as rancher, 184, 188; and strangers, 222
Hibbs, Edna, 231
Hibbs, Ellen, 162, 207, 231, 245, 355n10
Hibbs, Esther Leonard, 162, *196*, 218–19, 226–28, 241, 297; on canyon trails, 248; and dogs, 196; garden of, 207, 210–11; at Granite Creek, 204–5, *205*; on life in Hells Canyon, 203, 209, 213–14; on Kyle McGrady, 277; and radio, 236–37; as rancher, 184, 188, 197; on Ruth Sapp, 272; on school, 356n38; on strangers, 222

Hibbs, Glenn, 162, *184*
Hibbs, Lenora. *See* Barton, Lenora Hibbs
Hibbs, Martin, 162, *184*, 207, *227*, 231, 349n20; and mining, 120, 342n5; murder of, 226–28, 344n58
Hibbs, Mary. *See* Stickney, Mary Hibbs
Hibbs, Newton, 338n17
Hibbs, R. B., 342n4
Hibbs family, *174*, 184
Hickle, Walter, 315, 317
High Mountain Sheep Dam, 286, 293, 314–15
High Range, 206, 211; Basin, 168; Creek, 168
High Trail, *212*
Hill, Frank, 291
Hill Homestead, 166
Hilliker, J. A., 342n9
Hills, Frank, 292
Hilton, A. H. (Al), 261, *261*
Hiltsley, Agnes, 219
Hiltsley, Alberta, 229–30
Hiltsley, Bill, 219
Hiltsley, Frank, 229–30
Himmelwright, Fred, 116–17
Hitchcock, Maurice, 169
Hobach River, 32
Hogback Ridge, 185
holidays, 234–35
Hollandsworth, Lou, 168, 172
Hollandsworth, Polly Johnson, 168, 172
Home Below Hells Canyon (Jordan), 4, 167, 349n28
Homestead, Ore., 2, 33, 95, 100–101, 117, 257, 323n33, 336n45
Homestead Act, 151, 159
homesteading, 74, 114–15, 150–52, 159–61, 348n13–348n14, 349n2
Hoover Point, 322n20
Horn, Della, 335n56
Horrocks, Buster "Bub," 172, 190, 195, 202, 231, 292, 318
Horrocks, Cole, 183, 236, 243
Horrocks, Sharon. *See* Wing, Sharon Horrocks
Horrocks family, 182–83
Horse Creek, 47, 180, 326n49
Horse Heaven, 2, 184
Horse Mountain Lookout, 279
horses, 211, 237, 249, 320n22; and Nez Perce, 20, 22, 38, 63, 324n7; and ranchers, 196–97
Horseshoe Bend, 327n5
Hosnes, J. S., 335n56
Houser, S. T., 90
Houston, Jack, 279, 290–91
Howard, C. O., 303–6, 343n18, 344n22–344n23, 344n25, 344n28
Howard, M. S., 303, 305, 343n18
Howard, Oliver O., 331n33, 331n40; and Bannocks, 71–74, 331n35; and Nez Perce, 62–63, 65–68

Hubbel, Levy, 303, 305–6
Hubbell, J. E., 305, 343n18
Hudson's Bay Company, 43, 45, 326n35
Huesby, Henry, 147, 304
Huesby, J. A., 345n39
Huffman, Guy, 169, 179, 192, 217, 267–68
Hughes, Carl (Hezekiah), 80–81, 84–86, 333n25
Humphrey, Z. B. (Zack), 144–45, 147
Hunt, Wilson Price, 2, 32–36, 40, 323n39
Hunter, George, 67–68
Hunter, Ralph, 359n17
Huntington, Ore., 91–92, 94, 98, 100, 104, 123, 323n33
Hurd, Jerad S., 357n23
Husebye, Henry, 343n13
Hyatt, Mamie, *219*
Hyatt, Mary, 240

~: I :~

Idaho, 258–60, 264–66, *267–68*, 274, 276
Idaho Exploration and Copper Company, 120, 342n5, 342n7
Idaho Granite Company, 112, 346n54, 347n68
Idaho Power Company, 310–14, 362n19
Idaho Queen, 178; *I*, 288–89, 360n13; *II*, 288–89, 360n13; *III*, 289; *IV*, 289
Idaho Stone Company, 105
Idaho Territory, 49
Imnaha, 111–12, 114, *129*, *133*, *135*, *141*, 145, 254, 260, 283, 299, 345n40, 346n46; and accident on Salmon River, 134–35, 346n52; christening of, 345n39; and coal, 130, 345n43; construction of, 128; crew of, 132, 135–36, 345n41; and Eureka Mining, Smelting and Power Company, 112, 128, 137–38, 300, 346n57; in government service, 134, 300; maiden voyage of, 129–33, 345n41; salvage of, 137, 346n61; sinking of, 119, 135–38, 147, 346n57, 346n63
Imnaha Basalt, 8, 319n5
Imnaha Gold Mining Company, 116–18
Imnaha Mining Company, 305–6
Imnaha River, 8, 27, 46, 62, 105, *127*, 145, 149; and Bonneville, 47, 326n43; and ranchers, 162, 164–66, 175, 179, 181, 183, 185, 189
Imnaha Valley, 45–46
Indian Cave, 55, 329n35
Inland Empire Waterways Association, 310, 362n11
Inland Navigation Company, 283, 360n9
Iron Dyke Mine, 98–100, 336n43, 336n48
Iroquois, 41, 325n30
irrigation, 209–10
Irving, Washington: on Astor, 32–34, 37, 323n31, 324n48; on Hells Canyon, 2–3; on Mackenzie, 35, 324n48; on Nez Perce, 47, 327n54
Ives, Burl, 315, 317

~: J :~

J. N. Teal, 250
Jacks, Frank O., 187, 206, 211, 236, 297
Jackson, Henry, 312
Javits, Jacob, 363n48
Jefferson, Thomas, 27, 29
Jennings, Charlie, 94–95
Jensen, Fred, 164, 219–20
Johann, A. E., 289
Johnasse, Frank E., 342n5
Johnasse, Sam, 342n5
Johnson, Donald, 230–31
Johnson, Duane, 238, 241–42
Johnson, Gail, 166
Johnson, Greg, 166, *195*, 202, 211–12, 297; on dogs, 194–95; on HCNRA, 317; on life at Hells Canyon, 214; and planes, 291; on radio, 237; on ranching, 171, 173, 175–79, 181, 186, 191–92, 238; and school, 241–42; at Temperance Creek, 206, 209
Johnson, H. G., 303, 305, 343n18
Johnson, Hazel Welch, 166, 202, 205–7, 211–12, 216, 236, 242, 281, 287, 292; on life in Hells Canyon, 208–9, 212, 217–18, 233; as rancher, 173, 177–81, 191–92, 197, 200
Johnson, J. Ray, 271
Johnson, Jennie, 230–31
Johnson, John, 230–31
Johnson, Kenneth, 165–66, 202, 210–11, 218, 236, 285, 354n10; and planes, 291–92; as rancher, 166, 175, 177–78, 180–81, 191–92, 200; at Temperance Creek, 205–6
Johnson, Leonard, 166
Johnson, Mary, 168, 205
Johnson, Murland, 230–31
Johnson, Pete, *184*
Johnson, Slim, 168, *184*, 205
Johnson, Tom, *184*
Johnson Bar, 4, *41*, 174, 258, *259*, 300–301; Bartons at, 162, 349n20; Hells Canyon Lodge at, 278–80
Johnson Creek, 96
Johnson family, 267–68
Jonathan Bourne Company, 342n8
Jones, Ben, 34
Jones, Henry, 352n11
Jones, Jay, 352n11
Jordan, Grace, 167, 203–4, 213, 216, 224–25, 232, 243, 248; *Home Below Hells Canyon*, 4, 167, 349n28
Jordan, Len, 166–67, 204, 210, 213, 226–27, 232, 235, 253, 315–16, 363n49
Jordan family, 176, 181, *207*, 207–8, 241, 268
Jordan Valley, 72
Jorgenson, Fred, 359n17
Jorgenson, Victor H., Jr., 273
Joseph (Chief), 23, 47–48, 62, 65–66, 321n38, 331n30
Joseph Creek, 24, 47, 62, 73, 169, 326n49

Joseph Creek School, 242
Joseph Plains, *182–83*, *240*, 341n61; Nez Perce at, 63, 67; and ranchers, 168, 172, 174, 182–84, *184*, 217

~: K :~

Kamiah, Idaho, 322n7, 324n3, 325n14
Kamm, Jacob, 92, 94, 335n10
Kavanaugh, Andy, 340n37
Kennedy, Ted, 363n48
Kent, C. H., 335n11
Kernan, George, 335n56
Kerr, James, 92
Kettenbach, William F., 339n25, 347n65
King, C. L., 345n41
Kinney Creek, 7
Kirby Creek, 45, 326n41
Kirkwood, *12*, 210, 213; and boat service, 292–93; and canyon trails, 247; Dahlquists at, 349n29; Johnsons at, 166, 191; Jordans at, 167, 204, 207, 213, 349n28; lambing sheds at, *178*; and telephone service, 216, 354n10; Wilsons at, 167, *167*, 207
Kirkwood Bar, 4, 208, 248
Kirkwood Creek, 24, 167, *208*, 225, 247
Kjos, O. A., 347n65
Kleinschmidt, Albert, 90–92, 97, 319n8, 335n9, 336n49
Kleinschmidt, Carl, 91
Kleinschmidt Grade, 91, 99–100, 336n49
Knapper, Lou, *184*
Knight, M. V., 145, 147
Kohlhepp, Dorothy, 190
Kohlhepp, Morris, 190
Kootenai, 38, 324n7
Krebs, Sevella, 188
Kruger, George, 254
Kurry, Albert, 249, 358n49
Kurry Creek, 24, 69, 341n61
Kurry family, 60
Kuykendall, Elgin Victor, 326n49, 327n54

~: L :~

Ladd Metal Company, 99
Lake Bonneville, 10
Lake Idaho, 9
Landore, Idaho, 99, 336n49
Lanker, Drew, 300
Lapwai Creek, 36
Lapwai Reservation. *See* Nez Perce Reservation
LaRue, C. O. (Homer), 80–81, 84–86, 334n52
Lauserica, Ramon, 192
lava flows, 8–10

Lawyer's Creek, 28
LeClerc, Francois, 33–34
Lee Loi, 83
Leeper, Don, *176*
Lee She, 80, 82
Le Grand Coquin, 38–40, 325n24
Leland, Alonzo, 59, 72–73, 82, 104–5, 331n41
Leonard, Esther, *218*
Leopold, Aldo, 103
Let's Go, 258
Levy, William, 315
Lewis, G. W. (Cap), 104–5, 337n7
Lewis, Isaac R., 90, 335n2
Lewis, Meriwether, 27. *See also* Lewis and Clark expedition
Lewis and Clark expedition, 20, 27–30, *28*, 321n5, 322n9–322n11, 322n13, 322n20, 322n22, 324n8; and Nez Perce, 27–30, 321n2, 322n18, 326n46
Lewis River, 324n48
Lewiston, 128, *252*, 299, 338n15
Lewiston, Idaho, 1, 2, 7–8, 14, 48, *49*, 59–61, 87, 105, 319n1, 319n8, 327n1, 327n7, 329n52, 331n42, 333n37; boat landing at, 66, *178*, *266*; and boat service, 61, 115, 330n1, 358n41; and *Colonel Wright*, 53, 131; creation of, 49, 75; and ferry, 250, 329n53, 357n23; and granite, 111–12, 340n49, 347n68–347n69; and Haller, 4; and *Imnaha*, 128–29, *129*, 132–33, 135, 137–39, 300; and Indians, 72–73; and lime, 337n5; and mailboat service, 177–78, 193, 253, 258–59, 264–69, 271–74, 284–86, 290; and mining, 10, 75–76, 79–80, 82–84, 86, 103, 105, 107, 110–11, 116, 126–28, 327n5, 332n1, 332n23, 339n22, 339n28, 344n27, 345n32–345n33, 346n54; as mining supply center, 49–52, 113, 341n9, 341n61; and Mote, 143–45, 150; and *Mountain Gem*, 139; and Nez Perce war, 66, 68, 330n14; and *Norma*, 94, 96–97; and plane service, 291; and railroad, 91, 123, 150, 252, 345n39; and ranchers, 168, 180, 191, 193, 217–18, 251; and river highway, 50–51, 54, 61, 140, 258, 287; and river survey, 59, 104, 299, 337n10; road from, 329n53; and *Shoshone*, 55, 58; tourist trips from, 260, 278, 287, 289
Lewiston/Clarkston valley, 9
Lewiston Hill, *60*
Lewiston Normal School (Lewis-Clark State College), 112, 347n69
Lewiston Southern Navigation Company, 125, 137–40, 344n23, 347n65
Libby, E. H., 347n65
Libby, W. M., 299
Liebmann, A. G., 309–10
Life Magazine, 272–73
Lime Kiln Point, 81
Lime Point, 55, 57, 104, 130, 337n8–337n9
limestone, 103, 105, 319n4; at Grande Ronde River, 7, 104, 337n5, 337n7–337n9
Lindgren, Waldemar, 342n4
Lindsay, Halsted, 100
Lindsay, Theron, 100
Little Bar, 91–92, 176
Little Salmon River, 184, 323n45, 327n5
Lively, Lorenzo D., 304–5, 343n13, 343n18
Lloyd, Clive, 227

Lockley, Fred, 87
Logan, John, 359n17
Log Cabin Island, 81
Looking Glass, 321n39, 327n54
Lower Granite Dam, 325n25
Lower Imnaha Irrigation and Power Ditch, 151
Low Saddle, 179
lumber, 103, 329n52
Luoto, Ed, 270, 359n17
Luoto, Eino, 270
Lyda, Ellen, *183*
Lyons, Ed, 94

~: M :~

Mable, 98, 336n35
Mace Cabin, *212*
MacFarlane, Ed, 116, 255, *255*, 257, 257–63, 358n41, 358n45, 358n47, 358n54; and Ruth Sapp, 271–72; tourism business of, 260–61, 276
Mackenzie, Donald, 32–33, 35–43, 51, 323n45, 324n12, 325n21, 325n25–325n26; and Indians, 36, 39–41, 325n24, 325n30; Washington Irving on, 35, 324n48; nickname of, 38, 325n14
Macomb, Alexander, 43
Madden, Jim, 236
Madden Bar, 258
Madgwick, H. T., 104, 338n11
Madgwick, Harry, 338n15
Madison, G. A., 341n57
Magnesia Stone Company, 105, 338n15
Magnuson, Warren, 310, 312
Maguire, Jerry, 66
mailboat service, 1, *14*, 97, 108, *188*, 241, 249–50, 253, 259, 263–72, 283–85, 318; and Lewiston, Idaho, 177–78, 193, 253, 258–59, 271–74, 284–86, 290; and Pittsburg Landing, 178, 254, 257–59, 267–68, 285–86, 290; and ranchers, 175–78, 193; and *Saturday Evening Post*, 273–75; as tourist attraction, 276, 280
mail service, 108, 134, 144, 149, 155, 219, 226, 245–47, 253, 257–59, 263–65, 271, 290
Malaxa, Gus, 192–93, 292, 359n17
Malaxa, Jana Ulasia, 193
Malheur Reservation, 72, 74, 331n33
Mallory, Ben, 339n22
Mallory, Perry, 105, 338n19
Maloney Creek, 322n20
Mann Creek, 33, 323n28, 323n45
Mansfield, Mike, 312
Mansfield, Robert, 272
Marine History of the Pacific Northwest (McCurdy), 3
Marks, Albert, 220
Marshall, Bob, 222, 354n30
Martiartu, Toney, 192–93
Martin, Alec, 251

Martin, Clyde, 290–91
Martin, John, 335n56
Martin, K. J., 335n56
Martin, S. C., 257
Martin Bridge, 7
Maxwell, Anna, 166–67, 200
Maxwell, Dick, 166–67, 212, 232, 235, 248
Maynard, Hiram, 80–81, 84–86, 334n55
McCall, Tom, 316
McCam, John, 55
McCarthy, Patrick, 226, 228
McClaren, Joe, 264
McClellan, Robert, 32
McClure, James, 363n48
McCormick, James, 83
McCoy, Roy, 224, 253, 255
McCurdy, H. W.: *Marine History of the Pacific Northwest*, 3
McDonald, Ambrose, 345n41
McDuff, J. J., 110
McDuff Rapids, 322n13
McFarland, Bert, 346n61
McFarland, Ephraim, 345n41, 346n61
McFarland, H., 345n41
McFarland, Sandi, 19
McGaffee, Alfred (Fred), 165, 183, 201, 215, 222, 231, 235
McGaffee, Billy, 162, 165, 200, 227, 235
McGaffee, Everett, 231
McGaffee, George, 235
McGaffee, Iphigenia (Gene), 165, 203, 215, 222, 231
McGaffee, Mabel, 162, 165, 235
McGaffee, Murrielle. *See* Wilson, Murrielle McGaffee
McGaffee family, 172, 183
McGovern, George, 363n48
McGrady, Bob, 282, 359n1
McGrady, Florence, 263, 263, 267, 271, 271–72
McGrady, Kenneth, 281–82
McGrady, Kyle, 97, 258, 263, 263, 266, 267, 267–68, 268–69, 271, 274–76, 281–82, 288, 290; and draft, 270, 359n17; and lodge, 278–81; and media coverage, 271–76; and miners, 269–70; and Ruth Sapp, 271–72; tourism business of, 276–77
McGraw Creek Divide, 326n38
McKay, Douglas, 311
McMillan, Robert, 80–81, 84–87
McNabb, Marge, 287
McNabb, Oliver, 241–42, 272, 283–87, 284–86, 288, 360n9
Meadows, Idaho, 99
Meeds, Lloyd, 316
Merrill, J., 345n39
Metcalf, Lee, 312

Metropolitan Trust Company, 97–98, 100, 336n28
Meyell, Eric, 261
Meyers Creek, 210
Michler, Nathaniel, 59, 329n35, 329n44; on *Colonel Wright*, 53–54, 328n20; on *Shoshone*, 329n30, 329n34, 329n36
Miller, Chester, 141, 306
Miller, Eva Cool, 346n62
Miller, Grady, *186*, 351n51
Miller, James T., 92, 122, 128, 133, 137, 140, 304–6, 346n62; and boat, 344n22–344n24; and river transportation, 124–25, 344n21; and smelter, 343n18, 344n27
Miller, Joseph T., 303
Miller, Sebastian "Bas," 55, 57–58, 329n33
Millich, James, 91
mining, 77, 103–5, 122–23, 332n19, 345n33; at Anaconda ledge, 107, 339n27–339n28; at Battle Creek, 103, 116; at Birch Creek, 339n27; and boat service, 100, 269–70; at Cave Gulch, 110–11, 339n33, 340n37–340n38; at China Garden Creek, 340n38; by Chinese immigrants, 75–77, 79–80, 187, 332n1, 332n9, 332n11, 332n23, 333n28, 333n33; and gossans, 11, 319n12; in Grande Ronde district, 104, 338n11; at Grande Ronde River, 104–5, 338n21; and Lewiston, Idaho, 10, 49–52, 103; at Nez Perce Reservation, 25, 49; at Salmon Bar, 339n22; at Salmon River, 76, 112–13, 340n51; at Seven Devils Mountains, 51, 89–90, 97–99, 319n8, 327n5, 336n49; at Snake River, 103, 112–13, 340n51; and transportation, 116, 300, 341n69; and Umatilla, Ore., 328n14
missionary work, 25
Mitchell, William, 270
Mondale, Walter, 363n48
Monroe Creek, 323n28, 323n45
Monteith, John, 62–63
moonshine, 224–26
Morris, J. B., 347n65
Morrison, George, 338n14
Morrow, Alberta, 219
Morrow, Clyde, 219
Morse, Wayne, 311–13
Morton, Rogers, 363n48
Mote, Daniel Webster, 142–44, 147–51, 156–58, 187, 348n6, 348n12, 348n15; automatic writings of, 143–45, 147, 347n1; diaries of, 143, *148*, 152–54, *153*, 154–56, 348n2; and homesteading process, 150–52, 348n13–348n14; and mining, 145, 147, 348n9; as squatter, 160–61
Mountain Chief tunnel, 124, 127, *127*
Mountain Gem, 111, *138*, 138–40, 147, 252, 254, 260, 346n46, 347n65–347n66, 347n68
Mountain Queen Mine, 90
Mountain Sheep Dam, 286, 313–15
Mountain Sheep Rapids, 3, *135*; *Imnaha* at, 131–34, 346n46; obstructions at, 137, 299–300
Moxley, J. Q., 338n11
Mt. Mazama, 10, 16
Mt. St. Helen, 10
Murdoch, Angus, 122–23
Murie, Olaus, 312
Murray, James, 312

Murray, Washington, 51

~: N :~

National Park Service, 312
National River Bill, 316
Needle's Eye, 246, 248
Nehrhood, George A., 125, 137, 140, 145, 303–5, 344n25, 347n65, 348n7; and boat, 125, 344n22–344n24, 344n28; on sinking of *Imnaha*, 137–38, 346n63; and smelter, 343n18
Nelson, John, 270
Neuberger, Richard, 4, 242, 272–75, 311–13
New Meadows, Idaho, 179, 183–85, 327n5
New Tenio, 66
Newton, Henry, 270
Nez Perce, 17, 20, 47, 74, 220–21, 321n41, 324n8, 326n49, 332n45; bands of, 23–24, 38, 40, 62–63, 114, 326n45; and Blackfoot, 324n6; and Bonneville, 43, 46–48, 326n45, 326n48, 327n50; caches used by, 22–23, 67, 73, 321n34; and fishing, 22, 29–30, 320n28, 321n29, 322n13, 322n18; and historic period, 19–20, 22–23; and horses, 20, 22, 38, 63, 324n7; and Lewis and Clark expedition, 27–30, 321n2, 322n18, 326n46; and Mackenzie, 36–37, 40–41, 324n6, 324n9, 325n23–325n24; at reservations, 61–63, 69, 331n30; and seasonal cycle, 14–15, 20, 22; and Shoshone, 20, 321n40; society of, 20, 22–24, 320n23; at war, 38, 324n6, 324n9; and War of 1877, 24–25, 61–63, 65–68, 321n38, 330n14, 330n18
Nez Perce National Forest, 180
Nez Perce Reservation, 7, 23, 25, 49, 61–62, 69, 103, 337n2
Nixon, H. A., 112, 340n48
Nixon, Richard, 315, 363n48
Norma, 92, 94–97, 112–13, 128, 131, 299–300, 336n19–336n20, 336n22, 347n66; crew of, 94–97, 335n11
Northern Pacific Railroad Company, 91, 123, 345n45
North Fork, 37
Northwest, 73, 330n1, 331n40
North West Company, 32, 36, 40–41, 43, 323n23, 324n12, 326n35
Northwest Public Power Association, 312
Norwood, Gus, 312
Nyberg, Charlie, 242
Nyberg, Helen Brown, 242

~: O :~

Oakes, Bruce, 289
Oakes, Dick, 289
Ogre, 2
Ohadi Mining and Milling Company, 340n37
Olds Ferry, 54, 319n1
"Old Timer," 183, *185*
"Old Titus," 53
Oliver, Lester, 236, 359n17
Ollokut, 62, 65
Olney, Joe, 269–70
Olney, John, 266, 269–70

Olney, Lawrence, 269–70
Olson, John, 345n39
O'Mahoney, Joseph, 313
Onaidia, Joe, 193, 292
Onaidia, Marjorie Ulasia, 193
O-push-y-e-cut, 327n54
Ordway, John, 28–30
Oregon Board of Geographic Names, 3
Oregon Copper Company, 343n10
Oregon Railway and Navigation Company (OR&N), 91, 98, 123–24, 299, 338n15, 338n17; boats of, 112–13, 128, 139, 338n15
Oregon Short Line, 91, 335n6
Oregon Steam Navigation Company (OSN), 49, 52, 54, 328n14, 329n47, 330n1, 335n10; and competition, 52, 54–55; expedition by, 50–51, 327n4–327n5; route used by, 54, 328n25
Oregon Trail, 51
Oregon Washington Railroad and Navigation, 150, 348n12
Oregon Wool Growers, 192
Orofino, Idaho, 7
OSN. *See* Oregon Steam Navigation Company (OSN)
O'Sullivan, Patrick, 85–86
Oure, John, 345n41
Overbiling, Billie, 291–92
Owyhee Ferry, 54–55
Owyhee Mountains, 9
Oxbow, 9, 33, 68, 322n20, 326n38, 327n5
Oxbow Dam, 8, 12, 89, 100, 309, 311–14
Oytes, 72

~: P :~

Pacific and Idaho Northern railway (PIN), 91, 98
Pacific Fur Company, 32, 35–37, 40, 325n26
Pacific Northwest Power Company, 313–16
Pacific Telephone Company, 344n26
Packwood, Bob, 315–16, 363n48
Paiute, 14, 71–73, 325n27, 331n37, 331n40; at reservations, 74, 331n33
Palmer, A. Z., 335n56
Paradise Lake, 2
Parker, John, 272
Parks School, 241
Patterson, Paul, 311
Paul, Albert, 359n17
Payette Lake, 327n5
Payette River, 33, 327n5
Pea, Earl, 355n5
Peacock mine, 90, 97–98, 336n28
Pearcy, Edmund, 50–51, 327n4–327n5, 329n53
Peebles, John J., 321n1, 322n9, 322n11, 322n13
Pendleton Woolen Mills, 177–78, 268

Perkins, J. B., 339n25
Perry, George, 145, 348n6
Peterson, A. M., 258
Peterson, H. M., 305, 343n18, 347n65
Petri, Alice, 278–80
Petri, Henry, 278–80
petroglyphs, 18, 320n16
Pfost, Gracie, 312
Pickett, L. F., 261
pictographs, 18
Pierce, E. D., 25
Pierce, Idaho, 103
Pine, Frank, 359n17
Pine Creek, 9, 326n38; Valley, 55
Pine Flat, 58
Pinkham, Allen, 28, 30, 322n10
pithouses, 16
Pittsburg Landing, 7, 12, 22, 60, 114–15, 211, 230, 320n14, 330n24, 341n61, 341n69; and Bannock War, 73; and boat service, 134; and *Colonel Wright*, 54; and dams, 313; and ferry, 115, 240, 249–50, 358n49; and homesteading, 159, 161; and mailboat service, 178, 254, 257–59, 267–68, 285–86, 290; and mining, 82, 113–14, 116, 125, 344n24; and Nez Perce, 24, 62, 67, 69, 114; and OSN expedition, 51, 327n5; and plane service, 293; and ranchers, 167–68, 180; and river survey, 299–300; rock art at, 18, 320n14; and school, 240–41; and telephone service, 128, 216, 354n9–354n10; Wilsons at, 167, 180
Pittsburg Mining and Milling Company, 114, 341n64
Pittsburg Saddle, 69, 341n61
Pittsburg School, 240, 356n33
Plains Indians, 23
plate tectonic, 5, 7
Pleasant Valley Dam, 286, 313–14
Pocatello, Idaho, 43
Point Bluff, 151–52
Point Successful, 42, 326n31
Pollock Mountain, 184
Pomona flows, 8
Pony Bar, 166
portage, 52–53, 328n15
Porter, Sara, 335n56
Portland-Imnaha Copper Mining Company, 342n9
Portneuf, Idaho, 43, 326n35
Post Office Saddle, 46
Potvin, E. D., 339n28
Powder River, 45, 50, 53, 98, 327n9
Prater, Andrew, 343n19
predators: and ranchers, 197–99
"predatory animal contest," 238–39
prehistoric sites: in Hells Canyon, 16–17, 17, 320n4, 320n7
Prevost, Jean Baptiste, 34

Prohibition, 226, 355n51
Prospector, 116, 206, 257–58, 358n49
Pullman Mining and Milling Company, 108, 339n31
Pumpkin Seed, 264–65
Purgatory Lake, 2
Purviance, Norman M., 273

~: Q :~

Quartz Creek, 10

~: R :~

radio, 236–37
Ragtown, Idaho, 168, 209, 211
railroad, 97, 99–100, 103, 358n34; and boats, 112–13, 128, 139, 338n15, 345n45; and bridges, 92, 94, 150, 348n12; and Homestead, Ore., 100, 336n45; and Lewiston, Idaho, 91, 103, 123, 150, 252, 337n1, 345n39; and Northern Pacific Railroad Company, 91, 123, 345n45; and Oregon Short Line, 91, 335n6; and OR&N, 91, 98, 123–24, 299, 338n17; and OR&N's boats, 112–13, 128, 139, 338n15; and PIN, 91, 98; and ranchers, 184–85; and Seven Devils Mountains, 98–99, 336n38; and Union Pacific Railroad, 91–92, 94, 252–53, 358n33–358n34; and Union Pacific's survey, 99, 104–5; and Weiser, Idaho, 91, 98–99, 252
Rains, Servier M., 68
ranchers, 161, 171–72, 186, 200–202; and dogs, 194–96; and Forest Service, 166–67, 169, 171–72, 317, 349n29; and HCNRA, 166–67, 169–70; and horses, 196–97; and predators, 197–99; and ranch hands, 179, 187–94, 199, 352n11
Rankin, William "Billy," 114, 136–37, 187–88, 348n16, 358n34
Rapid River, 323n45
Rautenstrauch, Bill, 86
Ray, Dixie Lee, 316
Red Bluff, 54
Red Ledge, 336n49
Redmond, Jim, 284
Red Rock Pass, 10
Red Wolf, 48
Reed, Fred, 224
Reed, George, 224, 341n69
Reed, John, 32–33, 39
Reed, Simeon G., 54
religion, 233–34
Render, Luisa, 335n56
Rice, James, 151, 348n15
Rice Creek Canyon, 174
Riggins, Idaho, 7, 323n45, 327n5
River and Harbor Act, 134, 299
River Navigation Company, 288
Rivers, Dick, 193, 203, 224, 258, 287–90, 289, 318, 360n12, 361n21
Rivers, Swede, 290

Rmbole, E. W., 335n56
Robinson Gulch, 80–81, 333n27, 341n62
rock art, 17–19, 320n12
Rock Island arc, 29
rock shelter homes, 16
Rocky Canyon, 63
Rocky Mountains, 27
Rodgers, J. H., 335n4
Rogers, Al, 252
Rogers, George, 252
Rogers, Patty, 240
Rogersburg, Wash., 242, 251–54, 254
Rogers Mining, Milling and Smelter Company, 148–49, 348n11
"Root Digger" Indians, 326n36
Rosbold, Olof, 345n41
Ross, Alexander, 35–36, 42–43, 324n13, 325n27
Roupe, Bert, 251
Roupe, Jim, 251
Rowland, Archie, 258, 264
Ruby City, Idaho, 328n25
Ruckelshaus, William, 363n48
Rush Creek rapids, 258
Russell, Jim, *188*, 190
rustlers, 200–201

~: S :~

Sacramento River, 54
Saddle Creek, 164, *164*, 165, 208, *213*
Saddle Mountains, 9, 319n5
Salish, 23, 38, 43
Salmon Bar, 130, 339n22
Salmon City, 76
Salmon Falls, 60
Salmon River, 7, 9, 12, 28, *28*, *42*, 53, 58, *65*, *113*, 300; and Astor's expedition, 35–36, 323n45; Diversion Project, 309–10; and *Imnaha*, 131, 134–35, 137, 346n52; and Lewis and Clark expedition, 27, 29–30; and mining, 76, 112–13, 339n31, 340n51; and Nez Perce, 62–63, 66–69, 73; and OSN expedition, 50, 327n5; and ranchers, 168, 184–85; survey of, 51, 104; and transportation, 52, 328n13, 341n61
Salmon River Mining and Development Company, 112–13
Salt Creek, 332n11, 349n31
Salt Lake, 10
Salt Lake City, Utah, 52
Sam Yup Company, 79, 83
Sand Creek Lodge, *280*, 280–81, 360n24
Sandoza, T. F., 313–14
Sapp, George, 271
Sapp, Ruth, 271–72, 286
Saturday Evening Post, 242–43, 273–75, 293

Saunders, W. W., 339n22
Saylor, John, 315
Schaeffer Springs, 180
Schubert, F. C., 299–300
Schutz, L., 104, 338n11
Schwartz, Fred, 345n41
Scranton, John, 49–53, 60
Seton, Alfred, 37–40, 324n2, 324n5–324n6, 324n9, 325n21–325n25
Seven Devils Gorge, 3
Seven Devils Mountains, 2, 7, 9, 13, 35, *91*; and minerals, 51, 90, 327n5; mining at, 89–90, 97–99, 319n8, 336n49; and OSN expedition, 50, 327n5; and railroad, 98–99, 336n38; and ranchers, 183, *185*
Shahaptin River, 38
Shannon, Joseph, 359n17
Shawley, Stephen D., 321n5, 322n9, 322n11
Sheep Creek, 24, 179, 225, 247; Bartons at, 162, 165, 210
Sheepeater War, 74
sheep ranchers, 172, 181; Arams as, 188; Dahlquists as, 349n29; Dobbin as, 173, 175, 177, 179–80, 189, 192–93, 201; Johnsons as, 166, 171, 173, 175–81, 186, 191–92, 197, 200, 238; and lambs, 174–75, 178–79; and shearing, 175–76, *176*, 351n20, 351n24, 351n26; and Suicide Point, *179*; and summering, 179–81; and "Tight Squeeze," 179; and transportation, 175–76, 179, *180*, 181, 351n24; Bud Wilson as, 165, 167, 176, 179, 187, *188*, 190, 349n29, 351n20, 352n11; and wintering, 173, 175, 179; and wool, 174–78
Sherliln, C. A., 340n38
Shevlin, Frank, 219–20
Shevlin, Minnie Marks, 219–20
Shields, Lottie, 356n18
Shingle Creek, 183
Shirley, Buster, 165, 356n27
Shirley, Violet Wilson, 164–65, 201–2, 239, 296; on chores, 237–38; on dances, 235–36; on holidays, 234–35; on life in Hells Canyon, 203, 212–14; on mail service, 247, 259; on mother, 208, 213, 215, 233–34; on ranching, 185; and school, 241, 356n39
Shoshone, 14, 24, 38, 54, 71, 325n27; and Astor's expedition, 32–35, 41, 323n39; and Bonneville, 45, 326n36; and Nez Perce, 20, 321n40
Shoshone, 54–55, 57–59, 95, 131, 328n25, 329n30, 329n33–329n34, 329n36, 329n47
Shovel Creek, 300; Rapids, 299
sidehill gouger, 3
Sigler, Doris, 113
silver, 11, 89, 103, 319n12, 339n27–339n28, 339n33
Silver Valley, 103
Simmons, Ava, 270
Simmons, Ivan, 266
Simpson, William, 327n4
Sinke, Chalmers D., 276
Sis A Nim-Max Howit, 74, 332n45
Sitkus, Lawrence, 255
Sitkus, Leonard, 260
Six Lake Basin, 323n45

Slater, James, 84
Sluice Creek, 166
smallpox, 148
Smith, A. C., 321n34
Smith, Cyrus, 55, 57, 95, 329n33
Smith, Florence Winniford, 166, *230*, 240–41, 356n38
Smith, Francis, 270
Smith, Hugh, 316
"Snake Indians," 38, 321n6, 325n27
Snake River, 1, 2, 4, 7–10, 12, 28, *28*, *41–42*, 50, 73, *113*, *127*, 250, 255, *281*, 319n1, 319n8–319n9; and Astor's expedition, 32–33, 36, 323n45; boats on, 53–54, 58, 92, 98, 128; and Bonneville, 43, 45–48; and bridge, 92, 94, 336n49; canyon, 69, 103; and ferry, 329n53; and Lewis and Clark expedition, 27, 29, 324n8; and mining, 103, 112–13, 340n51; navigability of, 41–42, 50–51, 98, 116, 341n69; obstructions removed from, 124, 128, 133–34, 137, 257, 280–81, 285, 290, 300; and OSN, 49–51, 327n5, 328n25; portage on, 52; and ranchers, 175, 179, 183, 189; survey of, 30, 51, 59, 76, 104, 299–300; as transportation corridor, 52, 60, 328n13
Snake River Boat Company, 258
Snake River Plains, 41
Snake River Portage Company, 52
Snake River School, 240, 356n33
Snake River Transportation Company, 92, 94, 258–59, 360n9
Snow's Shanty, 329n36
Soldiers Meadow, Idaho, 105
Sommers Creek, 187
Southwick, Slim, 221–22
Spalding, Eliza, 25
Spalding, Henry, 25
Spangler, Clarence, 199
Spence, Joe, 293
Spencer, Dave, 184
Sperry, J. F., 341n57, 345n39
Spokane, 128, 143, 299, 331n40, 338n15
Spokane, Wash., 103
Spokane House, 325n14
Spray, 52
Spring Camp, 240
squatters, 160–61
Squaw Creek, 323n34, 326n41
Stainton, W. B., 129, 345n41
Stangle, Bud, 212, 291, 293
steamboat, 49, 53–54, 66, 92, 98, 105, 114, 300, 331n40, 351n24; and Eureka Mining, Smelting and Power Company, 123–24, 134, 343n18; in Lewiston, Idaho, 61, 103, 330n1
Steens Mountains, 72
Steiner, Julius, 342n9
Stephen, Evan, 220
Sterling, Bonnie, 204, 214, 287; and ranching, 179, 185–86, 190, 193
Sterling, Dick, 179, 190, 193, 204
Stickney, Mary Hibbs, 219, 349n20

Stickney, Ralph, 349n20
Stites, Idaho, 23, 125, 322n21, 323n45
Stone, Janie, 221, 224, 272; on life in Hells Canyon, 207, 209, 213, 215, 219–20
Stone, Ralph, 221
Stonebreaker, George, 116
Stratton, David, 81, 333n27
Street, H. B., 339n22
Stretchett, Clem, 3, 319n5
Strong, E. C., 339n25
Stuart, David, 37, 39
Stuart, Granville, 90
Stump, John F., 347n66
Stump, Thomas, 53–54, 328n21, 330n1, 347n66
Sturgill Bar, 94–95
Sugar Loaf Knob, 183
Suicide Point, 58, *179*, 247–48, *248*
Sully, Alfred, 66
Sulphur Creek, 168
Summit Creek, 116, 326n43
Summit Ridge, 51
Sundown, Jackson, 239
Superior Packing Company, 181
Supple, George, 128
Supple, Joseph, 344n22
Swallows Nest Rock, 2, 9, *60*
Swank, Gladys, 354n35
Swastika, 258
Sweeny, Charles, 338n19
Sweetwater Creek, 323n45
Symons, Thomas W., 30, 76, 104, 337n5, 337n10

~: T :~

Tammany Creek, 36
Taylor, Glenn, 310
tectonic plates, 5, 7
telephone service, 215–17, 354n4, 354n9–354n10; and Eureka Mining, Smelting and Power Company, 125, 128, 344n26
Temperance Creek, 10, 24, 291; Johnsons at, 166, 176, 205–6, 209, 268, 285, 287, 317, 354n10; Tituses at, 349n31, 354n19
Temperance Creek Livestock Company, 166
Temperance Creek Sheep Ranch, 171, 175–76
Ten Mile Creek, 251
Teton Pass, 32
"The Breaks," 183
The Dalles, Ore., 185, 250, 328n25, 357n25
Thiessen, Henry, 206
Thiessen, J. D., 341n69
Thirty-two Point Creek, 45

Thomas, Lowell, 276
Thomason, Mike, 115, 249
Thompson, A. W., 324n8, 325n14, 325n21, 325n25
Thompson, Rachel, 356n18
Thompson, S. Leslie, 133, 347n67
Thorn, Jonathan, 32
Thornbark Ridge, 74, 332n45
Three Creeks, 162, 210–11, 349n29
308 Review Report, 310–11
Thresher, Ben, 342n9
"Tight Squeeze," 179
Tillicum, 258
Timber and Stone Act, 348n2
Timothy (Chief), 48
Tippett, Biden, 284
Tippett, Don, 232
Tippett, Doug, 160, 169–70, 242, 317; on life in Hells Canyon, 220, 237; on "predatory animal contest," 238–39; on ranching, 171, 199
Tippett, James H. "Jidge," 169, 201–2, 233; as rancher, 172, 174
Tippett, Janie, 169–70
Tippett, Jessie Wilson, 169, 233, 238, 350n41
Tippett Land Company, 169–70
Titus, Bob, 269
Titus, Celia Wisenor, 167, 217–19, 349n31, 354n19
Titus, Jack, 167, 219, 223, 230, 267, 285, 349n31, 354n19; and ferry, 249–50
Titus, Vern, 349n31
Tolo Lake, 63
Toomey, Michael, 145
Tracy, H. C., 341n57
Train, Russell, 363n48
transportation: corridor, 52, 328n13; and ranchers, 175–79, *180*, 181, 351n24; river for, 52, 104, 110, 112, 116, 124–25, 134, 300, 328n13, 341n61, 341n69, 344n21, 346n50; and roads built, 91, 110, 126, 144, 167, 251, 329n53, 345n29, 346n50
Treasury mine, 339n33
Treaty of 1868, 71, 331n31
Trenary, George, 227
Triplett, Leslie, 270
Truman, Harry S., 310
Tsan, Liang Ting, 83
Tsui Yin, 82
Tucker, Gerald, 223, 330n9, 336n49, 357n6, 358n34; on Chinese miners, 332n11, 332n23; on *Imnaha*, 136–37
Tumelson, Tom, 263–64
Tussing, Annette, 363n47
Tuttle, G. A., *115*
Tuttle, J. F., 114, 341n61, 342n8
Twin Imps, 2
Twin Rock, 53

Twisted Hair, 27–28, 321n2

~: U :~

Udall, Stewart, 314–15
U&I, 358n41
Ulmann, Al, 316
Umatilla, 258, 300
Umatilla, Ore., 73, 327n9, 328n14, 328n25
Umatilla Indians, 71, 331n42
Umatilla Landing, 54
Umatilla Reservation, 69, 74
Union Pacific Railroad, 91, 252–53, 358n33–358n34; and bridge, 92, 94; survey by, 99, 104–5

~: V :~

Vallier, Tracy, 4–5, 326n38, 360n25; on Astor's expedition, 323n32, 323n34
Van Brundt, C. S., 341n57, 345n33
Vance, Hamilton, 145
Vandervater, Fred, 343n19, 344n27
Van Eaton, C. S., 275–76, 359n20
Van Pool, Clay, 292
Van Pool, David, 168
Van Pool, Erma, 217, 236, 350n35
Van Pool, Harold, 168–69, 236, 284, 359n17, 361n21; on life in Hells Canyon, 203, 214; as rancher, 183, 190–91
Van Pool, Heeman, 169
Van Pool, Sarah, 168
Van Pool, Tuppy, 168–69, 236
Van Pool family, 183–85, 201
Vansyckle, J. M., 53
Vaughn, Bert, 99
Vaughn, Frank, 80–81, 84–86
Vaughn, Jake, 99
Veranek, Carl, 100
Vest, Charles E., 335n56
Victor, Al, 229
Vincent, Joseph K., 83–84, 87, 333n37
Von Cadow, Leone, 277
Voorhees, F. D., 364n55

~: W :~

Waha, Idaho, 105, 110
Waha Landing, 129, 251
Walker, A. J., 345n41
Walker, Max, 212, 223, 226, 231–32, 236; on Dick Carter, 224–26; on murder of Martin Hibbs, 227–28; on ranching, 172, 181, 197–98
Wallace, Charles, 345n29
Wallace, George, 144
Walla Walla, 327n9

Walla Walla Valley, 41
Wallowa, 300
Wallowa County, 240, 329n53, 356n31
Wallowa Mountains, 7, 9, 74, 180–81
Wallowa River, 62, 326n49
Wallowa Trail, 74
Wallowa Valley, 62, 69, 185, 189
Wallula Junction, 73
Walters, Bill, 349n29
Wanapum: Basalt, 319n5; phase, 9
Wapshalee Creek, 50
Wapshilla Creek, 322n9–322n10
Wapshilla Ridge, 28–29, 29, 36, 322n10
Warnock, Alex, 356n27
Warnock, Ellen, 356n27
Warrens, Idaho, 103
Washington Public Power Supply System, 314–15
Waterspout Rapids, 11
Wauna, 264–65
Way-lee-way River, 47, 326n49
Weddle, Ferris, 316, 364n55
Weippe Prairie, 68–69
Weiser, Idaho, 4, 34, 319n8; and railroad, 91, 98–99, 252
Weiser, Peter, 28–30
Weiser River, 33–34, 50, 323n45
Wells, Merle, 321n1, 322n9, 322n11, 322n13
Wenaha, 188, 283–85, 284–85, 286, 287
West, Herbert G., 310
West Coast Portland Cement Company, 337n9
Western Union Mining and Developing Company, 343n10
Whipple, Stephen C., 62, 68
whirlpools, 229
White, Georgia Mae, 290
White, Green, 357n23
White, Len, 53, 335n16
White Bird, Idaho, 341n61, 349n29
Whitebird Creek, 323n45
White Bird Hill, 66, 341n61
White Monument mines, 90, 97, 99, 336n28
Wiggins, Robert, 3, 319n5
Wilcox, Scott, 338n17
Wild Goose, 254, 358n41–358n42
Wild Goose channel, 341n69
Wild Goose Mining and Milling Company, 107, 339n27–339n28
Wild Goose Rapids, 97, 299–300, 322n13; and copper, 105, 107; *Imnaha* at, 130, 133–34, 346n46; obstructions at, 124, 128; Pullman Mining and Milling Company at, 108, 339n31
Wild Goose Rapids Mining and Milling Company, 105
Wild Sheep Rapids, 11, 58

Wilkerson, Claude, 345n41
Wilkinson, William J., 303, 305, 343n18, 345n39
Willamette Transportation Company, 329n47
Williams, C. W., 92, 94
Willow Creek, 10, 179
Wilson, Aaron, 154, 346n59
Wilson, Allen, 162, 164, 199, *199*, 205, 222, 238–39, 241; and canyon trails, 246–47; in *Saturday Evening Post*, 242–43
Wilson, Billy, 237
Wilson, Buck, 219–20
Wilson, Bud, 162, 165, 167, *167*, *173*, *191*, 210, 248, 285, 354n10; and dogs, 194; and planes, 291–92; as rancher, 165, 167, 176, 179, *188*, 190, 352n11
Wilson, Charles, 164, 241
Wilson, Dan, 164, 241
Wilson, Darlene, 267
Wilson, Don, 164, 241
Wilson, Doris, 167, 188, 194, 216, 230; as rancher, 180, 190, 351n20
Wilson, Eliza, 219
Wilson, Ethel, 196, 203, 208–10, 213, 215, 232–33, 234, 238, 246; and religion, 233–34; and school, 241, 356n39; on strangers, 222–23
Wilson, Ether, 164–65
Wilson, Frank, 187, 268, 354n9
Wilson, Gary, 230
Wilson, Hazel Barton, 162, 164, 205, *241*, 242–43
Wilson, Helen, *167*
Wilson, Jack, 270
Wilson, James (Jimmy), *164*, 164–65, 226, 236, 237, 241–42, 246–47
Wilson, Jessie. *See* Tippett, Jessie Wilson
Wilson, John, 59
Wilson, Katherine (Kappy), 164, 232
Wilson, Kim, 162, 242–43
Wilson, Lem, 167, 188, 194, 198, 230, 291; as rancher, 167, 180, 351n20; and telephone service, 216, 354n10
Wilson, Marjorie. *See* Chadwick, Marjorie Wilson
Wilson, Minnie, 354n9
Wilson, Murrielle McGaffee, 165, 226, 235, 242, 248; on ranching, 172, 174, 196; as teacher, 225, 236, 241
Wilson, Pete, 162, 164–65, 209–10, 212, 218–20, 227, 230, 232, 238–39, 246; and canyon trails, 248–49; and dogs, 196; as environmentalist, 171; and holidays, 234–35; on life in Hells Canyon, 203; as rancher, 172–74, 185, 201–2; and religion, 234; and strangers, 222–23; and telephone line, 215
Wilson, Ray, 230
Wilson, Violet. *See* Shirley, Violet Wilson
Wilson family, 213, 214, 249; as ranchers, 164–65, 349n29; visitors to, 220–21
Winchester, Goldie, *117*, 117–18
Winchester, Sherman, 116–18, *117*
Wing, Sharon Horrocks, 195–97, 201, 292, 297, 317–18; on life in Hells Canyon, 216–17, 231, 243; as rancher, 172, 174, 182–83, 190

Winnemucca, 331n33
Winnemucca Reservation, 331n33
Winniford, Billy, 223
Winniford, Carmen. *See* Yokum, Carmen Winniford
Winniford, Eileen, *165*, 241
Winniford, Florence. *See* Smith, Florence Winniford
Winniford, Frank, 166
Winniford, John, *165*, 241
Winniford, Maxine, 241
Winniford, Mina, *165*, 166, 240–41
Winniford, Stella, 166, *219*
Winniford, Walter, *165*, 166, 241
Winniford, Willy, 166
Winniford, Wilma, *165*, *230*, 241
Winniford family, 166, *245–47*
Winslow, Stewart, 258
Winters, Bill, 352n11
Winters, Irene, 352n11
Wirth, Conrad L., 364n55
Wisenor, Estelle, 349n31
Wisenor, James, 211, 349n31
Wisenor, Rufus, 239–40, 349n31
Wisenor, Stella, 211
Wisenor, Wes, 349n31
Wolf, J. A., 345n41
Wolf Creek, 8, 33, 168, 323n28, 350n34
Wolfe, Don, 290–91
Wolper, Shorty, 234
Woolgrowers Warehouse Company, 177
Worden, T. H., 104, 338n11
Wright, George, 51–52
Wright, Thomas, 96, 329n52
Wundrum, Henry, 340n37, 340n39
Wundrum, Herman, 110–11, 340n36
Wundrum District, 340n36

~: Y :~

Yellow Boy mine, 339n33, 340n39
Yellowstone National Park, 319n1
Yellow Wolf, 66–67
Yokum, Carmen Winniford, 239, 241, 245, 259–62
Yo-mus-ro-y-e-cut, 326n48
Yu, Pung Kwang, 82–83

~: Z :~

Zig Zag Creek, *176*
Zimmerly, Albert L. "Bert," 201, 218, 282, 290–91
Zindell, Martin, 253

www.ingramcontent.com/pod-product-compliance
Lightning Source LLC
Chambersburg PA
CBHW080753300426
44114CB00020B/2725